ENERGY ECONOMICS AND TECHNOLOGY

Phillip G. LeBel is associate professor of economics at Montclair State College in Upper Montclair, New Jersey.

Phillip G. LeBel

ENERGY ECONOMICS AND TECHNOLOGY

THE JOHNS HOPKINS UNIVERSITY PRESS
Baltimore and London

Printed in the United States of America

The Johns Hopkins University Press, Baltimore, Maryland 21218
The Johns Hopkins Press Ltd., London

Illustrations by Hubert Johnson unless otherwise noted

Library of Congress Cataloging in Publication Data

LeBel, Phillip G.
Energy economics and technology.

Includes index.
1. Energy policy—Economic aspects—United States.
2. Energy development—Economic aspects—United States.
I. Title.
HD9502.U52L4 1982 333.79'0973 82-15183
ISBN 0-8018-2772-8
ISBN 0-8018-2773-6 (pbk.)

FOR CAROLYN, NATASHA, AND MELISSA

CONTENTS

LIST OF FIGURES

LIST OF TABLES

PREFACE

The ideas presented in this text are a product of a personal and professional interest. Like many individuals, I have been intrigued and concerned with the dramatic changes in the prices and uses of energy during the past decade. As I looked for answers to the many questions posed by the energy "crisis," I found it necessary to go beyond the more popular literature on the subject to a systematic investigation of the underlying economic and technical factors that shape energy decisions. When I extended that interest to the classroom, it seemed only natural that I should organize these ideas into a more structured form. Though the literature on energy has continued to grow at a dramatic rate, I hope that the concepts put forth here can at least serve as an introduction to the subject for both student and professional readers.

Among the particular reasons why I have chosen to write this book is a conviction that the policy issues posed by the events of the past decade are likely to remain with us for some time to come. Because the details of future energy policy issues may well be as varied as those of the recent past, I have therefore decided to employ a broadly based analytical framework that I think will be useful to readers in understanding and responding to these events as they arise.

Another reason why I have chosen to write this book is that unlike many areas of economic inquiry, energy policy choices depend on an understanding of both economic theory and the laws of physics. I have thus gone beyond an investigation of only the economics of energy to an explicit discussion of energy technology, and to the laws of thermodynamics, notions that economists have not often been prone to consider directly, but which I think are essential to making informed economic choices. At the same time, I have also tried to present key economic concepts in a way that can be understood by noneconomists and practitioners in energy, the quality of whose decisions depends critically on an understanding of how economics can affect the uses and limits of technology.

Finally, I have chosen to write this book because I have been encouraged to do so by numerous individuals, some of whom I would like to mention here. I would like to thank first of all Edwin F. Shelley, director of the Center for Energy Policy and Research of the New York Institute of Technology, with whom I first discussed this project and whose continued encouragement, suggestions, and constructive criticisms were often a source of inspiration. Second, for both their suggestions and their constructive criticisms, I would like to thank the following individuals who read various parts of the manuscript: Jill Kasle, Juanita Kreps, Sar Levitan, Richard D. Morgenstern, Owen Phillips, Irwin Price, Florence D. Shelley, Norman J. Singer, Theodore K. Steele, and Albert Wattenberg. They are, of course, blameless for any errors of fact or interpretation that I may have made. I am also grateful to Anders Richter, the editorial director of the Johns Hopkins University Press, for his encouragement in getting me to finish the manuscript in a timely fashion, and to Joanne Allen, whose editorial assistance did much to keep my use of the language of economics and technology from abusing the canons of written English. I would also like to acknowledge the administration of Montclair State College for providing financial assistance for completing some technical aspects of the book. Finally, I would like to thank my wife, Carolyn, and my daughter, Natasha, whose good humor and patience in seeing me through this project are far greater than words alone can express.

INTRODUCTION

Anyone who attempts to understand the recent energy crisis in the United States and the world often faces an uphill struggle. The reason for this predicament is relatively simple. Although the number of popular and technical publications on energy has increased, there has been almost no systematic introduction to the field of energy policy. Because energy policy is likely to become even more important in the coming years, there is thus a need to bring together in one volume the technological and economic bases of energy decisions.

Few issues demand an interdisciplinary perspective as does energy policy. It involves, after all, technology, economics, the natural environment, and thus the very basic foundations on which society must depend. Yet what is most central to the determination of energy policy is the economics through which all resources are priced and the underlying technology with which socially useful energy can be transformed. Indeed, it is only with an understanding of both technology and economics that well-informed choices can ever hope to become an integral element in the selection of appropriate energy policies.

Part I examines the significance of energy crises to economics, to public policy in general, and to energy policy in particular. Specifying these functional relationships at the outset will provide the reader with a conceptual perspective of the scope of energy policy alternatives. One way of appreciating the significance of energy policy alternatives is to look at past and projected uses of energy independently of the policies that have been and may still be made. By looking at the uses of energy is historical perspective, we can understand more fully the significance of energy crises to society and thus the importance of appropriate energy policies.

Appropriate energy policies depend directly on technology and economics. Part II examines in detail the technological dimensions of energy resource conversion, beginning with a survey of commonly used methods in the measurement of all energy flows, and the laws of thermodynamics that underlie them. With a knowledge of these physical principles, we can better interpret and assess explicitly the feasibility of fossil, nuclear, and renewable energy technologies. Indeed, only in so doing can we fully understand the economics through which technological decisions are transmitted.

Part III uses the information on energy technologies to examine the past and present pricing of energy resources. The focus of this section is to determine to what extent market forces and government policies have fostered an economically efficient allocation of energy resources. As will be seen, this assessment includes tests to determine the extent of competition in energy markets and the degree to which externalities have affected the allocation of resources.

Part IV integrates energy history, energy technology, and economic analysis into the design and implementation of present and future energy policies. Explicit energy policy criteria based on the framework of economic analysis and the underlying principles of physics are examined and compared. On the basis of such a comparison, we can evaluate the energy policies of the United States as well as those of other countries throughout the international economy.

Despite the interdisciplinary complexities of energy, the topics covered here can be understood by anyone with basic training in economics and a serious interest in the policy issues. All technical matters are translated into readily understandable language, and mathematical formulations are reinforced with numerical examples. Thus, energy policy choices can be made by a public much better informed than has been the case until now.

PART I

ENERGY CRISES AND PUBLIC POLICY

1

ECONOMICS AND ENERGY

1.1. THE SIGNIFICANCE OF ENERGY CRISES

Energy crises occur whenever there is a sudden and unexpected shift in the quantity of energy resources or in their prices or when there is a combination of these two factors. Energy crises usually have involved upward movements in prices as a result of a particular resource's being dramatically reduced in quantity under its previous schedule of prices or being less than proportionally increased in quantity under increased prices. Whether induced by changes in supply or in demand, energy crises can have widespread disruptive consequences. Since energy resources are an integral part of social and economic organization, the study of energy policy represents an important area of public policy.

Despite their significance, in the past the policy dimensions of energy received the greatest attention from environmental, consumer, and populist groups whose concerns have not always been translated into practice. The reasons for this long-term neglect, though hardly justified, are readily understandable. First, as indispensable as energy has been to society, historically it has accounted for a relatively small share of total resource use at any one time.[1] Second, when energy crises occurred in the past, they tended to disappear with comparably minor adjustments to economic and social organization. What distinguishes recent energy crises from those of the past is the growing complexity of energy decisions, that the cost of energy in the near term at least may claim a growing share of income, and that the economy may well be more affected by subsequent energy decisions than has been the case until now. Thus, future energy crises may be more severe than those of the past, and appropriate policies even more difficult to implement. The need for systematic analysis and policy formulation expands accordingly.

[1]Between 1947 and 1971 the cost share of energy in U.S. manufacturing averaged 4.48 percent (see E. R. Berndt and D. O. Wood, "Technology, Prices, and the Derived Demand for Energy," *Review of Economics and Statistics* 56, no. 3 [August 1975]:264). A comparable figure is used by Edward Hudson and Dale Jorgenson in their economic analysis reported in S. David Freeman, *A Time to Choose*, Final Report of the Energy Policy Project of the Ford Foundation (Cambridge, Mass.: Ballinger Publishing Co., 1974), p. 498. They list the cost share of energy in the GNP at 4.38 percent for 1975.

To illustrate the impact of an energy crisis, we need only to recall the 1973–74 oil embargo by members of the Organization of Petroleum Exporting Countries (OPEC) and the quadrupling of crude-oil prices which followed in the next three years.[2] The immediate cause of the embargo was clearly political: several Arab members of OPEC were concerned that U.S. and Western European support of Israel during the October Middle East war would once again cause defeat for Syrian, Egyptian, and Jordanian forces, much as had occurred in 1948, 1956, and 1967. The decision to impose an oil embargo was based on the expectation that external intervention in the Middle East could be minimized. To obtain broader support, the embargo was extended to Portugal, Rhodesia (now Zimbabwe), and South Africa, whose racial policies were anathema to other African and Third World countries. Though the embargo ended in 1974, the broader consequences of the energy crisis were only beginning to unfold.

Critical to the success of the embargo and to the quadrupling of oil prices was one key element: dependence. In 1973 the United States' share of energy from all sources represented 30 percent of world gross consumption. Of this U.S. gross energy consumption, 47 percent was supplied by petroleum. Thirty-five percent of all U.S. petroleum consumption depended on imported sources, and 25 percent of all oil imports came from Middle Eastern OPEC countries, notably Saudi Arabia, Iran, the United Arab Emirates, Kuwait, Iraq, and Qatar. Another 8 percent came from Algeria and Libya, both OPEC member countries, and from Egypt. The embargo by Arab OPEC countries—with the exception of Iran, which did not join the embargo but did press vigorously for the price increases that followed—amounted to 25 percent of U.S. oil imports, or 4 percent of total U.S. energy consumption from all resources.[3]

Despite the relatively small Arab OPEC share of U.S. gross energy consumption, the embargo nevertheless had a dramatic impact on the World economy. Although the Arab oil states terminated their embargo of the United States by March 1974, they joined other OPEC countries in a series of periodic price increases that have continued to affect the United States and other consuming countries even up to the present. The first visible sign of OPEC's influence was, predictably, the gasoline shortages and ominous queues of 1973, an economic disruption made even worse by a complex regulatory system which was totally unprepared for this sudden change. The shortage of gasoline soon affected production, non-energy prices, and na-

[2]Between 1 January 1973 and 1 January 1974 the posted price of Saudi Arabian thirty-four-degree-gravity oil, a conventionally used bench mark in OPEC pricing, went from $2.591 per barrel to $11.651. As of January 1981 it had reached $32.39 per barrel, which in inflation-adjusted terms was just under three times the January 1973 price. For an overview of the events of 1973 and the immediate aftermath of the OPEC embargo, see Raymond Vernon, ed., *The Oil Crisis* (New York: W. W. Norton and Company, 1976).

[3]The 4 percent share is derived from the product of the 47 percent, 35 percent, and 25 percent figures just cited. These shares are all taken from data in the appendix of ibid. and from energy trade figures compiled by the U.S. Department of the Interior, Bureau of Mines, *Minerals Yearbook* (Washington, D.C.: U.S. Government Printing Office, 1975).

tional unemployment. Between 1973 and 1975, the real Gross National Product, or GNP, fell by 3 percent and did not surpass the pre-embargo level until 1976. Unemployment, which stood at 4.9 percent in 1973, rose to 5.6 percent in 1974 and 8.5 percent in 1975, while 1973–74 consumer prices rose by over 11 percent within a year, the largest such increase then experienced since World War II. Moreover, as these events unfolded, they tended to destabilize an already precarious U.S. balance of payments, thereby accelerating an international decline in the value of the dollar, the currency on which so much of the world's trade had come to depend.[4]

The political events of 1973 may have been unique. Indeed, in 1979 the collapse of oil production and exports under the revolutionary Islamic regime of Ayatollah Khomeini led to a further doubling of the price of OPEC oil in world markets. Yet, even if OPEC and Middle Eastern political conflicts had been absent, it is fairly certain that the United States, and a number of other countries as well, would have faced an equally disruptive energy crisis sooner or later.[5] For the United States at least, the prospect of an energy crisis lay in the facts that reliance on petroleum as a primary energy resource was growing at a dramatic pace and that proven domestic reserves of petroleum had begun to peak. Since oil reserves were no longer growing as fast as domestic consumption, the United States began importing an increasing share of its oil from abroad. But as it did so, it entered a market in which many other countries were also increasing their demand for oil. The growth of world oil demand was beginning to exceed the growth of world oil production and reserves.

A useful way to understand these facts is to consider the world's energy resources and the patterns of energy consumption over time. Energy exists in many usable forms, such as light, heat, or mechanical operations. Part of society's energy consumption derives from finite and exhaustible stocks of resources, and part of it depends on "renewable" energy flows. As we shall see in chapter 4, no energy resources are strictly renewable, for if they were, we would be transcending a fundamental principle of physics, the Second Law of Thermodynamics. Nevertheless, for purposes of our present discussion, we can include in the list of energy resources the depletable fossil fuels coal, petroleum, and natural gas, depletable nuclear energy, and the "renewable" resources from the sun, water, and wind and from within the earth. All of these resources may be consumed in their primary forms, or they may be converted into the secondary form of electricity, as in the operation of hydroelectric dams and nuclear power plants. What they all have in common is the capacity to do work, which is essential to the operation of the economy.

[4]For additional data on the events of 1973–74, see Council of Economic Advisors, *Economic Report of the President, 1976* (Washington, D.C.: U.S. Government Printing Office, 1976), esp. pp. 83–90 and 128–52.

[5]One interpretation offered on the events of 1973 was that U.S. support of Israel was a primary cause of the Arab oil embargo, an argument which overlooks past U.S. energy policies and the various incentives that led to U.S. dependence on oil imported from the Middle East in the first place. For a discussion of the argument and the extensive counter-evidence, see C. F. Doran, *Myth, Oil, and Politics: Introduction to the Political Economy of Petroleum* (New York: Macmillan Publishing Co., 1977).

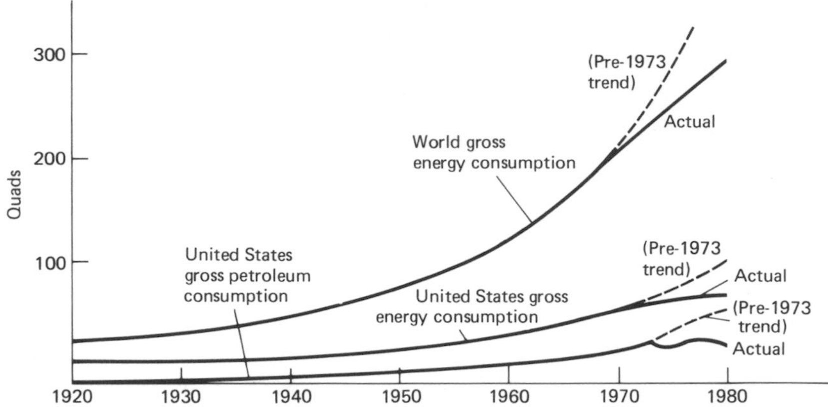

Figure 1.1. U.S. and World Gross Energy Consumption, 1920–80. Data from U.S. Department of the Interior, *Energy Perspectives 2* (Washington, D.C.: U.S. Government Printing Office, June 1976); World Bank, *World Development Report, 1981* (New York: Oxford University Press, 1981); and Sam H. Schurr and Bruce C. Netschert, *Energy in the American Economy, 1850–1975* (Baltimore: Johns Hopkins Press for Resources for the Future, 1960).

To facilitate the comparison of these energy resources, we can translate them into their heat energy equivalents by use of the term "quad."[6] A quad is 10^{15} British Thermal Units. A British Thermal Unit, or Btu, is the amount of heat required to raise the Fahrenheit temperature of one pound of 39.2°F water at sea level by one degree. Using this quad measure, figure 1.1 shows the growth of U.S. and world gross energy consumption based on the use of coal, petroleum, natural gas, hydropower, geothermal energy, and nuclear power. Although the United States' share of world energy consumption began declining as early as the 1920s, the increasing use of petroleum as a replacement for coal and wood suggests that future U.S. and world energy growth would depend more and more on petroleum resources. Yet, as noted in figure 1.2, although petroleum reserves have increased dramatically, in the 1960s their rate of growth was less than that of world petroleum consumption. Indeed, it was precisely this shifting pattern of reserves and consumption that lay behind an eventual energy crisis, whether OPEC were to initiate a shortage or not. The embargo of 1973 and the quadrupling of oil prices was simply an artificial mechanism for advancing the consequences of what would have occurred in any case.

The 1973 OPEC oil embargo pointed out the significance of the growing petroleum dependence in the economy of the United States and the world. It also pointed out that in the United States at least, past energy policies had led to continuing declines in the real price of oil and associated natural gas,

[6]The conversion units used in figure 1.1 and in subsequent examples are listed in the Appendix.

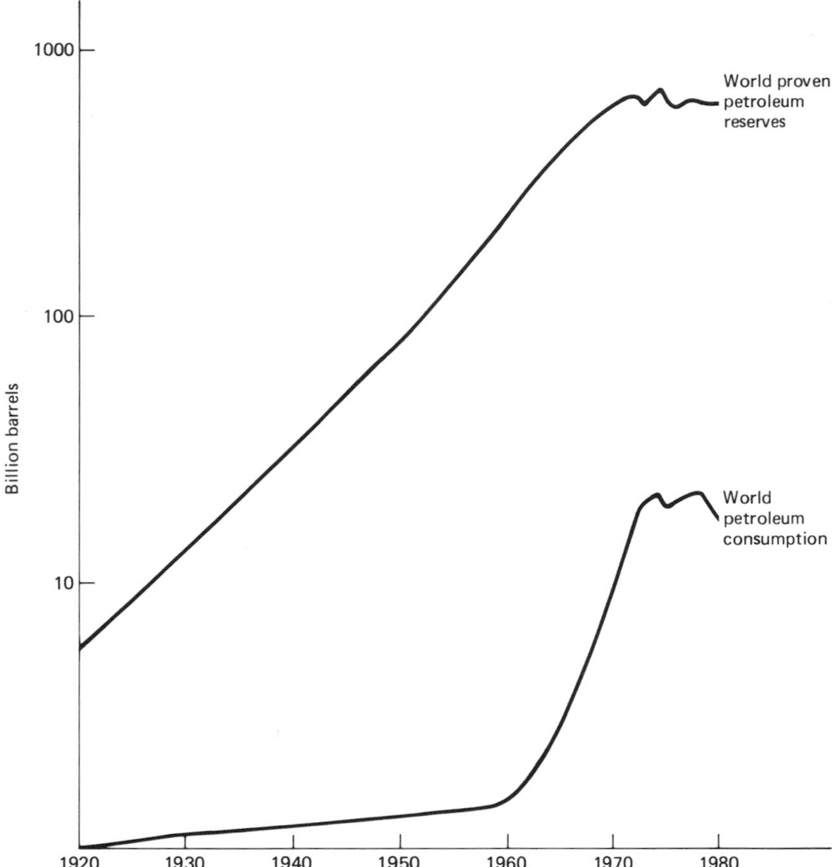

Figure 1.2. World Proven Petroleum Reserves and Consumption, 1920–80. The figures refer to published proven reserves and do not include ultimately recoverable reserves. Data from *Oil and Gas Journal* (Tulsa: Pennwell Publishing Co., selected years).

thereby encouraging the growth of consumption.[7] From the standpoint of supply, since the price of U.S. oil was falling below its domestic cost of replacement, the logical choice for exploration was in the world's least expensive source of discovery, the Middle East.[8] Yet, as the trends in figure 1.2 suggest, even as Middle East dependency grew, the decline in the real price

[7]The decline in the real price of oil was in both absolute and relative terms during the 1950s and most of the 1960s (see Robert S. Pindyck, "The Characteristics of the Demand for Energy," in *Energy Conservation and Public Policy*, ed. John C. Sawhill [Englewood Cliffs, N.J.: Prentice-Hall, 1979], pp. 22–45). More detailed data are reported in chapter 3.

[8]A summary comparison of worldwide development and operating costs in the 1960s in the United States, Venezuela, Africa, and the Persian Gulf States is found in M. A. Adelman, *The World Petroleum Market* (Baltimore: Johns Hopkins Press for Resources for the Future, 1972), p. 76. See also figure 15.2 below.

of oil worked gradually to discourage the more extensive patterns of exploration that would have been needed to keep up with demand.

Apart from dependency on imported oil, past U.S. energy policy also encouraged energy-intensive economic growth. The problem posed by energy-intensive growth is that without any corresponding emphasis on the technical efficiency of energy conversion, it leads to a rise in environmental pollution and, in the near term at least, to a more rapid exhaustion of the depletable energy resources on which the economy primarily depends. A simple way of measuring the energy intensity of an economy is to determine how much gross energy consumption is needed to produce a dollar's worth of output and then to trace this ratio through time. If energy intensity is declining, it will involve a smaller use of energy per dollar of output, a shift which in economic terms will be attributable to the higher price of energy relative to non-energy resources, to the form and extent of technical change, or to both.

The energy intensity of the U.S. economy since 1920 is summarized in figure 1.3. As can be seen, the long-term trend has been one of a gradual decline. Yet, from the mid-1960s up to the early 1970s this pattern was beginning to reverse itself as producers sought to substitute relatively inexpensive energy for non-energy resources. Indeed, one of the most visible symbols of

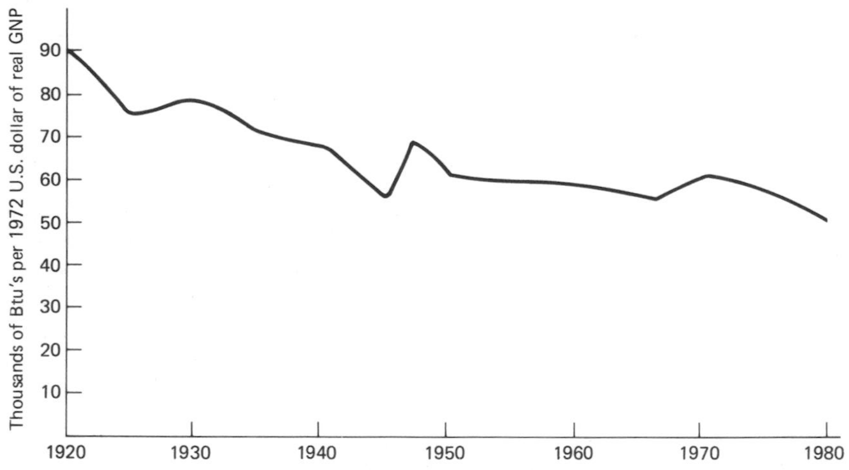

Figure 1.3. Energy Intensity in the U.S. Economy, 1920–80. Data from U.S. Department of Commerce, Bureau of Economic Analysis, *Long-Term Economic Growth, 1860–1970*, series A-7 and A-8 (Washington, D.C.: U.S. Government Printing Office, 1973); Council of Economic Advisors, *Economic Report of the President, 1981* (Washington, D.C.: U.S. Government Printing Office, 1981), p. 236; Schurr and Netschert, *Energy in the American Economy, 1850–1975*; U.S. Department of Energy, Energy Information Administration, *Annual Report to Congress II* (Washington, D.C.: U.S. Government Printing Office, 1979), table 1; idem, *Monthly Energy Review* (Washington, D.C.: U.S. Government Printing Office, September 1981), p. 4.

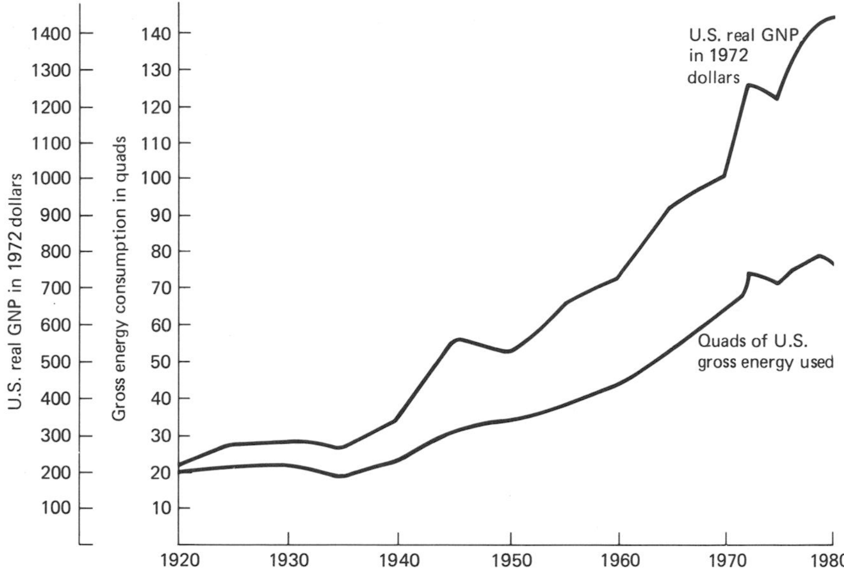

Figure 1.4. GNP and Energy Growth in the U.S. Economy, 1920–80. Data from Department of Commerce, Bureau of Economic Advisors, *Long-Term Economic Growth*; Council of Economic Advisors, *Economic Report of the President, 1918*, p. 236; Schurr and Netschert, *Energy in the American Economy*; Department of Energy, Energy Information Administration, Annual Report to Congress II, table 1; idem, *Monthly Energy Review*, September 1981, p. 4.

this shift was the decline in the fuel efficiency of U.S. automobiles in comparison with West European and Japanese alternatives.[9]

We might well ask why energy intensity is as important as energy dependence in assessing the overall significance of energy crises. The answer is found in the pattern of energy and economic growth over time. In any economy, as growth occurs, there will be structural change in patterns of consumption, as well as in the ways in which goods and services are produced. Given the degree of technical change and the role of relative prices in this process, one thing is clear: rising output is associated to some extent with growing energy use.

The evolution of energy and of the GNP of the U.S. economy is shown in figure 1.4. Although both technical change and relative prices have played a role in this pattern, it is clear that as the economy grows, so too will its demand for energy. The only way to separate the linkage between energy and

[9]The experience of the U.S. automobile industry illustrates the extent to which key sectors of the economy were, and still are, vulnerable to short-term energy-price shocks. As oil became scarce during the 1973 embargo, the sales of large cars plummeted, while fuel-efficient imports were being marketed at premium prices. What is also interesting is that the fuel-efficient import share of U.S. automobile sales tended to grow even while the real price of oil was declining, pointing to other factors that contributed to this position. For a comparative analysis, see J. R. Pierce, "The Fuel Consumption of Automobiles," *Scientific American* 234 (January 1975):34–44.

the economy is deliberately to reduce the degree of energy intensity, by an increase in the price of energy relative to non-energy resources, the promotion of energy-efficient capital structures, or both. Such a policy means that whatever level of economic production is reached, there is over time a larger and larger gap between this level of output and the amount of energy consumed. Unfortunately, in the period just prior to 1973, rising U.S. energy intensity only served to aggravate the adverse impact of the embargo beyond what it otherwise would have been.

The final element in assessing the significance of energy crises is population growth. Since most countries presently are faced with increases in population, their leaders usually seek to implement policies to promote economic growth and development. As long as population grows, the economy's production must expand at least as fast if living standards are to remain constant or improve. As a result, population growth rates tend to predetermine economic growth targets, which in turn predetermine growth requirements for energy as well as for other natural resources.

Given the degree of global dependence on depletable energy resources, the future growth of the world economy points to one basic conclusion: sooner or later the real price of depletable energy must rise.[10] Yet how quickly this price will increase in absolute and relative terms depends largely on the extent to which both conservation and renewable-resource technologies can serve as substitutes for depletable in energy resources. Because the eventual shift to a society based on renewable resources may not be a smooth one, how the transition is to be accomplished raises several questions regarding public policy: Can future energy crises be avoided? Will future economic growth be impaired? Will energy worsen existing problems of inflation and unemployment? Must the relationship between energy and economic growth imperil the environment? Can we adopt efficient energy policies that are consistent with social justice? Does the nature and use of energy require a substantial alteration in the prevailing mix of public and private decision making? Since all of these questions are tied intimately to energy technology and to the policies governing its use, we need first to define just what is meant by public policy in general and how it pertains to energy.

1.2. DEFINING PUBLIC POLICY

It has long been established that the best way to define public policy is not by what it purports to do but by what it accomplishes.[11] Of course, the fact that

[10]The long-term conversion of the economy from one based on a nonrenewable resource to one based on a renewable resource does not mean that there will be a physical exhaustion of its depletable energy resources. Rather, it means that the price of renewable energy alternatives will at some point be lower than the price of alternative depletable fuels such that a depletable energy resource is never entirely "consumed" unless artificially induced to do so by perverse policy decisions. For an exposition of the transition, see H. E. Goeller and A. M. Weinberg, "The Age of Substitutability," *Science* 191 (20 February 1976):683–89.

[11]Aristotle, in book 9 of the *Nichomachean Ethics*, stated the distinction in succinct terms: "It is not enough to know about virtue, then, but we must endeavor to possess it, and to use it, or to make any other steps that may make us good."

a particular policy has been effective by no means proves that it has been appropriate. Indeed, in order to define appropriate public policy, we must specify the criteria as well as the means by which we could justify a public rather than a private resolution of an issue in the first place.

Public policy comprises those actions that affect society as a whole. The institutional structure that gives rise to these decisions is what differentiates a democratic system from its alternatives. Regardless of the political structure, public policy stands in contradistinction to what may be considered private decisionmaking, that is, the rules, codes, and actions of individuals and small groups such as corporations, local religious or civic groups, or private social clubs. Though private institutions may establish differing rules of behavior, as they acquire greater size, these institutions tend to become more subject to the prevailing principles of social governance, even as they themselves may in turn exert a considerable degree of influence as to the nature and scope of those principles.

As the primary instrument of public policy, government performs two types of functions: the specification of ethical standards such as legitimacy and due process and the application of rules governing the behavior of the economy. Although the two categories overlap, we can at least draw some clear distinctions that are relevant to energy policy. For the present, we are most interested in the economic functions of governmental activity, for they bear most directly on the determination of specific energy policies.

In the United States at least, government performs five basic economic functions: (1) determination of laws governing economic organization and conduct; (2) maintenance of competition; (3) economic stabilization and growth; (4) an equitable distribution of income; and (5) reallocation of economic resources. Each of these functions will be considered in turn.

Laws governing economic organization and conduct cover such areas as the incorporation of businesses, bankruptcy, mergers, product safety standards, and other areas involving the production and exchange of goods and services.[12] In the United States these laws are designed to facilitate the orderly operation of market pricing in a capitalist economy. Though it is possible that society could function in their absence, their existence has been justified as a means of reducing the potential for fraud, monopoly, and other abuses. Indeed, such economic laws are common to virtually all economic systems, though they differ in their detail as to ownership and disposition rights.

Maintaining competition is a more obvious government function for private capitalist economics such as that of the United States. Drawing on a broad spectrum of economic models ranging from perfect competition to pure monopoly, economic analysis has shown the adverse behavioral and structural consequences that arise from imperfect market systems. The problem of imperfect competition is a multifaceted one, to be sure, but its eco-

[12]The origins of these rules are rooted directly in European, especially English, common law. For an overview of the historical origins of these laws and their economic rationale, see Joseph A. Schumpeter, *A History of Economic Analysis* (Oxford: Oxford University Press, 1954).

nomic consequences are clear: unless otherwise constrained and unless there are demonstrable economics of scale, imperfect competition leads to lower output and a higher level of prices for the goods and services that an industry produces than would be the case in a perfectly competitive economy.[13] Moreover, the limited number of firms in imperfectly competitive markets reduces consumer sovereignty by a decline in the number of available choices and by the concentration of advertising that these industries tend to use to ensure product loyalty and corporate dominance.[14] For the present, we need only to note the public mechanisms available for responding to these conditions.

In general there are three ways of responding to imperfect competition: regulation, antitrust, and nationalization.[15] Save for the postal system, the Tennessee Valley Authority, and a number of state-level public utilities, the United States, has thus far resisted any significant degree of public enterprise, unlike some Western European capitalist countries.[16] (Since our concern is essentially with the United States, we will defer any further consideration of nationalization until part IV.)

In contrast to its limited use of nationalization, the United States has made a much wider use of antitrust and regulation. Regulation of imperfectly competitive industries is found among numerous federal and state agencies, many with extensive jurisdiction.[17] Almost all regulatory statutes owe their origins

[13]The framework used in the economic analysis of imperfect competition is spelled out more fully in chapter 9. Though the question of monopoly is posed here in its traditional microeconomic terms, were imperfect competition to prevail universally in an economy, its macroeconomic consequences would be such that unless there were demonstrable economies of scale, for any given level of prices, the level of production would tend to be less than that which would be possible under a perfectly competitive economy, even under full employment. Moreover, this degree of inefficiency would also tend to understate the noneconomic distortions that could arise. For evidence on some of these distortions, see L. M. Salamon and J. J. Siegfried, "Economic Power and Political Influence: The Impact of Industry Structure on Public Policy," *American Political Science Review* 71 (November 1977):1026–43; W. G. Shepherd, "Market Power and Racial Discrimination in White Collar Employment," *Antitrust Bulletin* 14 (Spring 1969):141–61; and W. S. Comanor and R. S. Smoley, "Monopoly and the Distribution of Wealth," *Quarterly Journal of Economics* 89 (May 1975):177–94.

[14]A recent review of studies on the economic role of advertising is found in W. S. Comanor and T. A. Wilson, "The Effect of Advertising on Competition: A Survey," *Journal of Economic Literature* 17 (June 1979):453–76.

[15]Regulation encompasses the use of taxes and subsidies as well as controls on pricing and output. Moreover, it is applicable to both public and private enterprise, since a public enterprise could be just as monopolistic as a private one. There is also a fourth option deriving from the third: instead of nationalizing an existing monopolistic firm, the government could establish a competing public enterprise. This is one alternative that has been advocated to assist in the development of alternative energy resources and in the expansion of existing ones, particularly of federally owned deposits of petroleum, coal, and natural gas. For a United Auto Workers proposal to establish a Federal Energy Corporation similar to that proposed by the Carter administration, see *New York Times*, 22 August 1979, p. B-20.

[16]Though the United States has maintained a policy bias against public enterprise, this is not to say that public enterprise is unimportant (see W. G. Shepherd et al., *Public Enterprise: Economic Analysis of Theory and Practice* [Lexington, Mass.: Lexington Books, 1976]; A. H. Walsh, *The Public's Business: The Politics and Practices of Government Corporations* [Cambridge, Mass.: MIT Press, 1978]; and S. Holland, ed., *The State as Entrepreneur* [White Plains, N.Y.: International Arts and Sciences Press, 1973]).

[17]For a standard reference on the evolution, scope, and performance of regulation in the U.S. economy, see Alfred E. Kahn, *The Economics of Regulation*, 2 vols. (New York: John Wiley and Sons, 1970–71).

to the Interstate Commerce Act of 1887, which was used originally to regulate the railroad industry through control of prices and routings. The regulatory principle is simple: by control of both prices and routings, we can obtain the kind of market behavior among imperfectly competitive industries that is consistent with a perfectly competitive market, that is, larger output and lower prices than would occur in the absence of such regulation. In practice, however, regulation has produced some unusual outcomes. For example, given the deterioration of railroads under regulation during this century, decisions made by Congress in the 1970s to provide subsidies to the quasi-public Amtrak and Conrail systems marked a clear reversal of the original thrust of regulation when the principle was first established.[18]

Antitrust, the third anti-monopoly instrument, is essentially a federal government mechanism, with some delegation to state authorities.[19] The antitrust principle was first enunciated in the United States with the passage by Congress of the Sherman Act in 1890. It was later refined through the Clayton and Federal Trade Commission acts of 1914, along with a number of succeeding statutes. The antitrust remedy is a straightforward one: where monopoly exists, fines may be imposed for infractions; where monopoly persists, courts can order the divestiture of assets, to be allocated among several reorganized firms to restore a greater degree of competitive behavior.[20] Perhaps the most striking application of antitrust was the 1911 Supreme Court decision to dissolve the Standard Oil Company, which in the previous two decades had managed to achieve a nearly complete monopoly in the newly emerging petroleum industry.[21] As will be seen in chapter 9, although the petroleum industry has since become much more competitive, one of the newly created firms from the 1911 decision, Standard Oil of New Jersey, went on to become the Exxon Corporation, which today is the single largest firm in the world petroleum industry. Moreover, in the aftermath of the 1973 embargo, antitrust has once again been advocated as a response to the oil indus-

[18]Amtrak was created by the Emergency Rail Services Act of 1970 and began passenger service on 1 May 1971. In 1973 Congress passed the Regional Railway Reorganization Act, which established the U.S. Railway Association, a nonprofit, off-budget, government-sponsored rail system which was a consolidation of bankrupt freight railroads in the northeast, of which the Penn-Central was the largest. In turn, the Railway Association was authorized to sell debt instruments for purposes of making loans to the freight operating system, the Consolidated Rail Corporation, or Conrail.

[19]For background analysis, see S. W. Whitney, *Antitrust Policies,* 2 vols. (New York: Twentieth Century Fund, 1958); and A. D. Neale, *The Antitrust Laws of the United States*, rev. ed. (Cambridge, Mass.: Harvard University Press, 1970).

[20]The scale of antitrust actions is considerably broader than described here (see K. G. Elzinga and W. Breit, *The Antitrust Penalties* [New Haven: Yale University Press, 1976]).

[21]*U.S.* v. *Standard Oil of N.J.,* 221 U.S. 106(1911). A classic reference influential in the 1911 decision was the study by Ida M. Tarbell, *History of the Standard Oil Company* (1904; reprint ed., New York: Macmillan Publishing Co., 1925). See also J. H. McLean and R. W. Haigh, *The Growth of Integrated Oil Companies* (Boston: Harvard University Graduate School of Business Administration, 1954): G. S. Gibb and E. H. Knowlton, *The Resurgent Years, 1911–1927* (New York: Harper and Row, 1956); and John S. McGee, "Predatory Price Cutting: The Std. Oil (N.J.) Case," *Journal of Law and Economics* 1 (October 1958). McGee disputes the widely held notion that predatory price cutting was a factor in the rise of the Standard Oil Company.

try, even though it is now OPEC that is the principal monopolistic force in affecting recent oil price increases.[22]

In comparing the regulatory versus antitrust instruments, it should be noted in passing that some industries, such as broadcasting, telecommunications, and electric utilities, have been considered to be "natural monopolies." The presumption is that there are ever expanding economies of scale such that only a relatively large, or in some cases single largest, firm could achieve fully the lowest unit costs of production.[23] Where such conditions arise, the logical policy choice is to rely on regulation, public ownership, or both to ensure that the benefit of relatively low costs is shared effectively among consumers. However, as will be seen in chapter 9, in many areas of energy there are limits to these scale economies such that the actual size of firms under present and evolving energy technologies may not necessarily be the most efficient.

A third major economic function of government is stabilization. After the Great Depression of the 1930s it became clear that a developed capitalist economy like that of the United States would not necessarily sustain full employment over time in the self-correcting ways that classical theory had predicted. The policy response to this condition was an activist fiscal policy, the theoretical framework of which derived principally from the writings of John Maynard Keynes. Since then, subsequent research has defined more clearly the conditions under which fiscal policy will be effective. An important result of this work has been a revival of monetary policy and a defense of private market capitalism, a most prominent advocate of which has been Milton Friedman.

For all practical purposes, monetary and fiscal policy have now become the two primary instruments of stabilizing the economy. As a step in the confirmation of their roles, Congress passed the Employment Act of 1946, in which it accepted some degree of responsibility for maintaining reasonable levels of employment and price stability in the economy. Since then, Congress translated these objectives into more specific numerical targets by passing the Full Employment and Balanced Growth, or Humphrey-Hawkins, Act of 1978. In turn, since February 1979, Federal Reserve monetary policy has involved the announcement of monetary targets to Congress on a periodic basis so that in theory at least, monetary and fiscal policy might be more closely coordinated in achieving sustained macroeconomic stability.

A secondary function of economic stabilization policies is the promotion of economic growth. The linkage between macroeconomic policies and economic growth is a direct one: government policies influence the rate of savings and investment, which are central to the rate of capital formation, which in turn is an essential determinant to the rate of economic growth. The rele-

[22]Perhaps the most prominent restatement advocating antitrust to the petroleum industry is John M. Blair, *The Control of Oil* (New York: Pantheon Books, 1976).

[23]A perverse possibility is that over the whole range of market production the lowest unit costs will fail to be realized, in which cases subsidies become justified even under monopoly. Neither the measurement problems nor the resolution of them in this case is simple.

vance of economic growth to energy policy has already been noted; what follows from this relationship is that the capacity for future economic growth will depend to no small degree on the kinds of choices that are embodied in today's energy decisions.

In practice, though the combined use of monetary and fiscal policy has resulted in fewer and smaller fluctuations in unemployment and inflation than in any preceding era of U.S. history, these tools have been singularly unable to cope with many of the underlying structural problems of the economy, of which energy is an obvious example. Indeed, the performance of the economy during and following the 1973 OPEC embargo is a clear reflection of an underlying weakness of traditional monetary and fiscal policy. As is also evident, if monetary and fiscal policy are ever again to be as effective as they once were, one essential prerequisite will be the adoption of an appropriate energy policy, as succeeding chapters will demonstrate in detail.

A fourth economic function of government is the determination of an equitable distribution of income.[24] Because its application involves interpersonal value comparisons, it is one of the more difficult functions to translate into consistent economic policy. For example, to one individual *equitable* may mean absolute equality in the distribution of income, while to another it may mean reducing someone's income for social justice as long as it isn't yours. Though the theoretical and measurement issues extend beyond our present concerns, there is little doubt that the distribution of income is also a matter that is relevant to the determination of appropriate energy policies, as a simple illustration will show.

The routine economic functions of government depend obviously on the capacity to tax and the capacity to borrow. Apart from the impact of these activities on the form and level of the supply of money, as changes in these revenue sources take place, they have three principal types of effects: the degree of economic stability already noted, the composition of production, and the distribution of income. For the given mix of revenue sources in the U.S. economy, there is evidence that the combined impact of federal, state, and local government operations exerts some degree of progressivity on the distribution of income.[25] Setting aside whether the after-tax distribution of income is an appropriate one, consider the near-term consequences that may arise from an increase in the price of energy such as occurred in the aftermath of the 1973 embargo. Absent any considerations of the impact economic stability or the composition of production, the increase may well cause in the short term at least an adverse shift in the distribution of income, since poorer indi-

[24]*Distribution* refers here only to personal income rather than its function. The conventional economic criteria for this role are: that income distribution is a public good; that the income levels of the poor affect the utility of the rich; and that ethical considerations may transcend those that are considered to be economically efficient (see Lester Thurow, "The Income Distribution as a Pure Public Good," *Quarterly Journal of Economics* 85 [May 1971]: 327-36).

[25]See Joseph A. Pechman and Benjamin A. Okner, *Who Bears the Tax Burden?* (Washington, D.C.: Brookings Institution, 1974). Pechman and Okner found that when all federal, state, and local taxes plus the distribution of revenues are taken into account, the effective tax burden is slightly progressive.

viduals may be less capable of adjusting to these changes than the rich. As will be seen in subsequent chapters, one aspect of an appropriate energy policy is that whatever the measures used to affect the level and composition of energy use, it is essential that they not be used as a means of altering the distribution of income, since other more direct methods are already available.

The fifth economic function of government is the reallocation of resources. If government were somehow to disappear overnight, apart from the consequences on the production levels of goods and services, it is certain that the composition of production would be altered. The reasons for this alteration are tied directly to the pricing of goods and services, and by implication, to the taxes and subsidies that government uses to influence their production.

Many of the kinds of resources that have been affected by governmental reallocation share a common quality: if the pricing of these resources were determined solely by individual demand and supply, their equilibrium prices would be an inaccurate measure of their costs and benefits to society as a whole. Moreover, some of them would not even be produced at all. Even if we did not have to contend with the presence of monopoly, economic distortions could still arise from the market pricing of goods in a competitive industry.[26] Since a more detailed examination of these conditions is deferred until parts III and IV, we can at this point spell out the implications of these external economic consequences to the determination of appropriate energy policies.

In the United States the fuel consumption of automobiles accounts for over 12 percent of aggregate energy use.[27] Under conventional market pricing, the utility of the vehicle to its buyer is equal to its price and to the expected future fuel and maintenance costs from operation. To the producer, the price covers all stages of assembly and preparation, conventional sales and excise taxes, and an expected rate of return on invested capital. However, once the vehicle is acquired, its operation generates a certain amount of pollution into the environment in the form of rejected heat and particulate emissions. The pollution may affect both the consumer and producer directly, depending on their geographic locations and activities, and it will most certainly affect anyone in the region where the automobile is used. Thus, an external cost will have been imposed on a third party for which no compensation is likely to be awarded.

From the preceding example, the problem posed by external costs is at least intuitively obvious: when market pricing alone is used to determine the allocation of resources, since the private costs are less than the social costs, unless some corrective mechanism is introduced, the market price will be less than that which is socially optimal: that is, there will be an oversupply. The implication for energy policy is that if we wish to attain a socially optimal position by the equalization of private and social costs, the market price of au-

[26]The literature on the efficiency of market pricing is too extensive to cover in all of its dimensions here. A more detailed discussion is presented in chapters 13 and 14.

[27]R. F. Hemphill, Jr., "Energy Conservation in the Transportation Sector," in *Energy Conservation and Public Policy,* ed. John C. Sawhill (Englewood Cliffs, N.J.: Prentice-Hall, 1979), p. 80; and U.S. Department of Energy, Energy Information Administration, *Annual Report to Congress* (Washington, D.C.: U.S. Government Printing Office, 1980).

tomobiles will have to rise in real terms. It could do so by an increase in the price of fuel, by taxes on vehicles in proportion to their external costs, or by the use of mandated improvements in fuel efficiency. Since 1973 not only has OPEC assisted in raising the price of fuel but Congress has adopted mandatory fuel-efficiency standards by its passage of the Energy Policy and Conservation Act of 1975. Of course, had Congress adopted a tax on fuel in proportion to the increase already imposed by OPEC, these revenues would also have been available for domestic redistribution and reallocation, but this is a matter which will have to be deferred until part IV.

External costs are only one form of market failure. It is also possible that there may be external benefits accruing to third parties for which no price has been paid to the producer. In this case, since the private costs exceed the social costs, there will be an undersupply of the good from a socially optimal perspective. In those cases in which the external benefits cannot even be apportioned among individual consumers, such goods are known as pure public goods, in that the only way that they could be provided would be by direct financing from government. That the question of external benefits arises also in energy decisions can be seen in two additional illustrations.

Petroleum and natural gas exploration is an energy activity in which there may be significant external economies. As an example, suppose that a firm obtains the right to drill on a given plot of land or offshore. Fees are paid to obtain this right, either from a private landowner or from the government, and routine expenses are incurred in the purchase and utilization of capital equipment and labor. The first set of holes produce nothing. Then, after several such drillings, petroleum is discovered. Soon after this discovery, another firm acquires the rights to the plot just adjacent to the original discovery. With the knowledge of the first successful well, the second firm manages to drill a hole in the same deposit, but on the plot to which it has drilling rights. In the process, the second firm has received two external benefits for which it has not paid. First, it did not incur any initial dry-hole costs and thus was able to tap the petroleum deposit on its first drilling based on the knowledge and costs incurred by the first firm. Second, it was able to siphon away some of the petroleum that otherwise would gone to the initial firm. As a result, not only does the second firm profit from the sale of its petroleum but it receives benefits that could cause the initial firm to lose revenues.

In the reference terms of market failure, petroleum exploration of the type just illustrated exhibits an obvious external economy. Because some benefits from exploration may still flow to the original firm and some may go to the adjacent firm, petroleum exploration may be thought of as a quasi-public good. Short of any degree of outside intervention, each firm has an incentive in the short run to develop maximum rates of production, thereby shortening the long-run production horizon. In so doing, it leads to a short-term glut but a long-term undersupply that will be inconsistent with socially optimal conditions. In practice, there have been a variety of government policies over the years that have sought to minimize the extent of these external economies. As will be seen in parts III and IV, such policies as the use of prorationing and unitization of fields have often led to certain perverse effects as well, thereby pointing out the imperfect nature of many energy policy alternatives.[28]

As already pointed out, in some cases the benefits from a given activity are so diffuse that it is impossible to identify the benefit that any single individual receives. Since there would be no way to charge an individual for use of the good, such goods are privately unprofitable, despite the fact that society may derive benefits from their production. In such cases, government expenditures are essential if these goods and services are to be made available at all. When we consider the field of energy, it is clear that some activities do possess a pure-public-good quality. For example, in many areas of research, there are many energy technologies that are in such an early stage of development that no identifiable markets may be said to exist. At the same time, the progress of this research may do much to increase the range of energy policy alternatives and in so doing may reduce some of the uncertainty that exists within current energy markets. For example, the Brookhaven National Laboratory in Upton, New York, has undertaken a project involving a synchrotron light source in which extremely high-energy light can yield information on the behavior of electrons under conditions of superconductivity.[29] The importance of superconductivity is that it can greatly improve the technical efficiency of energy conversion, thereby yielding societal benefits in the long-term use of energy, and it is for this reason that government support could be justified. Similarly, we could say that had the United States had an appropriate energy policy in 1973, it is probable that society as a whole would have received a pure public benefit from a less severe energy shortage than the maldistribution of outcomes that actually resulted. Conversely, the absence of an appropriate energy policy in 1973 imposed a social cost on the economy in that it raised considerably the degree of uncertainty surrounding future energy supply.

The preceding discussion is an essential first step in defining the scope and significance of energy policy alternatives. However, because some questions in energy go beyond the conventional concerns of economics, it is useful at this point to illustrate in more direct terms the operational framework of energy policy decisions. We can then more readily understand the organization of the succeeding chapters.

1.3. THE DIMENSIONS OF ENERGY POLICY

If one quality is essential to an effective energy policy, it is a convergence of individual private interests with that of the community. Whether such convergence will produce in turn an appropriate and effective energy policy turns largely on the quality and quantity of information that is available and on the

[28]A good discussion of this problem and its impact on the energy intensity of the economy is found in Stephen L. McDonald, *Petroleum Conservation in the United States: An Economic Analysis* (Baltimore: Johns Hopkins Press for Resources of the Future, 1971), esp. the analysis in parts 1 and 3.

[29]*New York Times,* 16 November 1977, p. A-16.

capacity of economic and political institutions to undertake those adjustments that are necessary to its realization.

A useful way of illustrating the dimensions of energy policy decisions is with reference to an individual example. In the weeks just after the beginning of the 1973 OPEC oil embargo, apart from the emergence of the Project Independence Blueprint of the Nixon-Ford administration, one immediate action undertaken by Congress was the approval of construction of the trans-Alaska pipeline. Oil had been discovered in the Alaskan North Slope region during the 1960s. The purpose of the pipeline was to enable firms to transfer petroleum from Prudhoe Bay to the southern port of Valdez, where it would then be shipped by tankers to refineries within the lower forty-eight states. At the time, it was widely viewed as a symbol of relieving national dependence on uncertain Middle Eastern oil supplies and the threat of continuing oil embargoes. What the pipeline decision entailed was an eventual $7.7 billion expenditure based originally on a complex set of assumptions about technology, energy and non-energy prices, and associated economic policies, none of which remained fixed during the intervening three and a half years required to complete the project.[30]

First, in order to justify construction of the pipeline, estimates had to be made of the growth of domestic demand for petroleum and of the range of possible levels of supply from imported and domestic production. From these figures, an estimate had to be made regarding the probable or guaranteed price of North Slope oil and the share of that price which could be used to cover the construction and operating costs of the pipeline. From these figures, allowance then had to be made for inflation, uncertainty, and some adjustment for the potential environmental damage that might arise either to the permafrost of the Alaskan tundra over and through which the pipeline would pass or to the waters through which the oil eventually would be shipped. In turn, the effort to internalize environmental costs was tied directly to the technological basis for the decision: the thermostatic controls; supporting pylons; pipe material, thickness, and diameter; and the optimal speed at which the oil could be moved. Finally, the technical choices of the pipeline route had to take into consideration the various permits that would be needed, as well as the capacity of the consortium of firms to build and operate the system in a way that was both economically efficient to them and at a sufficiently competitive price to proceed.

There is little doubt that the Alaska pipeline has made a difference in U.S. domestic oil supplies. By 1980 its daily average flow of 1.6 million barrels a day amounted to just under 19 percent of total domestic production and 10 percent of domestic consumption.[31] At the same time, even though the price of domestically produced crude oil was deregulated in 1980, the Alaska pipeline and the North Slope oil that it carries are at best but one piece of the

[30] "Alaska Pipeline Flow Set to Start Tomorrow," ibid., 19 June 1977, p. 1.

[31] U.S. Department of Energy, Energy Information Adminstration, *Monthly Energy Review* (Washington, D.C.: U.S. Government Printing Office, May 1981), p. 6; and Chase Manhattan Bank, Chase Energy Economics, *The Petroleum Situation*, February 1981, p. 1.

complex energy decisions that U.S. policymakers have had to confront since 1973. Moreover, while Alaskan oil has grown in importance, it represents less than one-quarter of U.S. daily oil imports and less than 5 percent of aggregate primary consumption from all sources of energy. Since petroleum continues to account for approximately 45 percent of U.S. aggregate primary energy consumption, and since imported and potentially unsecure imported oil accounts for some 40 percent of all U.S. petroleum supplies, the United States is still almost as dependent on imported energy as it was in 1973. Thus, even though there have been periodic fluctuations in the price of OPEC oil, many of the underlying problems posed by the events of 1973 still remain. To appreciate their significance we can draw still further observations from the Alaska pipeline decision.

First, although the technology of the pipeline did anticipate many of the potentially adverse environmental costs that otherwise would have gone unchecked, what few observers took into account at the time was that the refining capacity in nearby California was oriented largely to the relatively low-sulfur crude oil then being imported from Indonesia to conform to the state's strict pollution standards. Thus, in order to make use of Alaskan high-sulfur crude, it had to be shipped through the Panama Canal to Gulf and eastern refineries or else face the prospect either of not being consumed or of being exported abroad as a perverse symbol of U.S. energy independence.[32] Since it was decided that the oil would be shipped through the canal to eastern refineries, the pipeline served ultimately as a fundamental lesson in the growing complexity of energy decisions and the need for a coherent energy policy.

Second, the construction of an oil pipeline in a remote region of Alaska pointed to the growing difficulty of increasing domestic energy supplies at relatively constant or falling real prices. As noted in figure 1.2, if the gap between the growth rates of consumption and reserves were to be closed, an increase in the price of oil would be inevitable. To do so, and to reduce somewhat the likelihood of a renewed OPEC embargo, depended partly on the willingness of the United States to increase its own oil price. It also depended on the extent to which an increase in the price of oil would at the same time pose adverse consequences on the domestic rate of inflation, the distribution of income, and the capacity of the economy for sustained economic growth without a recession, none of which had hitherto been significantly affected by the price of energy, since it had been falling mostly in real terms. Thus, not

[32]"Oil Glut Is Created by Alaska Pipeline," *New York Times*, 3 April 1978, p. 1. The complications from the Alaska pipeline decision have been even more complicated than described here. One complication was that Alaska oil tended to drive out of production California oil of comparable quality, thereby leading to a Federal Energy Administration decision to raise the entitlements of California producers ("Coast Oil Producers to Get Aid to Offset Alaska Flow," 19 December 1977, p. D-9). Since this reduced the West Coast demand for Alaskan oil, there were renewed proposals to construct a trans-Canada oil pipeline, which ironically had been one of the original proposals involving the Alaska pipeline decision in the first place ("Deciding on Alaskan Oil Line to Midwest," ibid., 13 January 1978, p. D-1). Then California became the first state to experience Federal Energy Administration-induced gasoline shortages in the spring of 1979 ("How Oil 'Glut' on Coast Became a Shortage," ibid., 6 May 1979, p. 18).

only did the United States lack a coherent energy policy, it did not even have the essential information needed to formulate such a policy.

Third, though increases in the real price of petroleum could assist in reducing the imbalance between its consumption and reserves, the practical question would be, By how much? To answer this question, we would need an indication of the capacity of the economy to substitute alternative sources of energy and to be more technically efficient in the energy that it consumes. Apart from the immediate alternatives on which the economy presently depends—natural gas, coal, and nuclear energy—the substitution possibilities for petroleum depend also on the forms in which these depletable energy resources could be consumed, that is, on the technology and economics of energy resources conversion. Thus, in the near term at least, the question of substitution must encompass not only these conventional fuels but also the extent to which the economy could efficiently produce shale oil, coal liquefaction, coal gasification, or breeder reactor technology. At the same time, it depends on whether these resources would be as competitive as the renewable-based alternatives of solar heatings and cooling, photovoltaic generation of electricity, wind, hydropower, geothermal power, and biomass resources, to name but a few. In sum, to determine to what extent the economy would continue to depend on both OPEC and petroleum energy required the adoption of a comprehensive energy policy. The basic dimensions of such a policy can now be described, for they anticipate the more detailed analysis that is to follow.

A comprehensive energy policy depends on three principal elements: technology, institutions, and economics. None of these elements functions in isolation. What links the institutional structure to technology is economics and the pervasive role of pricing. Each of these factors may be further defined.

The consumption of any energy resource is in its most fundamental sense a conversion of its form. Of the many potential energy resources, some are in forms that are readily compatible with current energy use in the economy, whereas others may require alternative storage and conversion before they can be so used. The conversion of these resources is governed in effect by the laws of thermodynamics, defining as they do the extent to which energy can be used efficiently. Moreover, it is this technical efficiency of energy resource conversion that is a major factor in the determination of economic efficiency and the use of market pricing within the economy. It enters into pricing by its impact on the environment and by the fact that some resources are exhaustible and others are not. Thus, the determination of energy policy requires an understanding of the physical principles that govern all energy conversion and of the associated technologies through which these principles are expressed.

Though energy may be governed by the laws of thermodynamics, it is the pricing of energy forms which will determine the mix and rate of consumption over time. From an economic perspective, an ideal objective of policy would be the provision of a sufficient amount of energy at a price that would enable society to satisfy its traditional concerns, that is, full employment, price stability, rising real per capita incomes, an equitable distribution of income, preservation of the environment, and an economically efficient industry which is at the same time a competitive one. As is obvious from historical experience alone, not all of these concerns may be attainable simultaneously. Indeed, each of them can be significantly affected by particular energy policies. What this implies is that in the determination of economic policy, the pricing of energy resources must be as economically efficient as possible. For this to be so, the markets through which these resources are priced must incorporate several basic qualities now often absent: an economic structure that conforms to competitive pricing criteria, compensatory adjustments for market failure where it arises, and an efficient incorporation of society's rate of time preference for present versus future energy use.

The third element in the determination of energy policy is, of course, the structure of institutions themselves. As is obvious from the examples thus far cited, whether OPEC, an integrated petroleum producer, or a federal or state regulatory agency, it is through a variety of complex and often conflicting sets of institutions that energy decisions are actually made. Indeed, it is these very institutions that determine both present energy use and the extent to which an economy is likely to experience continuing energy crises. The nature of these decisions, and the extent to which they conform to or conflict with technical and economic efficiency criteria in energy use, thus constitutes the basic dimensions of energy policy alternatives.

1.4. SUMMARY

Energy crises involve a sudden shift in the prices and the quantities of energy resources. They can cause widespread economic adversity, as the experience of the 1973 Arab OPEC oil embargo has shown. While each energy crisis may have its immediate political causes, it also points to an underlying economic change. Because energy decisions are increasingly complex, and because an economy depends critically on the availability of energy and its price, the study of energy resources represents an important area of public policy.

Energy policy can be understood best as a particular form of public policy. To understand the scope of energy policy, it is thus important to clarify the meaning of public policy. Although public policy is concerned ultimately with society's basic ethical standards, it is those standards affecting the economy which most directly pertain to energy policy decisions. There are five economic functions of public policy: (1) determination of laws governing economic behavior; (2) maintenance of competition; (3) economic stabilization and growth; (4) determination of an equitable distribution of income; and (5) the reallocation of economic resources. Though their impact on energy has been substantial and not always consistent, it is their reformulation in more rigorous terms that forms the basis of coherent energy policy.

The dimensions of any energy policy are a product of technology, economics, and the institutional structure through which energy decisions are made. The technological basis of energy policy decisions is shaped first and foremost by the laws of thermodynamics and by the technology in which these principles are embodied. Though the conversion of energy derives from these laws, it is the pricing of energy and its determinants that will establish the patterns of energy use in the economy. In the framing of energy policy decisions, it is therefore essential that the pricing of these resources be based on three fundamental criteria: (1) competitively equivalent markets; (2) social rather than private costs and benefits, and (3) an accurate reflection of society's rate of time preference for present versus future energy consumption. Finally, since energy decisions are determined through the institutional structure of society, the framing of appropriate energy policy must at the same time take into account the ways in which these decisions are made and the extent to which they are consistent with the technical and economic efficiency in the production and consumption of energy over time.

SUGGESTED READINGS

Clark, Wilson. *Energy for Survival.* Garden City, N.Y.: Doubleday Anchor Books, 1975.

Doran, C. F. *Myth, Oil, and Politics: Introduction to the Political Economy of Petroleum.* New York: Macmillan Publishing Co., 1977.

Eppen, Gary D., ed. *Energy: The Policy Issues.* Chicago: University of Chicago Press, 1975.

Mancke, Richard B. *The Failure of U.S. Energy Policy.* New York: Columbia University Press, 1974.

Vernon, Raymond, ed. *The Oil Crisis.* New York: W. W. Norton and Co., 1976.

2

ENERGY USE IN PERSPECTIVE

2.1. AN OVERVIEW OF PAST ENERGY USE

Energy crises are nothing new. Since the beginnings of civilization, economic and social progress throughout the world has depended on the advance of technology, and on energy technology in particular. Where change has been absent or slow, as world population growth has continued, it has invariably resulted in energy shortages, and thus in the eruption of energy crises. These crises have passed either by a diminution of population relative to available resources or by technological change. Technological change has manifested itself in the discovery of additional sources of energy, in the discovery of new forms of energy, or in a more efficient use of existing energy resources. This evolutionary pattern may be more clearly seen by looking briefly at the energy basis of civilization over time.

More than one million years ago, Paleolithic society functioned largely in the struggle against daily energy crises. With only rudimentary tools and practically nonexistent storage systems, an individual's biological survival dictated the hunting of animals and the gathering of plants on an almost daily basis. In those times as now, animals received their energy from plants, which in turn received their energy from the sun. Thus, Paleolithic society was critically dependent on solar energy. As we will see, this dependence has continued in a less obvious form down to the present.

Paleolithic society's greatest achievement was a capacity for human survival. Wars and pestilence helped keep population growth in check, though never to the extent that individuals could hope to escape the reality of the daily energy crisis. Indeed, when we think of the caloric energy spent by an individual just to hunt animals and gather food, the net energy balance was even more precarious.

Transcending the daily energy crisis of Paleolithic society came only with fundamental technological change: improved toolmaking, discovery of firemaking, and the advent of agriculture. Sharper axes and arrowheads led directly to greater reliability of tools, to be sure, but they also meant that a smaller amount of caloric energy had to be expended in the acquisition of food. Such improvements were made possible largely by firemaking, which up until then had been used mostly for heating. When considered with cooking, the heating and toolmaking applications of firemaking did not represent extraordinary increases in the wood used as fuel but rather were indicative of a more efficient use of heat.

Neolithic society incorporated these toolmaking and cooking changes and was distinguished from Paleolithic society by the emergence of agriculture. Agriculture was a profound transformation, of course, for it introduced geographic fixity in economic and social organization and thus made possible the kinds of specialization upon which all succeeding patterns of technological and economic advance have been built. Moreover, specialization made possible an ever-increasing sophistication in toolmaking, which led to the production of the many kinds of machines which have come to be taken for granted in contemporary society.

In addition to the energy transferred from the sun to people by plants and animals, energy consumption in Neolithic times consisted mostly of firewood. As in the Paleolithic era, Neolithic toolmaking technology was primitive at best, and there was considerable inefficiency in the use of available energy resources. Yet, toolmaking slowly improved, and with it came the kind of productive efficiency that was essential to the emergence of civilization. Since advances in the use of the sun's energy were particularly evident in the ancient civilizations of the Nile, Tigris and Euphrates, and Indus rivers, we can use examples from that period to illustrate the contemporary energy basis of society.

One change that accompanied the rise of ancient river civilizations was the discovery of metals. There is much evidence of the use of copper, then bronze (copper and tin), and then iron in the production of tools.[1] These metals made possible a greater and more accurate level of activity in agricultural production and did much to refine architectural technology. In agriculture, for example, the use of metals enabled farmers to make simple but durable plows, as is illustrated in many Egyptian hieroglyphs. Plow technology emerged from the initial application of metal to weapons and digging sticks. Digging sticks were then modified and adapted to oxen by use of elementary harnesses. This transitional process may still be seen in some countries today.[2]

The architecture of ancient civilizations provides ample evidence of increasing sophistication in tools, as well as growth in energy consumption. Durability of metals and the evolution of mathematical knowledge are clearly reflected in the precision with which the Great Pyramid of Cheops was constructed in Giza. Yet the Egyptians were still unable to harness the sun's

[1]For a more detailed discussion of the evolution of metal use, see Robert Maddin, James D. Muhly, and Tamara S. Wheeler, "How the Iron Age Began," *Scientific American* 237 (October 1977):122–31. This article points out the relative scarcity of copper and tin as a principal reason for the evolution of iron technology.

[2]This hierarchy could be considered a progressive one only under particular technological circumstances. It would be inapplicable, obviously, to crops such as rice or coffee. A good description of the transition from hoe to plow technology is found in Peter M. Weil, "The Introduction of the Ox Plow in Central Gambia," in *African Food Production Systems*, ed. P.F.M. McLoughlin (Baltimore: Johns Hopkins Press, 1970), pp. 230–63.

energy in ways that could mechanically expand the supply of usable energy in an efficient way. As a result, the Great Pyramid, like the Greek and Roman monuments that followed, was built with slave labor. The ancient Greek historian Herodotus estimated that the Great Pyramid alone took one hundred thousand men working three quarters of a year for twenty years to complete its construction, an awesome measure even by today's standards.[3]

Population continued to grow in ancient Egypt, interrupted occasionally by warfare and disease. The absence of any further dramatic changes in energy or tool technology in those times meant that forests were becoming increasingly denuded to satisfy fuel-consumption requirements, which in turn increased pressures on the use of slave labor. Since wood energy crises were becoming more and more aggravated, Egyptian frontiers began to expand southward, up the Nile, but as they did so, Egyptian rulers were less and less able to retain access to the Mediterranean, which had been partly responsible for the early success of Egyptian settlements. Though many factors contributed to the decline of ancient Egypt, few historians have given extensive consideration to the shortage of energy.

Neither civilization nor energy use ended with the collapse of ancient Egypt. Egyptian power was replaced in Africa by the kindgom of Meroë, then by Ethiopia and the successor states of the western savannah, while its Greek and Roman successors were emerging in the Mediterranean.[4] Since Greek and Roman civilization were both as dependent on slavery as ancient Egypt had been, they, too, eventually succumbed to external forces, but not before several technical advances critical to their longevity and to energy utilization had been made.

One of these was the wheel. In use since early Egyptian civilization, it was being applied to more and more complex tasks than the building of pyramids, chariot driving, and wine pressing. For example, beginning around 700 B.C., the pulley was developed to improve the mechanical efficiency in the moving of objects. Second, the Greek Archimedes, who is credited with development of the screw, soon made possible the use of screw presses. Despite these improvements, such machines still depended essentially on human, animal, or waterflow energy, which in those days as now was very much tied to the ability to use the sun's energy efficiently.

Advances in Greek energy technology also extended to wind power and to direct use of the sun. The Egyptians had known about sailing, as had the neighboring Phoenicians, but the Greeks made an enormous expansion in the use of sail power, as both their far-flung settlements and trading wealth have shown. Much of this success was due to improvements in nautical technology, as Greek ship design gradually began to reflect knowledge of the principles of hydrodynamics, first advanced by Archimedes.

[3]Herodotus, *The Histories*, bk. 2, trans. Aubrey de Sélincourt (Baltimore: Penguin Books, 1960), p. 151.

[4]A popular account of the decline of Egyptian civilization and of the rise of Meroë and the West African states of Ghana, Mali, and Songhaï is found in Basil Davidson, *The Lost Cities of Africa* (Boston: Atlantic-Little Brown, 1959), esp. chaps. 1-4.

Greek applications of direct solar energy extended to housing design as well as to war. The historian Xenophon noted in 400 B.C. that houses were being designed in such a way that the sun's heat would be minimized in summer and maximized in winter, mostly by the use of high porticoes on the south side. He also pointed out that such houses used low northern walls, to minimize the impact of winter winds.[5]

Information on Greek use of sunlight for warfare is only partly substantiated by historical accounts. The first reference comes from the Greek historian Galen, in the second century A.D. In his *De Temperamentis* he tells of Greek forces having used solar reflecting mirrors to set fire to a Roman fleet besieging Syracuse in 212 B.C.[6] The validity of this account is somewhat questionable, since it does not appear in the contemporary writings of either the Roman historian Livy or the Greek historian Plutarch.

One final development in ancient Greek energy technology occurred in Alexandria, Egypt, in the first century A.D. Hero, a Hellenistic inventor, assembled an "aeolipile," or sphere of Aeolus, a perforated cylinder that moved when steam heat was placed inside. It was used only as a toy by Hero and his contemporaries, but the principles of the steam engine were later refined by the Englishman Sir Isaac Newton in the seventeenth century, and steam became a principle form of energy in the early phases of the industrial revolution.

Taken together, the classical civilizations of Greece and Rome were still largely dependent on energy resources from the sun: for the wood they burned as fuel, for the crops they harvested for food, and for the winds used to move their ships.[7] Though they both made advances in household energy efficiency beyond what had existed along the Nile, as well as in the design of ships and machines, all of the technology was still rudimentary by current standards. Moreover, for the overwhelming number of routine tasks that were required during these times, technological change did not remove the slave basis of society. For reasons still debated by historians, steam power and concentrated sunlight never were applied to practical tasks. Had they been, perhaps these civilizations could have abolished slavery and still made the unusual achievements that they did. Instead, Rome first absorbed Greece and then took possession of the whole of the Mediterranean, after which it gradually fell to the weight of succeeding invasions from the north and, eventually, of the Arab conquests of the south during the seventh and eighth centuries.

If the Middle Ages in Europe have any meaning for energy, it is that ad-

[5]Xenophon's description is quoted in Marion J. Simon, *Your Solar House* (New York: Simon and Schuster, 1947), p. 15.

[6]See Aden Baker Meinel and Marjorie Pettit Meinel, *Power for the People* (Tucson: privately printed, 1970), p. 6.

[7]Despite impressive engineering feats in the construction of roads and aqueducts to serve elegant Roman cities, the Roman penchant for administrative efficiency did not overcome the still precarious balance of resources and population, as periodic accounts of famines attest. The ancient Roman historian Livy described two such incidents in his *Early History of Rome*, trans. Aubrey de Sélincourt (Baltimore: Penguin Books, 1961), pp. 173, 311. A. E. E. McKenzie, a modern historian, notes the absence of scientific genius among the ancient Romans, which may explain why Greek advances in technology often remained stillborn (see his *The Major Achievements of Science* [New York: Simon and Schuster Touchstone Books, 1973], p. 8).

vances in practical energy technology were almost nonexistent. As in Africa, Asia, and America, the Middle Ages in Europe were characterized by an inward, self-reliant pattern of economic and social organization, unlike the pattern in the classical civilizations of the Mediterranean or the emerging African kingdoms of Ghana, Mali, and Songhay. Under feudalism, European communities did experience a gradual increase in the number of water wheels, but serfs carried on many of the tasks that slaves formerly had performed, though on a much smaller scale, since living standards also had deteriorated. In fact, not until the revival of commercial activity and the growth of towns in the twelfth century did Mediterranean sail transport again reach the heights it had once enjoyed. Even after the twelfth century, right up through the seventeenth century, energy technology remained relatively unchanged, despite the many scientific discoveries that took place during the Renaissance.[8] Thus, as population once again began to increase in significant numbers, Europe soon faced the recurrent spectacle of energy shortages.

Fragmentary evidence does exist on the state of energy technology during the Middle Ages.[9] In 1005, Eilmer, an Anglo-Saxon Benedictine monk, is reported to have flown a glider six hundred feed from a tower of Malmesbury Abbey in England. Such achievement indicated a slow revival of interest in wind power, which Leonardo da Vinci later explored in detail during the Italian Renaissance of the sixteenth century. Elsewhere, in China, bamboo pipes are reported to have been used to tap natural gas for use in porcelain baking in 1013. Windmills began to appear in northern Europe in the twelfth century, by 1105 in France and by 1185 in Yorkshire, England, and expanded considerably in Spain, Portugal, and Holland during the fifteenth and sixteenth centuries. Cistercian monks in Milan are reported to have used city garbage and sewer water for fertilizer in 1150, anticipating modern recycling techniques by several centuries. Finally, coal became an increasing source of fuel in England by the late thirteenth and early fourteenth centuries. Pollution became so severe that King Edward I made it a capital offense to burn coal in the city of London.

One key factor prevented a more widespread development of energy technology from the Middle Ages up to the sixteenth century: the stagnation of scientific inquiry that had occurred since the fall of Rome. The Renaissance did much to revive interest in science, to be sure, but it was not until the seventeenth century that a fruitful union of practical applications and theory emerged, signaled first by the writings of such individuals as Leonardo da Vinci (1472–1519) and Copernicus (1473–1543). When we look at the contributions of Galileo (1564–1642), Johann Kepler (1571–1630), Francis Bacon

[8]In a recent work, Fernand Braudel describes how at one point in sixteenth-century Cairo the shortage of wood led to increasing dependence on scrub and animal dung, and how in November 1512 officers' kitchens ceased to function for lack of fuel (see his *The Mediterranean and the Mediterranean World in the Age of Philip II*, vol. 1 [New York: Harper and Row, 1972], p. 174). Similar conditions have been found more recently in the highland plateaux of Ethiopia and in India, Afghanistan, and Chad.

[9]A good chronology of the history of energy technology has been compiled and reported in Earl Cook, *Man, Energy, Society* (San Francisco: W. H. Freeman and Co., 1976), pp. 457–63.

(1561–1626), and Isaac Newton (1642–1727), to name but a few, it is clear that science was beginning to unfold many of the mysteries of the universe. Their discoveries were essential to the technological progress that followed.

In Europe as elsewhere, the emergence of modern science did not yet provide any change in the periodic cycle of energy crises. For England at least, traditional wood, water, and animal sources of energy could not keep pace with the growth of population and the consumption of natural resources. As a result, a serious energy crisis erupted around 1600.[10] It ended only when England shifted its energy base to coal, a profound transformation which is worth noting in brief detail.

England's geographic discoveries in Elizabethan times did much to stimulate population growth. Between 1534 and 1600, population increased by as much as 150 percent. Deforestation for fuel became so serious that shipbuilding, housing, and other industries were becoming endangered. Coal had been burned as early as in Roman times, but not until England began to experience such a wood energy shortage did coal become the predominant source of energy.

Apart from the relative scarcity of wood, several factors explain why coal was not used more abundantly until the sixteenth century. Chief among them was the smoke produced by coal burning. Second, coal had to be mined from the ground, which was physically more difficult than deforestation, since it required digging tunnels where air circulated poorly and flooding was commonplace. Third, coal could not be ignited as readily as wood and required a preparatory kindling.

These technological difficulties were overcome over the next two centuries, and in the process they paved the way for the industrial revolution. One initial step was the use of natural gas to ignite coal and to maintain high temperatures for more complete burning. Since some fumes were emitted even with this change, reverberating furnaces were introduced to reflect as much heat as possible while allowing for ventilation through chimneys. Another step was the processing of coke, which was used in the smelting of iron, copper, and tin. Once resmelting was added, iron ore production began to match the quality previously attained with the use of charcoal in preceding centuries. Finally, coal was applied to the generation of steam power, a new development pioneered by Thomas Newcomen and James Watt in England in the eighteenth century. Taken together, these modifications of coal technology helped to propel the English economy through its massive shift from an agrarian economy to an industrial one, which by the early nineteenth century was unparalleled in the world.

Mining of coal soon led to the discovery of natural gas and petroleum. Since geological transformations in the evolution of the earth produced all three of these fossil resources, it was only natural that gas and petroleum would be extracted from coal by a chemical process. The first discovery of

[10]John U. Nef, "An Early Energy Crisis and Its Consequences," *Scientific American* 237 (October 1977):141–51.

this sort came in 1688 when gas was distilled from coal, followed in 1694 with the extraction of oil from shale and cannel coal. Yet it was over one hundred years before any practical applications emerged. Beginning in 1792, coal gas was first used in lighting, and in 1815 commercial oil from shale retorting started in New Brunswick. Despite these discoveries, however, coal continued to be used primarily in the heating of homes and factories, as an industrial fuel for the production of goods, and as a fuel for steam power.

Knowledge of steam power has existed at least since the time of Hero of Alexandria. Yet, it was only in England, with the shift of coal and the scientific discoveries of the seventeenth century, that steam was considered practical for commercial use. Since steam is still an important form of energy, some of the principal events in its transformation to mechanical processes are also worth noting here.

Steam is generated by high-temperature evaporation of water. When induced in a contained space, it results in increased pressure from the agitation of molecules. It is not an energy resource per se, but rather a form of energy which is useful for the operation of machines. With the exception of isolated geothermal deposits in the earth's crust, steam heat has thus far been generated in significant amounts only by using depletable energy resources such as wood, coal, natural gas, petroleum, or nuclear energy.

The harnessing of steam to machines for practical purposes was first demonstrated by a water pump designed in 1698 by Thomas Savery of England. Savery's pump was grossly inefficient by modern standards, producing only approximately 1 percent of useful energy for each unit it consumed in the generation of steam.

Savery's pump was improved upon in 1705 by another Englishman, Thomas Newcomen. Newcomen's engine had about 2.5 percent efficiency. By means of a reciprocating-movement design, steam for the chamber passed into the piston cylinder, where it was then condensed by the spraying of cool water. The cool water helped to create a vacuum, which pulled the piston head forward and thereby moved the steam chamber back to the open position again.

Newcomen's engine became very successful in the first part of the eighteenth century. It was markedly superior to Savery's, and it satisfied the rapidly growing need for water pumps which the English shift to coal production had engendered. It was only surpassed by the modified engine of James Watt around 1769.

Watt's steam engine carried three improvements over the Newcomen engine. First, it used a double-injection piston. By having steam push the cylinder first inward and then outward in a rotating stroke, Watt's engine relieved some of the dependence on the water-condensing mechanism that had so limited the usefulness of the Newcomen engine. Second, a flyball governor attached to the drive shaft joint moderated the flow of steam into the piston openings. Third, a separate condenser chamber, for pressure adjustments, helped to moderate the temperature variation in the main cylinder. Taken together, the improvements in the Watt engine resulted in an efficiency twice that of Newcomen's.

Other modifications followed. In 1781, another Englishman, Jonathan Hornblower, developed the compound engine. This engine allowed rejected steam to pass into another cylinder in order to capture still more of the usable energy. Larger boilers and pistons then emerged, with growing applications to coal mining, textile mills, seagoing ships, and the development of railroads taking place in England, France, and the United States. Eventually, steam engines used in locomotives attained efficiencies as high as 23 percent, and until the 1950s many were still found in everyday use on spur lines in the United States.

Despite its relative inefficiency, steam power was a key to the industrial revolution, first in the powering of machines and later in the production of electricity. Like steam, electricity was found in nature. As early as 600 B.C. there was a curiosity about the properties of electricity, and the Greek philosopher Thales is reported to have produced static electricity by rubbing amber. He may well have experienced the same degree of amusement that today befalls a child who rubs his or her clothing before touching a metal door handle in dry winter air. Yet, as was the case with steam and Hero's aeolipile, electricity was to remain a mystery until the rise of science in the seventeenth and eighteenth centuries.

Electrical power derives from the release of charges. In nature, for example, an electrical storm occurs when disturbances in the atmosphere produce a charge of electrons which are drawn to another point with an opposite charge, a fact not lost on Benjamin Franklin and his contemporaries. In his famous kite-flying experiments in 1747 Franklin discovered the existence of these positive and negative forces and made a practical adaptation in the invention of the lightning rod, for fire protection in buildings. Yet, for electricity to be useful and reliable in machines, several additional needs had to be met, including the means for storage and current flows.

Induced electrical storage was first developed by Pieter von Musschenbrook, with the invention of the Leyden jar in 1745. The next development came in 1800, with Volta's construction of a galvanic cell which combined the storage principle of the Leyden jar with polarization charges which Franklin had discovered. Drawing on principles of magnetism that had been known since the twelfth century, the Englishman Michael Faraday found a way to generate electric current by magnetic induction in 1831. In the same year, Joseph Henry invented the first electric motor. Telegraphy, the telephone, refrigeration, electrolysis of metals, rail and road transport vehicles, radio and television, and numerous other inventions all flowed directly from these developments and provided further acceleration of the industrial revolution.

For all of the impact that electricity has had on society, it should be remembered that its production depends essentially on other energy resources. Today, for example, one method of producing electricity is by hydropower. Since such electricity production is water-based, it ultimately depends on the evaporative and condensation powers of the sun's rays in relation to the earth. Another method of generating electricity is by fossil fuel resources. Thomas Edison invented the first steam generator for producing electricity in New York with the opening of the Pearl Street power plant in 1882. A third and more recent method of generating electricity is the use of nuclear reactors to generate steam, which in turn moves the turbines that produce electricity. Regardless of the method, electricity, like steam, represents energy transformed, and as we will see, its usefulness is limited partly by the technical efficiency of energy conversion.

The next phase in the evolution of energy technology came with the adaptation of petroleum to the industrial revolution. More than any resource thus far described, petroleum has enabled the United States and other developed economies to function as high-energy societies. In simple terms, this means that in the last hundred years there has been an increase in total and per capita energy consumption unparalleled in human history. As noted in chapter 1, today this society is increasingly faced with the prospect of recurring energy crises, and thus what has been thought of as an endless industrial revolution may be reaching a plateau. Before this question is taken up in subsequent chapters, let us first look at the steps involved in the integration of petroleum into the industrial revolution.

Petroleum has been a known resource since the ancient Sumerians mined asphalt in 3,000 B.C. Until the Renaissance, it was thought of mostly as a building material or as having occasional medicinal applications. With the scientific discoveries of the seventeenth century, it began to be thought of differently. An oil well is reported to have been dug in Italy in the 1600s, and the kerosene used for lighting. Oil was also derived from retorting shale and cannel coal in England, as has been noted. Here, too, not much thought was given to its commercial applicability, for at that time too little was known about chemistry to yield any advantage.

Practical application of petroleum came with expanding research in fossil fuels during the nineteenth century. It received considerable stimulation following Edwin Drake's discovery of significant oil deposits at Titusville, Pennsylvania, in 1859. Improved refining techniques soon enabled the separation of higher- from lower-grade oil, so that grease, kerosene, gasoline, and other petroleum derivatives could be extracted for various uses.

Nothing accelerated the use of petroleum more than the development of the internal combustion engine. Down to the present day, this machine has remained the primary means of consuming petroleum energy; for that reason its evolution should be described in broad detail.

An internal combustion engine differs from its chief mechanical competitor, the steam engine, in that fuel is burned directly in the cylinder. The combustion of fuel creates the pressure for movement of the piston in a cylinder. The first practical internal combustion engine was built by the Frenchman Etienne Lenoir in 1860. Unlike its primary successors, the Lenoir engine operated by the combustion of illuminating gas rather than liquid fuel, a technological development which continues to be of interest even today.

The prototype of the gasoline engine came with the model built by the German inventors Otto and Langen in 1867. Crude by later standards, it nevertheless represented an important phase in the emergence of the first four-cycle engine, which Otto brought out in 1876. Though using a four-cycle engine, Otto's motor could not attain high speeds, mostly because of its poor compression ratio. The next phase—Gottlieb Daimler's high-speed gasoline engine of 1883—therefore was not surprising. Following that was the production of the gasoline automobile, first introduced by Charles Duryea in Springfield, Massachusetts, in 1892.

One modification of the internal combustion engine was introduced by the German inventor Rudolf Diesel, in 1894, and it now bears his name. Diesel engines do not rely on spark plugs for ignition and use lower-grade fuel than gasoline. Though Diesel had high hopes for the success of his engine, until now it has been used mostly in trucks and in only a few European and American automobiles.

At the beginning of the twentieth century, gasoline engines and to a much lesser extent diesel engines, faced two principal competitors: horse power and steam power. With the refinement of internal combustion technology, however, horses, and to a lesser extent steam, lost ground in primary energy-using sectors such as transportation. This shift was accelerated by several subsequent developments, notably rising urbanization and the introduction of mass assembly techniques by Henry Ford, which greatly lowered the retail price of automobiles.

The development of natural gas technology paralleled the rise of petroleum. The reason for its parallel development was that natural gas deposits often were found in the same geological seams as petroleum. While natural gas had been known and used as early as the eleventh century in China, only when the industrial revolution took place did its economic viability emerge. As early as 1818, for example, London Bridge was lighted by gas. By 1821 gas lamps were used in Baltimore, and their use rapidly spread to New York, Boston, and other American cities. Applications of natural gas to household heating and cooking, to industrial heating and manufacturing, and to a lesser extent to transportation have continued down to the present day. Yet, as the consumption of natural gas has expanded, so too has the knowledge that natural gas, like petroleum, is an exhaustible resource, as the shortage in the United States in the winter of 1977 served to note.

One final development in the evolution of energy use has been the emergence of nuclear power. Several steps signaled the potential of nuclear energy as a practical resource. First was the quantum theory of physics, advanced by the German physicist Max Planck in 1900. Planck's theory stated that all forms of radiant energy are emitted in discrete, indivisible units, or quanta, and that the energy of each unit is proportional to the frequency of the radiation. In simple terms, energy is atomistic in nature and varies only in multiples of this elementary unit, the quantum.

A second development was the mass-energy equation, $E = mc^2$, which the German physicist Albert Einstein used as part of his theory of relativity in 1905. In brief, the equation states that energy may be measured as the mass times the square of the speed of light. Planck had established that energy could be measured in terms of basic units, but it was Einstein's theory that revolutionized traditional perceptions of both energy and physics, as succeeding developments have proved.

Ultimately, the proof of Einstein's equation came with the development of controlled nuclear reactions. The first successful one occurred at the University of Chicago under the direction of Dr. Enrico Fermi on 2 December 1942. Three years later, one application of this new form of energy became clear with the United States' bombing of the Japanese cities of Nagasaki and Hiroshima. Since that time, the peaceful uses of nuclear power, mostly for production of electricity, have been very much entwined with widespread controversy over its destructive potential.[11] As a result, nuclear energy in the United States and elsewhere has not become the dominant form of energy generation that it originally was predicted to become.

In this brief overview of the evolution of energy technology, several generalizations emerge. First, until the industrial revolution, energy consumption per capita increased almost imperceptibly. Until that time, energy use was dependent largely on human, animal, water, and wood resources, and technological change in energy barely kept pace with population growth. Energy crises therefore were not uncommon experiences, causing geographic shifts in the economic bases of societies, economic instability, and not infrequently, the decline of particular civilizations. These crises were resolved only by a restoration of the balance between energy resources and population.

Second, with the rise of modern science in the seventeenth century, the evolution of machines made possible the harnessing of energy in such a way that significant increases in usable energy relative to population became attainable. The industrial revolution translated the growing stream of inventions to practical applications, thereby giving rise to these energy changes.

Finally, unlike earlier technological advances, the industrial revolution and modern economic growth have been sustained essentially by the production and consumption of depletable energy resources. This transformation has created the conditions for an inevitable increase in the real price of these resources. Not surprisingly, therefore, only with the reemergence of energy crises in modern times has there been a renewed appreciation of the energy problem in history.

2.2. ENERGY AND ECONOMIC GROWTH

Thus far, the evolution of energy consumption has been viewed essentially from a technological perspective. Yet to appreciate the significance of energy, the development of energy resources must also be examined in its economic context. By tracing the relationship of energy production, consumption, and technology to the structure of the economy, we can understand more clearly the linkages between energy and the economy.

[11]A critical popular account is McKinley C. Olson, *Unacceptable Risk: The Nuclear Power Controversy* (New York: Bantam Books, 1976). The issue of nuclear power is taken up in detail in chapters 6 and 12 of this volume.

Table 2.1. U.S. Gross Energy Consumption by Type, 1850-1980
(in quadrillion Btu's)

	Gross Energy Consumption							
Year	Coal	Petroleum[a]	Natural Gas	Nuclear	Hydro-power	Other[b]	Total	Per Capita[c]
1850	0.22	—	—	—	—	2.1	2.31	101
1860	0.52	—	—	—	—	2.6	3.12	97
1870	1.05	—	—	—	—	2.9	3.95	99
1880	2.05	0.1	—	—	—	2.9	4.95	100
1890	4.06	0.2	0.3	—	—	2.5	7.06	110
1900	6.84	0.2	0.3	—	0.3	2.0	9.64	128
1910	12.71	1.0	0.5	—	0.5	1.8	16.51	178
1920	15.50	2.6	0.8	—	0.8	1.6	21.30	186
1930	13.64	5.4	2.0	—	0.8	1.5	23.34	181
1940	12.54	7.5	2.7	—	0.9	1.4	25.04	181
1950	12.91	13.5	6.2	—	1.4	1.2	35.21	223
1960	10.10	20.1	12.7	—	1.7	0.8	45.40	247
1970	12.70	29.5	21.8	0.2	2.7	0.6	67.50	327
1971	12.00	30.6	22.5	0.4	2.9	0.4	68.80	330
1972	12.40	33.0	22.7	0.6	2.9	0.1	71.70	343
1973	13.30	34.9	22.5	0.9	3.0	0.1	74.70	355
1974	12.94	33.5	21.7	1.3	3.3	0.1	72.84	344
1975	12.83	32.7	19.9	1.9	3.2	0.1	70.63	331
1976	13.73	35.2	20.4	2.1	3.1	0.1	74.63	344
1977	13.99	37.2	19.9	2.7	2.5	0.1	76.39	350
1978	13.98	37.9	20.0	2.9	3.2	0.1	78.08	356
1979	15.15	37.0	19.9	2.8	3.2	0.1	78.15	353
1980	15.60	34.2	20.5	2.7	3.1	0.1	76.20	342

Sources: U.S. Department of Energy, Energy Information Administration, *Monthly Energy Review* (Washington, D.C.: U.S. Government Printing Office, May 1981); U.S. Department of the Interior, *Energy Perspectives* (Washington, D.C.: U.S. Government Printing Office, February 1975); idem, *Energy Perspectives 2* (Washington, D.C.: U.S. Government Printing Office, June 1976); U.S. Department of the Interior, Bureau of Mines, *Minerals Yearbook, 1977* (Washington, D.C.: U.S. Government Printing Office, 1977).

[a]Includes natural gas liquids
[b]Includes wood, geothermal, and waste energy gėneration
[c]Expressed in millions of British Thermal Units (MBtu's)

A first step in linking the evolution of energy to the economy is to compare the size distribution of energy resources over time to the pattern of economic growth. Rather than reconstruct a profile covering time since the beginning of civilization, we can begin in the period dating from the middle of the last century, for it was at that time, in the United States at least, that statistics on energy and the economy first began to be collected in a systematic fashion.[12] Table 2.1 lists U.S. consumption of energy by type for the period 1850–1980. Before we pass to a more detailed discussion of these data, a few clarifications should first be made. First, all energy consumption in table 2.1 has been derived by taking the physical consumption of various energy resources

[12]An excellent historical survey is Sam H. Schurr and Bruce C. Netschert, *Energy in the American Economy, 1850–1975* (Baltimore: Johns Hopkins Press for Resources for the Future, 1960).

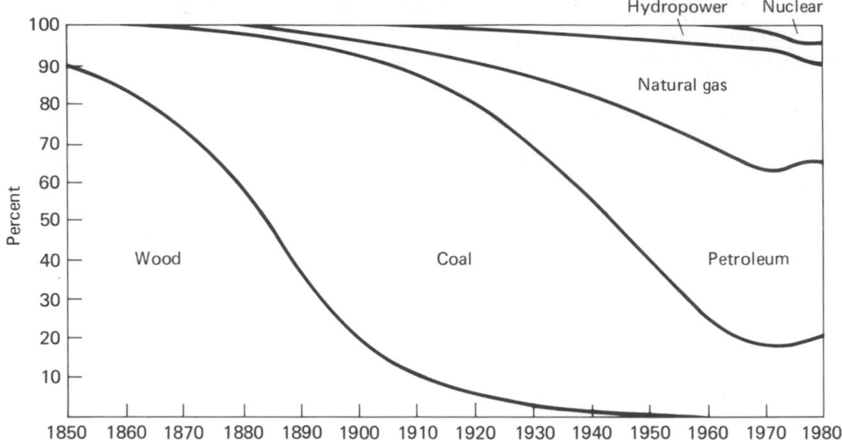

Figure 2.1. Distribution of U.S. Gross Energy Consumption by Type of Resource, 1850–1980. Data from Schurr and Netschert, *Energy in the American Economy*; and Department of Energy, Energy Information Administration, *Monthly Energy Review*, May 1981.

and standardizing their energy content, listed here in quadrillion Btu's.[13] Second, all consumption is based on gross units. Thus, gross consumption includes primary energy resource consumption, as well as the converted forms of steam and electricity, whose production depends on use of these resources. Third, gross energy consumption gives little notion of the technical efficiency of energy production, a matter that will be taken up in following chapters.

Two basic conclusions can be drawn from the data in table 2.1. One is that during the period 1850–1980 the United States experienced a large increase in its consumption of gross energy, on the order of just under 3 percent per year. This annual rate of increase, it should also be noted, generally exceeded the rate of growth of population by approximately 50 percent, such that gross energy consumption per capita was also on the rise, a not surprising phenomenon in light of the rapid industrialization taking place during this period. A second conclusion is that as gross energy consumption was increasing over the period, there was a fundamental shift in the types of energy resources being used. One useful way of understanding the significance of these changes is to show the shifts over time in the size distribution of the absolute amounts of energy by type of resource (see figure 2.1). As figure 2.1 shows, gross energy consumption was based initially on wood, then coal, then petroleum, then natural gas, and finally, in recent years, on a small but growing use of nuclear energy.

Despite these changes in the composition of U.S. energy consumption, not until the last twenty-five years did an energy crisis appear possible. The reasons for the absence of such a possibility lay in the fact that discoveries of new

[13]A *quad*, as noted in chapter 1, is 10^{15} Btu's.

energy resources continued to at least keep pace with increases in consumption. Moreover, the kind of technological change taking place during the industrial revolution was compatible with these discoveries such that the shift from wood to coal to petroleum and natural gas occurred almost without interruption in the growth of aggregate energy consumption.

If the United States did not face the prospect of an energy crisis until recently, an explanation is still needed to understand the shifts in the composition of energy resource use over the past century. The movement from wood to coal was based largely on the growth of population in the eastern part of the country, combined with increases in energy demand from the industrialization that was taking place. As land was settled, wood became relatively scarce, though not as scarce as it had become in England during the seventeenth century. In any case, since coal was plentiful in the Appalachian region, the eastern part of the country moved rapidly to a coal base, while the West and the South shifted more gradually.

The shift from coal to petroleum and natural gas was due mostly to the evolving pattern of industrialization rather than to any shortage of coal. For example, although industry was still able to use coal about as easily as petroleum or natural gas, households and transportation were increasingly oriented toward petroleum and natural gas, particularly for automobile and truck movement, household heating, and cooking. Thus, in this particular shift, the explanation lies in changes in the composition of final demand rather than in any technical conditions of production.

Once the economy had shifted to petroleum and natural gas, however, the crisis conditions discussed in chapter 1 soon began to emerge. There was some awareness of this possibility, though, and it was mostly in response to the growing dependence on petroleum and natural gas that nuclear energy was being promoted in the post–World War II era. Yet nuclear energy has been plagued with strategic and environmental controversy ever since the first commercial reactors were introduced, and for this reason it has not yet played the kind of role that many originally had envisioned.

Changes in the composition of the consumption of U.S. energy resources can also be traced to their end uses in the economy. Data on the distribution of energy resource consumption among the household and commercial, industrial, and transportation sectors of the economy during the period 1947–80 are shown in table 2.2. Since electricity is produced by energy resources, it is shown twice in the table, first as a form of energy consumption among the three end-use sectors of the economy, second to identify the energy resources used in its own production.

For the three energy-using sectors of the economy, there are variations in the transformation from the coal energy base to the petroleum and natural gas energy base. In the household and commercial sector, coal was the base for almost half of the net energy consumed in 1947, but it dropped most in relative terms, to 2 percent by 1975. Virtually all coal consumed in this sector has been used for space heating. Yet, while petroleum consumption expanded substantially in absolute terms, its relative share did not absorb much of the

Table 2.2. Sector Distribution of U.S. Energy Consumption, 1947–80

Sector	1947	1955	1960	1965	1970	1975	1976	1978	1980
				By Resource with Electricity Undistributed					
Household and commercial									
Petroleum	0.31	0.42	0.43	0.41	0.38	0.34	0.37	0.34	0.26
Coal	0.47	0.19	0.09	0.05	0.03	0.02	0.01	0.01	0.01
Natural gas	0.16	0.30	0.37	0.40	0.42	0.43	0.42	0.42	0.46
Electric[a]	0.05	0.09	0.11	0.14	0.18	0.22	0.20	0.22	0.26
Total	1.00	1.00	1.00	1.00	1.00	1.00	1.00	1.00	1.00
Amount[b]	7.17	9.45	11.42	13.79	16.99	17.27	18.35	18.24	16.52
Industry									
Petroleum	0.19	0.23	0.23	0.22	0.23	0.26	0.30	0.34	0.38
Coal	0.55	0.38	0.30	0.29	0.22	0.19	0.17	0.15	0.14
Natural gas	0.23	0.32	0.40	0.41	0.45	0.42	0.41	0.39	0.36
Electric[a]	0.04	0.07	0.08	0.09	0.10	0.12	0.12	0.12	0.12
Total	1.00	1.00	1.00	1.00	1.00	1.00	1.00	1.00	1.00
Amount[b]	13.30	15.10	16.00	18.80	22.70	22.10	21.73	22.74	23.42
Transportation									
Petroleum	0.65	0.92	0.96	0.96	0.95	0.96	0.96	0.97	0.97
Coal	0.34	0.05	—	—	—	—	—	—	—
Natural gas	—	0.03	0.03	0.04	0.05	0.03	0.03	0.03	0.03
Electric[a]	—	—	—	—	—	—	—	—	—
Total	1.00	1.00	1.00	1.00	1.00	1.00	1.00	1.00	1.00
Amount[b]	8.82	9.84	10.84	12.74	16.37	18.35	19.29	20.59	18.60
Electricity									
Petroleum	0.11	0.08	0.07	0.07	0.13	0.16	0.16	0.16	0.12
Coal	0.49	0.53	0.51	0.53	0.45	0.44	0.45	0.43	0.49
Natural gas	0.09	0.18	0.22	0.22	0.25	0.16	0.15	0.14	0.15
Hydropower[c]	0.31	0.21	0.20	0.19	0.16	0.16	0.14	0.14	0.13
Nuclear	—	—	—	—	0.01	0.08	0.10	0.13	0.11
Total	1.00	1.00	1.00	1.00	1.00	1.00	1.00	1.00	1.00
Amount[b]	4.26	6.60	8.26	11.08	16.24	20.08	21.45	23.42	24.81
				By End-Use Sector with Electricity Distributed					
Household and Commercial	0.28	0.30	0.33	0.34	0.36	0.37	0.37	0.36	0.36
Industry	0.45	0.44	0.42	0.42	0.39	0.37	0.37	0.38	0.40
Transportation	0.28	0.26	0.25	0.25	0.26	0.26	0.26	0.26	0.24
Total	1.00	1.00	1.00	1.00	1.00	1.00	1.00	1.00	1.00
Amount[b]	33.00	40.80	45.40	52.99	67.50	70.63	74.63	78.06	76.20

Sources: Computed from data in U.S. Department of Energy, Energy Information Administration, *Monthly Energy Review* (Washington, D.C.: U.S. Government Printing Office, May 1981), and in U.S. Department of the Interior, *Energy Perspectives 2* (Washington, D.C.: U.S. Government Printing Office, June 1976).

[a]Based on delivered rather than source electricity consumption

[b]In quadrillion (10^{15}) Btu's

[c]Includes net imports of electricity and electricity generation based on wood and waste resources

declining emphasis on coal. The reason for the apparent stability in the share of petroleum is that natural gas and electricity absorbed almost completely the shift from coal in the postwar period. In relative terms alone, natural gas's share of net energy increased by 150 percent, while electricity's share increased by 340 percent. Since absolute consumption in this sector more than doubled in the period 1947–75, the absolute consumption of natural gas and electricity expanded by even faster rates than did their shares.

One reason for the dramatic shift from coal to natural gas and electricity in the household and commercial sector was the pattern of construction in the postwar years. Housing was severely curtailed during World War II, and every effort was made to be self-sufficient in energy resources. In the postwar economic boom, however, there was much less concern for energy self-sufficiency. Since natural gas and electricity were then both cheaper and easier to use than coal, the growth of suburbia and commercial sprawl between cities eliminated almost completely any new demand for coal.

In industry, the shift from coal to petroleum and nataural gas was substantial, though less dramatic than in the household and commercial sector. Industrial production was closely wed to long-term capital investments, so that a shift from coal was not easily undertaken in the space of a decade or two. In the absence of accelerated depreciation allowances for resource conversion, there was not as much incentive to switch from coal. In fact, the growth of suburbs, while it resulted in a more energy-intensive lifestyle than had existed in the cities, did much to forestall some of the reaction to the adverse environmental impact of continued use of coal in heavily industrialized areas such as the northeastern United States. By the 1970s, however, suburban growth began to slow in many areas, partly because of difficulties in commuting from home to job. This change brought renewed concern over environmental pollution. Protective legislation was enacted soon thereafter.

There is one other explanation for the industrial sector's gradual shift from coal in the postwar era. Unlike the household and commercial sector, industry underwent a considerable expansion of capacity during World War II. Because of the wartime emphasis on energy self-sufficiency, much of the capital expansion continued to rely on coal rather than on the less certain supplies of petroleum and natural gas. With the end of the war, industry had considerable capacity in its plant and equipment to satisfy the postwar boom, and it was several years before new energy capital investments were required on a level such that any significant movement away from coal consumption became evident.

Because of the particular circumstances of industrial expansion during World War II, the shift from coal to other energy resources was much more gradual in the industrial sector than in the household and commercial sector. Coal's share of energy in the industrial sector dropped from a little over half in 1947 to just under one-fifth by 1975. Natural gas and electricity did increase their share of industrial energy consumption by sizeable amounts, though by much smaller margins than occurred in the household and commercial sector. Moreover, overall energy consumption expanded much less rapidly in the industrial sector than in the household and commercial sector, by only 1.83 percent a year as compared with the 3.19 percent annual rate of increase in energy consumption in the household and commercial sector.

Energy consumption changes in transportation were very much tied to two developments in the postwar era: the decline of rail transit and the resurgence of road and air transport. Automobile demand had been severely restrained during World War II, and in the postwar boom there was an increasing emphasis on the construction of a network of interstate highways. Such roads were essential to accommodate the explosion in vehicle use then under way. In addition, air travel received considerable stimulus from the technological advances in instrumentation, cabin pressurization, and speed that had been made during the war. Thus, the consumption of coal, which was used for one-third of transportation energy in 1947, all but disappeared by 1975. Behind this shift lay the conversion from coal to diesel fuel in locomotives, as well as the enormous increases in petroleum use in the vehicle and aviation industries.

Absolute consumption of energy in all forms in the transportation sector more than doubled in the period 1947–75. This expansion reflected not only the technological changes already noted but also the fact that regional economic integration into the national and international economy was taking place on an unprecedented scale. One indicator of this change was that during the 1950–75 period, domestic intercity traffic on railroads, highways, airways, inland waterways, and oil pipelines increased by over 90 percent, whereas real per capita GNP expanded by 60 percent.

Electricity consumption obviously depends on consumption of energy resources. Yet, as in other sectors of the economy, the means of production were also changing significantly in the 1947–75 period. Because of the growing share of electricity consumption's in the final demand for energy, the absolute amount of energy consumption involved in the production of electricity expanded faster than any of the energy aggregates thus far noted, by almost 400 percent in these twenty-eight years. However, although there was a slight decline in the coal share of energy resources used in electricity production, consumption of coal still rose over three times in the period because of the overall expansion of electricity consumption in the economy.

Of the other energy resources used in electricity production, hydropower increased by the smallest absolute amount, while the greatest absolute increases were found in natural gas (737 percent) and nuclear energy (889 percent since 1970). As may also be seen in table 2.2, except in its military applications, nuclear energy has been used exclusively in the generation of electricity, an application dictated essentially by economies of scale possible thus far only in electric utility plants.

If the sectoral patterns of U.S. energy consumption appear too abstract, one additional way of understanding their significance is in terms of the end uses of energy. Table 2.3 provides a breakdown of the end uses of energy in the United States for the early 1970s. As one might expect, transportation, space heating, industrial process steam, and direct heat accounted for over

Table 2.3. End Uses of Energy in the United States

End Use	Percentage of Total	Cumulative Percentage
1. Transportation (fuel, excluding lubricants and greases)	24.9%	24.9%
2. Space heating (residential, commercial)	17.9	42.8
3. Process steam (industrial)[a]	16.7	59.5
4. Direct heat (industrial)[a]	11.5	71.0
5. Electric drive (industrial)	7.9	78.9
6. Feedstocks, raw materials (commercial, industrial, transportation)	5.5	84.4
7. Water heating (residential, commercial)	4.0	88.4
8. Air conditioning (residential, commercial)	2.5	90.9
9. Refrigeration (residential, commercial)	2.2	93.1
10. Lighting (residential, commercial)	1.5	94.6
11. Cooking (residential, commercial)	1.3	95.9
12. Electrolytic processes (industrial)	1.2	97.1
13. Miscellaneous	2.9	100.0

Source: Stanford Research Institute, *Patterns of Energy Consumption in the United States* (Palo Alto: Stanford Research Institute, Stanford University Press, January 1972), p. 7.

[a]Includes some use for space heating, probably enough to bring total space heating to about 20 percent.

two-thirds of all end uses of energy. As noted in table 2.2, given that transportation has depended so heavily on petroleum, since transportation accounted for just under one-quarter of all end uses of energy, it is not surprising that the 1973 and 1979 OPEC oil price increases had the severe impact they did on the economy. More important, the end uses of energy also suggest that as the relative price of a particular energy resource such as petroleum undergoes a shift, it is likely to affect some sectors of the economy much more than others.

As noted in chapter 1, the energy crises of 1973 and 1979 were very much tied to dependence on petroleum in general and on OPEC oil in particular. We have seen how technology has helped to shape the demand for particular forms of energy; we can also illustrate this dependence in terms of patterns of energy production and consumption in the United States over time.

Table 2.4 summarizes the evolution of U.S. production and consumption energy balances for the period 1920–80. Curiously, until the 1950s the United States was a net exporter of energy resources to the rest of the world. Since that time it has been a net importer, with a 15–20 percent deficit in gross primary energy consumption in recent years.[14] The overwhelming cause of this deficit has been the growth in petroleum imports. In contrast, coal production has resulted in an exportable surplus in virtually every year since 1920, with hydropower and nuclear energy production just matching consumption. Thus, the United States not only has increased its reliance on petroleum and natural gas as principal energy resources but has done so by

[14]This deficit, it should be noted, is measured only to physical units and may not correspond directly to any dollar balances, given differences in domestic and international resource prices.

Table 2.4. U.S. Gross Energy Production, Consumption, and International Resource Adjustment, 1920–80
(in quadrillion Btu's)

	1920	1930	1940	1950	1955	1960	1965	1970	1975	1976	1978	1980
Petroleum												
Production	3.08	5.85	7.59	11.45	14.45	14.94	16.52	20.40	17.73	17.26	18.43	18.25
Consumption	2.63	5.40	7.53	13.49	17.52	20.10	23.24	29.50	32.70	35.09	37.97	34.20
Balance	0.45	0.45	0.06	−2.04	−3.07	−5.16	−6.72	−9.10	−14.97	−17.83	−19.54	−15.95
Natural gas[a]												
Production	1.05	2.50	3.75	6.84	10.53	14.14	17.65	24.15	22.02	21.83	21.73	22.02
Consumption	0.81	1.93	2.70	6.18	9.23	12.70	16.10	24.50	22.10	22.60	20.00	20.50
Balance	0.24	0.57	1.05	0.66	1.30	1.44	1.55	−0.35	−0.08	−0.77	1.73	1.52
Coal												
Production	16.46	13.99	12.81	16.65	12.75	11.14	13.40	15.25	15.39	15.87	15.04	18.91
Consumption	15.50	13.64	12.54	12.91	11.54	10.10	11.91	12.70	12.80	13.70	13.98	15.60
Balance	0.96	0.35	0.27	3.74	1.21	1.04	1.49	2.55	2.59	2.17	1.06	3.31
Hydropower[b]												
Production	2.36	2.34	2.23	2.62	2.36	2.50	2.06	2.70	3.17	2.98	3.03	3.03
Consumption	2.36	2.34	2.23	2.62	2.36	2.50	2.06	2.70	3.17	3.10	3.23	3.24
Balance	—	—	—	—	—	—	—	—	—	−0.12	−0.20	−0.21
Nuclear												
Production	—	—	—	—	—	0.01	0.04	0.23	1.84	2.00	2.98	2.70
Consumption	—	—	—	—	—	0.01	0.04	0.23	1.84	2.00	2.98	2.70
Balance	—	—	—	—	—	—	—	—	—	—	—	—
Total												
Production	22.95	24.46	26.38	37.56	40.09	42.73	49.67	62.73	60.15	59.94	61.20	64.87
Consumption	21.30	23.31	25.00	35.20	40.65	45.40	53.35	69.63	72.61	76.49	78.15	76.20
Balance	1.65	1.15	1.38	2.36	−0.56	−2.67	−3.68	−6.90	−12.46	−16.55	−16.95	−11.33

Sources: Sam H. Schurr and Bruce C. Netschert, *Energy in the American Economy, 1850–1975* (Baltimore: Johns Hopkins Press for Resources for the Future, 1960); U.S. Department of the Interior, Bureau of Mines, *Minerals Yearbook* (Washington, D.C.: U.S. Government Printing Office, selected years) U.S. Department of Energy, Energy Information Administration, *Monthly Energy Review* (Washington, D.C.: U.S. Government Printing Office, May 1981).

[a]Includes natural gas liquids

[b]Includes geothermal, wood, and miscellaneous

increasing its imports of these resources at a time when new discoveries were beginning to slow in relation to increases in consumption. As we have seen, that this dependence arose in the first place can be attributed to the impact of technology on the economy and to the relative pricing of these resources.

2.3. ENERGY CRISES AND STRUCTURAL CHANGE

As the preceding historical overview has shown, technological change has had important consequences for the ways in which energy is transformed in the economy. Because changes in energy technology also affect the economy, we can round out our understanding of the role of energy and energy crises in terms of the structural effects of energy on economic growth, inflation, unemployment, the environment, and the distribution of income.

At a macroeconomic level, we can trace several links between an energy crisis and its impact on the structure of the economy. If we begin by looking at the disparate causes leading to the English wood crisis in the seventeenth century and the OPEC crisis of 1973, it becomes apparent that an energy crisis may be accelerated by immediate political forces, but its underlying causes are clearly economic in nature. Thus, we need to look beyond the immediate political circumstances to the determinants of shifts in energy demand and supply.

The demand for energy is a derived demand, that is, it arises because of the level of income, tastes, and expectations concerning other goods and services whose production in turn depends on energy. Once the price of energy or of a particular energy resource goes up, consumers may attempt to switch to other energy resources or, as is often the case when such substitution possibilities may be limited by technical considerations, to reduce energy consumption. If technical improvements in energy efficiency can be achieved simultaneously with the increase in energy prices, it may be possible to maintain output and consumption at their previous levels, if not higher. Yet, as noted in chapter 1, in a growing economy like that of the United States, such improvements are most likely to occur only with new energy technologies. If historical evidence is a guide, this suggests that in the short run, as in 1973, a sudden shift in both energy prices and supplies can be absorbed only by altering other economic conditions. Such changes in turn will produce higher general prices as increased energy costs filter through the economy, an increase in unemployment as higher energy prices reduce the consumption of goods and services to some degree, or both. In turn, the effects of energy on inflation, unemployment, and economic growth are likely to alter to some degree the prevailing distribution of income.

Over the medium and longer term, the initial impact of energy price changes will then begin to work its way through the economy. Consumer lifestyles may be altered in the medium term, resulting in fewer automobile pleasure trips, more car pooling, and so on. Likewise, for those individuals about to purchase a car, fuel economy becomes more important than before, and a gradual shift toward smaller, fuel-efficient vehicles becomes evident.

On another level, higher energy prices have an impact on supply. In the short term, there may be few increases in production of energy resources because of capacity and other limitations. Over a longer term, however, higher prices encourage more production and exploration. Production increases are somewhat predictable in response to increases in prices, though to a lesser extent in relation to exploration. Yet, as we will see in chapter 3, the discovery of additional energy resources is subject to a number of unknowns.

We can further separate the supply impact of energy price increases into two categories. First is the impact of an overall increase in all energy prices by some amount, or percentage. In this case, there is likely to be some additional increase in the overall availability of energy supplies, with increases in a particular resource in some proportion to that resource's current and expected market price. A second impact is the relative shift that may occur as the price of a particular energy resource rises relative to that of others. For example, in the aftermath of the 1970 oil embargo, as oil prices rose, one secondary consequence was a shift away from petroleum to natural gas, a close substitute. Since the price of natural gas remained relatively constant over the next few years, the substitution of natural gas for petroleum shifted the demand for natural gas considerably. In the absence of any relative change in the price of natural gas, supplies did not increase by much in comparison with demand, and this regulated price arrangement did much to precipitate the natural gas shortage of 1977.

Apart from the absolute and relative consequences of energy price changes for production and consumption, relatively higher prices also stimulate research into alternative energy technologies. Such alternative energy technologies can involve more efficient ways of extracting and using existing resources or the development of alternative energy resources not currently in use. In the former category can be included secondary and tertiary recovery methods of petroleum and natural gas, conversion of coal into gas, conversion of coal into petroleum, extraction of oil from shale and tar sands, along with more efficient machines that are dependent on these fuels for their operation. In the latter can be included solar, wind, tidal, and geothermal energy, in addition to hydrogen, electricity storage, and nuclear fusion. The important consideration is that at some point these alternative technologies attain feasible mechanical efficiencies, and as prices of known energy resources rise, the alternatives become economic and begin to claim significant amounts of total production and consumption.

New energy technologies will also affect both household lifestyles and the organization of goods and services production. Just as the automobile helped revolutionize twentieth-century civilization, the particular mix of new energy resources over time can have an equally profound impact. Environmental quality, as well as the structure and efficiency of production, is likely to be affected. Put in the conceptual framework of energy policy, such changes may alter the nature and degree of externalities, as well as the extent to which energy resources are produced consistent with a perfectly competitive norm. In order to tie all of these elements into the design of energy policy, however, we first need to know more about the predictability of energy crises, a matter which is taken up in chapter 3.

2.4. SUMMARY

Energy use over time has had a critical influence on the pattern and stability of social and economic organization. Until the industrial revolution, societies depended mostly on human, animal, and wood energy resources, and living standards rose at a relatively slow pace. With the scientific discoveries of the seventeenth and eighteenth centuries, this pattern began to change, first by the substitution of coal for wood, then by refinement and integration of steam engine technology into the economies of western Europe and North America. Though the industrial revolution that followed increased the complexity of inventions and economic organization, only when electricity, petroleum, and natural gas entered into widespread use did the industrial revolution help to create the kind of society in which we now live.

In recent years, the recurrence of energy crises in the United States and in other countries has once again raised basic questions about the uses of energy and the appropriateness of energy policy. Preliminary to the design of any energy policy, however, are first need to examine the ways in which historical patterns of energy consumption and production can be used to predict energy crises.

SUGGESTED READINGS

Cottrell, Fred W. *Energy and Society.* 1955. Reprinted. Westport, Conn.: Greenwood Press, 1970.

Fisher, John C. *Energy Crises in Perspective.* New York: John Wiley and Sons, 1974.

McKenzie, A. E. E. *The Major Achievements of Science.* New York: Simon and Schuster Touchstone Books, 1973.

Mumford, Lewis. *Technics and Civilization.* New York: Harcourt Brace and World, 1934.

Schurr, Sam. H., and Netschert, Bruce C. *Energy in the American Economy, 1850–1975.* Baltimore: Johns Hopkins Press for Resources for the Future, 1960.

Sonenblum, Sidney. *The Energy Connections: Between Energy and the Economy.* Cambridge, Mass.: Ballinger Publishing Co., 1978.

3

PROJECTIONS OF ENERGY USE

3.1. METHODOLOGICAL CONSIDERATIONS

For economic policymakers, a knowledge of historical changes in energy technology and use is but an imperfect guide to the future. At the same time, because energy has become so important to the economy, policy choices must be made. Moreover, they must be based largely on the projection of these very historical conditions into alternative energy futures. This process, and the energy models used to derive these projections, is not intended to answer the normative question of what ought to be an appropriate energy policy; rather it is to be used to map out the many cause-and-effect relationships that policymakers are likely to confront. Thus, the purpose of energy models is to assist policymakers in arriving at the ultimate value judgments that they make when faced with a specific set of conditions. Energy policy criteria are spelled out in detail in part IV; at this point we can examine some of the ways in which alternative energy projections are made so that we may understand more clearly the role of technology and economics in arriving at appropriate policy choices.

To facilitate the formulation and operation of energy models, analysts often employ two simplifying conventions. One is the standardization of heterogeneous energy resources into a common accounting unit, especially when making projections at a macroeconomic level. For example, the U.N. world energy model uses units of coal equivalent for purposes of energy accounting and projections. In the United States, coal equivalents, oil equivalents such as millions of barrels per day, and British Thermal Units such as quads of Btu's all have been used in macroeconomic energy models. In contrast, microeconomic energy models often express energy quantities in their original units, depending on whether fuel-specific behavior or industry behavior is being examined. Though this procedure may appear unusual at first, the use of an energy *numéraire* makes it easier to analyze many of the questions that policymakers must address. For our present purposes, all energy units have been standardized into one or the other of the commonly used measures, based on conversion ratios listed in the Appendix.

The second convention is the specification of depletable energy resources in terms of known proven reserves. As we might expect, higher real prices of a resource generally elicit a larger quantity supplied of that resource. In the case of depletable energy resources, the relationship between price and quantity supplied derives from the degree of geologic assurance and the quantity that can be produced at that price, as can be seen in figure 3.1. As we move from the lower righthand corner to the left, resources that are considered unknown and speculative acquire greater geological certainty. As we move from the lower righthand corner to the top, reserves of varying degrees of geological uncertainty become subject to greater economic feasibility, that is, the risks of exploration become worth the effort in terms of the potential return. Though there is obviously a finite quantity of a depletable energy resource, only when the real price reaches a sufficiently high level is the prevailing degree of geological uncertainty likely to be reduced to a point where it can be estimated with confidence. What policymakers must anticipate is the precise shape of this depletable energy supply curve over time, and this is where energy forecasting models come to play a role.

Before we look at some of the more widely known energy forecasting models, it is useful to spell out in general terms the behavior of depletable energy resources in terms of alternative economic assumptions. In its simplest terms, the demand for energy derives from the demand for goods and services that depend on its use. Given a rate of aggregate economic growth, if a depletable resource comprises the sole source of economically useful energy, depending on the opportunities for conservation, the production of the

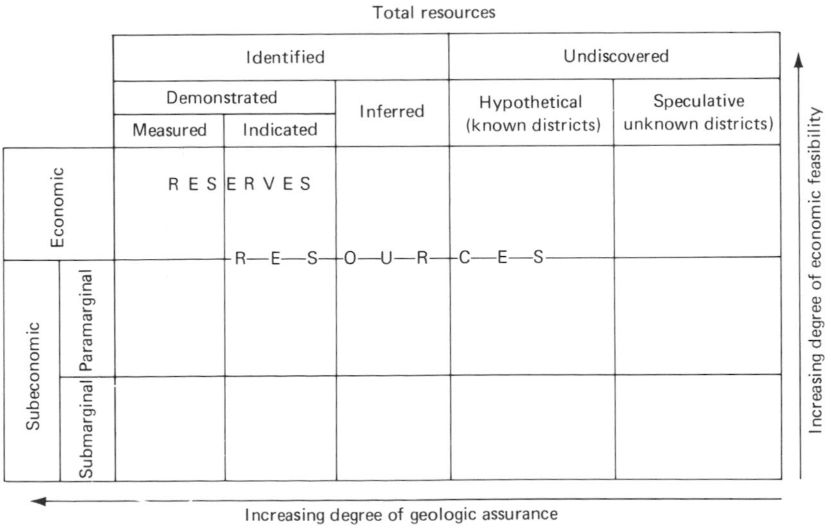

Total resources

		Identified			Undiscovered	
		Demonstrated		Inferred	Hypothetical (known districts)	Speculative unknown districts)
		Measured	Indicated			
Economic		RES	ERVES			
			R—E—S	O—U—R	C—E—S	
Subeconomic	Paramarginal					
	Submarginal					

Increasing degree of economic feasibility ↑

← Increasing degree of geologic assurance

Figure 3.1. Classification of Mineral Resources. Data from U.S. Geological Survey and U.S. Bureau of Mines, *Principles of the Mineral Resource Classification System of the U.S. Bureau of Mines and the U.S. Geological Survey*, Geological Survey Bulletin 1450-A (Washington, D.C.: U.S. Government Printing Office, 1976).

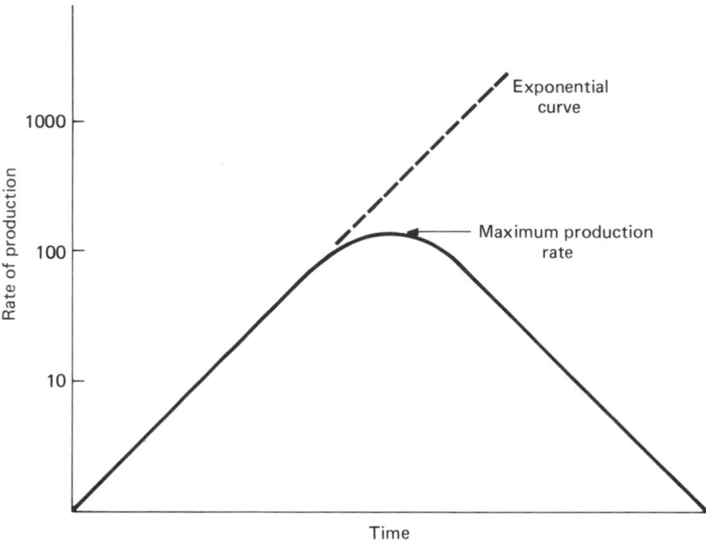

Figure 3.2. The Production of an Exhaustible Resource

resource will grow at some rate corresponding to the given rate of increase in income, as is illustrated in figure 3.2. Of course, what distinguishes a depletable energy resource from a renewable one is that its exponential growth pattern can not continue forever. Consequently, at some point the rate of production will tend to peak and then decline. It is at this point that conservation or the shift to renewable energy technologies, or both, must become more significant in the prevailing mix of energy resources if economic growth is to continue. Whether in fact such a transition can be accomplished without the eruption of an energy crisis is a key issue that policymakers must also confront, which again brings us back to the role of energy forecasting models.

A useful way to understand the dynamics in figure 3.2 is in terms of basic numerical comparisons. One way to express the historical pattern of growth is to derive the compound rate of increase in production, which may then be used to project future production rates. Thus, if initial production is p_0, in the following period (or year) it will be

$$p_1 = p_0(1 + r), \tag{3.1}$$

where r is the rate of increase. Similarly, for year t, production will be

$$p_t = p_0(1 + r)^t. \tag{3.2}$$

Under such compounding, the absolute increase in production is larger with each successive period, until the range of maximum production is reached.

We can also use the compound formula (3.2) to determine the number of years required for energy production and consumption to double or expand by any multiple of the original amount. Rearranging equation (3.2),

$$\frac{p_t}{p_0} = (1 + r)^t, \tag{3.3}$$

we can then take the logarithm of both sides,

$$\log(p_t/p_0) = t \log(1 + r), \tag{3.4}$$

and solving for t,

$$\frac{\log(p_t/p_0)}{\log(1 + r)} = t, \tag{3.5}$$

yields the basic solution. If we wish to know how many years are required for production (consumption) to double, equation (3.5) becomes

$$t = \frac{\log 2}{\log(1 + r)} = \frac{0.3010}{\log(1 + r)}. \tag{3.6}$$

Equation (3.6) can be used to determine the doubling period for any rate of increase. For values of r up to 12 percent, an approximate solution can be obtained by dividing 70 by the integer value of r. For example, if petroleum production were expanding by 5 percent a year, in 14 years it would double, and if by 10 percent a year, it would take only 7 years.

Another way of expressing the growth of production and consumption is to determine the continuous rate of expansion. In this case, production at period 5 can be expressed as

$$p_t = p_0 e^{rn}, \tag{3.7}$$

where n is the number of time periods (e.g., years), e is the base of natural logarithms (2.71828), and all other symbols have the same interpretation as in equation (3.1). The difference between equations (3.7) and (3.2) is that for longer time periods, continuous compounding will yield larger values than under the compound rate of (3.2). As an example, consider the level of production in period t, which is 25 years after the initial production of 10 per year has expanded at 5 percent a year. According to equation (3.2),

$$\begin{aligned} p_t &= p_0(1 + r)^t \\ &= 10(1.05)^{25} \\ &= 33.86, \end{aligned}$$

whereas according to equation (3.7), production would be

$$\begin{aligned} p_t &= p_0 e^{rn} \\ &= (10)(2.718282)^{(0.05)(25)} \\ &= 34.90. \end{aligned}$$

Given the long time period required for many energy projections, equation (3.7) may be a more appropriate measure than equation (3.2). In addition, using this type of formulation, we can also compute the total production of petroleum since the beginning. Cumulative production may be expressed as

$$(3.8) \qquad P_t = \int_{-\infty}^{t} p_0 e^{rn}\, dt = \left[\frac{p_0}{r}\right] e^{rn}.$$

As an illustration of equation (3.8), if initial production of petroleum were 10 per year and the rate of increase were 5 percent a year, after 25 years the total amount of production would be

$$P_t = \left[\frac{p_0}{r}\right] e^{rn}$$

$$P_{25} = \frac{10}{0.05}\,(2.718282)^{(0.05)(25)}$$

$$= 698.07 \text{ units.}$$

Equation (3.8) is central to the estimation of cumulative resource use. In addition to its use in calculating total resource production, it can also be used to determine total reserves and total discoveries. For accounting purposes, total discoveries must equal the sum of total production plus reserves:

$$(3.9) \qquad D_t = P_t + R_t.$$

Since total discoveries are limited by some finite amount, if conservation and renewable resource technologies were ruled out, aggregate economic growth would eventually lead to the depletion of the exhaustible energy resource. Moreover, as depletion approached, the price of the energy resource would tend to rise to such a point that it would claim an ever larger share of national output, and further economic growth would become impossible. Yet before we jump to the conclusion that Thomas Carlyle was right in calling economics the "dismal science," let us keep in mind the very restrictive assumptions on which this scenario has been based, namely, that conservation and renewable energy resource technologies would have no role to play and that the stock of depletable energy resources is known with both geological and economic certainty.[1] Fortunately, choices involving conservation, exploration, and renewable resource technologies do exist, but before we examine them further we need to complete our preliminary discussion of the properties of

[1]Thomas Carlyle was a nineteenth-century British historian who shared with economists of the period an interest in the causes and opportunities of economic growth. It was reading such ideas as the population-resources dilemma posed by Thomas Malthus (1766–1834) that led him to conclude that economics was the "dismal science."

depletable energy resources, particularly the question of the estimation of depletable reserves.

Figure 3.3 illustrates the separate movement of the three variables, cumulative discoveries, cumulative production, and proven reserves, given the aforementioned assumptions. As long as the rate of resource discovery exceeds the rate of production, total reserves will increase. Beyond some point, however, the rate of resource discovery will begin to slow, eventually falling behind the rate of production such that total reserves will peak and then decline. Mathematically,

$$\text{at } t_1\text{:} \quad \frac{dD}{dt} > \frac{dR}{dt} > \frac{dP}{dt} > 0,$$

$$t_2\text{:} \quad \frac{dD}{dt} = \frac{dP}{dt} > \frac{dR}{dt} = 0,$$

$$t_3\text{:} \quad \frac{dP}{dt} > \frac{dD}{dt} > \frac{dR}{dt} < 0,$$

With information on the rate of production and the rate of discovery, it is possible to derive both the total amount of reserves and the length of available time before all remaining reserves are exhausted. The most common method is to estimate the S-shaped cumulative discovery and production

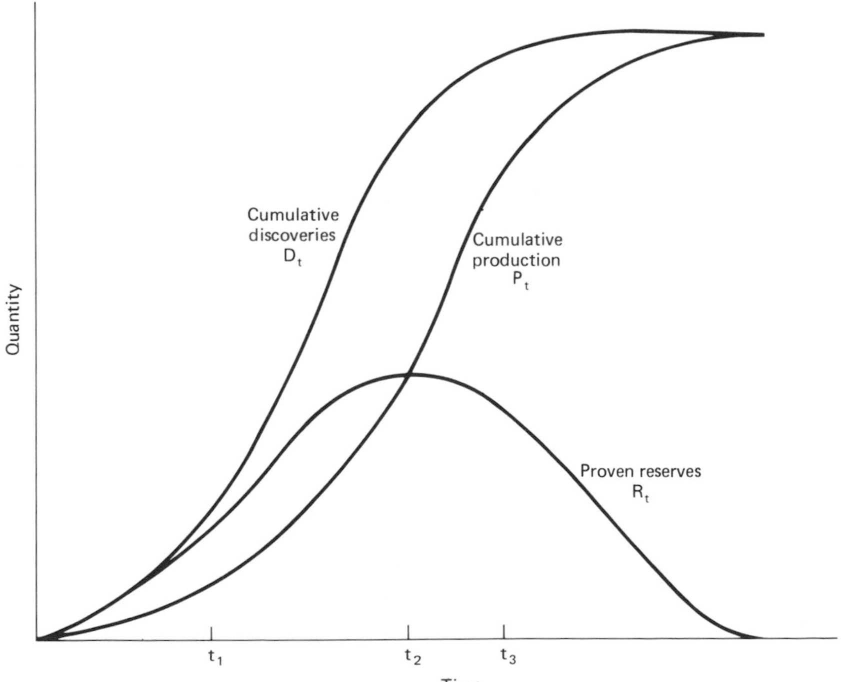

Figure 3.3. The Life Cycle of an Exhaustible Resource

curves by use of a logistic equation to compute the value of the upper asymptote. The logistic equation is of the general form

$$y = \frac{h}{1 + ae^{-bx}}, \tag{3.10}$$

where h, a, and b are parameters to be determined by the data and e is the base of natural logarithms. Translating equation (3.10) into the logistic curve for cumulative petroleum discovery gives

$$D_f = \frac{D_\infty}{1 + ae^{-rn}}, \tag{3.11}$$

in which D_∞ is the asymptotic finite value to which D_t will tend as the number of time periods, n, becomes infinite. Derivation of D_∞ can be determined by rearranging equation (3.11) as follows:

$$\frac{D_\infty}{D_f} - 1 = ae^{-rn}. \tag{3.12}$$

Taking the logarithm of both sides yields

$$\log[(D_\infty/D_f) - 1] = \log a - rn \log e. \tag{3.13}$$

A solution for equation (3.13) can be obtained by picking arbitrary likely values of D_∞ and inserting known values of D_f as a function of time. Then semi-logarithmic paper can be used to plot several estimates based on varying values of D_∞, and the one that best approximates a straight line is the solution.

A more precise method of estimating cumulative discoveries of a depletable energy resource is by statistical regression. Again, we choose several possible values of the level of cumulative discoveries, D_∞, based on historical trends. We can take each of these possible values and insert the historical values of cumulative discoveries, D_f, into the lefthand expression of equation (3.13) to derive a time-series set of data points, which can be used statistically to estimate values of the parameters, a and r. As an illustration, in table 3.1 five possible values of D_∞ for cumulative petroleum discoveries in the United States have been used to derive alternative data points for the period 1900–1980. When each of these sets was regressed as a function of time, the one that yielded the highest value of the coefficient of determination, $\bar{R}^2$, was $\log(200/D_f) - 1$.[2] The resulting equation is:

$$\log\left[\frac{200}{D_f} - 1\right] = 1.852919 - \underset{(0.00112)}{0.140586}{}^{t} \qquad \bar{R}^2 = 0.99898.$$

[2]The coefficient of determination ranges from zero to one. The bar over R indicates that the estimate has been adjusted for the number of degrees of freedom, which is determined by the number of independent variables and observations relative to the dependent variable. The number in parentheses under the coefficient of time is the standard error of estimate of the variable. Since we are concerned here more with applications, a reader interested in additional theory and interpretation should consult a standard text in econometrics (see, for example, Henri Theil, *Introduction to Econometrics* [Englewood Cliffs, N.J.: Prentice-Hall, 1978]).

Table 3.1. Estimation of Cumulative Petroleum Discoveries for the United States, 1900–1980

		Hypothetical Values of D_∞				
Year	D_f (in billions of barrels)	$\log \frac{160}{D_f} - 1$	$\log \frac{180}{D_f} - 1$	$\log \frac{200}{D_f} - 1$	$\log \frac{220}{D_f} - 1$	$\log \frac{240}{D_f} - 1$
1900	3.65	1.63181	1.68408	1.73074	1.77286	1.88126
1905	5.06	1.48601	1.53874	1.58574	1.62816	1.66681
1910	7.01	1.33895	1.39230	1.43982	1.48264	1.52162
1915	9.67	1.19162	1.24586	1.29408	1.33737	3.37692
1920	13.35	1.04080	1.09632	1.14555	1.18975	1.22987
1925	18.21	0.89134	0.94864	0.99926	1.04459	1.08563
1930	24.84	0.73570	0.79563	0.84828	0.89523	0.93761
1935	32.50	0.59363	0.65691	0.71213	0.76112	0.80514
1940	42.52	0.44137	0.50965	0.56863	0.62056	0.66693
1945	53.97	0.29328	0.36832	0.43229	0.48803	0.53743
1950	68.50	0.12573	0.21158	0.28324	0.34472	0.39857
1955	81.18	−0.01281	0.08540	0.16544	0.23300	0.29146
1960	96.20	−0.17835	−0.05993	0.03302	0.10954	0.17458
1965	109.24	−0.33286	−0.18859	−0.08049	0.00600	0.07809
1970	124.04	−0.53774	−0.34568	−0.21298	−0.11147	−0.02925
1975	140.85	−0.86659	−0.55603	−0.37680	−0.25031	−0.15246
1980	158.20	−1.94393	−0.86075	−0.57803	−0.40822	−0.28645

Sources: Based on odd-year estimates reported in M. King Hubbert, "Energy Resources," in *Energy Crisis: Danger and Opportunity,* ed. Victor John Yannacone, Jr. (New York: West Publishing Co., 1974), pp. 43–150; and on estimates published in *Oil and Gas Journal* (Tulsa: Pennwell Publishing Co., selected years).

Note: All data are hypothetical.

To verify that 200 billion barrels is the best estimate, we can insert the antilogarithm of the intercept term, a, and the estimated value of cumulative discoveries, $\hat{D}_\infty$ at 200, into the basic logistic equation (3.11). Since the denominator of (3.11) will not be significantly different from 1, the numerator, $\hat{D}_\infty$, represents the best estimate of cumulative discoveries and will tend to be far more accurate than by plotting data points graphically.

The significance of the estimate of ultimate cumulative discoveries is that when it is combined with cumulative production estimates, we can estimate not only the amount of remaining reserves but also how long it will take at current rates of production for this reserve to be exhausted. For example, cumulative production up to the present time can be computed from equation (3.8). If production in 1900 were 39.568 million barrels, and production increased through 1980 at a rate of 5.96 percent a year, using equation (3.8) we would obtain

$$P_{80} = \left[\frac{39.568}{(0.05965)}\right](2.718282)^{(0.05965)(80)}$$

$$= 78.376 \times 10^9 \text{ barrels.}$$

We can then subtract estimated cumulative production from estimated cumulative discoveries to obtain the amount of present reserves:

$$\begin{aligned} P_{80} &= D_{80} - P_{80} \\ &= (200 - 78.376) \times 10^9 \\ &= 121.624 \times 10^9 \text{ barrels.} \end{aligned}$$

From the estimate of present reserves, we can then use the growth rate of current production to determine how long time reserves will last before depletion. The equation is

$$(3.14) \qquad \begin{aligned} D_t - P_t &= \int_{-\infty}^{t} p_0 e^{rt}\, dt \\ &= \frac{p_0}{r}(e^{rn} - 1). \end{aligned}$$

Rearranging,

$$e^{rn} = \frac{(D_t - P_t)r}{p_0} + 1,$$

from which n can be computed by taking the natural logarithm of both sides:

$$\begin{aligned} rn &= \ln\left[\frac{(D_t - P_t)r}{p_0} + 1\right], \\ n &= \left(\frac{1}{r}\right)\ln\left[\frac{(D_t - P_t)r}{p_0} + 1\right]. \end{aligned}$$

By plugging in the 1980 values of r, P_t, p_0, and D_t, we obtain

$$\begin{aligned} n &= \frac{1}{(0.05969)}\ln\left[\frac{(121.624)(0.05969)}{3.052} + 1\right] \\ &= (16.75323)\ln(3.37868) \\ &= (16.75323)(1.21749) \\ &= 20.397 \text{ years.} \end{aligned}$$

As can be seen in equation (3.14), the remaining lifetime of exhaustible resources depends directly on the discovery rate and on the rate of growth of production. Should the production growth rate slow down relative to the rate of discovery, the remaining lifetime of the exhaustible resource is prolonged, and if the movement is in the opposite direction, it is shortened.

A slowdown in the rate of production growth is indicative of energy conservation, but only for the particular resource in question. It does not necessarily follow that overall energy use has become technically more efficient. For example, as we saw in chapter 2, the consumption of coal in the United States declined in relative terms throughout much of the twentieth century. Yet much of this slowdown was due to a shift to depletable petroleum and natural gas. Thus, we must keep in mind the degree of substitution opportunities when examining the behavior of depletable energy resources.

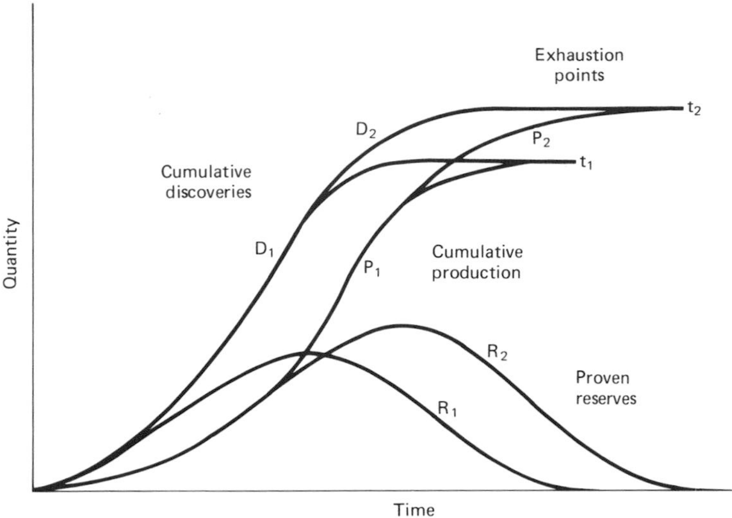

Figure 3.3.*a*. The Life Cycle of an Exhaustible Resource with Increased Supply

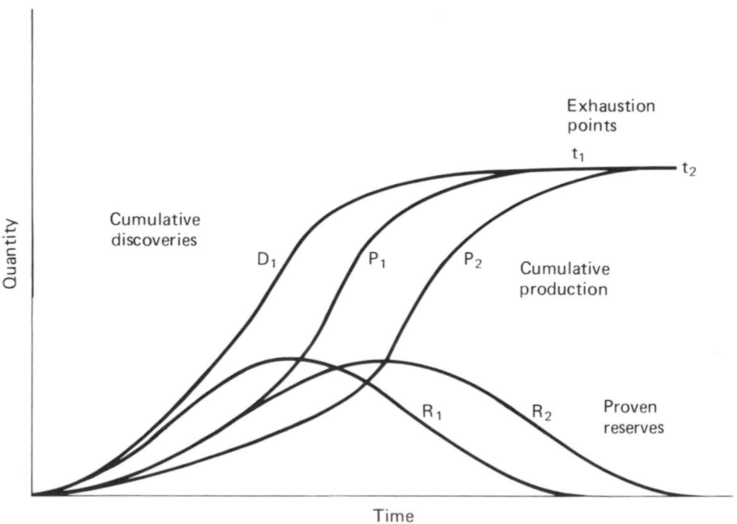

Figure 3.3.*b*. The Life Cycle of an Exhaustible Resource with Demand Restraint

An increase in the discovery rate may be due to chance, to technological change in exploration and extraction techniques, to an increase in the relative price of the particular energy resource, or to a combination of these factors. The net effect is to raise the discovery curve, just as a deterioration in any one of these factors would lower it. The significance of changes in both discovery and production rates is illustrated in figures 3.3.*a*, 3.3.*b*, and

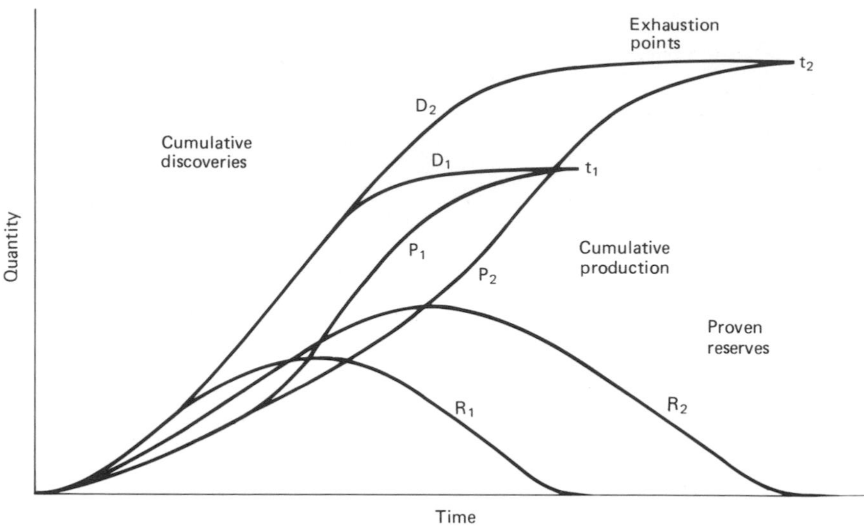

Figure 3.3.*c*. The Life Cycle of an Exhaustible Resource with Increased Supply and Demand Restraint

3.3.*c*. In figure 3.3.*a*, increased supply through a higher discovery rate and an unaltered production pattern will add to proven reserves and lead to higher cumulative production at a later point than under original conditions (t_2 instead of t_1). In figure 3.3.*b*, demand restraint lowers the rate of growth of production, thereby stretching out the unaltered ultimately proven reserve base from t_1 to t_2. In figure 3.3.*c*, a combination of a higher discovery rate and a lower production rate leads to cumulative production at a higher level and a later time period of exhaustion than would a higher discovery rate alone. Cumulative proven reserves also are increased beyond the pattern in 3.3.*a*, as is the time path of depletion. Because there are many possible variations, it is only by specifying the technology and relative prices of depletable energy within a broader forecasting model that we are likely to be able to make reasonable predictions about the future behavior of these resources.

3.2. THE STRUCTURE OF ENERGY FORECASTING MODELS

As we have seen, energy models usually are designed to illuminate the many causal relationships and choices that policymakers are likely to confront under real-world conditions. However, this is not to say that energy models have been especially successful in anticipating many of these choices. Yet since economic policies, and the criteria on which they are based, are so often derived from these models, it is important that we gain some insight into how they are constructed. We can then better appreciate some of the differences that underlie the alternative energy projections of the models to be discussed in section 3.3.

Macroeconomic models of energy have at their core a specification of the general energy-GNP relationship which we discussed in chapters 1 and 2. Since the demand for energy depends partly on the level of income and partly on the relative price of energy, if the latter is relatively stable, then this relationship can be expressed in functional terms as

$$E = f(Y), \tag{3.15}$$

where E is gross primary energy consumption and Y is the GNP. From this relationship, for a given rate in the growth of GNP we can project the future demand for energy. Yet as will be seen, the type of data used will significantly affect the accuracy of aggregate energy projections. Moreover, since the energy-GNP ratio has not been constant over time, some adjustment must be made to account for its variability.

Table 3.2 provides basic data on gross primary energy consumption, population, and the GNP in the United States for the period 1900–1980. As for the projections of depletable energy resource behavior discussed in section 3.1, one way to project the future demand for energy is by a time-series statistical regression.

To see how the choice of data can affect estimates of the energy-GNP ratio, three variants of equation (3.15) have been computed. The results of these equations are:[3]

$$E_{1900\text{-}1980} = 6.610434 + \underset{(0.00161)}{0.05077}Y_{5t} \qquad \bar{R}^2 = 0.984135, \quad n = 17, \tag{3.15.a}$$

$$E_{1950\text{-}80} = 5.905321 + \underset{(0.00152)}{0.05269}Y_t \qquad \bar{R}^2 = 0.975795, \quad n = 31, \tag{3.15.b}$$

$$E_{1970\text{-}80} = 40.03556 + \underset{(0.00350)}{0.02631}Y_t \qquad \bar{R}^2 = 0.847313, \quad n = 11. \tag{3.15.c}$$

Equation (3.15.a) is based on five-year observations of energy consumption and real GNP expressed in 1972 dollars for the period 1900–80; equation (3.15.b), on annual observations of energy and real GNP for the period 1950–80; and equation (3.15.c), on annual observations for the period 1970–80. Equation (3.15.a) states that for each billion-dollar increase in real U.S. GNP there will be a 0.05077 increase in quads of energy consumption. Equations (3.15.b) and (3.15.c) may be interpreted in the same fashion.

Another way of appreciating the importance of data to projections of future energy consumption is in terms of international comparisons. For example, suppose we had not yet experienced the effects of the doubling of the price of energy, as occurred in the case of OPEC petroleum during 1979–80. How could we estimate the long-term effects of a change in the relative price of energy on international demand? Figure 3.4 provides such a comparison, based on a thirty-nine-country sample of aggregate energy consumption and real Gross Domestic Product, or GDP, for three time periods, 1960, 1970, and 1975. Using equation (3.15), three regression estimates have been com-

[3]The numbers in parentheses are standard errors of estimate of the coefficients of Y.

Table 3.2. Energy, Population, and Economic Growth in the United States, 1900–1980

Year	(1) Gross Energy Consumption (in quads)	(2) Population (in millions)	(3) GNP (in billions of 1972 dollars)	(4) Per Capita GNP (in 1972 dollars)[a]	(5) Btu's per Dollar of GNP[b]	(6) MBtu's Per Capita[c]
1900	9.587	76.0	123.3	1,620	77,753.1	125.978
1905	13.212	83.8	154.7	1,846	85,404.1	157.661
1910	16.565	92.4	185.6	2,009	89,251.1	179.275
1915	17.764	100.5	192.4	1,914	92,328.5	176.756
1920	19.770	106.5	216.4	2,032	91,358.6	185.634
1925	20.880	115.8	277.2	2,394	75,324.7	180.311
1930	22.290	123.1	285.2	2,317	78,155.7	181.072
1935	19.110	127.3	260.8	2,049	73,274.5	150.118
1940	23.910	132.6	343.6	2,591	69,586.7	180.317
1945	31.500	140.5	559.0	3,979	56,350.6	224.199
1950	34.000	152.3	533.5	3,503	63,730.1	223.244
1951	35.100	154.9	576.5	3,722	60,884.6	226.598
1952	36.200	157.6	598.5	3,798	60,484.5	229.695
1953	37.300	160.2	621.8	3,881	59,987.1	232.833
1954	38.500	163.0	613.7	3,765	62,734.2	236.196
1955	39.700	165.9	654.8	3,947	60,629.2	239.301
1956	40.600	168.9	668.8	3,960	60,706.0	240.376
1957	41.600	172.0	680.9	3,959	61,096.0	241.860
1958	42.600	174.9	679.5	3,885	62,693.2	243.568
1959	43.600	177.8	720.4	4,052	60,521.9	245.219

1962	47.300	186.6	799.1	4,282	59,191.5	253.483
1963	49.200	189.2	830.7	4,391	59,227.2	260.042
1964	51.100	191.9	874.4	4,557	58,440.1	266.285
1965	53.300	194.3	925.9	4,765	57,565.6	274.318
1966	56.400	196.6	981.0	4,990	57,492.4	286.877
1967	58.300	198.7	1,007.7	5,071	57,854.5	293.407
1968	61.700	200.7	1,051.8	5,241	58,661.3	307.424
1969	65.000	202.7	1,078.8	5,322	60,252.1	320.670
1970	66.900	204.9	1,075.3	5,248	62,215.2	326.501
1971	68.300	207.1	1,107.5	5,348	61,670.4	329.792
1972	71.600	208.8	1,171.5	5,609	61,139.1	342.912
1973	74.600	210.4	1,235.0	5,870	60,404.9	354.563
1974	72.700	211.9	1,217.8	5,747	59,697.8	343.086
1975	70.600	213.6	1,202.1	5,628	58,730.6	330.524
1976	74.000	215.1	1,274.7	5,926	58,052.9	344.026
1977	75.800	217.8	1,337.6	6,169	56,668.7	348.025
1978	78.080	219.4	1,399.2	6,377	55,856.2	355.879
1979	78.150	221.1	1,431.1	6,461	54,574.8	353.460
1980	76.201	222.8	1,480.7	6,646	51,462.8	342.015

Sources: Sam H. Schurr and Bruce C. Netschert, *Energy in the American Economy, 1850–1975* (Baltimore: Johns Hopkins Press for Resources for the Future, 1960); U.S. Department of the Interior, *Energy Perspectives 2* (Washington, D.C.: U.S. Government Printing Office, 1976); U.S. Department of Energy, Energy Information Administration, *Monthly Energy Review* (Washington, D.C.: U.S. Government Printing Office, May 1981); U.S. Council of Economic Advisors, *Economic Report of the President* (Washington, D.C.: U.S. Government Printing Office, 1981).

[a]Computed by dividing items in colums (3) by those in column (2)

[b]Computed by dividing items in column (1) by those in column (3)

[c]Computed by dividing items in column (1) by those in column (2)

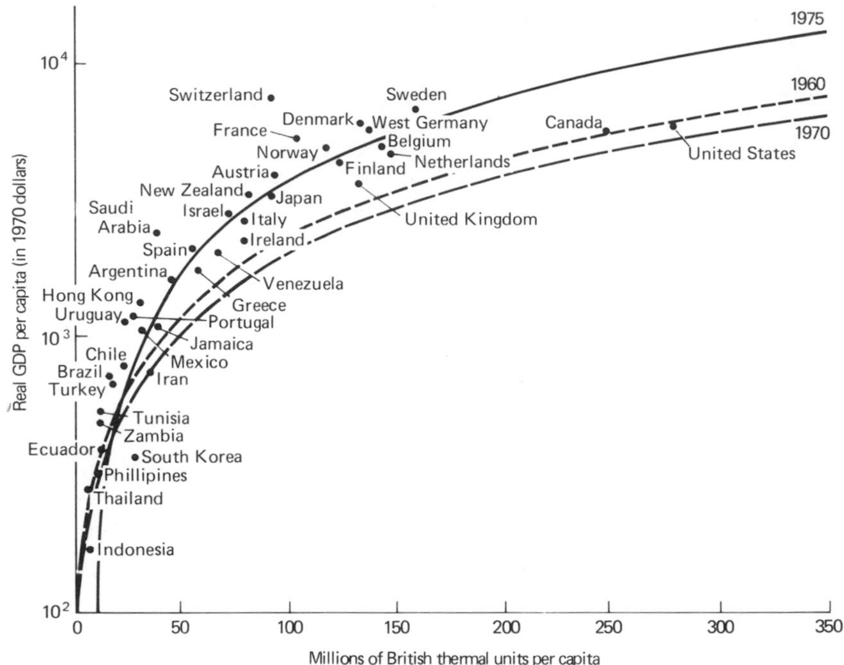

Figure 3.4. International Comparisons of Energy Consumption and Real Gross Domestic Product, 1960, 1970, 1975. Individual country observations are for 1975. Data from United Nations, *Statistical Yearbook, 1976* (New York: United Nations Publications, 1976); and idem, *National Accounts*, vol. 2, *Statistical Tables, 1976* (New York: United Nations Publications, 1976).

puted to determine the relationship between energy and real GDP for the three separate years. The results of these equations are:

$$(3.15.d)\quad E_{1960} = -5.10665 + \underset{(0.00396)}{0.04051Y} \qquad \bar{R}^2 = 0.731515,\ n = 39,$$

$$(3.15.e)\quad E_{1970} = -7.12354 + \underset{(0.00294)}{0.04849Y} \qquad \bar{R}^2 = 0.877351,\ n = 39,$$

$$(3.15.f)\quad E_{1975} = 6.17130 + \underset{(0.00232)}{0.02255Y} \qquad \bar{R}^2 = 0.710170,\ n = 39.$$

It is interesting that the level of income exerts approximately the same magnitude of influence on international energy consumption as it does in the United States alone. During the period 1960–70, the international price of energy was declining in real terms. Accordingly, there was a much higher increase in energy consumption per unit increase in real income in 1970 than there was in 1960. However, in the aftermath of the quadrupling of OPEC oil prices in 1973–74, there was a decline in the international energy intensity of 1975 to a level below that in 1960, and below that estimated for the United States alone in equation (3.15.c).

The international comparisons of figure 3.4 enable us to make a further observation regarding the energy-income relationship. We can think of each of the three curves shown in figure 3.4 as an indirect reflection of the technical efficiency of energy conversion at a given moment in time. Because the U.S. energy–GDP relationship in 1975 was below the estimated curve for 1975, the United States was less technically efficient in its consumption of energy than the sample of thirty-nine countries as a whole. For example, in 1975 the United States had a real per capita GDP of $6,623 and a per capita level of gross energy consumption of 274.9 MBtu's. If the United States had been as energy intense as the estimated sample as a whole, it would have consumed only 155.5 MBtu's per capita to produce its per capita GDP of $6,623; that is, its energy consumption would have been less than 60 percent of its actual level, with no reduction in real income. Similarly, had the United States' degree of technical efficiency of energy been as high as that of the sample as a whole, its actual consumption of 274.9 MBtu's per capita would have enabled it to have a real per capita Gross Domestic Product of $11,917, or 80 percent higher than it actually had in that year. Thus, when we consider both different time periods and international comparisons of energy and income, it is clear that there can be a much broader degree of flexibility than there might at first appear to be.

We can now complete our elementary forecasting model by combining the information from the estimating equation (3.15) with a projected rate of economic growth. For purposes of discussion, let us assume that the level of real GNP will continue to increase at its 1900–1980 historical rate of 3.15 percent. Using equation (3.2), the level of real GNP in the year 2000 would be

(3.2.a)
$$\begin{aligned} Y_{2000} &= 1{,}480.7(1.0315)^{20} \\ &= \$2{,}753.29 \text{ billion.} \end{aligned}$$

Inserting the estimated 2000 level of real GNP in equation (3.15.a) yields a projected level of gross primary energy consumption of approximately 146.39 quads of energy, while for equations (3.15.b), (3.15.c), (3.15.d), (3.15.e) and (3.15.f) the estimated levels of energy consumption would be 150.98, 112.47, 106.43, 126.38, and 68.26 quads, respectively, a wide variation indeed.[4]

As we might suspect, there are several problems in using the preceding simple macroeconomic energy forecasting model. First is the problem of data to be used in the projections. Though all three equations used to estimate the demand for energy in the United States show some tendency for energy intensity to continue its historical decline, the question is which is more representative of future conditions. There does not appear to be much difference between the five-year, very long coefficient of income in (3.15.a) and the thirty-year annual coefficient of income demand in (3.15.b). What distinguishes these two equations from (3.15.c) is that it was during the 1970s that

[4]It should be noted that the last three figures were derived from an international cross section of energy and GDP, rather than energy and GNP. Since GDP is strongly correlated with GNP but is slightly smaller, the last three estimates contain a slight upward bias when applied to the United States.

the relative price of energy rose by such unprecedented proportions, as can be seen in figure 3.5. Thus, the increase in real energy prices during the 1970s reduced the historical rate of aggregate energy demand to approximately half of its preceding rate, much as we have seen in the international comparison of equation (3.15.f).

A second difficulty with our simple macroeconomic energy forecasting model is that GNP is assumed to continue to grow at its historical rate. Since some energy is needed to produce a unit of GNP, as the relative price of a resource changes, it can in turn affect the potential growth of GNP and its

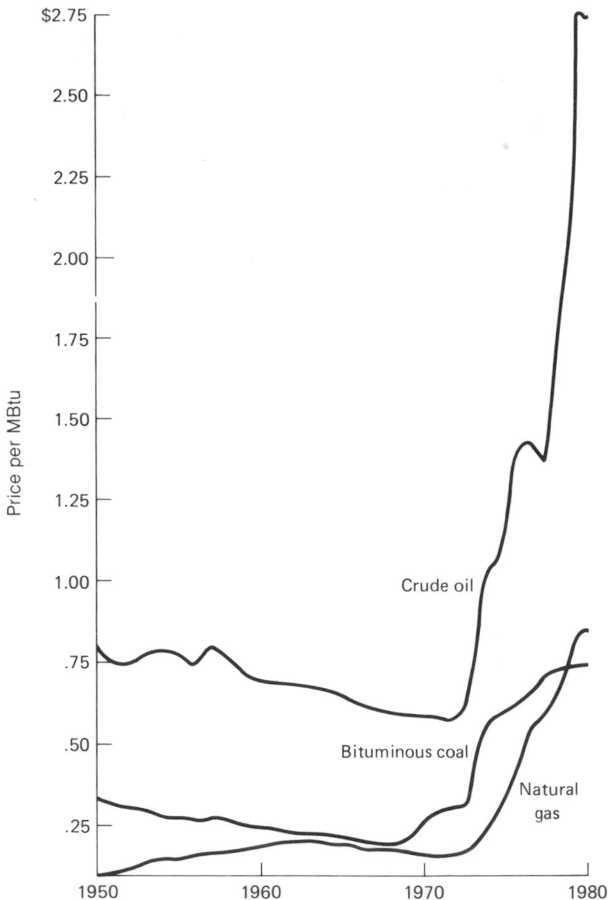

Figure 3.5. Constant-Dollar Prices of Fossil Fuels in the United States, 1950–80. Figures are in 1972 dollars per MBtu. Crude-oil prices are based on delivered refinery purchases, composite of all sources. Bituminous coal prices are based on deliveries to steam-electric utility plants. Natural gas prices are based on average wellhead values of domestic production. Data from Department of the Interior, *Energy Perspectives 2*, p. 98; and from Department of Energy, Energy Information Administration, *Monthly Energy Review*, May 1981, pp. 76, 88–89.

composition, much as changes in the quantity and quality of other inputs can do. What is needed therefore is a specification of the linkages between inputs and outputs, or as economists would call it, a macroeconomic production function within the aggregate forecasting model. We could then better predict the impact of changes in relative prices on the actual and potential growth of GNP, on inflation and unemployment rates, on the environment, and on the distribution of income.

A third difficulty derives directly from the second: energy intensity tells us relatively little about the sectoral allocation of energy resources or of their composition. Ultimately, we are interested in knowing not only future levels of aggregate energy demand but also the composition of energy balances. We could then predict the effects of an increase in GNP on the composition of energy demand, on domestic production of energy, and thus on international energy trade. To be useful, these changes should also be identified by resource and by sector, as in the configuration presented in tables 2.1 and 2.2.

Finally, even if a macroeconomic forecasting model had the aforementioned level of detail, we would need to identify the instrumental variables that policymakers could use to affect energy alternatives. These instrumental variables are the same ones discussed in section 1.2. They include: public regulation, subsidies, taxation and spending, and monetary controls over the level of credit and interest rates. If these instrumental variables were specified accurately in the model, then we could examine by simulation the separate effects of alternative choices that policymakers might have to confront, thereby simplifying the task of making energy policy decisions.

If simplified energy forecasting models are limited, how do more complex models differ? Figure 3.6 illustrates several key linkages in many macroeconomic energy models. In such models there are three basic types of variables: exogenous variables, independent of the model; instrumental variables, independent within the model; and endogenous variables, dependent on the first two types of variables. Endogenous variables can be further classified according to whether they function as policy objectives or serve as links between independent and policy variables. Rather than undertake an extensive examination of the many possible configurations that such models could assume, it would be more useful to summarize the broad types of relations characterized in figure 3.6.

For forecasting and policy purposes, most energy models include only those exogenous variables that have exhibited a significant influence on past energy decisions. Thus, OPEC pricing and production decisions bear clearly on the determination of U.S. crude-oil prices. In addition to market supply and demand, government decisions also influence input prices. The government instruments shown are the same kinds of tools discussed in chapter 1. They include general spending and taxation, monetary controls over credit and interest rates, and tax and pricing regulation of utilities. Once producer prices determine the level and composition of GNP, we can derive simultaneously the level of consumer prices, the rate of unemployment, and the level of aggregate energy demand. When combined with the level of international ex-

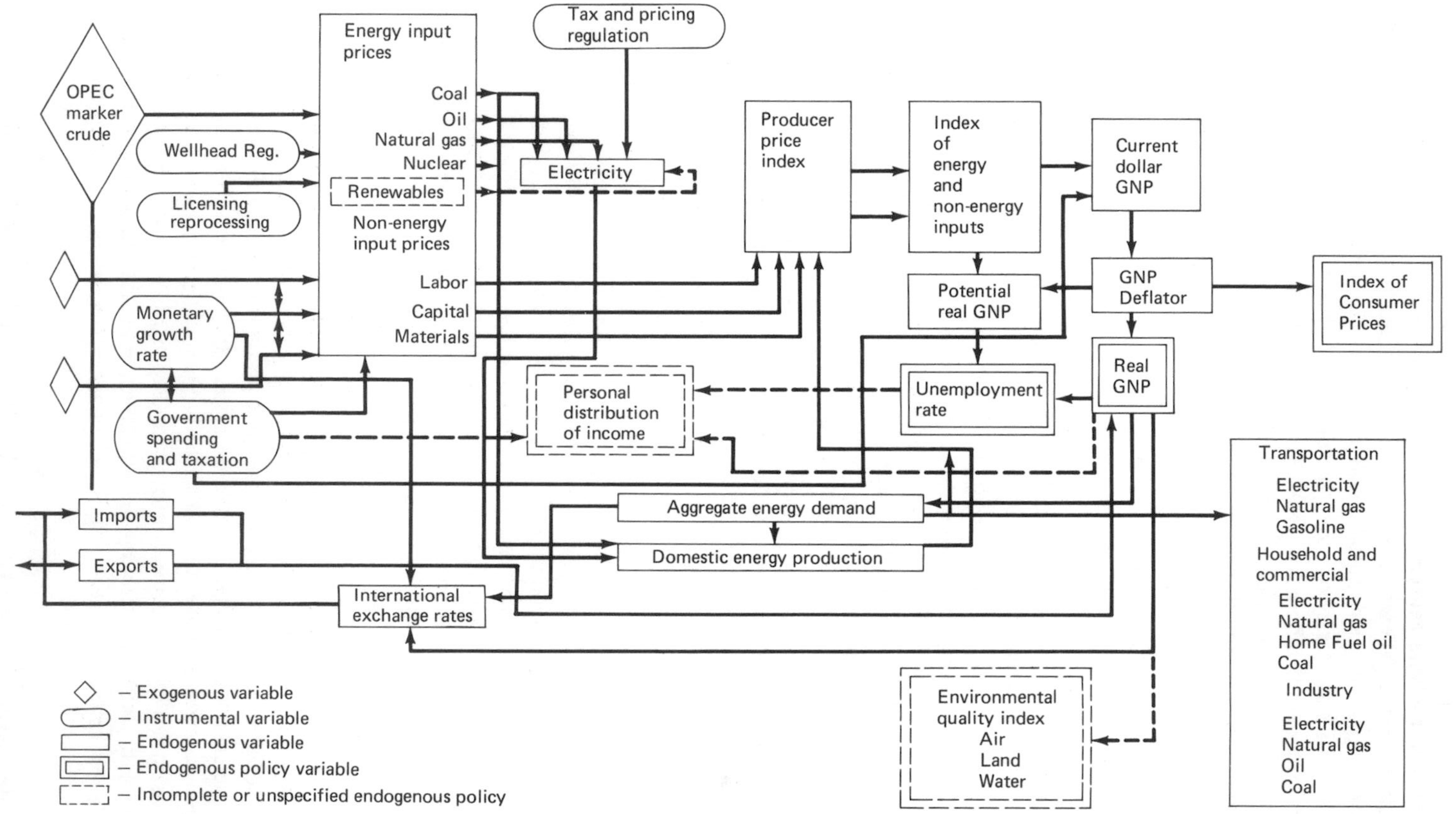

Figure 3.6. Key Linkages in Energy Forecasting Models. Adapted from Knut Anton Mork, ed., *Energy Prices, Inflation, and Economic Activity* (Cambridge, Mass.: Ballinger Publishing Co., 1981), pp. 64–65.

change rates, the interactions between aggregate energy demand and supply will then determine to what extent there will be imported energy dependence, as well as the distribution of delivered energy resources by sector and by type.

Despite the complexity of many recent macroeconomic energy forecasting models, they have often failed to predict accurately alternative energy futures, particularly the impact of rising energy prices on economic growth, on inflation, and on the distribution of income. Though there are many specific reasons for the divergent predictions of individual models, most of them share several general weaknesses which merit brief elaboration.

One of the most basic problems in any energy forecasting model is the quality of data. As we saw even in the simple energy model discussed previously, past trends are not readily indicative of future conditions. Thus, it was logical that pre-1973 forecasting models discounted largely the role of OPEC in world oil pricing and production decisions, since there was no observable statistical evidence to the contrary. On the other hand, with the substantial increases in U.S. domestic energy prices resulting from regulatory reforms and elimination of all remaining controls over domestic crude-oil production in 1980, the ability of OPEC to exercise the kind of influence that it did in 1973 and in 1979 is diminished substantially. This is, in effect, the classic problem of nonreplicability of an experiment that confronts all social-science investigation. The only way to minimize this weakness would be to simulate the effects of unobserved low-probability alternatives within the model. Yet the number of low-probability events may be large and therefore relatively costly to undertake. Thus, even when econometric models use weighted data and adaptive expectations formulations, there is an inherent tendency for them to reflect past or present conditions rather than anticipate unorthodox outcomes.[5]

Closely related to the problem of data is incomplete specification of variables within forecasting models. As we have seen, one underlying issue confronting policymakers is the rate and extent of a shift from depletable energy resource utilization to renewable energy technologies and conservation under alternative patterns of economic growth and relative energy prices. The difficulty is that the rate of introduction of new technologies may be tied not only to the relative price of existing resource technologies and conservation but also to uncertainties surrounding their costs. With but experimental estimates of these costs rather than observed market prices, there is considerable potential for underestimating or overestimating the likelihood of alternative mixes of depletable and renewable energy technologies for the future.

Figure 3.6 also illustrates another example of incomplete specification of variables, shown here as the set of linkages between government policies, alternative energy–GNP configurations, and the distribution of income. As will be shown in part IV, choices in energy policy can not be readily separated from their effects on the distribution of income. Yet many models of energy

[5]For a discussion of these techniques and their rationale, see Theil, *Introduction to Econometrics.*

tend to concentrate on the mix and level of energy balances, even though these choices may carry significant but ignored consequences on the distribution of income.

A third difficulty in macroeconomic energy forecasting models is that the market prices on which they depend may fail to reflect their associated social costs and benefits. Typical of this problem are the effects of energy-conversion choices on the environment suggested in figure 3.6. As an example, one way of reducing U.S. dependence on uncertain supplies of OPEC oil is by an accelerated program of synthetic fossil fuels production proposed during the Carter administration. As will be seen in chapter 5, shale oil, tar sands, coal gasification and liquefaction technologies all represent major alternatives to both OPEC and limited domestic supplies of conventional oil and gas. Yet each of these technologies carries unpriced environmental costs in the form of air, water, and land pollution. Thus, while they might appear economically competitive in a market price-forecasting model, they could distort substantially the choice of an optimal energy policy. With all of these caveats in mind, then, let us now turn to the specifics of several key energy forecasting models.

3.3. FORECASTING ALTERNATIVE ENERGY FUTURES

Energy forecasts are not new.[6] What distinguishes recent ones from those in the past is that they are more comprehensive and far greater in number than ever before. Instead of presenting an exhaustive list of these forecasts or attempting to analyze each one in detail, our concern at this point is with a comparison of basic conclusions from several key studies. The findings of these studies, and the underlying assumptions that give rise to their differences, anticipate the analytical framework of the technology and economics of energy presented in subsequent chapters.

Tables 3.3 and 3.4 list several forecasts of future U.S. energy consumption. These forecasts, made over a time span of almost twenty years, provide projections of energy consumption for varying dates over a thirty-year period. The large variation in estimates is not surprising, but what is particularly interesting is that most of the studies project future energy consumption to rise above present levels, even under assumptions of low to moderate economic growth and varying degrees of effort to promote energy conservation. Given the present U.S. dependence on depletable energy resources and on imported

[6]One of the most famous early energy forecasts was *The Coal Question*, a study made in 1865 by William Stanley Jevons on the expected lifetime of English coal reserves. Jevons predicted their exhaustion in a matter of a few decades, which of course has not yet occurred because of the emergence of alternative energy resources and energy conservation opportunities. A more recent study with similar dire predictions is the 1972 Club of Rome's *The Limits to Growth*. Far more sophisticated, its computerized model combined an examination of resource depletion with population growth, economic growth, and environmental degradation. Its pessimistic conclusions have since been criticized for failing to take into account the role of relative prices and opportunities for technical substitution (see Donella Meadows et al., *The Limits to Growth* [New York: Universe Books, 1972]).

Table 3.3. Forecasts of U.S. Gross Energy Consumption, 1980, 1985, 2000, 2010 (in quadrillion Btu's)

Study	1980	1985	2000	2010
Landsberg et al. (1963)	79.19	89.23	135.16	—
U.S. Department of the Interior				
(1972)	96.00	116.60	191.90	—
(1975)	—	103.50	163.40	—
Ford Foundation Energy Policy Project (1974)				
Historical growth	100.00	115.00	187.00	—
Technical fix	88.00	92.00	123.00	—
Zero energy growth	85.13	88.00	100.00	—
Project Independence Blueprint (1974)				
Base case	86.30	102.92	147.00	—
Conversion	82.20	94.16	120.00	—
FEA, *National Energy Outlook* (1976)				
Low growth	80.23	90.72	—	—
High growth	85.40	105.64	—	—
United Nations (1976)				
Reference case	86.50	102.90	—	—
Edison Electric Institute (1976)				
Moderate growth	—	—	161.00	—
Institute for Energy Analysis (1976)				
Low growth	—	—	101.40	—
High growth	—	—	125.90	—
National Energy Plan (1977)	—	97.00	—	—
Stanford Research Institute (1977)				
Base case	—	—	143.20	—
Low growth	—	—	109.40	—
Electric Power Research Institute (1977)				
High case	—	—	196.00	—
Conservation case	—	—	146.00	—
Workshop on Alternative Energy Strategies (1977)				
Low growth	—	—	115.10	—
High growth	—	—	132.00	—
Brookhaven National Laboratory/Dale Jorgenson Associates (1978)				
Base case	—	—	138.50	—
National Research Council, National Academy of Sciences (1979)[a]				
Low growth	—	69.25	66.73	65.10
High growth	—	94.29	144.28	191.60
Resources for the Future (1979)				
Low growth	—	80.52	95.00	—
High growth	—	89.50	145.00	—
The Global 2000 Report to the President (1980)				
Low growth	—	90.00	129.70	—
High growth	—	102.00	141.30	—
Ross and Williams (1981)				
Low growth	—	73.04	67.83	64.00
Business and usual	—	80.09	93.00	102.00
Actual consumption	76.20	—	—	—

Sources: Hans H. Landsberg, Leonard L. Fischman, and Joseph L. Fisher, *Resources in America's Future* (Baltimore: Johns Hopkins Press for Resources for the Future, 1973), p. 857; U.S. Department of the Interior, *United States Energy through the Year 2000* (Washington, D.C.: U.S. Government Printing Office, 1972 and 1975); Ford Foundation Energy Policy Project, *A Time to Choose* (Cambridge, Mass.: Ballinger Publishing Co., 1974), pp. 28, 76, 111; Federal Energy Administration, *Project Independence Blueprint* (Washington, D.C.: U.S. Government Printing Office, 1974), pp. 17, 431,A-1; idem, *National Energy Outlook, 1976*

Table 3.4. Forecasts of U.S. Energy Consumption by Resource, 1985, 2000, 2010
(in quadrillion Btu's)

Resource	Landsberg et al.	Ford Foundation Energy Policy Project			National Academy of Sciences		Ross and Williams[d]
		High case[a]	Environmental Protection	Zero growth	High growth[b]	Low growth[c]	
				1985			
Coal	0.1804	0.1738	0.1522	0.1591	0.2875	0.2383	0.1779
Conventional	—	—	—	—	(0.1929)	(0.1970)	—
Liquid synthetics	—	—	—	—	(0.0691)	(0.0269)	—
Gas synthetics	—	—	—	—	(0.0255)	(0.0144)	—
Petroleum	0.3720	0.4348	0.4457	0.4205	0.3900	0.4357	0.4080
Natural gas	0.3480	0.2696	0.3043	0.3068	0.2184	0.2231	0.2307
Shale oil	0	0	0	0	0.0080	0	0
Tar sands	0	0	0	0	0	0	0
Nuclear	0.0693	0.0870	0.0543	0.0568	0.0458	0.0387	0.0322
Renewables	0.0303	0.0348	0.0435	0.0568	0.0503	0.0642	0.1512
Total	1.0000	1.0000	1.0000	1.0000	1.0000	1.0000	1.0000
Amount in quads	89.23	115.00	92.00	88.00	94.29	69.25	68.93
				2000			
Coal	0.1329	0.2086	0.1789	0.1800	0.3741	0.2649	0.1705
Conventional	—	—	—	—	(0.2086)	(0.2198)	—
Liquid synthetics	—	—	—	—	(0.1076)	(0.0292)	—
Gas synthetics	—	—	—	—	(0.0579)	(0.0159)	—
Petroleum	0.3919	0.3476	0.4187	0.3900	0.2998	0.3950	0.3630
Natural gas	0.3145	0.1925	0.2967	0.2900	0.1503	0.1572	0.1382
Shale oil	0	0	0	0	0.0149	0	0
Tar sands	0	0	0	0	0	0	0
Nuclear	0.1398	0.2139	0.0244	0.0300	0.0954	0.0626	0.0396
Renewables	0.0209	0.0374	0.0813	0.1100	0.0655	0.1203	0.2887
Total	1.0000	1.0000	1.0000	1.0000	1.0000	1.0000	1.0000

2010							
Coal	—	—	—	—	0.3826	0.2366	0.1659
Conventional	—	—	—	—	(0.2197)	(0.2366)	—
Liquid synthetics	—	—	—	—	(0.0992)	0	—
Gas synthetics	—	—	—	—	(0.0637)	0	—
Petroleum	—	—	—	—	0.2516	0.3702	0.2596
Natural gas	—	—	—	—	0.1169	0.1244	0.0872
Shale oil	—	—	—	—	0.0157	0	0
Tar sands	—	—	—	—	0	0	0
Nuclear	—	—	—	—	0.1555	0.0860	0.0453
Renewables	—	—	—	—	0.0777	0.1828	0.4420
Total	1.0000	1.0000	1.0000	1.0000	1.0000	1.0000	1.0000
Amount in quads	—	—	—	—	191.60	65.10	64.00

Sources: Hans H. Landsberg, Leonard L. Fischman, and Joseph L. Fisher, *Resources in America's Future* (Baltimore: Johns Hopkins Press for Resources for the Future, 1963); Ford Foundation Energy Policy Project, *A Time to Choose* (Cambridge, Mass.: Ballinger Publishing Co., 1974); Philip Handler, *Energy in Transition, 1985–2010* (San Francisco: W. H. Freeman and Co., 1980); and Marc H. Ross and Robert H. Williams, *Our Energy: Regaining Control* (New York: McGraw-Hill Book Co., 1981).

[a] The case of high economic growth and high imports

[b] Estimates for 1985 and 2000 have been interpolated from 1980 data and estimates for 2010, based on a high-energy-consumption scenario

[c] Estimates for 1985 and 2000 have been interpolated from 1980 data and estimates for 2010, based on a scenario of low energy consumption and accelerated conservation

[d] Estimates for 1985 and 2000 have been interpolated from 1980 data and estimates for 2010, based on an accelerated-energy-conservation scenario

supplies of petroleum, these studies thus suggest two basic conclusions: (1) that the real price of energy relative to other resources is likely to rise in the future; and (2) that if dependence on imported energy resources remains as high as it did during the 1970s, then increases in the price of depletable energy could occur at the kind of crisis speed as they did in the past. Yet with recent stability and even some decline in recent international petroleum prices, we must ask whether the conditions that prevailed at the time these studies were made are comparable to those we are likely to confront during the coming decades. To answer this question, we need first to disaggregate the projections of table 3.3 by resource and by sector.

One way of approaching the question of comparability is to look at some of the projections of table 3.3 in terms of specific sources of energy. Table 3.4 provides a breakdown of estimated gross energy consumption by resource for several of the projections cited in table 3.3. Given the historical dependence of the United States on imported supplies of petroleum, the figures of table 3.4 show that there are two basic alternatives: accelerated diversification of supplies and vigorous energy conservation. As a bench mark, the 1974 Ford Foundation's estimated high-growth case illustrates the consequences of continuing high rates of economic growth with no deviations in the then historical patterns of energy production and consumption. Petroleum would continue to take a larger share of total energy consumption, with attendant implications on imported energy dependence. Yet even under what was then considered a moderate program of conservation, environmental protection, and continued use of nuclear energy, the degree of dependence on petroleum would not change much in relative terms. In contrast, the 1979 National Academy of Sciences study took a more optimistic view of the potential of synthetic fossil fuel technologies and the potential for energy conservation. In the high- and low-growth scenarios of the National Academy of Sciences

(Washington, D.C.: U.S. Government Printing Office, February 1976), pp. G-15, G-17, G-20, G-23; Philip Handler, *Energy in Transition, 1985–2010* (San Francisco: W. H. Freeman and Co., 1980); United Nations, *United States Energy through the Year 2000,* rev. ed. (New York: United Nations Publications, 1975), based on Department of the Interior, *United States Energy through the Year 2000*; Edison Electric Institute, *Economic Growth in the Future* (New York: McGraw-Hill Book Co., 1976), p. 193; Institute for Energy Analysis, Oak Ridge Associated Universities, *U.S. Energy and Economic Growth, 1975–2010* (Oak Ridge, Tenn.: Institute for Energy Analysis, September 1976); Office of the President, *National Energy Plan* (Washington, D.C.: U.S. Government Printing Office, 1977), p. 96; Stanford Research Institute, *Fuel and Energy Price Forecasts,* vols. 1 and 2, Report EPRI EA-433, prepared for the Electric Power Research Institute (Menlo Park, Calif.: SRI, 1977); Robert T. Crow, "Demand 77," *EPRI Journal,* December 1977, pp. 20–23; Workshop on Alternative Energy Strategies, *Energy Supply-Demand Integrations to the Year 2000* (Cambridge, Mass.: MIT Press, 1977); David J. Behling and Edward Hudson, *Policies for Energy Conservation: Potentials, Mechanisms, and Impacts* (Upton, N.Y.: Brookhaven National Laboratory, 1978); Resources for the Future, National Energy Strategies Project, *Energy in America's Future: The Choices before Us* (Baltimore: Johns Hopkins University Press for Resources for the Future, 1979), p. 10; Council on Environmental Quality and the Department of State, *The Global 2000 Report to the President: Entering the Twenty-First Century* (Washington, D.C.: U.S. Government Printing Office, 1980), pp. 167, 179; and Marc H. Ross and Robert H. Williams, *Our Energy: Regaining Control* (New York: McGraw-Hill Book Co., 1981), pp. 30, 200.

[a]Figures for 1985 and 2000 are interpolated

study shown here, gross energy consumption is projected at lower levels than those of the Ford study, with conventional and synthetic coal fuels reducing some of the historical dependence on petroleum and natural gas, and on imported petroleum in particular. However, in a more recent study, physicists Marc Ross and Robert Williams suggest that the synthetic route may not be necessary and that diversification and energy conservation can be achieved simultaneously by a more substantive shift to renewable energy resource technologies than any of these studies had considered possible. Indeed, Ross and Williams conclude that by 2010, real U.S. GNP could rise by an historical rate of 2.7 percent to reach a level over twice what it was in 1980, but with gross energy consumption at 16 percent less than the 1980 level of 76 quads.

Another way to understand the energy projections of table 3.3 is in terms of the sectoral distribution of energy consumption. Table 3.5 provides such a breakdown for the same studies and time periods cited in table 3.4. What is significant here is that depending on the level and form of energy consumption, there can be substantial variations in its sectoral distribution in the economy, even as the degree of energy import dependence and intensity of energy consumption may be affected. For example, in the three alternative scenarios of the 1974 Ford Foundation study, the share of energy in the transportation sector varies according to the extent to which liquid fuels such as gasoline will continue to be provided by conventional petroleum supplies and on the degree to which fuel conservation by vehicles can be achieved. In contrast, the emphasis on synthetics and conservation in the 1979 National Academy of Sciences study suggests that while energy conservation is possible, synthetic fossil fuels can maintain or even increase the share of transportation energy consumption beyond its current point. On the other hand, the shift to renewables and conservation embodied in the Ross and Williams projection suggests a much smaller variation in the transportation share of energy than either the Ford or the National Academy of Sciences study. In effect, then, the form and level of consumption can have significant consequences for the sectoral distribution of energy in the economy, as we have seen in this simple comparison of forecasts for the transportation sector.

If energy choices were as simple and as elegant as the alternative projections of tables 3.4 and 3.5 seem to suggest, the task of formulating an appropriate energy policy would be relatively simple. Unfortunately, there are tradeoffs in each of these scenarios, the specifics of which may not always be readily apparent. A good example is the trade-off between energy security and environmental protection. As is shown in one of the National Academy of Sciences scenarios, the current U.S. dependence on imported petroleum could be relieved by an accelerated program of development of synthetic fossil fuels, much as was proposed by the Carter administration. Yet whether one is considering gasification or liquefaction of coal, shale oil, or tar sands, experience with currently available production technologies points to significant environmental costs that may accompany a greater use of these resources. Technical inefficiency in converting these resources from their natural state into usable energy forms thus threatens to pollute drinking water at a faster rate, to reduce food production by removal of agricultural topsoil,

Table 3.5. Forecasts of U.S. Energy Consumption by Sector, 1985, 2000, 2010
(In quadrillion Btu's)

Sector	Landsberg et al.	Ford Foundation Energy Policy Project: High case	Ford Foundation Energy Policy Project: Environmental Protection	Ford Foundation Energy Policy Project: Zero growth	National Academy of Sciences: High growth[a]	National Academy of Sciences: Low growth[b]	Ross and Williams[c]
				1985			
Residential/commercial	0.2869	0.3287	0.3493	0.3610	0.2899	0.2753	0.3408
Industry	0.4330	0.4502	0.4367	0.4302	0.3941	0.4331	0.4032
Transportation	0.2801	0.2211	0.2140	0.2088	0.3160	0.2916	0.2560
Total	1.0000	1.0000	1.0000	1.0000	1.0000	1.0000	1.0000
Quads	89.23	115.00	91.60	88.10	94.29	69.25	68.93
Import share	0.0744	0.2260	0.1520	0.1300	0.1920	0.2020	—
Real GNP[d]	—	2,150	2,114	2,114	1,658	1,604	1,611
Energy intensity[e]	—	53,488	43,330	41,675	56,870	46,044	42,814
				2000			
Residential/commercial	0.2292	0.2753	0.2919	0.3580	0.2599	0.2230	0.2988
Industry	0.4619	0.5190	0.5089	0.4700	0.4310	0.5311	0.4546
Transportation	0.3089	0.2057	0.1992	0.1720	0.3091	0.2459	0.2466
Total	1.0000	1.0000	1.0000	1.0000	1.0000	1.0000	1.0000
Quads	135.16	187.00	123.00	100.00	144.28	66.73	65.93
Import share	0.1127	0.1980	0.1300	0.1300	0.1646	0.1980	—
Real GNP[d]	—	3,484	3,353	3,361	2,584	2,024	2,402

2010							
Residential/commercial	—	—	—	—	0.2407	0.1891	0.2719
Industry	—	—	—	—	0.4559	0.5965	0.4891
Transportation	—	—	—	—	0.3034	0.2144	0.2390
Total	1.0000	1.0000	1.0000	1.0000	1.0000	1.0000	1.0000
Quads	—	—	—	—	191.60	65.10	64.00
Import share	—	—	—	—	0.1436	0.1875	—
Real GNP[d]	—	—	—	—	3,472	2,468	3,135
Energy intensity[e]	—	—	—	—	55,184	26,402	20,415

Sources: Hans H. Landsberg, Leonard L. Fischman, and Joseph L. Fisher, *Resources in America's Future* (Baltimore: Johns Hopkins Press for Resources for the Future, 1963); Ford Foundation Energy Policy Project, *A Time to Choose* (Cambridge, Mass.: Ballinger Publishing Co., 1974); Philip Handler, *Energy in Transition, 1985–2010* (San Francisco: W. H. Freeman and Co., 1980); and Marc H. Ross and Robert H. Williams, *Our Energy: Regaining Control* (New York: McGraw-Hill Book Co., 1981).

[a]Estimates for 1985 and 2000 have been interpolated from 1980 data and estimates for 2010, based on a high-energy-consumption scenario

[b]Estimates for 1985 and 2000 have been interpolated from 1980 data and estimates for 2010, based on a scenario of low energy consumption and accelerated conservation

[c]Estimates for 1985 and 2000 have been interpolated from 1980 data and estimates for 2010, based on an accelerated-energy-consumption scenario

[d]In billions of 1972 U.S. dollars

[e]In Btu's per 1972 U.S. dollar of GNP

and to increase the incidence of respiratory and cancer fatalities from higher air emissions associated with their use. The question then becomes one of deciding to what extent an additional degree of energy security is worth an additional degree of environmental degradation, and to what extent market pricing can by itself yield an economically efficient solution.

Another possible route to energy security is by an accelerated use of nuclear energy. Among others, both the Ford and National Academy of Sciences studies considered this option as a way of enhancing energy security but without imposing some of the environmental costs associated with a greater use of conventional and synthetic fossil fuels. The difficulty here is that nuclear power imposes its own kinds of risks. Some of these risks are related to the environment, as was evident in the 1979 reactor accident at Three Mile Island in Middletown, Pennsylvania, and in the problem of long-term storage of highly radioactive wastes from routine reactor operation. Moreover, nuclear fuel wastes and some types of nuclear fuel cycles involve significant amounts of plutonium, the principal ingredient in nuclear weapons. Thus, even if nuclear reactor technologies were relatively safe and even if there were a relatively safe waste storage technology, by accelerating the development of commercial nuclear power, we might be acquiring an additional degree of energy security by increasing the probability of nuclear weapons proliferation, thereby jeopardizing national security. To answer these questions, we need therefore to understand how nuclear energy is converted, stored, and priced.

A third example of an energy trade-off is the relationship of energy prices to the distribution of income. Poor people tend to spend a higher share of their income on energy than do the rich, even though their absolute consumption of energy may be smaller. If we seek to reduce the degree of dependence on imported energy by increasing the price of energy to stimulate conservation, as in the imposition of a tax on gasoline, there may be an adverse effect on the income of the poor, particularly if they face fewer opportunities for conservation than do the rich. The question then becomes: To what extent can we rely on demand restraint to achieve energy security and protection of the environment and at the same time prevent a significant redistribution of income? As in the two supply-side scenarios just discussed, market supply and demand forces could be used to weigh energy security against the distribution of income or against energy conservation and environmental protection. Yet whether market forces will be sufficient for such choices to be made depends largely on the degree of efficiency of the market place, that is, on whether there is adequate information available to producers and consumers; on the technical laws of energy conversion; and on the extent of competition. The price, income, and substitution elasticities that economists use to measure the responsiveness of energy demand and supply to market-pricing forces provide one way of answering these questions. We will consider them in detail in chapters 9 and 10.

A fourth example of an energy trade-off is the extent to which society should accelerate its consumption of depletable energy resources rather than shift to a renewable resource based economy, and the extent to which such a shift affects the opportunities for continued economic growth. To be sure, this issue is tied to questions of energy security, to environmental protection, to the distribution of income, and to the efficiency of market supply-and-demand forces. At the same time, renewable resource technologies are also governed by and sensitive to the laws of energy storage and conversion, particularly in that the natural forms of renewable energy resources do not correspond to the forms in which the modern economy consumes the bulk of its energy resources. Thus, the extent to which one could adopt a particular consumption mix of depletable and renewable energy resources depends essentially on the capacity for substitution and on economic efficiency.

A final example of an energy trade-off is the balance between domestic energy pricing and international economic growth and development. Much of the relatively high historical energy intensity of the United States has been due to a domestic policy of cheap energy based on regulated pricing and production subsidies. It may have promoted an equitable distribution of income and economic growth, but it also fostered environmental pollution and dependence on uncertain supplies of imported energy. Now that both OPEC and the United States have raised the real price of energy, they have brought about increases in inflation and a potential slowdown in continued economic growth. In turn, lower economic growth and higher inflation affect not only the United States but also the developed and developing economics. Thus, the choice of specific energy prices and technologies can affect the prevailing degree of international economic equilibrium.

What, then, do these forecasts of alternative energy futures show us? Basically they suggest that continued economic growth is possible under a broad variety of energy options. To choose the energy-intensive growth of the past is likely to accelerate the consumption of depletable energy resources, to risk higher environmental pollution, to perpetuate dependency on uncertain supplies of imported energy, and to involve a much greater use of nuclear power than has been the case until now. On the other hand, economic growth could also be achieved by a less-energy-intensive "soft energy path" that makes much greater use of energy conservation and renewable resource technologies. Of course each of these alternatives, and the many others that lie between, carries important implications for the potential rate of economic growth, for future rates of inflation and unemployment, and for the personal distribution of income. In effect, what these scenarios provide is a useful starting point for the determination of specific energy choices. The many trade-offs of these alternative energy futures are distinguished by the underlying principles of energy conversion, the ways alternative energy resources are priced, and, ultimately, the policy criteria used to guide the allocation of energy resources. It is to these matters that we now turn.

3.4. SUMMARY

Projections of energy production and consumption all depend on past data. Despite imperfections in the use of historical information to predict the future, it is essentially through the use of quantitative models that consistent forecasts may be made, and appropriate policy choices adopted.

Quantitative models of energy vary widely in both scope and methodology. From elementary models of compound and continuous growth, it is possible to derive estimates of aggregate energy use and a breakdown by resource and by sector within the economy. Since the economy depends largely on depletable energy resources, these models must therefore link the behavior of production, consumption, and reserves to the level of energy use within the economy. Yet for these projections to be of use, we need to incorporate the influence of other economic variables, notably sectoral models of the economy that combine monetary and fiscal policy instruments. By so doing, we can better formulate the many trade-offs that are inherent in specific energy policy choices.

SUGGESTED READINGS

Barney, Gerald O. *The Global 2000 Report to the President.* Report prepared by the Council on Environmental Quality and the Department of State. Vols 1 and 2. Washington, D.C.: U.S. Government Printing Office, 1980.

Freeman, S. David. *A Time To Choose.* Final Report of the Energy Policy Project of the Ford Foundation. Cambridge, Mass.: Ballinger Publishing Co., 1974.

Handler, Philip, coord. *Energy in Transition, 1985–2010.* San Francisco: W. H. Freeman and Co., 1980.

Landsberg, Hans H. *Energy: The Next Twenty Years.* Report sponsored by the Ford Foundation and administered by Resources for the Future. Cambridge, Mass.: Ballinger Publishing Co., 1979.

Lovins, Amory B. *Soft Energy Paths: Toward A Durable Peace.* Cambridge, Mass.: Ballinger Publishing Co., 1977.

Ross, Marc H., and Williams, Robert H. *Our Energy: Regaining Control.* New York: McGraw-Hill Book Co., 1981.

Searl, Milton, ed. *Energy Modeling: Art, Science, Practice.* Working Papers for a Seminar on Energy Modeling, 25–26 January 1973. Washington, D.C.: Resources for the Future, March 1973.

Schurr, Sam H. *Energy in America's Future: The Choices before Us.* Study prepared for the Resources for the Future National Energy Strategies Project. Baltimore.: Johns Hopkins University Press for Resources for the Future, 1979.

Stobaugh, Robert, and Yergin, Daniel, eds. *Energy Future.* Report of the Energy Project at the Harvard Business School. New York: Random House Publishers, 1979.

Wilson, Carroll L. *Energy: Global Prospects 1985–2000.* Report of the Workshop on Alternative Energy Strategies (WAES). New York: McGraw-Hill Publishing Co., 1977.

PART II

TECHNOLOGICAL DIMENSIONS OF ENERGY RESOURCES

4

THERMODYNAMICS IN ENERGY SYSTEMS

4.1. THE EARTH'S ENERGY SYSTEMS

Of the many factors governing the feasibility of energy policy decisions, the thermodynamic principles governing energy transformations are among the least understood. Though part of this lack of understanding could be attributed to some of the purely theoretical concerns of the physical sciences, it is an inexcusable condition where these same thermodynamic principles bear so directly on the determination of contemporary energy policy. In the discussion that follows, a brief introduction to these principles provides a basis for examining both present and future energy technologies, as well as the economic decisions appropriate to their use.

Energy is anything that makes it possible to do work. Moreover, energy can exist in many forms: thermal, electrical, chemical, magnetic, and nuclear, to name but a few.[1] While all of these forms of energy exist in nature, they often require transformations in order to become economically useful.[2] What is needed to understand the many types of energy and their transformations into useful forms is an energy accounting system based on stocks and flows.

With the exception of nuclear resources, most of the earth's energy derives ultimately from the sun. It does so mainly through the heat and light that the sun emits daily toward earth, as well as through the sun's historical impact on the evolution of the earth's geological and atmospheric composition. As a result, the earth possesses at any one time both new flows of energy and whatever stocks it has been able to capture and store from past solar energy flows.

Solar energy is generated continuously in the sun's core by thermonuclear fusion. With core temperatures reaching as high as 25 million degrees Celsius (45 million degrees Fahrenheit), the fusion of hydrogen atoms produces

[1]These forms may be either kinetic or potential. Since many economic uses of energy require energy storage capacity, potential energy is of particular interest in the determination of alternative energy resource utilization.

[2]Whether kinetic or potential, many energy resources are converted into a secondary energy form, such as nuclear and hydropower in the generation of electricity.

lighter helium atoms, and the loss of mass becomes the energy emitted by the sun. Since the sun is in a spatial vacuum, with no conduction or convection channels connecting it to earth, solar energy reaches the earth only by radiation, which is measured in photons. These photons, or quanta of light, may be further converted into watt-hours, quads, or any other standard unit of energy accounting.

Energy is released from the sun at the rate of 3.46×10^{25} watts. Of this amount, 5.00×10^{-9} percent, or $173{,}000 \times 10^{12}$ watts (173 trillion kilowatts), travels the 93-million mile distance to reach earth at a rate of just over eight minutes per emission. Of the solar energy reaching the earth's atmospheric boundary, 30 percent ($52{,}000 \times 10^{12}$ watts) is reflected away in the form of short-wave-length radiation. The remaining 70 percent is absorbed by the earth through a variety of biophysical mechanisms, and most of it is quickly reemitted into space in the form of long-wave-length radiation. (All of these mechanisms are summarized in figure 4.1.)

Of all solar energy reaching the earth's surface, almost two-thirds is accounted for by direct conversion to heat. Almost one-third is in the form of evaporation and precipitation patterns. Winds, waves, and convection currents account for just over a third of 1 percent, and photosynthesis absorbs a third of 0.01 percent. To appreciate the magnitudes in this distribution, in 1975 world gross primary energy consumption was about 250 quads. This represents approximately twenty-four minutes' worth of the solar radiation reaching the earth's atmospheric boundary every day. Yet the direct use of solar energy in society accounted for only a minute fraction of the world's annual energy consumption, since practically all of the 250.1 quads were provided from the depletable fossil energy resources coal, petroleum, and natural gas.

Despite the flow of radiant solar energy from the earth, some storage does occur. One mechanism is the temporary storage of evaporation and precipitation energy in water and ice forms. Another is the somewhat more substantial storage resulting from photosynthesis in plants.[3] Photosynthesis is vital to the earth not only for the oxygen that plants produce but also for its role in fossil fuel creation. However, all of the earth's presently known fossil fuels were created from past plant growth and major climatic and geological changes which have since ceased to occur as they once did. Thus, although some plants store energy in such forms as wood and peat, there is currently no significant natural production of the common fossil fuels coal, petroleum, and natural gas, at least in relation to their rates of consumption.

Geological transformation in the evolution of the earth also created forms of energy other than the sun, including thermal and nuclear energy.[4] Thermal energy is released as cooling of the earth produces fissures in the form of earthquakes, volcanoes, hot springs, rock convection, and steam flows. Nu-

[3]Despite the smaller daily flow of photosynthetic as opposed to evaporation and precipitation energy, storage in plants is much more substantial by virtue of this mechanism.

[4]Magnetic energy is another of these forms, though limited in its potential use by its storage and conversion properties as well as by its relative scarcity.

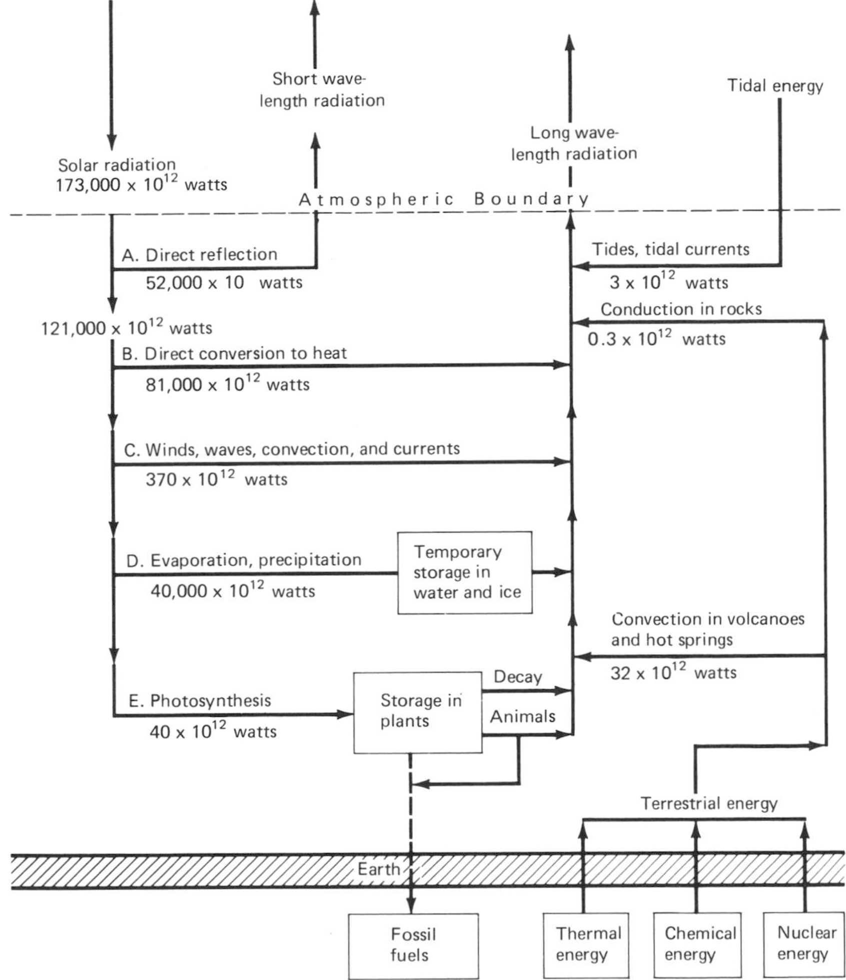

Figure 4.1. The Earth's Energy Flows. Adapted from M. King Hubbert, *Energy Resources* (Washington, D.C.: National Academy of Sciences, National Resources Council, 1962), reprinted in idem, "The Energy Resources of the Earth," *Scientific American* 224 (September 1971): 60–70.

clear energy has been produced mostly by controlled reactions, though there is evidence that natural nuclear reactions have occurred in the evolution of the earth.[5]

Gravitation serves as a conversion mechanism for energy resources, as in the production of electricity from falling water. Moreover, water movement is also influenced by the gravitational force of the moon, thereby producing the

[5]A natural nuclear fission reaction occurred in the region of Gabon several million years ago (see George A. Cowan, "A Natural Fission Reactor," *Scientific American* 235 [July 1976]: 36–47).

tidal flows of rivers and oceans. For all liquid flows caused by gravitation, unless blocked by natural or artificial barriers, such as dams, there is no enduring energy storage, since all energy flows are released by evaporation and precipitation cycles into long-wave-length radiation.

Taken together, the flows of figure 4.1 underline the earth's dependence on the sun for many of the naturally and socially produced forms of energy. In order to understand why the available energy resources of the economy are not used in proportion to their frequency in nature, it is necessary to take into account how these resources are stored and converted into useful forms.

4.2. ENERGY STORAGE AND ENERGY CONVERSION

Patterns of energy use in society depend partly on the structure of relative prices and partly on the storage and conversion properties of individual energy resources. At this stage we can express the storage and conversion properties of energy resources by use of elementary quantitative relations. As will be seen, we can quantify energy storage and conversion for both daily solar flows and those forms of energy that have been stored and converted from the past.

Energy storage will always be accompanied by energy conversion. For example, solar radiation is captured in evaporation and released by precipitation, with temporary storage taking place in water and ice. For energy storage to take place over larger periods of time, there will be a corresponding increase in the magnitude of energy conversion. One of these larger conversion patterns is photosynthesis, which is a chemical transformation essential to active plant energy storage as well as to the past creation of coal, natural gas, and petroleum fossil fuels.

Chemical energy is obtained by a rearranging of molecules in which some of the bonding electrons of a given compound are released, hence the term "electrochemical energy." This rearranging may occur when compounds are combined to form new ones or when they are broken down. For example, we can express the energy stock accumulation arising from photosynthesis in plants as

$$CO_2 + H_2O + \text{Energy} \rightarrow C_x(H_2O)_y + O_2, \tag{4.1}$$

where CO_2 is carbon dioxide, H_2O is water, and $C_x(H_2O)_y$ is a carbohydrate group which is part of the molecule of starches and sugars, e.g., sugar is $C_{12}(H_2O)_{11}$.

In fostering plant growth, photosynthesis thus provides potential energy. If we consider the process of plant growth over the life span of the earth, those plants that did not decay were covered by sediment such that the water, oxygen, nitrogen, and miscellaneous plant products were separated from the carbon, reaching an initial carbon purity stage of peat (13,912,800 joules/kg), followed by eventual mixed deposits of coal (27,825,600 joules/kg), natural gas (46,007,100 joules/kg), and crude petroleum (53,368,236 joules/kg).

Photosynthetic forms of energy storage can also be reversed at any time, as they often are by animal digestion or by combustion. In these cases, the transformation defined in equation (4.1) is switched. Thus, oxidation, which can be obtained by animal digestion or by combustion, can be represented by

(4.2) $$C_x(H_2O)_y + XO_2 \rightarrow (CO_2)_x + (H_2O)_y + \text{Energy}.$$

Variants on the energy transformation of equation (4.2) include not only the combining of carbon and oxygen to produce carbon dioxide and energy but also the combining of hydrogen and oxygen to produce water and energy:[6]

(4.2.a) $$C + O_2 \rightarrow CO_2 + \text{Energy},$$

(4.2.b) $$H + O_2 \rightarrow H_2O + \text{Energy}.$$

Thus, carbon and hydrogen are both fuels, but they produce separate by-products.

Combustion and digestion are only two ways that chemical energy can be obtained. Metals also can undergo transformations, releasing energy in the process. For example, zinc and copper placed in sulphuric acid and water release electrical energy, which is what occurs in the operation of a battery.

The operation of a battery is straightforward: when a zinc strip is dipped into sulphuric acid, some of the zinc dissolves into a zinc sulphate solution, thereby leaving a negative electron charge on the zinc strip. Similarly, when a copper strip is dipped into sulphuric acid, some of the copper dissolves into a sulfate solution, leaving the copper strip with a negative charge, but smaller than that of the zinc strip. When a connecting rod is attached between the zinc and copper strips and the sulfate is allowed to pass through a porous wall between the two strips, the flow of sulfate enables a smooth discharge of electrons to occur. The smooth discharge of electrons is electricity, and it may be used to illuminate a bulb, start a motor, or activate any mechanical process to which it has been adapted.[7] Commercially produced batteries often use lead, lead peroxide, and sulphuric acid to achieve this transformation.

It is also possible to apply electrochemistry to electroplating, as in chromium plating of steel bumpers on automobiles, and to electrolysis, as in the refinement of aluminum from aluminum oxide. In these cases, differences in electric charges are used either to attach one metal to another or to separate one compound from a larger one.

Thermal energy derives from the release of heat from the earth. It occurs

[6]Natural gas and natural gas liquids are also energy resources that yield energy in a similar fashion. Thus:

$$\text{Methane } CH_4 + 2O_2 \rightarrow CO_2 + 2H_2O + \text{Energy}$$

and

$$\text{Sulfur } S + O_2 \rightarrow SO_2 + \text{Energy}.$$

The specific energy obtained from these reactions is based on oxidation of a gram of the element. Carbon yields 94.03 kilocalories; hydrogen, 68.37 kilocalories; and methane, 210.8 kilocalories.

[7]Despite negative charges on the two strips, the one with smaller value (copper) cannot resist as much as can the other (zinc), and the stronger charge is automatically drawn to the weaker one. Electricity can, of course, also be produced by hydropower and fossil and nuclear energy.

as steam heat and as conduction from radioactive decay in rocks located deep below the surface. All of these heat sources are by-products of the formation of the earth in the solar system, generally thought to be a result of a large explosion billions of years ago. As the earth cooled from this "cosmic bang," the temperature of the surface began to fall, leaving a mass of heat energy trapped under the surface.

Natural release of thermal energy occurs whenever continued cooling of the earth causes sufficient contraction of the earth's mantle such that enough pressure is built up to create fissures in the form of earthquakes, volcanoes, and hot spring eruptions. It has been estimated that overall, the average flow of daily thermal energy amounts to 0.063 watts per square meter, a figure which combines both conduction energy in rocks and volcanic and hot spring energy of steam, as is suggested by the flows listed in figure 4.1.[8] While thermal energy may be of considerable potential, its storage within the earth is highly diffused, leaving only scattered natural fissures and those created for use in the economy. In short, the conversion of thermal energy to useful forms requires sufficient storage concentrations in one location, a matter which will be discussed in greater detail in chapter 7.

Another pattern of energy transformation shown in figure 4.1 is gravitational. Gravitational energy stocks and flows will alter as the potential energy storage of liquids is allowed to flow toward a lower elevation. In quantitative terms, the potential energy of a given mass may be expressed as

$$P = mgh \text{ joules,} \tag{4.3}$$

where P is potential energy, measured in joules; m is the mass of the object, measured in kilograms; g is acceleration due to gravity (9.8 meters per second squared); and h is the height the object can potentially fall, measured in meters. As an example, if one kilogram of water falls 200 meters, it will release the energy equivalent of 19,208 joules, or just over 18 Btu's. Unless some mechanism is used to restore this potential, as in evaporation and precipitation of water using solar energy, the potential energy from gravitation will diminish with each successive flow. As will be seen, this condition also carries considerable consequences in the design and implementation of appropriate energy policies.

One other major form of energy storage and conversion is nuclear. This type of energy derives from the rearrangement of the protons and neutrons in the nucleus of atoms, which leads to a complete restructuring of one element into another as heat energy is released. Since nuclear energy involves a much greater transformation than do chemical energy processes, a correspondingly larger amount of energy is obtained from a given amount of fuel. Indeed, we can think of chemical energy transformations as linear and additive, as in equations (4.1) and (4.2), whereas nuclear energy is exponential and multiplicative.

Nuclear energy can be obtained by the fission or fusion of atomic particles. The basic relations in nuclear energy are contained in Einstein's equation

[8]This figure is an average. It does not follow that every square meter will possess this flow, since some fissures will be considerably greater and others may be much less.

(4.4) $$E = mc^2,$$

where m is the mass of the particle and c is the speed of light (3×10^8 meters per second). Though from a physical perspective fission or fusion conceivably could take place with any atomic structure, it is desirable to start with an element which has a relatively heavy atomic weight but which also possesses in a purified form a degree of instability (radioactivity) such that the effort required to produce the nuclear reaction is as small a proportion of the energy released as possible. At present, of the varying isotopes of uranium, ^{233}U, ^{235}U, and ^{238}U, only ^{235}U is abundant enough in nature and endowed with these properties. It is thus no surprise that ^{235}U is the most widely used nuclear fuel for the commercial generation of electricity in municipal power plants.

Uranium is obtained from uranium oxide, U_3O_8. By weight, 85 percent of U_3O_8 is pure uranium, and of this amount, 99.3 percent is ^{238}U. Although ^{238}U can be bombarded with neutrons in a reactor to create a fission chain reaction, much less effort is needed to create such a reaction with ^{235}U. Since ^{235}U contains only 0.7 percent of pure uranium, it is often enriched to reach a concentration level of 3–4 percent before being placed in a nuclear reactor.

Nuclear fission occurs when sufficient quantities of enriched uranium are arranged close enough to each other for a chain reaction to take place. At an enrichment level of 3–4 percent, this critical mass of uranium is just unstable enough that it begins a process of radioactive decay. In so doing, the ^{235}U absorbs a neutron particle and then splits into more stable elements such as strontium and xenon, thereby releasing neutrons plus heat energy. In equation form, this particular fission reaction can be expressed as [9]

(4.5) $${}^{235}_{92}U + {}^{1}_{0}n \rightarrow {}^{90}_{38}Sr + {}^{136}_{54}Xe + 10{}^{1}_{0}n + \text{Heat Energy}.$$

Since the isotope of each atomic particle possesses a specific weight, or atomic mass unit (amu), we can derive the loss of mass from the nuclear reaction by subtracting the terminal amount of mass from the initial amount and then convert this loss into the equivalent amount of energy released by inserting the mass loss into equation (4.4). Thus, for the reaction shown in equation (4.5), the loss of mass from fission is

		Sr-90	89.9073		
U-235	235.0439	Xe-136	135.9072	Heat	
1 neutron	1.0087	10 neutrons	10.0867	Energy	0.1514
	236.0526 amu =		235.9012 amu		+ 0.1514 amu,

(4.5.a)

[9]Equation (4.4) is only one of hundreds of possible fission reactions. Depending on the type of neutron bombardment in a controlled reaction, we can obtain such isotope products as krypton, barium, cesium, palladium, to name but a few. However, the amount of heat energy released depends on the type and stability of the resulting isotopes. Thus, some nuclear reactions can be substantially more powerful than others by margins ranging as high as 50 percent in mass losses alone.

where 1 amu has a value of 1.6603×10^{-27} kg.[10] In the case of equation (4.5.a), the atomic mass unit loss of 0.1514 corresponds to 2.5137×10^{-28} kg, which can then be converted into energy as follows:

$$(4.4.a) \qquad E = (2.5137 \times 10^{-28}) \times (3 \times 10^{8} \text{ meters per second})^{2}$$
$$= 2.2623 \times 10^{-11} \text{ joules}$$
$$= 2.1469 \times 10^{-14} \text{ Btu's.}$$

As a comparison, if 1 percent of the 2.6×10^{24} atoms in one kilogram of uranium were to fission in a chain reaction, the total energy released would amount to:

$$(4.4.b) \qquad E = (0.01)(2.6 \times 10^{24})(2.2623 \times 10^{-11} \text{ joules})$$
$$= 5.88198 \times 10^{11} \text{ joules}$$
$$= 5.58063 \times 10^{8} \text{ Btu's.}$$

These 10 grams of fissioned uranium would thus provide an amount of energy equivalent to over 96 barrels of crude oil, or 21.5 tons of bituminous coal.

Nuclear fusion follows the same principle embodied in equation (4.4). Unlike fission, however, fusion involves the joining of atoms in order for heat energy to be released. The principle behind fusion energy is simple: elements with relatively loose bonds are brought together to produce a combined element with stronger bonds and a smaller atomic mass. Since the resulting element contains a smaller mass than the combined mass of the fusing elements, there is a corresponding release of either energy alone or energy plus residual atomic particles.

At present the only known natural process of nuclear fusion occurs in stars such as the sun. However, in recent years laboratory experiments have moved in the direction of controlled nuclear fusion. Most of these experimental reactions rely on the use of deuterium (^{2}H) and tritium (^{3}H) as the heavy hydrogen isotopes most susceptible and plentiful to produce more stable forms such as helium (^{4}He). The transformation equations of such a fusion reaction may be expressed as follows:

$$(4.6) \qquad {}^{6}Li + n \rightarrow {}^{4}He + {}^{3}H + \text{Heat Energy}$$

and

$$(4.7) \qquad {}^{2}H + {}^{3}H \rightarrow {}^{4}He + n + \text{Heat Energy.}$$

In equation (4.6) the relatively stable but weak bonded element lithium (^{6}Li) combines with one neutron to produce the more stable element helium (^{4}He) plus the unnatural element tritium (^{3}H) and thereby releases energy. In turn, the tritium is then combined with deuterium (^{2}H) to produce still more helium (^{4}He) and additional heat energy. Two stages are involved, since the combination of the unnatural element tritium with deuterium is essential to

[10]One atomic mass unit, or amu, is equal to 1.6603×10^{-24} g.

obtain the largest possible combination of released heat energy.[11] To provide a comparison with other energy resources, we can say that the element deuterium is found in one out of every 6500 atoms in sea water. The energy from one cubic meter of sea water is 11.388×10^9 Btu's, which is equivalent to just under 2,000 barrels of crude oil or over 430 short tons of anthracite coal. By extension, a cubic kilometer of sea water, which represents just one-billionth of the earth's supply at any one time, contains the equivalent of approximately $2{,}000 \times 10^9$ barrels of crude oil, a figure not significantly different from present proven world reserves.

As the above examples suggest, energy can be stored or converted by any number of chemical, thermal, gravitational, or nuclear processes. Yet not all of these processes can be utilized in society with the same degree of ease. Indeed, as has already been pointed out, the composition of current energy consumption by type of resource bears little resemblance to the distribution of available energy resources in nature. Part of the explanation for this puzzling disproportionality lies in the technical efficiency of energy production and consumption. To measure that efficiency, we must take into account the laws of thermodynamics.

4.3. THE INPUT-OUTPUT EFFICIENCY OF ENERGY FLOWS

Whether by natural or by human interaction, the conversion of energy is governed by fundamental physical principles. One of these principles is the First Law of Thermodynamics. Simply stated, it postulates that the quantity of energy in the universe is constant.[12] In other words, energy can be neither created nor destroyed, even as it is converted from one of its many forms to another.

A useful way of understanding the significance of the First Law of Thermodynamics is to consider the historical context from which it arose. As noted in chapter 2, during the eighteenth and nineteenth centuries the economies of western Europe and North America experienced vast transformations as a result of the growth of industrialization and urbanization. Distributive considerations aside, this process was accompanied by unparalleled increases in both aggregate and per capita income. From a philosophic perspective, many saw these changes as extensions of the eighteenth-century Enlightenment notion of human progress and the perfection of society. In turn, scientists

[11]The amount of energy released by the reaction in equation (4.6) is 7.67999×10^{-13} joules, and that in equation (4.7), 2.81599×10^{-12} joules. The combined net energy transformation is 3.58399×10^{-12} joules, and the combined equation to produce this amount is

$$D + 6Li = 2^4He + 3.58399 \times 10^{-12} \text{ joules},$$

or

$$3.401215996 \times 10^{-15} \text{ Btu's}.$$

[12]Since Einstein's discovery of relativity, the First Law of Thermodynamics can be stated more accurately: the sum of all energy and mass in the universe is constant. The significance of this statement becomes more obvious if we consider such technologies as solar satellites, which are discussed in chapter 7.

sought ways to determine whether such changes were in fact real or only apparent. One of these individuals was the American expatriate Benjamin Thompson, later known as Count Rumford, the founder of the Royal Institution in London.

Thompson's problem was to account for the stocks and flows of energy in mechanical processes. In his early investigations, he relied on the measurement of heat energy used in the boring of a brass cannon. Until Thompson's time, it was widely thought that heat was an invisible fluid, known as "caloric," which was able to expand solids and fluids to create steam, a not terribly surprising conclusion in light of the rise of steam technology then under way. However, it was also thought that in the case of a process such as a two-horsepower boring machine the chips would be hotter than the barrel, since the bore would somehow squeeze the "caloric" out of the barrel as it removed the chips. What Thompson discovered, however, was that the temperature in the chips was the same as that in the barrel, even when boring took place in water. The caloric theory was thus rejected. In addition, however, Thompson came close to formulating the First Law of Thermodynamics when he noticed the loss of efficiency in the conversion of energy from chemical (horses eating fodder) to mechanical (the horse-driven cannon-boring machine) to heat. It remained for his successors to derive a specific quantitative formulation.

One of Thompson's successors was the Englishman James P. Joule. Joule combined the laws of motion with energy into the formal statement of the First Law of Thermodynamics.[13] In quantitative terms, the law can thus be expressed as

$$Q_1 = W + S_2 - S_1, \tag{4.8}$$

where Q_1 is the input energy of a work process, W is the energy used to accomplish work, S_2 is the terminal amount of energy outside the work process, and S_1 is the initial amount of energy outside the work process ($S_2 \geq S_1$). In other words, the amount of input energy must equal the sum of the energy used to accomplish a task and the energy rejected by that process.

The work energy used in a given natural or mechanical process may not necessarily be the same as the original input energy. For example, gasoline contains potential heat energy. When it is burned, it releases this energy into a flow which may then be used to provide mechanical energy. The mechanical energy derives from the movement of the pistons within the cylinder caused by the combustion of gasoline, and as the pistons move, a crankshaft transfers this mechanical energy to the wheels to provide motion. Conversely, it is also possible to use gasoline to produce gasoline, as in the operation of an oil refinery. However, in all cases, the total level of input energy will always exceed the amount of end-use energy, since some of the input energy will be rejected as heat into the environment.

[13]The three basic laws of motion derive largely from the classical mechanics of Isaac Newton: (1) every body continues in its state of rest, or of motion with a constant velocity in a straight line, unless acted upon by some external force; (2) change of momentum is proportional to the force and to the time during which it acts, and is in the same direction as the force; (3) to every action there is an equal and opposite reaction.

Unused energy is stored through either natural or mechanical processes, as in the photosynthetic accumulation of solar energy and in the production of gasoline stocks, respectively. However, not all energy forms are so conveniently stored. Indeed, most solar energy occurs in the form of long-wavelength radiation flows into the atmosphere. Though not impossible, it can be difficult to capture relatively high concentrations of these flows for practical applications within the economy. Thus, in the case of equation (4.8), if one is concerned with the end uses of energy, it is desirable that work energy (W) be in as high a proportion to input energy (Q) as possible. The actual ratio represents the input-output efficiency of the given process and is expressed as

$$\text{End Use Efficiency} = \frac{W}{Q_1}. \tag{4.9}$$

On the other hand, if the energy used to accomplish work involves the intermediate conversion and storage of energy for subsequent use in a work process, then it is desirable to have as small a ratio of work energy to input energy as possible, assuming, of course, that the stored energy is in a form that can be readily used when needed. If this is in fact the case, then from equation (4.8) we can express the efficiency of energy storage as

$$\text{Energy Storage Efficiency} = \frac{S_2 - S_1}{Q_1}. \tag{4.10}$$

From equation (4.10), if follows that the higher the degree of storage efficiency, the smaller will be the amount of work needed to convert input energy into a usable stored form. It also indicates that all end uses of energy in the economy must be based on flows, whereas intermediate forms may require conversion into stocks. This enables us to express First Law efficiency in both kinetic and potential terms, namely:

$$\text{End Use Efficiency} = \frac{W_{\text{kinetic}}}{Q_1} \tag{4.9.a}$$

and

$$\text{Useful Energy Storage Efficiency} = \frac{W_{\text{potential}}}{Q_1}. \tag{4.9.b}$$

In this way, regardless of intermediate or end uses, the energy storage originally referred to in equation (4.8) can now be thought of as rejected energy flows.

Each of the variants of equation (4.9) can now be used to account for both energy flows and their efficiency in and across time. Energy use varies widely throughout the U.S. economy. One way of appreciating this variation is to measure the energy consumption requirements to produce a unit of output. A sample of these energy consumption requirements for various products in the U.S. economy is listed in table 4.1. However, we cannot conclude from

Table 4.1. U.S. Average Energy Consumption Requirements for the Production of Selected Materials

Material	MBtu's per Ton
Rock Derivatives	
Porcelain	80.00
China	40.00
Glass	
Plate and bottles	14.00–18.00
Technical	54.00
Handmade	80.00
Cement	13.10
Tile	4.00
Bricks	1.00–6.00
Metals	
Titanium	481.90
Aluminum	269.40
Recycled	10.00
High-grade steel	202.00
Copper	71.70
Zinc	50.20
Lead	44.00
Steel	43.00
Recycled	8.80
Petroleum derivatives	
Polypropylene	144.50
Polyethylene	137.50
Polyvinyl chloride	102.60
Polystyrene	45.20
Natural fibers	
Paper	23.00
Lumber	9.93
Foodstuffs	
Fresh/frozen, packed fish	117.08
Butter	98.90
Cheese, natural and processed	95.10
Beef sirloin	85.20
Chicken	38.30
Scotch whiskey	28.40
Roast coffee	20.60
Bread, standard white loaf	16.60
Oranges, fresh	15.00
Milk, fluid	13.60
Cane sugar, granulated	11.90

Sources: Stanford Research Institute, *Patterns of Energy Consumption in the United States* (Palo Alto: Stanford Research Institute, Stanford University Press, January 1972); A. B. Makhijani and A. J. Lichtenberg, "An Assessment of Residential Energy Utilization in the U.S.A." (Berkeley: University of California, 1972); J. M. Fowler, *Energy and the Environment* (New York: McGraw-Hill Book Co., 1975), p. 88; and A. J. Fritsch, L. W. Dujack, and D. A. Jimerson, *Energy and Food* (Washington, D.C.: Center for Science in the Public Interest, 1975).

this information that one product is more energy-efficient than another, since the products themselves are so heterogeneous.

A more accurate comparison of energy efficiency is between the measurement of the energy output per unit of energy input of a given process and the measurement of the energy input of a non-energy output over time. Since electricity and food energy are good examples, each will be considered in turn.

Commercial electricity in the United States is produced almost exclusively by large-scale public and private generating plants. These plants use coal, oil, natural gas, nuclear energy, and hydropower in varying combinations to produce heat, which is then used to create pressurized steam. In turn, the steam is used to rotate the blades of turbines which generate electricity. In the case of hydropower, falling water is used directly to rotate the turbine blades.

The energy flows of a typical 1,000-megawatt power plant are shown in figure 4.2. As can be seen, when water recycling and steam losses are taken into account, the net delivered output of 77.4 million kilocalories per hour requires a gross primary energy input of 325 million kilocalories per hour, which gives a system conversion efficiency of 23.82 percent, which is obtained by multiplying together all of the efficiencies at each stage of conversion. At any one time, however, the actual First Law efficiency is likely to be even less than the given system efficiency, since no adjustment has been made for physical deterioration of plant equipment, and the loss of efficiency that this entails, or for the energy required to produce the plant equipment in the first place.[14]

As a second example, data on the input-output structure of energy flows in U.S. animal agriculture for the years 1955, 1965, and 1970 are listed in table 4.2. Here our measure of First Law efficiency is more akin to equation (4.9.b), since animal outputs are equivalent to stored energy, which is then used either in the production of additional animal energy or directly consumed—eggs, for example.

Several observations can be drawn from table 4.2. First, if one computes the energy equivalent of animal outputs, the First Law efficiency is relatively low in all three years, especially when compared with the system efficiency of electricity production noted in figure 4.2. Second, the input-output energy efficiency of U.S. animal agriculture has been falling, from almost 10 percent in 1955 to just under 8 percent in 1970. This decline in technical efficiency seems at first paradoxical, especially when compared with traditional measures of agricultural productivity such as output per acre or output per person. Obviously, much of this traditional productivity has been in the form of an extraordinary energy subsidy in the form of fertilizers, pesticides, and mechanization of farms over the past several decades. The third observation derives directly from the second: as we have seen in preceding chapters, be-

[14]Each of these adjustments could reduce the hourly conversion efficiency by as much as 50 percent, leaving net efficiency in the neighborhood of 10–15 percent.

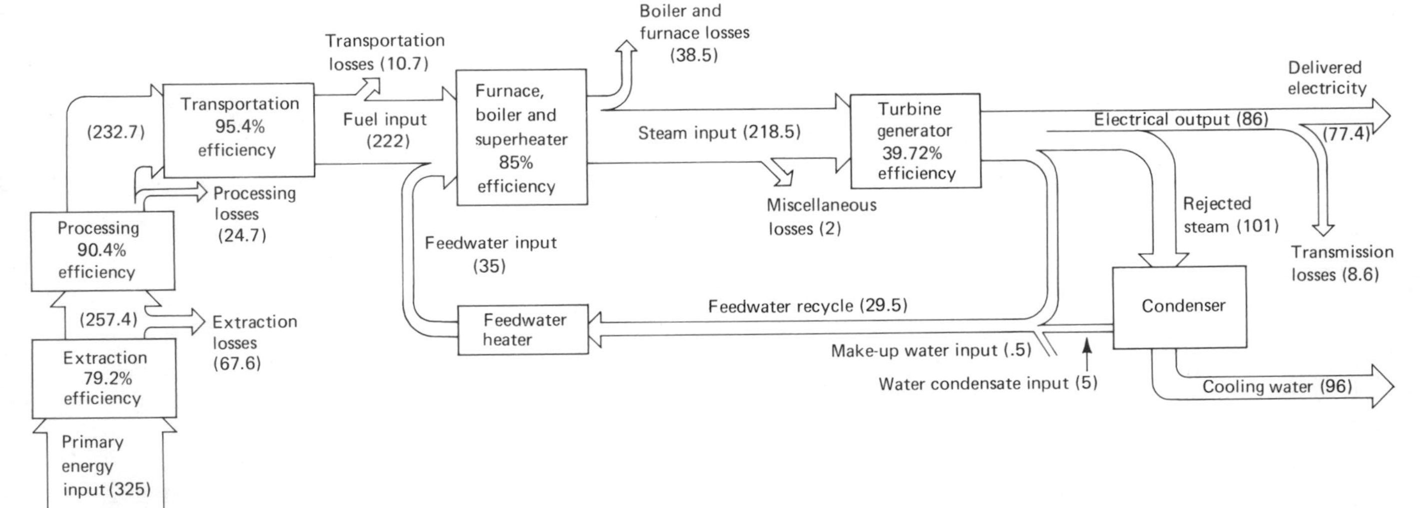

Figure 4.2. The Input-Output Structure of Large-Scale Electrical Power Generation. The figure is based on a modern, 1,000-megawatt coal-fired plant. All energy flows are shown in millions of kilocalories per hour. Adapted from Earl Cook, *Man, Energy, Society* (San Francisco: W. H. Freeman and Co., 1976), p. 37.

Table 4.2. The Input-Output Structure of Energy Flows in U.S. Animal Agriculture, 1955, 1965, 1970

Energy Form	1955	1965	1970
Input (E_1)			
Concentrates	425.6	556.8	617.6
Harvested roughage	211.2	240.0	249.6
Pasture	339.2	470.4	473.6
Total	976.0	1267.2	1340.8
Output (E_2)			
Beef	16.83	23.22	26.85
Veal	1.07	0.69	0.40
Pork	20.07	20.34	24.52
Lard	10.88	8.36	7.65
Lamb	0.91	0.78	0.66
Chickens	1.37	2.54	3.31
Turkeys	0.59	1.10	1.27
Eggs	5.99	6.08	6.34
Milk	36.35	36.63	34.50
Edible offal	1.17	1.20	1.30
Total	95.23	100.94	106.80
Conversion Efficiency (E_2/E_1)	0.09757	0.079656	0.079654

Source: U.S. Department of Agriculture, *Agriculture Statistics* (Washington, D.C.: U.S. Government Printing Office, 1956, 1966, 1971). Data are reproduced in Earl Cook, *Man, Energy, Society* (San Francisco: W. H. Freeman and Co., 1976).

Note: Input and output figures are in 10^{12} kilocalories.

cause the relative price of energy was falling during the period shown in figure 4.2, agriculture tended to become more energy-intensive than it might have done otherwise. Finally, the First Law tells us relatively little of the potential degree of technical efficiency that could be obtained in the production of agricultural or other goods and services. To answer this question we need to define the Second Law of Thermodynamics.

4.4. THE ENTROPY LAW AND ENERGY UTILIZATION

The First Law of Thermodynamics tells us that for any natural or mechanical process, the energy transformation that occurs will never be 100 percent efficient. Perpetual motion machines are thus an impossibility, just as is the proverbial "free lunch." The First Law instills rigor in energy accounting; a logical question, then, is, to what extent can energy transformations approach 100 percent efficiency? The answer is found in the Second Law of Thermodynamics, also known as the Entropy Law.

The Second Law of Thermodynamics states that left to itself, every system changes in such a way that it will approach a final state of rest. Translated into energy terms, there is an irreversible pattern in all energy transformations which leads to an eventual position of zero usable energy. To better understand the theoretical and practical significance of this law, we can examine the historical context from which it arose.

As we have seen, the evolution of steam technology was a primary factor in the emergence of the industrial revolution. It also stimulated the scientific inquiry into energy use which led to the First Law of Thermodynamics. However, as industrial production relied increasingly on evolving energy technologies, there was a growing concern over the limits to improving steam technologies. The result of the research efforts that followed was the Second Law of Thermodynamics.

One of the first discoveries to lead to the Second Law was made by the French engineer Sadi Carnot in 1824. Intrigued by the increasing uses of steam technology in coal production, transportation, and other areas, he noted that the sucessful operation of a steam engine was governed by the particular juxtaposition of high-temperature heat with low-temperature heat, that is, of steam heat with the cooler heat from the condenser. Specifically, the proportion of energy input that could be transformed into work depended on the difference between the temperatures in the hot and cold parts of the engine. The higher the temperature difference, the greater would be the potential work obtained. If no temperature difference existed, no work would be possible, regardless of the amount of energy input into the system. For Carnot and his successors the design of efficient engines depended on the concentration of as great a temperature difference between two parts of a system as possible, a principle that has become enshrined as Carnot efficiency. In mathematical terms, it can be expressed as

(4.11) $$\chi \leq 1 - \frac{T_2}{T_1},$$

where T_1 is the temperature of input energy, T_2 is the temperature of rejected energy, and χ is equal to W/Q_1.

The linkage between the First and Second Laws of Thermodynamics is straightforward. First Law efficiency is derived from equation (4.8), as follows:

(4.8.a) $$Q_1 = W + \Delta S,$$

where Q_1 is the input energy of a work process, W is the energy used to accomplish work, and ΔS is the energy rejected by the work process, as measured by the change in the stock of energy outside of the work process ($S_2 - S_1$). By dividing Q_1 into each side of equation (4.8.a), we get

(4.12) $$1 = \frac{W}{Q_1} + \frac{\Delta S}{Q_1}.$$

Rearranging terms results in

(4.13) $$\frac{W}{Q_1} = 1 - \frac{\Delta S}{Q_1},$$

in which the lefthand side is in the general form of equations (4.9.a) and (4.9.b). From equation (4.13) we can further specify the change in rejected energy as

(4.14) $$\Delta S = \frac{S_2}{T_2} - \frac{S_1}{T_1},$$

which by definition is greater than or equal to zero. Equation (4.14) can be rearranged to isolate the energy and temperature relations as follows:

(4.15) $$\frac{S_2}{T_2} - \frac{S_1}{T_1} \geq 0,$$

(4.16) $$\frac{S_2}{T_2} \geq \frac{S_1}{T_1},$$

(4.17) $$\frac{S_2}{S_1} \geq \frac{T_2}{T_1}.$$

From equation (4.17) it is clear that the growth of rejected energy is minimized when the temperature of newly rejected energy of a given transformation is as low a fraction of its input energy as possible. This conclusion is the same as the Second Law Carnot efficiency equation (4.11).

As an illustration of the Second Law of Thermodynamics, consider a steam engine that is to be used to produce electricity. It is designed to take 1,000-degree Kelvin input energy at a rate of 25 kilocalories per second, with a rejected energy rate of 20 kilocalories per second at 400 degrees Kelvin. From the First Law we can compute initially the rated power of the engine design as

(4.8.b) $$W = (Q_1 - \Delta S)\lambda,$$

where λ is the kilocalorie per second/kilowatt electricity conversion factor (=4.187). Thus:

$$W = (25 - 20)(4.187)$$
$$= 20.94 \text{ kilowatts.}$$

From equation (4.9) we can also derive the First Law efficiency of the machine as

(4.9.c) $$\frac{W}{Q_1} = \frac{(25 - 20)}{25}$$
$$= 0.25, \text{ or 25 percent.}$$

Let us now compare the actual efficiency of the machine with its theoretical maximum. From the Second Law defined in equation (4.11), the theoretical maximum efficiency of this machine would be:

(4.11.a) $$= 1 - \frac{T_2}{T_1}$$
$$= 1 - \frac{400}{1000}$$
$$= 0.60, \text{ or 60 percent.}$$

Because the actual efficiency is less than half of the theoretical efficiency, we thus have an indication of the potential energy conservation that could be achieved by use of an alternative design configuration.

There are many alternative designs that could be used to improve energy conservation. Although each additional degree of technical efficiency would be more difficult to obtain than the preceding one, let us consider what the rated power of a machine such as the one that we have been describing would be if it were to operate at its Second Law theoretical maximum. One possibility would be that if the input energy rate were the same, in order to reach the Second Law efficiency limit, the rejected energy rate would have to be

(4.9.d) $$\frac{(25 - X)}{25} = 0.60,$$

$$X = 10 \text{ kilocalories per second.}$$

Now using the theoretical limit value of rejected energy at a rate of 10 kilocalories per second, the machine could achieve a rated power of

(4.8.c) $$\begin{aligned} W &= (Q_1 - \Delta S)\lambda \\ &= (25 - 10)(4.1487) \\ &= 62.8 \text{ kilowatts.} \end{aligned}$$

Alternatively, if we were not able to produce a machine that had a 60 percent First Law efficiency, then if we could still obtain input energy at a rate of 25 kilocalories per second, it would no longer be necessary to use such high-temperature input energy. Thus, if the rejected energy rate were still 10 kilocalories at 400 degrees Kelvin, as long as we could obtain an input energy rate of 25 kilocalories, we should use the lowest-temperature steam that would still yield this input rate. If it were possible to achieve Second Law efficiency, the required temperature would be

(4.11.b) $$0.25 = 1 - \frac{400}{T_1}$$

$$T_1 = 533.33 \text{ degrees Kelvin.}$$

In effect, we should either choose a temperature differential between input and output energy within the limits of what is needed to satisfy what is thermodynamically possible with the given design configuration or else switch to a thermodynamically more efficient machine. To do otherwise would involve an excessive use of input energy which would be converted into work and which thus would be rejected into the environment as thermal pollution. That so little attention has been given to Second Law efficiency in the past can be attributed to a traditional preoccupation of producers and consumers with First Law efficiency and, ultimately, to the relative pricing of energy. As long as energy has been relatively cheap, there has been little reason for engineers, architects, and other energy decisionmakers to make use of the energy technologies most appropriate to their tasks.

As the preceding example suggests, the Second Law of Thermodynamics enables us to assess the extent to which actual efficiency of an energy transformation process can attain its theoretical maximum. The Second Law also serves to point to an underlying consequence of all energy use, namely, the degradation of socially available energy. Entropy, the term used to characterize this process, was first noted by the German physicist Rudolf Clausius in 1865. It was subsequently refined and applied to non-energy questions by Ludwig Boltzmann and others.[15]

The measurement of entropy derives directly from equation (4.8) and is accounted for as the change in the storage of rejected energy. In practical terms, as has been noted, the entropy of the universe is always rising or is constant, depending on the actual efficiency of a given energy transformation.

Low-entropy states are those which are relatively ordered, or structured. In energy terms, this means that the socially useful energy that can be obtained from such states is relatively high; compare, for example, the technical ease with which one can extract useful energy from fossil fuel deposits with the difficulty of using nuclear fission or fusion. However, as entropy increases with the growth in the number of energy transformations, absolute differences in temperature of energy forms tend to diminish, thereby leading to a uniform and stable temperature distribution characterized by nineteenth-century physicists as the "heat death" of the universe. Along that transformation path lie the technical choices for energy utilization that must be made by society, recognizing that each attempt to recycle and recapture rejected energy forms cannot be perfectly efficient.

Measurement of the degree of entropy follows directly from the work of Clausius and Boltzmann.[16] Mathematically, the degree of entropy can be expressed as

$$Z = k(\ln W), \tag{4.18}$$

where k is Boltzmann's constant, which has a value of 1.38×10^{-23} joules per degree of Kelvin temperature, and W is the ordinal measure of the degree of disorder arising from a given macrostate. A macrostate is defined by the number of possible combinations obtained from $W = N!/N_1!N_2! \cdots N_m!$, where N represents the number of particles and m represents the number of microstates. In effect, the rejected energy of a particular energy transformation, which we denoted as ΔS is equation (4.8.a), may be thought of as a sub-

[15] A good discussion of the significance of this process is found in Nicholas Georgescu-Roegen, *The Entropy Law and the Economic Process* (Cambridge, Mass.: Harvard University Press, 1971), esp. chaps. 5–9.

[16] The literature on entropy is extensive and includes several conditional measures based on the status of particles in distinguishable versus undistinguishable states. Classical thermodynamics is based on distinguishable particles with no restriction and is the form used in the Clausius-Maxwell-Boltzmann formulation presented here. The Bose-Einstein formulation is based on indistinguishable particles with symmetric wave features, e.g., photons and deuterons, whereas Fermi-Dirac formulations are based on indistinguishable particles with antisymmetric wave functions, e.g., electrons and protons. Each of these formulations is examined and contrasted in detail in V. Kadambi and Manohar Prasad, *An Introduction to Energy Conversion* (New York: John Wiley and Sons, Halsted Press, 1976).

set of Z. We can thus express the global consequences from a given energy transformation: with each energy transformation, there is a tendency for the number of possible states in which the total energy of the universe can be distributed to increase. Because the number of states can increase, it is more difficult to capture and utilize that energy, since its distribution becomes increasingly dispersed, or chaotic. The degree of chaos, in turn, is a function of the number of states, or combinations. For example, if there are four types of energy resources and only two possible states in which this energy can be transformed, or grouped, the number of combinations will be

$$W = \frac{N!}{N_1!\,N_2!\,\cdots\,N_m!} = \frac{4!}{2!\,2!\,0!\,0!} = \frac{24}{4} = 6. \tag{4.19}$$

If, on the other hand, the number of states increases from two to four, the number of possible combinations is enlarged significantly:

$$W = \frac{4!}{1!\,1!\,1!\,1!} = 24. \tag{4.20}$$

The corresponding degrees of entropy from equations (4.19) and (4.20) will be, respectively:

$$Z = k(\ln W) = (1.38 \times 10^{-23})\ln 6 = 2.472 \times 10^{-23} \tag{4.19.a}$$

and

$$= (1.38 \times 10^{-23})\ln 24 = 4.385 \times 10^{-23}. \tag{4.20.a}$$

Clearly, then, as each energy transformation occurs, either in nature, as in photosynthetic accumulation, or in the economy, as in the consumption of gasoline, the degree of entropy will tend to increase. In graphic terms, the degree of entropy increases over time and approaches the maximum, or heat death, as in a cumulative probability density such as the one illustrated in figure 4.3.

Figure 4.3 also provides an illustration of the lesser-emphasized Third Law of Thermodynamics, which states that the entropy change of a given energy

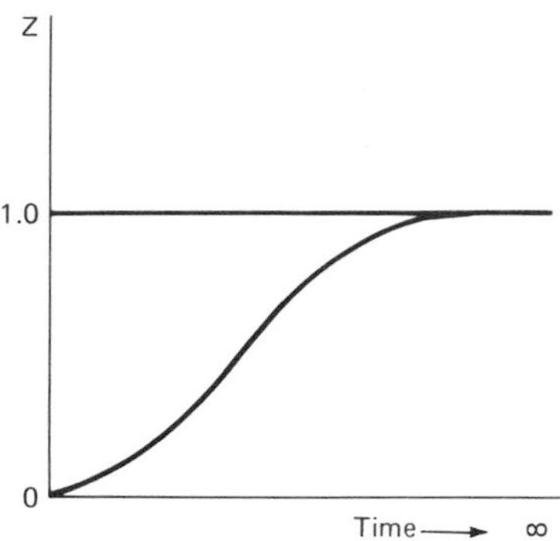

Figure 4.3. A Cumulative Probability Density Function for the Third Law of Thermodynamics

transformation at the absolute zero of temperature is zero.[17] Moreover, although certain local energy transformations, such as electrical transmission, can acquire superconductive, or extremely efficient, properties at temperatures approaching absolute zero, it is impossible to reduce any system to the absolute zero of temperature in a finite number of operations. Thus, as figure 4.3 shows, entropy approaches a maximum along the upper asymptote as time approaches infinity. The final equilibrium, or heat death, of the universe is never completely attained.

4.5. IMPLICATIONS OF THERMODYNAMICS FOR ENERGY POLICY

The laws that govern energy transformations are critical to the choice of alternative energy policies. As this point, we can identify two basic ways in which these laws bear on that choice.

First, there is a direct link between the principles of energy conversion and the problem of environmental pollution. As can be deduced from the equations in sections 4.3 and 4.4, environmental pollution can be characterized first and foremost as the product of thermodynamically inefficient conversions of energy. Carbon dioxide, sulfur dioxide, particulate, and thermal pollution all derive from technically inefficient conversions of energy resources. If we were able to achieve higher temperature differentials in energy conversions, and if we were to use energy-conversion technologies with First Law efficiencies close to or equal to their Second Law limits, then the share of rejected energy in the environment would be far smaller than is now the case.

[17]The Third Law is also known as Nernst's heat theorem, named after the German physicist Walter Nernst (1864–1941). Mathematically, the Third Law can be expressed as

$$\lim_{T \to 0} [\partial (\Delta g)/\partial T] = \lim_{T \to 0} [\partial (\Delta h)/\partial T] - \lim_{T \to 0} (\Delta s),$$

where Δg is Gibb's measure of the energy change adjusted for the degree of mechanical pressure and Δh is the change in enthalpy, the heat content per unit of mass of constant mechanical pressure.

Environmental pollution can be classified further into two classes: unavoidable and avoidable. Unavoidable pollution can be thought of as the energy that will be rejected into the environment after all other choices have been examined and the technically most efficient one has been adopted. There is an element of relativity in this definition in that technological necessity is to a certain extent subjective and in that technology is not fixed over time. Nevertheless, if we assume that it is necessary to provide a certain rate of production of a resource such as electricity and that there are several ways in which to satisfy this production, there is still likely to be some degree of environmental pollution, since the Second Law temperature differential essential to 100 percent technical efficiency of conversion can not be infinite. In other words, there is no ice cream in the sun, just as there is no free lunch.

Although some environmental pollution is inevitable if an economy is to function, it does not follow that the actual degree of pollution is unavoidable. Energy choices can be ranked in terms of their degree of harm to the environment. Since this is the realm in which human intervention is both possible and desirable, it is necessary to find ways in which the prices that are used to guide the allocation of resources will be consistent with technically efficient choices involving the conversion of energy. As we saw in chapter 1, there are tax and regulatory instruments that can be used to promote environmental protection. Ultimately, then, the problem of environmental protection is one of finding the socially least costly way of generating the least degree of environmental pollution from a given level of economic activity, a question which we will pursue at several points in subsequent chapters.

The second way that the laws of thermodynamics bear on the choice of alternative energy policies is in terms of the irreversibility of choices. Given the current dependence of the world economy on depletable energy resources, with each additional unit of consumption, entropy tends to reduce the quality of socially useful energy for each successive generation. To be sure, the conversion to a society based on renewable resources remains an inevitable choice at some point in the future. Yet if we make technically efficient use of depletable energy resources today, the economically useful lifetime of these resources can be extended further into the future. What is also significant is that in making such choices, we also promote a higher degree of environmental protection than would otherwise be the case. Thus, if technically efficient choices can also be made to be economically efficient ones, then some of the policy trade-offs posed in chapter 3 might not be as severe as they at first appear to be. The next step in arriving at these choices, then, is to examine the technological basis of energy decisions in terms of current and alternative energy resources.

4.6. SUMMARY

Energy exists in many forms. Although the sun is the ultimate source of all presently known energy resources, resources are not used in proportion to their frequency in nature. Economic factors may contribute to this disparity, but it depends partly on the laws of thermodynamics.

The First Law of Thermodynamics provides a basic accounting mechanism for energy stocks and flows. The Second Law enables us to measure the technical efficiency of given energy transformation and to account for the eventual degradation of useful energy. These two laws can be applied in turn to the specific measurement of alternative energy technologies, as well as to the assessment of appropriate energy policies.

The principles of thermodynamics have two basic implications for energy policy decisions. One is that there is an inverse relationship between the technical conversion of energy and environmental pollution. Although the Second Law of Thermodynamics dictates some degree of environmental pollution if economic activity is to occur, there is a wide variation between the prevailing degree of pollution and what is technically necessary for such economic activity. The second implication is that by virtue of the Second Law, energy conversions move along an irreversible path. Irreversibility of energy conversion and the continuing degradation of the environment affect the quality of future energy choices. Thus, resources conservation is a central question in arriving at energy policy decisions.

SUGGESTED READINGS

Bueche, Frederick J. *Introduction to Physics for Scientists and Engineers.* 3d ed. New York: McGraw-Hill, 1980.

Cook, Earl. *Man, Energy, Society.* San Francisco: W. H. Freeman and Co., 1976.

Georgescu-Roegen, Nicholas. *The Entropy Law and the Economic Process.* Cambridge, Mass: Harvard University Press, 1971.

Kadambi, V., and Prasad, Manohar. *An Introduction to Energy Conversion.* Vol. 1. New York: John Wiley and Sons, Halsted Press, 1976.

5

FOSSIL FUEL RESOURCES

The fossil fuels petroleum, natural gas, and coal provide the bulk of the world's present energy consumption. This has not always been the case, and it is not likely to be so in the future, but the present dependence on these resources is of critical significance for at least two basic reasons. First, as noted in chapter 4, all of the earth's presently known stock of fossil fuels arose from past geological transformations. Fossil fuels thus exist in fixed quantities which become crucial as our present consumption of them expands. Second, as noted in chapters 2 and 3, in an increasingly complex economy based on specialization, both the production and consumption of goods and services have resulted in a high degree of dependence on these resources. To better understand the technological basis of this dependence, we will examine in the following sections how various fossil fuel resources are converted into their end-use forms. We will then be able to see more clearly the relationship between the principles of thermodynamics and the economics of these resources.

5.1. PETROLEUM

Petroleum is currently the most widely used fossil fuel in both the U.S. and the world economy. It accounts for just under half of U.S. gross energy consumption, and its share has tended to rise almost without interruption throughout the twentieth century.[1] Its practical appeal is straightforward: it is a relatively low-entropy resource, and it can be transformed into a wide variety of useful products. This transformation begins at the stage of exploration and extraction.

5.1.1. Exploration and Extraction

We saw in chapter 3 how estimates of cumulative production and consumption rates can be used to determine the level of proven reserves of a depletable energy resource. Unfortunately, the degree of confidence that we could at-

[1]As table 2.1 shows, petroleum represented approximately 45 percent of U.S. gross energy consumption in 1980. In 1925 dependence on petroleum was less than 20 percent.

tach to the level of estimated reserves is not as high as the statistical estimates of these logistic curves alone would suggest. Indeed, until those reserves are actually withdrawn into production, geological estimates will vary according to changes in the level of information, in exploration and production technology, and in the relative price of the resource. How, then, does the technology of petroleum exploration and extraction affect the estimation of proven reserves of a depletable energy resource such as petroleum?

It is now well established that crude oil and natural gas are found almost exclusively in sedimentary rock formations. The reason for this pattern is that as the plant and animal life of millions of years ago perished from the earth's climatic changes, sedimentary accumulations such as shale, limestone, and sandstone provided the necessary sealing off of fossils to prevent oxidation. Sedimentary accumulation also facilitated their gradual transformation into liquid and gas hydrocarbons as heat and pressure conditions evolved.

Earthquakes and other, more gradual shifts in geological structures have resulted in the migration of oil and natural gas through porous rocks into relatively impervious traps of varying size. A field containing one or more of these trapped deposits may vary in size from as few as 2.6 square kilometers to as many as 260, through the average has recently been about 5. Discovery of deposits depends on the methods used in exploration; three of the most widely used techniques deserve brief explanation.

One of the most common methods of exploration is gravity surveys. Differences in the earth's gravity field indicate variations in the subsurface density of rocks. Where less than average densities are found, there is a correspondingly higher probability that oil and natural gas deposits are present. Since natural gas is the lightest of the mineral elements in fossil fuel deposits, it is generally trapped under the ceiling of a dome or fault of a relatively impervious rock such as shale or limestone. Below the natural gas will be the petroleum, if it is there at all, followed by water if it is present, and the relatively porous sedimentary sandstone through which the oil and natural gas passed as they moved geologically toward the surface. Were the natural gas able to reach the surface, it would become diffused into the air until a stable pressure equal to the earth's atmospheric pressure were reached. Similarly, petroleum reaching the surface would also expand, though up to the density of comparable liquids at that level. In any case, where these deposits exist in significant quantitites, they can be detected with some precision by gravimetric instruments by virtue of their lower relative density.

A more accurate method of exploration is seismographic testing. In this technique, the release of small explosive charges at different angles into the ground from a given source makes it possible to determine the subsurface rock structure and position. When a seismic wave emitted by an explosion reaches a different rock density, the wave is reflected back to the earth's surface. Simple trigonometry makes it possible then to derive the subsurface rock depths and angles. Those areas with significant geological faults or folding patterns are the ones most likely to contain oil and natural gas.

The third method of petroleum and natural gas exploration is the use of magnetometers. In this technique, registered deviations in normal magnetic fields of common geological formations point to subsurface areas which have a less than average density and which are likely to contain trapped deposits of petroleum and natural gas. As in gravity and seismic analysis, however, there is no guarantee that deviations in magnetic field patterns can provide conclusive evidence of deposits. Thus, there remains a margin of uncertainty that can be eliminated only by exploratory drilling.

Drilling is a significant element in petroleum exploration and extraction operations. Its importance arises not only from the risk of dry holes but also because of the depths to which relatively solid rock must be drilled before a viable deposit can be tapped. Thus, in practice, the decision to drill is weighed against the expected reduction in uncertainty from additional gravity and seismic tests. Established statistical methods governing data frequencies and sample size assist in reducing the degree of uncertainty in these decisions.[2]

A corollary factor in drilling decisions is the expected pressure of an estimated deposit. Obviously, the greater the pressure, the easier it is to extract the oil or natural gas from the well. The two determinants governing pressure are the depth of deposits and the contractionary force on a pool exerted by shifts in the earth's geological plates. Once pressure from a successful well begins to fall as a result of continuing extraction, the slower flow of oil raises operating costs to a point where further withdrawal becomes uneconomical to the firm, and the well is capped and abandoned. To extend the useful life of a well, secondary and tertiary recovery methods must be used (both are discussed further in section 5.4.1).

Data on twentieth-century U.S. domestic petroleum and natural gas exploration and production are shown in tables 5.1 and 5.2. As we might expect, the number of drillings has varied largely with the real price of oil. In figure 3.5 we saw that the constant dollar price of crude oil in the United States declined generally throughout the period from 1950 to the early 1970s. Thus, the 1955 level of over 55,000 drillings per year was not surpassed until 1980, when it topped 60,000. Yet despite the recent price increases wrought by OPEC and federal deregulation, the United States is not likely any time soon to see the era of easy oil that it once widely enjoyed.

To illustrate the problem of future U.S. petroleum supplies, let us look further at the data in tables 5.1 and 5.2. Despite technological improvements in exploration methods and increases in the real price of oil, new discoveries in the continental United States have begun to slow in relation to past performance. Although the dry-hole percentage of wells drilled has fluctuated somewhat inversely to technological change and to the real price of oil, it has become relatively cheaper to discover new oil by exploring in hitherto in-

[2]For a practical application of exploration techniques under uncertainty, see Arthur W. McCray, *Petroleum Evaluations and Economic Decisions* (Englewood Cliffs, N.J.: Prentice-Hall, 1975); and J. M. Ryan, "Limitations of Statistical Methods for Predicting Petroleum and Natural Gas Reserves and Availability," *Journal of Petroleum Technology*, March 1966, pp. 281–87.

Table 5.1. U.S. Domestic Crude-Oil and Natural Gas Exploration, 1900–1980

Year	Oil and Natural Gas Wells Drilled	Dry Holes Drilled as Percentage of Total Wells Drilled	Offshore Wells Drilled as Percentage of Total Wells Drilled	Total Drilling Depth (in millions of meters)	Average Depth per Well (in meters)	Average Cost per Well (in 1972 constant dollars)	Average Cost per Meter Drilled (in 1972 constant dollars)	End-of-Year Proven Reserves of Crude Oil (in billions of barrels)
1900	17,069	19.8%	—	—	—	—	—	2.90
1910	15,013	18.3	—	—	—	—	—	4.50
1920	34,029	21.9	—	—	—	—	—	7.20
1930	20,827	29.6	0.2%	24.1	915	—	—	13.60
1940	29,161	24.2	0.4	28.0	1,128	—	—	19.02
1945	24,482	30.0	0.5	28.4	1,253	—	—	20.83
1950	42,173	35.4	0.8	48.7	1,188	—	—	25.26
1955	55,207	37.2	1.0	69.7	1,412	—	—	30.01
1960	44,133	39.8	1.2	56.8	1,288	$63,578	$5.00	31.61
1965	39,596	40.3	2.6	54.5	1,376	63,966	4.80	35.12
1970	27,177	39.7	3.9	41.8	1,536	73,400	5.20	39.01
1975	36,960	35.3	2.8	54.2	1,466	99,795	7.64	32.16
1976	38,941	33.8	2.6	56.2	1,445	101,545	7.83	30.94
1977	44,982	32.7	2.8	64.3	1,429	106,697	8.03	29.50
1978	47,057	34.5	3.0	69.2	1,471	120,283	8.96	27.80
1979	49,743	31.6	3.2	72.6	1,460	129,537	9.69	27.05
1980	60,845	29.7	4.5	86.7	1,425	—	—	26.40

Sources: For the years 1900–1940, see E. DeGolyer and L. W. McNaughton, *Twentieth Century Petroleum Statistics* (Dallas, 1949). For the years 1940 to the present, see American Petroleum Institute, *Petroleum Facts and Figures* (Washington, D.C.: American Petroleum Institute, annual); idem, *Basic Petroleum Data Book*, vol. 1, no. 2 (Washington, D.C.: American Petroleum Institute, 1980); U.S. Department of Energy, Energy Information Administration, *Monthly Energy Review* (Washington, D.C.: U.S. Government Printing Office, May 1981).

hospitable or environmentally delicate areas such as Alaska and along the continental ocean shelf. Offshore drilling began off the Louisiana coast as early as 1947, and the petroleum now being extracted from Prudhoe Bay in Alaska was discovered as recently as 1968. Thus, even though there are continental areas that have yet to be explored intensively, the offshore percentage of drillings has tended to rise, as has the average depth per well drilled (see table 5.1). Greater depths in more remote areas mean higher real costs per well drilled and per depth of well drilled. Consequently, while there has been an increase in the real price of oil, the level of proven reserves in the United States has tended to decline from a peak of over 39 billion barrels in the early 1970s to approximately 26.4 billion by 1980. Even though Alaskan oil may yet prove to add another 10–15 billion barrels, and even though additional discoveries are likely to result from the current expansion of continental and offshore exploration which could shift upward the end-of-year proven reserves of crude oil, the studies cited in chapter 3 have generally concluded that even under sharply higher real oil prices, the likelihood of discovering

Table 5.2. U.S. Domestic Crude-Oil Production, 1900–1980

Year	Number of U.S. Operating Wells (in thousands)	Annual Domestic Oil Production (in billions of barrels of crude oil)	Daily Output per Well (in barrels)	Offshore Share of U.S. Domestic Production	Import Share of U.S. Domestic Consumption	Offshore Share of U.S. Domestic Consumption
1900	79	0.063	2.7	—	—	—
1910	149	0.209	3.9	—	—	—
1920	268	0.442	4.5	—	—	—
1930	331	0.898	7.4	—	—	—
1940	389	1.350	9.6	—	—	—
1945	416	1.710	11.3	—	—	—
1950	566	1.970	11.8	1.0%	16.42%	0.84%
1955	524	2.480	13.2	2.4	19.64	1.93
1960	591	2.580	12.0	4.5	28.05	3.24
1965	589	2.850	13.3	8.5	32.18	5.77
1970	531	3.520	18.0	16.4	34.38	10.76
1975	500	3.060	16.8	16.3	48.64	8.37
1976	508	2.970	16.3	15.5	53.53	7.20
1977	509	3.100	16.7	14.4	53.92	6.64
1978	508	3.161	17.0	13.0	53.77	6.01
1979	516	3.121	16.5	12.5	51.24	6.09
1980	527	3.138	16.3	11.9	46.78	6.33

Sources: For the years 1900–1940, see E. DeGolyer and L. W. McNaughton, *Twentieth Century Petroleum Statistics* (Dallas, 1949). For the years 1940 to the present, see American Petroleum Institute, *Petroleum Facts and Figures* (Washington, D.C.: American Petroleum Institute, annual); idem, *Basic Petroleum Data Book*, vol. 1, no. 2 (Washington, D.C.: American Petroleum Institute, 1980); U.S. Department of Energy, Energy Information Administration, *Monthly Energy Review* (Washington, D.C.: U.S. Government Printing Office, May 1981).

another Texas or Alaskan North Slope giant oil field in the United States is relatively small.[3]

If domestic discoveries of oil have tended to slow even as the real price of oil has risen, so too has domestic production. Indeed, in 1980 U.S. domestic oil production went up slightly for the first time in a decade, to 3.138 billion barrels, but it was still some 10 percent below the 1970 peak of 3.520 billion barrels. Moreover, daily output per well has not yet surpassed its early 1970s peak of 18 barrels. Thus, even though offshore oil has tended to account for a higher share of domestic production and consumption, total production has not kept pace with the growth of imported oil consumption (see table 5.2).

[3]For a recent assessment, see H. William Menard, "Toward a Rational Strategy for Oil Exploration," *Scientific American* 244 (January 1981):55–65.

Taken together, then, tables 5.1 and 5.2 point to one basic conclusion: increases in the real price of oil can raise the level of domestic proven reserves, domestic rates of production, and output per well, but in the short run at least they are not likely to remove the kind of precariousness in oil balances that the United States experienced throughout the 1970s. What makes this so critical is that petroleum can be refined into so many useful products on which the economy now depends.

5.1.2. Refining and Distribution

Regardless of location, the technology of petroleum refining and distribution has followed a well-defined pattern of evolution.[4] Early refining methods relied only on the application of heat to permit separation of the denser petroleum forms from the lighter ones. In this process, crude oil is passed through pipe coils of a furnace into a fractionating tower. When released into the tower, those compounds with the highest proportion of hydrogen to carbon molecules are converted into vapor and separate by weight into differing products as cooling within the tower converts them back into liquid form. Gasoline is the lightest of these products and emerges at the top of the tower, where it is drained off into collection containers. Below the gasoline collector level are found naptha, kerosene, gas oil, and the solid residues lubricating oil and asphalt.

The difficulty with the straight-run distillation process is that depending on the quality of the crude oil, the highest percentage of gasoline to be found is about 20 percent. Consequently, as changes in consumption altered the demand for petroleum by-products, there was a need to develop auxiliary methods of changing the proportions of these end products of crude-oil distillation.

The first modification in petroleum refining came with the introduction of thermal and catalytic cracking technology in the 1930s. Thermal cracking involves subjecting heavier petroleum refining products such as gas oil to pressurized heat. When the molecules of these heavier products break down and are fed into a fractionating tower, they yield the same by-products as does the refining of conventional crude oil. This recycling could raise the gasoline share of the original crude from its initial limit of 20 percent to as high as 45 percent.

The problem with thermal cracking was that lighter end products such as gasoline tended to recombine in high-compression motors, leading to knocking and incomplete combustion. One solution to this problem was to apply a catalyst in the cracking process which would prevent a subsequent recombination under pressure. The thermal and fluid cracking processes were based on the original catalytic system developed by Eugene Houdry in 1936. Since

[4]A general discussion of petroleum exploration and refining technology is found in Olin T. Mouzon, *Resources and Industries of the United States* (New York: Appleton-Century-Crofts, 1966), esp. chap. 4. For a more technical exposition, see Park J. Jones, *Petroleum Production*, vol. 1 (New York: Reinhold Publishing Co., 1946).

then they have become universally applied throughout world petroleum refining plants.[5]

In functional terms, catalytic technology can be classified into several basic categories. Polymerization involves the aggregation of similar molecules into larger ones. Alkylation involves the aggregation of dissimilar molecules into larger ones. Isomerization involves the rearrangement of atoms of a given molecule to produce different textural properties. These processes have become especially important with the growth of non-fuel end uses of petroleum in recent years, particularly in the development of plastics, fertilizers, and polyesters. Moreover, the development of these by-products has been even further accelerated by the use of hydrogenation, which has enabled refiners to upgrade lower-yield fuels such as distillate oils.[6] Finally, catalytic reforming has assisted in the development of the aromatic character of many petroleum by-products, an essential consideration involved in their detection in transport and storage systems. A graphic summary of the flow processes of a typical refinery is shown in figure 5.1.

Petroleum distribution depends partly on the distance between deposits and their end-use location, partly on the number and location of refineries, partly on the end form of petroleum products, and finally on the technology of transport. In general, as noted in table 5.2 and in chapters 2 and 3, the tapering off of new domestic discoveries of petroleum within the United States has led to increasing reliance on the importation of petroleum from abroad to various coastal refineries, where its products are then transported to their ultimate points of consumption.

Several trends in petroleum refining and distribution in the United States can be seen in the data in table 5.3 and in figures 5.2 and 5.3. First, as the final demand for petroleum products in the United States has changed, so too has the composition of refinery output. In the early 1900s, before the development of thermal and catalytic cracking techniques, domestic refining output consisted mostly of distillate and residual fuel oil, followed by a substantial share allocated to kerosene, then an important product in household and industrial lighting and heating systems. Gasoline accounted for just over 10 percent of refinery output, and this share was roughly half of its then possible upper limit from simple distillation technology. In succeeding years, the demand for distillate and residual fuel oil grew, but not nearly as fast as the demand for gasoline and other products. Thus, the distillate–residual fuel oil share of total output fell from over half of refinery output in 1900 to just under a third by the 1970s. In addition, with the growth of electricity usage, the demand for kerosene fell considerably, and

[5]A more detailed discussion of the evolution of refining technology is found in H. F. Williamson et al., *The American Petroleum Industry, 1899–1959*. (Evanston: Northwestern University Press, 1963), esp. chap. 4.

[6]Hydrogenation involves the infusion of hydrogen to raise the combustion property of lesser-grade by-products. By expanding the range of mixes through this process, greater flexibility is achieved in matching final demands to resources, though there is an energy cost with each conversion, which will have an impact on its relative price.

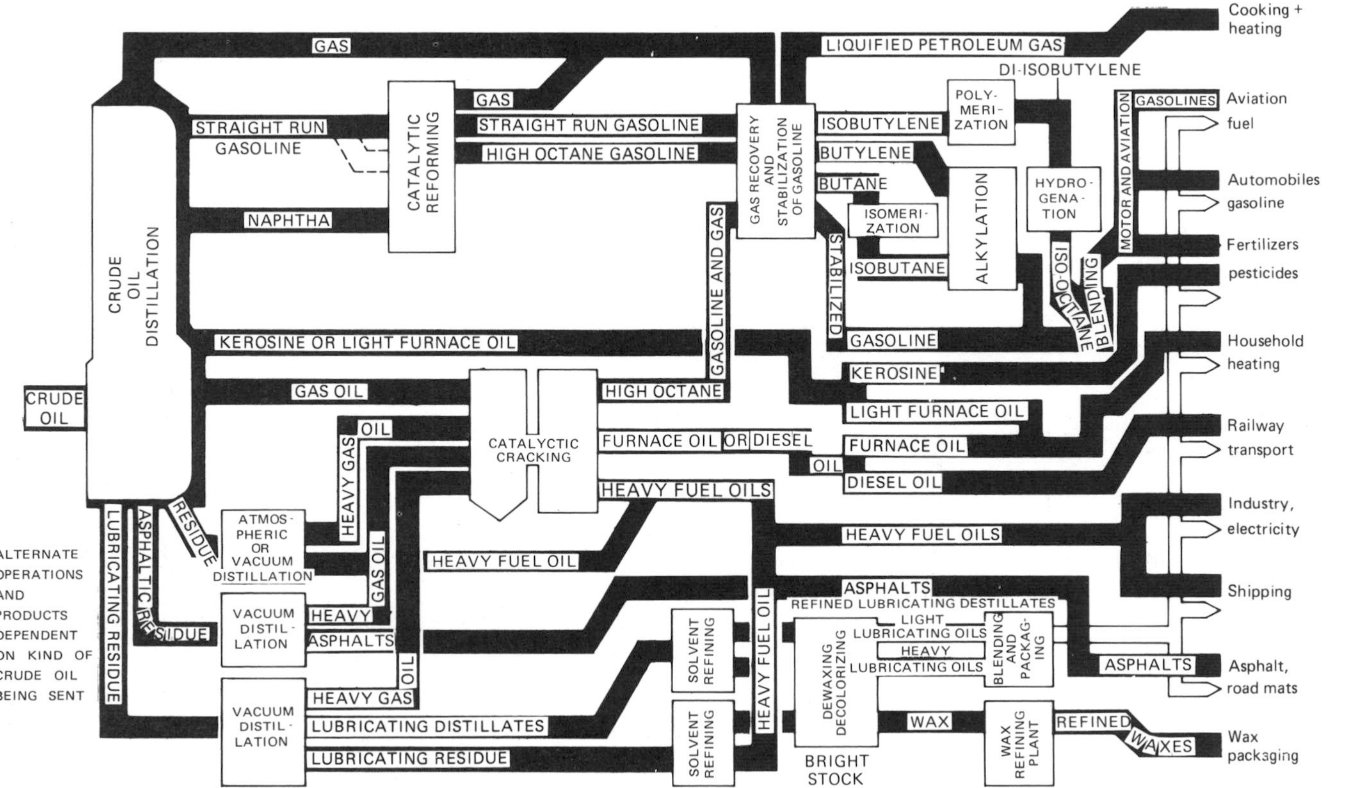

Figure 5.1. Petroleum Flows through a Modern Refinery. Adapted from Olin T. Mouzon, *Resources and Industries of the United States* (New York: Appleton-Century-Crofts, 1966).

Table 5.3. The Evolution of U.S. Domestic Refinery Capacity, 1900–1980

Year	Number of Refineries in the United States	U.S. Domestic Refining Capacity (in millions of barrels per year)	U.S. Petroleum Consumption (in millions of barrels per year)	Average Annual Domestic U.S. Refining Capacity (in millions of barrels)	Ratio of Domestic Petroleum Consumption to Domestic Refining Capacity	U.S. Domestic Share of World Oil-Refining Capacity
1900	70	41	40	0.59	0.96	80%
1910	156	176	174	0.89	0.99	78
1920	472	473	454	1.00	0.96	76
1930	512	895	971	1.90	1.08	68
1940	556	1,694	1,285	3.05	0.76	60
1945	413	1,935	1,662	4.68	0.86	53
1950	357	2,444	2,181	6.85	0.89	47
1955	318	3,074	2,802	9.67	0.91	41
1960	311	3,624	3,611	11.65	0.99	36
1965	286	3,933	4,202	13.75	1.07	32
1970	279	4,407	5,365	15.80	1.22	28
1975	287	5,537	5,958	19.28	1.08	24
1976	291	5,646	6,391	19.40	1.13	23
1977	302	6,063	6,727	20.08	1.10	23
1978	285	6,223	6,838	21.84	1.10	22
1979	291	6,260	6,544	21.51	1.05	22
1980	297	6,468	6,420	21.78	0.99	22

Sources: U.S. Department of Commerce, Bureau of the Census, *Statistical Abstract* (Washington, D.C.: U.S. Government Printing Office, selected years); idem, *Historical Statistics, Colonial Times to 1970* (Washington, D.C.: U.S. Government Printing Office, 1976); *Oil and Gas Journal* (Tulsa: Pennwell Publishing Co., selected years); U.S. Department of Energy, Energy Information Administration, *Monthly Energy Review* (Washington, D.C.: U.S. Government Printing Office, May 1981).

the kerosene share of refinery output dropped from just over a quarter of all refinery output to just over 1 percent in recent years. Moreover, though the absolute production of lubricants rose, its share of total output fell from almost 10 percent to just over 1 percent by the early 1970s.

Two other trends in figure 5.2 are worth noting. One is that with the emergence of commercial jet aviation after World War II, refinery output moved quickly to accommodate this new source of demand for petroleum production. The other is that increased knowledge of petroleum chemistry facilitated the application of refinery by-products to such new fields as fertilizers, pesticides, synthetic fabrics, and plastics, as indicated by the "all other" category.

The shift in domestic refining output also was accompanied by several changes in the scale and location of refining plants. Until the 1950s most of the growth of domestic petroleum consumption was satisfied by new discoveries of domestic reserves. Accordingly, the number of domestic refineries grew in rough proportion to the growth of domestic discoveries and demand, with a gradual decline setting in by the late 1950s.

The eventual decline in the number of U.S. domestic petroleum refineries was facilitated by two structural shifts then under way. One was the rise in worldwide petroleum discoveries relative to those in the United States, especially in the period following World War I. With the dramatic discoveries in the Middle East, refinery capacity expanded in those areas closest to the fields.

The other shift was the use of large-scale operations. In the United States, as elsewhere, the average annual capacity of refineries grew considerably with new advances in technology. As table 5.3 shows, the average capacity of a U.S. domestic refinery increased from just over half a million barrels in 1900 to over 20 million barrels by the late 1970s. Economic considerations aside, such large-scale operations have been necessary for the processing of many petroleum by-products. This is especially true for those products requiring material inputs found only in a small proportions of a barrel of crude petroleum.

Despite the growing diversity of refining operations, the end uses of petroleum have exhibited a well-defined pattern, as can be seen in figure 5.3. The most important shift has been the increase in the share of petroleum consumption allocated to transportation, with a corresponding decline in the shares going to industry, household, and commercial use. The most obvious

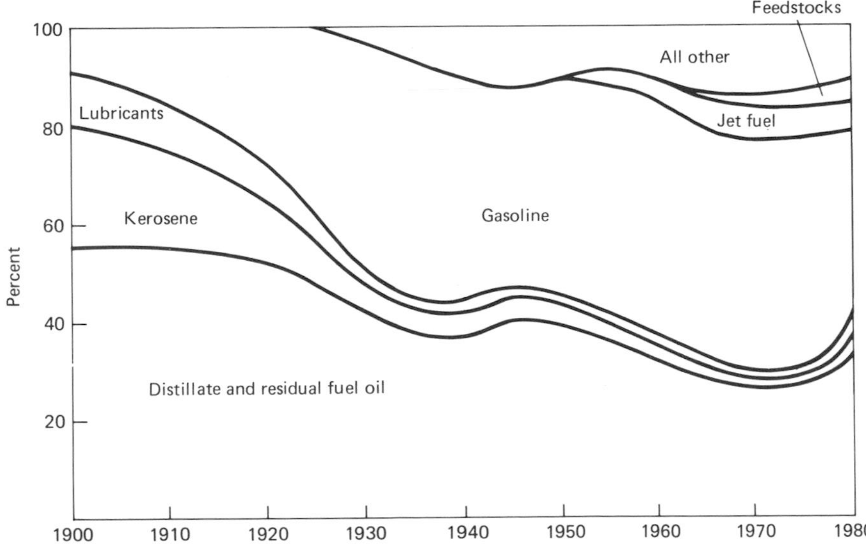

Figure 5.2. Composition of U.S. Domestic Refinery Output, 1900–1980. "All other" includes wax, coke, asphalt, still gas, liquid gas, and residual non-energy by-products such as plastics and polyesters. Data from U.S. Department of Commerce, Bureau of the Census, *Statistical Abstract* (Washington, D.C.: U.S. Government Printing Office, selected years); and idem, *Historical Statistics, Colonial Times to 1970*, vol. 1 (Washington, D.C.: U.S. Government Printing Office, 1976).

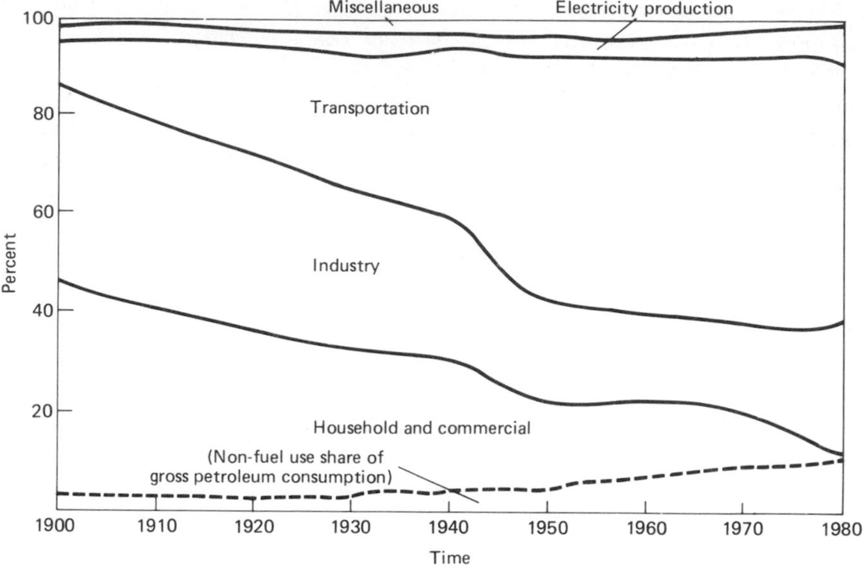

Figure 5.3. Sector Distribution of U.S. Petroleum Consumption, 1900–1980. Data from Department of Energy, Energy Information Administration, *Monthly Energy Review*, 1974–80; Department of the Interior, *Energy Perspectives 2*; and Department of Commerce, Bureau of the Census, *Historical Statistics, Colonial Times to 1970*, vol. 1.

reason for this pattern is the increasing yield of gasoline from refining and its use by road and airline transportation systems. At the same time, much of the decline in other sectors' usage of petroleum is attributable to the growth of natural gas and electricity consumption, as noted in chapter 2. Because natural gas has become so important to the U.S. economy, we should take a closer look at the technology of its production.

5.2. NATURAL GAS

Natural gas is the second most widely used fossil fuel in the U.S. economy and is third, after coal, in the world. As of 1980, natural gas accounted for just over one-quarter of all U.S. gross energy consumption. Though this is slightly less than its one-third peak share of 1970, natural gas use has expanded dramatically in this century, especially as a substitute resource for coal. As with petroleum, the transformation of natural gas into its many end uses begins with exploration and extraction.

5.2.1. Exploration and Extraction

Natural gas is the product of geological and climatic influences on plant and animal fossils now long extinct. As with the creation of petroleum, these transformations took place within sedimentary rock formations in which surface accumulations sealed off dead plants and animals in such a way that oxidation could not occur. In turn, heat and pressure transformed these fossil deposits into solid coal, liquid petroleum, and natural gas. Because these geological and climatic shifts were of such an enormous magnitude, they also provided a varied dispersion of natural gas deposits. As a result, natural gas is found not only where there are petroleum and coal deposits but also in fields where there are no other fossil resources. Moreover, roughly 70 percent of all natural gas is found either in isolated fields or in petroleum fields in which its extraction is not significantly affected by oil production.[7]

Exploration for natural gas is based on the same kinds of methods as those used in petroleum research. Distinguishing natural gas deposits from petroleum deposits is based initially on tests such as those to detect differences in gravity and magnetic-field strength. Ultimately, however, estimates of natural gas deposits, like estimates of petroleum deposits, can be verified only by exploratory drilling.

Basic data on recent U.S. domestic natural gas exploration are presented in table 5.4. Not surprisingly, the number of well drillings has increased at a substantial rate in recent years, in general proportion to the growth of demand and to increases in the real price of natural gas pointed out in figure 3.5. To be sure, expanded drilling has added to reserves, but not in proportion to production. Consequently, as in the case of domestic petroleum, increases in the real price of natural gas have not been sufficient to offset declines in the level of proven reserves.

Natural gas is extracted with the same kind of technology used in petroleum extraction. The most important difference is that natural gas must be kept under pressure once it reaches the surface. In addition, natural gas flows may require further modification before transfer to ultimate points of consumption can proceed.

Natural gas wells are of three basic types. A dry well is the simplest and most desirable, since it involves the least physical change once the natural gas is brought to the surface. A gas condensate well is one in which the lowering of underground pressure by continuing extraction often results in the conversion of the natural gas into a liquid condensate form. Such condensate wells usually contain natural gas liquids such as gasoline, with as many as ten to seventy-five barrels per 28,000 cubic meters. The extract is thus a wet gas that must be separated once it reaches the surface, since many of the end uses of natural gas require purity of liquid or gas flows.

A third type of natural gas well is the crude-oil well, in which the gas is trapped in the upper portion of a deposit. This casing head, or cap, gas is also wet, by virture of the incomplete separation of liquid hydrocarbons. Though it may be of the same quality as that found in a condensate well, its extraction is governed by the yield from petroleum extraction. In practice, where the petroleum of such a field commands a higher price per Btu, the gas may be left in the ground as a means of maintaining the maximum feasible

[7]Mouzon, *Resources and Industries of the United States*, p. 134.

Table 5.4. U.S. Domestic Natural Gas Exploration, 1900–1980

Year	Number of Wells Drilled	Total Depth of Drillings (in millions of meters)	Average Depth per Well Drilled (in meters)	Average Cost per Well Drilled (in 1972 U.S. Constant Dollars)	Average Cost per Meter of Wells Drilled (in 1972 U.S. Constant Dollars)	Proven End-of-Year Reserves (in trillions of cubic meters)
1900	—	—	—	—	—	0.132
1910	—	—	—	—	—	0.244
1920	—	—	—	—	—	0.448
1930	—	—	—	—	—	1.288
1940	2,000	—	—	—	—	2.380
1945	3,000	—	—	—	—	4.116
1950	3,000	4.176	1,392	—	—	5.169
1955	4,000	6.065	1,516	—	—	6.229
1960	5,262	8.876	1,687	$137,116	$7.72	7.345
1965	4,772	8.083	1,694	120,978	6.83	8.021
1970	3,844	7.046	1,833	140,375	7.58	8.141
1975	7,654	13.237	1,729	179,885	9.97	6.384
1976	8,904	14.762	1,658	176,419	10.15	6.048
1977	11,380	18.136	1,594	188,660	10.84	5.852
1978	12,930	21.184	1,638	206,663	11.83	5.824
1979	14,673	22.161	1,510	225,903	12.90	5.519
1980	15,730	23.421	1,489	—	—	5.409

Sources: U.S. Department of the Interior, Bureau of Mines, *Minerals Yearbook* (Washington, D.C.: U.S. Government Printing Office, selected years); American Petroleum Institute, *Basic Petroleum Data Book* (Washington, D.C.: API, 1981); U.S. Department of Energy, Energy Information Administration, *Natural Gas Production and Consumption Annual,* 1980; idem, *Monthly Energy Review* (Washington, D.C.: U.S. Government Printing Office, October 1981).

natural pressure on extracting the petroleum. Depending on both technology and relative prices, the natural gas may then be extracted once petroleum flows have become uneconomical. Furthermore, in some cases, the original natural gas may be diluted or augmented by additional injections of other gases or fluids, as occurs in secondary and tertiary recovery methods of petroleum extraction.

5.2.2. Refining and Distribution

Natural gas consists of hydrogen, methane (CH_4), carbon dioxide (CO_2), nitrogen (N_2), and certain hydrocarbons. Though it is possible to obtain gas by-products such as methane, butane, and propane from crude-oil refining, the energy input necessary to extract these compounds in useful quantities is inherently more resource-intensive than the processing of natural gas itself. Indeed, it is for this reason that petroleum gas by-products of distillation are usually further transformed into such liquid or solid forms as ammonia, methyl alcohol, formaldehyde, plastics, acetones, nylon, polyesters, and polyethylenes. At the same time, given the differences in quality among natural gas deposits, invariably some degree of refining is essential to the transformation of natural gas into technically and commercially viable products.

One method of refining natural gas is compressing and cooling. Depending on temperature and pressure conditions, natural gasoline can be separated, along with butane and propane hydrocarbons, leaving a relatively pure methane gas. One difficulty with this method is that the proportions of propane and butane in the gasoline are often too high to yield gasoline stability at atmospheric temperature and pressure. Another is that the residual methane may not have a sufficiently high Btu value per unit of volume to be commercially viable, particularly if too much hydrogen is released by the compression and cooling. Indeed, the compression and cooling technique carries the same kind of limitation as the simple distillation method of crude-oil refining, namely, the instability of desired by-products and the relatively low yields thus obtained. Consequently, more recent methods have generally displaced compressing and cooling natural gas plants from their once preeminent role.

Another method of natural gas refining is liquid absorption. In this process, natural gas is passed through an oil absorber unit whose flow is countercurrent to the flow of the natural gas. The liquid hydrocarbons such as butane, propane, and natural gasoline can then be removed from the oil by traditional distillation. Though distillation adds to the extraction cost, it results in a much higher degree of purity in the liquid by-products as well as in the residual methane.

A third method of natural gas refining is charcoal absorption. Natural gas is passed through activated charcoal rather than through oil. The activated charcoal, which is positioned in a tower, collects the liquid hydrocarbons, which are then separated from the charcoal by the injection of live steam. Since the liquid hydrocarbons have different weights, this procedure serves as a modified form of distillation which provides a much higher yield than possible with liquid absorption techniques alone. Taken together, both liquid and charcoal absorption methods account for around three-quarters of all natural gas refining in the United States. [8]

Natural gas products are distributed generally from refining plants to regional marketing centers by an interstate pipeline system, the extent of which is shown in table 5.5 Though some natural gas is transported by rail, and a smaller share by truck, pipelines today carry over two-thirds of all domestically produced natural gas and practically all supplies of imported natural gas.[9]

With the exception of the period of the Great Depression, natural gas end use has followed a fairly clear pattern of evolution (see figure 5.4). In general, as its refining technology has improved, natural gas has become increasingly

[8]Ibid., p. 140.

[9]For an overview and assessment of liquified natural gas transport technology, see Elisabeth Drake and Robert C. Reid, "The Importation of Liquefied Natural Gas," *Scientific American* 236 (April 1977):21–29.

Table 5.5. U.S. Domestic Natural Gas Production, 1900–1980

Year	Natural Gas Wells in Place	Annual Marketed Domestic Natural Gas Production (in billions of cubic meters)	Daily Output per Well (in cubic meters)	Offshore Share of U.S. Domestic Natural Gas Production	Import Share of U.S. Natural Gas Consumption	Offshore Production Share of U.S. Natural Gas Consumption	Natural Gas Pipeline Capacity (in thousands of kilometers)
1900	10,123	7	1,895	—	—	—	—
1910	19,264	14	1,991	—	—	—	—
1920	27,135	23	2,322	—	—	—	—
1930	42,731	55	3,526	—	—	—	—
1940	53,880	77	3,915	—	—	—	—
1945	59,134	113	5,235	—	—	—	499
1950	64,900	176	7,430	0.1%	—	0.11%	623
1955	71,475	263	10,081	1.4	0.10%	1.50	800
1960	90,761	358	10,807	3.4	1.29	3.59	1,015
1965	111,680	449	11,015	5.9	2.98	6.12	1,236
1970	117,000	614	14,378	14.7	3.90	15.08	1,469
1975	132,000	591	12,267	21.2	4.91	22.65	1,577
1976	137,000	566	11,319	21.5	4.83	21.55	1,588
1977	148,000	576	10,663	22.7	5.18	23.65	1,606
1978	157,474	563	9,796	25.6	4.92	25.93	1,631
1979	169,891	566	9,128	26.5	6.19	26.17	1,658
1980	—	570	—	—	4.95	—	1,684

Sources: U.S. Department of the Interior, Bureau of Mines, *Minerals Yearbook* (Washington, D.C.: U.S. Government Printing Office, selected years); U.S. Department of Commerce, Bureau of the Census, *Historical Statistics, Colonial Times to 1970*, vol. 1 (Washington, D.C.: U.S. Government Printing Office, 1976); U.S. Department of Energy, Energy Information Administration, *Natural Gas Production and Consumption Annual*, 1980; idem, *Monthly Energy Review* (Washington, D.C.: U.S. Government Printing Office, October 1981).

competitive with other fuels, especially coal. In addition, as petroleum refining has focused on higher yields of gasoline and aviation fuel, natural gas has become a more competitive substitute for fuel oil in household and commercial heating, as well as in the production of electricity. Thus, whereas in 1900 over two-thirds of U.S. natural gas supplies went to industry, the industrial share of natural gas consumption has since dropped to less than half. Since the absolute level of consumption of natural gas in the industrial sector has grown during this period, the nonindustrial market for natural gas has increased at a much faster rate.

What, then, is likely to be the potential for natural gas in the future? As can be seen in tables 5.4 and 5.5, as the price of natural gas has risen in recent years, there have been intensified efforts to increase the level of domestic proven reserves. At the same time, in the near term at least, higher real prices have thus far failed to slow the decline in domestic proven reserves, as has been the case of domestic petroleum production and discovery rates. Though there may yet be significant quantities of natural gas in such deep deposit zones as the overthrust belt of the western United States and in mixed-water offshore deposits, the price of natural gas may have to rise to substantially higher levels in comparison with other fuels before these resources become economic. Since conventional and synthetic coal represent two of these alternatives, we can round out our discussion of fossil fuels with an examination of coal production technology.

5.3. COAL

Coal is presently the third most widely used energy resource in the U.S. economy. Having replaced wood as the single largest energy resource by 1885, it retained its primary role until displaced by petroleum in 1951. Though natural gas became the second most widely used resource in 1958, coal remains a far from insignificant resource for both present and future energy consumption. In fact, based on present-day technology and prices, coal accounts for well over four-fifths of U.S. proven nonrenewable energy resources. Yet as we will see, under present and evolving conversion technologies, coal poses unique problems that limit its potential demand within the economy.

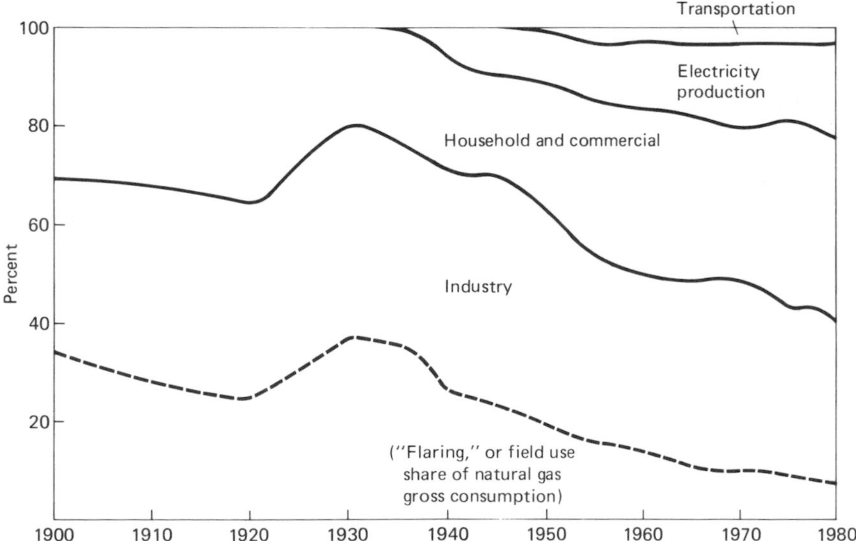

Figure 5.4. Sector Distribution of U.S. Natural Gas Consumption, 1900–1980. "Flaring" includes pumping, extraction, field losses, and plant fuel uses. Data from Department of Energy, Energy Information Administration, *Monthly Energy Review*, 1974-80; Department of the Interior, *Energy Perspectives 2*; and Department of Commerce, Bureau of the Census, *Historical Statistics, Colonial Times to 1970*, vol. 1.

5.3.1. Exploration and Extraction

As a fossil fuel, coal owes its origins to some of the basic geological processes that led to the formation of petroleum and natural gas. Coal is distinguished from these other fuels by two unique problems. One is that as a solid, coal must be mined. Mining can be dangerous to worker health, and it poses significant environmental costs.[10] The second problem is that because there are many impurities within coal deposits, combustion creates additional environmental risks to plant and animal life in the form of carbon dioxide, sulfur dioxide, and nitrogen oxide emissions. Coal is, in a word, dirty.

Coal deposits vary substantially in terms of purity and energy content. Figure 5.5 illustrates this variation among present proven U.S. coal fields. The quality of coal in these deposits ranges from lignite to anthracite, with sub-, medium-high-volatile, and low-volatile bituminous grades in between. Anthracite is the hardest of these coals. Though it does not have the highest energy content among all types of coal (20–24 MBtu's/ton), it has long been considered one of the most desirable because of the relative absence of impurities. However, it has also been one of the least plentiful of known recoverable deposits, amounting to approximately 1 percent on a Btu basis. In contrast, bituminous coal has a slightly higher energy content (20–26 MBtu's/ton) and is far and away the most abundant of presently recoverable types of coal, representing 64 percent on a Btu basis. Sub-bituminous coal is softer, has an even lower energy content (15–20 MBtu's/ton), and represents roughly one-sixth of presently known deposits. Lignite is the softest of all, has the lowest energy content (10–14 MBtu's/ton), and accounts for one-fifth of presently recoverable deposits.

The greatest single impurity in coal is sulfur. In the geographic terms of figure 5.5, Midwestern coal has the highest sulfur content, followed by Appalachian Eastern and then Western coal deposits. For example, approximately 60 percent of Midwestern coal contains sulfur deposits of 3 percent or more by weight. In contrast, one-fifth of Appalachian coal contains concentrations of sulfur at 3 percent of weight, whereas only 1 percent of Western coal is so concentrated. Though there are other impurities in coal, it is sulfur that has caused the greatest problems in terms of environmental and health costs. When high-sulfur coal is burned, sulfur dioxide is ejected into the environment. When sulfur dioxide comes into contact with water, sulfuric acid is formed. Unless otherwise treated, coal emissions that interact with environmental precipitation thus become what is known as acid rain.[11] Given

[10]For discussions of the environmental effects of stripmining and technical alternatives, see National Academy of Sciences, *Rehabilitation Potential of Western Coal Lands*, Report to the Energy Policy Project of the Ford Foundation (Cambridge, Mass.: Ballinger Publishing Co., 1974); and Genevieve Atwood, "The Strip-Mining of Western Coal," *Scientific American* 233 (December 1975):23–29.

[11]Current environmental standards call for no more than 1.2 pounds of sulfur dioxide (SO_2) per million Btu's of heat generated by coal in new electricity generating plants. Coal with 24 MBtu's per ton cannot contain more than 0.7 percent sulfur by weight, a factor which has created pressures for shifting from relatively high-sulfur Appalachian coal to lower-sulfur deposits in Alaska, New Mexico, Arizona, Montana, Wyoming, Colorado, and North Dakota.

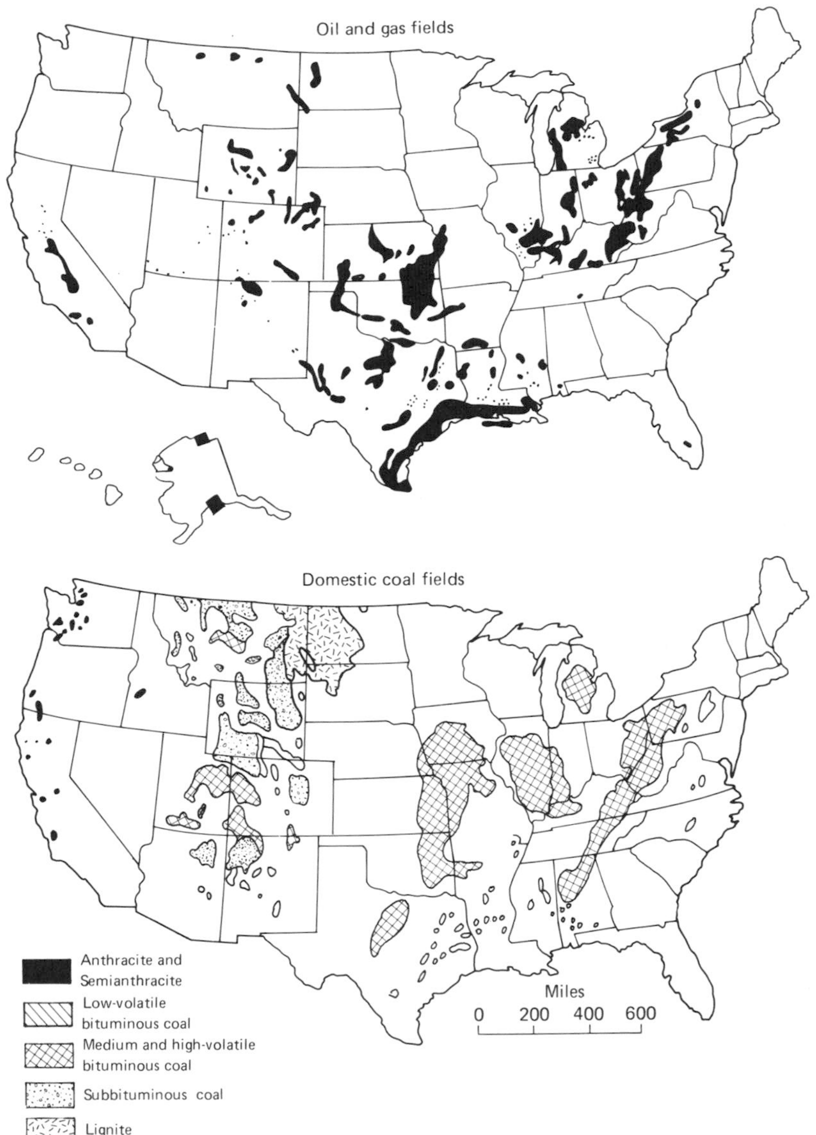

Figure 5.5. Geographic Distribution of U.S. Conventional Fossil Resource Deposits. Map of oil and gas fields adapted from Department of the Interior, *Energy Perspectives* 2, p. 91. Map of domestic coal fields adapted from ibid., p. 111.

For a discussion of the problem of acid rain, see Gene E. Likens, Richard F. Wright, James N. Galloway, and Thomas J. Butler, "Acid Rain," *Scientific American* 241 (October 1979):43–51. One important finding of the authors is that building higher smokestacks tends to convert the acid rain from a local problem into a regional one. Thus, scrubbers or similar types of technologies of the kind discussed in section 5.3.2 are likely to be more effective solutions.

that mining still serves as the principal method of coal extraction and that coal contains such harmful impurities, how is it transformed into the useful energy forms on which the economy depends?

Coal deposits can exist at at least the same depths as those of petroleum and natural gas, deriving as they do from common fossil sources. Throughout the twentieth century, most domestic coal production has been in bituminous coal, as is illustrated in table 5.6. Though anthracite is an environmentally cleaner fuel, its share has fallen as changes in the demand for coal have stimulated production toward more plentiful and relatively more accessible bituminous supplies. As a result, anthracite coal, which accounted for as much as half of all production in the mid-nineteenth century, has steadily dropped in the twentieth century to its presently insignificant level of less than 1 percent.

A second pattern in domestic coal production is that as coal consumption

Table 5.6. U.S. Coal Production, 1900–1980—Basic Data

Year	Production of Anthracite, Bituminous, and Lignite (in millions of short tons)	Bituminous and Lignite Share of Total Coal Production	Number of Bituminous Mines	Output per Bituminous Coal Mine (in short tons)	Average Value of Bituminous Coal Mined (in 1972 dollars per minemouth short ton)
1900	262.79	78.87%	3,754	55,208	—
1910	417.11	83.37	5,818	59,771	—
1920	568.67	85.57	8,921	54,546	—
1930	534.78	87.06	5,891	79,032	—
1940	512.26	90.22	6,324	73,088	—
1945	630.86	91.56	7,033	82,130	—
1950	560.39	92.95	9,429	55,244	$8.14
1955	490.02	94.82	7,856	59,143	6.65
1960	434.33	95.79	7,865	52,900	6.83
1965	526.96	97.18	7,228	70,848	5.97
1970	612.98	98.36	5,601	107,647	6.85
1975	654.64	98.97	6,168	105,123	15.32
1976	684.91	98.99	6,161	110,159	14.71
1977	697.21	99.12	6,077	114,729	14.17
1978	670.16	99.15	6,229	107,587	14.52
1979	781.13	99.15	6,000	130,188	14.44
1980	835.40	99.15	6,300	132,603	15.12

Sources: U.S. Department of Commerce, Bureau of the Census, *Historical Statistics, Colonial Times to 1970,* vol. 1 (Washington, D.C.: U.S. Government Printing Office, 1976); U.S. Department of Energy, Energy Information Administration, *Monthly Energy Review* (Washington, D.C.: U.S. Government Printing Office, May 1981); President's Commission on Coal, *Coal Data Book* (Washington, D.C.: U.S. Government Printing Office, February 1980).

Table 5.7. The Evolution of U.S. Coal Mining Technology, 1900–1980

Year	Surface Share of All U.S. Coal Mining	Mechanically Cleaned Coal as Percentage of All Coal	Mechanically Loaded Coal as Percentage of All Coal	Room-and-Pillar Mining as Percentage of All Underground Coal Mining	Shortwall Continuous Mining as Percentage of All Underground Coal Mining	Longwall Continuous Mining as Percentage of All Underground Coal Mining	Mechanical Mining as Percentage of All Underground Coal Mining	Mining Fatalities per Million Worker-Hours of Production	Nonfatality Injuries per Million Worker-Hours of Production
1900	0.22%	2.13%	—	78.0%	—	—	78.0%	—	—
1910	0.35	3.84	—	79.0	—	—	79.0	—	—
1920	1.67	3.16	—	80.0	—	—	80.0	—	—
1930	4.17	8.30	10.05%	81.0	—	—	81.0	—	—
1940	9.68	22.20	35.40	88.4	—	—	88.4	1.65	68.75
1945	18.94	25.60	56.10	90.8	—	—	90.8	1.11	59.58
1950	24.11	38.48	69.40	91.8	1.2%	—	93.0	0.90	52.00
1955	25.04	58.69	84.60	88.1	8.0	—	96.1	1.00	45.00
1960	31.67	65.74	86.30	67.8	27.4	—	95.2	1.20	42.00
1965	35.24	64.88	89.20	53.9	42.7	—	96.6	1.00	45.00
1970	43.85	53.65	97.20	46.1	50.1	2.1%	98.3	1.00	44.00
1975	54.84	41.20	98.50	32.0	63.4	3.1	98.5	0.42	30.00
1976	56.63	40.50	99.00	31.0	63.9	3.6	98.5	0.37	38.00
1977	59.53	40.00	99.20	29.7	65.2	4.1	99.0	0.33	38.00
1978	60.34	41.23	99.30	30.0	65.0	4.1	99.1	0.30	38.00
1979	61.00	42.43	99.45	31.0	64.0	4.2	99.2	0.29	38.00
1980	62.20	45.60	99.50	32.0	63.0	4.2	99.2	0.28	38.00

Sources: U.S. Department of Commerce, Bureau of the Census, *Historical Statistics, Colonial Times to 1970*, vol. 1 (Washington, D.C.: U.S. Government Printing Office, 1976); U.S. Department of Energy, Energy Information Administration, *Monthly Energy Review* (Washington, D.C.: U.S. Government Printing Office, May 1981); President's Commission on Coal, *Coal Data Book* (Washington, D.C.: U.S. Government Printing Office, February 1980).

has been displaced to a significant extent by petroleum and natural gas, the number of mines has varied significantly in response to changes in relative energy prices. Yet within this fluctuation there has been a gradual trend toward higher output per mine, a reflection of not only changes in relative prices but also economies of scale and technological change.

In general, all mining operations can be grouped into three basic categories: underground, surface, and auger. Underground mining is the most traditional type, even though it accounts for less than 40 percent of current production (see table 5.7). Underground mining can be classified further as to the direction of digging and excavation. A shaft mine uses a direct, vertical elevation technique. It is the deepest type of mine, and it must use the greatest degree of artificial support systems, particularly air and temperature circulation controls. Slope mines have entry passageways positioned on a downward angle from the processing plant. And in drift mines, unprocessed coal is transferred from higher-elevation mine entrances to lower-elevation plants by means of chutes and conveyors.

In surface mining, the topsoil, or overburden, is stripped away, and the exposed seams are excavated directly. In area surface mining, large-scale excavations involving a relatively flat terrain are common, particularly in the Midwest. Contour mining involves excavation on slopes that vary from ten to fifteen degrees above horizontal and, usually, smaller-scale operations than in the case of area strip mining. Mountaintop removal methods are used when the terrain varies by twenty degrees or more from horizontal.

Auger, or bore, mining is a variant of strip mining. Statistics on this type of production are usually included in surface production figures. What distinguishes auger mining from strip mining is that by using core removal techniques, there is a potentially less destructive alteration of the environment. However, since most coal seams are substantially wider than they are deep, auger mining is at best a compromise form of strip mining.

The dilemma of coal mining methods is straightforward. On the one hand, strip mining is far safer in terms of its working environment than underground methods. On the other hand, strip mining tends to impose higher costs on the environment in terms of permanent alteration of land. Indeed, it may preclude a return of land to its former use even when elaborate reclamation may be undertaken. How this dilemma has been dealt with thus far can be seen in table 5.7.

First, to reduce underground accidents, coal mining has become much more capital-intensive over the years. The percentage of mechanically cleaned coal rose steadily until 1960; then it began a gradual decline as chemical cleaning displaced some of this process. Second, almost all coal is now mechanically loaded from mines to transport systems. Moreover, the simple room-and-pillar method has been replaced largely by shortwall continuous mining methods, and to some extent by longwall machines. Under shortwall methods, a coal seam with a face of up to 150 feet and 1,000 feet long is scraped continuously by machines while a movable shaft protecting miners permits the overburden to fall safely behind them. Longwall methods are based on the same principle but involve coal seam facings of up to 600 feet and 4,000-foot lengths. The net effect of mechanization of coal mining has been to reduce worker injury and fatality rates. Yet, whether strip or underground mining methods are used, coal still imposes many external costs on human safety and the environment. How these costs are priced and how this affects the competitive role of coal will be taken up in chapter 12.

5.3.2. Refining and Distribution

Compared with petroleum refining, coal refining is relatively simple. In essence, it involves the reduction of impurities so that the combustion of relatively pure carbon can attain the consistency and minimal pollution conditions essential to its demand. Yet to say that coal refining is simple is not to say that it is as technically successful as other forms of energy refining.

Three basic technologies can be used to refine coal. The simplest and oldest is water leaching. It often takes place at mine sites rather than at final destination points because of the ease with which it can be done at that stage.

Basically, water leaching involves the feeding of coal and oxygen into a leaching solution to permit the dissolution of sulfur. Wet coal is then separated from the sulfur before shipment to consumers, and iron sulfate and pure sulfur are extracted as marketable by-products. The problem with the simple leaching process is that a considerable amount of sulfur remains in the coal.

A second technique is fluidized bed combustion. Whether first leached or not, crushed coal and limestone (calcium carbonate) are fed into a pressurized steam chamber. The steam facilitates the formation of calcium oxide and calcium sulfate. These compounds are then periodically removed from the bed. Rejected gas from the chamber passes through a particulate removal cycle before transfer to a heat recovery unit within the basic coal burning unit. This leaves the relatively pure coal to be removed from the chamber, dried, and then fed to the basic coal burning unit.

The third technique is flue gas desulfurization, or the limestone wet scrubbing process. In this method, a limestone slurry is fed into a chamber in which rejected energy and particulates of untreated coal combustion have been fed. An effluent hold tank collects the calcium sulfate and calcium oxide by-products, and the remaining cleansed effluent is discharged into the atmosphere through conventional smokestacks. The difficulty that these cleansing techniques have posed is that the benefits to be gained accrue to society at large, but the costs of installation and operation fall directly on the producer. Thus, market pricing may not in itself provide the appropriate incentives to reconcile this divergence in private and social costs.

As we have seen, there is some degree of coal preparation at mine sites themselves. One reason for this is that the breaking of coal into smaller pieces is essential for its transportation to final consuming points. The transportation of coal to end users is done mostly by rail, though this form of transport has dropped from over 80 percent of all shipments in 1940 to its present share of approximately 65 percent. Roughly 2–3 percent of coal production has always ben consumed at the mine, but in recent years coal processing plants have accounted for a rising share of all production. They now account for approximately 10 percent of total output. The remaining distribution of coal production has been by water and motor vehicle transport, with each of these modes claiming approximately one-tenth of total coal distributed.

The distribution of coal end uses is summarized in figure 5.6. The most important shift has been in its specialization in the production of electricity. Whereas only 5 percent of coal production went to produce electricity in 1900, almost 80 percent was so allocated in 1980, and this amounted to half of all primary energy consumption in the electricity generation sector of the economy.

The second and third most important shifts in coal end uses have been its almost virtual elimination in transportation and a substantial decrease in its use by household and commercial units. Perhaps the greatest single factor behind the decline of coal in transportation has been the shift from coal to

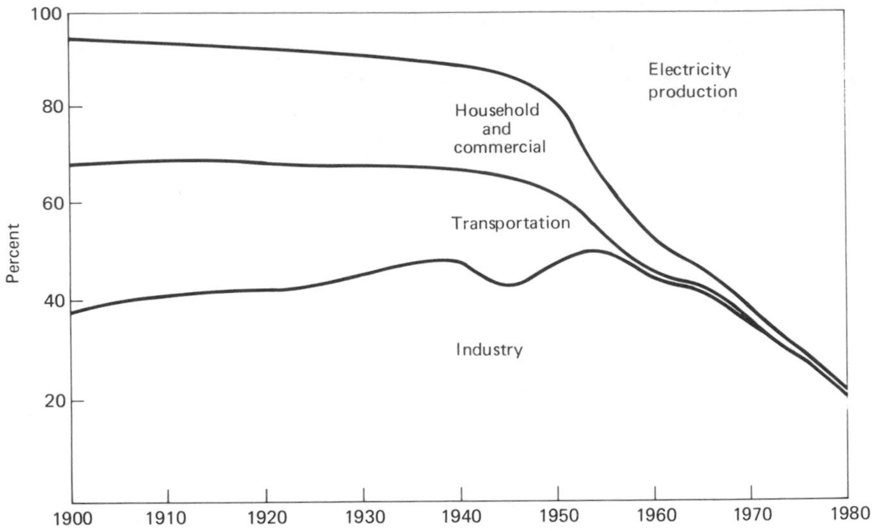

Figure 5.6. Sector Distribution of U.S. Coal Consumption, 1900–1980. Data from Department of Energy, Energy Information Administration, *Monthly Energy Review*, 1974–80; Department of the Interior, *Energy Perspectives 2*; and Department of Commerce, Bureau of the Census, *Historical Statistics, Colonial Times to 1970*, vol. 1.

diesel and electric trains. To be sure, its decline has also been hastened by the decline in railway transit relative to motor vehicle and air transit in general, but it was in the 1950s that coal-fired trains began to disappear rapidly from railroad systems. As to household and commercial use of coal, the decline here has been due largely to its replacement by petroleum and natural gas, even though the growth of electricity consumption partly obscures the continuing significance of coal in this sector.

5.4. TECHNOLOGICAL ALTERNATIVES IN FOSSIL FUELS

The United States' experience with fossil fuels is a curious one. From an early reliance on coal, its most abundant nonrenewable resource, it has gradually shifted its consumption to petroleum and natural gas, both of which represent but a small fraction of domestic and world reserves. As has been seen, apart from relative prices, technology has played an important role in the production and consumption possibilities of all of these resources. Consequently, before any assessment is made of the stock of fossil reserves, we must take into consideration recent and projected technological change in fossil fuel production and utilization.

Technological change in fossil fuel production and utilization can be viewed from two basic perspectives. One is the extent to which technology affects the overall level of energy consumption, that is, the kind of efficiency already specified in the discussion of thermodynamic efficiency in chapter 4. A second, related category of technical change is the extent to which a given resource can be converted into alternative usable forms. It is with both of these perspectives in mind that we can now proceed with the analysis of current and future technological changes and their impact on fossil resource utilization.

5.4.1. Secondary and Tertiary Recovery Methods

Fossil fuel extraction traditionally has been undertaken by drilling, or in the case of coal, by mining. However, in the case of petroleum and natural gas, once the earth's natural underground pressure begins to fall from continued extraction, the marginal cost of extraction begins to rise, eventually reaching a point where it is no longer economical to continue operations. This often means that up to 70 percent of the petroleum or natural gas may be left underground.

One way of increasing the yield from petroleum and natural gas deposits is by secondary and tertiary recovery methods. In secondary recovery, the underground pressure of a deposit trap is raised by injection of air, gas, or water. Obviously, in the case of natural gas recovery, the only feasible method is the use of water. The reason is that air and gas would tend to mix with the existing petroleum and natural gas deposits, thereby requiring more extensive treatment once extraction has taken place.

A second way of increasing the yield from deposits, a way which applies only to petroleum, is by tertiary recovery methods. In this procedure, the viscosity of petroleum can be lowered by the injection of steam, heat, or chemicals. Thicker crude oil can then travel more quickly to the surface.

Taken together, secondary and tertiary recovery methods have raised the yield of petroleum deposits alone from around 25 percent in the 1940s to over 30 percent in the 1970s.[12] In the 1980s the yield will undoubtedly reach 40 percent or higher, and it may well be applied extensively to natural gas extraction as well.

The net result of secondary and tertiary recovery technology is to narrow the gap between proven recoverable reserves and ultimate deposits. Depending on relative prices, it may raise the estimate of economically recoverable reserves as well. However, because each extra unit of oil or gas extracted requires greater quantities of supplementary energy to compensate for the loss of a well's natural pressure, in terms of the Second Law of Thermodynamics, the net energy yield is not as great as when extraction first began.

Mining is not subject to secondary and tertiary recovery methods, at least in the sense that these methods apply to petroleum and natural gas extraction. In fact, the continuous mining shortwall and longwall methods discussed previously yield a greater percentage of coal extracted from a deposit than the older room-and-pillar method. The reason for such higher extraction rates is that in a conventional mine the pillars themselves consist of coal. Unless the mining operation is moving toward exhaustion from its farthest

[12] For a discussion of recovery methods and their effects on reserves, see A. R. Flower, "World Oil Production," ibid., 238 (March 1978):42–49.

point away from the entrance, these pillars must remain in place if workers and equipment are to circulate efficiently. Thus, whereas some 50–60 percent of the coal in a deposit could be extracted by the room-and-pillar method, by the shortwall technique, the yield rises to 70–85 percent. By longwall methods, it can reach 75-90 percent. Of course, since both of these methods involve the subsequent collapse of overburden, they thereby impose environmental costs of the kind already noted for strip mining techniques.

One recent development in coal processing technology also deserves mention at this point. Although extraction technology may not change dramatically beyond its present dimensions in the immediate future, the method of transport may. Two forms of transport now emerging are unit trains and slurry pipelines. Railroads have continued to carry the bulk of coal productions. It has been suggested that slurry pipelines containing pressurized water and pulverized coal could transport coal much more cheaply in energy terms than could conventional trains. Although estimates on efficiency comparisons vary, one of the largest constraints in expansion of slurry pipelines is water consumption necessary for efficient operation. In the western United States, where many of these pipelines have been proposed, water is relatively scarce and has thus far inhibited large-scale expansion.

Unit trains are the railroads' response to slurry pipeline proposals. Unlike conventional rail transport, unit trains operate on a continuous circuit basis between mine and a single customer, often an electric utility. Such trains may have as many as 110 cars and deliver as much as 2.6 million tons of coal a year over the comparable distances envisioned in slurry pipelines, and with considerably more efficiency than conventional rail systems.[13] Whether either of these transport technologies will become viable, however, will depend partly on the convertability of coal and substitute resources into readily usable forms, a matter to which we now turn.

5.4.2. Coal Liquefaction, Shale Oil, and Tar Sands

With the growth of world petroleum consumption, diminishing returns to domestic exploration and extraction have stimulated a renewed interest in the conversion of other fossil fuels into the readily usable forms derived from petroleum refining operations. One of these methods is coal liquefaction.

Coal liquefaction is not new. It was undertaken in Germany during the Second World War, and it has been used on a limited basis in South Africa for over twenty years. Based on present-day technology, the physical conversion yield is on the order of from 1.5 to 3.5 barrels of liquid products and from 112 to 280 cubic meters of natural gas per ton of coal.[14] When these figures are translated into energy equivalents, the gross First Law efficiency may reach 70 percent. When the energy consumption requirements for liq-

[13] E. D. Griffith and Alan W. Clarke, "World Coal Production." ibid., 240 (January 1979):38–47.

[14] A good summary analysis of coal liquefaction technology is found in Neil P. Cochran, "Oil and Gas from Coal," ibid., 234 (May 1976):24–29.

uefaction are also included, the net conversion efficiency may still be as high as 60 percent.

One way of appreciating the significance of coal liquefaction is to compare the current consumption of petroleum with its coal equivalent. In 1980 the United States consumed approximately 5.9 billion barrels of oil and 687.4 million tons of coal. At an average conversion rate of 2.5 barrels of oil per short ton of coal, if the rate of coal production were increased by 752.6 million to 1.44 billion tons a year, coal liquefaction of this additional coal could satisfy virtually all of the 1980 imported-oil requirements of the United States. Of course, such a doubling of production could hardly be accomplished in such a short period of time, nor would such liquified coal necessarily be available at a competitive price, particularly if we take into consideration the social costs of production of existing technologies. Yet in light of uncertain supplies of OPEC oil, at some point even the social cost of coal conversion becomes economic. Coal liquefaction and its sister technology, coal gasification, thus continue to attract interest as part of national energy policy.

The technology of coal liquefaction is governed largely by the chemistry of coal and the resulting liquid by-products. Because the natural formation of coal eliminated most of the original water, coal has a relatively low ratio of hydrogen atoms to carbon atoms in comparison with the ratio found in liquid petroleum. Specifically, the ratio in coal is 0.8 to 1.0, and that for oil, 1.75 to 1.0. Consequently, coal liquefaction methods all involve the addition of hydrogen up to the ratio found in petroleum if the resulting products are to have the useful properties of natural petroleum.

There are four basic methods of coal liquefaction. One of them, carbonization, involves heating coal with hydrogen in the absence of air so that tar and gas are released. The tar and gas are then separated by modified distillation techniques to yield the more commonly desired products substitute natural gas, liquid petroleum, gasoline, and residual fuel oil. In direct hydrogenation, the second of these technqiues, coal is fed into a heating chamber as slurry, or crushed coal with water. To facilitate the liquefaction, a catalyst such as cobalt molybdenum may also be added before the resulting liquid is distilled into the desired end products. In the third method, the Fisher-Tropsch synthesis, coal is first gasified by combustion with oxygen and steam (its hydrogen source). The gas is then passed over a catalyst to yield both gas and liquid petroleum by-products. In the fourth method, a solvent such as xylene (itself a hydrogen-endowed petroleum by-product) is injected into a coal slurry to facilitate the dissolving reaction. As the slurry passes into the dissolving chamber, both fresh and recycled hydrogen are added under relatively high temperature and pressure. Distillation then permits the extraction of water, sulfur, fuel gases, product oil, and residual solid fuel. Figure 5.7 illustrates one version of this technique under development during the Carter administration. Since none of these techniques is mutually exclusive of any other, some advocates have proposed that maximum conversion efficiencies could be obtained by combining them.[15]

[15]Ibid. Cochran's article considers what such hybrid refineries might involve.

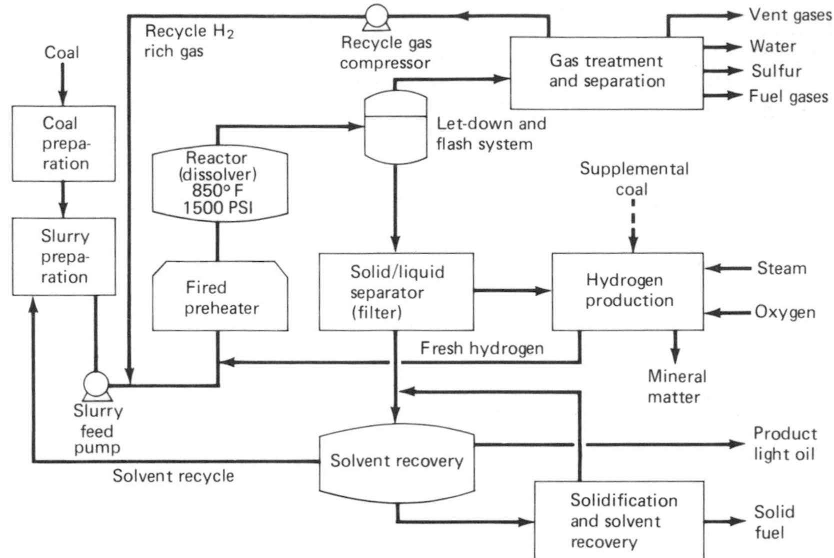

Figure 5.7. Solvent-Refined Coal Liquefaction Technology. Adapted from President's Commission on Coal, *Coal Data Book* (Washington, D.C.: U.S. Government Printing Office, February 1980), p. 181.

The feasibility of widespread coal liquefaction depends largely on the capacity to expand coal production and on the price of competitive energy substitutes. At the same time, coal liquefaction, like the basic technology used in its primary extraction, is relatively dirty. Consequently, even if the prices of domestic and imported petroleum were to rise well above those of coal liquefaction, such substitution might not prove to be as economically efficient to society as a whole as the market price alone would tend to suggest.

Another factor that may affect the implementation of coal liquefaction technology is the feasibility of substituting shale oil and tar sand resources. In each of these types of deposits, petroleum generally exists in liquid form, with a few key differences from conventional petroleum. In the case of shale oil, petroleum is embedded in shale rock. Unlike conventional deposits, however, shale oil is not concentrated into relatively accessible traps or pools. As a result, the extraction of shale oil involves a more fundamental alteration of the deposit source, much as occurs in coal mining. Indeed, shale oil extraction can be thought of as a hybrid process halfway between mining and conventional drilling. Exploration has shown that the density of shale oil deposits varies from 10 gallons per short ton of shale to as high as 240 gallons. By weight, these figures translate into a range from 3.8 percent to over 90 percent. Obviously, the lower the density of oil, the higher will be the extent of mining activity as part of the overall conversion technology.

The conversion of shale oil into useful forms requires mining, retorting, and upgrading. Depending on the relative costs of locally available inputs such as water and transport, mining and retorting can be separated

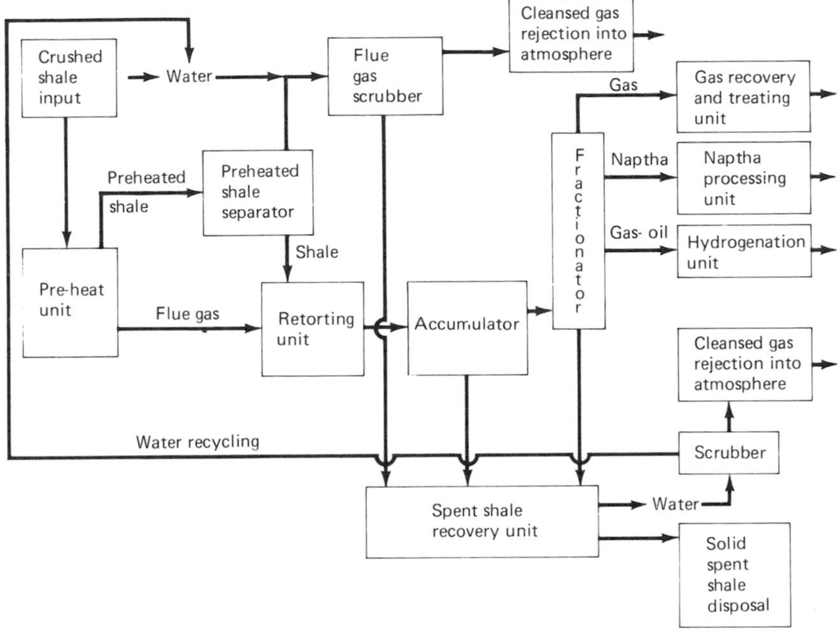

Figure 5.8. Shale Oil Basic Conversion Technology. Adapted from T. F. Yen, *Science and Technology of Oil Shale* (Ann Arbor: Ann Arbor Science Publishers, 1976), p. 48; and T. Healy, *Energy and Society* (San Francisco: Boyd and Fraser Publishing Co., 1976), p. 109.

geographically or integrated at the mining site itself. When extraction and retorting-upgrading are undertaken at the mine site, the conversion is known as *in situ* recovery. Conversely, when shale oil is first mined and then shipped to another destination for retorting and upgrading, the process is known as *ex situ* recovery. Though shale oil can be mined by conventional methods similar to those used in coal extraction, some have suggested the use of unorthodox techniques such as bioleaching to dissolve the solid shale mineral structure.[16]

Figure 5.8 illustrates the basic stages of shale oil conversion technology. Once the shale oil has been dissolved and crushed, it is preheated to permit the reduction of impurities such as sulfur through use of a separator and flue gas scrubber of the kind used in conventional coal processing. The preheated, separated shale is then passed through a retorting unit to separate the kerogen and other organic compounds from the crushed rock. The shale is then passed through an accumulator and a fractionating tower, after which gas, naptha, and oil may be extracted. In turn, hydrogenation and related upgrading steps alter the composition of these products to conform to their conventional petroleum and natural gas counterparts. Finally, the spent

[16]T. F. Yen, *Science and Technology of Oil Shale* (Ann Arbor: Ann Arbor Science Publishers, 1976), esp. chaps. 1 and 2.

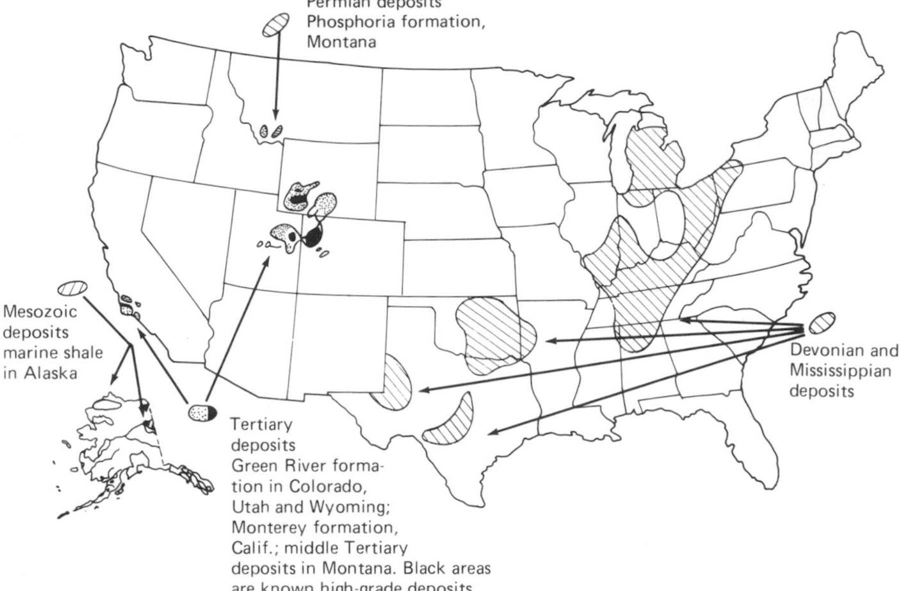

Figure 5.9. Geographic Distribution of Shale Oil Deposits in the United States. Adapted from Yen, *Science and Technology of Oil Shale*.

shale rock is passed through a recovery unit, where water is cleansed and recycled, and the residual spent shale is redeposited at the mine or at an alternative disposal site. Yet as sophisticated as shale oil technology has become, there are still significant environmental costs in terms of land displacement, water consumption and pollution, and air emissions. These social costs should, of course, be included in any assessment of the economic potential of shale oil resources in comparison with conventional competitive alternatives.

Shale oil deposits in the United States are estimated to be well in excess of presently known petroleum deposits (their geographic distribution is shown in figure 5.9). Some of the richest known deposits are located in the Green River formation in Colorado, Utah, and Wyoming. When these and other domestic deposits are added together, the total oil equivalent may be as high as 168 trillion barrels.[17] Though only a fraction is likely to be recoverable based on the current level of technology and prices, in terms of energy content, the yield would be equivalent to over twenty times the amount of domestic coal deposits, over nine hundred times the energy content of domestic petroleum deposits, over 95 percent of all known domestic fossil and nuclear energy deposits together, and it would be roughly fifty times the world stock of these same finite resources. Obviously, as the prices of conven-

[17]Ibid., p. 8. Yen notes that 80 percent of these resources are found in relatively low-density deposits, i.e., with between five and ten gallons per ton of shale rock.

tional petroleum and natural gas increase in real terms over time, even the social costs of shale oil could make it competitive.

Another resource that could affect the implementation of both coal liquefaction and shale oil technology is tar sands. Tar sands contain petroleum in sandstone deposits, in much the same patterns as shale. Two key differences that distinguish this resource, however, are that the petroleum is solidified as tar and that sandstone is more amenable to decomposition than is shale rock.

The United States is not known to possess substantial deposits of tar sands.[18] The best-known world deposit of tar sands is the Athabasca field in Alberta, Canada, and commercial production has been underway at this field as the post-1973 price of OPEC oil has risen. The size of this deposit may be as large as 600 billion barrels of oil equivalent. In energy terms, this represents 0.33 percent of all known U.S. domestic fossil and nuclear energy deposits and almost fifty times the 1980 level of U.S. gross primary energy consumption, as can be seen in the reserve estimates of Table 5.8.

Tar sands can be extracted by mining, much as in shale oil recovery. Recovery can thus be undertaken by *in situ* techniques, or by surface mining. Underground extraction must also be accompanied by heat injection, as in underground fires, emulsion, or steam injection, which could then lower the viscosity to permit a relatively smooth flow to nearby collection pools for conventional pressurized elevation to the surface. Once tar sands are extracted, their refining is similar to that of shale oil and conventional petroleum, since they all have generally the same hydrocarbon structures.

5.4.3. Synthetic Gas from Coal and Other Resources

Just as petroleum can be obtained from coal, shale oil, and tar sands, so too can natural and synthetic gas.[19] As figures 5.7 and 5.8 illustrate, as the distillation of petroleum from a coal or shale oil deposit proceeds, natural gas is also released. This gas can be captured for subsequent upgrading and distribution, and depending on the relative prices of end products, it may make more sense to increase conversion temperatures to increase the yields of natural and synthetic gas from primary solid fossil fuels. Based on the kinds of technology illustrated in figures 5.7 and 5.8, natural gas yields can vary between 100 and 300 cubic meters per short ton of processed coal, with comparable figures for shale oil and tar sands. However, because synthetic gas involves extraction from relatively impure natural resources, the social costs may be substantially higher than their conventional domestic, or even imported, counterparts. Thus, although synthetic gas could also become economically competitive, we should base any comparison on the social costs and benefits rather than on private market prices alone.

[18]U.S. tar sand deposits are mostly in Utah and are estimated at approximately 20 billion barrels.

[19]For a more detailed exposition, see Harry R. Perry, "The Gasification of Coal," *Scientific American* 230 (March 1974):19–25.

Table 5.8. Estimates of U.S. and World Fossil Energy Reserves

	United States				World[a]		
	Standard units	Quads	Btu distribution	As percent of world reserves	Standard units	Quads	Btu distribution
	Known Recoverable Reserves[b]						
Petroleum	26.4[c]	153	2.63%	5.3%	566.0[c]	3,225.0	9.47%
Natural gas	191.0[d]	196	3.38	9.6	2,230.0[d]	2,299.0	6.75
Natural gas liquids	6.0[d]	35	0.60	2.4	363.0[d]	1,456.0	4.28
Bitumens	2.5[e]	14	0.24	9.4	26.7[e]	107.9	0.30
Coal	218.4[f]	4,980	85.76	33.5	651.7	14,858.0	43.65
Shale oil	74.0[g]	429	7.39	1.0	8,612.0[h]	10,352.0	30.41
Tar sands	—	—	—	—	300.0[i]	1,740.0	5.11
Total		5,807	100.00%	17.17%		34,036.9	100.00%

Petroleum	156-377[c]	438-1,056	0.04-0.10%	3.78-9.10%	2,000.0[c]	11,600	0.07%
Nataural gas	800-1,360[d]	825-1,402	0.08-0.14	6.16-10.46	13,000.0[d]	13,403	0.08
Natural gas liquids	21-36[d]	122-209	0.01-0.02	1.44-2.46	2,120.0[d]	8,503	0.05
Bitumens	15[e]	87	0.01	13.53	160.2[e]	643	0.004
Coal	1037-1789[f]	23,644-40,789	2.37-4.01	8.75-15.10	11,850.0	270,186	1.71
Shale oil	168,000[g]	974,400	97.48-95.71	6.28	2,676,011.0[h]	15,520,863	98.06
Tar sands	20[i]	116	0.01	3.33	600.0[i]	3,480	0.02
Total	—	999,632-1,018,059	100.00%	6.32-6.43%	—	15,828,678	100.00%

Sources: Data on petroleum resources are from the American Petroleum Institute, *Basic Petroleum Data Book* (Washington, D.C.: API, 1981), through December 31, 1980. World petroleum resources are based on V. E. McKelvey, "World Energy Resources and Reserves," *Public Utilities Fortnitely* 25 (September 1975): 27-33. Data on natural gas resources are from the American Gas Association, through December 31, 1980. Data on bitumens are from Paul Averitt, "Coal Resources of the United States, January 1, 1974," Geological Survey Bulletin 1412 (Washington, D.C.: U.S. Government Printing Office, 1975). Data on U.S. coal resources are from U.S. Bureau of Mines, Geological Survey Bulletin 1412, 1975. World coal resources are based on National Coal Association, *Coal Facts* (Washington, D.C.: National Coal Association, 1977), p. 71. Data on U.S. shale oil resources are from T. F. Yen, *Science and Technology of Oil Shale* (Ann Arbor: Ann Arbor Science Publishers, 1976), p. 8. World shale oil estimates are extrapolated from data in ibid., chap. 1. Data on tar sands are from Earl Cook, *Man, Energy, Society* (San Francisco: W. H. Freeman and Co., 1976), p. 100.

[a]Inclusive of the United States, the USSR, and the People's Republic of China, unless otherwise noted

[b]Known recoverable reserves are approximately half of demonstrated recoverable reserves

[c]Petroleum resources are listed in billions of barrels, and their Btu equivalent is derived on the basis of 5,800,000 Btu's per barrel

[d]Natural gas resources are in trillions of cubic feet, and their Btu equivalent is derived on the basis of 1,031 Btu's per cubic foot

[e]Bitumens are listed in billions of barrels, and their Btu equivalent is derived on the basis of 4,011,000 Btu's per barrel

[f]U.S. coal resources are listed in billions of short tons, and their Btu equivalent is based on a weighted average of anthracite, bituminous, and lignite, all down to a depth of 305 meters

[g]Shale oil resources are listed in billions of barrels of oil equivalent, and their Btu content is derived on a basis of 5,800,000 Btu's per barrel. Eighty percent of these deposits contain less than ten gallons per ton of shale

[h]This is an estimate only. No firm data have been reported

[i]Tar sands are listed in billions of barrels of oil equivalent, and their Btu content is based on 5,800,000 Btu's per barrel

[j]Ultimate recovery is based on long-term significant shifts in relative prices and technology

5.5. U.S. AND WORLD FOSSIL RESERVES

As we saw in chapter 3, there is a significant difference between proven reserves and ultimately recoverable deposits of a depletable energy resource. To be sure, the ratio of proven reserves to ultimately recoverable deposits depends on the relative price and on the state of energy-conversion technology. Though there are still many economic and technological uncertainties, we should take stock at this point of the relative order of magnitude of U.S. and world depletable fossil reserves.

Data on U.S. and world proven and ultimately recoverable deposits of fossil fuel resources are listed in table 5.8. If we consider only presently recoverable reserves, the United States possesses a relative abundance of coal. It exceeds by a factor of ten the next most abundant resource, shale oil. The reason why this is so important is that petroleum accounts for almost one-half of all U.S. primary energy consumption, while coal accounts for just under one-seventh. Moreover, this disparate pattern also exists in terms of world proven energy resources and patterns of consumption; it is even more pronounced if we compare the distribution of ultimately recoverable resources with the distribution of current energy consumption. As we will see in part III, it is essentially the pricing of these resources and the given state of technology which has caused this disproportionality to arise and which must inevitably be altered as time goes by.

5.6. SUMMARY

In the United States and throughout the world, petroleum, natural gas, and coal account for over nine-tenths of all energy production and consumption. Because petroleum and natural gas are technologically easier to extract and convert to useful energy forms, as well as less destructive to the environment, they have gradually displaced coal from its once preeminent position as the world's principal energy resource. Despite the reduction of fatalities associated with coal production and consumption, coal has still presented serious disadvantages in relation to its two closest competitors. These differences are found in production, transport, and flexibility of end uses.

Increasing reliance on petroleum and natural gas as substitutes for coal has contributed to diminishing returns to exploration in the United States. The trend of declining reserves, which has also occurred among other economies in the world, is likely to become more aggravated and universal in the future as the consumption of these fuels continues to rise.

Technological change can influence the efficiency of fossil energy conversion. In so doing, it can affect the degree of technical substitution of fossil energy with non-fossil energy, and with non-energy resources in the economy. Secondary and tertiary recovery methods can offset to some extent the impact of declines in the marginal rate of discovery, as can the implementation of energy-efficient technologies that consume the final demand products of petroleum and natural gas refining. In addition, the implementation of coal liquefaction and gasification technologies can contribute substantially to the supply of conventional petroleum and natural gas, even though the production of these synthetic fuels may not be as energy-efficient as conventional extraction and refining. Finally, as the price of petroleum and natural gas begins to rise in response to diminishing returns to exploration and rising consumption, less accessible fuels such as shale oil and tar sands may also come to play a role.

Though fossil fuel production is ultimately governed by both economics and technology, current estimates of fossil reserves in the United States and abroad show a marked disproportionality to their patterns of consumption. Shale oil, one of the most abundant fossil resources, is an insignificant element in current consumption, whereas coal, the second most abundant, is falling rapidly in order or importance. Instead, the United States and other world economies have developed a growing dependence on the relatively scarce fossil resources petroleum and natural gas. Such a dependence cannot continue for long, as recent events have begun to demonstrate in world petroleum and natural gas markets.

SUGGESTED READINGS

Hobson, G. D., and Tirafsoo, E. N. *Introduction to Petroleum Geology.* 2d ed. London: Scientific Press, 1981.

McCray, Arthur W. *Petroleum Evaluations and Economic Decisions.* Englewood Cliffs, N.J.: Prentice-Hall, 1975.

Mouzon, Olin T. *Resources and Industries of the United States.* New York: Appleton-Century-Crofts, 1966.

Yen, T. F. *Science and Technology of Oil Shale.* Ann Arbor: Ann Arbor Science Publishers, 1976.

6

NUCLEAR ENERGY RESOURCES

Few issues in energy policy are as controversial as the utilization of nuclear power. Though the origins of the commercial uses of nuclear energy derive ominously from its original military application to the destruction of Hiroshima and Nagasaki in 1945, nuclear power has long been proposed as a feasible alternative to the world's growing dependence on fossil fuels. Indeed, since the Second World War the United States has had one of the more ambitious programs to develop commercial nuclear power. It has involved substantial subsidies such as the Price-Anderson Act, which limits the liability of nuclear electric utilities in the event of a reactor accident and subsidizes the cost of the insurance provided, and several research programs designed to accelerate the development of breeder and other alternative nuclear technologies. However, in light of the 1979 nuclear reactor accident at Three Mile Island and continuing concern over reactor safety, nuclear power as of 1980 accounted for less than 4 percent of all primary energy consumption in the United States and in other countries of the world economy. To understand both the potential and the risks of nuclear power, an examination of nuclear technology is essential.

6.1. THE NUCLEAR FUEL CYCLE AND ELECTRICITY GENERATION

As noted in chapter 4, nuclear energy derives from the basic mass-to-energy relation expressed in Einstein's equation, $E = mc^2$. Because it is exponential and multiplicative rather than linear and additive as in fossil fuel energy, the yield per unit of mass is substantially larger in nuclear transformations. As an example, where one barrel of petroleum contains 5,800,000 Btu's, its weight equivalent of fissioned uranium contains 8.4763×10^{12} Btu's, or around 1,461,442 times the amount found in petroleum. The intuitive appeal of such a powerful resource has been of no small consequence in considering its application to commercial energy production and utilization.

Though fusion of atoms may become practical within the next few years, the most common method of obtaining nuclear energy is by nuclear fission. The key to the choice of an element to be fissioned lies in its binding energy and its potential instability. All elements contain potential energy bound in the particular structure of each atomic unit. The amount of this energy depends on the arrangement and number of electrons and on the protons and neutrons of the nucleus, known collectively as nucleons. The binding energy tends to increase as the number of nucleons becomes larger. However, for nuclear fission to be possible, it is desirable to have not only a high degree of binding energy but also a requisite degree of instability, a quality which is rare in nature but possible to attain through enrichment techniques.

Whether from nature or by human intervention, beyond some point, the potential binding energy among elements attains a maximum, as in iron, after which it will begin to decline as the number of nucleons becomes greater. Within this declining range one can find not only some of the rarest elements known but also those that are so heavy with nucleons that they contain the kind of fissionable instability which can be relatively easily converted into energy.

If we plot the values for the degree of potential energy and the atomic weight of elements in the periodic table, the result is the curve of binding energy.[1] The curve of binding energy based on forty-five elements of the periodic table is shown in figure 6.1. As can be seen, some of the most common elements in nature, such as helium and oxygen, have relatively few nucleons, even though their binding energy may be high. Consequently, the most likely candidates for fission are the heavier elements, within the upper right portion of the curve. They have not only a high degree of potential energy but also the desired degree of instability. As figure 6.1 shows, these elements include two isotopes of natural uranium, ^{235}U and ^{238}U. Uranium has thus become one of the most commonly used elements in the commercial application of nuclear fission technology.[2]

For its use to be technically feasible, uranium must first be mined, then purified and usually enriched before implantation in a nuclear reactor. This process, the subsequent removal of fission by-products, and the possible reprocessing of the uranium, is known as the nuclear fuel cycle. Though the cycle will vary somewhat according to the type of reactor, the more common elements can be described at this point.

Uranium is usually found in low concentrations of host rocks as uranium oxide, U_3O_8. Since the discovery of uranium in 1789, subsequent exploration and extraction have shown that more than 95 percent of all uranium oxide deposits are found in sandstone; the reason for this pattern is not clear. Given the relatively low concentrations, which are often 0.1 percent or less,

[1]The periodic table groups elements by both atomic number and weight. With the exceptions of aluminum, potassium, cobalt, and nickel, the higher the atomic number of an element, the higher will be its atomic weight. The arrangement of elements by atomic number is based on the number of nuclear protons and the extranuclear electron structure; the atomic weight is a function of the proton and neutron nuclear structure and is expressed as an index in relation to the atomic weight of the oxygen atom.

[2]Two other fuel isotopes are thorium, ^{232}Th, and plutonium, ^{239}Pu. Thorium is found in pitchblende, carnotite, and to a certain extent in uranium and titanium ore. Thorium is a natural radioisotope; plutonium is artificial and produced from uranium, ^{238}U.

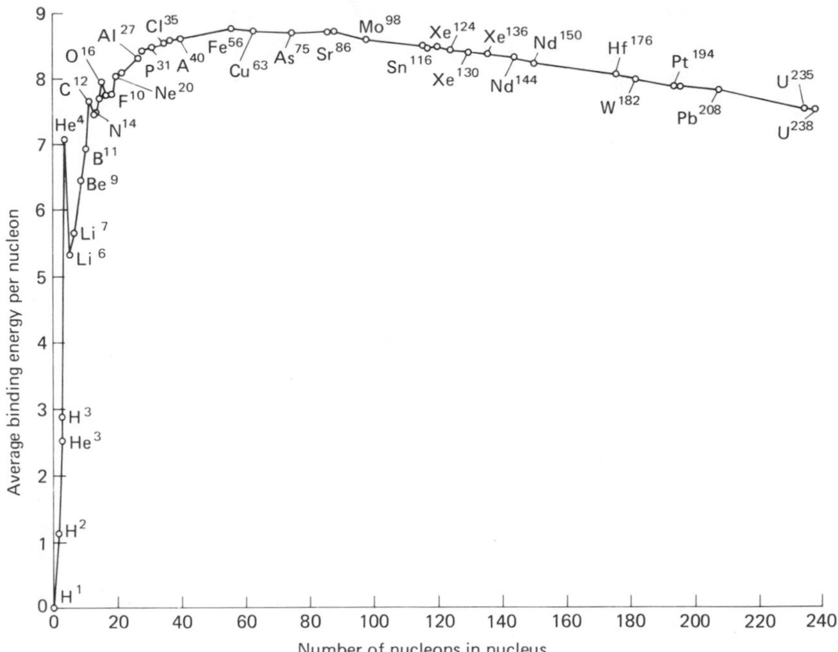

Figure 6.1. The Curve of Binding Energy. Adapted from Richard Wilson and William J. Jones, *Energy, Ecology, and the Environment* (New York: Academic Press, 1974), p. 146.

the first step following excavation of uranium oxide deposits is to separate the sandstone from them. This is done both mechanically and chemically, and the result is known as yellowcake, a concentrate containing approximately 80 percent uranium oxide and 20 percent sandstone or residual rock.

Increasing the concentration of uranium oxide from 0.1 percent to 80 percent involves the rejection of a substantial amount of host rock. In comparative terms, it involves the mining of between 500 and 800 tons of ore for every ton of yellowcake milled. To facilitate milling operations, rejected rock, or tailing, is sold periodically to the construction industry for use in the fabrication of cement blocks. Unfortunately, uranium ore tailings contain radioactive radon gas, an environmental hazard of growing concern as uranium production expands.[3] This risk and others within the nuclear fuel cycle are examined in detail in section 6.5.

Though concentrated beyond its natural state, uranium yellowcake cannot be used directly in a nuclear reactor. Instead, it must be refined by convert-

[3]The Tennessee Valley Authority, the largest single producer of electricity in the United States, traditionally has taken the tailings from uranium oxide deposits and recycled them for use in non-energy applications such as concrete blocks. Recently, the Alabama Department of Public Health began tests to determine if the 50,000 to 70,000 tons of radioactive slag used to make the blocks represents a significant health hazard (see "An Unwelcome Alabama Guest: Radioactive Gas in Many Homes," *New York Times*, 16 March 1979, p. 1).

ing it into uranium hexafluoride (UF_6), which is a solid compound at room temperature but which vaporizes at 57°C. This gaseous conversion property is important, since it facilitates the enrichment process that follows.

Despite the relatively high proportion of uranium in the hexafluoride concentrate, only a fraction is suitable for nuclear fission. Within the concentrate are three natural uranium isotopes: ^{238}U, ^{234}U, and ^{235}U.[4] By weight, 99.283 percent of natural uranium is ^{238}U, 0.711 percent is ^{235}U, and 0.006 percent is ^{234}U. Because it can be easily moderated by water, ^{235}U is the most desirable of the three, so much so that light water reactors are the most common type of commercial nuclear technology now in use. However, because all of the natural isotopes of uranium exhibit identical chemical behavior, the only way that they can be separated to obtain a sufficiently enriched quantity of ^{235}U is by physical means.

Currently, four methods are used to enrich the proportion of ^{235}U from its 0.711 percent level to the 2–3 percent necessary for use in a reactor. The process most widely used in the United States is gaseous diffusion. In this technique, uranium hexafluoride is raised to a sufficiently high temperature to convert it into a gaseous state. It is then passed through a porous barrier, which enables the lighter molecules, containing ^{235}U, to move more quickly than the heavier ones, containing ^{238}U. The efficiency of each passage is so slight that the process must be repeated as often as 1,250 times in order to attain the commercial-grade ^{235}U concentration of 2–3 percent.[5] As of 1980, virtually all uranium enrichment in the United States had been by this process.

A second enrichment process uses a gas centrifuge.[6] In this technique, at speeds of up to 400 meters per second, the spinning of the gaseous uranium hexafluoride causes the heavier ^{238}U to move to the outer wall of a centrifuge, leaving the ^{235}U near the center for extraction and chemical treatment. Despite the fact that gas centrifuge technology uses only about 4 percent of the energy involved in comparable enrichment via gaseous diffusion and has been technically demonstrated since 1940, early inefficiencies in gas centrifuge technology led to its abandonment in favor of gaseous diffusion. Now that centrifuge technology has been improved, it may soon replace gaseous diffusion. URENCO, a public consortium formed by the United Kingdom, West Germany, and the Netherlands, has already used its two pilot facilities to move into the construction of commercial gas centrifuge plants, and this has stimulated renewed interest within the United States.

The third and fourth methods of uranium enrichment use aerodynamic

[4]There are fourteen isotopes of uranium, but only three of them are found in nature.

[5]The fuel must be passed through as many as 4,000 times if the military-weapons grade of 90 percent ^{235}U is to be attained. In all types of enrichment, the energy required for upgrading the proportion of ^{235}U is measured in separative work units, or SWU's. For an assay of 0.2 percent ^{235}U, the production of 1 kilogram of 3 percent ^{235}U requires 5.5 kilograms of natural uranium and 4.3 SWU's (see Spurgeon M. Keeny, Jr., *Nuclear Power Issues and Choices*, Report of the Nuclear Energy Policy Study Group [Cambridge, Mass.: Ballinger Publishing Co., 1977], p. 400).

[6]For a more detailed discussion, see Donald R. Olander, "The Gas Centrifuge," *Scientific American* 239 (August 1978):37–43.

and laser technologies, respectively. In aerodynamic enrichment, a gaseous mixture of hydrogen and uranium hexafluoride is forced through a jet nozzle in a semicircular path to achieve a centrifugal separation of ^{235}U from ^{238}U. In laser enrichment, concentrated light is used to differentially excite the uranium hexafluoride molecules of ^{235}U and ^{238}U. Of these two methods, only the aerodynamic process has reached commercial feasibility in West Germany, Brazil, and South Africa.[7]

Once uranium has attained a commercial-grade enrichment level of 2–3 percent, the next phase of the nuclear fuel cycle is to convert the uranium hexafluoride back into a solid and to combine it with oxygen to yield uranium dioxide (UO_2), which is a powdery metal. To facilitate pre-fission handling and transport, the uranium dioxide is then usually compressed into small pellets about one and one-quarter centimeters in diameter, and half that in length for light water reactors. The pellets are then stacked and encased in a metallic rod about 366 cm long. Each rod is clad with a noncorrosive metal such as zirconium before being inserted into an assembly grid of like rods to precipitate a chain reaction.

As a controlled nuclear reaction proceeds, it gradually consumes the enriched ^{235}U. Commercially useful heat is released while radioactive fission by-products accumulate within the fuel assembly core. Consequently, beyond some point, the loss of ^{235}U necessitates the removal of the spent fuel and its fission by-products. As figure 6.2 shows, this spent fuel is available for reprocessing into a form sufficiently enriched for subsequent use in a reactor, as well as for the extraction of isotopes that can be used for other purposes, for example, in medicine and in industrial research. Once this reprocessing has been completed, the residual fission products constitute radioactive waste, which must be stored for relatively long periods of time if potential damage to the environment is to be minimized.

Data in table 6.1 provide an indication of the order of magnitude involved in several stages of the U.S. commercial nuclear fuel cycle. From a production perspective, it is clear that although there are inventory lags between each stage and demand, the relative scarcity of natural uranium requires the mining of substantial amounts of ore to obtain sufficient quantities for refining and enrichment. For example, in 1980 almost 900 tons of ore were needed for every ton of milled ore. In turn, only one-quarter of each milled ton was needed to attain the degree of uranium concentration necessary for conversion into uranium hexafluoride and the subsequent conversion into uranium dioxide pellets.

Fuel represents a relatively small share of nuclear energy costs; capital and maintenance account for the remainder. Despite the relative insignificance of fuel costs, however, until recently nuclear power consumed more electrical energy than it produced.[8] The reason for this net energy consumption was

[7]Keeny, *Nuclear Power Issues*, p. 400.

[8]For a relatively recent study of positive net energy flows from nuclear power, see Ralph M. Rotty, A. M. Perry, and David B. Reister, "Net Energy from Nuclear Reactors" (Institute for Energy Analysis Report IEA-75-3, Oak Ridge Associated Universities, Oak Ridge, Tenn., November 1975).

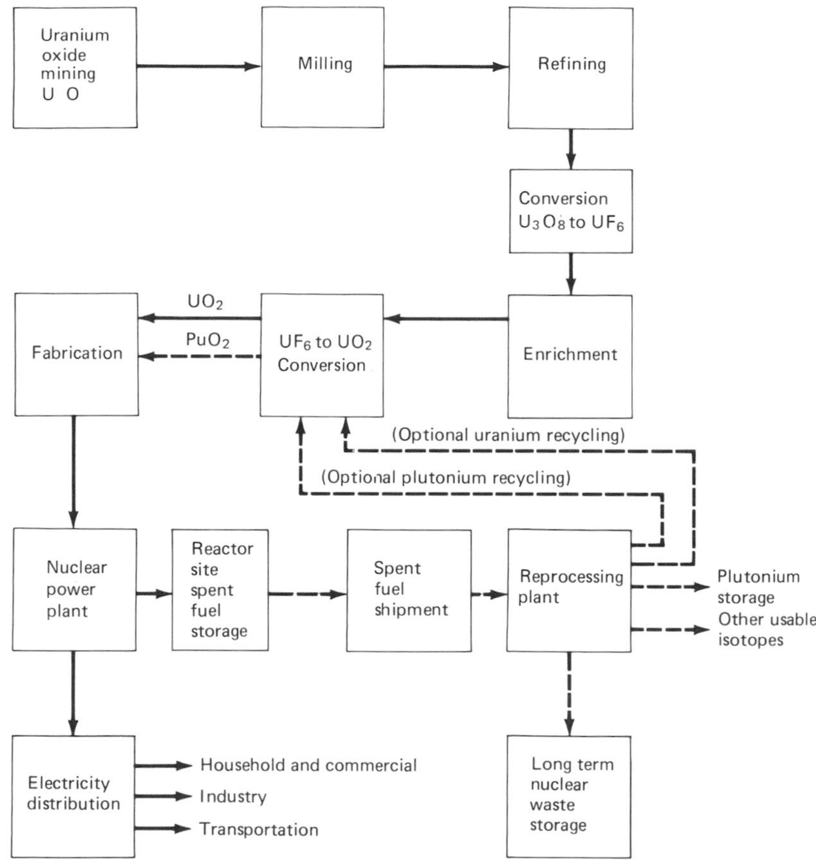

Figure 6.2. The Nuclear Fuel Cycle. Adapted from S. S. Penner, ed., *Energy and Energy Policies*, vol. 3 (Reading, Mass.: Addison-Wesley Publishing Co., 1976), p. 81.

that gaseous diffusion enrichment was—and continues to be—relatively energy-intensive, that reactor control systems also required considerable amounts of energy, and that reprocessing of fuel played such a small role in the U.S. commercial nuclear power industry.

Of the spent fuel from U.S. commercial reactors, relatively little is currently recycled.[9] A principal reason for limited reprocessing is that enriched by-products such as plutonium present complex safety and security considerations. As a result, reprocessing capacity has not increased in proportion to overall uranium use, and storage of radioactive wastes has become a growing

[9]As of 1980, the only operable nuclear recycling plant in the United States was the Allied Chemical Corporation unit in Barnwell, South Carolina. Because reprocessing had been halted by the Carter administration, this unit had requested a government subsidy. For a more detailed discussion of reprocessing, see W. P. Bebbington, "The Reprocessing of Nuclear Fuels," *Scientific American* 235 (December 1976):30–41.

Table 6.1. The U.S. Nuclear Fuel Cycle in the World Economy, 1956–80

Year	U.S. Production of Uranium Ore (in millions of short tons)	Uranium Oxide "Yellowcake" Mill Production (in short tons)[a]	Production of Refined Uranium Oxide (in short tons)	Radioactive Waste Discharge from Commercial Reactors (in short tons)	Year-End Inventory of Commercial Radioactive Waste (in short tons)	World Uranium Oxide Mill Production (in short tons)[b]	U.S. Share of World Uranium Oxide Mill Production
1956	3.500	6,000	2.65	—	—	14,470	41.47%
1957	3.695	8,640	10.72	—	—	23,470	36.81
1958	5.178	12,560	49.61	—	—	36,450	34.46
1959	6.934	16,390	128.53	—	—	36,250	45.21
1960	7.970	17,646	98.77	—	—	41,140	42.89
1961	8.041	17,399	138.12	—	—	36,300	47.93
1962	7.052	17,010	141.76	—	—	34,600	49.16
1963	5.645	14,218	114.85	—	—	31,100	45.72
1964	5.674	11,847	130.56	—	—	26,700	44.37
1965	4.362	10,442	170.01	—	—	20,800	50.20
1966	4.329	10,590	315.02	—	—	19,500	54.31
1967	5.272	11,250	187.48	—	—	19,100	58.90
1968	6.448	12,340	427.09	—	—	23,000	53.65
1969	5.904	11,610	768.10	—	—	23,100	50.26
1970	6.324	12,900	1,017.76	73.83	177.42	24,000	53.75
1971	6.279	12,300	2,316.40	121.22	212.69	23,900	51.46
1972	6.418	12,900	1,759.89	265.58	478.27	25,600	50.39
1973	6.537	13,200	2,778.14	164.20	642.47	25,700	51.36
1974	7.116	11,500	4,908.31	500.31	1,142.77	24,600	46.75
1975	7.365	11,600	2,501.54	602.79	1,745.57	26,400	43.94
1976	8.917	12,700	3,570.48	804.46	2,439.83	23,606	53.80
1977	10.236	14,900	3,444.85	1,045.80	3,595.83	27,399	54.38
1978	14.300	18,500	3,023.00	1,244.10	4,791.60	40,000	46.25
1979	15,010	18,730	3,482.00	1,529.00	6,320.60	45,455	41.21
1980	16.750	21,850	5,302.18	1,540.00	7,260.00	53,656	40.72

Sources: U.S. Department of Energy, Energy Information Administration, *Annual Report to Congress* (Washington, D.C.: U.S. Government Printing Office, 1980); idem, *Statistical Data of the Uranium Industry* (Washington, D.C.: U.S. Government Printing Office, 1981).

[a]Based on plant recovery rates

[b]Exclusive of Austria, Brazil, Czechoslovakia, Finland, East and West Germany, Hungary, India, Israel, Japan, People's Republic of China, USSR

problem.[10] As an illustration of the waste problem, a typical 1,000-megawatt light water nuclear plant operating at 80 percent capacity will consume annually around 200 tons of nuclear fuel and will generate between 30 and 40 tons of radioactive waste. If we take into consideration the growth of nuclear reactor plants, the cumulative radioactive waste generation from commercial

[10]The waste storage referred to here is only in reference to commercially generated waste and does not include the accumulated waste from weapons production.

operations alone has reached a level approaching 8,000 tons, with some additional 3 million cubic meters of low-level radioactive waste.

Until now, high-level wastes have been stored mostly in the states of Washington, South Carolina, and Idaho. Low-level waste storage has been more dispersed, including the dumping of waste cannisters off the Delaware-Maryland coast during the 1964–70 period. The issues raised by this phase of the nuclear fuel cycle are examined in greater detail in section 6.5; at this point, we can proceed to trace the use of nuclear power to the end uses of electricity.

Following the inauguration of the first commercial nuclear reactor at Shippingport, Pennsylvania, in 1957, plant capacity expanded rapidly to accommodate the growth in aggregate electricity consumption. Much of this expansion was greeted with a degree of enthusiasm. In fact, in the years prior to 1973, many predicted that by the year 2000 the United States would have an array of around 1,000 commercial nuclear reactors, which together would account for half of the then projected 2 million megawatts of total electricity capacity in the United States.[11] Since then, however, optimism has been tempered considerably, especially in light of the increase in real energy prices and in the operational safety questions surrounding the use of nuclear power.

The present significance of nuclear power can be seen in table 6.2 and figures 6.3 and 6.4. First, as electricity consumption has expanded, the fastest growth has taken place in the household and commercial sectors. In fact, as pointed out in chapter 2, as of 1980, 26 percent of all household and commercial energy use was in the form of electricity, as was 12 percent of industrial energy use. Yet, because of the level of overall industrial energy use relative to other sectors, it has remained the single largest consumer of electricity. Second, while nuclear power represented under 4 percent of all U.S. primary energy consumption as of 1980, its share in electricity production stood at almost 11 percent. Third, while nuclear power has relieved some of the dependence on fossil fuels, were its capacity tripled to replace the relatively scarce fuels petroleum and natural gas, it would conserve 19 percent of 1980 natural gas consumption but less than 8 percent of aggregate petroleum use. Thus, commercial nuclear power does not yet perform the kind of strategic role in aggregate energy use now performed by petroleum. To understand the risks of the expansion of nuclear power, we need to take a closer look at how energy from the nucleus is transformed ultimately to its electrical end uses.

6.2. NUCLEAR FISSION

In a nuclear fission reaction, the splitting of an atom releases heat energy, which in turn is used to generate steam. The steam moves the rotors of a tur-

[11]For one such projection, see Glen T. Seaborg, "On Misunderstanding the Atom," *Bulletin of the Atomic Scientists* 27 (September 1971). See also M. Carasso, et al., "The Energy Supply Planning Model, PB-245 382 and PB-245 383" (Springfield, Va.: National Technical Information Service, 1975). The Carasso study, which was prepared under a contract to the Bechtel Corporation, estimated that by 1985 there would be 140 operational reactors in the United States.

Table 6.2. U.S. Nuclear Power Plant Capacity, 1957-80

Year	Commercially Licensed Reactors[a]	Aggregate Nuclear Reactor Capacity (in net megawatts)	Average Capacity (in net megawatts per reactor)	Production of Electricity from Nuclear Reactors (in billions of kilowatt-hours)	Nuclear Share of Total Electricity Production	Nuclear Share of Total Primary Energy Consumption
1957	1	90	90.0	0.1	0.1%	0.0024%
1958	1	90	90.0	0.2	0.1	0.0046
1959	1	90	90.0	0.2	0.1	0.0112
1960	2	290	145.0	0.5	0.1	0.0397
1961	3	465	155.0	1.7	0.2	0.0528
1962	4	730	182.5	2.3	0.3	0.0690
1963	7	942	134.6	3.2	0.4	0.0684
1964	9	917	101.9	3.3	0.3	0.0732
1965	10	933	93.3	3.7	0.4	0.1046
1966	11	1,840	167.2	5.5	0.5	0.1408
1967	10	1,805	180.5	7.7	0.6	0.2155
1968	10	2,792	279.2	12.5	0.9	0.2279
1969	13	4,102	315.5	13.9	1.0	0.3456
1970	16	5,150	321.9	21.8	1.4	0.5942
1971	21	8,472	403.4	38.1	2.4	0.8058
1972	26	13,028	501.1	54.1	3.1	1.1869
1973	35	20,049	572.8	83.3	4.5	1.6728
1974	44	29,690	674.8	114.0	6.1	2.6049
1975	54	38,568	714.2	172.5	9.0	2.7389
1976	57	41,129	721.6	191.1	9.4	3.5273
1977	65	47,023	723.4	250.9	11.8	3.5290
1978	71	49,385	695.6	269.6	12.3	3.7717
1979	71	54,600	769.0	255.4	11.4	3.4799
1980	75	57,800	770.7	251.1	11.0	3.5485

Source: U.S. Department of Energy, Energy Information Administration, *Monthly Energy Review* (Washington, D.C.: U.S. Government Printing Office, May 1981), pp. 6, 64, 74.

[a]Including those shut down for safety and/or refueling; exclusive of military and laboratory research reactors

bine that produces electricity. In order for this process to attain technical efficiency, enough enriched uranium dioxide must be placed together to reach a stage known as a critical mass, that is, a sufficient concentration to precipitate fission by the emission of neutrons and their interaction with the uranium nucleus.

In all reactors the nuclear fuel must be sealed and moderated if the fissioned energy is to be produced in a smooth and controllable fashion. For this purpose, all reactors have control rods that can be inserted in the nuclear fuel core assembly unit (see figure 6.5). These control rods are usually made of a highly absorbent material such as boron or cadmium steel, which can con-

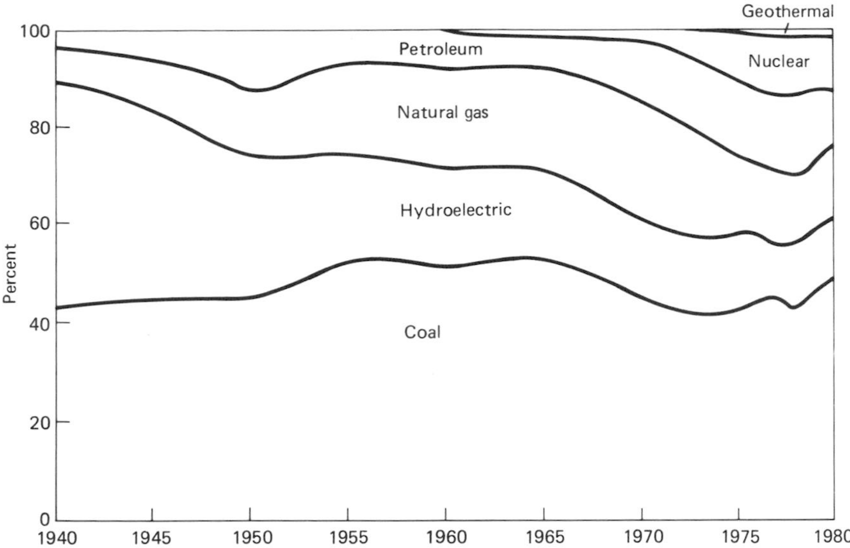

Figure 6.3. Frequency of Primary Energy Inputs in U.S. Electricity Production, 1940–80. Data from Federal Power Commission, *Consumption of Fuel for Production of Electric Energy* (Washington, D.C.: U.S. Government Printing Office, selected years); Department of Energy, Energy Information Administration, *Annual Report to Congress III* (1980); idem, *Monthly Energy Review*, September 1981; Department of the Interior, *Energy Perspectives 2.*

tain the emission of neutrons. Electric neutron counters are used to determine the position of the control rods within the fuel assembly units. When the control rods are fully inserted among the nuclear fuel assemblies, as when a refueling shutdown is required, there is no longer enough neutron emission to sustain nuclear fission, and the reactor ceases to generate heat. Moreover, to assist in the moderation, fuel assembly and control rod units are also immersed in a circulating liquid or gas, which serves to cool the reactor to a desirable temperature level.[12]

The chamber within which controlled fission takes place is known as the reactor pressure vessel. With stainless and carbon steel walls as thick as 27 centimeters, the pressure vessel must be strong enough to contain the emission of neutrons. It must also be capable of maintaining sufficient water pressure and temperature, both of which are essential to the controlled chain reaction. To minimize the danger of radioactive emission beyond the pressure vessel, this unit is further housed in a biological shield of reinforced concrete with walls up to 3 meters thick. Only a small section of the vessel is not surrounded by this shield, in order to permit the movement of control rods and periodic refueling.

[12]It should also be noted that refueling can be done only by shutting a reactor down completely, a process which contributes significantly to the cost of nuclear electricity because it reduces the load factor.

To provide additional protection from radiation, the reactor pressure vessel and its surrounding biological shield are placed in a containment structure that is made of steel-lined reinforced concrete some 60 meters tall and over a meter in thickness. Within the containment structure is also housed a steam generator with a water-circulating system that is joined by pipes to an external electricity generator.

6.2.1. Light Water Reactors

Though there is a substantial variety in available fission technology, the most widely used system in the United States is the light water reactor. All light water reactors use ^{235}U as fuel and are so called to distinguish them from heavy water, gas, and liquid metal reactor alternatives. In addition, light water reactors may be further classified into boiling water and pressurized water systems. Their principal operating characteristics are shown in figure 6.6.

In a typical 1,000-megawatt boiling water reactor, the reactor vessel control rods may be inserted from below, as shown, or from above, into the 100-ton fuel core. Water pumped into the vessel is heated by fission to a temperature of 300°C, under a pressure of 700,000 kilograms per square meter (1,000 lb/in^2), and passes as steam from the reactor vessel to an electricity turbine outside the containment structure. If the reactor is operating

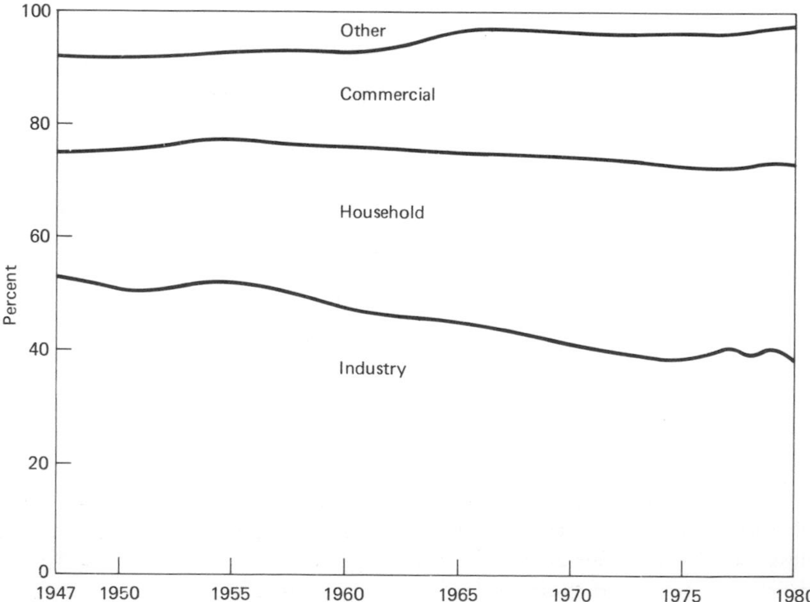

Figure 6.4. Sector Distribution of U.S. Electricity Consumption, 1947–80. Data from Department of Energy, Energy Information Administration, *Annual Report to Congress III*; and idem, *Monthly Energy Review*, September 1981.

at normal capacity, once steam passes through the generating turbine, it enters a condenser, where it is then converted back into water by cooling water circulating through sealed pipes.

One potential disadvantage of the boiling water reactor is that the steam passing from the reactor vessel may be contaminated by radioactivity, particularly if the cladding metal surrounding the fuel pellets is not thoroughly sealed. However, under its relatively low pressure, the boiling water reactor is less likely to experience an explosive breakdown. Furthermore, the fact that steam is produced within the reactor is also an advantage in that steam will inhibit the fission process even more than water.

In contrast to the boiling water reactor, pressurized light water reactors do

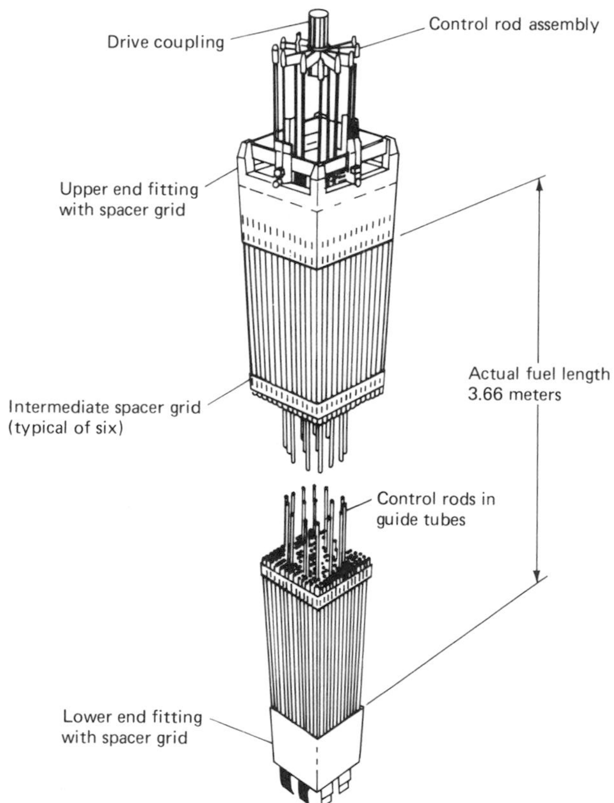

Figure 6.5. The Structure of a Nuclear Assembly Core. A single fuel rod may contain around 250 fuel pellets. Forty-nine fuel rods constitute an assembly, and several hundred assemblies are joined to form the reactor core. A typical 1,000-megawatt reactor may contain as much as a ton of fuel in some 8 million fuel pellets joined in 30,000–40,000 fuel rods. Adapted from *The Environmental Impact of Electric Power Generation: Nuclear and Fossil* (Harrisburg, Pa.: Pennsylvania Department of Education, 1973), reproduced in J. M. Fowler, *Energy and the Environment* (New York: McGraw-Hill, 1975), p. 277.

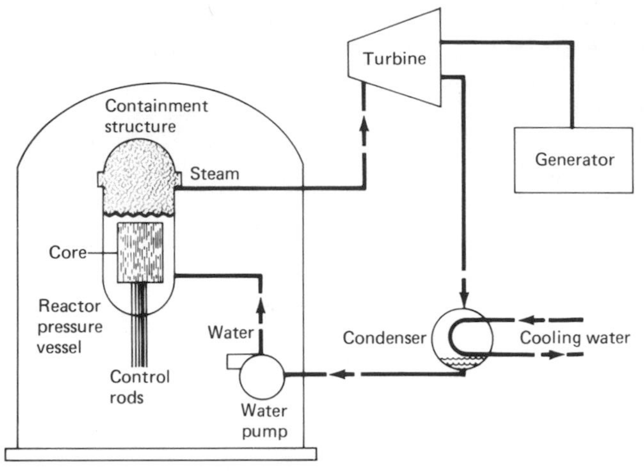

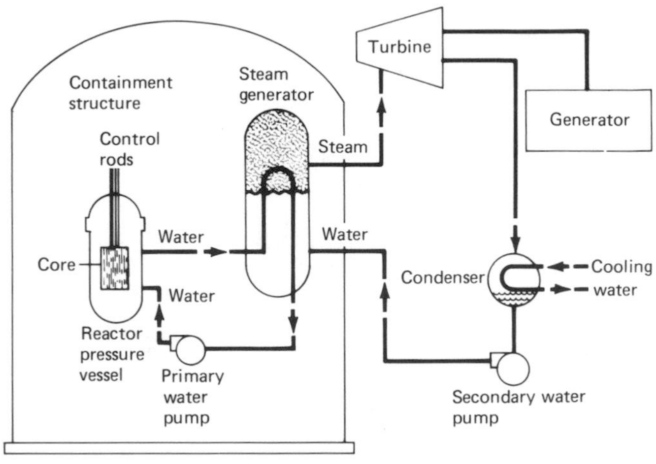

Figure 6.6. The Structure of a Light Water Reactor. *Top*, the boiling water reactor power system; *bottom*, the pressurized water reactor power system. Adapted from Spurgeon M. Keeny, Jr., *Nuclear Power Issues and Choices*, Report of the Nuclear Energy Policy Study Group (Cambridge, Mass.: Ballinger Publishing Co., 1977), pp. 394–95.

not produce steam directly within the reactor pressure vessel. Instead, the water in the vessel is raised to a higher average temperature, around 330°C, and is kept in a liquid state by raising the average pressure to around 1,400,000 kilograms per square meter (2,000 lb/in^2). This highly pressurized water then passes through a steam generator which is fed water from a secondary circuit. The heat from the pressurized water in the pipe is sufficient to raise the temperature of the water in the generator (which is at lower

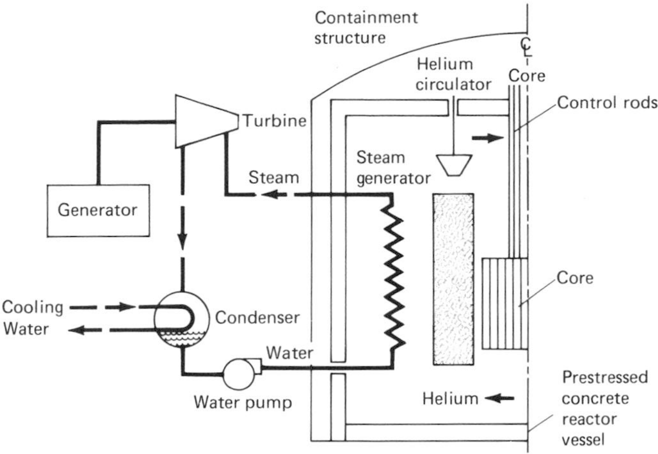

Figure 6.7. The Structure of a High-Temperature Gas-Cooled Reactor. Adapted from Keeny, *Nuclear Power Issues and Choices*, p. 397.

pressure) to create steam. The steam then passes through turbine rotors, which generate the electricity, just as it does in boiling water nuclear reactors and in fossil fuel steam-generating plants. As in the boiling water system, once steam emerges from the turbine, it is then condensed back into water by a third water circuit.

One notable advantage of the pressurized water reactor is that the water circulating through the reactor vessel does not mix with the water used in the steam generator. Thus the turbine is less likely to have radioactive contamination transmitted by the steam. However, the higher pressure and lack of steam within the reactor vessel represents a more explosive potential should any of the safety systems fail, particularly since higher temperatures increase the corrosion rate of the fuel rods and the vessel metal.

6.2.2. High-Temperature Gas Reactors

A problem common to light water reactors is that the water coolant tends to absorb a significant number of neutrons emitted by the uranium fuel, particularly if the water contains any impurities. As a result, the wastage of neutrons tends to lower the operational efficiency of commercial light water reactors below the potential of their fuel. One way of avoiding this loss is to use a high-temperature gas-cooled reactor, the structure of which is illustrated in figure 6.7.

At present there are only two commercial high-temperature gas reactors in the United States.[13] One is the Peach Bottom, Pennsylvania, 40-megawatt

[13]With the exception of these two reactors, all commercial nuclear energy in the United States in 1980 was generated by light water reactors. Light water reactors account for three-fourths of world nuclear power, with the rest accounted for by heavy water and high-temperature gas models. For an exposition of the latter, see Harold M. Agnew, "Gas-cooled Nuclear Power Reactors, *Scientific American* 244 (June 1981):55–63.

reactor, which began operation in 1967, the other is the 350-megawatt reactor at St. Vrain, Colorado, which began operation in 1974. In these high-temperature gas reactors, graphite is used as a moderator in the control rods, and helium gas is used as a coolant. Under temperatures reaching as high as 800°C, the helium converts piped water passing through the reactor pressure vessel into steam. The steam attains temperatures of over 500°C under a pressure of up to 1,015,000 kilograms per square meter (1,450 lb/in^2), a level higher than that found in light water reactors and thus yielding higher thermodynamic efficiency. In fact the high-temperature gas reactor's efficiency of 40 percent is equal to that of the most efficient fossil fuel plants.

One factor affecting the thermodynamic efficiency of high-temperature gas reactors is the mix of fuel. As in light water reactors, enriched ^{235}U still serves as the principal fuel. However, the enrichment level is raised from 80 percent to 90 percent uranium oxide concentration. To compensate for the marginal energy enrichment requirement, ^{232}Th (thorium) is also added to the reactor during its initial phase of operation. The function of the thorium is to facilitate the production of the artificial radioisotope ^{233}U, which may also be used as a fuel in reactor reloadings. At present, however, this fuel breeding cycle has not been implemented on a commercial scale by high-temperature gas reactor utilities.

Despite the potentially superior thermodynamic efficiency of the high-temperature gas reactor, it has not yet emerged as a competitive alternative to the light water reactor. Economic considerations aside, one of the principal factors governing the efficiency of gas reactors is their implied breeder fuel cycle. For reasons discussed in detail in section 6.3, U.S. energy policy has shown a reluctance to undertake a widespread production of commercial breeder reactors. As will be seen, the reasons for this reluctance are more closely tied to safety and security considerations rather than to a concern for the economically efficient production of electricity, at least for the short term.

6.2.3. Heavy Water Reactors

All the reactor technologies thus far discussed share a common dependency on relatively enriched ^{235}U. As has been demonstrated, because of its low natural concentration and associated degree of scarcity, enrichment of ^{235}U is a delicate and cumbersome process. However, unlike light water or high-temperature gas reactors a heavy water, or deuterium oxide, reactor can use natural unenriched uranium as a fuel. Moreover, unlike light water and high-temperature gas reactors, a heavy water reactor can be refueled without a complete reactor shutdown.

The structure of the heavy water reactors is illustrated in figure 6.8. Known also as the CANDU, or Canadian-deuterium-uranium reactor, after the country which pioneered its commercial application, it possesses several unique features.[14] First, although boron or cadmium steel control rods func-

[14]For a description and comparative assessment of the CANDU system, see Hugh C. McIntyre, "Natural-Uranium Heavy-Water Reactors," ibid., 233 (October 1975):17–27.

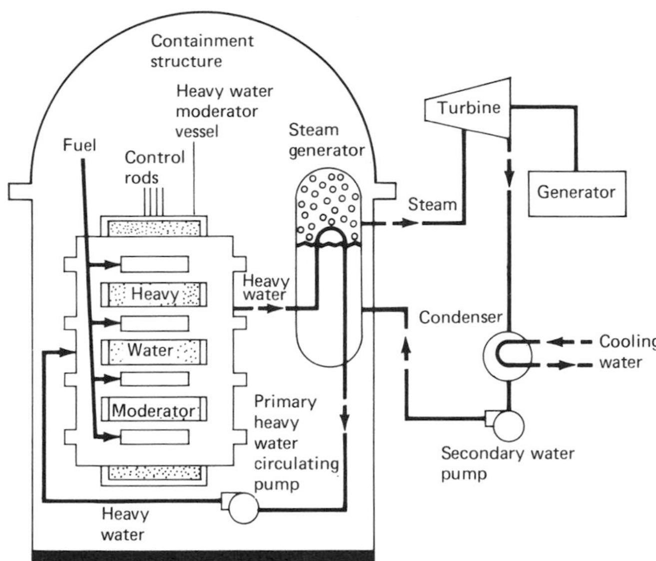

Figure 6.8. The Structure of a Heavy Water Reactor. Adapted from Keeny, *Nuclear Power Issues and Choices*, p. 396.

tion in much the same way as in other reactors, the heavy water reactor's coolant flows through several hundred individual pressurized tubes containing the natural uranium fuel. These pressurized tubes are kept immersed in a room-temperature unpressurized reactor vessel containing additional heavy water as a coolant.

Second, the fissioning of natural uranium fuel heats the heavy water to a temperature of around 310°C. Under a circulating pressure of 1,010,000 kilograms per square meter (1,450 lb/in^2), the heavy water converts ordinary light water in steam at a temperature of 250°C, with a pressure of 399,000 kilograms per square meter (570 lb/in^2). Under these conditions, electricity production from steam passing through turbine rotors and its subsequent condensation back into water from a third light water circuit coolant yields a first law thermodynamic efficiency of approximately 35 percent. Although the heavy water reactor's efficiency is less than that of a high-temperature gas reactor or a modern fossil fuel plant, it does compare favorably with that of light water plants.

The reason why natural uranium can be used in the heavy water reactor is straightforward. All nuclei can absorb neutrons in varying degrees. When a nucleus of ^{235}U splits, it releases on the average 2.5 neutrons. For a smooth reaction to occur, the moderating and cooling elements and the reactor vessel must be designed in such a fashion that only one neutron survives the uranium fuel, to precipitate another in an orderly chain reaction.

In light water reactors, because ordinary water has such a large neutron-capture cross section (which is mostly because of its impurities), it is essential that the uranium fuel be enriched, so that enough neutrons will be available to precipitate a sustained nuclear reaction. In contrast, the neutron-capture cross section of a deuterium, or heavy water, reactor is only one-six-hundredth that of a light water reactor, it thus permits the use of natural unenriched uranium as fuel. Though enriched uranium could also be used in a heavy water reactor (in which case it would tend to function as a breeder reactor), one distinct advantage of the heavy water reactor is that the use of unenriched uranium could obviate a complex and costly phase of the conventional nuclear fuel cycle.

As already noted, with the exception of two high-temperature gas reactors, the United States relies almost exclusively on light water nuclear power plant technology. Apart from radioactivity and design limitation considerations, one principal reason why the apparently superior CANDU system has not been adopted more widely throughout the world is that deuterium is relatively scarce. Its natural abundance in hydrogen oxide is 0.0148 percent, or about one deuterium molecule for every 6,800 molecules of light water. Thus, although, a heavy water reactor does not require enriched uranium, it does require a comparable enriched water equivalent.

The basic method of obtaining heavy water is by distillation. The reason for this is that heavy water has a slightly higher boiling point than light water: 101.52°C as opposed to 100°C, at normal atmospheric pressure. Based on current CANDU reactor design, around one ton of heavy water is needed for each additional megawatt of installed capacity. Since the United States presently has no significant domestic demand for heavy water, domestic production has been mostly for research and export markets. Under current conditions, a substantial increase in production would have to take place before heavy water could accommodate any significant share of present U.S. nuclear electricity generation demand.[15] Since economic considerations are also important to such a decision, we can defer any further evaluation of the heavy water reactor at this point and look at the breeder reactor alternative.

6.3. THE BREEDER REACTOR

As noted in chapter 4, the First Law of Thermodynamics states that the sum of useful and rejected energy from a given transformation must equal the energy available to a process. In other words, for a machine able to attain 100 percent efficiency, the useful energy could not exceed the available input energy. Against this principle stands the paradoxical notion of a breeder reactor, that is, a nuclear reactor which produces more fuel than it consumes. To resolve this apparent inconsistency we need to take a closer look at the nuclear fission process.

In conventional fission reactors of the kinds already discussed, a moderator such as boron, helium, or water serves to sustain a chain reaction by ab-

[15]Historically, a considerable share of U.S. heavy water sales has gone to Canadian nuclear reactor firms, that is, until Canadian disatisfaction arose with contract procedures, after which Canada constructed its own plant, in Bruce, Ontario, in 1973. U.S. sales of heavy water reached a peak of 976 short tons in 1968 but fell to as low as 2 short tons by 1976.

sorbing all but one neutron per emission from each nuclear division. If the moderator permits more than one neutron to be released for each reaction, additional fuel is created even as some of the original fuel is consumed. If more than two neutrons are released, then more fuel will be created than is consumed, hence the name breeder reactor.

The nuclear fuel created by the fission of one nucleus of ^{235}U is not another nucleus of fissile ^{235}U. Instead of being absorbed by the reactor's moderating element(s), the surplus neutron(s) emitted from an initial fission of a ^{235}U nucleus will be absorbed by other isotopes within the nuclear fuel core. These other isotopes are not readily suited for use as a nuclear reactor fuel, but they become suited once they have absorbed surplus neutrons from the fissioning of the ^{235}U fuel. The two principal types of breeding reactions are known as slow and fast and are so designated by the supplementary fuels used in the reaction of ^{235}U.

In a slow, or thermal, neutron breeder reaction, a relatively abundant natural element such as thorium, ^{232}Th, is mixed with the enriched uranium dioxide fuel. Thorium is a suitable element not only because of its abundance relative to ^{235}U but also because it is one of the heavier elements, with a considerable degree of binding energy.[16] However, although thorium isotopes are radioactive, that is, unstable, by itself a thorium isotope does not yield the kind of steady-state chain reaction that is possible with ^{235}U. Instead when a surplus neutron is emitted by the fission of a ^{235}U nucleus, it is absorbed by the ^{232}Th. The beta emission then converts ^{232}Th into the relatively unstable isotope ^{233}Th. At this point, a beta particle, or energetic electron, is emitted by the ^{233}Th, which transforms one of the neutrons of the ^{233}Th into a proton. This, the ^{233}Th becomes protoactinium (^{233}Pa), another radioactive isotope. In turn, the ^{233}PA also releases a beta particle, thereby converting its nuclear structure into ^{233}U, an artificial isotope of uranium but one that is as well suited as is ^{235}U to use as fuel in a reactor. In other words, it is radioactive and has a high degree of binding energy, but it is stable enough for recycling into a nuclear reactor via enrichment of the spent fuel from the original ^{235}U reaction.

In a fast neutron breeder reactor, the net release of a neutron from the fission of a ^{235}U nucleus results in the neutrons being absorbed by the relatively abundant ^{238}U already present in the enriched fuel core.[17] When the ^{238}U captures a surplus neutron, it becomes the unstable isotope ^{239}U. The ^{239}U then emits a beta particle. Just as in the ^{233}U conversion process of thermal breeders, a neutron is then transformed into a proton. This transformation in turn converts the ^{239}U into the radioactive element neptunium, ^{239}Np. Since neptunium is also radioactive, when it releases a beta particle, the con-

[16]Though not shown in figure 6.2, throrium, ^{232}Th, is very close to ^{235}U on the curve, as is suggested by its atomic weight. For this reason it is a technically appealing fuel, particularly in that it is relatively abundant in nature.

[17]As pointed out in section 6.1, 99.283 percent of natural uranium consists of ^{238}U. Enrichment raises the proportion of ^{235}U from 0.711 percent to between 2 percent and 3 percent, and with only an insignificant fraction in the form of ^{234}U, over 96 percent of the enriched fuel will still be ^{238}U.

version of one of its neutrons into a proton changes the isotope into plutonium, ^{239}Pu. The plutonium is readily suitable as a reactor fuel, containing as it does a relatively high degree of binding energy and the requisite degree of stability for processing as fuel through the enrichment phase of the nuclear fuel cycle described in figure 6.2.

While plutonium is also produced by conventional fission reactors, it constitutes a relatively small proportion of spent fuel. The reason for this is the presence of a fuel moderator in conventional fission reactors. By implication, such a fuel moderator will be largely absent in a fast neutron breeder reactor. That plutonium is one of the most toxic radioactive substances and that it is also the principal element used in the production of nuclear weapons suggests some of the limitations of the fast neutron breeder, matters which are examined in section 6.5. Before these questions are addressed, however, let us return to the original question raised by breeder technology, that is, whether it is consistent with the laws of thermodynamics.

We are in a position to resolve the thermodynamic paradox of breeder reactors. In terms of ^{235}U, the First Law is still substantiated, particularly if we trace through the useful heat applied in the production of electricity via water to steam conversion, as well as the accompanying rejected heat from this process and its subsequent condensation into water. The same is also true for both the slow and fast neutron breeders, that is, the production and consumption of ^{233}U and ^{239}Pu, respectively. The only difference is that we are allowing specifically for the degree of fission possible from a natural uranium isotope, ^{235}U, and the necessity to create the artificial isotopes in order to use their binding energy in a technically efficient manner. In effect, the breeding of artificial nuclear fuels is perfectly consistent with the First and Second Laws of Thermodynamics. The energy input will still match or exceed the useful energy output obtained by nuclear electricity generation.

6.3.1. Slow Neutron Breeder Technology: Light Water, Gas-Cooled, and Molten-Salt Reactors

Several types of slow neutron breeder reactors have been under study for a number of years. In light water and gas-cooled reactors, the reactor fuel core, moderating elements, and control rods are much the same as in conventional fission reactors. The difference is that thorium, ^{232}Th, is added to the enriched ^{235}U. The neutron absorption by the moderating elements is slightly less than in conventional reactors, and net neutron emission allows the creation of ^{233}U in much the way that has already been described. As spent fuel is reprocessed, enriched ^{233}U can then be used as reactor fuel in a high-temperature, gas-cooled conventional fission reactor (with 90 percent enriched ^{235}U and ^{232}Th), in a light water breeder reactor (with ^{232}Th), and in a molten-salt breeder reactor (with ^{232}Th).[18]

The molten-salt breeder reactor uses graphite tubes to moderate the flow

[18]For a summary of alternative nuclear fuel configurations, see Keeny, *Nuclear Power Issues*, p. 393.

of neutrons. However, much as in conventional heavy water fission reactors, the fuel is passed through these graphite tubes as a molten salt fluoride. In addition, the core is surrounded by a blanket of thorium fluoride, which also serves to contain the emission of neutrons. The advantage of this system is that core temperatures as high as 650°C can be attained, thereby yielding higher thermal efficiency in the generation of steam than conventional fission reactors. In addition, as in heavy water technology, there can be continuous refueling rather than the required periodic shutdown characteristic of conventional light water and high-temperature gas reactors.

The principal disadvantage of the molten-salt breeder reactor, and of other slow neutron breeder reactors as well, is that its breeding ratio is not significantly above unity. A breeding ratio is a measure of the amount of fissile product that is created per amount of fissile product consumed. A breeding ratio of 1.05, for example, depending on average reactor operating time and efficiency, means that it would take 20–21 years to create enough fuel to operate an additional reactor.

At present there are no slow neutron commercial breeder reactors in operation in the United States. There have been proposals to convert operating conventional reactors such as the one at Shippingport, Pennsylvania, to light water thermal breeder capability, but most efforts of the Atomic Energy Commission and its successor, the Nuclear Regulatory Commission, have been devoted to the promotion of fast breeder technology. As will also be seen, even here there have been problems with the use of breeder technology.

6.3.2. Fast Neutron Breeder Technology: Gas-Cooled and Liquid-Metal Fast Breeder Reactors

Fast neutron breeder reactors are distinguished from their slow neutron counterparts principally by the absence of a moderating material within the reactor fuel core. As already noted, with no moderator, the fission will generate substantial amounts of fuel as fertile isotopes absorb free neutrons. To maximize neutron absorption by fertile isotopes, the reactor core is surrounded by a blanket containing fuel rods made of spent fuel from conventional reactors. Such spent fuel consists primarily of depleted-strength ^{235}U and ^{238}U.

The fuel of fast neutron reactors is a mixture of recycled ^{239}Pu and ^{238}U. The ^{239}Pu may be obtained from enrichment reprocessing of conventional reactor spent fuel or from slow neutron thermal breeders in operation. As has been described, in a fast neutron reaction, the fissile ^{239}Pu will release neutrons which will convert ^{238}U into more ^{239}Pu. Moreover, the original fission of enriched ^{239}Pu will release heat energy that can produce steam sufficient to generate electricity, as happens in conventional fission reactors.

There are basically two types of fast neutron breeder reactors. The gas-cooled breeder reactor uses helium as a coolant and is distinguished from its nonbreeding counterpart by the absence of ^{235}U as its fuel (as well as by the absence of the moderator). However, although a gas-cooled breeder would yield technically competitive thermal efficiency, radioactive gas presents recycling problems. Consequently, thus far the United States has placed greater emphasis on the liquid-metal fast breeder reactor alternative.

A functional profile of a liquid-metal fast breeder reactor is illustrated in figure 6.9. Liquid sodium heated by the fission of ^{239}Pu is transferred from the reactor vessel to a heat exchanger containing a separately circulating flow of liquid sodium, in much the same fashion as the circulation system in conventional pressurized light water reactors. Next, ordinary water passing in tubes through the secondary liquid-sodium flow is converted to steam, which is then used to turn the rotors of a turbine that generates electricity. The steam then passes through a condenser cooled by a secondary ordinary-water source, where it is then recycled back through the secondary liquid-sodium chamber.

One appealing feature of the liquid-metal fast breeder reactor is that it can use as much as 60–70 percent of enriched uranium fuel, in contrast to the 2 percent average of conventional light water reactors now in operation. Second, because liquid sodium has such a high boiling point, reactor temperatures can attain a level as high as 620°C, which, when the heat exchangers are taken into account, results in the production of steam at temperatures approaching 540°C. The First Law efficiency would be about 40 percent, a figure higher than that for all light water reactors now in use but equal to that of conventional high-temperature gas-cooled reactors and fossil fuel electrical plants.

On the other side, the opaque quality of liquid sodium presents considerable difficulty in establishing efficient reactor monitoring systems for refueling and maintenance operations. Another difficulty is that sodium is extremely explosive when exposed to air or water. Third, should sodium attain its boiling point (880°C), bubbles in the sodium would accelerate the

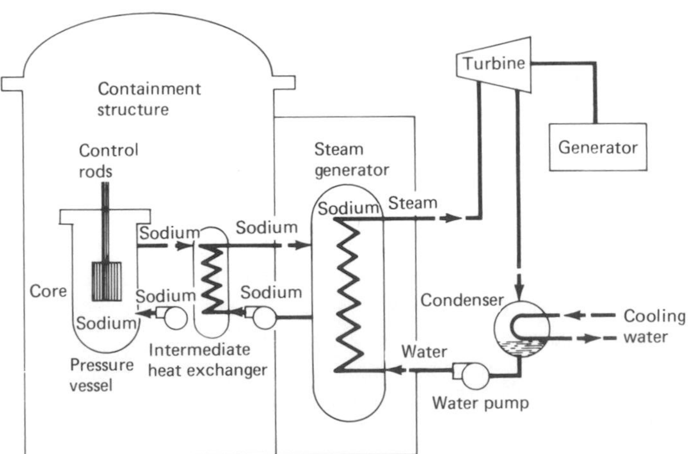

Figure 6.9. The Structure of a Liquid-Metal Fast Breeder Reactor. Adapted from Keeny, *Nuclear Power Issues and Choices*, p. 398.

transmission of neutrons rather than slow them down as conventional water reactor systems do. Moreover, at ordinary temperatures, sodium becomes a solid, which means that refueling and maintenance must be done under heating conditions not required in any other type of reactor, which further complicates the plumbing. Finally, the essential quality of fast neutron breeders is their speed, which is an advantage when all systems are functioning properly but can be a disaster when they are not. Whereas slow neutron reactors will fission at a rate of once every 10^{-4} seconds, a fast breeder will do so every 10^{-8}, or ten-thousand times as fast, thereby raising complex questions about the efficiency of reactor safety and control systems.

The first U.S. commercial fast breeder reactor to come into operation was the Enrico Fermi station at Lagoona Beach, near Detroit, Michigan, in January 1966. After a number of start-up problems had been resolved, it finally reached 10 percent of its 200-megawatt capacity in October of that year. On October 5 the core began to heat up beyond normal, and the reactor was soon closed down by emergency cooling systems. The problem with the Fermi reactor was that several cooling tubes had become clogged. Because of the radioactivity within the core, it was 1970 before it was possible to repair the original damage from the events of 1966. The Fermi reactor continued to function poorly, and as of 1978 it was welded shut to contain permanently the radioactive material still within its core.

Despite the Fermi reactor experience, breeder technology retains considerable appeal for one basic reason: theoretically, it can increase the useful life of existing uranium resources by a thousand times more than conventional fission technologies. Though concern over nuclear weapons proliferation has made the U.S. Congress uncertain as to whether to complete the Clinch River experimental liquid-metal fast breeder reactor at Oak Ridge, Tennessee, countries such as France have accelerated efforts to develop advanced breeder models, particularly the 1,200-megawatt French Superphénix reactor at Creys-Malville.[19] At the same time, other potentially more attractive nuclear technologies, such as nuclear fusion, could obviate much of the concern over nuclear weapons proliferation.

6.4. THE POTENTIAL OF NUCLEAR FUSION TECHNOLOGY

In chapter 4 we saw that energy can be obtained either by the fission of atoms or by their fusion. When two atoms are fused, their separate weights exceed the weight of the single resulting atomic element, and the mass that is lost is converted into energy. Until now, only uncontrolled forms of fusion have taken place: the release of energy from the sun and the implosion of hydro-

[19]For a popular account of the Fermi reactor experience, see John G. Fuller, *We Almost Lost Detroit* (New York: Ballantine Books, 1975). For an analysis of the Clinch River type of breeder that led to a slowdown of development efforts, see Thomas B. Cochran, *The Liquid Metal Fast Breeder Reactor: An Environmental and Economic Critique* (Baltimore: Johns Hopkins University Press for Resources for the Future, 1974). For a discussion of French efforts to develop breeder technology, see Georges A. Vendryes, "Superphenix: A Full-Scale Breeder Reactor," *Scientific American* 236 (March 1977):26–35.

gen atoms into helium in a hydrogen bomb.[20] Although the energy released from a fusion reaction will range between 2 percent and 12 percent of that of a fission reaction, fusion still represents an enormous potential resource when compared with its fossil fuel alternatives.

As illustrated in figure 6.1, controlled nuclear fission is best obtained from the elements that have both a high degree of binding energy and the requisite degree of instability. However, these same heavy isotopes are the least likely candidates for nuclear fusion, since the fusion of heavy atoms is much less likely to yield a stable isotope. Instead, the appropriate range of fusion elements is to be found at the opposite end of the spectrum. While these elements may have less binding energy per nucleus, they are also considerably easier to fuse than heavier elements, requiring as they do relatively less input energy for a given transformation.[21] That the fusing and fused elements are at the lower end of the periodic table also indicates that the emission of radioactivity common to all fission reactions is largely minimized. Indeed, among all presently known forms of fusion, the only radioactive isotope produced is tritium (^3H).

The energy yield from a nuclear fusion reaction is in the region of 98,000 kilowatt hours per gram, or the equivalent of 335 MBtu's. Were the U.S. economy to be sustained somehow by fusion power alone, its 1980 annual consumption of primary deuterium-tritium fuel would amount to only 227.46 metric tons. Since this represents but a fraction of a percent of the earth's heavy-water supply, if fusion technology were successful, it could provide one of the most abundant energy resources ever developed.

Despite the potential benefits from nuclear fusion, research efforts thus far have been unsuccessful in achieving a controlled fusion reaction which could yield net energy output. In brief, the problem with achieving a controlled fusion reaction is that two typical atoms of, say, ordinary hydrogen (^1H) will not fuse when brought into close contact at normal temperatures. The reason for this resistance is simple enough: atomic nuclei are surrounded by circulating electrons which carry a negative charge. In order to overcome that electrical resistance, the two elements must be heated to temperatures at least as high as 50 million degrees C, which is hotter than the temperature of the core of the sun itself.

[20]To be exploded, a hydrogen bomb has first to be charged by an uncontrolled nuclear fission reaction.

[21]To provide an indication of the potential energy from nuclear fusion, six typical transformation equations are listed here:

$$^2H + {}^2H \rightarrow {}^3H + {}^1H + 6.1192 \times 10^{-16} \text{ Btu's } (= 6.4480 \times 10^{-13} \text{ joules}) \quad (6.1)$$

$$^2H + {}^2H \rightarrow {}^3H + n + 4.9652 \times 10^{-16} \text{ Btu's } (= 5.2320 \times 10^{-13} \text{ joules}) \quad (6.2)$$

$$^2H + {}^3H \rightarrow {}^4He + n + 2.6724 \times 10^{-15} \text{ Btu's } (= 2.8159 \times 10^{-12} \text{ joules}) \quad (6.3)$$

$$^2H + {}^3He \rightarrow {}^4He + {}^3H + 2.7863 \times 10^{-15} \text{ Btu's } (= 2.9359 \times 10^{-12} \text{ joules}) \quad (6.4)$$

$$^6Li + n \rightarrow {}^4He + {}^3H + 7.2883 \times 10^{-16} \text{ Btu's } (= 7.6799 \times 10^{-13} \text{ joules}) \quad (6.5)$$

$$^2H + {}^6Li \rightarrow 2\,{}^4He + 3.4012 \times 10^{-15} \text{ Btu's } (= 3.5839 \times 10^{-12} \text{ joules}) \quad (6.6)$$

The three variables necessary to achieve a controlled fusion reaction are temperature, density, and confinement time. Though there are several ways to combine these variables in a fusion reactor, the British physicist J. D. Lawson has determined the necessary conditions for their success. The Lawson criterion is:

$$n\tau > 10^{14} \text{ atoms/second/cm}^3, \tag{6.7}$$

where n is the number of particles per cubic centimeter and τ is the confinement time, in seconds. To appreciate the significance of the Lawson criterion, we should note that most container, or reactor, vessels could not withstand the pressures necessary for fusion beyond a very limited period of time. Consequently, the objective in fusion technology is to raise the density of the fuel to as high a level as possible, thereby lowering the necessary time for fusion. For example, if we were able to achieve a density of 10^{26} particles per cubic centimeter, only 10^{-12} seconds would be needed for fusion to occur: 10^{14} is the product of 10^{26} and 10^{-12}. Since such particle densities exceed most feasible technologies, lower densities are considered with correspondingly longer confinement times. Usually this means that average particle density will range between 10^{14} and 10^{15} per cubic centimeter and that containment time will vary between 1.0 second and 0.1 second, respectively.

The technologies for generating fusion energy are varied. At present, however, only two of them show promise of ultimate practical application: magnetic confinement and laser fusion. In magnetic confinement technology, since the temperatures necessary to sustain a fusion reaction would melt ordinary reactor vessels, basic fuel such as deuterium-tritium is suspended in a high-temperature gas which is circulated by a magnetic field. The gas is so hot that it is electrified, that is, it contains free electrons and electrically charged atoms, or ions, which are essential to the fusion process. Gas that has attained an electrical state is known as plasma, and is so called to distinguish it from the properties of gas under ordinary temperatures.

An illustration of a magnetic confinement fusion reactor is shown in figure 6.10. This type of reactor, which is also known as a Tokamak, or large current, reactor, after its Soviet developers, has been used in U.S. plasma physics research at Princeton University. In a magnetic confinement reactor, magnetized coils assist in the passage of plasma at high speeds in a circular pattern. Once the plasma state has been attained, the atomic fuel becomes part of the plasma, and the nuclei can fuse into helium (or tritium, depending on the type of reaction). The neutron energy released by this reaction is then available for the conversion of water to steam, which in turn can be used to turn the rotors of a generator, much as occurs in fission reactors and fossil fuel plants.

Of all recent efforts to attain the conditions stipulated by the Lawson criterion, the Princeton magnetic confinement reactor has come the closest. In early August 1978 the Princeton reactor attained a temperature of more than 60 million degrees Centigrade, a level significantly higher than neces-

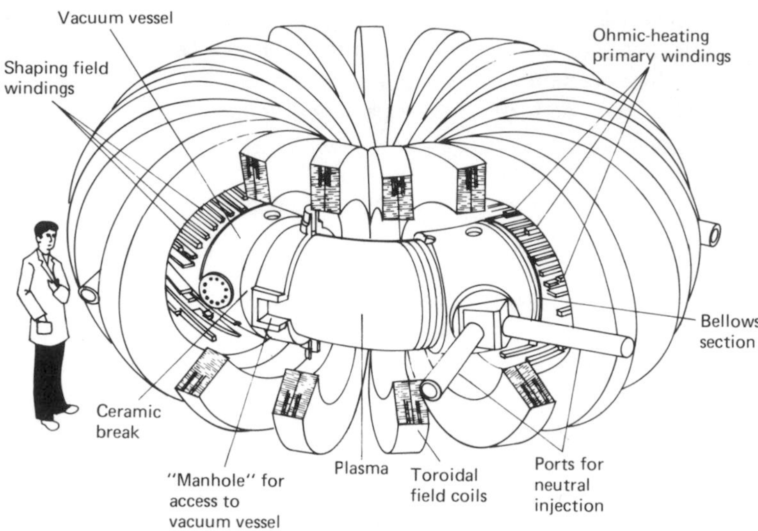

Figure 6.10. The Magnetic Confinement Fusion Reactor. Adapted from Energy Research and Development Association, *Fusion Power by Magnetic Confinement*, ERDA 11 (Washington, D.C.: U.S. Government Printing Office, 1972), reprinted in Penner, *Nuclear Energy and Energy Policies*, vol. 3, p. 333.

sary to sustain a fusion reaction.[22] However, while temperatures have reached new peaks, the Tokamak reactor has not yet succeeded in producing a sustained fusion reaction, nor has it achieved the positive net energy output essential to its success as a commercial system.

Variations on magnetic confinement fusion reactors include magnetic mirror plasma confinement and what is known as the theta-pinch confinement system. In a magnetic mirror confinement system, the passage of plasma through two magnetic field coils causes the charged fuel particles to be suspended in between the mirror, or magnetic, regions, thereby permitting fusion to occur within a relatively isolated space, unlike the rotating plasma space of the conventional magnetic confinement system. While a magnetic mirror reactor can attain fuel densities several times that of a Tokamak type of reactor, as well as considerably higher temperature, its reflective system is difficult to control on a sustained basis. In a theta-pinch reactor, such as the Scylla machine at the Los Alamos, New Mexico, Scientific Laboratory, plasma is magnetically contained in a rod-like form within a cylinder. Particle densities are considerably higher than in either the Tokamak or Mirror systems but are achieved at a cost of a much smaller confinement time.

In contrast to magnetic confinement fusion is the inertially confined fusion reactor. The two outstanding examples of this type of reactor which are cur-

[22]U.S. Makes Major Advance in Nuclear Fusion," *Washington Post*, 1 August 1978, p. 1. One variant of the Princeton Tokamak is the stellerator, which has additional helical windings which impose a steady-state quality to the magnetic confinement in contrast to the circular movement within the Tokamak.

rently under development are laser and particle beam fusion. Laser fusion reactors are the best known of inertially confined fusion systems, since they have shown the greatest promise of attaining the kind of efficiency thus far demonstrated by Tokamak style reactors.[23] In a laser fusion reactor, extreme concentrations of multiple light beams, with strengths up to 1 million joules per nanosecond (one-billionth of a second) per gram, are able to convert up to 30 percent of the energy of a 1-millimeter-diameter fuel pellet contained within the center. The force of the laser beams would initially compress the fuel pellet to a density consistent with the Lawson criterion, thereby permitting a release of heat energy as helium emerges from the fusion process.

One difficulty with laser technology is that it has attained only a 2–3 percent input efficiency, that is, an overwhelming amount of the energy emanating from the laser beams fails to focus critically on the fuel pellet. An alternative that has been proposed is the use of particle beam accelerators.[24] Particle beam research has provided partial demonstration of the feasibility of this technique, but there is still a considerable difficulty in containing the electron flow within the reactor pressure vessel. Vacuum and low-temperature superconductivity methods are also under consideration, but at present it appears that particle beam fusion reactors are much less technically developed than their laser or magnetic confinement counterparts.

Magnetic and inertially confined fusion technology represents a potentially powerful alternative for the generation of electricity in the coming years. At the same time, because of the difficulties already cited and because the technology for coupling fusion reactors to electrical power plants has yet to be developed, it will be some time before nuclear fusion can become a practical alternative to present-day resources. Thus, technological change and the relative pricing of energy will determine the role of commercial nuclear fusion in the mix of future energy resources.

6.5. NUCLEAR RESERVES AND NUCLEAR RISKS

As in the case of fossil fuel resources, there is an inverse relationship between the frequency of alternative nuclear technologies now in use and the frequency of primary energy reserves on which these technologies depend. For example, nuclear fusion technology would make use of one of the most abundant energy resources, but nuclear fission depends on one of the rarest natural elements now known. Indeed, it is partly for this reason that there has been continuing interest in breeder reactor technology. How large, then, are U.S. commercial nuclear energy reserves?

The geographic distribution of U.S. uranium and thorium deposits is shown in figure 6.11. Most deposits are concentrated in the West and the Southwest, though changes in relative prices could make other regions more competitive than they have been. To be sure, higher real prices in recent

[23]For a detailed description, see John L. Emmett, John Nuckolls, and Lowell Wood, "Fusion Power by Laser Implosion," *Scientific American* 232 (June 1974):24–37.

[24]See Gerold Yonas, "Fusion Power with Particle Beams," ibid., 239 (November 1978):50–61.

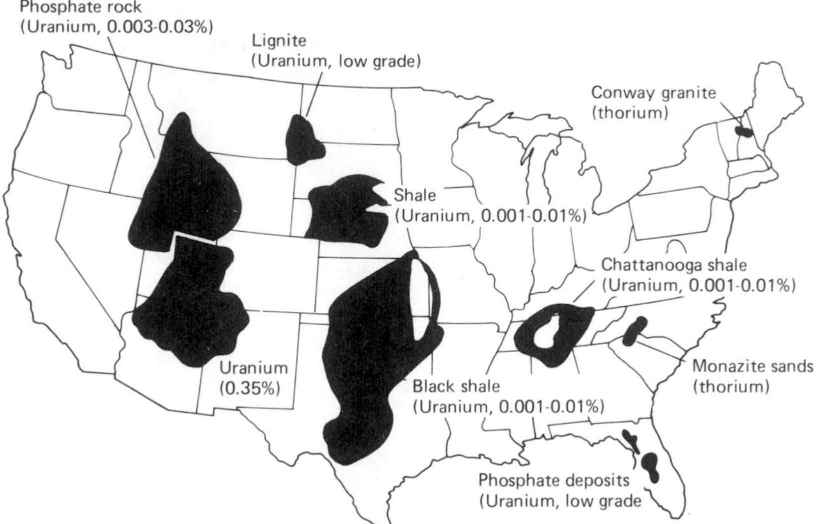

Figure 6.11. Geographic Distribution of U.S. Uranium and Thorium Deposits. Adapted from M. King Hubbert, "Nuclear Energy and the Fossil Fuels," in American Petroleum Institute, *Drilling and Production Practice* (New York: API, 1956), p. 25, reproduced in Cook, *Man, Energy, Society*, p. 299.

years have increased the level of proven nuclear energy reserves. As of 1980, presently recoverable reserves of uranium yellowcake amounted to approximately 645,000 short tons, while thorium reserves amounted to approximately 218,000 short tons. In comparison with fossil fuels, the economically useful life of nuclear energy under current prices is roughly eighty years, or somewhat greater than that of petroleum and natural gas but far less than that of coal. Yet even if nuclear energy reserves were stretched by a shift from conventional fission reactors to breeder technologies, there are risks peculiar to commercial nuclear power that tend to limit its potential as an alternative to petroleum and natural gas.

Three principal areas of risk are associated with the commercial expansion of nuclear power. The first area of risk is in the operational safety of reactors and the possibility of major catastrophe, such as a reactor meltdown. Second is the risk associated with the processing of uranium and allied fuels at various stages of the nuclear fuel cycle, including the long-term disposal of nuclear wastes. Third is the risk of nuclear theft and terrorism arising from the spread of nuclear weapons production capability within the United States and abroad. The factor that links all of these risks together is the pollution potential of nuclear power, especially radioactive pollution.

All conventional methods of producing electricity generate polluting by-products. They do so by their inherent thermodynamic inefficiency. To place the technological potential of nuclear energy in a proper perspective, we should thus compare the degree of pollution of a conventional nuclear power plant with its available counterparts.

Apart from the relative scarcity of nonrenewable fossil fuels, one factor detracting from their use is the impact of particulates on the health of a community. Table 6.3 illustrates the comparative enviromental impact of alternative fossil and nuclear-based electricity generating technologies. Coal tends generally to impose higher death rates and workdays lost per unit of electricity generated than do other alternatives. Moreover, unless otherwise constrained by the use of the fluidized bed combustion and scrubber technologies discussed in chapter 5, a single 1,000-magawatt coal plant could cause up to 75,000 cases of chronic respiratory disease per year, twice that many asthma attacks, and up to ten times that number of worker-days of aggravated heart-lung disease symptoms, not to mention the increase in children's respiratory disease and several dozen premature deaths. In contrast, no such costs arise from the operation of nuclear power plants, which is one reason for the appeal of this technology. However, as we will see, nuclear power carries its own unique forms of risks, which must then be weighed against those of coal and alternative electrical generating technologies, including renewable ones not shown here.

A second area of comparison between nuclear energy and its conventional counterparts is the degree of thermal pollution. While thermal pollution engenders less obvious and immediate consequences, it can be very significant to the environments in which electrical power plants function. Both light water nuclear reactors and conventional power plants have a Second Law thermodynamic efficiency ranging between 33 percent and 40 percent, with new fossil plant efficiency generally exceeding that of comparable nuclear reactors. In fossil fuel plants, rejected heat is emitted through smokestacks, as well as carried away by circulating water condensers. Because of the protective shields used in the operation of nuclear power reactors, their thermal pollution in the air is significantly less than that of comparable fossil fuel plants. Consequently, the water discharge will be greater by a factor as large as three to one. Moreover, the temperature of the water discharge may also be higher than in fossil plants. One estimate places the flow of rejected water from a 1,000-megawatt reactor at 1.34×10^9 cubic meters per year, with an average temperature of 7°C above the cooling water source from which it has been taken.[25] The significance of this temperature difference and of the magnitude of the flow may be substantial when measured in terms of the bacteriological and aquatic stabilization capacity of water sources under these conditions.

Of all the sources of pollution thus far noted, none can compare with radiation in its potential impact. Although some coal deposits are known to contain traces of radioactivity, the principal source of radioactivity in the generation of electricity derives from nuclear reactors. To understand the significance of radioactivity, we need first to spell out briefly how it is measured and transmitted into the environment.

[25]H. C. Hottel and J. B. Howard, *New Energy Technology: Some Facts and Assessments* (1971; reprint ed., Cambridge, Mass.: MIT Press, 1974), pp. 235–36.

Table 6.3. Comparative Environmental Impact of 1,000-Megawatt Electric Energy Systems

	Air Emissions			Water Discharges				Solid Waste			Land Use		Occupational Health	
System[a]	Tons ($\times 10^3$)	Curies ($\times 10^3$)	Severity[b]	Tons ($\times 10^3$)	Curies ($\times 10^3$)	Btu's ($\times 10^{13}$)	Severity[b]	Tons ($\times 10^3$)	Curies ($\times 10^3$)	Severity[b]	Acres ($\times 10^3$)	Severity[b]	Deaths	Workdays lost ($\times 10^3$)
Coal														
Deep-mined	383.0	—	5	7.33	—	3.05	5	602	—	3	29.4	3	4.00	8.77
Surface-mined	383.0	—	5	40.50	—	3.05	5	3,267	—	5	34.3	5	2.64	3.09
Oil														
Onshore	158.4	—	3	5.99	—	3.05	3	—	—	1	20.7	2	0.35	3.61
Offshore	158.4	—	3	6.07	—	3.05	4	—	—	1	17.8	1	0.35	3.61
Imports	70.6	—	2	2.52	—	3.05	4	—	—	1	17.4	1	0.06	0.69
Natural gas	24.1	—	1	0.81	—	3.05	2	—	—	0	20.8	2	0.20	1.99
Nuclear	—	489	1	21.30	2.68	5.29	3	2,620	1.4	4	19.1	2	0.15	0.27

Source: Council on Environmental Quality, *Energy and the Environment* (Washington, D.C.: U.S. Government Printing Office, 1974), p. 14.

[a]Operating at a 0.75 load factor with low levels of environmental control or with generally prevailing controls

[b]0 = none, 1 = negligible, 2 = small, 3 = moderate, 4 = significant, 5 = serious

Radiation signifies the transmission of heat or light energy under varying wave lengths. The shorter the wave length, the greater will be the energy contained in each quantum. While radiation occurs naturally throughout the universe, when it is concentrated, it has ionizing potential, that is, the capacity to remove the electrons with which it comes into contact. Because nuclear fission involves the splitting of relatively heavy atomic elements, its ionizing radiation can be substantial, long-term, and potentially destructive over time.

There are three forms of ionizing radiation: alpha particles, beta particles, and gamma rays. An alpha particle consists of two protons and two neutrons and is the nucleus of a helium atom. Because it has no orbiting electrons, it carries a positive charge. While it generally can be shielded by relatively thin materials such as paper, should it be inhaled, its ionization could be carcinogenic to the body. In contrast, beta particles consist only of electrons. They thus are lighter, can travel faster, and penetrate more deeply than alpha particles. While beta particles could penetrate depths of up to one and a quarter centimeters in a metal such as aluminum, their ionizing capability is not as great as that of alpha particles. Gamma rays are high-energy photons with no electric charge that travel at the speed of light. Though they have little ionizing strength by themselves, their speed greatly stimulates ion-producing particles within objects. Moreover, their penetration ranges up to several centimeters in a highly absorbent shield such as lead.

Individual radioisotopes vary in the kinds of radiation they emit, as can be seen in a representative sample listed in table 6.4. With the exception of carbon-14, all of the isotopes shown are direct fission by-products from conventional fission reactors.[26] The halflife of these isotopes indicates the length of time required for the original amount of radioactivity to drop to half. As with any kind of logarithmic progression, it would take roughly ten halflives for the strength of any one radioisotope to reach 0.1 percent of its original level; for plutonium, for example, it would take as long as 24,300 years. It is also worth noting that these rates of radioactive decay are independent of temperature and pressure conditions and can be altered only by fission or fusion reactions to produce isotopes of different halflives.

The danger of radioactivity is that it can cause cancer, genetic defects, and other physical disorders over prolonged periods of time. Several measures of radiation have been developed over the years. They cover a spectrum ranging from a pure rate of emissions, measured in curies, to the biological absorption rate of individuals, measured in rems or millirems.[27] The term "rem" derives from "roentgen-equivalent man" and refers to the amount of roentgens absorbed in a single dose by one individual. A roentgen is equal to one

[26]Carbon-14 is a relatively stable radioisotope. It is close to the lower end of the periodic table and is not directly affected by conventional fission reactions of uranium isotopes, though it does have widespread research applications outside of the production of energy.

[27]A curie is a rate of emissions independent of its intensity and is equal to the disintegration of 3.7×10^{10} nuclei per second. A rad—radiation-absorbed dose—is the amount of radiation per absorption tissue and is equal to 100 ergs, or 10^{-5} joules, which is 2.7×10^{-2} Kwh of energy per gram of absorbing material.

Table 6.4. Fission-Product Radioisotopes

Element	Atomic Number	Half-life	Radiation Emitted[a]
Iodine-129	53	17,000,000 yrs.	β, γ
Technetium-99	43	500,000 yrs.[b]	e^-, $\gamma \rightarrow \beta$
Plutonium-239	94	24,300 yrs.	α, β, γ
Carbon-14	20	5,580 yrs.	β
Cesium-137	55	30 yrs.	β,γ
Strontium-90	38	29 yrs.	β
Plutonium-241	94	13 yrs.	α, β, γ
Krypton-85	36	9.4 yrs.[c]	e^-, β, $\gamma \rightarrow \beta$, γ
Promethium-147	61	2.3 yrs.	β
Cerium-144	58	1.6 yrs.	β, γ
Ruthenium-106	44	1.0 yr.	β
Zirconium-95	44	65 days	β, γ
Strontium-89	38	54 days	β
Ruthenium-103	44	39.8 days	β, γ
Niobium-95	41	35 days[d]	$e^- \rightarrow \beta$, γ
Tellurium-129	52	34 days[e]	β, γ
Cerium-141	58	32.5 days	β, γ
Praseodynium-143	59	13.8 days	β, γ
Barium-140	56	12.8 days	β, γ
Iodine-131	53	8 days	β, γ
Zenon-133	54	5.3 days[f]	e^-, $\beta \rightarrow \beta$, γ
Lanthanum-140	57	40 hrs.	β, γ
Rhodium-103	45	57 mins.	e^-
Praseodynium-144	59	17 mins.	β
Rhodium-106	45	30 secs.	β, γ

Source: Adapted from Clark Goodman, "Science and Technology of the Environment" (Houston: University of Houston, 1972), reprinted in John M. Fowler, *Energy and the Environment* (New York: McGraw-Hill, 1975), p. 479.

[a] e^- = internal electron conversion; α = alpha particles, for elements with atomic number ≥ 82; β = beta particles, or fast electrons; γ = gamma rays

[b] Preceded by 5.9 hours of isomeric internal transition

[c] Preceded by 4.4 hours of isomeric internal transition

[c] Preceded by 90 hours of isomeric internal transition

[e] Isomeric internal transition, followed by a 72-minute half-life

[f] Preceded by 2.3 days of isomeric internal transition

electrostatic unit per 0.001293 grams of air and carries 2.0933×10^9 electrons. A thousand millirems equal one rem.

Radiation stems from a variety of sources. Data on U.S. whole-body dose rates for 1970 (in table 6.5) show that almost two-thirds emanated from natural sources, with the remainder generated mostly by medical diagnostic testing from x-rays. Because commercial nuclear power accounted for a very small share of man-made radiation, the estimates of table 6.5 suggest that nuclear power has been a relatively safe technology. To determine just how safe it has been, though, we need to look at nuclear reactor safety systems, and at the studies that have been made of them.

Commercial reactors have a variety of mechanisms designed to ensure a relatively smooth generation of power. As noted in section 6.2, these include reinforced concrete shields for the reactor pressure vessel and its surrounding containment structure, electric neutron counters to adjust fuel control rods, as well as a variety of temperature and pressure gauges. Moreover, all reactors also have emergency core cooling systems, which provide secondary safeguards should early warning mechanisms fail.

Despite these safety systems, reactor accidents have taken place, though none yet has been as serious as a fuel core meltdown. The most notable of these accidents are the Enrico Fermi incident of 1966; a fire in the control room at the Browns Ferry reactor in Athens, Alabama, in 1975; an argon explosion at the Donald C. Cook reactor in Waterford, Connecticut, in December 1977; a radioactive water leak at the Hanford reactor in Richland, Wash-

Table 6.5. Estimates of Annual Whole-Body Dose Rates in the United States, 1970

Source of Radiation	Average Dose Rate[a] (millirems per year)
Natural	
Environmental	
Cosmic radiation	45.0 (30.0–130.0)
Terrestrial radiation	60.0 (30.0–115.0)[b]
Internal radioactive isotopes	25.0
Subtotal	130.0 (61.9%)
Man-made	
Environmental	
Global fallout	4.0
Nuclear power	0.003[c]
Medical	
Diagnostic	72.0
Radiopharmaceuticals	1.0
Occupational	0.8
Miscellaneous	2.0
Subtotal	80.0 (38.1%)
Total	210

Sources: Spurgeon M. Keeny, Jr., *Nuclear Power Issues and Choices*, Report of the Nuclear Energy Policy Study Group (Cambridge, Mass.: Ballinger Publishing Co., 1977), p. 163; National Academy of Sciences, "The Effects on Populations of Exposure to Low Levels of Ionizing Radiation," Report of the Advisory Committee on the Biological Effects of Ionizing (Washington, D.C.: NAS, 1972); and Klement et al., "Estimates of Ionizing Radiation Doses in the United States, 1960-2000," U.S. Environmental Protection Agency (Washington, D.C.: U.S. Government Printing Office, 1972).

Note: Values in parentheses indicate the range over which average levels for different states vary with elevation.

[a]The dose rate is the annual amount of radiation due to all preceding nuclear power generation activities; the dose commitment is the total amount of radiation eventually delivered, over an assigned period of time, due to a given amount of electricity generated by nuclear means

[b]The range of variation is attributable largely to geographic difference in the content of potassium-40, radium, thorium, and uranium in the earth's crust

[c]This figure rose to about 0.023 millirems per year in 1975

ington, in December 1977; an explosion at the Vermont Yankee reactor in Vernon, Vermont, in March 1978; and most recently, the loss-of-coolant accident at the Three Mile Island reactor near Harrisburg, Pennsylvania, in March 1979. Following each of these incidents, investigations have been undertaken into their causes and risks, as well as to recommend solutions and improvements.[28] Of all the studies thus far produced, perhaps the most notable has been the Nuclear Regulatory Commission's 1975 Reactor Safety Study, WASH-1400, known also as the Rasmussen report, after its principal investigator.

WASH-1400 focused primarily on the probability of a large-scale reactor accident.[29] Such a catastrophe would be the failure of major safety systems, which would lead to the meltdown of the fuel core. This condition is also known as the China syndrome, since it would presumably be so hot and radioactive that it would start a gradual descent into the ground once all shielding had been destroyed. Depending on early evacuation warnings, it would cause up to ten-thousand early fatalities, with an upper limit of 100,000 latent cancers spread out over a period of thirty years and an assorted number of related glandular and genetic disorders of a lesser magnitude. In calculating these outcomes, the study estimated that the probability of such a worst-case accident would be one chance out of a thousand per reactor-year using actuarial data alone, and would be one chance in twenty-thousand reactor-years if prevailing safety standards were applied. In more immediate terms this translates into one core meltdown every two-hundred years for every one-hundred reactors in operation. In sum, the study concluded that this risk, though real, was far less than that arising from automobile deaths, fires, natural disasters, and traditional sources of human disease.

WASH-1400 has been subject to numerous criticisms. The most important ones can be listed in summary form.[30] First, WASH-1400 did not completely

[28]For a summary, see *New York Times*, 15 April 1979, p. 26. See also John G. Kemeney, *Report of the President's Commission on the Accident at Three Mile Island* (Washington, D.C.: U.S. Government Printing Office, October 1979). The Kemeney report attributed most of the cause of the accident at Three Mile Island to human failure stemming from inadequate training and supervision by the utility and by the Nuclear Regulatory Commission. For two defenses of nuclear reactor safety, see Harold W. Lewis, "The Safety of Fission Reactors," *Scientific American* 242 (March 1980):53–65; and Steven A. Fetter and Kosta Tsipis, "Catastrophic Releases of Radioactivity," ibid., 244 (April 1981):41–47.

[29]For a summary of WASH-1400 and related safety studies, see D. Bodansky and F. H. Schmidt, "Safety Aspects of Nuclear Energy," in *The Nuclear Power Controversy*, ed. A. W. Murphy (Englewood Cliffs, N.J.: Prentice-Hall, 1976), pp. 8–54. In such a major accident, the most intensive emission is considered to be 750 rem; in more remote regions, the effects would decline in intensity at a rate corresponding to approximately 3 percent per mile, so that at a distance of 250 miles, the dose would be 1 rem, and at over 300 miles it would drop to the 150-millirem level. Of course, the intensity of this dosage would also be determined by evacuation notification time and wind and rain conditions.

[30]See A. B. Lovins and J. H. Price, *Non-Nuclear Futures* (Cambridge, Mass.: Ballinger Publishing Co., 1975), pp. 23–29, 57–64. See also Daniel F. Ford and Henry W. Kendall, "Catastrophic Nuclear Reactor Accidents," in *The Nuclear Fuel Cycle*, by the Union of Concerned Scientists (Cambridge, Mass.: MIT Press, 1975), pp. 70–119.

specify all potential sources of reactor failure, including those arising from mechanical malfunctioning, design errors, and human incompetence and sabotage. Second, it did not spell out the interdependence of multiple failure possibilities, nor did it include any assessment of them. Third, though medical research has established a casual relationship between radiation and disease, WASH-1400 relies on as yet incompletely verified rates of transmission. Fourth, though WASH-1400's methodology can assign comparative risk, it is inadequate to predict absolute risk. Fifth, it uses linear extrapolations of accident rates by assuming a learning curve which could compensate for previously unspecified and underestimated sources of failure. Finally, it bases its linearity assumptions on relatively sparse data in relation to comparison sources of risk.

Perhaps the most telling criticism of WASH-1400 is that it was disowned by the Nuclear Regulatory Commission in January 1979, well before the incident at Three Mile Island. As will be seen in part III, the costs inherent in these risks must be included in any assessment of the comparative economic efficiency of alternative modes of electrical generation.

A second major area of risk in commercial atomic power arises from the processing of nuclear fuel. Although radioactivity becomes more concentrated with each stage of preparation, the most hazardous phases are the reprocessing and disposal of nuclear wastes. The dilemma is that reprocessing involves the separation of plutonium, ^{239}Pu, as one of the potentially reusable fuels essential to a viable long-term nuclear industry but that plutonium is one of the most toxic substances yet known and is the principal ingredient in the production of nuclear weapons. Short of widespread reprocessing and breeder technology, the United States is thus faced with a growing problem of waste disposal.

Several long-term nuclear disposal solutions have been proposed.[31] At one level there are several unfolding options involving containerization of wastes which could render their risk independent of storage sites. These include reinforced concrete, steel alloys, and high-strength glass, among other materials. Second, given some choice of container materials, there are three possible site options: deep storage in a stable geological layer such as salt, concentrated aboveground storage to be guarded by an elite security system, and ejection into outer space via garbage rockets. The difficulties presented by each of these include the criticisms of reactor safety already noted, plus the incremental costs of disposal. Though the United States is presently leaning toward a deep-mine solution, it has made no final decision regarding long-term disposal. What is pertinent to energy policy is that the costs of any disposal must be included as part of the costs of nuclear electricity production.

The third major area of risk in commercial atomic power is the potential

[31]For a supportive evaluation of disposal alternatives, see B. L. Cohen, "The Disposal of Radioactive Wastes from Fission Reactors," *Scientific American* 236 (June 1977):21–31. Cohen recommends deep storage of wastes as the technically most viable solution for an expanding nuclear power industry.

for nuclear theft and nuclear terrorism.[32] Recent experience has firmly established that U.S. and world exports of reactors and fuels have enabled individual countries to obtain nuclear weapons capability. Apart from the risks and desirability of legitimate nuclear proliferation, there is also the potential for nuclear theft and nuclear terrorism. Nuclear theft and terrorism could be used in a variety of ways: contamination of air, water, and food supplies or, more dangerous, fabrication of nuclear bombs. Though there have been no proven cases of nuclear terrorism, present safeguards such as the International Atomic Energy Agency are as weak as all other international agencies in the protection of populations from terrorism. In terms of energy policy, although nuclear weapons proliferation originated independently of commercial nuclear power, the accumulation of wastes and the issue of breeder technology add a third area of costs to be considered when evaluating the competitive economic position of commercial nuclear power.

What, then, can be said of the potential for commercial nuclear power as an alternative to the environmental, international security, and relative scarcity problems surrounding conventional fossil fuels? First, because commercial nuclear power is used exclusively for the production of electricity, even if it posed no risks of its own, it could ease the dependence on depletable fossil fuels only to the extent that they are used to generate electricity. As we have seen, as of 1980 an all-nuclear electricity generating industry would represent a reduction in gross petroleum consumption of less than 10 percent and a reduction of natural gas consumption of under 15 percent. Thus, the principal source of potential savings would be as a substitute for coal, with a reduction in its consumption of up to 80 percent. If such savings were technically feasible, coal could then be applied more readily to the production of synthetic fossil fuels. Yet, as we have seen, though synthetic fuels could reduce dependence on conventional petroleum and natural gas, they would also impose serious risks to the environment and to human health. Thus, nuclear power offers no easy solutions to the questions of energy security and environmental protection.

Second, should there be a significant expansion of commercial nuclear power based on conventional fission technology, it would undoubtedly cause a considerable increase in the cost of nuclear fuel and in the nuclear fuel share of total commercial nuclear power costs. Though proven reserves of commercial nuclear resources would undoubtedly increase under higher real prices, in order to remain competitive with alternative electricity technologies, commercial nuclear power would quickly be faced with an expansion of its own unique risks, namely, reactor operating safety, reprocessing, and the potential for nuclear theft and terrorism. Certainly the inclusion of redundancy in reactor safeguard design does not necessarily compensate for errors in human judgment, as the accident at Three Mile Island so clearly demon-

[32]See D. J. Rose and R. K. Lester, "Nuclear Power, Nuclear Weapons, and International Stability," ibid., 238 (April 1978):45–57. See also L. Schienman, "The Nuclear Safeguards Problem," in Union of Concerned Scientists, *The Nuclear Fuel Cycle* (Cambridge, Mass.: MIT Press, 1975), pp. 120–37; and Keeny, *Nuclear Power Issues*, pp. 271–99.

strated. Moreover, even if operating reactors were relatively safe, the higher real costs of nuclear fuel would undoubtedly create pressures for nuclear fuel recycling and the expansion of breeder reactor technology. In turn, each of these changes in the nuclear fuel cycle would create additional prospects for nuclear accidents in the transportation of radioactive fuel and for nuclear theft and terrorism to arise. Moreover, as it now stands, the nuclear fuel cycle still leaves unresolved the problem of the long-term disposal of nuclear fuel wastes.

Third, when the substantial public subsidies used to develop commercial nuclear power over the past several decades are added to the commercial and environmental costs of nuclear power, conventional nuclear energy may not be as economically competitive as currently available alternative technologies or even as the fusion and renewable energy technologies now under development. In sum, then, the economic role of commercial nuclear power depends ultimately on the relative price of energy, and whether that price is an economically efficient one.

6.6. SUMMARY

Nuclear power has been a rapidly growing and complex energy technology. Its principal commercial use is in the production of steam which is used to generate electricity. Since historically most electricity has been produced by fossil fuels, nuclear power has been seen as a way of accommodating the rapid increase in electricity consumption without accelerating the depletion of nonrenewable and environmentally polluting fossil fuels.

Nuclear energy can be obtained either by fission or by fusion. Although both reactions are possible in the uncontrolled form of nuclear weapons, thus far only fission has established a controlled-reaction technical capability. Of several fuels that can be used in a conventionally controlled fission reaction, the most readily available is uranium, and its ^{235}U isotope. Its preparation involves several stages of refinement and disposal which are known as the nuclear fuel cycle.

Nuclear fission energy can be obtained from several types of reactors. These include the boiling and pressurized water reactors, the high-temperature gas reactor, the heavy water reactor, and comparable variants of the breeder reactor, which can generate more fuel than it consumes. With the exception of experimental breeder technology and two high-tempeature gas reactors, virtually all commercial U.S. nuclear power is provided by roughly equal shares of boiling water and pressurized water reactors. As yet, emerging nuclear fusion technologies such as magnetic confinement, laser, and particle beam systems have not demonstrated a capacity for sustained controlled reactions. It may take a few decades before technological problems are sufficiently resolved to place them as competitive alternatives.

The expansion of commercial nuclear power is contingent on a number of considerations. Under conventional technology, fissile uranium resources face a nonrenewable geological horizon as short as eighty years, with possibly half that amount in economic terms unless commercial breeder technology is adopted on a broad scale. In turn, the expansion of breeder technology raises important safety questions regarding the operation of nuclear power as a whole and breeder technology in particular. First, as in any new technology, the safety of nuclear reactors may have been overestimated. Second, the processing of nuclear fuel, especially nuclear wastes, involves the potential for nuclear weapons proliferation, the use of breeder technology, and the long-term disposal of nuclear wastes. Third is the question of nuclear theft and nuclear safeguards. Since there are attendant risks in all of these questions, they should be included in any assessment of the comparative economic efficiency of nuclear power.

SUGGESTED READINGS

Bupp, Irvin C., and Derian, Jean-Claude. *Light Water: How the Nuclear Dream Dissolved.* New York: Basic Books, 1978.

Keeny, Spurgeon M., Jr. *Nuclear Power Issues and Choices.* Report of the Nuclear Energy Policy Study Group. Cambridge, Mass.: Ballinger Publishing Co., 1977.

Murphy, A. W., ed. *The Nuclear Power Controversy.* Englewood Cliffs, N.J.: Prentice-Hall, 1976.

Penner, S. S., ed. *Nuclear Energy and Energy Policies.* Vol. 3. Reading, Mass.: Addison-Wesley Publishing Co., 1976.

Union of Concerned Scientists. *The Nuclear Fuel Cycle.* Cambridge, Mass.: MIT Press, 1975.

Willrich, Mason, and Taylor, Theodore B. *Nuclear Theft: Risks and Safeguards.* Cambridge, Mass.: Ballinger Publishing Co., 1974.

7

RENEWABLE ENERGY RESOURCES

No stock of energy is renewable. If it were, we would not be governed by the laws of thermodynamics, nor would we be likely ever to have an energy crisis. Yet, despite the laws of thermodynamics and the presence of energy crises, there are energy resources that may be thought of as "renewable." How would this be so? A "renewable" energy resource is always based on the flows of energy from a finite and depletable stock. In chapter 4, we saw that all of the earth's energy flows derive their power from the sun and from the gravitational force of the moon. Because the sun's energy is so vast, and likely to last for billions of years at its present rate of emission, the earth is endowed with many and varied "renewable" energy resources. The relevant question for energy policy is, to what extent can these energy flows be transformed into economically useful forms? The first step in answering this question is to define in the broadest terms the dimensions of renewable energy technology.

By definition, renewable energy resources do not include exhaustible stocks of fossil and nuclear fuels. They do include hydropower and solar, biomass, geothermal, wind, and tidal power. Some of these energy forms provide a continual release of energy into the environment which is ultimately dissipated from the earth in the form of long-wave-length radiation. Others may be converted into temporary energy storage forms such as water, ice, and biomass, though they are eventually depleted through natural forces within the biosphere. For renewable energy technologies to be technically efficient, they must possess at least four basic capacities: for storage, conversion, concentration, and transportation with ease.

One basic requirement of renewable energy technology is a capacity for energy storage. This is important because the economy's rates of consumption do not often correspond to the natural rate of emission of renewable energy flows. Thus, while the amount of available renewable energy may be sufficient for a given task, it may have to be converted into a stock before it can be used.

Another basic requirement of renewable energy technology is the capacity to convert natural flows into the ultimately usable forms desired by society. As an illustration, hydropower and tidal power are gravitational, but most end uses of energy in the economy are mechanical, thermal, or electrical.

Thus, renewable energy may require not only conversion into a stock but also a conversion of its form.

A third basic requirement of renewable energy technology is the capacity to concentrate energy flows. Many routine functions of energy within the economy call for energy flows at a higher level than those found among the natural flows of renewable energy resources. While many renewable energy resources contain enormous potential in the aggregate, they must be sufficiently concentrated and moderated if they are to be successful in the roles now performed by fossil and nuclear fuels.

Finally, renewable energy technology must be able to transport energy to its point of end use. Just as renewable energy flows may require storage, so too they may need to be transported from their points of origin to ultimate points of consumption. That many renewable flows are dispersed suggests that storage, conversion, and transport are simultaneous requirements if renewable energy technology is to be successful. Indeed, when we contrast all of these characteristics of renewable energy resource technologies with those of exhaustible resource technologies, it is not so surprising that the world's economy should have drawn so heavily and for so long on finite energy supplies. Since exhaustible energy stocks are now faced with potentially diminishing economic returns, we need to determine how the diverse types of renewable energy resources can be converted into usable energy forms.

7.1. HYDROPOWER

As noted in chapter 4, of the solar radiation reaching the earth, 23 percent is converted into evaporation and precipitation energy flows. With a power of $40{,}000 \times 10^{12}$ watts, it would take just over two hours for the flow of this energy to equal the world's 1980 level of gross primary energy consumption, at approximately 306.97 quads.[1] In theory at least, this means that the 1980 annual flow of evaporation and precipitation energy could sustain the 1980 rate of world gross primary energy consumption for almost four thousand years. However, as we will see, the useful energy that can be extracted from hydropower is a much more modest amount than this comparison suggests.

Historically, hydropower has been used mostly in the generation of mechanical energy. The most common application of this energy was in the development of water mills. Water mills rely on the gravitational potential of falling water to turn water wheels connected to millstones. In turn, the millstones are used to crush grains into flour. Although evidence of water mills dates to as early as ancient Rome, most mills were crude and inefficient by thermodynamic standards. Some mills, such as the seventeenth-century Ver-

[1]Nineteen eighty world gross primary energy consumption reached a level of approximately 145 million barrels per day of oil equivalent, or 306.965 quads. If one watt equals a time rate of energy expenditures of 1 joule per second, and 10^{18} joules are equal to 1 quadrillion Btu's, then it would take 25 seconds of $40{,}000 \times 10^{12}$ watts to yield 1 quad, and 7,674.71 seconds to obtain the 1980 level of world gross energy consumption of 306.965 quads. Dividing through by minutes and hours yields 2.13 hours.

sailles waterworks at Marly-la-Machine, France, did attain capacities as high as 56 kilowatts, but the greatest expansion of hydropower came as a result of the industrial revolution of the nineteenth century and the emergence of commercial electricity demand.[2] Since that time, hydropower has been used almost exclusively for the generation of electricity among the more developed countries, and it is spreading to the developing world as well.

The appeal of electrical energy is straightforward. It is clean, easily transported over long distances, and can be used to produce light, sound, and mechanical and thermal energy with relative conversion efficiency. However, as has been noted, most electricity has been produced by environmentally polluting fossil and nuclear resources. The practical question for hydropower is thus the extent to which it can sustain present and future electricity demand, particularly as alternative nonrenewable resources are economically depleted.

Despite the theoretical potential of world hydropower, only that proportion which is transformed naturally into gravitational flows is readily suited for conversion into mechanical, electrical, or thermal forms within the economy. Offshore, this energy exists in tidal and hydrothermal form; on land it is found in net flows as part of the earth's precipitation-evaporation cycle. Since tidal and hydrothermal energy are discussed in section 7.4, our concern at this point is with land-based hydropower potential, and with that of the United States in particular.

Figure 7.1 illustrates the average precipitation-evaporation flows within the contiguous United States. Within these flows, there is a positive net precipitation flow on land, of which around 11 percent is channeled through the agricultural, industrial, and residential sectors of the economy. Including that which is absorbed into underground water deposits, or aquifers, the runoff from land passes eventually toward the ocean. In turn, there is a positive net evaporation of water from the ocean, which together with net water flows on land constitutes the hydrologic equilibrium of the environment.

To translate the continental water runoff into energy terms, we need to specify an appropriate hydropower accounting framework. Regardless of end use, hydropower capacity is governed by three variables: volume, height, and gravity. The potential energy from any water flow can be expressed as equal to the product of these variables:

$$E = mgh, \tag{7.1}$$

where E is the number of joules per liter,[3] m is the metric volume, in liters, g is the acceleration of gravity, 9.8 meters per second squared, and h is the height of the waterfall, in meters. When equation (7.1) is expressed per unit

[2]The forerunners of mechanical hydropower were aqueducts and canals. For a discussion of their role in history, see Norman Smith, "Roman Hydraulic Technology," *Scientific American* 238 (May 1978):154–61; and John S. McNown, "Canals in America," Ibid., 235 (July 1976): 116–24.

[3]At atmospheric density and pressure, 1 liter of water weighs 1 kilogram. This mass is used in the derivation of hydroelectric power estimates.

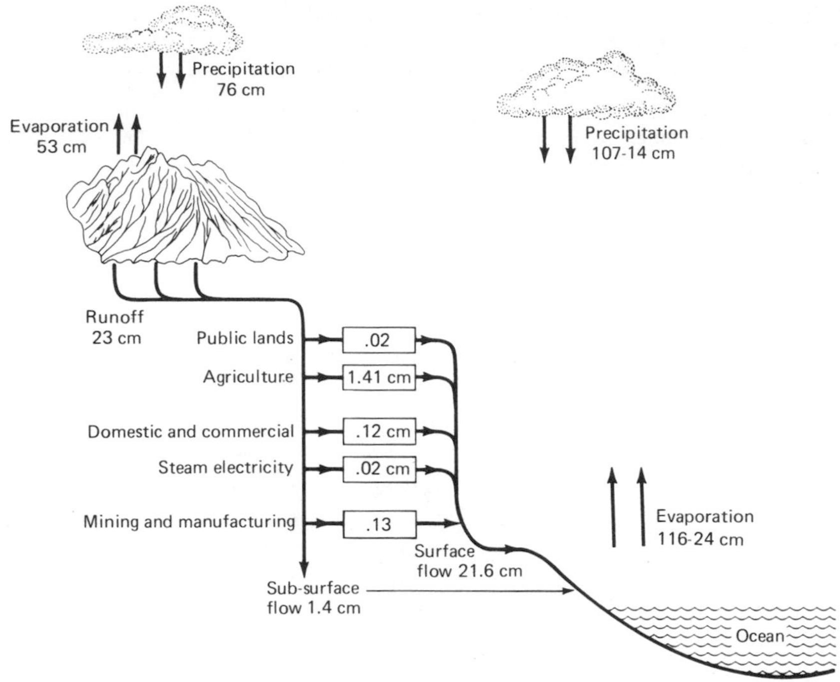

Figure 7.1. Average Annual Water Rates for the Contiguous United States. Data from U.S. Water Resources Council, *The Nation's Water Resources* (Washington, D.C.: U.S. Government Printing Office, 1968).

of time, for example, in seconds, the energy is measured in terms of watt power:

$$\frac{E}{dt} = W. \tag{7.2}$$

When (7.2) is further adjusted for conversion losses, the result is net power:

$$\frac{\alpha E}{dt} = W_n. \tag{7.3}$$

If we take from figure 7.1 the annual land runoff figure of 23 centimeters, this converts into a flow of 7.29×10^{-3} cubic meters per second.[4] Since the United States has 9,160,454 square kilometers of land area, the aggregate water flow is around 66,779 cubic meters per second. When this flow is adjusted for differences in elevation, the level and distribution of population, and the degree of concentration in water drainage sites, it yields a gross theo-

[4]Twenty-three centimeters per year is equal to 23 cubic centimeters per square centimeter of land, or 0.23 cubic meters per square meter. The runoff for each square kilometer is 2.3×10^5 cubic meters per year, which when divided by 31,536,000 (the number of seconds in a year) yields 7.29×10^{-3} cubic meters per second.

Table 7.1. Hydroelectricity in the United States, 1900–1980

Year	Hydroelectric Capacity (in net gigawatts)	Hydroelectric generation (in thousands of gigawatt-hours)	Hydroelectric as a Percentage of All Electricity Generation	Installed Hydro-electric Capacity as a Percentage of Ultimate Capacity
1900	0.5	2.786	70.2%	0.3%
1910	1.2	8.626	48.9	0.6%
1920	3.2	18.779	34.3	1.6
1930	8.6	35.870	34.2	4.3
1940	11.2	50.131	33.4	5.6
1945	15.9	84.747	35.9	7.9
1950	18.7	100.685	29.3	9.4
1955	25.0	116.236	20.7	12.5
1960	32.0	149.000	17.7	16.0
1965	44.0	196.981	17.0	22.0
1970	55.0	250.610	15.3	27.5
1971	55.0	269.582	15.0	27.5
1972	56.0	273.003	14.7	28.0
1973	62.0	272.000	13.8	31.0
1974	64.0	301.010	15.3	32.0
1975	66.0	300.020	14.4	33.0
1976	68.0	284.132	13.9	34.0
1977	68.0	220.143	10.4	34.0
1978	71.0	280.419	12.7	35.5
1979	71.2	279.783	12.4	35.6
1980	71.4	276.021	12.1	35.7

Sources: U.S. Department of Energy, Energy Information Administration, *Monthly Energy Review* (Washington, D.C.: U.S. Government Printing Office, May 1981); Federal Power Commission, *Annual Summary of Capacity, Production, and Fuel Consumption* (Washington, D.C.: U.S. Government Printing Office, selected years); and Sam H. Schurr and Bruce C. Netschert, *Energy in the American Economy, 1850–1975* (Baltimore: Johns Hopkins Press for Resources for the Future, 1960).

retical hydropower capacity of around 200,000 megawatts, or as it is conventionally expressed, 200 gigawatts.[5]

The significance of the theoretical capacity of U.S. hydropower can be seen in table 7.1. With 1980 installed capacity at 71.4 net gigawatts, hydropower accounted for just over 12 percent of overall U.S. electricity production from all resources. At the same time, the expansion of hydropower to its ultimate capacity faces two fundamental limitations. Both of these limitations, and the response thereto, merit brief descriptions as they pertain to the role of hydropower in aggregate energy policy.

One constraint affecting all hydroelectric use is that electricity cannot be stored except by conversion to an alternative energy form. Yet there is a need to store energy because electricity consumption varies substantially within any given day and throughout the week, as can be seen in figure 7.2.

One way of accommodating variable electricity consumption rates is to install enough hydroelectric and nonrenewable resource capacity to satisfy peak demand periods. Though this could be achieved with nonrenewable-

[5]Federal Power Commission, *Hydroelectric Power Reserves of the United States* (Washington, D.C.: U.S. Government Printing Office, 1972), p. x.

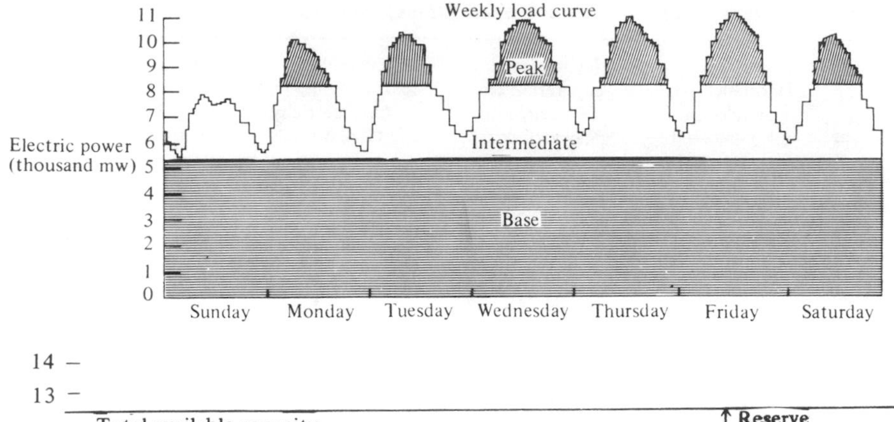

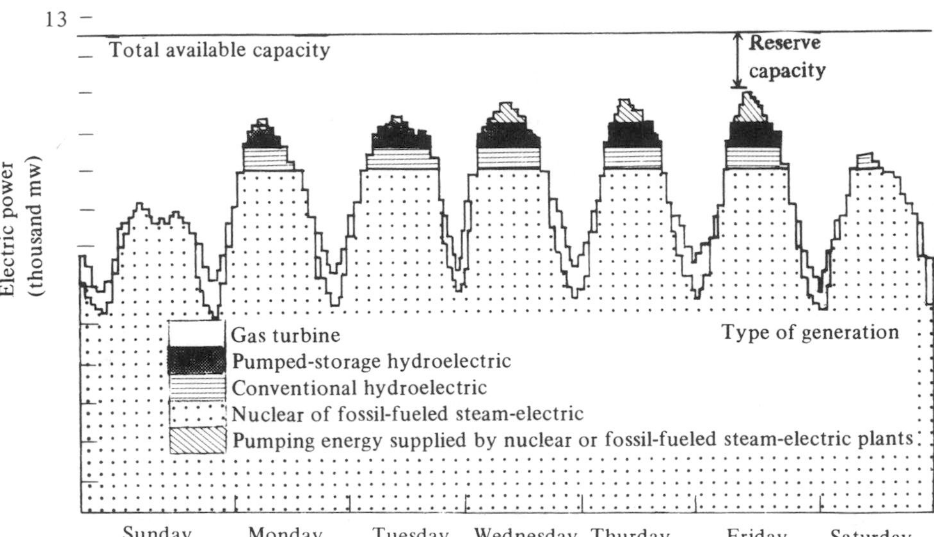

Figure 7.2. Typical Electricity Power Loads of Central Generating Plants and Sources of Reserves. *Top*, by type of load; *bottom*, by type of generation. From Federal Power Commission, *The 1970 National Power Survey* (Washington, D.C.: U.S. Government Printing Office, 1971), reprinted in Fowler, *Energy in the Environment*, pp. 111, 114.

resource generating capacity alone, a technically more efficient method is the use of pumped-storage systems. In a pumped-storage unit, a hydroelectric generator is connected to a conventional fossil or nuclear electric generating system. The nonrenewable resource generating system has some degree of excess capacity which is available during off-peak hours. Because these nonrenewable-resource generators are likely to attain their greatest thermodynamic efficiency by operating close to their peak capacity on a continuous basis, the excess capacity can be used to operate electrical pumps to lift downstream water into a storage reservoir for use by the hydroelectric generating system to which it is connected. Thus, because the hydroelectric unit can combine its regular water flow with that from the pumped-storage reservoir during peak demand periods, it reduces some of the need to install additional nonrenewable backup systems.

As figure 7.2 shows, pumped-storage systems have accounted for as much as 5 percent of all electrical generating capacity in the United States. Despite the potential for an even larger share in the future, as is noted below, there are particular costs associated with the use of pumped-storage and conventional hydroelectric generating systems. One implication for energy policy is that there is a need to adopt a more extensive use of time-of-day and peak-load electricity pricing than has been the case until now.

Another constraint affecting the expansion of hydroelectric capacity is that the dams and reservoirs essential to the operation of electric generators will alter substantially the original natural environment. Some of these alterations may be beneficial, as in the expansion of local navigation, fishing, and recreation, but others will add to social costs. Of the many types of costs associated with hydroelectric power expansion, six of the most important ones can be briefly noted here. One is that hydroelectric dams accumulate silt, which eventually reduces the hydroelectric potential. In turn, silt-flow blockage may hamper downstream soil fertility, particularly in areas where fertilizers and other energy subsidies are relatively scarce.[6] Moreover, controlled flows may also adversely affect downstream alkalinity, especially for those flows that feed into ocean currents. Fishing also may be adversely affected; although some reservoirs can be stocked with certain species, species that are dependent on migratory patterns, such as salmon and the Tennessee snail darter, may not be able to propagate. In addition, while artificial reservoirs may contribute to the expansion of agricultural irrigation, by their creation they also remove some of the original upstream land through permanent flooding. Finally, hydroelectric power systems will also affect the aesthetic value of a natural environment, particularly in that future expansion may bear directly on hitherto unaltered natural water systems.

Two important conclusions emerge from the preceding discussion of hydropower. First, while hydroelectric power does not generate as much pollution as do fossil and nuclear power plants, even if it were expanded to its ultimate technical capacity, it could not even provide for current levels of electricity consumption, let alone allow for any future growth. As a point of comparison, in 1980 the approximately 595.9 gigawatts of installed electric capacity from all resources was used to generate 2,286,000 gigawatt-hours in the United States. Now if the 1980 installed hydroelectric capacity of approximately 71.4 gigawatts were expanded to the theoretical limit of 200 gigawatts, it would amount to at most 34 percent of the 1980 installed electric capacity from all resources. Moreover, even if technical efficiency of installed hydroelectric capacity were increased by some of the options already noted, it

[6]The Aswan Dam in Egypt is a case in point. Blockage of Blue Nile flows from Ethiopia not only has reduced natural fertilization considerably but also has contributed to downstream soil alkalinity. For a discussion of the problem in the western United States, see Arthur F. Pillsbury, "The Salinity of Rivers," *Scientific American* 245 (July 1981):55–65.

would still make only a marginal contribution to expanding the hydroelectric share of overall capacity. It would thus do little to permit any reduction in the prevailing degree of dependence on nonrenewable resources or to accommodate any significant growth of long-term electricity demand.

The second conclusion is that while the technical efficiency of all electricity generation can be increased through the use of pumped-storage backup systems, the attainment of this efficiency is very much dependent on the adoption of economically efficient pricing policies. These policies include peak-load and time-of-day pricing and the specification of the social costs and benefits from hydropower and nonrenewable-resource electrical generating technologies. Since these economic questions are spelled out in detail in parts III and IV, we can now turn to a second major form of renewable-resource technology, solar energy.

7.2. SOLAR ENERGY

Of the many types of renewable energy resources, one of the most important is direct solar radiation. The reasons for its importance are simple enough: first, direct solar radiation is by far the largest of all renewable energy flows, and second, its light and thermal form can be readily used not only for conventional heating, cooling, and lighting but also for the direct generation of electricity. To understand these transformations, we need first to take stock of how direct solar radiation can be measured.

As noted in chapter 4, solar energy reaching the earth's atmosphere is emitted at a rate $173{,}000 \times 10^{12}$ watts. Because this flow stems from a process of continuous fusion within the sun, the light and heat energy are dispersed into space as radiation, within a distribution illustrated in figure 7.3. As can be seen, most of this energy lies within wave lengths of between 0.3 and 1.2 microns. Once it has been filtered by passage through dust and gases of the earth's atmosphere, even though its frequency distribution is not appreciably altered, the amount of direct solar energy reaching the surface is reduced to roughly half of its original amount. For all practical purposes, this radiation must then be measured in terms of its density per unit of surface area.

The area of the diametral plane of the earth is 1.27×10^{14} square meters. If this area receives solar energy at a rate of $173{,}000 \times 10^{12}$ watts, the flow reaching the earth's atmosphere is around 1,360 watts per square meter. After atmospheric filtration has been taken into account, this flow is reduced to an average of 638 watts per square meter.[7] When this radiation density is further multiplied by time, the result is the amount of potential solar energy

[7]Figure 4.1 shows the direct heat of solar energy as 8.1×10^{16} watts. When this is divided through by the 1.27×10^{14} square meters of the earth's diametral plane area, the direct solar energy flow yields 638 watts per square meter. As figure 4.1 also shows, the difference in atmospheric solar radiation and direct solar radiation on the earth is accounted for by direct reflection, winds, waves, convections and currents, evaporation and precipitation, and photosynthesis.

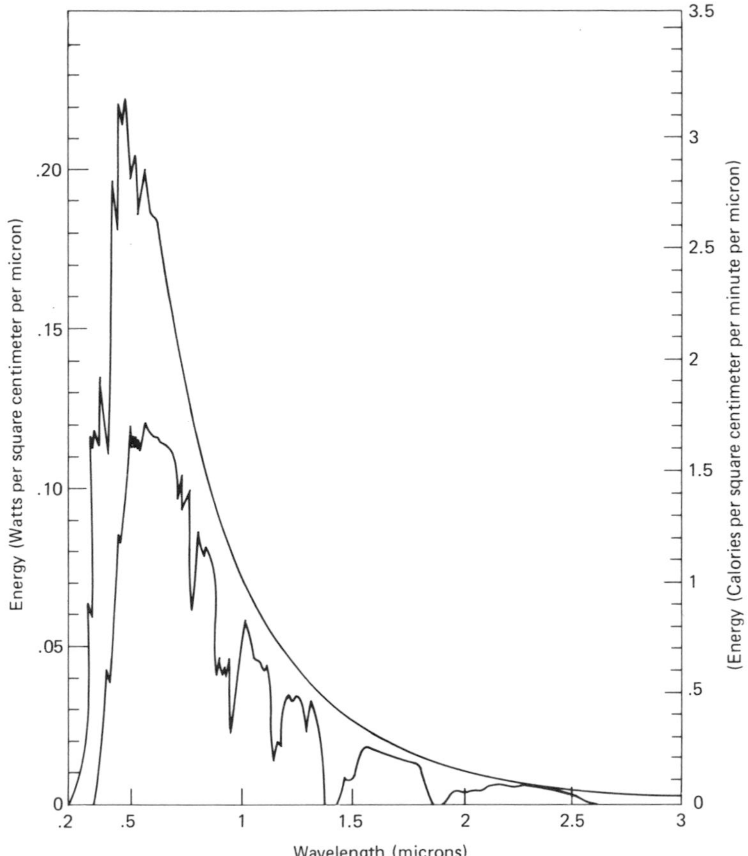

Figure 7.3. The Earth's Spectral Distribution of Solar Radiation. The outer distribution refers to solar radiation reaching the earth at the top of its atmosphere. The inner distribution refers to solar radiation reaching the ground, and takes into account the absorbing effects of water vapor, carbon dioxide, oxygen, nitrogen, ozone, and particles of dust. Data are based on a solar constant of 1.95 calories per square centimeter per minute. Adapted from D. M. Gates, "The Flow of Energy in the Biosphere," in *Energy and Power*, edited by the editors of *Scientific American* (San Francisco: W. H. Freeman and Co., 1971), p. 47; Farrington Daniels, *Direct Use of the Sun's Energy* (New York: Ballantine Books, 1974); and M. P. Thekaekara, "Data on Incident Solar Radiation," in *Solar Cells*, ed. Charles E. Backus (New York: IEEE Press, 1976), p. 3.

per unit of area, and can be expressed in watt-hours, Btu's, or any other standard unit of energy such as those listed in the Appendix.

Given its relatively northern position, the United States receives on the average 180 watts per square meter of surface area, the variation of which is illustrated in figure 7.4.[8] When this average flow is multiplied by the area of

[8]The 180-watt figure is derived by multiplying the cosine of the angle of the United States to the diametral plane to the sun, that is, 630 × cos 180°, which means that the United States is on an average angle of 73.40° to the sun.

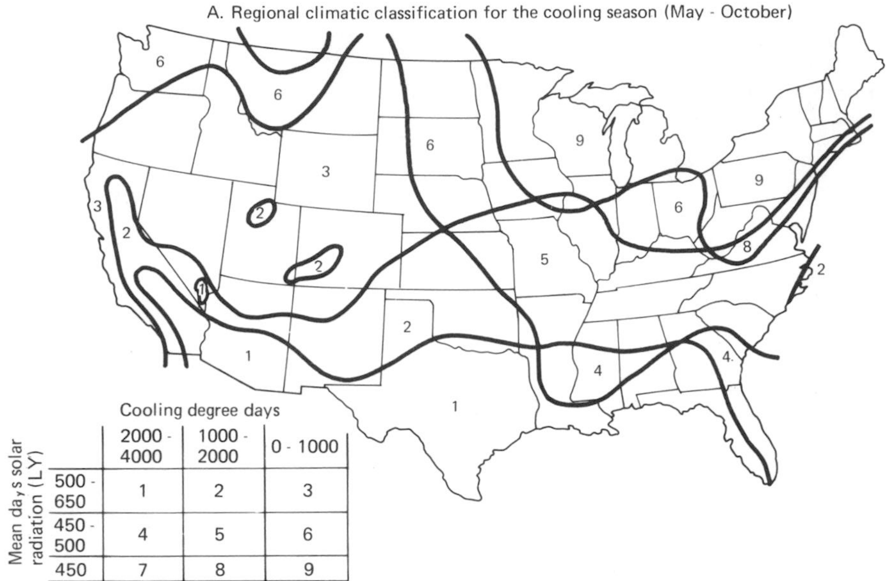

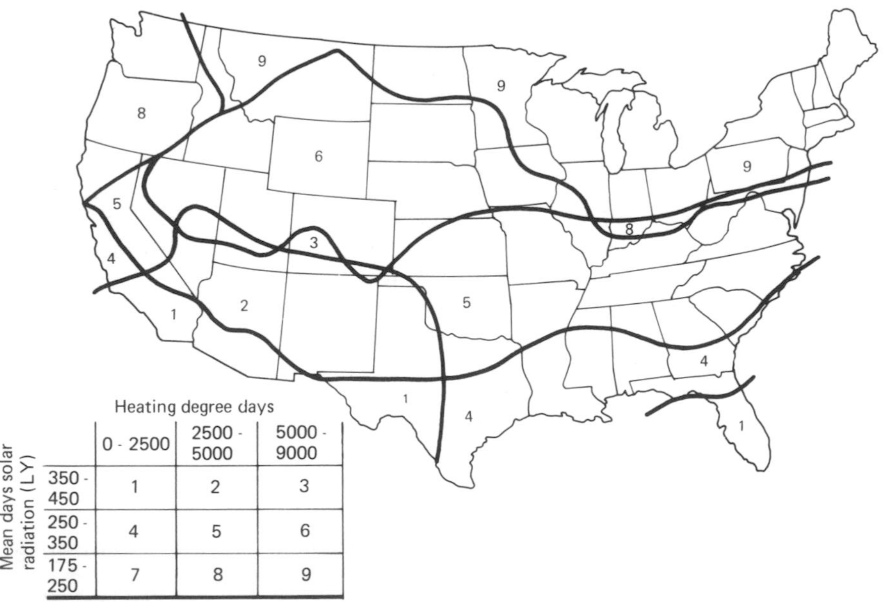

Figure 7.4. Seasonal Insolation and Heating-Cooling Variations within the United States. From Ian R. Jones, "Solar Heating and Cooling of Buildings," in *Proceedings of the Workshop on Solar Heating and Cooling of Buildings*, coord. F. A. Iachetta (Washington, D.C.: National Science Foundation, 1975), pp. 23–24.

the United States, aggregate surface solar radiation amounts to a rate of 1650×10^{12} watts. Allowing for seasonal and nocturnal variations, if solar radiation is released at this rate for only half of any average year, then the annual flow would provide the following total amount of energy:

$$(7.4) \qquad E = 1{,}650 \times 10^{12} \text{ watts} \times \frac{8{,}760 \text{ hours per year}}{2}$$

$$= 7.227 \times 10^{18} \text{ watt-hours.}$$

From equation (7.4), since one watt-hour is equal to 3.413 Btu's, the theoretically available solar energy in the United States amounts to 2.4666×10^{19} Btu's, or 24,700 quads. Thus in one year, direct solar radiation could provide 325 times the amount of energy presently consumed from all conventional resources. Moreover, the annual flow of this solar energy amounts to over four times the level of U.S. presently known recoverable fossil reserves listed in table 5.8 and 8 percent of its conventional fission technology nuclear energy reserves listed in table 6.4. In theory at least, then, solar energy resources could defer until far into the future any immediate concern over the economy's present dependence on depletable energy resources.

Although solar energy potential is relatively high, it does not necessarily follow that this energy can be readily converted into useful forms desired by society. In fact, using present-day technology, solar energy conversion into thermal and electrical forms is only around 10 percent efficient, which reduces the practical potential of available solar energy to just over thirty-two times the 1980 level of aggregate primary energy consumption. Even with this degree of inefficiency, though, with only 3 percent of the land area of the United States applied to collection and conversion, solar radiation could provide enough energy to sustain the 1980 level of aggregate energy consumption from all other energy resources used in that year.[9]

From a technically adjusted perspective, it should also be noted that not every region within the United States could expect to generate the same amount of solar energy. Indeed, when the variations illustrated in figure 7.4 are converted into the quantitative estimates of table 7.2, the regional potential of solar energy can be more clearly understood. As an example, if New England receives on the average 1,181 Btu's per square foot per day, the theoretical annual amount of energy available with a 10 percent collection and conversion efficiency would be:

$$(7.5) \qquad E = 1{,}181 \,(\text{Btu/ft}^2/\text{day}) \times 365 \,(\text{days}) \times 1.7549 \times 10^{12} \,(\text{ft}^2 \text{ of land in New England}) \times 0.10 \,(\text{efficiency})$$

$$= 75.65 \times 10^{15} \text{ Btu's, or } 75.65 \text{ quads.}$$

[9]If solar energy were 100 percent efficient, it could provide about 325 times the 1980 level of primary energy consumption. Thus to provide the amount of 1980 primary energy, only 1/325 of the land area would be needed. In turn, if solar technology were only 10 percent efficient, then ten times this amount of land would be needed, i.e., 10/325, which reduces to 3.08 percent of the area of the United States. Since practical collection would be limited essentially to land areas, and since land area represents 97.84 percent of all of the United States, this means that about 3.15 percent of total land would be needed for this purpose.

Table 7.2. Average Solar Insolation and Degree Days, by Census Region

Region	Annual		Maximum (July)		Minimum (January)		Average degree days
	$Wh/ft^2/day$	$Btu/ft^2/day$	$Wh/ft^2/day$	$Btu/ft^2/day$	$Wh/ft^2/day$	$Btu/ft^2/day$	
New England	346	1,181	540	1,843	130	444	6,500
Middle Atlantic	346	1,181	551	1,881	140	478	6,000
East North Central	356	1,215	572	1,952	151	515	7,000
West North Central	389	1,324	659	2,249	194	662	6,000
South Atlantic	442	1,509	572	1,452	248	846	4,000
East South Central	421	1,406	572	1,952	205	700	4,200
West South Central	464	1,584	659	2,249	281	959	1,800
Mountain	464	1,584	702	2,396	238	812	6,000
Pacific	421	1,406	702	2,396	162	552	2,400

Source: Federal Energy Administration, *Project Independence Blueprint* (Washington, D.C.: U.S. Government Printing Office, November 1974), p. A-1-9.

Note: Insolation is the amount of solar radiation per unit of horizontal surface over a period of time.

Equation (7.5) shows a substantial energy potential, but it also assumes that 100 percent of all land would be used for collection and conversion. If New England were to set aside only the average 3 percent of land suggested by the national solar equivalence requirement, then the region could be provided with 2.2695×10^{15} Btu's, or 52 percent of its regional consumption of 4.3268×10^{15} Btu's in that year. If New England increased its collection area to 5.7 percent of its land, then solar energy could provide 100 percent of its primary energy consumption for that year, a percentage that is still within practical limits in light of the less than average population density of that region.

In contrast to solar-scarce New England stand the southwestern and mountain regions of the United States. In these regions, solar energy intensity attains a level of 1,584 Btu's per square foot per day. With 14.5 percent of the U.S. population, these regions consumed about 10.97×10^{15} Btu's of aggregate primary energy in 1980. Were these regions to use 3 percent of their land area to collect and convert solar radiation at 10 percent efficiency, based on the kind of computation shown in equation (7.5), the available energy from direct solar power would be 5.65 times the amount regionally consumed from alternative resources in that year. Moreover, such solar energy would also be equivalent to over 80 percent of all primary energy consumption of the United States in 1980. Thus, to provide an amount of solar energy just equal to their conventional resource consumption of 1980 would require the setting aside of only 0.53 percent of their land area. To be sure, this relatively low percentage, and the somewhat higher figure for New England, might be even lower were collection and conversion efficiency to rise above the average 10 percent rate. To understand why solar energy has been so inefficient, we need to take a closer look at present-day collection and conversion technology.

Although solar radiation provides essential light energy on a daily basis, it is the rejected energy from this radiation that constitutes the principal resource of potential solar energy technology. The two areas where this resource shows the greatest potential application are in heating and cooling, and in the direct generation of electricity. Each of these applications will be considered in turn.

Heating is the oldest known solar technology. Apart from the temporary incident radiation to the body from a day at the beach, or the glee with which a child generates solar combustion by concentrating sunlight on paper or leaves with a magnifying lens, only recently has solar heating emerged as a potentially viable technology for residential and commercial use on a widespread scale. One principal reason for the slow development of commercial solar heating is that it has been difficult to develop a mechanism for storage of solar heat once sunlight is no longer available, such as on cloudy days and throughout the night.[10] How this is resolved is best seen by looking at the operation of typical solar heating systems.

[10]The lack of commercial applications has long been an issue of interest to economic historians and students of the history of technology. Apart from the reputed military use of mirrors by Archimedes in 212 *b.c.*, in the eighteenth century, Georges Buffon used 168 six-inch

The simplest type of solar heating technology is based on the use of flat-plate collectors. A flat-plate collector is made of a highly heat-absorbent and heat-conducting material such as copper or aluminum tubing and is usually painted flat black to reduce as much as possible any reflection of incoming radiation.[11] To reduce heat loss further, the collector is sealed in a container with a glass or plastic transparent top to permit maximum absorption. Within the collector tubing, water or air from a storage tank circulates and absorbs heat from the tube as it is returned to the storage tank. Depending on the insulation within the collector and the storage tank, temperatures as high as 65°C (149°F) can be attained. Maximum temperatures depend in turn on both the initial ambient temperature and on collector efficiency. The largest increase in temperature from a basic flat-plate collector system is generally around 40°C.

Heat storage is a function of both container insulation and the collector fluid. When a 40°C temperature change is attained, water can store up to 1.67×10^5 joules (158.48 Btu's) of energy per kilogram.[12] To determine the required amount of water storage, consider a typical 140-square-meter (that is, a 1,500-square-foot) residential structure that consumes around 800 million joules (759,200 Btu's) of energy per day for space and water heating. If the residence utilizes a solar collector with an efficiency of 500 watts per square meter, then over the course of a seven-hour day, the energy per square meter of collector space would be 3,500 watt-hours, or 12.6×10^6 joules.[13] The collector space needed to sustain 100 percent of daily space and water heating would thus be:

$$(7.6) \qquad A = \frac{8 \times 10^8 \text{ joules of daily consumption}}{12.6 \times 10^6 \text{ joules }/\text{m}^2/\text{day}} = 63.49 \text{ m}^2.$$

square mirrors to ignite wood two hundred feet away. Nicolas de Saussure (1740–99) developed a solar oven that could provide temperatures up to 320°F. Antoine Lavoisier (1743–94) used an alcohol-filled lens to melt platinum at 3,190°F. The Swedish-American John Ericsson built nine solar hot-air engines adaptable to steam production between 1860 and 1883. In 1872 a solar desalination plant at Salinas, Chile, combined 51,200 square feet of collectors with windmills to provide fresh water at a rate of one pound of water per square foot of glass collector per day. In 1913, Philadelphia engineers Frank Shuman and C. V. Boys built a 13,269-square-foot collector in El Maâdi, Egypt, to operate a 100-horsepower engine to pump irrigation from the Nile river. For a description, see Wilson Clark, *Energy for Survival* (Garden City, N.Y.: Doubleday Anchor Books, 1975), chap. 6.

[11]The performance capacity of a flat-plate collector can be defined as $k = \epsilon \cdot \tau \cdot \alpha - \Omega (T - Ta)$, where ϵ is the solar intensity of the plane of the collector, i.e., watts per square meter, τ is the transmittance of the coverplates, α is the absorptivity of the absorber plate, Ω is the coefficient of upward loss of the absorber plate to the ambient air, T is the mean temperature of the plate, and Ta is the ambient temperature (see H. C. Hottel, "Solar Energy," *Chemical Engineering Progress*, July 1975, pp. 53–65).

[12]One kilogram of water (equal to one cubic meter) has a specific heat of 1,000 calories per degree of Centigrade temperature. If a 40°C temperature change results from solar heating, the amount of heat storage is 4×10^4 calories per kilogram. Since there are 4.184 joules per calories, the amount of energy stored is $(4.184) \times (4 \times 10^4)$, or 167,360 joules, i.e., 1.67×10^5 joules per kilogram of water.

[13]One joule is equal to one watt-second. Thus, 3,500 watt-hours multiplied by 3,600 seconds per hour yields 12.6×10^6 joules.

Since the area of the residential structure is 140 square meters, if the collectors were placed on an angle facing south, they would take up well under half of the available roof space.[14]

The volume of water necessary to sustain daily energy consumption is determined by dividing daily consumption by the thermal capacity of water. In the example thus far illustrated, the necessary water storage is:

$$(7.7) \qquad V = \frac{8 \times 10^8 \text{ joules of daily energy consumption}}{1.67 \times 10^5 \text{ joules /kg of water storage}}$$

$$= 4{,}790 \text{ kg}$$

$$= 4.79 \text{ cubic meters of water}$$

$$= 1{,}264 \text{ gallons of water.}$$

The difficulty raised by solar space and water heating is that the intermittent flow of the sun's energy may be insufficient to assure a steady supply for residential requirements. Although water storage can allow for variation throughout a twenty-four-hour period, the capacity of the solar collector system and the water storage may have to be enlarged beyond daily energy consumption, or an auxiliary conventional energy source may have to be integrated into the system. Though sustained cloud cover can last for as long as a week, the probability that it will occur is relatively small. Thus, if a three-day cloud capacity is built in, a solar collector system could approach 100 percent sufficiency for space and water heating. In the example thus far cited, it means that a threefold expansion of capacity would call for a 3,792-gallon water storage tank, which is larger than most conventional water systems now in use but not exceptional to either residential or commercial heating technology.

Technical efficiency of flat-plate solar heating systems can be increased by changes in both the storage medium and the collectors themselves. In lieu of water, the most common medium now in use, some storage systems rely on hot rocks or eutectic salts, as solids through which water or air will circulate to and from solar collectors. Loosely packed rocks are used for air-circulating systems and avoid the problem of freezing inherent in winter water storage. At the same time, the thermal capacity of rocks is only around 40 percent that of water, and in terms of units of energy storage, the quantity of rocks will have to be 2.5 times the stored-energy equivalent of water.

[14]Collector roof space is, of course, determined also by the angle of optimum efficiency. The higher the optimal angle, the greater must be the height of the collector, though the smaller will be the share of horizontal roof space required. If 63.49 square meters are used, then 7.968 meters represents the hypotenuse of the reflection angle. If a 45° angle is the optimum one for efficiency, then the amount of horizontal roof space needed can be computed as $\cos A = x / 7.968$; that is $\cos 45° = x / 7.968$, or $0.707107 = x / 7.968$, which gives 5.634227 meters as the value of x. Since the collection area is 7.968 square meters, the roof area will be 5.634227 meters squared, or 31,744, 512, which is 22.6 percent of the 140 square meters of horizontal roof space. A tripling of collector space on a 45° angle would take up 68 percent of horizontal roof space.

Eutectic salts are salts which can circulate in a liquid form to collect heat and which will cool into a solid within a storage medium, thereby releasing a liquid such as water which can readily transmit energy for space and water heating. One type of eutectic salt is sodium hydrate, $Na_2SO_4 \cdot 10\ H_2O$. When crystallized into a solid, sodium hydrate separates into sodium sulfate, Na_2SO_4, and water, 10 H_2O. The sodium hydrate–sulfate transition occurs at 32.3°C and can absorb or release energy equivalent to a 50°C change in temperature from solar collectors. Although the thermal capacity is thus higher than that of water, sodium hydrate and allied eutectic salts have thus far also presented problems in the storage phase because of the somewhat rigid stratification of the solid's cyrstalline structure.[15]

The efficiency of flat-plate collectors can be increased by two elementary modifications. One is the use of additional panes of glass or plastic over the collectors in order to reduce heat loss into the atmosphere.[16] However, each additional pane reduces losses at a declining marginal rate, so that a zero-loss collector becomes both technically and economically impossible. As a result, most multipane collectors generally do not have more than three or four cover plates.

Another method of improving collector efficiency is by using collector angle-adjusting mechanisms to maximize the inflow of solar radiation. Although many collectors are attached at a fixed angle to a building, several variations can be used to attain optimal collection. One is using corrugated collector surfaces and retaining the collector's basic fixed angle. Some loss is still engendered by this process, however, and it is not as efficient as altering the collector angle itself. Collector angles can be adjusted on a daily or seasonal basis using either manual or self-adjusting mechanisms operated by solar or auxiliary power. Of course, as each of these alterations is incorporated into design, collector costs are increased, thereby reducing the cost-effectiveness of solar energy.

[15]See Martin Goldstein, "Some Physical Chemical Aspects of Heat Storage," in United Nations, *Proceedings of the United Nations Conference on New Sources of Energy* 5 (New York: United Nations, 1964):411–17; and H. G. Lorsch, "Thermal Energy Storage for Solar Heating," *ASHRAE Journal*, November 1975, pp. 47–52.

[16]Black-body radiation loss is given at 5.67×10^{-8} watts per square meter; it is known also as the Stefan-Boltzmann constant, after its discoverers. If a black-body collector attains a temperature of 65°C using an ambient temperature of 0°C, then the heat loss can be derived from the following:

$$\lambda = \frac{\rho\,(\text{black-body net reflectivity per degree Kelvin})\,(T^4 - T\text{ ambient})}{1 + n(\text{the number of panes})}$$

$$= (5.67 \times 10^{-8})\,(338^4 - 273)$$

$$= 740 \text{ watts per square meter.}$$

Increasing the number of panes to 3 reduces heat loss to

$$\lambda = \frac{(5.67 \times 10^{-8})(338^4 - 273)}{4}$$

$$= 185 \text{ watts per square meter,}$$

or a reduction of 75 percent of the loss from an uncovered collector (see Jerrold H. Krenz, *Energy: Conversion and Utilization* [Boston: Allyn and Bacon, 1976], pp. 219–27).

Flat-plate collectors suggest considerable versatility. Not only can they be used as a sole source of space and water heating but they can be connected to auxiliary systems and provide for cooling, as can be seen in a few basic configurations illustrated in figure 7.5. In system 1, solar collectors are complemented by a conventional power source such as fuel oil, gas, or electricity and are used to provide heating, hot water, and cool air conditioning by absorption. In system 2, only space and water heating are provided by solar collectors; cool air conditioning is supplied by a separate electrical source. In system 3, energy still provides thermal input, but a heat pump is used to raise thermodynamic efficiency as energy flows are passed to space, hot water, and cooling systems. Since the heat pump is discussed in chapter 8, we can now turn to the technology of focusing collectors, a solar source with significant industrial potential.

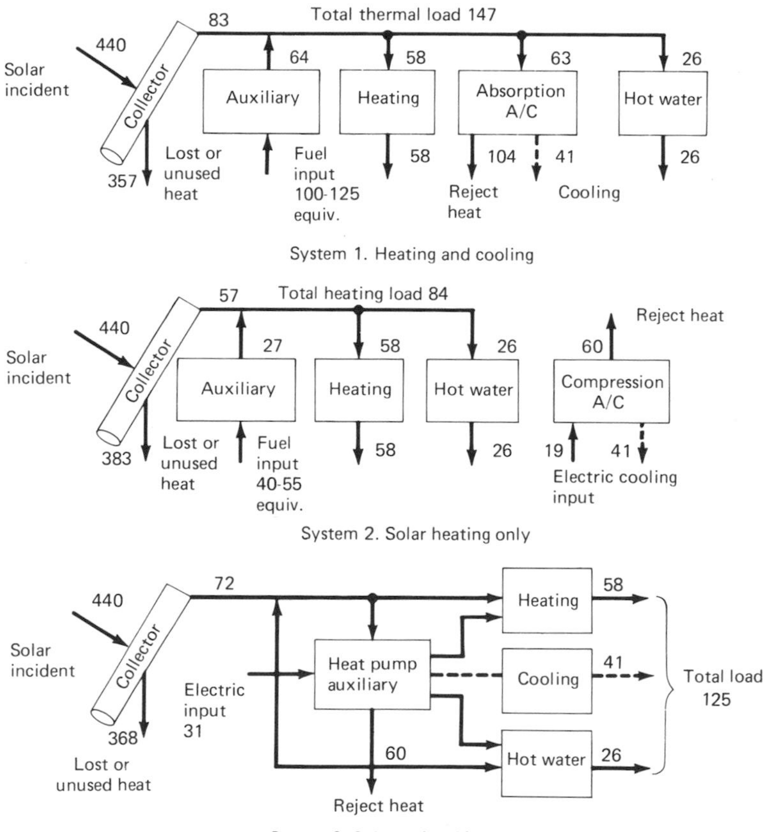

Figure 7.5. Residential Solar Energy Systems. The figure is based on an 800-square-foot collector. Numbers are in millions of Btu's per year. From Albert Weinstein, "Technical and Economic Considerations for Solar Heating and Cooling of Buildings: A Report by Westinghouse Heating Electric Corporation," in Iachetta, *Proceedings of the Workshop on Solar Heating and Cooling of Buildings*, p. 37.

Although flat-plate collectors technically can accommodate a substantial share of residential and commercial space, hot water, and cooling demand, much higher temperatures are needed for industrial energy usage. One way to accommodate these needs is by the use of focusing collectors. Focusing collectors rely on cylindrical or spherical parabolic surfaces to concentrate naturally diffused solar radiation on a specific surface. Since the direct solar radiation must be reflected from primary concentrators to a central collector, there is some energy loss due to concentrator light absorption and from dispersion of reflected energy about the central collector region. Despite reflector losses as high as 10 percent, focusing collectors can compensate by using a relatively large number of collectors.

The net radiated power of a focusing collector system can be expressed as

$$P_{\text{net}} = \epsilon\tau\alpha - \Omega(T - Ta) - Ce\sigma T^4, \tag{7.8}$$

where ϵ is the solar flux received by a single concentrating reflector, measured in watts per square meter; τ is the transmittance of the cover plate of a single concentrator; α is the absorptivity of the cover plate of a single concentrator; Ω is the coefficient of upward loss of energy from concentrator to ambient air; T is the mean temperature of the concentrator plate, in Kelvin degrees; Ta is the ambient temperature, in Kelvin degrees; C is the concentration ratio of absorber collector area to concentrator reflector area; e is the emissivity of the solar absorber; σ is the black-body net reflectivity per degree Kelvin, known also as the Stefan-Boltzmann constant (5.67×10^{-8}); and T^4 is the fourth power of the Kelvin temperature of the absorber. As a simple illustration of equation (7.8), if the incident solar radiation (ϵ) is 500 watts per square meter, the transmittance-absorptivity product of a concentrator is 0.81, no upward loss is produced by a concentrator, the concentration ratio is 50 (i.e., $C = 1 / 50$), emissivity is 5 percent, and the absorber temperature is 600°C, then the net power per concentrator area will be 372 watts. The advantage of a focusing collector now becomes evident. If a sufficient number of concentrators is provided, enough power can be generated to produce steam for a modern electricity generating plant, the most likely area of application. As an example, in order to generate enough power for a solar plant on the 1,000-megawatt scale typical of fossil and nuclear plants, the amount of collector space needed would be around 2.6 square kilometers.[17] In many of the solar-rich, population scarce desert regions of the southwestern United States, such solar power plants have long been considered; and a 10-megawatt pilot plant near Barstow, California, is scheduled to begin operations in the near future.

After heating and cooling, the second major area of solar energy technology is the direct generation of electricity. Whereas a focusing collector can be used to generate steam heat for central electricity power plants, solar electricity production can be obtained by the direct conversion of radiation energy to electricity. The collector-convertor mechanisms used in this process

[17]One thousand megawatts is equal to 1 billion watts. When divided by the net wattage per concentrator, 372, the result is 2,688,172 square meters, which is 2.6 square kilometers, or 1,0376 square miles.

are known as photovoltaics. Photovoltaic cells are a type of semiconductor, that is, a crystalline solid such as silicon, germanium, or gallium which has electrical conductivity greater than that of insulators but not as efficient as that found in metals. Since silicon is the most common basic type of photovoltaic semiconductor now in use, the first step in understanding this technology is to spell out briefly how solar cells are able to generate electricity.

Silicon atoms normally have fourteen electrons per atom. Of these fourteen, four are available to interact with other atoms.[18] These available electrons can combine with other elements to form compounds or they can interact with other silicon atoms in a process of crystal stabilization. Whenever an interactive electron moves, it leaves a "hole" into which other electrons are free to move. The movement of these electrons is the same as that found in a direct electrical current.

Though there are several ways in which silicon crystals can be used to generate an electrical current, what they all share in common is the application of thermal energy. In the case of photovoltaic cells, when silicon absorbs units of light energy, or photons, the temperature of the absorbing crystal is raised to a point where an electrical current can be generated. To enhance this process, photovoltaic cells usually consist of silicon that is bonded to another material which contains a relative surplus or shortage of interactive electrons. For example, when silicon is bonded to phosphorus, which has five interactive electrons, it is known as a negative, or *n*-type, semiconductor. In turn, silicon bonded to boron, which has only three interactive electrons, has a relative shortage of interactive electrons and is known as a positive, or *p*-type, semiconductor.

As photons are absorbed by silicon, they build up energy to move the interactive electrons between the silicon and the bonding surface. Voltage builds up to the point where the *n*-layer can push any additional electrons into the *p*-layer—the voltage is approximately 0.65 volts. When a circuit joining the silicon and the bonding material is attached, as photons are absorbed by the silicon, a net flow of electrons is released into the circuit.

Photovoltaic efficiency under conventional technology is only around 10–11 percent. The reason for this relatively low level of efficiency is that the electron gap between the free electrons of silicon and a bonding material requires a relatively strong flow of photons. Such stronger radiation is found within the ultraviolet end of the spectrum rather than along the infrared band. Recent work in semiconductor bonding does point to the possibility of attaining ultimate efficiencies as high as 25 percent, but so far these cells still depend largely on silicon, a difficult material to mass-produce with sufficient purity.[19]

[18]For a more detailed discussion, see Bruce Chalmers, "The Photovoltaic Generation of Electricity," *Scientific American* 235 (October 1976):34–43.

[19]See Krenz, *Energy Conversion*, chap. 7, esp. pp. 241–51. The 25 percent efficiency figure is approached when gallium arsenide and cadmium tellurium are used. One recent development is the possibility of using amorphous semiconductor technology. For a description regarding the technology and its inventor, Sanford Ovshinsky, see "Cheaper Solar Energy Proclaimed by Inventor," *New York Times*, 1 December 1978, p. D-1.

Potential applications of photovoltaics include the terrestrial generation of electricity on a decentralized basis, as well as the use of solar-powered satellites. As one proponent has advocated, solar satellites might be used to collect the higher-intensity energy above the earth's atmosphere and then to transmit this energy via microwaves to receiving stations on earth for regional distribution.[20] Despite the successes of space exploration, this proposal has been considered one of the least economic of all photovoltaic alternatives. Indeed, one of the fundamental limitations of all photovoltaic systems is that although they can achieve competitive technical efficiency, they have not yet become economically competitive with alternative modes of electricity generation.

7.3. BIOMASS ENERGY RESOURCES

Of all renewable energy resources dependent on the daily flow of the sun's energy, one of the least abundant derives from photosynthesis in plants. At the same time, as all students of biology can attest, photosynthesis is critical to practically all forms of life. The significance of photosynthesis lies, of course, in the oxygen–carbon dioxide cycle of the atmosphere, as well as in the storage of energy within animal and plant organisms. Photosynthesis is one of the oldest means of energy storage, but with the expansion of scientific knowledge, it has taken on added importance in the development of appropriate energy policies. Today, resources directly or indirectly dependent on photosynthesis are known commonly as biomass energy resources, and they represent another alternative to the current world dependence on economically depletable fossil and nuclear fuels.

The storage of solar energy by photosynthesis takes place at a rate of 4×10^{13} watts. Though this flow represents but 3.305×10^{-4} percent of the direct solar energy reaching the earth, when a calculation of the kind shown in equation (7.4) is performed, the potential energy from biomass is approximately 598×10^{15} Btu's per year, or just under twice the 1980 level of world aggregate consumption of 306.97 quads from all other energy resources.[21] This is not as substantial a ratio as that found in direct solar radiation, but it does suggest a significant alternative resource, especially among developing countries with a relative abundance of solar energy and a scarcity of fossil and nuclear fuels. Since a more detailed exposition of photosynthesis is beyond the scope of this book, we can at this point mention some of the more widely used and promising forms of biomass energy resources.

The most obvious form of biomass energy is food from agriculture. By and large, with the expansion of scientific knowledge, agricultural production

[20]Peter E. Glaser, "Power from the Sun: Its Future," *Science* 5 (22 November 1968):857–61.

[21]If we assume that only one-half of the year is used to collect solar energy via photosynthesis, then equation (7.4) applied to biomass becomes

$$
\begin{aligned}
(7.4a) \qquad E &= 4 \times 10^{13} \text{ watts} \times \frac{8{,}760 \text{ hours per year}}{2} \\
&= 1.7520 \times 10^{17} \text{ watt-hours per year} \times 3.413 \text{ Btu's per watt-hour} \\
&= 5.97957 \times 10^{17} \text{ Btu's.}
\end{aligned}
$$

throughout the world has been able to sustain an expanding population with rising per capita consumption. Though this has not been true in every country, and though it will not necessarily be so in the future, to the extent that it occurs, it depends on the capacity to innovate in three principal ways: organizational efficiency of existing inputs, improvements in the genetic efficiency of plants and animals, and augmentation of natural photosynthetic energy from other sources of supply. In the United States, all three types of innovation have occurred simultaneously, so that the United States generally has enjoyed a surplus position, as may be seen in table 7.3.

Several generalizations can be drawn from table 7.3. First, following a peak in 1950, the amount of farmland in the United States has been declining at a rate of roughly 0.4 percent per year, a trend reflective of both enclosure via urban sprawl and past federal government efforts to subsidize farm income through the soil bank program. Second, the decline in farmland has been accompanied by an even more dramatic reduction in the farm population, at a rate of almost 2 percent a year, as part of the broader pattern of urbanization and industrialization. Third, despite some variations in the nutritional intake of the population, overall food consumption has been well above established minimum health standards, so much so that the United States has been largely in the position of being a net exporter of agricultural products.

Changes in relative prices have undoubtedly played a major role in influencing the behavior of agricultural inputs and outputs in the U.S. economy. At the same time, table 7.3 suggests that the historical gains in agricultural productivity may be considerably more difficult to sustain in the future. The reason for this difficulty is straightforward: given the relative constancy of natural photosynthetic energy, most of the increases in output have been derived by the increase in fossil-based energy inputs, namely, a greater use of mechanized energy in the form of tractors and harvesters, and in the use of petrochemical fertilizers. To be sure, there have also been gains from improvements in the genetic quality of plants and animals, and in production economies of scale. Yet, unless genetic breakthroughs on the order of the Green Revolution of the 1950s and 1960s can be sustained at an ever larger level, the cost of fossil-fed food energy is likely to rise relative to other goods and services less dependent on these resources, much as has been the recent U.S. experience. What this suggests, then, is that if economic growth is to be based on a continuing decline in the agricultural share of national output, the technical efficiency of energy conversion in agriculture will have to rise at a sufficient rate to compensate for the increase in the real cost of fossil fuels. Agriculture thus depends on energy policy choices.

Apart from food energy production, firewood is the oldest known biomass energy resource. As noted in chapter 2, until the industrial revolution, it was the single largest energy resource used in the world economy, as it still is in some isolated areas of the developing world today. The principal constraints imposed by an accelerated use of firewood are: a reduction in one of the most universal building materials, acceleration of soil erosion, climate dehydration, and reduction of plant oxygenation essential to atmospheric equilib-

Table 7.3. Energy and Agriculture in the United States, 1900–1980

Year	Total Farmland (in millions of acres)	Farm Population (in millions)	Number of Farms (in thousands)	Average Farm Size (in acres)	Acres per Farm Population	Maximum Photosynthetic Energy on All Farmland (in trillions of kilocalories)	Number of Tractors on Farms (in thousands)	Fertilizer Consumption of Farms (in thousands of short tons)	Fertilizer Consumption per Acre of Farmland (in pounds)	Ratio of Agricultural Exports to Agricultural Imports	Daily Per Capita Consumption of Food Energy (in calories)
1900	839	29.4	5,737	146	28.5	6.74	—	2,730	6.50	2.27	—
1910	879	32.2	6,406	137	27.2	7.06	1	5,547	12.62	1.10	3,499
1920	956	32.0	6,518	147	29.9	7.67	275	6,354	13.29	1.13	3,274
1930	987	30.5	6,546	151	32.4	7.92	775	7,278	14.75	0.79	3,435
1940	1,061	30.5	6,350	167	34.7	8.52	1,545	8,336	15.72	0.60	3,350
1950	1,202	23.0	5,648	213	52.3	9.65	3,394	20,345	33.85	1.03	3,260
1960	1,176	15.6	3,963	297	75.4	9.44	4,685	24,900	42.35	1.13	3,140
1970	1,103	9.7	2,954	373	113.7	8.86	4,619	39,775	72.12	1.20	3,300
1975	1,086	8.8	2,808	387	123.4	8.72	4,467	42,500	78.26	2.25	3,250
1976	1,084	8.3	2,778	390	130.6	8.70	4,434	49,100	90.59	2.19	3,380
1977	1,081	7.8	2,752	393	138.6	8.68	4,402	51,600	95.47	1.76	3,380
1978	1,052	6.5	2,370	444	161.9	8.45	4,370	47,500	90.30	1.99	3,440
1979	1,049	6.2	2,330	450	169.2	8.43	4,350	51,100	97.43	2.08	3,500
1980	1,047	6.1[a]	2,309	453	171.6[a]	8.41	4,360[a]	51,300[a]	97.99	2.04[a]	3,520[a]

Sources: U.S. Department of Agriculture, Economic Research Service: *Farm Population Estimates for 1910–70* and *Farm Population Estimates,* annual. U.S. Department of Agriculture, Statistical Reporting Service: *Number of Farms, 1910–1959*; *Land in Farms, 1950–1959*; *Number of Farms and Land in Farms, 1959–1970*; *Farm Numbers,* annual supplements; *Agricultural Statistics,* annual; Commercial Fertilizers: Consumption in the United States, annual; *The Balance Sheet of the Farming Sector,* annual; and *Farm Income Statistics,* annual—all published by the U.S. Government Printing Office, Washington, D.C.

[a]Preliminary data

rium. What may still provide a margin for expansion is a more deliberate use of selective forest management techniques.[22]

One limitation of wood biomass is that it is relatively heavy per unit of energy, that is, about 16,500 Btu's per kilogram, in contrast to a conventional alternative such as crude petroleum's 50,634 Btu's per kilogram. Consequently, in its original form, wood biomass possesses a serious disadvantage in terms of transportation. As one alternative, wood biomass could be converted near its source to methyl alcohol (CH_3OH), known also as methanol, which could be used as a gasoline substitute or additive as in gasohol, an antifreeze, a general solvent, or a denaturant.[23] As another alternative, wood biomass could also be used directly as a fuel to distill other biomass products with a relatively higher energy content per unit of volume. Sugar cane and the hevea rubber plant of Malaysia are but two examples of such biomass alternatives.

One other potential application of biomass energy is the direct production of hydrogen. As will be seen in chapter 8, hydrogen is appealing because of its relative abundance in nature, because it can be readily consumed as a substitute for many of the fossil and nuclear uses now operating within the economy, and because its combustion generates mostly water as the principal by-product of the heat energy released. In brief, whenever photosynthesis occurs, hydrogen normally serves to reduce the amount of carbon dioxide intake of plants in order to produce sugar. Instead of this sequence, if a plant absorbing light for photosynthesis receives a reduction in its carbon dioxide input, it will generate a greater amount of hydrogen. There are limits to the hydrogen-producing capacities of plants, to be sure, but as alternative and economically depletable resources become more expensive over time, such modified natural mechanisms may come to play a significant role in the future.

7.4. HYDROTHERMAL AND GEOTHERMAL ENERGY RESOURCES

Other sources of renewable energy are those found naturally in water and within the earth, known, respectively, as hydrothermal and geothermal energy. Hydrothermal energy derives from the temporary storage of direct solar radiation in water. In contrast, geothermal energy is released as steam heat through volcanoes, hot springs, and other fissures in the earth's mantle. Although geothermal energy is not dependent on daily solar radiation, its solar origin and relative abundance still enable one to classify it as a renewable

[22]The two dimensions of forest management, or silviculture, are (1) the selection of optimal growth species and (2) selective cutting on a periodic basis. For a recent discussion, see Stephen H. Spurr, "Silviculture," *Scientific American* 240 (February 1979):76–91.

[23]One gallon of methanol contains about 84,000 Btu's, in contrast to the 126,000 Btu's per gallon of gasoline. However, the combustion efficiency of methanol is higher than that of gasoline, and gasohol mixtures with up to 25 percent methanol can be used with only minor modifications of engines. When gross energy inputs and outputs of methanol are computed, the 172,000 Btu's of inputs yield 134,000 of output, of which 84,000 are in the methanol, and the remainder in fiber by-product, thus yielding a first law thermodynamic efficiency of 77.9 percent.

energy resource. Since neither of these resources may be sufficiently concentrated nor in forms suitable for ultimate consumption by society, we need to examine how they can be so transformed.

Water comprises over 70 percent of the earth's surface. For a yearly average surface temperature of 20°C, 2.4×10^6 joules of energy are needed to evaporate one kilogram of water. From figure 7.1, if ocean water evaporates at an annual rate of 120 centimeters, then 1.2 cubic meters, or 1,200 kilograms, of water per square meter will be evaporated. At this rate, the solar energy input per square meter of surface is the product of these two terms, of 2.9×10^9 joules per square meter. When averaged throughout a year, this would be equivalent to a power of around 92 watts per square meter.

In practical reference terms, it would take just over one hundred hectares, or 10.87 square kilometers, to obtain the equivalent of one 1,000-megawatt power plant, assuming, of course, no conversion losses. For the world as a whole, its 358 million square kilometers of sea water alone thus contain the annual potential of approximately 984,768 quads, or over three thousand times the 1980 global rate of aggregate primary energy consumption of approximately 306.97 quads. Although this energy is essential to plant and animal life on land and on sea, as well as for its provision of the gravitational hydropower already noted in section 7.1, it would take just over 0.03 percent of that energy to sustain the 1980 level of world energy consumption. The area involved to provide this equivalent amount of energy would be 111,605 square kilometers, which in absolute terms is large but in comparative terms is equal to approximately 1 percent of the land area of the United States, or roughly the size of Indiana. Moreover, even if conversion efficiency were only as high as one-third, a tripling of the required water area would still be a feasible alternative.

Hydrothermal power plants function on well-established principles, as can be seen in figure 7.6.[24] In an open-cycle plant, differences between surface water and deep water as large as 15°C are sufficient to boil water essential to the flow of steam to turn the rotors of an electricity-generating turbine. Since surface-water temperatures are below the normal boiling point, when a vacuum pump is used to reduce atmospheric pressure to around 3 percent of its normal level, that is, down to 0.46 pounds per square inch of area, boiling can be achieved. However, the reduced pressure of the steam requires that its volume to the turbine be almost four thousand times that of a conventional power plant. Thus, while an open-cycle plant does not require any artificial fluids, its net energy is generated only at a Second Law thermodynamic efficiency of around 3 percent, well below the 33–40 percent found in conventional fossil and nuclear power plants.

In a closed-cycle hydrothermal plant, a boiler utilizes a recirculating vaporizing fluid such as ammonia, propane, or freon. When such a fluid is passed through the boiler, it absorbs heat and is vaporized so that it can turn the

[24]Hydrothermal power also has had a long list of advocates, dating back to the Frenchman Jacques d'Arsonval in 1881, and the French engineer Georges Claude in Cuba in 1930.

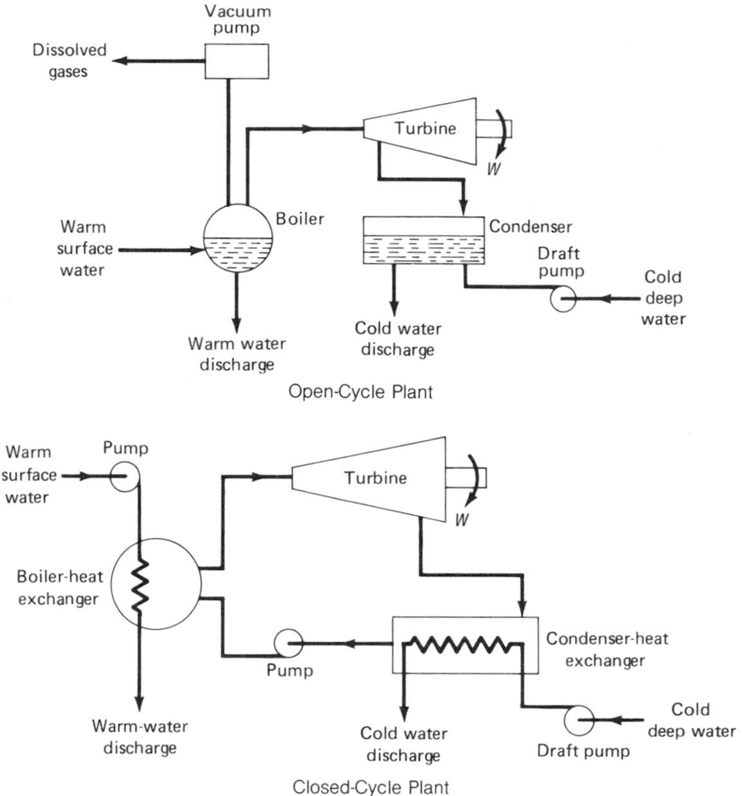

Figure 7.6. The Structure of a Hydrothermal Electricity Plant. *Top*, an open-cycle plant; *bottom*, a closed-cycle plant. Adapted from Jerrold H. Krenz, *Energy: Conversion and Utilization* (Boston: Allyn and Bacon, 1976), pp. 273, 275.

rotors of the electricity turbine, after which it is recondensed by cold deep water. The advantage of a closed-cycle plant is that the vapor pressures of ammonia and propane are about ten times those of a conventional power plant. However, large heat exchangers are necessary to attain the comparable net energy flows of both a conventional power plant and that of an open-cycle system.

As already noted, hydrothermal generating plants represent a significant source of renewable energy. Not only could they be used to generate electricity for distribution to conventional power grids already in place but they could also be used for energy storage and conversion, as in the production of hydrogen. At present there are four experimental hydrothermal power plants, each with a net power capacity of between 100 and 400 megawatts. Aside from economic considerations, the principal technical constraints involved in the expansion of hydrothermal plants are: biofouling (that is, loss of operational efficiency because of water impurities); corrosion of generating, distribution, and mooring equipment; jurisdictional issues surrounding plant sitings; and alteration of the hydrologic equilibrium of the environment. Each of these factors must be included in any assessment of the economic efficiency of hydrothermal power.

Geothermal energy is released from within the earth at a rate of around 0.063 watts per square meter. On a global level this translates into a power rate of 3.2134×10^{13} watts, which over a year's time would provide 2.81498×10^{17} watt-hours, or 960.7 quads. Most of this energy results from the cooling of magma within the earth's core; the remainder comes from the thermal by-product of the dcecay of natural radioisotopes such as ^{238}U (uranium), ^{232}Th (thorium), and ^{40}K (potassium). A quick reflection on the alternative sources of energy already noted shows that this is a far smaller power source than that available from direct solar radiation, gravitational hydropower, or even hydrothermal power. Indeed, 960.7 quads per year would amount to only 3.13 times the 1980 level of world energy consumption from conventional fossil, hydro-, and nuclear power sources. Nevertheless, there are certain areas where geological fissures release steam at higher than average rates, as can be seen in figure 7.7 Within these regions, geothermal energy can be used on a significant scale for direct space and water heating, as well as for the generation of electricity.

The flow of geothermal energy is in four basic forms: dry and wet steam, hot brine, and hot rock. Hot rocks contain the greatest energy abundance, followed by hot brine, wet steam, and dry steam, respectively. This same ranking also reflects the relative difficulty of tapping and utilizing these energy flows within the economy.[25] Thus, dry steam, the least abundant, is also the form most readily suited for consumption within the economy. In fact, of all developed sources of geothermal energy, only dry steam (in Italy, California, and Japan) and wet steam (in New Zealand and Mexico) have been brought into any significant degree of commercial use. As of 1975, the electric power capacity of all of these operations amounted to 1,172 megawatts, a level just over the size of one modern fossil or nuclear power plant, and only 3.647×10^{-5} percent of ultimate geothermal capacity.

With the famous springs in Bath, England, geothermal energy use dates back to the Romans. Presently, the cities of Reykjavik, Iceland; Boise, Idaho; and Klamath Falls, Oregon, are among those that rely partly on geothermal energy for residential heating. However, the greatest application of geothermal energy lies in the generation of electricity.

Like hydrothermal plants, geothermal plants function according to well-known principles (see figure 7.8). In a dry-steam plant, geothermal energy is used to convert a closed water flow into steam for the generation of electricity. In turn, the steam is condensed back into water by an alternative cool water source or other cooling medium. In an open-cycle system, wet steam,

[25]Hot rock is found at depths of 3,050 meters (10,000 feet), dry steam at 2,440 meters (8,000 feet), hot brine at 370 meters (4,500 feet), and wet steam at 915 meters (3,000 feet). Hot rock reaches temperatures up to 400°C; hot brine, temperatures of 240°C; wet steam, 230°C; and dry steam, 200°C. Thermodynamic efficiency, combined with relative purity and depth of drilling, yields these rankings.

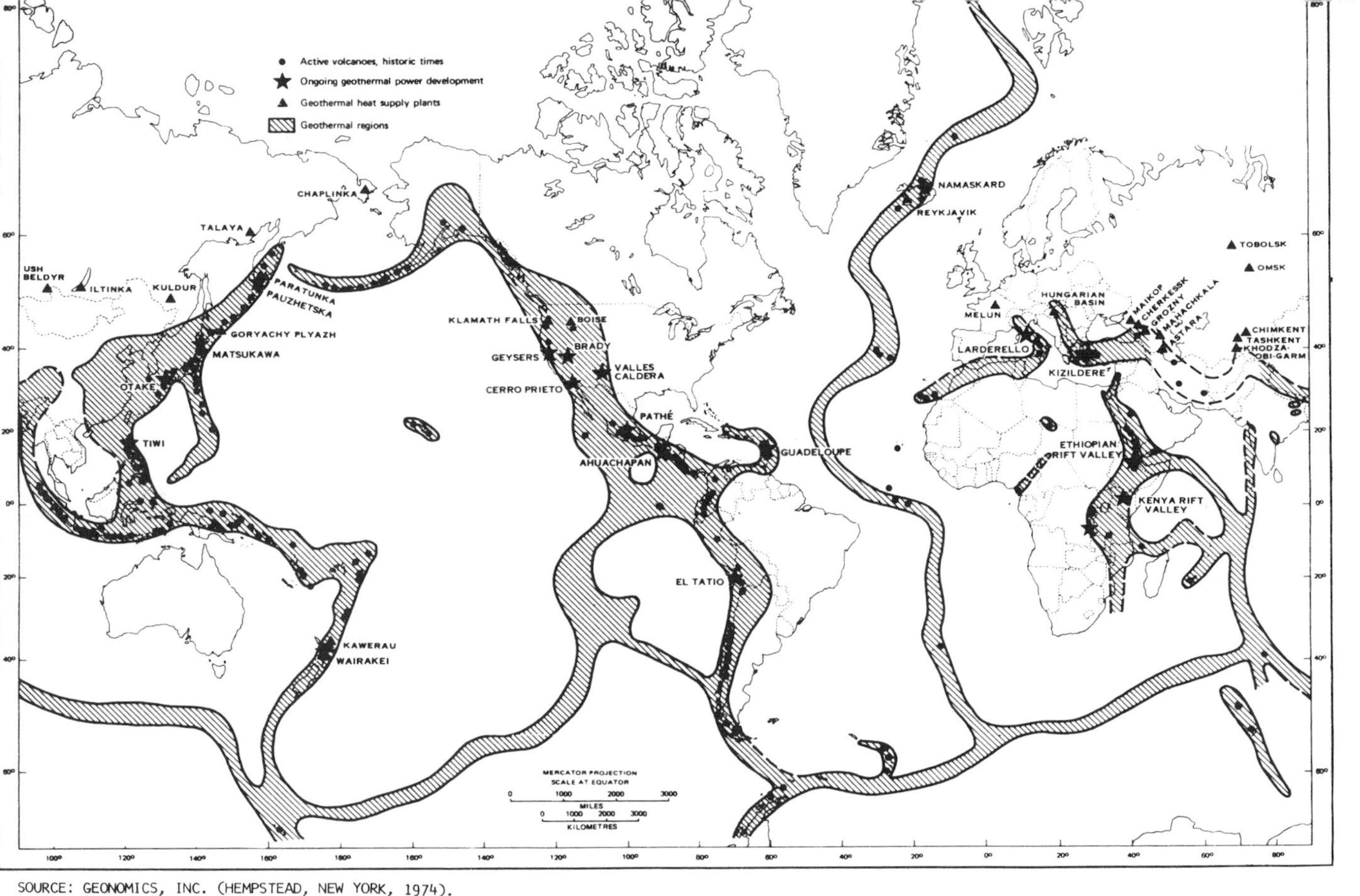

SOURCE: GEONOMICS, INC. (HEMPSTEAD, NEW YORK, 1974).

Figure 7.7. Geothermal Regions of the World. From the Futures Group, *A Technology Assessment of Geothermal Energy Resource Development* (Washington, D.C.: National Science Foundation, 15 April 1975), p. 220.

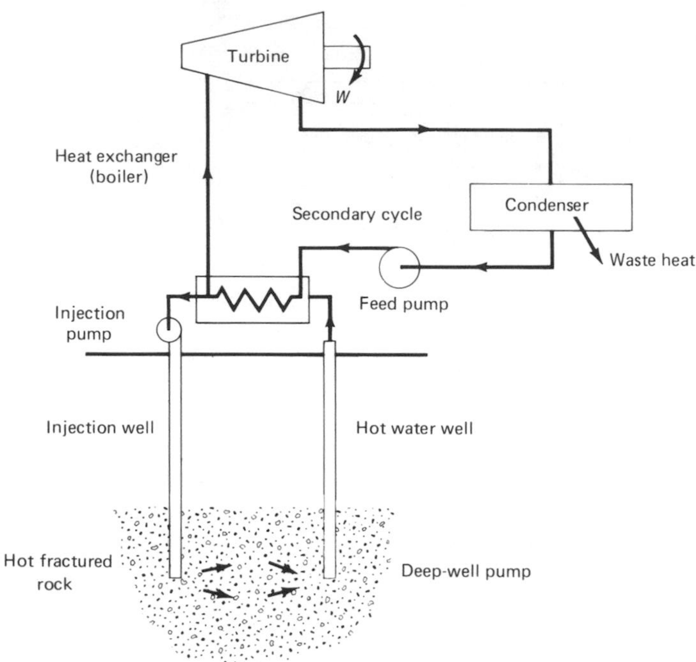

Figure 7.8. The Structure of a Closed-Cycle Geothermal Electricity Plant. Adapted from Krenz, *Energy: Conversion and Utilization*, p. 291.

which generally contains impurities such as sulfur, is first cleansed via a centrifugal separator. High-pressure, purified steam then serves as a direct source of generator power, while hot water rejected by the separator can be recycled and injected in a second stage as low-pressure steam. Second Law thermodynamic efficiency of such multistage systems can reach as high as 28 percent, which is just under that of alternative conventional modes of electricity generation already noted.

Expansion of geothermal electricity generation involves several technical considerations. First, the purification of geothermal energy invariably releases quantities of hydrogen sulfide gas, which is both noxious and corrosive. Second, higher water intake levels are needed to compensate for the lower thermodynamic efficiency of geothermal plants in comparison with their conventional counterparts. Unless it is reinjected into the ground, as is done at such plants as the Geysers' in California, alternative water uses are reduced, and atmospheric moisture increased. Third, acceleration of geothermal releases may also increase the probability of seismic disturbances, especially in earthquake-prone regions such as California. Against these constraints and their associated social costs stand the environmentally polluting qualities of conventional power plants and their economically depletable resource base, factors that add much to the potential economic efficiency of geothermal energy.

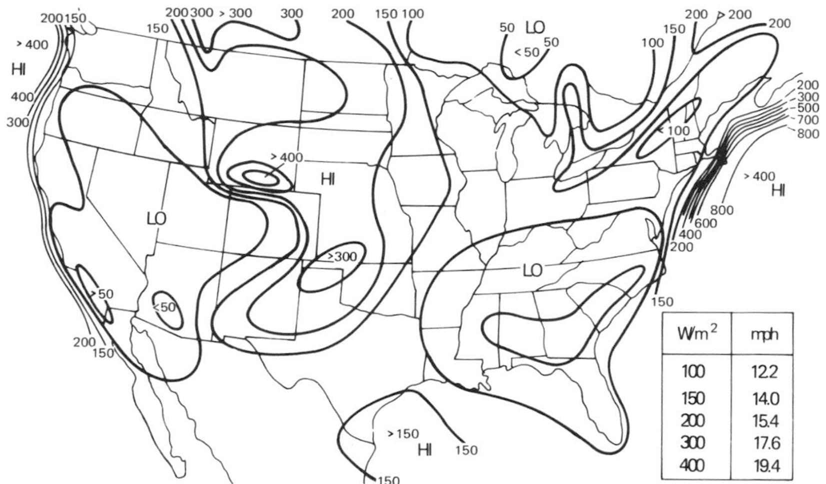

Figure 7.9. The Distribution of Wind Energy Potential in the United States. From J. W. Reed, "Wind Climatology," in *Second Workshop on Wind Energy Conversion Systems*, ed. F. R. Eldridge, NSF-RA-N-75-050 (Washington, D.C.: National Science Foundation, 1975), pp. 319, 325, reprinted in David R. Inglis, *Wind Power and Other Energy Options* (Ann Arbor: University of Michigan Press, 1978), p. 50.

7.5. WIND ENERGY

As any reader of Don Quixote can attest, wind power does much to stir one's imagination. Indeed, wind power once formed the principal mode of water transport, as well as provided a substantial share of mechanical energy in favorable regions such as the Netherlands and in the Iberian peninsula itself. However, the difficulty with wind power is its inconstancy, a factor which is all too well known to any sailor and which has inhibited its much broader application until now.

Of the direct solar radiation absorbed by the earth within its atmosphere, around 20 percent is converted into winds, waves, convection, and currents. Of this amount, winds account for around 2×10^{13} watts.[26] When this rate is converted into its annual potential of 597.57 quads, it represents an energy source that is just under two times the 1980 level of world energy consumption from conventional resources. The relevant question at this point is, to what extent can this wind potential be used as an alternative to the present world dependence on its economically depletable conventional resources?

The U.S. distribution of wind energy potential is illustrated in figure 7.9. When regional differences are taken into account, estimates of the net potential for the United States as a whole range between 1.29×10^{12} and 1.54×10^{12} kilowatt-hours per year, a capacity which in theory at least could satisfy

[26]This estimate is based on Palmer C. Putnam, *Power from the Wind* (New York: Van Nostrand Reinhold Co., 1948), p. 209. Putnam's work is considered a classic in the field.

approximately two-thirds of all electrical consumption in the United States during 1980.[27] To determine the number of windmills necessary to attain that capacity, we need to spell out briefly the measurement of power from an individual windmill.

The power of any windmill is a function of several basic variables, namely, air density, volume, velocity, rotor diameter, and the pitch of the blades. In its simplest terms, the power is equivalent to the difference between kinetic energy entering the windmill and that which passes from its exhaust stream. As the following will show, there is an upper limit consistent with the laws of thermodynamics that prevents any windmill from converting 100 percent of any wind flow to a usable energy form.

As a first step in the measurement of wind power, the kinetic energy of an airflow can be expressed as

$$E = \tfrac{1}{2}\rho V^2 \text{ joules per cubic meter,} \tag{7.9}$$

where ρ is the density of air, that is, its kilogram unit mass divided by its cubic-meter volume,[28] and V^2 is the square of the meters-per-second velocity of air. In turn, when a volume of air moves one meter, we can derive the available power per square meter of air as

$$\begin{aligned} P &= EV \\ &= \tfrac{1}{2}\rho V^3 \text{ watts per square meter.} \end{aligned} \tag{7.10}$$

However, not all wind energy can be converted to power, nor in the case of rotary windmills can it be expressed in simple cubic-meter blocks. Consequently, equation (7.10) can be thought of as a level of gross flow of wind energy that must be adjusted downward to determine available energy from a cylindrical air flow passing through a windmill's rotors. Thus, equation (7.10) can be redefined as

$$P = 2\pi r^2 \rho V_e^3 a(1 - a)^2, \tag{7.11}$$

where πr^2 is the cylindrical volume of air, in cubic meters; ρ is the density of air; V_e^3 is the cube of the velocity of entering air; and a is the axial interference of the windmill rotors, defined by the pitch of the blades, as well as their number, width, and thickness. When the rate of change in power is computed as a function of axial interference, it is possible to determine the

[27]U.S. Library of Congress, Science Policy Research Division, *Energy Facts* (Washington, D.C.: U.S. Government Printing Office, 1973); and Joseph M. Savino, ed., *Wind Energy Conversion Systems: Workshop Proceedings* (Washington, D.C.: National Science Foundation, June 1973).

[28]The density of air is defined as the kilogram-denominated atomic number of the mass, which is divided by its cubic-meter volume. The volume of air is determined by the product of 8.3144×10^7 ergs per molecule degree Centigrade (which is the ideal gas constant) and the absolute temperature, which is then divided by the atmospheric pressure, measured in newtons. As an illustration, if 20°C air with an atmospheric pressure of 1.01×10^5 newtons per square meter is available, the volume of air will be 24.1 cubic meters. Since the kilogram-denominated atomic number of air is approximately 29, the density of air at this pressure and temperature is 1.2 kilograms per cubic meter, or 29/24.1.

most efficient degree of axial interference needed to obtain the maximum power from a given wind flow.[29] It turns out that this occurs when the coefficient, a, has a value of ⅓, which when inserted into equation (7.11) yields

$$P_{max} = 2\pi r^2 \rho V_e^3 \, ⅓ \, (1 - ⅓)^2 \tag{7.12}$$
$$= (8/27) \, \pi r^2 \rho V_e^3.$$

The theoretical net efficiency of a given windmill is then defined as the ratio of its maximum output to its actual output, or:[30]

$$\Omega = \frac{P_{max}}{P_{actual}} \tag{7.13}$$
$$= \frac{8/27 \, \pi r^2 \rho V_e^3}{1/2 \pi r^2 \rho V_e^3}$$
$$= 16/27 = 0.5926 = 59.3 \text{ percent.}$$

Because of mechanical limitations in energy conversion, actual efficiency of any windmill generally will not exceed half of the maximum, which translates into a more typical rate of 29.7 percent.

As an illustration of the preceding principles, consider the power of a windmill that has a radius of 12 meters, a wind velocity of 8 meters a second (17.9 miles per hour), and a density of 1.2 kilograms per cubic meter of air. Using equation (7.12), the maximum power would be 82.36 kilowatts, of which actual efficiency would attain around half that rate, or 41.18 kilowatts.[31] Similarly, if we have data on wind velocity, it is possible to determine the required radius of a windmill. Once this has been compared with mechanical stress capabilities of building materials, we can also derive the number of windmills needed to attain a desired amount of power. To continue the example, if it turned out that the actual rotor radius was the most technically efficient (which it is not), then in order to satisfy the approximately 620.2 million-kilowatt electricity capacity of the United States in 1980, we would need about 15.1 million windmills, a figure far in excess of the estimated capacity of wind power already noted, and likely to cause Don Quixote to roll over in his grave. However, if we adopted the ceiling wind-power figure of 1.54×10^{12} kilowatt-hours already cited, then this capacity could be accomplished with a much more modest number of windmills, in the neighborhood of 4.3 million. What is even more to the point, though, is that present-day proposals would call for much greater sizes and the use of combined-cycle windmills such that the required number could be well under 1 million.

Several types of windmills are illustrated in figure 7.10. Some of them, such as the Savonius / ϕ-Darrieus combination windmill, can attain efficiencies of as high as 35 percent. While windmill proposals have extended across a

[29]The partial derivative of power with respect to the coefficient, a, yields a quadratic, which when set equal to zero results in a most efficient value of a, at 1/3: $dp/da = 1 - 4a + 3a^2 = 0$.

[30]The denominator expression is a redefinition of equation (7.10), in which the volume of air is based on a cylindrical flow, as it is in the efficiency equation (7.11).

[31]$P = (8/27)\,\pi \times 1.2 \times (12)^2 \times (8)^3 = 82.36$.

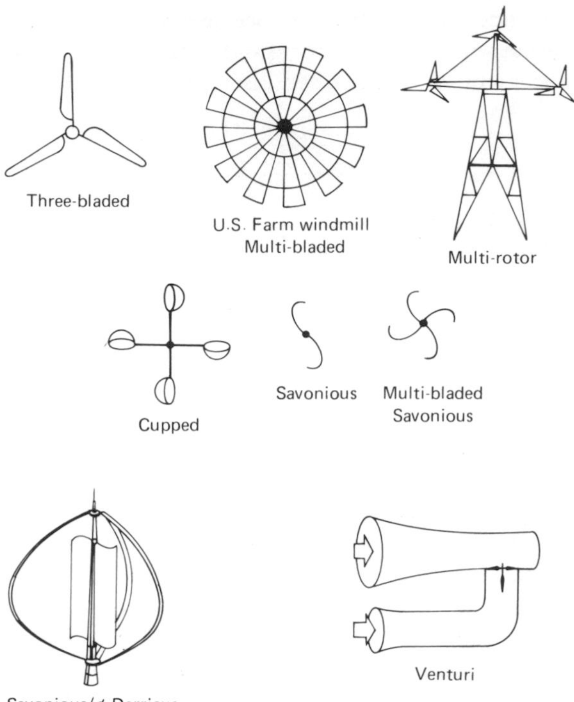

Figure 7.10. Alternative Windmill Configurations. From National Science Foundation, Division of Advanced Energy and Resources Research and Technology, *Wind Machines* (Washington, D.C.: U.S. Government Printing Office, October 1975), pp. 18–19.

broad range of applications from individual residential systems to large-scale electricity-generating units, they all have in common the substitution of this renewable energy resource for the fossil and nuclear fuels presently depended upon. Economics aside at this point, what they all lack is both a constant flow of power and a means of energy storage. For these reasons, most applications now under consideration involve the conversion of wind energy from its mechanical or electrical kinetic forms to the various kinds of stored-energy modes illustrated in figure 7.11. Since these alternative storage mechanisms are analyzed in chapter eight, we can now turn to the last major renewable energy resource, tidal power.

7.6. TIDAL POWER

Tidal power, the variation in water elevation of rivers and oceans, is caused by solar and lunar gravitational forces as the earth rotates on its axis and revolves around the sun. As pointed out in chapter 4, though not on the scale of direct solar radiation, tidal power is nevertheless a significant renewable energy resource. With a power rate of 3×10^{12} watts, it could provide in a year's time about one-third of the world's 1980 level of energy consumption from existing conventional resources. Like other renewable resources, however, tidal power is kinetic energy. Given that its flow is not always constant, it must be converted into an alternative stored energy form if it is to be economically competitive.

Despite the theoretical potential of tidal power, in most large open bodies of water the effects are so dispersed that the available energy is relatively inconsequential. In fact, only where there is a significant flow of water through a narrow passage can tidal variations become significant enough to consider technical applications. This means that the net power potential from tidal

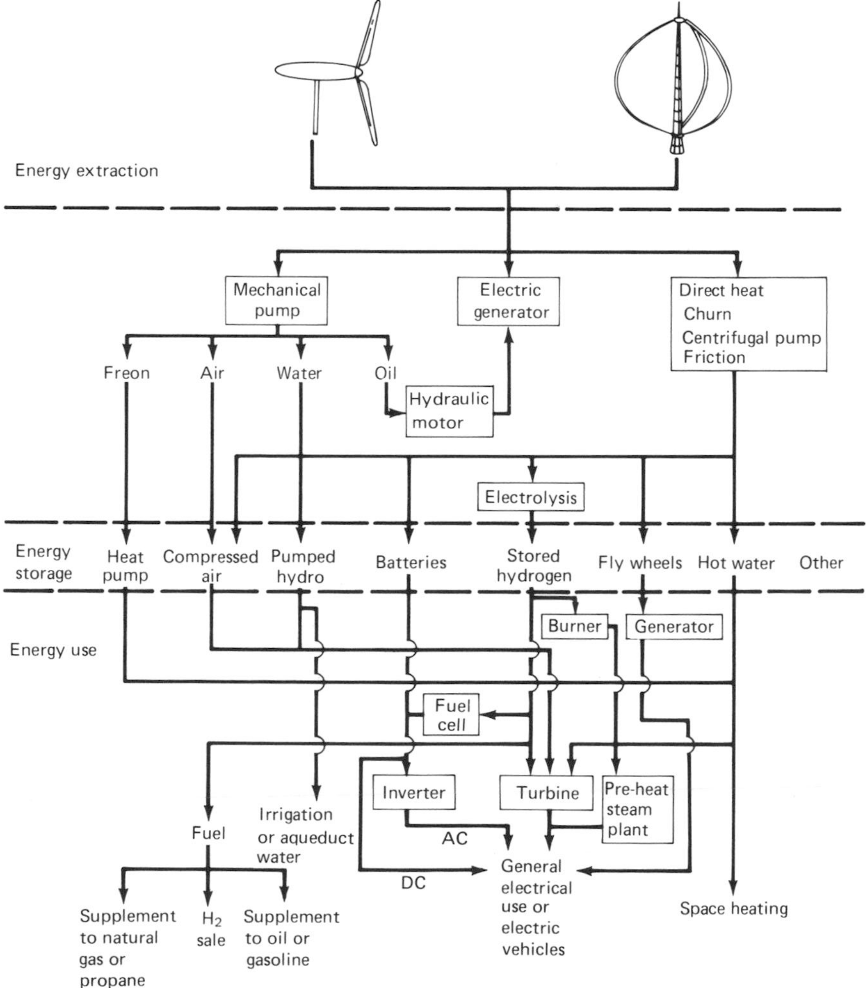

Figure 7.11. Wind Energy Alternative Applications. From National Science Foundation, Division of Advanced Energy and Resources Research and Technology, *Wind Machines*, p. 34.

power may be no greater than 10^{12} watts.[32] For all practical purposes, it also means that the most universal application of tidal power is likely to be the generation of electricity, since electricity can be readily transported and converted into a stored-energy form. Within this context we can identify briefly how tidal power is measured and discuss some of the applications already adopted or currently under consideration.

The strongest gravitational force affecting the tides is the moon. Typically, in a given period of twenty-four hours and fifty minutes, there are two high and two low tides. Since this period is greater than a day, the timing of the highs and lows will oscillate around a cycle that is completed every fourteen and three-quarter days. Larger variations in this pattern occur when the sun and the moon act together. When their gravitational force is in the same direction, it corresponds to the time of the new moon. When in the opposite direction, it corresponds to the time of the full moon. As these positions shift in cyclical fashion, the conversion of the tidal flows into electricity requires that the water pass through the rotors of a generator placed in a dam, or barrage, at the mouth of a stream.

In more systematic terms, tidal power is a function of the volume of water, the variation in height, and the gravitational constant. We can express the potential energy from these variables as

$$dE = yg\rho A dy \tag{7.14}$$

where y is the height of a tidal dam, in meters; g is the gravitational constant, 9.8 meters per second squared; ρ is the density of water, 1.025×10^3 kilograms per cubic meter; A is the surface area of the tidal passage water, in square meters; and dy is the vertical distance of the tidal range, in meters. If the tidal dam has perfectly vertical sides, then the maximum energy available is determined as

$$E_{max} = \tfrac{1}{2}\, g\rho A(dy)^2. \tag{7.15}$$

Over a period of twenty-four hours and fifty minutes, there will be four tidal flows; this enables us to measure the amount of power generated as

$$P = \frac{4[\tfrac{1}{2} g\rho A(dy)^2]}{8.92 \times 10^4 \text{ seconds}}. \tag{7.16}$$

As an illustration, if a water basin has a surface area of 5 kilometers by 15 kilometers, and a tidal range of 2 meters, then the daily power from this system would be 65,910,000 watts, or 65.91 megawatts.[33] When this figure is adjusted downward to around one-quarter of this level, to reflect the actual thermodynamic efficiency, the actual power would amount to 16.48 megawatts.

[32]This estimate is provided by W. H. Munk and G. J. F. MacDonald, *The Rotation of the Earth* (Cambridge: Cambridge University Press, 1960), p. 219.

[33]In this equation, power is computed as

$$\frac{4/2(1.025 \times 10^3)(9.8)(7.5 \times 10^7)(2)^2}{8.92 \times 10^4} = 65{,}910{,}000 \text{ watts.}$$

Table 7.4. Dimensions of World Tidal Power Sites

Site	Tidal Range, R (m)	Basin Area, A (km^2)	Power, P (MeW)	Dam Length, L (m)	L/A (m/km^2)	L/P (m/MW)
La Rance, France[a]	11.4	22.0	160.0	725.0	33.0	4.5
Kislogrub, U.S.S.R.[a]	4.0	2.0	1.8	30.5	15.0	16.9
Brest, France	6.4	92.0	211.0	3,640.0	40.0	17.3
Chausey, France	12.4	610.0	5,252.0	23,500.0	39.0	4.5
Severn, England	11.5	50.0	370.0	3,500.0	70.0	9.5
Pasamaquoddy, Maine, U.S.A.	7.5	120.0	378.0	4,270.0	36.0	11.3
Bay of Fundy, Cobequid, Canada	11.0	700.0	4,743.0	8,000.0	11.4	1.7

Source: R. C. Dorf, *Energy, Resources, and Policy* (Reading, Mass.: Addision-Wesley Publishing Co., 1978), p. 282.

[a]Operational

Several types of tidal power plants can be used to obtain the maximum degree of efficiency from a given site. In a single-basin plant, water is accumulated during the rising tide and released through the generators when the basin tide has reached a maximum height in relation to the surrounding water. Greater efficiency is achieved with a two-way flow system, in which reversible generators produce electricity with the tidal flow in each direction. The most complex of all systems is a two-way flow system operating on a double basin. The second basin stores water for generating electricity during peak periods, much like the pumped-storage hydroelectric system discussed in section 7.1. When all of these configurations are taken into account, the practical question for energy policy is, to what extent do they determine the most feasible sites for the construction of tidal power plants?

Table 7.4 lists some of the most efficient sites for tidal power plants throughout the world. As is indicated, thus far only two of these plants have been constructed, and they are far from the largest. The underlying economic dimensions of these plants are suggested in the ratios of dam length to water basin area and of dam length to actual power output. Clearly, the lower these ratios, the lower will be any capital and operating costs. While such sites as the Passamaquoddy, Maine, basin's 378 megawatts would represent but a fraction of the approximately 620.2 gigawatts of installed capacity of the United States as of 1980, they could still become economically competitive with locally available alternatives. Ultimately, then, it is the relative pricing of resources based on their social costs and benefits that will determine the mix of renewable and depletable energy resource technologies.

7.7. SUMMARY

Renewable energy resources are among the oldest and most abundant yet least used in the U.S. and world economies. The appeal of renewable energy resources is that in their relative abundance they do not constitute an eco-

Table 7.5. U.S. Annual Gross Renewable Energy Potential

Renewable Resource	Watts	Distribution
Hydropower	2.0×10^{11}	0.0001
Direct solar energy	1650.0×10^{12}	0.9989
Biomass energy[a]	3.7×10^{9}	2.24×10^{-6}
Hydrothermal power[b]	9.5×10^{11}	0.0006
Geothermal energy	5.8×10^{11}	0.0003
Wind energy	1.4×10^{11}	0.0001
Tidal energy	1.0×10^{10}	6.05×10^{-6}
Total[c]	1.7×10^{15}	1.0000 (= 100%)

Note: Unless otherwise noted, all estimates are those identified in the chapter.

[a]Derived by multiplying the rate of photosynthetic energy by the gross amount of U.S. farmland, in square meters, as computed from table 7.3

[b]Determined by multiplying the amount of hydrothermal energy per square meter by the 200-mile offshore water equivalent of the ocean coastline of the United States

[c]1.49×10^{19} watt-hours per year; $50{,}826 \times 10^{15}$ Btu's, or 50,826 quads, per year

nomically exhaustible stock of energy. What has discouraged a much greater use of these resources until now is that they are all based on kinetic flows which do not always match the rates of consumption in the economy. Moreover, renewable energy resources do not often exist in forms that correspond to the patterns of energy demand within the economy.

Technology can convert both the forms and the rate of production of renewable energy flows into patterns that are compatible with the structure of energy use in the economy. As has been seen, this means essentially the storage of gravitational and thermal energy, the production of electricity, and the implied conversion of renewable electricity production into alternative forms of energy storage. All of these technologies have demonstrated a competitive thermodynamic efficiency, and some of them, such as photovoltaic cells, may provide an even larger advantage in the next few years.

In comparison with fossil and nuclear fuels, renewable energy resources are found in relative abundance. As can be seen in table 7.5, the Btu equivalent of renewable energy each year is 8.5 times the presently known recoverable stock of fossil fuel reserves listed in chapter 5, and 127 times the presently known recoverable stock of nuclear energy reserves under conventional fission technology. What this suggests is that beyond some point, the relative importance of renewable energy resources must inevitably increase.

Two basic considerations affect the accelerated use of renewable energy resources. One of them is economic, which is discussed in part III. The other is the capacity for energy storage and conversion. Many of these storage and conversion systems are already in use in conventional energy consumption. Beyond these systems are still other types of storage and conversion that will ultimately affect the economic efficiency of renewable energy resources. A closer examination of these alternative storage and conversion technologies is taken up in chapter 8.

SUGGESTED READINGS

Daniels, Farrington. *Direct Use of the Sun's Energy.* New York: Ballantine Books, 1974.

Gray, T. J., and Gashus, O. K., eds. *Tidal Power.* New York: Plenum Press, 1972.

Inglis, David R. *Wind Power and Other Energy Options.* Ann Arbor: University of Michigan Press, 1978.

Knight, H. G., Nyhart, J. D., and Stein, R. E. *Ocean Thermal Energy Conversion.* Lexington, Mass.: Lexington Books, 1977.

Meinel, Aden Baker, and Meinel, Marjorie Pettit. *Applied Solar Energy: An Introduction.* Reading, Mass.: Addison-Wesley Publishing Co., 1976.

Milora, S. L., and Tester, J. W. *Geothermal Energy as a Source of Electric Power.* Cambridge, Mass.: MIT Press, 1976.

Robertson, E. E. *Bioconversion.* Philadelphia: Franklin Institute Press, 1977.

8

ALTERNATIVE ENERGY STORAGE AND CONVERSION TECHNOLOGIES

Virtually all of the many forms of energy now consumed within the economy depend ultimately on three primary sources: the fossil fuels of coal, petroleum, and natural gas; nuclear power; and renewable energy resources. At the same time, as both the laws of thermodynamics and historical energy use have shown, the use of any of these fuels involves considerable inefficiency. The laws of thermodynamics rule out the possibility of 100 percent efficiency, but much of the actual inefficiency is attributable to chosen modes of energy storage and conversion. What is needed, therefore, is a closer examination of the role of energy storage and conversion in the attainment of technical efficiency in energy use.

A desirable characteristic of any energy resource is that it be in as low an entropy state as possible. Indeed, much of the historical attraction of fossil and nuclear fuels has been that they possess this orderly property to a considerable degree. However, since these resources do not everywhere correspond to the end uses of energy within the economy, it is in their storage and conversion phases that so much of the economy's energy inefficiency arises. Since the world economy is presently so dependent on economically depletable resources, these storage and conversion qualities take on a particular importance in the determination of appropriate energy policies.

As long as it is in either a solid, a liquid, or a gas stock form, energy can be stored by one means or another. When it is converted into a flow, as in light or electricity, no storage is possible except by temporary transformation into an alternative stock form. Many of the conventional storage modes of energy are already obvious: gasoline stocks, coal deposits, pipeline natural gas, to name but a few. It is also possible to store liquid and gas fossil fuel by compression, to store mechanical energy by the use of flywheels, and to store electrical-to-chemical energy in batteries as well as in hydrogen (all of these are summarized in table 8.1). Since these mechanisms are not as widely used as are conventional storage systems, we will examine them here in terms of their potential for raising the level of current energy conservation.

Table 8.1. Capacities of Alternative Energy Storage Systems

System	Maximum Energy Storage Density (in watt-hours per Kg)
Air Compression	7.7
Flywheel	
Aluminun alloy	21.0
4340 steel	33.2
Maraging steel	48.0
E-glass	190.0
Carbon fiber	215.0
S-glass	265.0
PRD-49 ("Kevlon")	350.0
Fused silica	870.0
Battery	
Aqueous electrolyte	
Lead-acid	34.6
Nickel-iron	45.5
Nickel-iron	55.0
Nickel-zinc	66.4
Nickel-hydrogen	80.5
Zinc-bromide	89.1
Zinc-chloride	90.9
Organic	
Lithium-sulfur	225.0
Lithium-bromide	229.0
High-temperature	
Sodium-sulfur	142.0
Lithium-tellurium-tetrachloride	232.0
Aluminum-chlorine	296.0
Lithium-sulfur	318.0
Metal-air	
Cadmium	119.0
Iron	253.0
Zinc	279.0
Manganese	304.0
Chromium	542.0
Sodium	747.0
Calcium	943.0
Titanium	983.0
Magnesium	1,405.0
Aluminum	1,690.0
Lithium	2,748.0
Berylium	3,701.0
Hydrogen	7,725.0

Source: R. F. Post and S. W. Post, "Flywheels," *Scientific American* 229 (December 1973): 20; R. C. Dorf, *Energy, Resources, and Policy* (Reading, Mass.: Addison-Wesley Publishing Co., 1978), p. 362; and S. W. Angrist, *Direct Energy Conversion*, 3d ed. (Boston: Allyn and Bacon, 1976), pp. 45–53.

The second stage in which the technical efficiency of energy use is critically affected is in the conversion of one form of energy to another. Perhaps the greatest change occurs in the conversion of any fossil or nuclear resource into electricity. Under conventional technology, central generating plants consume hydro-, fossil, and nuclear power to generate electricity, which in turn is distributed to its end uses as light, thermal, sound, and mechanical energy. Beyond this system, and the emerging use of photovoltaic cells noted in chapter 7, four technologies are of general interest to energy conversion, and to electricity production in particular: the heat pump, waste recycling, magnetohydrodynamics, and fuel cells. Following an analysis of alternative storage mechanisms, each of these conversion technologies will be discussed in turn.

8.1. COMPRESSION ENERGY STORAGE

The principle of compression energy storage can be readily understood in reference to fossil fuels and the laws of thermodynamics. One of the properties that makes petroleum and natural gas economically useful as combustion fuels is that they exist generally in naturally pressurized, underground deposits. Because they are so pressurized, the energy needed for their extraction is relatively small, at least in the early stages. Moreover, in the case of natural gas, pressurization at the surface level is essential if enough energy is to be concentrated per unit of mass for relative ease of transport and consumption. In fact, as noted in chapter 5, in the case of long-distance transfers between points of extraction and consumption, the storage of natural gas under such compression as to yield a liquefied form has made the use of imported natural gas in the United States and other major consuming countries more attractive.[1] Thus, a higher energy density per unit of volume already governs many conventional applications of energy utilization within the economy.

Though conventional compression mechanisms are essential to present levels of efficiency in the use of fossil fuels, there are several alternative applications which could raise these levels closer to their thermodynamic limits. One of them is the use of mechanical compression during off-peak periods of electricity generation.

As noted in chapter 7, the variation in electricity consumption throughout the day, week, and season requires that a considerable degree of slack be built into each conventional large-scale generating plant. Peak-load pricing and the use of pumped-storage hydropower are two ways to accommodate the variation in electricity consumption rates. However, short of significant changes in the structure of the economy's patterns of production and consumption, even with the use of pumped-storage auxiliary systems, hydropower generation could at best meet only a fraction of electricity generation requirements. The reasons are simple enough: first, too few sites are suited for the expansion of hydroelectric and pumped-storage systems, and second, environmental constraints aside, ultimate hydroelectric capacity would amount to only 35 percent of the 1980 installed capacity from all conventional resources.

Alternative compression storage for the generation of electricity can be

[1] See Elizabeth Drake and Robert C. Reid, "The Importation of Liquefied Natural Gas," *Scientific American* 236 (April 1977):21–29.

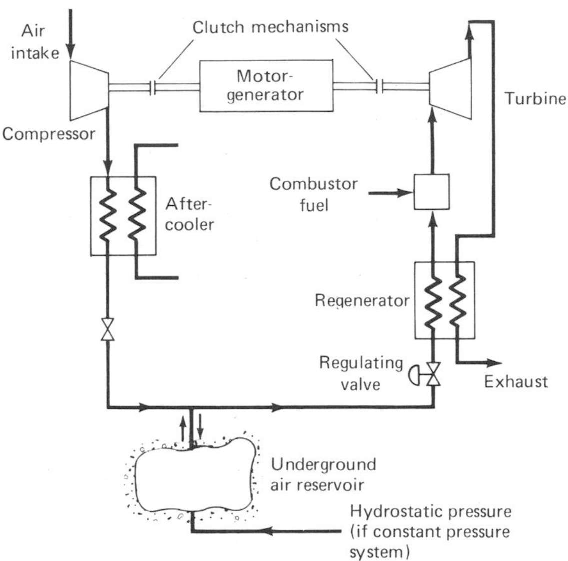

Figure 8.1. A Compressed-Air Energy Storage System. Adapted from S. W. Angrist, *Direct Energy Conversion*, 3d ed. (Boston: Allyn and Bacon, 1976), p. 61.

achieved with air or with any gas that is suitable for the operation of an electrical generator. Since gases are either relatively rare or more useful as energy resources themselves, the most likely candidate for compression is air itself. In a compressed-air storage system of the kind illustrated in figure 8.1, a conventionally fueled compressor is used to pump air into a large-scale container. A regulating valve releases the compressed air through a regenerator, where it can then be mixed with a combustor fuel to attain the maximum heat and pressure needed to drive an electrical turbine. Compressed air would be accumulated during off-peak hours and released during maximum-use periods, much as occurs in a pumped-storage hydroelectric system.

The key factor in a compressed-air system is the availability of a storage container. Though containers could be constructed, the easiest solution would be to make use of the many types of underground cavities already in place. They include dissolved salt caverns, porous underground reservoirs, depleted gas and oil fields, and abandoned mines already suitably dispersed for an efficient integration into present patterns of electricity energy distribution. Constant pressure within these cavities could be provided by hydrostatic adjustment, that is, the shifting of underground water deposits that are generally not critical to the surface variation in the earth's hydrologic equilibrium.[2]

[2]The hydrologic equilibrium illustrated in figure 7.1 does not show the many lags involved in the evaporation-precipitation cycle. There are large, deep-level deposits of water that are not frequently recycled through evaporation-precipitation, even though they may well move within underground circulation systems. For a discussion of the behavior and potential uses of these underground water deposits, or aquifers, see R. B. Ambroggi, "Underground Reservoirs to Control the Water Cycle," *ibid.*, 236 (May 1977):21–27.

Within the United States at least, there are presently no known air-compression electricity-generating systems. However, studies have been undertaken on the technical feasibility of such systems. For the United States and other countries, as depletable energy resources are consumed, and the relative prices of those resources increases over time, compressed-air electricity-generating systems are likely to become economically competitive. Just how significant these systems could become depends not only on the relative price of energy but also on the magnitude and distribution of underground cavities, for which no known comprehensive survey has yet been undertaken.[3]

8.2. FLYWHEEL ENERGY STORAGE

Another area of inefficiency in energy use is in the acceleration and deceleration of motors from their optimal levels of operation. As urban automobile commuters know all too well, fuel efficiency is drastically affected by traffic conditions that lower average operating speed. The inefficiency encountered in conventional electricity generation is yet another example. For both of these forms of consumption, flywheels could substantially reduce the amount of energy that is now rejected into the environment.

The flywheel is one of the oldest known machines. The energy-storage principle behind it is fairly straightforward. The centrifugal, or outward directional, force of a rotating wheel is stored within its circular mass as inertial energy. The amount of this energy will vary according to the square of the speed of rotation, or velocity, and the tensile, or resistance, strength of the material from which the wheel is made.[4] Thus, a higher velocity of rotation will store more energy per unit of mass, but the upper limit of energy storage is that amount of energy which will cause the wheel material to disintegrate.

Until recently, most flywheel designs used commonly available high-strength steel for short-run, stop-and-go regenerative braking systems. The problem with steel and other relatively heavy materials is that their density is so great that the tensile-strength limit is reached at a lower rotation velocity than is the case with more lightweight materials. Thus, the potential gain in energy efficiency from flywheel storage would be substantially reduced by the need for conventional energy inputs to transport the flywheel and the vehicle over any significant distance. However, with the development of high-tensile-

[3]The most extensive studies thus far have been concerned with the storage of strategic petroleum reserves and the disposal of nuclear wastes (see B. L. Cohen, "The Disposal of Radioactive Wastes from Fission Reactors," *ibid.*, 236 [June 1977]:21–31).

[4]Flywheel energy storage can be determined from the equation, $E = (0.5)Iw^2$, where I is the moment of inertia and w is the angular velocity in radians per second. The moment of inertia is defined as $I = cMR^2$, where M is the total mass, in grams per cubic centimeter, R^2 is a linear dimension such as the radius, and c is a tensile-stress-adjustment coefficient of the material based on its configuration. In turn, tensile strength, T, which is the force divided by the area, can then be used to define the maximum energy-storage density as follows: $E_{max} = (0.5)Iw^2_{max} = 0.5(cMR^2)(2T/\rho R^2)$, where ρ is the density. Then $E_{max} = CMT/\rho$, and since $M = \rho V$, $E_{max} = cVT$.

strength lightweight materials such as aromatic polyamides, flywheel technology can be applied to a much broader array of energy storage problems.[5]

Aromatic polyamides derive their tensile strength from the alignment of individual fibers parallel to each other. They are bonded together with an epoxy and have densities well below those of metals with comparable tensile strength, generally by a factor of four or five to one. The energy storage of fibers ranges between 100 and 1,000 watt-hours per kilogram, or in conventional energy units, of between 155 and 1,552 Btu's per pound. To appreciate the storage capacity of fibers, it should be noted that conventional flywheels made of a high-quality metal such as maraging steel have a storage capacity of only about 48 watt-hours per kilogram. However, to fully understand the potential of flywheel technology, we need to see how it could be integrated into the existing and evolving structure of energy use in the economy.

As an illustration of the application of flywheel technology, consider the problem of efficiency accompanying electricity generation and automobile use. In the case of electricity, to avoid the cumbersome reliance on auxiliary power plants or pumped-storage hydropower, flywheels could be integrated within existing power plant systems to accumulate energy during slack periods and to release it during peak demand times. How such a system would work can be understood in reference to the power plant flywheel illustrated in figure 8.2.

An electrical power plant flywheel of the type illustrated in figure 8.2 would weigh 100–200 tons and would have a peak power-storage capacity of 20,000 kilowatt-hours. To ensure its optimal operating efficiency, the flywheel would be housed in a vacuum chamber using an inert gas such as helium as a circulating medium. At the top of the flywheel, the rotor would move within a generator-motor. During off-peak hours, the flywheel generator-motor would operate as a motor using power from the central power plant to store energy. In peak periods, the flywheel generator-motor would switch over to a generator mode, to release the stored energy into the electrical distribution system already being fed by the conventional power plant's capacity of 1,000 megawatts. In essence, the flywheel would enable the conventional generating plant to operate closer to its peak capacity on a continuous basis, which would make the most efficient use of its primary energy and which could also lower the average cost of electricity.

As an illustration of flywheel technology, consider the operation over a typical daily cycle of a 1,000-megawatt power plant system such as that illustrated in figure 7.2. During the twelve-hour daytime period, electricity demand reaches 13,500 megawatt-hours; during the twelve-hour night period it falls to 5,800 megawatt-hours. The problem is how to handle the daytime peak excess demand of 1,500 megawatt-hours. If peak demand were handled by a pumped-storage hydroelectric system, depending on height and velocity conditions, required water storage could be as large as 30–40 reservoir acres.

[5]Many of these high-strength lightweight materials are a direct by-product of space-exploration programs (see Henry R. Clauser, "Advanced Composite Materials" *ibid.*, 229 [July 1973]).

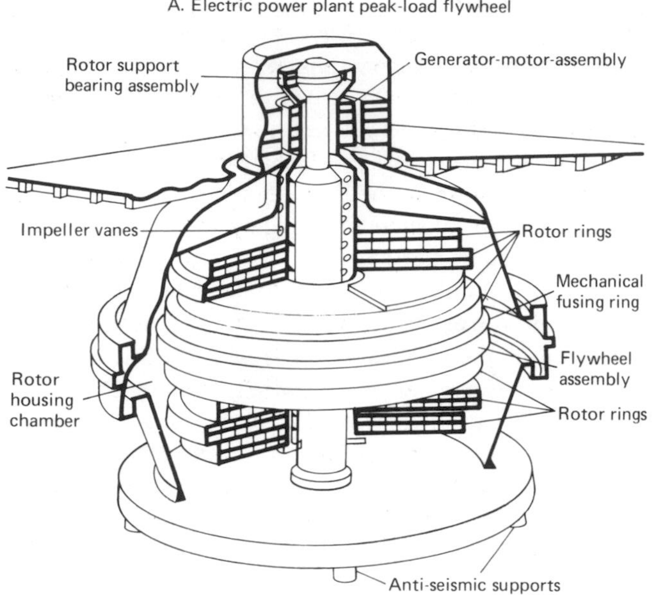

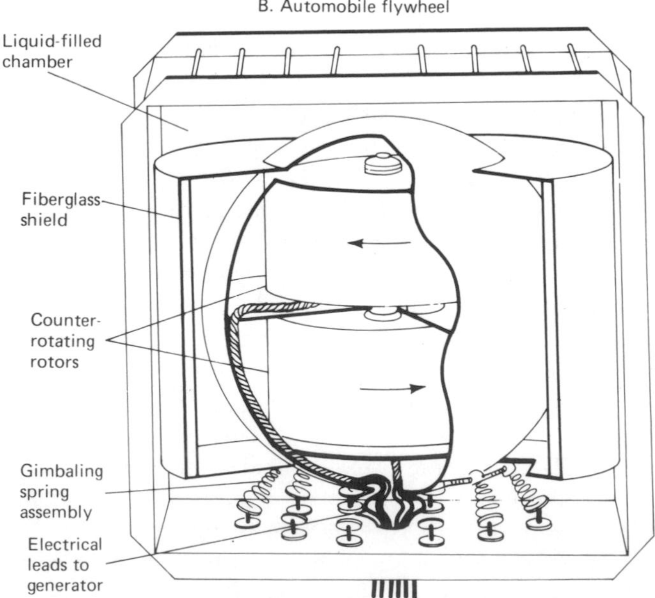

Figure 8.2. Alternative Applications of Flywheel Energy Storage. Adapted from R. F. Post and S. F. Post, "Flywheels," *Scientific American* 229 (December 1973):22.

On the other hand, seventy-five 20-megawatt-hour flywheel storage units would require only 3.75 acres and could be charged with off-peak slack capacity without having to install another generating unit. The system's load factor could thus be raised from 74 percent to 80 percent, and as long as the capital cost of flywheel storage were less than the capital cost of an additional generating unit, thermodynamic efficiency would be higher and average costs would be lowered.

A second illustration of flywheel technology may be seen in reference to transportation. Surprising as it may seem, some forms of transportation have already made use of flywheels on a limited scale. For example, a conventional internal combustion engine usually employs a flywheel attached to its driveshaft in order to conserve the amount of primary energy needed to move the pistons. In addition, in Switzerland and in San Francisco, flywheels have been used to operate electric buses. The charging of the buses comes from an overhead power line which stores power in the flywheels and releases it until a new supply is needed. The difficulty with both of these applications is that they rely on conventional steel flywheels, where storage capacity is limited, as has already been noted. What is worth examining, therefore, is how some of the fiber-composite flywheels with higher storage capacities could make a significant difference in the use of primary energy consumption.

As noted in chapter 2, in 1980 the transportation sector of the U.S. economy consumed about one-quarter of all primary energy. Ninety-six percent of the transportation sector's energy came from petroleum, and this amount represented almost 60 percent of petroleum consumption in the economy as a whole, of which around half was supplied by imports. Most of the transportation sector's consumption of petroleum is in the form of gasoline, with the remainder in the form of lubricants and plastics.

It is widely known that a typical automobile converts only 20–25 percent of its gasoline energy into power; the remainder is rejected into the environment as thermal and particulate pollution.[6] It is also widely known that automobile engine efficiency can be and is being improved through changes in engine and body design. Various alternative engine designs—ranging from the conventional fuel combustion Otto cycle, the compression-ignition Diesel, the vapor-cycle Rankine cycle, the Stirling cycle, and the closed- and open-cycle Brayton gas turbine engines—have been available for some time. Ignoring at this point some of the engineering issues involved in these alternative engines, if primary reliance shifted from the conventional Otto engine to the open-cycle Brayton gas turbine, engine fuel efficiency would rise from 30 percent to 44 percent, representing an increase of about 50 percent. In turn, by reducing the weight of automobiles and shifting toward greater use of aerodynamic design, depending on weight standards and automobile accessories, another 60–70 percent increase in fuel efficiency could be obtained.

[6]For a more detailed discussion, see D. Wilson, "Alternative Automobile Engines," *ibid.*, 239 (July 1978):39–49; and John R. Pierce, "The Fuel Consumption of Automobiles," *ibid.*, 234 (January 1975):34–44.

Taken together, these measures could raise the fuel efficiency of the U.S. automobile fleet from its 1980 average of just over fourteen miles per gallon to between thirty and forty miles per gallon by the end of the decade, with new models achieving an average approaching 60 miles per gallon.

Setting aside for the moment alternative methods of raising petroleum fuel efficiency in automobiles, consider the effect of a fiber-composite flywheel to power a comparable electric vehicle. A 2,200-pound 40-miles-per-gallon petroleum vehicle under the optimum chagnes just described would be able to travel 600 miles at 60 miles per hour on one tank of 15 gallons of fuel. Based on the conversion data in the appendix, if one gallon of gasoline contains on the average 125,000 Btu's, the total energy consumed per tank would be 1,875,000 Btu's, or 9,375 Btu's per mile. Since one watt-hour equals 3.413 Btu's, a single 30-kilowatt-hour flywheel unit of the kind illustrated in figure 8.2 could store 102,390 Btu's. Unlike a conventionally powered automobile, however, an electric vehicle of comparable weight and speed could travel much farther per unit of energy consumed because of its greater efficiency in the conversion of electrical to mechanical energy.[7] Consequently, a flywheel electric vehicle of the same curb weight as a conventional vehicle could use one 30-kilowatt-hour storage unit to travel between 75 and 150 miles on one charge, depending on whether urban or country driving were the norm, as well as on the degree of road angles and related conditions, or at a rate of as little as 683 Btu's per mile. If the flywheel were contained within a vacuum, the storage charge could last unused for a period of up to six months, and recharging could be done at special electric fuel station outlets, or through residential installation systems, including, where feasible, photovoltaic cells.

To appreciate the potential of flywheel technology let us make a simple comparison. In 1980 some 154.41 million vehicles in the United States traveled roughly 2,025.16 billion miles and consumed some 140 billion gallons of gasoline with an aggregate energy content of approximately 18 quads. Now, if instead of using internal combustion engine technology, the U.S. automobile fleet were to consist only of flywheel electric vehicles powered by 30-kilowatt-hour charges, they could travel approximately 75 miles per charge, that is, they would consume approximately 1,366 Btu's per vehicle mile. Thus, to travel 2,025.16 billion miles, they would consume 2.766 quads, or 15.38 percent of the energy that would have been used by conventionally powered vehicles. However, let us also assume that this electricity would be provided from conventional generating plants with an average conversion efficiency of 33 percent. Thus, an electricity generating plant would have to consume three times the primary energy per Btu of electrical energy made available to flywheel vehicles. If electricity plants were to do this, then the gross primary energy consumption needed for flywheel vehicles would be 8.299 quads, or

[7] See R. F. Post and S. F. Post, "Flywheels," *ibid.*, 229 (December 1973):17–23. The authors base one comparison on a 13.3-miles-per-gallon, 15-gallon, 2,200 pound, 200-mile-per-tank conventional automobile and a flywheel electric vehicle of the same weight which would employ regenerative braking, improved aerodynamic design, and other factors that would enable it to obtain a mileage equivalent to 250 miles per gallon.

46.14 percent of conventional petroleum consumption in transportation. If we adjust further to allow for transmission losses of energy at 10 percent, and allow for the (unamortized) energy equivalent of the petrochemical energy contained in the flywheels themselves at 3.00 quads, this would yield a level of required gross primary energy consumption of 12.2211 quads, or 68 percent of the 1980 level of petroleum consumption in the transportation sector.[8] For the economy as a whole, a switch to flywheel vehicles would thus represent a reduction in gross petroleum energy consumption of 17 percent, and a reduction of aggregate energy consumption of about 8 percent. Given that flywheels would normally have a useful lifetime of more than one year, gross energy savings in subsequent years could reach as high as 30 percent of the 1980 level, depending on replacement demand for flywheels and increases in the number of vehicles, with even higher savings if flywheel vehicle efficiencies were to achieve the average potential of 150 miles per charge, or 683 Btu's per mile.

To be sure, fuel efficiency in conventional gasoline-powered vehicles has shown dramatic improvement in recent years. Indeed, some designs now promise to deliver 50–60 miles per gallon.[9] Yet even at that level, flywheel-powered vehicles could still become competitive, particularly if they utilized the kind of fiber-composite technology that has been under development, for they would be capable of achieving fuel-equivalent efficiencies of as high as 180 miles per gallon. What could make flywheels even more competitive is that as electric vehicles, they would be environmentally cleaner than petroleum fuel vehicles, and far less dependent on a relatively scarce and insecure resource such as petroleum, since there are many alternative fuels that can be used to produce electricity. Lacking thus far have been both economic incentive and the associated expansion of the technological capacity to make advanced flywheel systems economically competitive with their conventional alternatives.

8.3. BATTERY ENERGY STORAGE

One factor that may affect the utilization of flywheels in areas such as automobiles is battery-storage technology. Unlike flywheels, batteries contain no moving mechanical parts and rely generally on non-fossil materials for their construction and operation. Batteries also have a long record of use throughout the economy, including an early role in establishing electric-vehicle technology. Thus far, a more substantial use of batteries in the economy has been limited by the relatively small energy-storage capacity of the most economical type of battery now in use, namely, the lead-acid battery. To

[8]Based on the estimates given in note 7, the energy content of fiber is estimated at 63,117 Btu's per pound. Each vehicle is estimated to require approximately 308 pounds of fiber for a flywheel unit, or 19,444,447 Btu's per vehicle. When this figure is multiplied by the approximately 154.41 million vehicles, we get approximately 3.00 quads of energy.

[9]See Charles L. Gray and Frank von Hippel, "The Fuel Economy of Light Vehicles," *ibid.*, 244 (May 1981):48–59.

understand the potential of battery storage, our concern is thus first to examine the operation of conventional systems and then to explore potential and emerging alternatives.

As noted in chapter 4, batteries produce electricity from chemical reactions. Two differing materials such as copper and zinc serve as electrodes, or points, where electrons are shifted into a circuit by a connecting wire. The flow of electricity is facilitated by the electrolyte, or the chemical with which each electrode is permitted to interact.[10] For practical purposes, as long as no current is being drawn off, as in the ignition of an automobile engine, the battery is thus capable of storing potential electricity in chemical form. Such electrochemical transformations can be achieved either with dry cells—as found in flashlights, radios, and other easily transported equipment—or with wet cells of the kind found in automobiles.

Conventional storage batteries, which rely on commonly used materials, have been economical to produce, though limited in their capacity. These batteries typically do not have more than 25–30 watt-hours per kilogram of weight. For this reason, while they are competitive with conventional metal flywheels, they cannot readily compete on a large scale with major conventional storage modes such as stocks of liquid or gas fossil fuels. The role of batteries may be changed by the shift to higher-storage-efficiency technology, now under development. Four types of higher-storage-efficiency batteries are of particular interest: aqueous electrolyte, organic, high-temperature, and metal-air.[11] Each of these will be considered in turn.

Of the principal types of alternative batteries, aqueous electrolyte systems resemble most closely the conventional lead-acid wet cell. The difference is that instead of lead, other, less common materials are needed to yield higher storage efficiencies. The technical trade-offs involved include the operating temperature range, charge retention, limits of recharging cycles, and transmission capability.[12] Many of these batteries are possible in theory, but the ones of greatest practical potential are those based on nickel and zinc as electrodes, with bromide, cadmium, iron, hydrogen, and chloride serving as electrolytes. The energy-storage density of these alternative batteries ranges from 45 watt-hours to 91 watt-hours per kilogram, well above the capacity of conventional batteries already noted. However, implicit in these gains is also

[10]A typical lead-acid battery uses lead oxide, lead, and hydrogen sulfate to produce electricity, lead sulfate, and water, as follows:

$$PbO_2 + Pb + 2\,H_2SO_4 \rightarrow 2\,PbSO_4 + 2\,H_2O.$$

[11]One type of battery absent from this list is the nuclear cell. Nuclear batteries rely on the release of heat from radioactive decay to product electricity. Thermoelectricity, known also as radioisotope thermoelectric generation, or RTG technology, has been used thus far only in rarefied applications such as the Atomic Energy Commission's Systems for Nuclear Auxiliary Power (SNAP) program. Apollos 11 and 12 utilized plutonium batteries in lunar exploration, and the Pioneer exploration of Jupiter relied on four 30-watt units (see J. M. Fowler, *Energy and the Environment* [New York: McGraw-Hill, 1975], p. 310).

[12]A more detailed discussion with reference to research in each of these alternatives is presented in S. W. Angrist, *Direct Energy Conversion,* 3d ed. (Boston: Allyn and Bacon, 1976), pp. 44–55.

the potentially higher relative cost, which ultimately will govern the degree of their commercial utilization on a large scale.

Organic batteries differ from aqueous electrolyte cells in that they rely to a much greater extent on non-metals for energy storage and conversion. Typical batteries of this kind are lithium-sulfur, with a storage density of 225 watt-hours per kilogram, and lithium bromide, with 229 watt-hours per kilogram. Their capacities are clearly larger than those of aqueous electrolyte batteries, though they generally suffer from low discharge-charge rates and more limited life cycles.

One way of attaining a higher storage density is by raising the average operating temperature of batteries. In high-temperature batteries, temperatures as high as 300°C permit the attainment of sufficiently high storage densities to compensate for reduced discharge-charge and life-cycle capacities. Typical examples of high-temperature batteries are lithium-tellurium-tetrachloride, with 232 watt-hours per kilogram; aluminum-chlorine, with 296 watt-hours per kilogram; and lithium-sulfur, with 318 watt-hours per kilogram. The difficulty with these high-temperature batteries is that they have greater sealing problems, greater corrosion, and fewer recharging cycles than do other alternatives.

The fourth type of alternative battery is the metal-air battery. In metal-air batteries, a metal serves as a negative electrode, and a gas using oxygen from the air serves as the positive electrode. Of all the types of batteries thus far discussed, metal-air batteries have the highest storage density. They range from 119 watt-hours per kilogram in cadmium-air batteries to 3,701 watt-hours per kilogram in beryllium-air batteries and thus can in theory at least exceed the storage capacity of the alternative fiber-composite flywheels, noted in section 8.2. The principal difficulty with metal-air batteries is that corrosion is more acute than in other systems. In order to minimize this corrosion, metal-air batteries must generally rely on relatively rare materials known as noble metals, which are the most resistant to corrosion. Moreover, the energy required to refine non-common metals is also a deterrent to development, as may be recalled from the data in table 4.2.

8.4. HYDROGEN ENERGY STORAGE

Ever since the discovery of hydrogen by Henry Cavendish (1731–1810) in 1776, scientists have considered ways in which hydrogen could be used to store energy. Yet only in the twentieth century has the practical potential of hydrogen been demonstrated. Indeed, as the 1937 Hindenburg disaster in Lakehurst, New Jersey, made sufficiently clear, though lighter than air, hydrogen is certainly a highly combustible element. Interesting enough, in the years following the Hindenburg explosion the prospects for widespread hydrogen utilization have become greater than ever, for reasons which are spelled out below.

The significance of hydrogen energy storage can be demonstrated with reference to a few of its fundamental properties. First, since it constitutes one-half of each molecule of water, it is one of the most abundant elements in nature. It is thus potentially inexpensive in comparison with other modes of energy storage. Second, its energy-storage density is higher than that of all fossil fuels and the alternative storage modes thus far described, as can be seen in table 8.2. In fact, its storage density is exceeded only by that found in nuclear energy. Third, hydrogen can be transported readily in liquid or gas forms, which are compatible with existing energy technology in the economy. Fourth, while the production of hydrogen from water yields useful oxygen, its principal by-product from combustion is also water, a welcome alternative to the current pollution from fossil fuel combustion. Finally, against all of these advantages is the fact that the production of hydrogen from water must itself consume a primary form of energy, a consideration of no small consequence in a thermodynamic universe.

Setting aside for the moment the process of producing hydrogen from water, consider some of the specific ways in which hydrogen can be used in the economy. In the residential sector, for example, hydrogen gas can everywhere be substituted for the currently utilized natural gas. With only minor modifications, it can also be used as a substitute for other fossil fuels as well. Since water is the principal combustion by-product, buildings using hydrogen fuel for heating could attain a 30 percent greater energy efficiency by eliminating the flue system now essential to fossil fuel utilization. Moreover, water released from hydrogen combustion could also provide humidity, which now is often provided by deliberate open-air drafts.

As a second illustration, hydrogen can also be used as a fuel in conventional transportation systems, especially those now dependent on internal combustion engines using fossil fuels. In this case, for hydrogen fuel to be technically efficient, it must be converted to a liquid form, which calls for a cryogenic process capable of inducing temperatures as low as −253°C. In its liquid form, hydrogen has the same energy-storage density per unit of weight as in its gaseous state, except that its volume is reduced by 615 times. One cubic meter of liquid hydrogen contains 7,142,857 Btu's, in comparison with 15,357,142 Btu's per cubic meter of methanol and 29,642,857 Btu's per cubic meter of gasoline. In a typical gasoline automobile, which has a fifteen-gallon tank and gets fifteen miles per gallon, the total energy consumption per tank would be 1,875,000 Btu's (at 125,000 Btu's per gallon), or 8,333 Btu's per mile. In a liquid hydrogen–fueled vehicle this amount of energy would require a storage space 4.15 times that of a gasoline tank, though the hydrogen would weigh only one-third the amount of gasoline. Thus, as long as the extra tank weight did not exceed the difference in fuel weight, if design constraints could be accommodated, then a hydrogen–fueled vehicle could be just as energy-efficient in gross terms as its gasoline counterpart.[13] Moreover, apart from some controllable smog-producing nitrogen oxide emis-

[13]By gross terms is meant only the end-use efficiency. Source efficiency would have to add the energy consumption per gallon of refined gasoline, and for hydrogen, the energy consumption needed in its production from air by electrolysis.

Table 8.2. Energy Efficiency of Product Recycling in the U.S. Economy

		Energy Needed to Produce:			
		One Short Ton		1980 Domestic Consumption	
Industry	1980 Domestic Consumption (in millions of short tons)	With Conventional Technology (in millions of Btu's)	With Recycling Technology (in millions of Btu's)	With Conventional Technology (in Btu's)	With Recycling Technology as Half of Production (in Btu's)
Aluminum	6.9	269.4	10.0	1.858×10^{15}	0.963×10^{15}
Plastic	19.3	99.0	2.7	1.911×10^{15}	0.981×10^{15}
Raw steel	80.0	43.0	8.8	3.440×10^{15}	2.072×10^{15}
Newsprint	11.5	22.8	17.6	0.262×10^{15}	0.232×10^{15}
Glass containers	14.0	15.6	14.4	0.218×10^{15}	0.210×10^{15}
Paperboard	63.7	6.5	3.3	0.329×10^{15}	0.312×10^{15}
Total	—	—	—	8.018×10^{15}	4.770×10^{15}

Sources: A. B. Makhijani and A. J. Lichtenberg, "An Assessment of Residential Energy Utilization in the U.S.A." (Berkeley: University of California, 1972); R. S. Berry and H. Makino, "Energy Thrift in Packaging and Marketing," *Technology Review*, February 1974, pp. 33–43; D. Hayes, "Repairs, Re-Use, Recycling—First Steps toward a Sustainable Society" (Washington, D.C.: World Watch Institute, September 1978); and U.S. Department of Commerce, *1981 Industrial Outlook* (Washington, D.C.: U.S. Government Printing Office, January 1981).

Note: 1980 primary energy consumption was 76.201×10^{15} Btu's, or 76.201 quads.

sions, a hydrogen vehicle would vastly reduce the amount of air pollution now due largely to gasoline vehicles.

As the Hindenburg incident suggests, a natural concern connected with the use of hydrogen is the danger of spontaneous or uncontrolled combustion. To be sure, in its gaseous state, hydrogen is highly combustible, more so in fact than the gasoline or natural gas it might possible replace. For example, at atmospheric pressure, gasoline requires 0.25 millijoules to ignite, and methane 0.28, but hydrogen needs only 0.02 millijoules. In more immediate terms, since a single match could ignite gasoline, only one-tenth of that energy would be needed. However, when liquid or gas hydrogen leaks from a container, it dissipates much more quickly into the atmosphere than gasoline because of its lighter weight. Consequently, whereas hydrogen might ignite more readily than alternative fuels, its explosive potential is actually much less. The advantage of hydrogen in this context becomes obvious, especially when one considers its use as an automobile fuel.

A more serious problem in the use of hydrogen is that in order to extract it from water, there must be an expenditure of another form of energy. Indeed, the necessity of energy consumption in order to extract hydrogen is a major reason why hydrogen is classified as an energy-storage mechanism rather than as a form of primary energy. Since the thermodynamic efficiency of hydrogen energy conversion is critical to the efficiency of hydrogen end uses, we also need to take into account the principal methods by which it is done.

The most common method of hydrogen energy production from air is by electrolysis. In electrolysis, an electrical current is passed through water via inert electrodes. As the passage of the current dissociates the water, hydrogen collects at the cathode, and oxygen passes to the anode.[14] In the United States, electrolytic production of hydrogen has taken place mostly in large-scale plants with gross conversion efficiencies of 60–70 percent and net efficiencies of 30–40 percent. For example, in 1980, hydrogen production in the United States reached a level of 2.715 billion cubic meters, almost all of which was used as liquid hydrogen rocket fuel for space exploration and scientific research.[15] In fact, despite its large absolute amount, 2.715 billion cubic meters of hydrogen would amount to 3.15×10^{13} Btu's, or 0.04 percent of the aggregate primary energy consumption in the United States in 1980. In other words, hydrogen energy production in the United States at present does not represent a significant alternative energy resource.

The expansion of conventional electrolysis on a significant scale to produce hydrogen would clearly generate additional constraints on alternative uses of electrical power. However, several methods not currently in use could be applied to keep hydrogen-electricity demand at a minimum. The first method would be to use off-peak central-power-plant capacity to generate hydrogen.

[14]The electrolysis equation is: $H_2O \rightarrow H_2 = (0.5)\ O_2 + 68$ kilocalories per mole.

[15]The largest liquid-hydrogen storage tank in the world is at the J. F. Kennedy Space Center in Cape Canaveral, Florida. It has a capacity of 900,000 gallons, which is equivalent to 37.7×10^9 Btu's, and represents about 73 percent of the world's pumped-storage hydroelectric-equivalent capacity (see D. Gregory, "The Hydrogen Economy," *Scientific American* 229 [January 1973]: 13–21).

As in the case of pumped hydropower, compressed-air, flywheel, and battery storage, hydrogen production from central generating plants would result in an increase in the operating efficiency of large-scale power plants to levels much closer to their thermodynamic limits. Beyond these methods, it would also be possible to utilize hitherto underutilized renewable energy resources to generate electricity for hydrogen electrolysis, or for the storage of energy in the alternative modes already cited.

As an illustration of alternative storage systems, figure 8.3 shows how wind power could be used to store energy in batteries, in hydrogen, and in flywheels for subsequent retrieval in response to industrial and consumer demand. In the case of hydrogen energy, in its gas or its liquid form it could be used directly in the ways already described, or it could be integrated into a fuel cell which would use it to produce electricity. Similarly, photovoltaic cells could also be used to generate electricity for hydrogen energy storage, as could the hydrothermal, geothermal, and tidal renewable energy resources discussed in chapter 7. In fact, hydrogen plus battery storage may well be essential in converting many of the intermittent renewable energy flows into usable storage modes for efficient integration into the economy.

Beyond electrolysis, there are a few other means of producing hydrogen from water. One of them is photolysis, which is the dissociation of water by intensive ultraviolet radiation. The difficulty in making practical use of ultraviolet radiation for this purpose is that in its natural intensity it is obviously inadequate. Thus, it can only become effective if it is concentrated by powerful x-ray machines, which themselves consume large amounts of electrical and hence primary energy, thereby reducing the potential energy gain. Fusion reactors of the kind described in chapter 6 might be possible sources of radiation, but as has been noted, fusion technology does not promise any immediate possibility for widespread use in ways that alternative energy resources are capable of doing.

A second alternative method of hydrogen production is by thermal dissociation. In order for this method to be feasible, however, temperatures as high as 2,500°C are needed, temperatures which are well above anything now commercially possible. Consequently, thermal dissociation is only a theoretical transformation with no immediate practical possibility. Finally, there is the production of hydrogen by the bioconversion method discussed in chapter 7. Bioconversion hydrogen production is relatively easy to implement, and its energy consumption requirements are even less than those of electrolysis because of the conversion efficiency of photosynthesis. The principal limitation of bioconversion hydrogen production is that it can be undertaken only on a limited scale governed by the efficiency of photosynthesis and by the alternative demands for biomass energy within the economy. Indeed, bioconversion hydrogen cannot readily compete even with conventional electrolysis once these basic considerations have been taken into account. In sum, electrolysis remains as the most efficient technology for the production of hydrogen from water. Its expansion can be readily undertaken by the use of both off-peak electrical power plant capacity and by the renewable energy

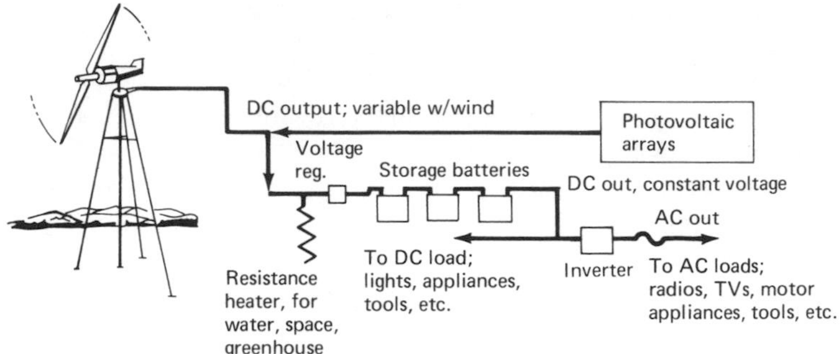

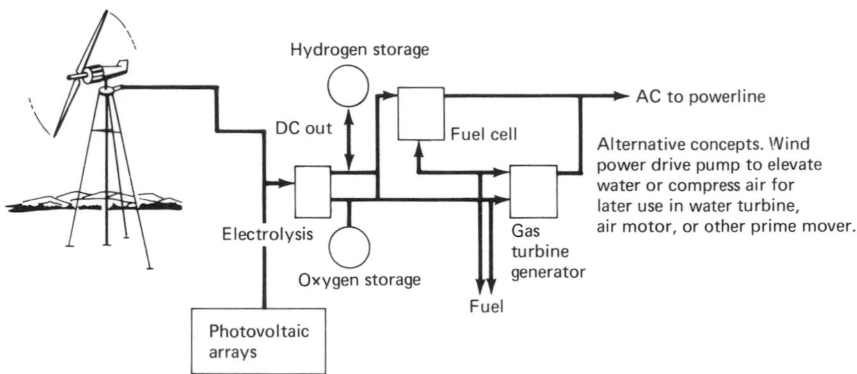

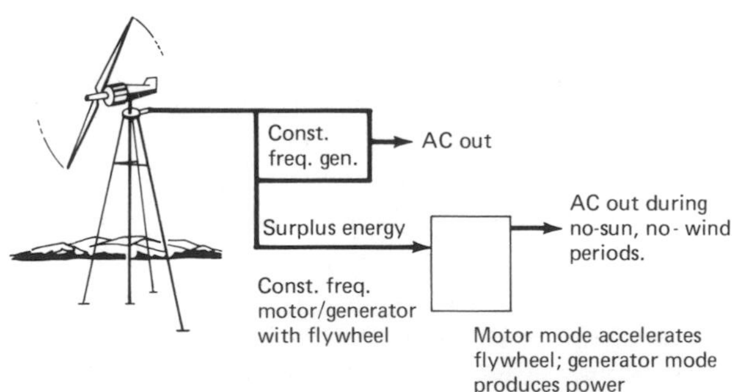

Figure 8.3. Alternatives for Converting and Storing Wind Energy. From National Science Foundation, Division of Advanced Energy and Resources Research and Technology, *Wind Machines*, p. 39.

resources already noted. Whether and how much it should be done can be determined by economic considerations, which are covered in parts III and IV.

8.5. HEAT-PUMP TRANSFER TECHNOLOGY

A major factor influencing the utilization of alternative energy storage technologies is the efficiency of energy transfer and conversion. As we have seen, the conversion of primary energy to electricity in conventional power plants often rejects as much as two-thirds of that energy into the environment as thermal and particulate pollution. In addition, where intermittent flows of renewable energy are concerned, for these resources to become technically competitive requires an efficient mechanism for energy storage and conversion. As will be seen below, there are several alternative transfer and conversion technologies that may well raise the efficiency of current energy use much closer to its thermodynamic limits. One of the most important of these technologies is the transfer system of the heat pump.

As its discoverer, Lord Kelvin, noted in the mid-nineteenth century, a heat pump functions according to the reverse principle of a heat engine. To understand how this could be so, we need to apply the laws of thermodynamics (see chapter four) to a closer view of the functions of heat engines.

In figure 8.4, a heat engine such as the kind found in a gasoline-powered automobile ignites fuel inside a high-temperature reservoir, or cylinder. The combustion of fuel releases pressurized heat to produce mechanical energy, or work, by the turning of a crankshaft which moves the wheels for locomotion. As the Second Law of Thermodynamics shows, only a fraction of the incoming high-temperature heat can be converted into work, with the remainder rejected into the environment through an exhaust as thermal pollution. Since Second Law, or Carnot, efficiency is determined by the difference between input and rejected energy, in a perfect heat engine the temperature of the rejected energy will be the same as that found in the environment, that is, equal to the ambient temperature.

As a reverse heat engine, a heat pump uses a vacuum to transfer heat from a low-temperature reservoir to a high-temperature one, as occurs in the operation of a refrigerator or air conditioner. In a heat pump, a compound such as freon, ammonia, or isobutane circulates continuously between a near vacuum chamber and a compressor. Within the compressor chamber it is a liquid at ambient, or room, temperature. As it circulates in the near vacuum, it expands into a gas, thereby absorbing heat from the low-temperature reservoir, which is then passed to a high-temperature reservoir, where it is released as the gas is compressed back into a liquid. If the heat pump were reversible—one of the properties originally recognized by Lord Kelvin—then in the winter it could take heat from the cooler outside air and warm a room, and in the summer it would function in its opposite role as an air conditioner.

The significance of a heat pump is now obvious: the transfer of energy is more efficient than the conversion of its form. Thus, in the winter a reversible heat pump will be more energy-efficient than conventional alternatives such

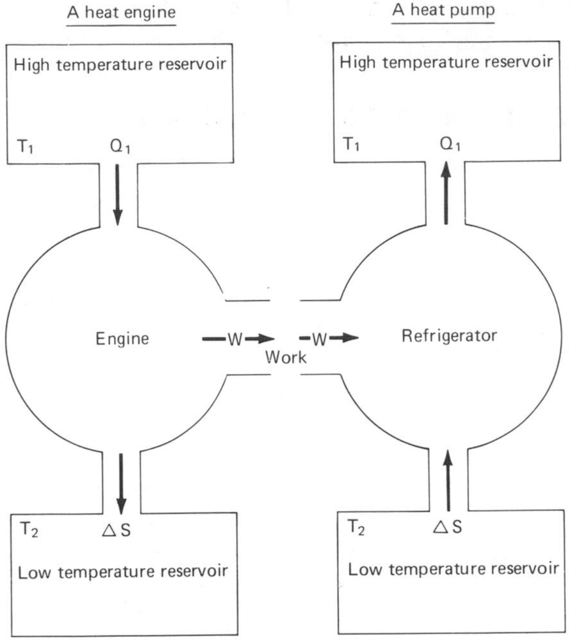

Figure 8.4. Reversibility in Heat Engines. Adapted from V. Kadambi and M. Prasad, *An Introduction to Energy Conversion*, vol. 1 (New York: John Wiley and Sons, Halsted Press, 1976), pp. 72–74; and Cook, *Man, Energy, Society*, p. 43.

as steam or electrical heat. In more specific terms, we can determine the comparative efficiency of a heat pump by deriving first its Second Law efficiency and then its Coefficient of Performance. From equation (4.11) we recall that the definition of Second Law efficiency is

(8.1)
$$\chi \equiv \frac{W}{Q_1} = \left(1 - \frac{T_2}{T_1}\right)$$
$$\equiv \left(\frac{Q_1}{W}\right)\left(1 - \frac{T_2}{T_1}\right),$$

where W is the amount of energy converted into work, Q_1 is the amount of input energy, T_2 is the absolute temperature of the outside cool air, and T_1 is the absolute temperature of the inside warm air. In turn, the Coefficient of Performance is defined as

(8.2)
$$C.O.P. = \frac{Q_1}{W} = \frac{\chi}{[1 - (T_2/T_1)]},$$

where temperatures are listed on the Kelvin scale. As an illustration, if the outside temperature is 1°C, the inside temperature is 15°C, and χ is 0.35, then the *C.O.P.* will be 7.00. In effect, by its transfer of ambient heat, the heat pump provides an energy output that is seven times its input. Despite the apparent contradiction of the First Law of Thermodynamics, this efficiency exceeds 100 percent because instead of a produced stock of energy's being converted into another form, as occurs in a conventional heat engine, "free" environmental thermal energy is being transferred.

One factor that limits the use of heat-pump technology is relatively large temperature differences such as those found in extremely cold climates. As can be seen in equation (8.2), the greater the difference between the inside and outside temperatures, the lower will be the heat pump's efficiency. When the efficiency falls below 1, the heat pump operates basically as an electrical resistance heater.

Widespread adoption of heat-pump technology could make a substantial difference in aggregate primary energy use. In the United States, around 18 percent of all primary energy is used to provide space heating; in 1977 this amounted to 13.67 quads. If heat pumps had an efficiency as low as 1.5, they could provide energy savings of 50 percent for space heating and reduce aggregate primary energy consumption by as much as 9 percent. Despite this advantage, when commercial production of heat pumps began in the 1930s, demand was restricted by inadequate compressor technology and faulty design. Since then, improvements in compressor technology and rising fuel prices have brought about a revival in heat-pump demand that may become substantial in the coming years.[16]

8.6. WASTE RECYCLING

As the environmental concerns of the 1970s have shown, the United States generates a considerable amount of waste for each unit of final demand. The pricing of resources plays a major role in their utilization, but as the cost of exhaustible energy resources increases, waste recycling becomes more practical. In turn, the technical efficiency of energy use is raised closer to its thermodynamic limits.

The energy impact of waste recycling is twofold. First, as non-energy materials are recycled, a smaller energy input is required for their conversion into usable products than in conventional production. Second, some wastes can be used directly as energy resources. Both of these impacts merit further examination.

As pointed out in chapter 4, the energy-input requirements of the diverse products of the U.S. economy vary significantly. At the same time, since many of these products are generated continuously with virgin materials, by

[16]By 1970 an estimated 11 percent of electrically heated homes in the United States had heat pumps (see Eric Hirst and John C. Moyers, *Potential for Energy Conservation through Increased Efficiency of Use,* testimony before U.S. Senate, Committee on Interior and Insular Affairs, March 1973, p. 15).

recycling waste materials, it is possible to attain significant reductions in primary energy use, as may be seen in table 8.2. When these figures for the energy input per ton of product using conventional and recycling technologies are multiplied by the annual level of consumption, the gross primary energy needed for their production can then be derived. For 1980, using conventional technology alone, the 8.018 quads of primary energy needed to produce the output of the six industries in table 8.2 would be equivalent to 10.5 percent of the 76.2 quads of gross primary energy consumption among all industries. Were these same six industries to use 50 percent recycling, as illustrated in the last column, the resulting 4.77 quads of energy consumption would represent a 41 percent savings in energy use in these sectors alone, and savings of almost 5 percent in gross primary energy consumption for the economy as a whole.

Actual 1980 production in the six industries listed in table 8.2 did rely on recycling technology in varying degrees. However, it was on average less than half of the 50 percent comparison level of the last column.[17] Yet if a 50 percent level of recycling were to operate throughout all manufacturing industries of the economy, net energy savings in this sector alone could rise to 6–10 quads of energy a year.[18] As we have noted in other comparisons of this type, what is essential to the realization of this degree of energy conservation is the relative pricing of resources and the extent to which these prices can be made to reflect the costs and benefits of conservation to the economy as a whole.

Beyond the energy-saving potential of materials recycling, wastes can also serve as direct sources of energy. To do so they must be organic, that is, they must be derived from plant and animal by-products discarded from the economy. In the United States at least, these organic wastes represent a significant potential resource appropriate to national energy policy.

Table 8.3 shows some of the principal yields found in commonly disposed organic materials in the U.S. economy. As can be seen, the aggregate annual energy potential from these organic wastes as of the early 1970s was on the order of 15 quads. That this is a significant source of energy can be understood by comparing it with the 1980 level of aggregate primary energy consumption of 76.1 quads. While the potential supply of waste energy in any given year thus amounts to approximately one-fifth of all primary energy consumption, much of the waste is so dispersed and mixed that only a fraction can be used readily within the economy. Thus, a more relevant comparison is of the recoverable supply, which in the early 1970s amounted to

[17]In 1977, the share of production accounted for by recycling was estimated as: aluminum, 6 percent; iron and steel, 19.2 percent; glass, 2 percent; newsprint, 5 percent; paperboard, 3 percent; and plastics, less than 1 percent (see Denis Hayes, "Repairs, Re-Use, Recycling—First Steps toward a Sustainable Society" (Washington, D.C.: World Watch Institute, September 1978]).

[18]In 1978, value added in manufacturing among the six sectors listed was under 23 percent of all manufacturing. Based on a rough dollar-to-energy relationship, this suggests that 3–4 times the energy savings thus far cited could be obtained by comparable recycling at a 50 percent level in all manufacturing.

Table 8.3. U.S. Annual Energy Potential from Organic Wastes

Organic Material	Total Waste Generation[a]		Recoverable Wastes[b]	
	Millions of short tons	Percent	Millions of short tons	Percent
Manure	200	22.73%	26.0	19.08%
Urban refuse	129	14.66	71.0	52.09
Logging, wood residue	55	6.25	5.0	3.67
Agricultural crop and food wastes	390	44.32	22.6	16.58
Industrial wastes	44	5.00	5.2	3.82
Municipal sewage	12	1.36	1.5	1.10
Miscellaneous	50	5.68	5.0	3.67
Total	880	100.00%	136.3	100.00%

Source: L. L. Anderson, *Energy Potential from Organic Wastes: A Review of the Quantities and Sources,* U.S. Bureau of Mines Information Circular no. 8549 (Washington, D.C.: U.S. Government Printing Office, 1972).

[a]1. 10^9 barrels of oil = 5.8×10^{15} Btu's
2. 8.8×10^{12} cubic feet of natural gas = 9.1×10^{15} Btu's
Total 14.9×10^{15} Btu's
= 14.9 quads

[b]1. 170×10^6 barrels of oil = 9.86×10^{14} Btu's
2. 1.36×10^{12} cubic feet of natural gas = 1.40×10^{15} Btu's
Total 2.38×10^{15} Btu's
= 2.38 quads

2.38 quads, or about 4 percent of primary energy consumption from conventional sources. When recyclable organic wastes such as wood and paper are subtracted from this estimate, the energy potential still amounts to about 3 percent of aggregate primary consumption. Moreover, the entropy principle noted in chapter 4 suggests that as the economy grows more complex over time, this share is likely to rise. When compared with the rising consumption of economically depletable conventional fuels, waste energy will thus become even more important in the future.

From its diverse forms and locations, organic waste can be converted into useful energy in a variety of ways. One of the most obvious is incineration to provide thermal energy for direct heating as well as steam for the generation of electricity. In many developing countries where fossil and biomass wood energy resources have become scarce, animal wastes have long provided a routine source of fuel. In more developed countries, the problem is less one of supply than of composition, particularly since both water and inorganic materials may be present in significant quantities from conventional collection methods. In order for refuse energy technologies to function properly on a continuous basis within an incinerator and without the need for supplementary fuel, organic wastes must normally contain less than 50 percent water and more than 25 percent combustible organic material.[19] Despite dif-

[19]L. L. Anderson, *Energy Potential from Organic Wastes: A Review of the Quantities and Sources,* U.S. Bureau of Mines Circular No. 8549 (Washington, D.C.: U.S. Government Printing Office, 1972).

ficulties in attaining these properties, two pilot facilities, one in Chicago and the other in Hempstead, New York, have advanced toward commercial operation since the 1973 OPEC oil embargo.[20]

One obvious factor limiting a more widespread use of garbage-to-fuel plants is the complexity of refuse preparation required for continuous operation. In lieu of these preparations, a second possibility is to undertake partial separation of refuse and then to combine the semicombustible refuse with combustible conventional fuels such as coal, petroleum, or natural gas. At present, one such incinerator using 20 percent refuse and 80 percent coal has recently begun pilot operations in Saint Louis, Missouri.

A third application of organic wastes is the production of synthetic fuels, in particular oil and biogas. In essence, organic wastes are subjected to temperature and pressure conditions that result in the conversion of solids into combustible oil or gas. Hydrogenation, pyrolysis, and anaerobic digestion are three principal methods by which synthetic fuels from waste can be produced; each of these merits brief explanation.

In hydrogenation, organic waste is heated for as long as an hour at temperatures of up to 380°C and under pressures as great as 250 times the normal atmospheric level. Within a reactor vessel, carbon monoxide, steam, and an alkaline catalyst such as sodium carbonate convert the carbon content of the waste into oil at a rate of about 1.25 barrels per ton of dry waste. It is because of the combination of the hydrogen with the carbon that this process is known as hydrogenation. However, because the oil yield is relatively small and requires pressurization at significant levels, thus far hydrogenation has been considered an inferior method in comparison with pyrolysis, the most common method now under consideration for large-scale conversion.

Pyrolysis is the thermal decomposition of matter in the absence of oxygen. It differs from hydrogenation in that it is done in the absence of oxygen and can be achieved using atmospheric pressure. The energy yield is approximately 1 barrel of oil per ton of refuse, slightly less than that in hydrogenation. Though pyrolysis can be implemented with several known systems, none of them has completely eliminated the problem of char accumulation within the reactor vessel; thus, periodic cleaning is required, which reduces the possibility of continuous operation as occurs in conventional fossil and hydroelectric power plants.

Anaerobic digestion, the third method of synthetic fuel production from wastes, is the simplest though perhaps the least used system in the United States. Table 8.4 illustrates the potential of this technology, showing the specific energy yields obtainable from common animal wastes based on fermentation at room temperatures. In anaerobic digestion, bacteria are cultivated for as long as a week in a waste digestor to break down organic refuse into acids, alcohols, and aldehydes. In turn, these compounds then dissolve,

[20]For a description of the Hempstead facility, see Karen W. Arenson, "French Recycling Plant on L. I.," *New York Times*, 11 July 1978, p. D-1. The facility has been closed since 1980 because of noxious fumes and improper functioning.

thereby releasing methane (CH_4), carbon dioxide (CO_2), and solid residue. The resulting methane is a low-energy gas of about 600 Btu's per cubic foot, which is roughly 60 percent of the energy content of conventional natural gas from existing fossil fuels. It should be noted that biogas plants have already become commercially competitive in many developing countries, such as India and Korea. As economically depletable natural gas increases in cost, biogas is also likely to become more competitive in such areas as the midwestern United States as well.[21]

8.7. MAGNETOHYDRODYNAMICS

Electricity is traditionally produced from hydro power, fossil power, and nuclear power resources. Falling water or pressurized steam is used to turn the rotors of a generator, which in turn produces electricity. When nontraditional renewable resources such as tidal and wind energy are used to produce electricity, the process is essentially the same. In fact, of all of the methods thus far described, only photovoltaic technology does not rely on an electrical generator. However, both photovoltaic and other methods of electrical generation have in common a relatively low conversion rate; thus they result in a significant loss of energy.

One factor that may alter significantly the efficiency of electricity generation is magnetohydrodynamics. Magnetohydrodynamics can be defined as the properties of a conducting fluid within a magnetic field. Unlike conventional electrical generation or photovoltaics, with a magnetohydrodynamic generator, electricity can be produced with a theoretical conversion efficiency as high as 80 percent and with practical operating efficiency as high as 60 percent, which is 50 percent higher than the most modern fossil fuel plant and over twice as high as the theoretical limiting efficiency of photovoltaic cells.[22]

The relative efficiency of magnetohydrodynamic, or MHD, generators can be best understood with reference to the Second Law of Thermodynamics. As has been shown, the higher temperature difference between two reservoirs (such as those illustrated in figure 8.4), the greater will be the efficiency in the conversion of energy. To attain high-temperature differences, a conventional fuel such as coal, natural gas, or petroleum is first burned in a compressed-air chamber. Gas heat in the burner is "seeded" with an ionized alkali metal such as potassium or cesium, which makes the gas electrically conductive. The ionized gas, or plasma, is then released from the burner through a focusing nozzle to enable it to pass efficiently through a superconducting magnet. As it passes through the magnet the electrical current produced within the electromagnetic field is strong enough to be drawn off to a

[21] For a more detailed description of practical biogas technology, see Peter Maynell, *Methane: Planning a Digester* (New York: Schocken Books, 1978). See also W. Vergara and D. Pimentel, "Fuels from Biomass," in *Advances in Energy Systems and Technology*, ed. Peter Auer, vol. 1, (New York: Academic Press, 1978), pp. 125–73.

[22] Angrist, *Direct Energy Conversion*, p. 341.

Table 8.4. Biogas Production from Anaerobic Fermentation at Room Temperature

	Production per Unit Weight of Dry Solids				Percentage of Gas Composition after 21 Days		
	24 Days		80 Days				
Raw Material	ft^3/lb	m^3/kg	ft^3/lb	m^3/kg	CH_4 (Methane)	H_2 (Hydrogen)	CO_2 (Carbon Dioxide)
1. Cow dung	1.00	0.063	3.30	0.210	60.0%	1.1%	34.4%
2. Cow dung + 0.4% cane sugar	1.10	0.070	3.30	0.210	57.6	2.1	38.4
3. Cow dung + 1% ashes	0.98	0.061	3.00	0.190	60.4	2.9	34.4
4. Cow dung + 2.4% fresh leguminous leaves (25% dry matter, 2.31% nitrogen)	1.00	0.063	3.20	0.200	61.6	4.0	32.0
5. Cow dung + 1.2% sarson oil cake (94% dry matter, (4.74% nitrogen)	1.00	0.063	3.30	0.200	67.7	—	30.4
6. Cow dung + 1% cellulose	1.30	0.084	3.30	0.210	52.8	—	44.0
7. Cow dung + 0.4% casein (12.6% nitrogen)	1.40	0.087	3.50	0.220	64.0	2.4	32.0
8. Cow dung + 1% cane sugar + 1% urea (44.5% nitrogen)	1.40	0.087	4.20	0.260	68.0	—	30.6
9. Cow dung + 1% cane sugar + 1% calcium carbonate	1.50	0.091	3.90	0.240	70.0	—	28.0
10. Cow dung + urine (4% solids) at 20 ml/100 g (15 fl oz/lb)	1.40	0.087	3.90	0.240	67.0	—	32.0
11. Cow dung + 0.4% charcoal	1.00	0.065	2.60	0.160	65.6	—	32.0
12. Cow dung + 20% dry, non-leguminous leaves (1.71% nitrogen)	1.30	0.081	3.50	0.220	68.0	0.6	28.0

Source: National Academy of Sciences, *Methane Generation from Human, Animal, and Agricultural Wastes* (Washington, D.C.: National Academy of Sciences, 1977), p. 69.

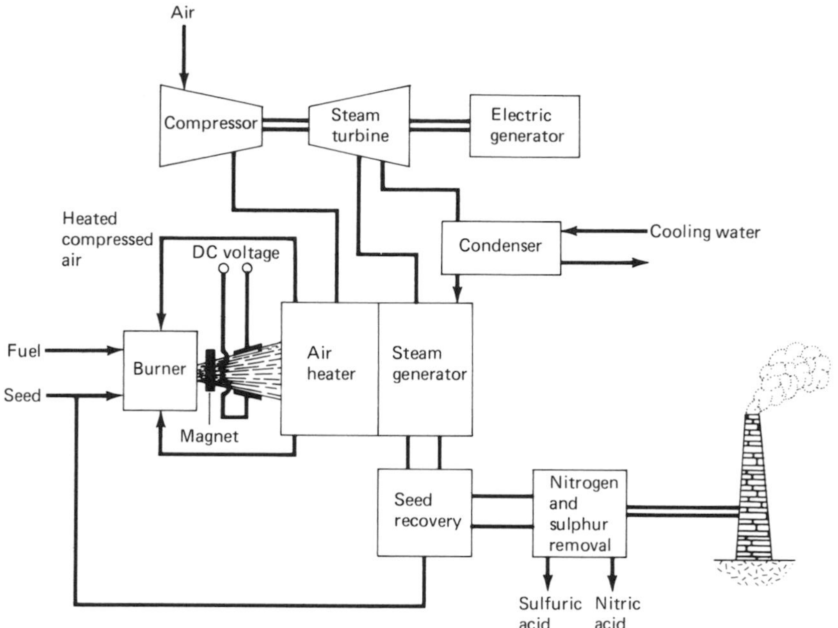

Figure 8.5. A Combined Magnetohydrodynamic-Steam Power Plant. Adapted from Healy, *Energy and Society*, p. 312.

direct-current external circuit and converted by an alternator into a conventional alternating circuit.

Given operating temperatures as high as 2,700°C, MHD generators also reject heat at relatively high temperatures. In order to make the most efficient use of the rejected energy, most practical MHD generator configurations are designed with a topping cycle such as the system illustrated in figure 8.5. In this particular arrangement, direct current is produced by the MHD generator. Rejected heat is then used to produce steam to operate a turbine for supplementary electricity generation, as occurs in conventional steam-based electrical production. Based on such a topping cycle, MHD generators could thus be integrated into all conventional fossil fuel plants now in use as well as into commercial electricity fission reactors of the kinds discussed in chapter 6.

The appeal of MHD technology is that it raises electrical power generation much closer to the Second Law, or Carnot, efficiency: a small amount of input energy would be needed per unit of electricity generated, and by extension, the more complete combustion would greatly reduce the amount of pollution now produced by conventional fossil fuel plants.[23]

[23]For a 1,000-megawatt power plant using coal with 3 percent sulfur content, the daily pollution would be on the order of: particulates, 33 tons; sulfur oxide, 450 tons; nitrogen oxides, 80 tons. With a MHD generator, the daily pollution of a unit of comparable capacity would be: particulates, 3 tons; sulfur oxides, 3 tons; nitrogen oxides, 4 tons. The combined reduction in pollu-

Thus far several limitations have restricted a more widespread commercial utilization of magnetohydrodynamic generators. Four of them can be noted here. One is that the magnets needed to operate MHD generators are relatively difficult to produce, particularly for modern power plants with average capacities of one gigawatt each. A second, more serious limitation is that MHD generators have not yet been able to operate for relatively long periods of time because of faster metal corrosion under high temperatures. Third, metal fatigue also increases as seeding materials penetrate the walls of generators, thereby reducing the technical life cycle of plants. Finally, the most efficient seeding materials are also some of the rarer elements and thus are difficult to procure. MHD generators thus require efficient seed-recovery cycles of the type illustrated in figure 8.5, a system which until now has made only limited progress.

To date, MHD generators have been used only in laboratory research.[24] In time, the problems already noted may be solved, thereby moving MHD technology closer to an economically competitive position. Since progress in this direction clearly involves economic considerations, research in MHD technology is an important element in the determination of national energy policy.

8.8. FUEL-CELL TECHNOLOGY

Ever since the fuel cell's discovery by Sir William Grove in 1839, this first cousin of the battery has held much promise as an efficient generator of electricity. Although practical fuel-cell technology dates from the work of Francis Bacon at Cambridge University in the 1930s, it was largely the expansion of the U.S. space-exploration program during the 1960s that led to the production of usable prototypes. Indeed, the historic manned lunar landing of July 1969 was facilitated partly by three fuel cells that provided 6.6 kilowatts of electrical power. At this point we need to have a basic understanding of how fuel cells generate electricity and how they could be integrated within the economy.

Unlike the storage of electrical energy in chemical form within batteries, fuel cells provide a continuous generation of electricity from an externally supplied chemical fuel.[25] Though many chemicals can be used, virtually all fuel cells function on the electrochemical conversion process illustrated in figure 8.6. A fuel such as hydrogen enters the cell near a negatively charged porous electrode, or anode. The anode and its companion porous electrode,

---

tion would thus be on the order of 98 percent. These and other details are found in "Environmental Pollution Control through MHD Power Generators," mimeographed (Everett, Mass.: AVCO Everett Research Laboratory, September 1970).

[24]In March 1971 the Soviet Union inaugurated a 25,000-kilowatt MHD natural-gas generator. Similar models have been under development in West Germany and in Japan. In the United States, most experimental work in MHD generators has been undertaken by AVCO Everett Research Laboratory in Everett, Massachusetts.

[25]A general description of fuel-cell technology is given in Arnold P. Fickett, "Fuel-Cell Power Plants," *Scientific American* 238 (December 1978):70–76.

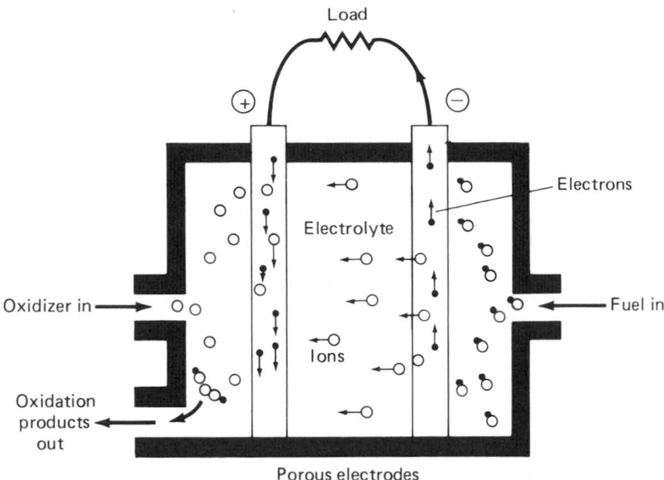

Figure 8.6. The Structure of a Fuel Cell. Adapted from Angrist, *Direct Energy Conversion*, p. 354.

the positively charged cathode, are both immersed in an electrolyte, or conversion fluid, which is used to transmit ions (nonstable elements or compounds). To facilitate the generation of electricity, an oxidizing agent such as oxygen in air is also fed into the cell. When the hydrogen comes into contact with the anode, it loses electrons and releases the residual of positively charged hydrogen ions. If the electrolyte is acidic, the hydrogen ions migrate to the cathode, where they react with electrons and oxygen to form water.[26] Electrons released by the ionization of hydrogen are then released from the anode as an electrical current. In effect, the fuel cell functions in the opposite direction of electrolysis, taking as it does two separate elements to form a single compound such as water and generating an electrical current in the process. Conducting wires attached to the fuel cell can then distribute the electricity in much the same fashion as occurs in conventional electricity transmission.

The conversion efficiency of fuel cells compares favorably with that of all conventional fossil, nuclear, and renewable electrical technologies and at the same time avoids some of the technical problems associated with a MHD generator of comparable efficiency. In the case of the typical hydrogen-oxygen fuel cell, between 0.6 and 0.85 volts can be supplied per cell, with a conversion efficiency of 83 percent and an average operating efficiency of about 60 percent.[27] In addition, by virtue of their conversion efficiency, fuel cells generate only minimal environmental pollution, which in the case of hydro-

[26]If the electrolyte is alkaline, hydroxyl ions ($OH-$) migrate to the anode. Other configurations include the migration of carbonate ions (CO_3—) to the anode in a carbonate-salt electrolyte and the migration of oxide ions (O—) from the cathode to the anode in a solid oxide electrolyte (see Angrist, *Direct Energy Conversion*, pp. 352–418).

[27]On a more precise level, the first law efficiency of a fuel cell is determined by the ratio of useful work to heat released, in which useful work is further defined as the Gibbs free-energy charge. For a hydrogen-oxygen cell this translates into: (56.62 kcal/mole)/(68.30 kcal/mole) =

gen-oxygen units consists essentially of water, carbon dioxide, and waste heat. Since fuel cells are relatively quiet, modular (they can be stacked into multi-megawatt configurations or paired to residential use), and transportable, they can be used as backup systems for central generating plants, or on a decentralized basis even within large urban communities. In comparison with the environmental pollution posed by fossil fuel plants and by radioactive releases from nuclear reactors, the minimal amount generated by fuel cells gives them a particular advantage in terms of urban siting. Moreover, on a decentralized basis, rejected heat from fuel-cell units could also be captured and used to provide space heating for buildings in which the fuel cells were operating. In sum, improvements in energy efficiency from fuel cells could be obtained in at least three principal ways: higher conversion efficiency, reduction in transmission costs by on-site generation, and topping off of industrial, commercial, and residential heating consumption by recycling of rejected heat.

Despite the apparent superiority of fuel-cell technology over conventional alternatives, a number of constraints have prevented the broadly based commercialization that we might expect. One of the most important is the problem of fuel itself. In section 8.4 we saw how the most efficient mode of hydrogen energy production necessitates the consumption of primary and secondary energy via electrolysis. Not only is electrolysis the reverse process of fuel-cell operation, but the primary energy needed to produce the electricity for electrolysis has been based invariably on conventional fossil, hydro-, and nuclear power. With the exception of hydropower, these technologies rarely approach their 35–40 percent Second Law conversion efficiencies. Consequently, absent any substantive change in these technologies such as MHD generators, or any of the other renewable technologies discussed in chapter 7, the most likely justification for hydrogen-fuel-cell utilization would be through off-peak hydrogen storage from central power plant generation, as has been noted already. The net efficiency of fuel-cell technology would be reduced from 60 percent to about 40 percent, or roughly equal to that which is available from conventional technolgies already in place. Under such an operation, fuel cells could still provide some net gains in overall primary energy use in that they could permit conventional power plants to operate closer to their thermodynamic limits.

As an alternative to hydrogen, other materials could be used to operate fuel cells with comparable conversion efficiency. Among them are natural gas, gasified coal, biomass methane, and biogas.[28] While all of these gas fuels share common properties appropriate to efficient energy conversion in

---

0.83. Actual conversion losses from materials conductivity lower this limit to an operational efficiency of about 60 percent (see R. C. Dorf, *Energy, Resources, and Policy* [Reading, Mass.: Addison-Wesley Publishing Co., 1978], p. 358).

[28]This list is far from exhaustive. Ammonia, hydrazine, calcium hydride, and hydrogen oxide are among other hydrogen-based fuels. In addition, it is also possible to use biochemical cells, in which organic transformations provide sufficient wastes in the form of ammonia, ethanol, and hydrogen to sustain fuel-cell operations.

fuel cells, they do not possess equal energy efficiencies in their preparation. For example, since coal gasification requires energy conversion at the outset, the net gains may not be materially higher than those of hydrogen. The input energy necessary to biomass methane is somewhat less than that necessary to gasified coal, but is substantially larger than that needed in biogas preparation. To be sure, all of these gases require far more energy in their preparation than does natural gas, yet natural gas is much closer in relative terms to economic exhaustion. Clearly, then, relative prices have an important role to play in the selection of appropriate fuels.

A second problem in fuel-cell technology is that as in battery-storage systems, electrolyte materials are subject to deterioration and require periodic replacement. Though this is not an insuperable difficulty, it does weigh significantly in the ultimate economic efficiency of fuel-cell technology. Indeed, since large-scale utilization of fuel cells has yet to take place within the U.S. economy, it is clear that pricing and national energy policy are key factors in any eventual change from current energy patterns.

8.9. TOTAL ENERGY SYSTEMS

At several points in the discussion so far, reference has been made to combined-cycle technologies. Combined-cycle, or co-generation, technologies form the basis of what are known as total energy systems. Essentially, the design of total energy systems involves the matching of every possible energy flow from a conversion technology to its technically most efficient task. Although many energy technologies are not included in the present survey, we can nevertheless draw on existing examples to illustrate the potential of total energy systems.[29]

One of the best-known examples of a total energy system is industrial co-generation. As we have seen, the First Law efficiency of a conventional fossil or nuclear power plant does not generally exceed 40 percent. This means that 60 percent of the energy input is rejected into the environment as heat or particulates. Under industrial co-generation, rather than so much waste's being permitted to occur, decentralized fossil electricity-generating units are used at industrial—or group residential, as the case may warrant—sites to generate electricity. These decentralized generating units may be individually owned or owned by a centralized public utility, and they function as a com-

[29]Among some of these alternatives are: thermionic generators, thermoelectric generators, electrokinetic convertors, piezoelectric convertors, and electric synthesizers. A thermionic generator releases electrons from metals under confined heating, with temperatures reaching as high as 1,600°C; for use as a heat engine, laboratory efficiencies as high as 25 percent have been attained. A thermoelectric generator is another heat engine that relies on temperature differences between two conductor junctions to build up voltage; tests at Bell labs on a solar generator have attained only about 2 percent efficiency. An electrokinetic convertor relies on pressure differences among fluids to build up voltage for electric current. Piezoelectric converters use the same pressure principles applied to crystalline solids. An electric synthesizer adjusts the speed of an electric motor to the optimal requirements of a given task, much as occurs in the case of a variable-speed drill.

plement to, or in some cases a substitute for, central-power-station generating units. In turn, the rejected steam from a decentralized co-generating unit can be upgraded by a boiler unit to function as industrial process steam, or to provide steam heat in building radiator systems. Whatever the configuration, the thermodynamic efficiency of the total energy system of the industrial site is raised under co-generation, since the need for supplementary energy to provide the industrial process steam or building steam heat is reduced in proportion to the amount of rejected steam captured from the electricity-generating unit for re-use, or "topping off." Moreover, to the extent that the combined cycle operates more closely with variations in the decentralized demand for electrical and thermal energy, the thermodynamic efficiency of the regional or national energy system is enhanced. Indeed, if the Second Law efficiency of a central-station electricity-generating plant were 35 percent and that of the steam boiler of a separate industrial process were 25 to 28 percent, on-site industrial co-generation of both steam and electricity could yield a combined-cycle Second Law efficiency of up to 50 percent, especially when transmission and distribution losses from central-station electricity generation are included as the alternative.

Co-generation has yet to become a significant element in U.S. commercial energy systems. In contrast, many countries in Europe have utilized co-generation for decades, with correspondingly higher levels of energy conservation than those achieved in the United States. Not surprisingly, the relative absence of co-generation in the United States is one reason why the U.S. economy has the relatively high historical energy intensity of the kind that we saw in figure 3.4. Once again, the relative pricing of energy has been a major reason for this difference in the choice of specific energy technologies and in comparative energy intensity.

We can conclude our discussion of total energy systems with reference to a few other examples of the potential for energy conservation. Throughout the discussion, we have looked at energy storage and conversion choices mostly in terms of specific, and at times seemingly unrelated, technologies. Yet as they become economically competitive, they will most likely emerge as combinations and variations of each other. Moreover, the concept of total energy systems embraces more than decentralized co-generation. It also involves the optimal use of existing energy technologies. Thus, there is considerable potential for energy conservation just by increasing the level of insulation in buildings, by using optimal thermostatic controls, and by maintaining and driving existing vehicles in energy-efficient ways which most of us have come to view as familiar. Taken together, these everyday energy choices and the use of some of the alternative systems that we have examined could quite easily make it possible to achieve the kind of low-energy continuing real economic growth envisioned in some of the projections enumerated in chapter 3.

It would be ideal if energy conservation could be achieved at constant or falling real costs. Yet simple economic logic suggests that raising real energy prices is the most likely way to bring about these changes. Indeed, energy conservation may turn out to be one of the most important of all of the alternative sources of energy in the United States during the next several years, but much will depend on the interplay of energy pricing and energy technologies. Now that we have looked at the spectrum of energy technologies, let us examine these choices from an economic perspective.

8.10. SUMMARY

Technical efficiency of energy use depends critically on storage and conversion technology. At the same time, much of the present use of conventional fossil and nuclear fuels is inefficient by thermodynamic standards. What can raise the efficiency of conventional and renewable energy technologies closer to their thermodynamic limits is the use of alternative storage and conversion methods.

Beyond present patterns of energy storage are four basic systems which could significantly raise the efficiency of primary energy use: compressed air, flywheels, batteries, and hydrogen. Compressed air could store mechanical energy in unused underground reservoirs when central power plants operate at less than peak capacities and release that energy for electricity production when demand increases. Batteries could store electrical energy in chemical form from both conventional electrical power plants and from alternative renewable energy resources. Higher-density energy storage batteries not now in use could raise this storage capacity even further. Flywheels can store mechanical energy for subsequent conversion into electricity. Flywheel technology is one of the oldest known energy-storage mechanisms, but with the development of fiber-composite flywheels, storage densities far exceeding compressed-air and all practical battery configurations could be used to raise central-power-plant operations closer to their thermodynamic limits. Flywheels could also facilitate the use of renewable energy resources as well as the development of flywheel vehicles in transportation. Finally, hydrogen can be used not only in the production of electricity but also as a fuel for areas (such as transportation) that are now so dependent on liquid fossil fuels. It is also environmentally superior to conventional fuels in that its principal by-product from combustion is water.

Another way of increasing energy efficiency is by use of alternative conversion technologies. Of several possible technologies, four basic ones can make significant differences in present energy use: heat pumps, waste recycling, magnetohydrodynamics, and fuel cells. Heat pumps seem to defy the laws of thermodynamics in that they draw on the heat of low-temperature reservoirs to increase the temperature of high-temperature reservoirs such as buildings in winter. As long as temperature differences are not extreme, heat pumps are far superior to conventional fossil and electrical-resistance heating. A second alternative, waste recycling, can improve energy efficiency in two ways. When commonly used materials such as metals and plastics are recycled, substantial reductions in energy use can be achieved. Moreover, organic wastes can themselves be used as fuels in a variety of ways, ranging from supplementary resources for the operation of steam power plants to the production of synthetic gas. A third alternative, magnetohydrodynamics, relies on the high-temperature conversion efficiency of plasma fluids to convert combustible fuels into electricity. MHD generators could also be combined with central power plants to raise total operating efficiency. The fourth alternative is fuel cells. Fuel cells convert hydrogen-based fuels into electricity by chemical transformations that avoid the limitations of conventional heat engines. Fuel cells are modular and can be used in conventional power plants as well as in decentralized energy systems.

Raising the efficiency of energy use increases the need for multiple-energy technologies. Though none of these systems is technically unconstrained, thermodynamic efficiency does call for the design of appropriate total energy structures. Through the co-generation of power, these total energy systems can bring together the most efficient combinations of technologies for the performance of chosen energy tasks. In turn, the choice of individual technical combinations depends on the role of economics and on energy policy in particular.

SUGGESTED READINGS

Angrist, S. W. *Direct Energy Conversion*. 3d ed. Boston: Allyn and Bacon, 1976.

Auer, Peter, ed. *Advances in Energy Systems and Technology*. Vol. 1. New York: Academic Press, 1978.

Dickson, Edward M., Ryan, John W., and Smulyan, Marilyn H. *The Hydrogen Energy Economy*. New York: Praeger Publishers, 1977.

Hottel, H. C., and Howard, J. B. *New Energy Technology*. 1971. Reprint. Cambridge, Mass.: MIT Press, 1977.

National Academy of Sciences. *Methane Generation from Human, Animal, and Agricultural Wastes*. Washington, D.C.: National Academy of Sciences, 1977.

Williams, R. H. *The Energy Conservation Papers*. Cambridge, Mass.: Ballinger Publishing Co., 1975.

PART III

THE ECONOMICS OF ENERGY RESOURCES

9

THE STRUCTURE OF ENERGY RESOURCE PRODUCTION

As we saw in parts I and II, projections of future energy use depend on several key factors. Aside from the relative price of resources, the level of aggregate economic activity, and the technical laws governing energy storage and conversion, one key factor likely to affect future energy use is the extent to which energy markets are economically efficient. For economists and economic policymakers, economic efficiency is determined essentially by the extent to which the allocation of resources conforms to a perfectly competitive market structure. Indeed, whether one should apply any of the procompetitive policy instruments noted in chapter 1 depends fundamentally on how competition is measured. A more rigorous policy definition of competition is presented in chapter 13. At this point, we can examine the question of economic efficiency in energy markets in terms of four basic measures, namely, the elasticity of supply, economies of scale, concentration ratios, and the degree of profitability.

9.1. A REFERENCE FRAMEWORK FOR ENERGY SUPPLY DECISIONS

The production of any good depends fundamentally on its costs and on the price at which it can be sold. In the case of energy resources, the supply curves that embody these relationships are as varied as are the many types of energy already discussed. Insofar as energy policy is concerned, the basic economic question on the supply side is the extent to which output varies directly with changes in the price of energy. To answer this question, we must specify the number of producers and how they are organized, the input-output structure of production, and the role of technological change. First we need to spell out an analytical frame of reference.

Figures 9.1.*a*, 9.1.*b*, and 9.1.*c* provide a conceptual framework that underlies all energy supply decisions. In the short-run static condition shown here, figure 9.1.*a* identifies the choice of inputs in the production of energy, figures 9.1.*b* and 9.1.*c* translate the chosen production levels of individual

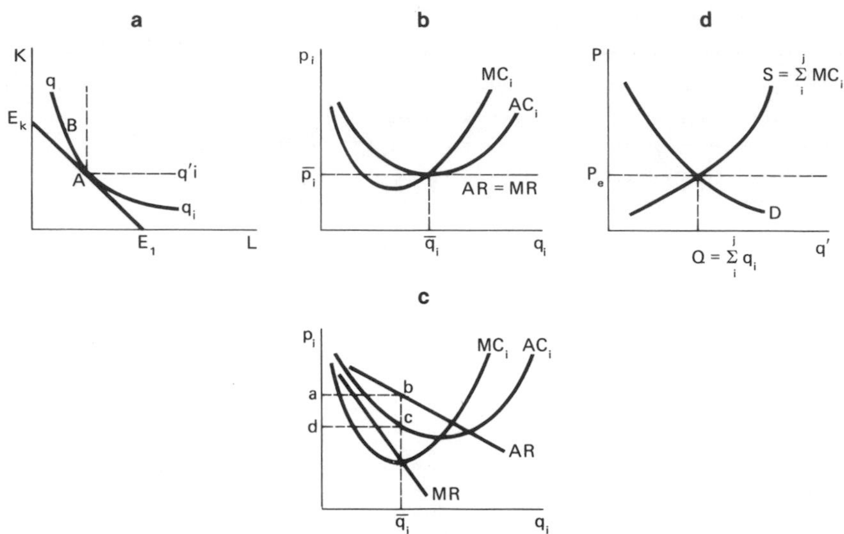

Figure 9.1. The Simple Geometry of Short-Run Energy Supply Decisions: **a.** producer input efficiency; **b.** producer output efficiency (perfect competition); **c.** producer output efficiency (imperfect competition); **d.** static market equilibrium.

firms into their corresponding curves, and figure 9.1.*d* brings together the individual producer costs to form market supply and its relation to the demand for the particular energy product.

In any given time period, an individual energy producer will tend to choose within its budgetary limits the most efficient combination of inputs to generate a given level of energy output. The number and proportions of inputs will differ according to the particular resource and its associated production technology, but for purposes of illustration, these inputs can be classified generally as capital (K) and labor (L), as is shown in figure 9.1.*a*. To be sure, the prices of these inputs could vary according to the amounts purchased by each producer. However, if the quantities of capital and labor represent only relatively small shares of the total use of these inputs within the economy, then for each firm the prices may be thought of as given and invariant to its decisions. The slope of the budget constraint, E_kE_l, is thus the ratio of the unit price of labor to that of capital.[1] In more practical terms, the slope of the budgetary constraint indicates the importance of relative prices to the choice of any particular combination of inputs in energy production.

Despite the great variety of possible input combinations within a given budgetary constraint, a producer is interested primarily in that particular

[1]Since E_kE_l is an isocost relationship that defines the varying proportions of inputs which can be obtained from a given expenditure limit, its slope can be expressed in more formal and conventional terms as the ratio of the budgetary constraint, or total cost (TC), divided by the unit price of capital, to the total cost of labor divided by its unit price: slope of E_kE_l = $(TC/r)/(TC/w) = -w/r$, where w = the unit wage rate and r = the unit price of capital per unit of time.

combination which yields the greatest level of output, since it is also the least expensive. What determines this choice is the firm's available energy-production process, and the extent to which input substitution can be undertaken with the given level of technology.

A firm's energy-production function specifies the alternative input combinations that correspond to its various levels of output. If these relationships are well defined, then we can derive for any one level of output the range of input alternatives that are essential to the determination of optimum input efficiency. In figure 9.1.*a* one typical set of these alternative inputs, or isoquants, is illustrated as qq_i. Simple inspection shows that in this case the optimal level of operation is at point A, since it involves the largest degree of output consistent with the firm's budget constraint.[2]

As we might suspect, the shape of the firm's energy production function is crucial to the attainment of its optimal input efficiency. To see how this is so, consider the impact of a change in relative prices. If the price of labor increases relative to that of capital, the slope of the budgetary limit will increase, thereby increasing the relative possible share of capital while reducing that of labor. If the production function is of the type illustrated by qq_i, it also suggests a new optimum input combination at a point of tangency somewhere to the left, as in position B, if that is where the new tangency is found.[3]

To proceed with the conceptual framework of figure 9.1, once an energy-producing firm has chosen an optimal input combination, the next question is whether it can economically produce a particular level of output such as the qq_i of figure 9.1.*a*. The answer lies in the joining of its fixed and variable inputs to derive a cost-of-production function which can then be compared with the price at which any particular level of output can be sold (fig. 9.1.*b*).[4]

[2]In more formal terms, given a generalized production function $Q = f(x_1, x_2)$, where x_1 and x_2 are two inputs of the kind illustrated in figure 9.1.*a*, and a budget constaint $C = p_1x_1 + p_2x_2$, where C is the total cost and p_1 and p_2 are the respective input prices, the maximum optimal combination of x_1 and x_2 can be determined from the Lagrangian function, $L = f(x_1, x_2) - \lambda(p_1x_1 + p_2x_2 - C)$. Differentiating with respect to each input yields

$$\partial L \,/\, \partial x_1 = \partial f \,/\, \partial x_1 - \lambda p_1 = 0; \partial L \,/\, \partial x_2 = \partial f \,/\, \partial x_2 - \lambda p_2 = 0,$$

which when rearranged gives

$$\frac{\partial f}{\partial x_1} \,/\, p_1 = \frac{\partial f}{\partial x_2} \,/\, p_2 = \lambda = (\partial f/\partial x_1) \,/\, (\partial f/\partial x_2) = p_1/p_2,$$

that is, the ratio of the marginal rate of technical substitution of input 1 to input 2 is equal to the ratio of input prices of input 1 to input 2.

[3]The degree of flexibility in attaining these alternative points of efficiency is the elasticity of substitution. In more formal terms, the elasticity of substitution can be expressed as

$$\sigma_{kl} = -\left[\frac{\Delta(Q_k/Q_l)}{(Q_k/Q_l)} \Bigg/ \frac{\Delta(r_k/r_w)}{(r_k/r_w)}\right] = -\left[\frac{\Delta \log(Q_k/Q_l)}{\Delta \log(r_k/r_w)}\right].$$

[4]Determination of this efficiency calls for the joining of price and elasticity information from the firm's demand curve to its particular production function. In empirical studies involving energy, economists have utilized a range of production functions which approximate varying degrees of the elasticity of input substitution, the properties of which are too complex to consider

The conventional rule of profit maximization indicates that the energy firm will select a level of output $\overline{q}_i$, which is where its marginal cost of the last unit produced just equals the marginal revenue from its sale.

As we can see, the equilibrium position of an energy producer in figure 9.1.*b* is based on a perfectly competitive market. Since the producer can exert no significant degree of control over the price or the output, not only does the marginal revenue (*MR*) equal the marginal cost (*MC*) but the average cost (*AC*) equals the average revenue (*AR*). However, we need only to think of OPEC to note that there are imperfectly competitive energy markets in which producers can control a significant share of output and prices. Under these conditions, average and marginal revenue are downsloping, as is shown in figure 9.1.*c*. Profit maximization by an imperfect competitor follows the same rule as in perfect competition, but with the result that an optimal level $\overline{q}_i$ will now be a lower output and at a higher price than would be the case for the perfect competitor. The result is the accumulation of excess profits, as denoted by the rectangle *abcd*. To be sure, where imperfect competition does exist, there is economic inefficiency in the short-run allocation of energy resources.

The third stage of figure 9.1 is the determination of market equilibrium (fig. 9.1.*d*). As can be seen, unless there is external intervention, as in the regulation of price or output (which of course can and does occur), the market equilibrium will be the individual producer output which just matches consumer demand at the market's clearing price.

The energy production decision framework thus far depicted refers only to the short run. These same conditions hold true for the long run as well, except that in the long run variables formerly considered fixed are in a position to shift, in patterns which are illustrated in figure 9.2.

Like short-run energy production decisions, long-run energy production decisions involving inputs are governed by the firm's budget constraint and the relative price considerations already noted. However, relative prices are now influenced by two additional variables: technological change and economies of scale. In the case of economies of scale, a firm may be able to double its output with a less than proportional increase in its inputs, shown in figure 9.2.*a* by the shift in the isoquants from qq_1 to qq_2. Such economies may be due to the operating scale of machines, as in the case of some electrical generators. At the same time, there is no foreordained pattern of scale economies in all sectors of production. In fact, in some cases there may also be diseconomies of scale, as illustrated by the outward shift of the firm's energy production isoquant from qq_2 to qq_3. Where these diseconomies exist, they point to a restructuring of the individual energy industry, particu-

---

in detail here. The principal types of these functions and their associated substitution elasticities are the Leontief Input-Output Model ($\sigma_k = 0$); the Cobb-Douglas production function ($\sigma_{kl} = 1$); the CES, or Constant Elasticity of Substitution throughout all ranges of production function ($\sigma_{kl} = 0 - \infty$); and the VES, or Variable Elasticity of Substitution production function, of which the most common form is the Translog production function ($\sigma = 0 - \infty$).

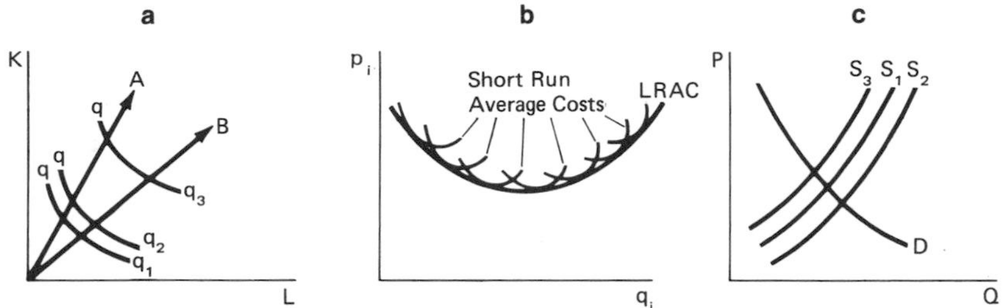

Figure 9.2. The Simple Geometry of Long-Run Energy Supply Decisions; **a.** producer input efficiency; **b.** producer output efficiency; **c.** dynamic market equilibrium.

larly if maximum economic efficiency is an integral component in energy policy.

Technological change in energy production has already been described in some detail in chapters 5–8. In diagrammatic terms, the economic consequences of these decisions may also be reflected in the relative efficiency of energy inputs. As one possibility, greater output may be obtained from the same level and proportions of inputs, in which case such technological change is considered unbiased, or neutral. On the other hand, if there is an improvement in only one input, as in the capital good of figure 9.2.*a*, capital goods then become relatively less expensive and the firm's expansion path over time will be one that is capital-intensive and labor-saving, as is illustrated by pattern *A*. If the reverse is true, the shift will become labor-intensive and capital-saving, causing the expansion path to shift from its movement along *A* to a movement along *B*.

Technological change and the pressure or absence of economies of scale alter the firm's long-run average cost curve (*LRAC*), shown here in figure 9.2.*b*. Where technical efficiency is increasing, the firm's short-run average cost curves will move along the declining segment of the long-run average cost curve. Where such change is absent or counteracted by the production of a depletable energy resource, a more likely position is the movement along the upward-sloping portion of the long-run average cost curve. Finally, when the cost curves of an individual energy-producing firm are aggregated throughout the industry, we can measure the impact on the market equilibrium by tracing the shifts of the industry's supply curve relative to its demand.

Each of the preceding examples provides an illustration of the operational framework of energy supply decisions. To be sure, the price of energy depends ultimately not only on the cost of production but also on the demand for energy, on the extent to which energy production is taxed or subsidized, on economic uncertainty and the risks inherent in exploration and development, and on whether the allocation of energy resources is governed principally by the interaction of supply and demand or is affected by government regulation. Since we are concerned here only with the question of competition, let us now use the foregoing framework to look at four empirical measures of producer competition.

9.2. AN OVERVIEW OF ENERGY SUPPLY RESPONSES

One way of looking at the question of producer competition is in terms of the elasticity of supply. For a competitive market and a given period of time, a one-unit relative change in the price of a resource should elicit a greater relative change in quantity supplied than it would in a market where competition is limited or absent. In more formal terms, the price elasticity of supply that is used to make such comparisons can be defined as the relative change in quantity supplied per relative change in its price, that is:

$$\epsilon_s = \left(\frac{\Delta Q}{Q}\right) \Big/ \left(\frac{\Delta P}{P}\right) = \frac{\partial Q}{\partial P}\left(\frac{P}{Q}\right), \tag{9.1}$$

where Q is the quantity supplied and P is the price. Since the value of ϵ_s ranges from zero to infinity, equation (9.1) provides an ordinal scale with which to rank alternative market supply curves, and the industries that lie behind them, from least to most competitive. Similar comparisons could be made based on estimates of the cross-price elasticity of supply, where Q would refer to the quantity supplied of one industry and P would refer to the price of a competitive alternative. Though there are several ways in which equation (9.1) could be expressed for purposes of empirical estimation, because there have been relatively few studies of energy supply elasticities thus far, let us concentrate on the interpretation of available findings.

Table 9.1 provides summary estimates of short- and long-run price elasticites of supply for the primary energy fuels petroleum, natural gas, coal, and uranium. Though some of these estimates pertain to U.S. domestic resources and others are based on international data, they suggest several basic conclusions.

First, as we might expect, short-run price elasticities of supply for each of the four primary energy resources are lower than long-run estimates. Thus, given sufficient time to alter the scale and technology of their operations, producers are likely to be more responsive to changes in relative energy prices than in the short run.

Second, despite greater relative flexibility, the long-run elasticity-of-supply estimates suggest that the real price of these resources might have to increase during the 1980s at rates at least comparable to those of the 1970s if some of the more energy-intensive scenarios of chapter 3 are to be fulfilled. The question then becomes one of deciding whether such comparable changes in energy prices would serve as a satisfactory indicator of the behavior of competitive energy markets or whether they would be indicative of some broader phenomenon.

The basic difficulty with using supply elasticities as a measure of producer competition is that they reveal none of the determinants which give rise to these differences, of which competition is but one. For example, the irrevers-

Table 9.1. Estimates of Primary Energy Price Elasticities of Supply

Fuel	Short-Run Price Elasticities	Long-Run Price Elasticities
Petroleum	0.110891–0.140704[a]	0.67–0.34; 0.41502–0.367935[a]
Natural gas	0.042154	0.3026–0.2700; 0.3529–0.1911[c]
Coal	0.142407	0.31506–0.20808
Uranium	1.21[b]	

Sources: On short-run estimates of price elasticity for petroleum, see M. A. Adelman and H. D. Jacoby, "Alternative Methods of Oil Supply Forecasting," in *Advances in the Economics of Energy and Resources,* ed. R. S. Pindyck, vol. 2 (Greenwich, Conn.: JAI Press, 1979), p. 19. On short-run estimates for natural gas and coal, see Federal Energy Administration, *National Energy Outlook, 1976*, (Washington, D.C.: U.S. Government Printing Office, February 1976), p. G-22. On uranium estimates, see J. B. Gordon and M. L. Baughman, "The Economics of the Throwaway Nuclear Fuel Cycle," in *Advances in the Economics of Energy and Resources*, ed. R. S. Pindyck, vol. 1 (Greenwich, Conn.: JAI Press, 1979), p. 224. On long-run estimates for petroleum, see Paul L. Eckbo, "A Basin Development Model of Oil Supply," in Pindyck, *Advances,* vol. 2, p. 54. On long-run estimates for natural gas and coal, see FEA, *National Energy Outlook, 1976*, pp. 139 and G-2 (reference case), respectively.

[a]These estimates are based on North Sea discoveries; thus the conditions are not directly comparable to those in the United States

[b]This estimate is based on reserves only, and not on actual production, as of 1 January 1977, within a price range of ten to fifteen dollars per pound of U_3O_8

[c]Data are for 1985, using 1975 constant dollars per thousand cubic feet within a price range of $1.00–2.80

ible nature of entropy would suggest that the long-run elasticity of supply would tend to be lower in an industry based on depletable energy resources than it would in an industry based on nondepletable resources. Thus, to conclude that depletable-energy-resource industries were less competitive than other industries on the basis of supply elasticities alone would be an insufficient test. For this reason, let us look at alternative measures of producer competition as they apply to these same energy resources.

9.3. PETROLEUM AND NATURAL GAS

Few industries in the U.S. economy are as large and as complex as the petroleum and natural gas industries. In the 1980 annual list of the largest 500 industrial firms published by *Fortune* magazine, twenty of the first fifty are petroleum corporations.[5] The 1980 sales of these firms accounted for 55 percent of the sales by all firms in the top fifty and 29 percent of the sales among all of the 500 firms and had a market value equivalent to over 18 percent of the U.S. 1980 Gross National Product. Given the size of these petro-

[5]*Fortune 500*, 4 May 1981, pp. 224–25. Sales are often considered as a good measure of firm concentration in that they correlate well with assets and stock equity. For tests of the appropriateness of alternative indices, see S. S. Shalit and U. Sanker, "The Measurement of Firm Size," *Review of Economics and Statistics* 59 (August 1977):290–98.

leum firms, two questions come immediately to mind: Do they enjoy economies of scale that could justify their relative size? and Are they monopolistic to such an extent that economic efficiency and social welfare are reduced to a level below what we would expect to find in a perfectly competitive market?

Economies of scale generally are defined in terms of the nonproportional relations between changes in inputs and outputs. The can be more rigorously and empirically usefully defined as existing when for a fixed set of input prices and cost minimization, average costs decline as the scale of output is increased (see figure 9.2.*b*).[6] In the case of petroleum, the measurement of these scale economies is complicated by the fact that there is extensive vertical integration throughout the stages of exploration, extraction, refining, and distribution. Hence, there are two possible sources of scale economies: those within a given stage of production and those over several stages of production. Each of these will be considered in turn.

One difficulty facing petroleum and natural gas firms is that there may be significant benefits accuring to other than the principal firm engaged in exploration. As pointed out in chapter 1, these external economies arise from the fact that drilling by one firm increases the knowledge of deposit size and affects the decision by other firms to proceed with drilling in adjacent tracts. Absent any coherent policy by governments or lessors of exploratory tracts, the logical response of exploratory firms is to attempt to reduce these external economies by engaging in exploration as large-scale as possible, given geological information, budgetary constaints, and the expected selling price of the crude oil, natural gas, or derived fossil fuel products. Such practices, known commonly as unitization when extraction feasibility is taken into consideration, have long characterized petroleum and natural gas exploration.

Internalization of discovery benefits from large-scale drilling does not prove that there are economies of scale in exploration. For example, unless there is a significant skew in the distribution of geological information to large-scale exploratory firms, a small firm can discover as large a deposit from a single well-placed hole as it could from a greater number of exploratory drillings over a larger tract. Given that depths and pool sizes have not varied substantially over time, the first conclusion to the scale-economies question is that they do not generally exist in exploration. What does exist is an internalization of benefits from large-scale drilling. The implication for energy policy is that the total costs may be so high as to serve as barriers to potential new entrants.

Just as exploration does not yield returns to scale, neither does extraction. Extraction costs are governed by the variables already cited in chapter 5, namely the size of the pool, the depth and pressure of the deposit, labor, and

[6]See Giora Hanoch, "The Elasticity of Scale and the Shape of Average Costs," *American Economic Review* 65 (June 1975):492–97. Hanoch's formulation allows for the fact that expansion may not move along a fixed ray of the kind illustrated in figure 9.2.*a* but may in fact shift in response to both technical change and changes in relative input prices. Such shiftability in the output expansion path is known as non-homotheticity, after R. Shepherd, *Cost and Production Functions* (Princeton, N.J.: Princeton University Press, 1953).

the costs of extraction equipment.[7] Since a given pool contains a finite quantity of the resource, each additional amount extracted lowers the pressure on the remainder, thereby creating an inevitable rise in cost. Though secondary and tertiary recovery methods help raise the yield, they also add to costs, since the marginal rate of extraction necessitated additional capital expenditures in the first place. In his 1972 study of the world petroleum market, Morris Adelman put it succinctly: "The more a given deposit is developed, the higher—almost certainly—will be the cost of additional development. Production cost always rises as a function of greater output."[8]

In contrast to the constant or increasing average costs associated with petroleum and natural gas exploration and extraction, there is some evidence of the presence of scale economies in petroleum refining. To determine the extent of scale economies in any industry, economists have developed three techniques: survivor studies, statistical cost analysis, and engineering process analysis. Of these three, the survivor method, that is, the study of survival over time of large firms as opposed to small firms, is considered a relatively weak test for scale economies because its highly aggregated approach fails to identify many important underlying determinants, with the result that conflicting conclusions may emerge.

A stronger test for scale economies is statistical cost analysis. In this approach, aggregate data on industry inputs and outputs are used to estimate industrywide production functions of the kinds referred to in section 9.2. One such study, by Hildebrand and Liu in 1957, used a modified constant elasticity of substitution production function for the petroleum and coal pro-

[7]In more formal terms, a firm should undertake additional exploration and extraction as long as the present value of expected future revenues from each additional unit exceeds the present value of the capital and operating costs. The present value of expected revenues is based on a weighted function of past prices, current market prices, public policy, inflation, and uncertainty. It can be expressed as $PV_r = \int_0^t R_t d_t = \int_0^t (p_t q_t) e^{-rt} dt$, where R_t equals revenues per time period, p_t is the price, q_t is the production quantity, r is the discount rate, t is the number of production time periods under consideration from the particular exploration and production investment, and e = the base of natural logarithms. Once inflation and uncertainty have been taken into account, the price per unit (e.g., one barrel), can be expressed as a weighted constant: $p_t = p_c$. The production profile is based on a declining rate of production as pressure falls in the reservoir: $q_t = q_0 e^{-at}$, where a = the rate of decline over the production horizon, as determined by engineering and geological data. The present value of the return can then be redefined as $PV_r = p_c q_0 \int_0^t e^{-(r + a)t} dt$. The present value of capital is expressed as $PV_c = k \int_0^t e^{-rt} dt = k((1 - e^{-rt})/r)$. As an example, if a barrel of crude oil can be sold at \$0.10 (p_c), the initial annual production rate is 1,364,954 barrels (q_0), the uncertainty adjusted rate of time discount is 10 percent (r), the production decline rate is 5 percent a year (a), a twenty-year production investment horizon is contemplated, and the undiscounted capital cost is \$100,000, then the present value of the investment is exactly equal to the present value of the costs, at \$864,664.72. If there are no better investment opportunities for the \$100,000, then the investment expenditures should be undertaken. To verify that this is optimal, the per-barrel cost of capital can be computed from $c' = k[1 - e^{-rt}/r]/q_0[1 - e^{-(a + r)(t)}/a + r] = k/q_0 [(a + r)/r][(1 - e^{-rt})/(1 - e^{-(a + r)(t)})]$, which turns out to be \$0.10, or just equal to the selling price of the crude oil per barrel (p_c). It should be emphasized however, that this privately efficient market choice may be socially suboptimal. For an elaboration of investment decisionmaking in petroleum, see M. A. Adelman, *The World Petroleum Market* (Baltimore: Johns Hopkins Press for Resources for the Future, 1972), pp. 50–52.

[8]Ibid., p. 21.

ducts industry.[9] The study concluded that for this combined industry there were constant, rather than decreasing or increasing, costs to scale. Two reasons may account for their finding only constant returns: first, they treated petroleum and coal together, and second, their estimates do not isolate refining from other stages of production.

The most reliable method, engineering process analysis, is also the one with the strongest evidence of scale economies in refining. Pioneered many years ago by Bain (1956), engineering process analysis utilizes highly detailed, direct engineering data obtained from individual firms to identify the choice of scale in single and multiplant operations.[10] Using this method, economists have generally followed Bain's framework by comparing engineering estimates of the minimum-optimal-scale, or MOS, plant with the actual sizes found throughout the industry. The MOS plant is at that level where any scale opportunities have been exhausted. If plants exceed this level, either they have constant returns to scale (the most likely condition for actual observation) or they may be in the increasing-cost range. Economists have also used the MOS criterion to determine by what percentage average costs would rise if a plant were constructed with a capacity at some stipulated fraction of the MOS bench mark, that is, to identify a point to the left of the industry's minimum average cost level. Similarly, we can also compare the industry share of four hypothetical MOS plants with the actual share of output by the prevailing four largest firms. If the share of the four largest MOS plants is less than the share of the actual four largest, the implication is that the industry's four largest firms (or whatever bench-mark comparison has been adopted) could be restructured with no significant increase in the industry's average cost of production.

Results of studies of MOS petroleum refining capacity for the United States are given in table 9.2. In each of the studies, engineering and interview data were assembled to obtain comparable statistical estimates of refineries being contemplated or actually under construction. The list of costs is not strictly comparable in all cases (for example, Bain included transport costs, but Pratten and Scherer did not), but Scherer (1975) has concluded that the variation in definitions is not significant enough to dismiss the relative uniformity of conclusions among the three studies. What these studies point to is significant: there are economies of scale in petroleum refining; these economies have increased gradually over time in response to the size of the market and to technological change; at the same time, MOS refineries would call for plants roughly one-quarter the size of the four largest plants during each period of observation.

Several criticisms have been raised regarding the use of engineering process analysis to measure the presence of scale economies, the most important of which can be briefly summarized here. First, engineering studies cannot

[9]G. H. Hildebrand and T. C. Liu, *Manufacturing Production Functions in the United States, 1957* (Ithaca: Cornell University Press, 1965), p. 108.

[10]J. S. Bain, *Barriers to New Competition* (Cambridge, Mass.: Harvard University Press, 1956).

Table 9.2. Estimates of Minimum-Optimal-Scale Plant Capacity in U.S. Petroleum Refining

Study	MOS Plant Capacity as Percentage of National Capacity	Four-Firm MOS Ratio	Four-Firm Actual Ratio	Percentage Elevation of Unit Costs at One-Third MOS
Bain (1956)[a]	1.75 (=122,500 bbl/d)[b]	7.00	37.00[c]	—
Pratten (1971)[d]	2.00 (=210,526 bbl/d)[b]	8.00	33.00[e]	—
Scherer et al. (1975)	1.90 (=200,000 bbl/d)[b]	7.60	33.00[e]	4.8%

Sources: J. S. Bain, *Barriers to New Competition* (Cambridge, Mass.: Harvard University Press, 1956), pp. 72, 84; C. F. Pratten, *Economies of Scale in Manufacturing Industry* (Cambridge: Cambridge University Press, 1971), pp. 269–77; and F. M. Scherer, A. Beckenstein, E. Kaufer, and R. D. Murphy, *The Economics of Multi-Plant Operation: An International Comparisons Study* (Cambridge, Mass.: Harvard University Press, 1975), chap. 3.

[a]MOS estimates are based on integrated petroleum refining operations and use coastal location data for the early 1950s

[b]Crude-oil refining capacity of one MOS plant, in barrels per day, corresponding to the MOS share of national capacity

[c]For 1947

[d]Estimates based originally on U.K. data, then scaled up to U.S. market data by a factor of five

[e]For 1967

adequately represent the organizational and entrepreneurial characteristics of individual refining operations. Second, there may be financial scale economies such as lowered risk charges to large-scale firms. Third, costs may differ among firms because of differences in the demand for their outputs. Fourth, interview data on plants may well fit engineering specifications, but they do not necessarily separate multiplant and market classifications in ways that are appropriate to industrial organization analysis. While it is true that engineering data cannot directly represent organizational differences among firms—and there have been few attempts to measure them directly in concert with engineering data—it is also true that engineering data can be viewed as at least partial proxies to these influences. If there are financial economies of scale accruing to large firms, to the extent that they exist, there is market failure within the industry as a whole, since such economies of scale will result in a skewed distribution of risk toward smaller firms. Moreover, economies of scale can also serve as a barrier to entry for potential refiners. The problem posed by differences among firms in the demand for products could be significant, except that most refinery products are relatively homogeneous within classes. Thus, to the extent that differences in demand arise, they may be attributable to differences in advertising, for which research efforts thus far do not point to any definitive conclusions.[11] As to the incompatibility of engineering and economic data, one can always find fault with research im-

[11]For an overview of the role of advertising, see H. M. Mann, "Advertising, Concentration, and Profitability: The State of Knowledge and Directions for Public Policy," in *Industrial Concentration: The New Learning,* ed. H. J. Goldschmid, H. M. Mann, and J. F. Weston (Boston: Little, Brown and Co., 1974), pp. 15–54.

perfections, but this is equally true of the converse proposition, that is, that there is inherent optimality in the prevailing scale of refining. Before any further conclusions can be drawn, however, we must also look beyond refining to distribution and then take account of the possibility of economies of scale to integrated firms.[12]

Petroleum and natural gas distribution encompasses both wholesale and retail activities. On the wholesale level, the extent of scale economies turns largely on the question of the efficiency of pipeline and allied rail, vehicle, and marine distribution systems to and from refineries. On the retail level, it is cast essentially as the extent to which products are more efficiently distributed within relatively large or small outlets, such as gasoline stations and home fuel oil dealers.

Among alternative ground energy transportation systems, pipelines have played an increasingly important role in petroleum and natural gas distribution. For example, of 1980 refinery receipts, approximately 58 percent came by pipeline, 40 percent by water, and 2 percent by truck and rail; on the output side, 71 percent of refinery products were shipped by pipeline, 13 percent by water, 12 percent by truck, and 5 percent by rail. There is evidence that scale economies to petroleum and natural gas are found in pipelines and in tankers. In the case of pipelines, for example, Moore (1959) found that for a daily flow of 125,000 barrels per day over a distance of 1,000 miles, systems with outside diameters of up to 30 inches required only around 5 percent of the hydraulic horsepower needed for a pipeline roughly half this size.[13] Since then, subsequent research has shown that over time there have been continuing returns to scale, with new projected pipeline capacities reaching outer diameters of 48 inches. Because the capital and operating costs of these pipelines tend to be relatively large as well, with the exception of governments, it is principally the largest petroleum firms that have been involved in their construction and operation. From a structural point of view, this has given large firms potential leverage over smaller competing firms, particularly in light of the rising share of pipeline distribution involved in all petroleum transport. However, whether in fact this has been used to advan-

[12]There are two types of integration, vertical and horizontal. Vertical integration refers to the fusing within a firm of the several stages of transformation of a production, as in the case of petroleum firms engaged in exploration, extraction, refining, and distribution. Horizontal integration refers to a single firm's acquiring larger shares of the market within which it is operating, and acquiring larger shares of competitor resource markets, as in the expansion of petroleum firms into natural gas, shale oil, coal, or uranium industries. For more rigorous statements of the theoretical characteristics associated with vertical integration and economies of scale, see W. J. Baumol, "On the Proper Cost Tests for Natural Monopoly in a Multiproduct Industry," *American Economic Review* 67 (December 1977):809–22; and M. L. Greenhut and H. Ohta, "Vertical Integration of Successive Oligopolists," *ibid.*, 69 (March 1979):137–41. Baumol contends that economies of scale are neither necessary nor sufficient for monopoly to be the least costly form of productive organization in that the cost of producing a sum of outputs by a single firm may be less than the costs of producing them separately. Baumol has labeled such conditions as economies of scope rather than economies of scale.

[13]W. T. Moore, "Economies of Scale: Some Statistical Evidence," *Quarterly Journal of Economics,* May 1959. The Alaska pipeline has a 48-inch diameter.

tage can only be answered by a broader perspective that includes the conduct of petroleum firms, which is covered in subsequent sections.

There is also evidence of scale economies in the use of tankers. In assessing these returns, Adelman (1972) has pointed out that the principal impetus to the construction of large tankers in the first place was the closure of the Suez Canal following the 1967 Middle East war and that by no means did the increase in size lead to dominance by large petroleum firms.[14] Moreover, since the reopening of the canal, it is not clear whether supertankers will retain a competitive edge in international transport, especially in North American and European markets. Hence, their scale economies may be smaller than once thought.

Beyond these two areas of potential scale economies in petroleum and natural gas distribution, there is no conclusive evidence of scale economies in gasoline, home fuel oil, or allied areas of retail marketing. Since these industries are also among the least capital-intensive, it is not surprising that they should have some of the greatest degree of flexibility in terms of market entry. Given that all of the various stages of petroleum and natural gas supply thus far discussed do not present a uniform presence or absence of scale economies, what is now needed is to determine if there are such scale economies to vertical integration within the industry as a whole.

Vertical integration is as significant a characteristic of the petroleum industry as is its relative size. In their 1959 study of the U.S. petroleum industry, DeChazeau and Kahn noted that vertically integrated firms accounted for 59.8 percent of domestic and 99.6 percent of foreign crude-oil production, 83.1 percent of crude-oil pipeline deliveries, 96.2 percent of domestic refining, 61.4 percent of terminal and bulk plant sales, and 58 percent of service-station gasoline sales.[15] Though these proportions have since been reduced as a result of recent OPEC nationalizations and lesser structural changes, the largest firms outside those of Eastern Europe and China are still integrated ones.[16]

[14]Adelman, *World Petroleum Market*, chap. 4. See also Z. S. Zannetos, "Some Problems and Prospects for Marine Transportation of Oil in the 1970's" and J. G. Hale and R. J. Deam, "Oil Transportation Studies," in *Energy: Demand, Conservation, and Institutional Problems*, ed. M. S. Macrakis (Cambridge, Mass.: MIT Press, 1974), pp. 403–16 and 417–424, respectively. Zannetos notes that though tanker fleets have been largely funded by major oil firms, there is no dominance of ownership. Hale and Deam quote a 40 percent ownership share of oil tankers by international oil firms and have noted that beyond a 50,000 deadweight ton size, freight rates have not shown any significant variation, suggesting that economies of scale may not extend beyond this level of capacity.

[15]M. DeChazeau and A. E. Kahn, *Integration and Competition in the Petroleum Industry* (New Haven: Yale University Press, 1959), pp. 22–23. For more recent comparisons, see W. S. Measday, "The Petroleum Industry," in *The Structure of American Industry*, ed. W. Adams, 5th ed. (New York: Macmillan Publishing Co., 1977), pp. 130–63.

[16]Integrated firms are also known as "majors," and nonintegrated firms are known as "independents." The seven largest fully integrated firms are Exxon, Shell, BP (British Petroleum), Gulf, Texaco, Mobil, and Chevron (Standard Oil of California); CFP (Compagnie Française des Pétroles) and ENI (Ente Nazionale Idrocarburi) are next in the rankings but are significantly smaller than the first seven. Since the nationalizations by OPEC, many national companies, such as NIOC (National Iranian Oil Company), ARAMCO (Arabian-American Oil Company), IPC (Iraq Petroleum Company), and SONATRACH (Algerian National Oil Company), have

The presence of scale economies to vertical integration requires that there be an average cost advantage at least equal to the net level obtainable from summing of all stages of production. This phenomenon may also be described as synergy; that is, the whole must be greater than the sum of the parts. However, unlike the relatively obvious technological advantages accruing to large-scale refining, whether scale economies exist among integrated firms can not be readily measured with conventional statistical tests. The reason for this difficulty is simple enough: once we consider integrated processes, the number of possible sources of scale economies may be difficult to identify among the many inputs and outputs of such large-scale operations.

Despite the measurement difficulties associated with joint production, the most likely sources of scale economies extend to activities thus far excluded from consideration: aggregate financial efficiency and the level and quality of research and innovation. Each of these possibilities will be considered in turn.

The sources of aggregate financial efficiency to a firm are most likely to be found on two basic levels: (1) the extent to which integrated operations lower a firm's average costs by a reduction in the number of financial transactions and (2) the ability of integrated firms to reduce the degree of risk attendant with several stages in the fuel-supply chain. To the extent that these financial economies exist, we would expect to find lower costs per unit of final output among these firms as opposed to the unit cost of final output from a comparative chain of nonintegrated firms. Though the intuitive logic of this proposition may be strong, the evidence in petroleum and natural gas is at best indirect. For example, in a study of all industry manufacturing firms among the 1963 *Fortune* 500, Carter (1977) formulated an efficiency test for vertical and horizontal integration.[17] His results indicated that the rate of return on equity to vertically integrated industries was at least 8.6 percent higher than that for all firms taken together. Unfortunately, since there was no disaggregation by industry, the significance of vertical integration to petroleum and natural gas in particular can not be determined. In addition, a profitability measure is at best a proxy for scale economies, unless we are able to give explicit consideration to differences in product costs among differing types of firms. Finally, profitability does not by itself distinguish the degree of regulation by type of firm. Since profitability is also a factor in the determination of market power, further consideration is deferred until the discussion of market conduct.

If evidence on returns to scale among petroleum and natural gas firms is inconclusive, it is equally so in the area of research and innovation. As a hypothesis, the argument can be stated as follows: because research and development is laden with uncertainty, it is inherently risky; relatively large expenditures are initially necessary if new innovations are to be brought

---

become major producers even though as yet they do not have the refining and distribution facilities of the major western oil firms.

[17] J. R. Carter, "In Search of Synergy: A Structure Performance Test," *Review of Economics and Statistics* 59 (August 1977):279–89.

forth; only larger firms are in a position, by virtue of their size, to undertake these expenditures. The proposition is, of course, an old one, long associated with Joseph Schumpeter (1942) and more recently reiterated by J. K. Galbraith in *The New Industrial State* (1967).[18] Against this proposition, however, is the possibility that innovations may not be cost-effective to consumers, that their diffusion may be restricted or give rise to monopoly returns from the operation of the patent system or that the most significant innovations may not even originate among the largest firms.

Relatively few studies have focused on the direct returns to innovation from large-scale firms in the petroleum industry. Of these, three merit a brief discussion of their findings. In their previously noted investigation, DeChazeau and Kahn (1959) noted that although there were undoubtedly some financial scale returns to integrated petroleum firms, many of the major innovations in the industry were as often as not first developed by relatively small firms in search of competitive advantage. Turning to more recent evidence, Teece (1979) undertook a quantitative investigation of the extent of research and development expenditures by size of firms in the petroleum industry.[19] He found a statistically significant linkage between firm size and the level of expenditures in three categories: basic, development, and applied research; and he attributed this pattern to the lower capital costs and greater diffusibility of innovations throughout several production stages of integrated petroleum firms. However, expenditures in each of these areas are at best a proxy for the qualitative impact of innovations. For this reason, it is also worth noting a third study of the influence of firm size on innovation, undertaken by Markham, Hourihan, and Sterling (1977).[20] The authors found that in the two key areas of shale oil and coal conversion, petroleum firms received 80.2 and 46.0 percent, respectively, of all patents granted to developers of these technologies. However, although the influence of petroleum firms appears to be significant, their data also show that 65 percent of shale oil patents and 55 percent of coal conversion patents went to firms smaller than the largest five within the petroleum industry. Moreover, shale oil and coal conversion patents represented just over 1 percent of the total patents received by petroleum firms for all innovations during this period, which suggests that most innovations have been focused on improvements in conventional fuels rather than these synthetics. On balance, then, when scale economies to integrated firms are added to those available to individual production stages

[18]J. Schumpeter, *Capitalism, Socialism, and Democracy* (New York: Harper Publishers, 1942). Schumpeter argued that while perfect competition may be an appropriate analytical model for static economic efficiency, it is wholly inadequate for dynamic efficiency. J. K. Galbraith updated this argument in *The New Industrial State* (Boston: Houghton Mifflin, 1967) by attributing most innovational capacity to the large firm's "technostructure," or research and engineering capability. This point has been much debated by economists.

[19]D. J. Teece, "Integration and Innovation in Energy Markets," in *Advances in the Economics of Energy and Resources,* ed. R. S. Pindyck, vol. 1 (Greenwich, Conn.: JAI Press, 1979), pp. 163–212.

[20]J. W. Markham, A. P. Hourihan, and F. L. Sterling, *Horizontal Divestiture and the Petroleum Industry* (Cambridge, Mass.: Ballinger Publishing Co., 1977), pp. 65–88.

alone, the accumulated evidence does suggest moderate advantages from large-scale production. Since the very largest firms may exceed the size necessary to realize these scale economies, what is also needed is an assessment of the behavior of the petroleum and natural gas industry as a whole.

The question underlying the conduct of the petroleum and natural gas industry is essentially whether it is a competitive one. One basic test for imperfect competition (see figure 9.1.*c*) is the extent to which firm profit maximization leads to lower output and higher prices than would be the case under perfect competition, that is, differences in profitability among firms. At the same time, firm behavior is also influenced by knowledge of and response to prevailing public policies such that this particular test alone is rarely sufficient proof. Thus, several corollary tests have also been devised: concentration ratios, the relationship of concentration to vertical and horizontal integration, joint exploration and production ventures that might be collusive, advertising, and pricing practices among firms. The significance of advertising and vertical integration have already been noted, and pricing, taxes, and regulation are covered in chapter 11. This leaves for consideration the degree of concentration, profitability, horizontal integration, and joint ventures.

Concentration ratios are measures of the market shares accounted for by the largest firms in the industry.[21] Outside of pure monopoly and duopoly, no concentration ratio provides rigid proof of imperfect competition. Hence, empirical evidence must be judged in a comparative framework, that is, against all industries, against other individual industries, or as indirect evidence which must be combined with other tests of behavior. Within this context, table 9.3 provides a sample of all-industry and individual-industry concentration ratios within the United States for the 1947–72 period. Among all manufacturing industries, which together account for less than half of the U.S. Gross National Product, the incidence of concentration of the largest fifty and two hundred firms shows a gradual increase during the 1947–72 period. However, there are significant differences from this trend among individual energy and non-energy industries. With the exception of concrete block and fur goods, concentration among the four largest firms exceeded generally the all-industry levels of the largest fifty. Also, concentration appears to have increased slightly in natural gas and in petroleum production and to have dropped slightly in petroleum refining and gasoline retailing. In essence, these energy industries can be characterized as moderate oligopolies with some degree of market power.

A closer view of concentration trends in the domestic petroleum industry is provided in table 9.4. Overall, the largest degree of concentration lies principally in refining and in reserves, regardless of the number of benchmark firms used, while the greatest degree of competition is found in exploration. The asymmetry between oil reserves and drilling suggests that although entry

[21]Concentration ratios may be based on output, sales, employment, assets, or any related index that correlates with the size of firms (see Shalit and Sankar, "The Measurement of Firm Size").

Table 9.3. Concentration Ratios in Manufacturing in Selected U.S. Industries, 1947–72

Market Share of Shipments by the Largest:	1947	1954	1958	1963	1967	1970	1972
	All Manufacturing Industries						
50 firms	17%	23%	23%	25%	25%	24%	25%
200 firms	30	37	38	41	42	43	43
	Selected Industries						
4 firms							
Aircraft	—	55	62	58	76	73	69
Automobiles	95	98	99	99	93	93	93
Bottled liquors, except brandy	—	67	61	58	53	—	51
Cigarettes	—	82	80	—	—	—	84
Coal production	—	17[a]	—	—	27[b]	—	30
Concrete block	—	5	4	4	—	5	5
Fur goods	3	4	5	5	5	6	7
Natural gas pipeline sales	—	23[a]	—	22[c]	—	25	25
Newspapers	21	18	17	15	16	16	17
Petroleum							
Gas retail	—	31	31	31	31	31	29
Production	19	19	19	24	29	33	29
Refining	37	33	32	34	33	33	33
Roasted coffee	—	45	46	54	57	—	64
Storage batteries	62	65	64	60	60	59	58
Tires	—	—	—	70	70	72	73
Uranium mining and milling	—	—	—	—	57	—	56

Source: U.S. Department of Commerce, Bureau of the Census. *Concentration Ratios in Manufacturing, 1972,* Special Report Series MC72(SR)-2 (Washington, D.C.: U.S. Government Printing Office, October 1975).

[a]1955

[b]1965

[c]1961

barriers to exploration may be few, larger firms have more often than not been able to internalize their discoveries by selected drilling in relatively large tracts. The post-1972 data also point to moderately continuing decreases in the concentration of refining and crude-oil reserves, even though the levels in these areas are still above the all-industry fifty-firm ratios listed in table 9.3.

On a global scale, concentration ratios among firms and in geographic regions outside of Eastern Europe and China reveal changes comparable to those found in the United States (see table 9.5). First, on both a regional and global scale, there were clear declines in the degree of concentration in production, refining, and crude-oil reserves during the 1953–72 period. Moreover, this decline is reflected in the distribution of world crude-oil tanker capacity, despite the substantial switch to the very large crude-oil carriers constructed following the closure of the Suez Canal during the 1967 Middle East war. To be sure, some of these changes reflect the nationalizations undertaken by OPEC cited earlier. At the same time, they point to the one factor that made it possible for OPEC to succeed as it has, namely, the decreasing ability of world-market firms to control effectively the various stages of international petroleum production, refining, and distribution. Though governmental policies (or a lack of them, as is often the case) have also played a role, the essential point here is that the degree of competition undoubtedly has been enhanced by the decline in global concentration from its early post–World War II levels.

As noted in chapter 5 petroleum and natural gas exploration is based on common methods. Not surprisingly, many, though not all, of the same firms engaged in petroleum production also produce natural gas. In tables 9.6, 9.7, and 9.8, concentration ratios in natural gas sales by producers to interstate pipeline firms show a marked reversal of the declining trends gener-

Table 9.4. Concentration Ratios in the U.S. Petroleum Industry, 1926–80

Source	1926	1935	1947	1952	1954	1955	1960	1963
								Domestic Oi
Largest 4 firms	—	—	—	—	—	—	—	—
Largest 8 firms	—	—	—	—	—	—	—	—
Largest 15 firms	—	—	—	—	—	—	—	—
Largest 20 firms	—	—	—	—	—	—	—	—
								Domestic Crude
Largest 4 firms	—	—	—	19.6%	—	18.8%	26.5%	—
Largest 8 firms	—	—	—	32.6	—	31.1	43.8	—
Largest 15 firms	—	—	—	43.8	—	41.7	58.7	—
Largest 20 firms	—	—	—	49.3	—	46.2	63.0	—
								Domestic Crude
Largest 4 firms	—	38.0%	32.0%	—	—	32.9%	—	34.0%
Largest 8 firms	—	58.0	59.0	—	—	57.5	—	56.0
Largest 15 firms	—	—	—	—	—	76.4	—	77.3
Largest 20 firms	—	—	—	—	—	82.2	—	82.0
								Domestic Marketin
Largest 4 firms	35.0%	30.8%	—	—	31.2%	—	—	—
Largest 8 firms	56.4	48.6	—	—	54.0	—	—	—
Largest 15 firms	71.0	64.0	—	—	—	—	—	—
								Producer Shares of Prove
Largest 4 firms	—	—	—	—	—	—	—	—
Largest 8 firms	—	—	—	—	—	—	—	—
Largest 20 firms	—	—	—	—	—	—	—	—

Sources: Petroleum Information Corporation, *Resume of Oil and Gas Operations,* vol. 1 (Denve Petroleum Information Corporation, 1974–80); J. G. McLean and R. W. Haigh, *The Growth of In tegrated Oil Companies* (Boston: Harvard University Graduate School of Business Administration 1954), pp. 104, 332; M. DeChazeau and A. E. Kahn, *Integration and Competition in the Petroleum In dustry* (New Haven: Yale University Press, 1959), pp. 30–31; Federal Trade Commission, *Th Petroleum Industry: Structure and Conduct* (Washington, D.C.: U.S. Government Printing Office 1973), tables 1-3; T. D. Duchesneau, *Competition in the U.S. Energy Industry* (Cambridge, Mass. Ballinger Publishing Co., 1975), pp. 37, 44, 45; *National Petroleum News Factbook Issue* (New York

ally found in petroleum sales. Unfortunately, most recent economic investigations of natural gas supply have focused on the efficiency of its regulation by the Federal Power Commission rather than on the underlying degree of efficiency resulting from changes in producer concentration. However, despite increases at the production level, natural gas concentration ratios have continued to be lower than those for crude-oil production or petroleum refining. Moreover, as we will see, when considered together, petroleum and natural gas have tended to be far less concentrated than several of the key industries noted in table 9.3. Since concentration ratios are presumed to be positively correlated with profitability, let us look at this third test of economic efficiency.

1965	1970	1971	1972	1973	1974	1975	1976	1977	1978	1979	1980
)rilling Completions											
—	—	—	—	—	9.0%	8.5%	6.9%	7.4%	6.1%	6.0%	5.4%
—	—	—	—	—	13.7	12.9	11.4	11.9	10.2	9.5	8.8
—	—	—	—	—	18.9	18.1	15.4	16.9	14.8	13.6	12.8
—	—	—	—	—	22.0	20.1	17.5	19.3	16.6	15.6	14.8
)il Production											
28.9%	32.5%	32.7%	32.6%	32.7%	32.2%	32.2%	30.4%	29.4%	28.5%	28.5%	29.7%
45.8	50.1	51.3	51.3	51.9	51.5	51.0	48.9	48.7	49.4	48.2	48.6
60.5	65.9	69.8	69.7	70.8	70.8	70.4	68.4	67.3	68.3	66.4	67.3
65.3	70.2	73.8	72.9	74.4	74.5	72.8	72.1	72.5	73.0	70.9	71.5
)il Refining Capacity											
—	32.9%	34.3%	33.1%	34.2%	32.9%	32.7%	32.7%	31.9%	28.0%	25.6%	22.9%
—	58.1	60.5	59.0	61.3	58.9	53.9	57.0	55.4	48.3	45.4	39.7
—	78.9	85.8	79.4	86.1	83.3	76.2	79.8	77.8	67.0	61.6	55.4
—	86.2	93.9	87.4	93.3	91.4	83.6	87.9	83.5	72.7	65.3	61.0
f Gasoline											
—	30.7%	29.6%	29.0%	29.3%	29.9%	29.2%	29.5%	29.2%	28.5%	28.8%	28.9%
—	55.0	53.2	51.6	51.5	51.9	50.0	50.1	49.3	49.4	49.8	50.1
—	73.9	72.1	70.6	69.7	69.0	65.9	64.8	65.1	65.7	65.9	66.2
)omestic Crude-Oil Reserves											
—	37.2%	—	—	—	35.1%[a]	—	—	—	—	—	—
—	63.9	—	—	—	54.2[a]	—	—	—	—	—	—
—	93.6	—	—	—	73.1[a]	—	—	—	—	—	—

/IcGraw-Hill Publishing Co., 1978–80); U.S. Department of Energy, Energy Information Administra-ion, *Monthly Energy Review* (Washington, D.C.: U.S. Government Printing Office, March 1981); *Oil nd Gas Journal* (Tulsa: Pennwell Publishing Co., 1965, 1971–80); U.S. Bureau of the Census of the ubcommittee on Antitrust and Monopoly of the Subcommittee on the Judiciary, U.S. Senate, pt. 1, *:oncentration Ratios in Manufacturing, 1963* (Washington, D.C.: U.S. Government Printing Office, 966), p. 21; American Enterprise Institute, Proceedings of the January 1977 Conference, *Horizontal)ivestiture* (Washington, D.C.: American Enterprise Institute, 1977).

[a]Data furnished by W. S. Moore, Management Analysis Center, Cambridge, Mass.

Table 9.5. Concentration Ratios in the World Petroleum Industry, by Firm and Region, 1953–80

	1953	1972	1974	1976	1980
	World Crude-Oil Production				
Market share of the largest:					
4 firms	69.0%	49.2%	40.8%	39.3%	39.0%
7 firms	87.1	70.9	58.2	55.8	50.8
8 firms	91.0	75.1	62.2	59.2	53.6
15 firms	97.4	87.1	70.2	67.0	66.1
Regional share of the seven largest firms in:					
Africa	92.0	47.0	—	—	95.0
Far East	94.0	71.0	—	—	78.0
Latin America	81.0	73.0	—	—	82.0
Middle East	92.0	83.0	—	—	85.0
Ratio of crude-oil production to crude-oil refining capacity by:					
7 largest firms	1.198	1.275	—	—	1.888
All firms	0.995	0.874	—	—	0.579
	World Crude-Oil Refining Capacity				
Market share of the largest:					
4 firms	63.5%	38.3%	—	—	17.5%
7 firms	75.5	48.7	—	—	24.3
8 firms	78.5	50.8	—	—	26.0
15 firms	86.7	61.2	—	—	33.3
Regional share of the seven largest firms in:					
Africa	32.0	30.0	—	—	56.0
Far East	77.0	34.0	—	—	30.0
Latin America	67.0	51.0	—	—	64.0
Middle East	98.0	63.0	—	—	75.0
West Europe	65.0	55.0	—	—	43.0
	World Proven Crude-Oil Reserves				
Market share of the largest:					
4 firms	73.5%	46.7%	—	—	—
7 firms	91.8	69.6	—	—	—
8 firms	95.8	74.6	—	—	—
15 firms	98.6	87.4	—	—	—
Geographic shares held by the 7 largest firms in:					
Africa	89.0	25.0	—	—	—
Far East	94.0	74.0	—	—	—
Latin America	77.0	60.0	—	—	—
Middle East	94.0	83.0	—	—	—
	World Tanker Capacity				
Market share of the largest:					
4 firms	22.0%	14.0%	—	—	—
7 firms	29.0	20.0	—	—	—
8 firms	30.0	21.0	—	—	—
15 firms	35.0	24.0	—	—	—

Table 9.5.—*Continued*

	1953	1972	1974	1976	1980
Thousand deadweight tons of:					
Largest 7 firms	9,841	41,547	—	—	—
World	34,523	218,890	—	—	—

Sources: N. Jacoby, *Multinational Oil* (New York: Macmillan Publishing Co., 1974), pp. 183, 186, 188, 192–94, 199, 203 (based on data in *Clarkson's Tanker Register* and *Skinner's Oil and Gas International Yearbook*); *International Petroleum Encyclopedia* (Tulsa: Pennwell Publishing Co., selected years); and *Oil and Gas Journal* (Tulsa: Pennwell Publishing Co., selected years).

Note: Global market shares and regional market shares are exclusive of Canada, Eastern Europe, the USSR, and the People's Republic of China.

A profitability test of industry behavior has two appealing features, namely, that it can be readily computed and that it can be easily interpreted in terms of elementary economic theory. In general, as is illustrated in figure 9.1, the greater the degree of competition, the lower will be the profitability to an individual firm. By extension, the lower the profitability to an individual firm, the lower will be the profitability of the industry as a whole. Where competitive conditions prevail, investment patterns over time will tend to equalize differences in the risk-adjusted average profitability among industries to a rate that is consistent with society's rate of time preference for future versus persent goods. Moreover, even where imperfect competition and alternative ownership and organizational modes exist, economic efficiency is still maximized by policy choices equivalent to those derived from perfectly competitive behavior.

Equalization of profitability is often confused with two other measures: the absolute level of profits and the absolute size of firms. To be sure, in the petroleum industry, the firms already noted are certainly large in comparison with those in other industries; the same is true for its average levels of profits. However, a singular focus on firm and profit size ignores the size of the

Table 9.6. Market Share of Purchases from U.S. Natural Gas Producers by Interstate Pipeline Firms, 1955–78

Purchase by	1955	1961	1965	1970	1972	1978
Largest 4 firms	22.8%	21.5%	23.2%	25.3%	24.5%	23.6%
Largest 8 firms	35.1	32.4	37.7	42.8	42.0	34.8
Largest 15 firms	47.8	45.7	52.8	60.4	58.7	47.6
Largest 20 firms	53.7	52.8	59.8	67.5	66.7	52.8

Sources: Leslie Cookenboo, Jr., "Competition in the Field Market for Natural Gas," *Rice Institute Monograph in Economics* 44 (January 1958): 48; Federal Power Commission, *Sales by Producers of Natural Gas to Interstate Pipeline Companies* (Washington, D.C.: U.S. Government Printing Office, June 1962, June 1966, June 1970, June 1974); Martha A. Brannan, *Market Shares and Industry Company Data for the U.S. Energy Market, 1950–1978* (Washington, D.C.: American Petroleum Institute, 1979).

Table 9.7. Market Share of Sales by U.S. Natural Gas Producers to Interstate Pipeline Firms, 1955, 1972

Producer	1955	1972
Phillips	8.74%	4.76%
Standard of Indiana	5.54	5.25
Humble	4.58	
Union[a]	3.95	3.78
Cities Service	3.67	
Shell[b]	3.26	4.86
Magnolia	2.80	
Chicago Corporation	2.57	
Exxon		8.99
Gulf Oil		5.37
Texaco		4.63
Mobil		4.36
Total for top 8	2.05 trillion ft^3	6.19 trillion ft^3
Total for all producers	5.85 trillion ft^3	14.74 trillion ft^3

Source: Federal Power Commission, *Sales by Producers of Natural Gas to Interstate Pipeline Companies* (Washington, D.C.: U.S. Government Printing Office, June 1974).

[a]Called Union Oil in 1972

[b]Called Shell Oil in 1972

market, as well as whether there may be economies of scale of the kinds already noted.

The profitability of a firm or industry can be measured in a variety of ways. What these ways have in common is the derivation of a rate of return using some measure of the level of profits, such as net income divided by an investment denominator: sales, invested and borrowed capital, fixed and gross assets, or equity. To be sure, whatever measure is used will be governed by prevailing accounting practices and by the degree of taxation and regulation

Table 9.8. Net Natural Gas Reserves, 1973

Producer	Reserves
Exxon	10.42%
Gulf Oil	3.80
Sohio	2.92
Shell Oil	2.89
El Paso	2.69
Cities Service	2.06
Sun Oil	1.80
Tenneco	1.66
Total for top 8	70.6×10^{15} ft^3 (= 28.24%)
Total for all producers	250.0×10^{15} ft^3

Source: Federal Trade Commission, *The Structure of the U.S. Petroleum Industry: A Summary of Survey Data,* prepared for the chairman, Special Subcommittee on Integrated Oil Operations of the Committee on Interior and Insular Affairs, U.S., Senate, 94th Cong., 2d sess. (Washington, D.C.: U.S. Government Printing Office, 1976), p. 54.

to which the firm and industry have been subjected. Since these matters are taken up in chapter 11, our concern at this point is to determine whether a standard measure of profitability under actual conditions is indicative of higher than average profitability in all industries. Where such higher than average profitability exists, it indicates that the prevailing degree of competition is less than that which is necessary to realize the economies of scale already noted.

Table 9.9 lists two common measures of profitability in the U.S. petroleum industry. From a sample of fifteen firms, the rate of return to assets reveals a long-term decline in profitability that is consistent with the parallel data on the rate of return to equity shown below, and with the trend toward deconcentration already noted in tables 9.4 and 9.5. In addition, disaggregation of these two rates of return by firm size points also to a trend toward equalization of profitability among firms. Thus, as deconcentration has occurred, the earlier, somewhat monopolistic returns of the largest firms have been reduced to levels much closer to the industry's overall average. While greater competition is one of the factors contributing to this change, government policies and OPEC have also played a role, especially in the period since World War II, as will be seen in chapters 11 and 15.

Table 9.9 also indicates that the rate of return to equity in petroleum is not significantly different from the comparable rates of return found in all manufacturing, mining and smelting, and in all trade. Of course, since these rates are unweighted, their homogeneity neither confirms nor denies that the economy is a competitive one, except to suggest that in the long run petroleum is as competitive as are these other industries under this criterion. The exception to this evolving pattern of deconcentration and competition is the extraordinary increase in the rate of return to petroleum firms after the quadrupling of oil prices by OPEC in the aftermath of the 1973 Middle East war. Although this coincidence of events suggests collusion between the petroleum industry and OPEC, it would be premature to draw such a conclusion until the energy-pricing mechanisms of chapter 11 have been fully spelled out.

Horizontal integration and joint ventures are two additional tests that can be used to determine the extent of competition in the petroleum industry. The hypothesis is that the greater the degree of joint ventures and horizontal integration into product substitutes, the higher will be the price in all affected areas, and output will be restricted to an imperfectly competitive profit maximization level, as in figure 9.1.*c*. This hypothesis is also one that is often presented in the context of exchange and processing agreements, joint pipeline activities, and the extent of interlocking directorates. Although pricing is not discussed until chapter 11, we can combine the available evidence on profitability with that which is found in each of these alternative areas.

There is ample evidence of horizontal integration by petroleum firms into alternative fuel industries. Much of this integration has taken place over the past twenty years. A useful way of assessing its significance is to look at the

Table 9.9. Measures of Profitability among U.S. Petroleum Firms, 1917–80

Rate of Return	1917	1929	1945	1955	1966	1970	1972	1974	1976	1978	1980
To assets[a]											
First 4 firms	14.7%	7.7%	5.5%	6.9%	8.4%	6.9%	6.1%	9.1%	6.1%	5.8%	9.8%
Second 4 firms	11.6	5.8	8.3	7.8	7.3	5.8	5.7	8.3	7.2	6.7	8.9
Third 4 firms	9.9	7.2	6.2	6.0	5.8	4.4	4.9	9.1	5.7	6.6	10.6
Top-15-firm mean	13.0	7.3	6.4	7.0	7.6	6.2	5.6	8.9	6.3	6.0	9.7
To equity[b]											
First 4 firms				13.2[c]	12.5[d]	11.6	10.5	17.9	12.3	11.9	21.7
Second 4 firms				12.3[c]	9.8[d]	9.2	9.5	16.9	12.5	15.2	19.0
Third 4 firms				12.3[c]	10.2[d]	8.9	9.6	16.2	13.0	13.6	25.6
Top-15-firm mean				12.0[c]	11.3[d]	10.6	9.9	17.4	12.5	13.1	21.6
To equity											
All manufacturing			17.0[e]	14.9	14.2	10.8	12.1	15.2	15.0	15.0	16.6
Mining and smelting			16.0[e]	13.0	13.9	8.5	10.7	24.5	16.5	19.8	23.2
All trade			18.3[e]	10.9	13.7	11.7	11.8	13.5	14.7	15.3	14.1

Sources: Forbes Magazine, 15 September 1977; *National Petroleum News Factbook, Issue* (New York: McGraw-Hill, selected years); American Petroleum Institute, *Basic Petroleum Data Book* (Washington, D.C.: API, selected years); *Fortune 500*, selected years.

[a]Based on a sample of the fifteen largest firms, ranked by assets. Within each group of four firms, the rate of return is weighted by the level of assets among the four

[b]Rates of return to equity by firm are weighted within each class by equity; all-industry rates of return to equity are unweighted

[c]Computed as pre-tax profits divided by assets for calendar year 1954

[d]Computed as net profit as a percentage of invested capital

[e]Refers to 1947

partial-correlation coefficients between firm rankings of oil and a substitute industry, based on a common measure such as firm ranking in production or reserves. If we use firm rankings in production for the period of the mid-1970s, we will see that the partial correlations between oil and oil and gas firms are as high as 0.96 but those between oil firms and oil, gas, coal, uranium, and geothermal firms decline to approximately 0.80. In effect, then, there is a relatively high degree of horizontal integration among various energy industries.

Despite relatively high interindustry rank correlations of producing firms, we should also consider the degree of horizontal integration in terms of reserves. The reason for considering reserves rather than production ranks alone is that the former are more indicative of future behavior than is production alone. Moreover, to the extent that we are contemplating the introduction of stronger competitive policy measures, we should also look at industry structure and behavior within a dynamic framework. Based on the index of reserves, the partial correlation of firm holdings by rank is still as high as 0.95 between oil and natural gas. This is not surprising in light of the fact that petroleum and natural gas are frequently joint products of exploration, as we saw in chapter 5. More significant is the fact that when we look at the rank correlations for oil and the combined ranking of firm holdings of oil, gas, coal, uranium, shale oil, and geothermal deposits, the coefficient declines to −0.13, which is to say that there is no significant pattern of common holdings of reserves of these resources.

Another way of assessing horizontal integration is to look directly at concentration ratios in production and reserves, based on alternative definitions of the energy industry. Table 9.10 illustrates to what extent varying definitions of industry production and reserves are concentrated at the four-, eight-, and twenty-firm levels. As in our measurement of partial-correlation coefficients of firm rankings, the degree of firm concentration for these various definitions of the energy industry is significant. However, before we draw any conclusions, three qualifications should be pointed out. First, since there are less than perfect rank correlations, the degree of aggregate energy concentration for such industry definitions as fossil fuels is still below the degree of concentration for any single fossil fuel alone. That this is so can be seen by comparing the data of section I in table 9.10 with the corresponding concentration ratios in production with oil in table 9.4, with natural gas in tables 9.6, 9.7, and 9.8, and with coal in table 9.12. Second, as in the measurement of rank-correlation coefficients, when we define the energy industry in broader terms, the degree of concentration also tends to decline, as shown here in sections II and III of table 9.10. Third, the federal government owns or controls access to as much as one-half of many alternative fuels, such as shale oil and coal.[22] Consequently, whether concentration ratios alone can serve as a proxy measure for competition at this level depends as much on

[22]Richard L. Gordon, "Coal—The Swing Fuel," in *Energy Supply and Government Policy*, ed. R. J. Kalter and W. A. Vogely (Ithaca: Cornell University Press, 1976), p. 213.

Table 9.10. Interindustry Concentration Ratios in Production and Reserves

	Concentration Ratios of the Largest:			
	4 Firms	8 Firms	20 Firms	25 Firms
I. Production by leading U.S. fossil fuel producers in:				
1955	11.0%	19.7%	31.1%	38.2%
1970	21.2	34.9	54.8	58.5
1974	19.1	31.5	49.6	—
II. Market shares of private reserve holdings for 1974 based on industry definitions as:				
Oil	26.0	41.7	61.4	—
Oil, gas	25.1	39.2	59.0	—
Oil, gas, coal	19.1	31.5	49.6	—
Oil, gas, coal, uranium	18.4	29.7	47.8	—
III. Market shares of private and public reserve holdings for 1975 based on industry definitions as:				
Oil	27.3	42.2	56.9	—
Oil, gas	26.2	40.3	59.9	—
Oil, gas, coal	15.2	23.7	37.6	—
Oil, gas, coal, uranium	15.1	23.6	38.1	—
Oil, gas, coal, shale oil, uranium	10.9	17.8	29.0	—
Oil, gas, coal, shale oil, uranium, geothermal	10.9	17.4	29.0	—

Sources: T. D. Duchesneau, *Competition in the U.S. Energy Industry* (Cambridge, Mass.: Ballinger Publishing Co., 1975), pp. 94–95, J. W. Markham, A. P. Hourihan, and F. L. Sterling, *Horizontal Divestiture and the Petroleum Industry* (Cambridge, Mass.: Ballinger Publishing Co., 1977), pp. 11, 22.

specific government leasing decisions as on the structure of the industry, or on the behavior of firms themselves.

If concentration ratios of horizontally integrated industries are lower than those of a single-fuel industry alone, then there is no a priori basis for concluding that horizontal expansion is inherently anticompetitive. In pursuing this test of competition, economists usually have combined the degree of concentration in horizontally aggregated industries with the extent to which alternative energy resources can function as directly competitive substitutes for each other, as in home fuel oil versus natural gas or electricity for residential and commercial heating. As we will see in chapter 10, interfuel competition can be measured in terms of cross-price demand elasticities and in terms of price elasticities of substitution. The higher the cross- and substitution-price elasticities of demand, the greater will be the degree of interfuel competition. At this point, we can note that for all of the fuels listed in table 9.10 that are produced in currently significant commercial quantities, their long-run price and substitution elasticities of demand are all higher than their short-run ones. What this suggests is that horizontal integration appears on the surface at least to be inimical to competition. However, as long as concentration ratios in horizontally integrated industries remain lower than those of a single-fuel industry alone, and as long as there is no long-run tendency for either of these concentration ratios to increase over time, then even with relatively high degrees of interfuel substitution, horizontal integration may actually strengthen rather than weaken energy competition.

Evidence from studies of joint ventures is much less clear as to its impact on competitive behavior. The areas in which joint ventures have been documented include offshore lease acquisitions, exploratory drilling, ownership and production from oil and gas leases, pipeline ownership and operation, and exchange and processing agreements. From these various areas, studies of domestic leasing and exploration by Mead (1968), Markham (1970), Wilson (1972), and Wilcox (1974) all point to a common interpretation: that the presence of joint ventures arises from attempts by firms (1) to reduce the overall degree of market risk and (2) to minimize the potential external benefits of the kinds already noted.[23] As to international activity, Adelman (1972) and Wilkins (1975) found that as often as not, joint ventures at least up to 1973 functioned periodically as a monopsonistic device whereby exploration firms could obtain collectively lower contract costs in leasing, a conclusion which bears more directly on the subsequent monopolistic behavior of OPEC than on the behavior of the exploratory firms themselves.[24]

Apart from the efficiency (or inefficiency) of regulation by the Federal Power Commission, although there have been cases of monopolistic practices, the result has often been the expansion of alternative pipeline facilities by competing joint ventures, since pipelines do exhibit economies of scale in their operation. Moreover, the rate of return to pipeline companies has been found to be not significantly higher than comparable rates of return in other industries. As to exchange and processing agreements, the evidence points to similar behavior. DeChazeau and Kahn (1959) noted that these agreements gave monopolistic advantages to integrated firms, but Johnson et al. (1975) found no consistent pattern in recent experience to confirm such widespread practices.[25] Unfortunately, statistical tests on both pipelines and processing and exchange agreements have been difficult to formulate and assess. Thus, these two activities cannot serve as adequate measures of imperfect competition.

We are now in a position to answer in summary form the questions posed originally, namely, whether there are economies of scale that could justify the

[23]W. J. Mead, "The Structure of the Buyer Market for Oil Shale Resource," *National Resources Journal* 8 (October 1968); J. W. Markham, "The Competitive Effects of Joint Bidding by Oil Companies for Offshore Leases," in *Industrial Organization and Economic Development,* ed. J. W. Markham and G. Papanek (Boston: Houghton-Mifflin, 1970), pp. 122–33; J. Wilson, Testimony submitted to the Subcommittee on Antitrust and Monopoly of the Senate Judiciary Committee, 93d Cong., 1st sess., pt. 1, 1972; S. Wilcox, "Entry and Joint Venture Bidding in the Offshore Petroleum Industry" (Ph.D. diss., University of California, Santa Barbara, 1974).

[24]Adelman, *World Petroleum Market,* pp. 86–88; Mira Wilkins, "The Oil Companies in Perspective," *Daedalus,* Fall 1975, pp. 159–78.

[25]DeChazeau and Kahn, *Integration and Competition in the Petroleum Industry,* pp. 185–86; W. A. Johnson, R. E. Messick, S. Van Vactor, and F. R. Wyant, *Competition in the Oil Industry* (Washington, D.C.: Energy Policy Research Project, George Washington University, 1975).

relative size of petroleum and natural gas firms and whether these industries are competitive. There are undoubtedly economies of scale in petroleum and natural gas. These economies of scale are found separately in refining, in pipelines, and to a limited extent in the financing and research activities of vertically integrated firms. At the same time, there are indications that the sizes of the very largest firms exceed those levels essential to the realization of these economies, even though they may be operating in the constant-returns range of their average cost curves. As to competition in the petroleum and natural gas industry, available evidence suggests that the imperfect competition that once characterized the industry has gradually dissipated over the years as a result of rising interfirm competition, the rise of OPEC, and the impact of government energy policy. Whether the prevailing degree of competition in petroleum and natural gas warrants more competitive policy measures depends on the impact of past and current government actions, on the costs and benefits of the various pro-competitive policy instruments noted in chapter 1, and on the extent to which they are likely to be effective within a dynamic international economic framework.

9.4. COAL

In comparison with the petroleum and natural gas industry, the U.S. coal industry is relatively small. In the 1980 *Fortune 500* list of the largest U.S. industrial firms, only one was primarily a coal producer, and its sales represented but 0.1 percent of total sales by the largest 500 firms during that year.[26] As noted in chapter 5, although over the past five decades the coal industry has lost its once preeminent role to petroleum and natural gas, as one of the most abundant energy resources available to the U.S. economy, it is still an important one. The questions at this point is the same as the case of petroleum and in natural gas: Are there economies of scale in coal? and Is the industry a competitive one?

One distinguishing feature of the coal industry is that it functions less as a national industry than it does as a regional one. The 4,000 or so firms that operate some 6,200 mines are dispersed throughout twenty-nine producing states, and for the most part, production is marketed within readily identifiable regions. Thus, while national comparisons may be interesting, they are much less meaningful than regional ones. Wherever possible, this distinction will be employed here in drawing inferences about both scale economies and the degree of competition.

Coal is an energy resource in which there are measurable economies of scale. Though the conversion of coal into its conventional end uses involves far fewer transformations than does the conversion of petroleum, the evidence of scale economies in coal extends to its two basic stages, extraction and distribution. Each of these will be considered in turn.

[26]*Fortune 500,* 4 May 1981. The two largest coal producing firms of 1980 were owned by non-coal firms, while the third largest firm ranked 131st on the *Fortune 500* list.

Table 9.11. Estimates of Scale Economies in U.S. Coal Mining, 1973–75: Minimum Efficient Size and Minimum Average Cost as a Function of Overburden Ratio for Surface Strip Mines and of Seam Thickness for Deep Shaft Mines

	Annual Production Rate (in tons)	Average Cost (in 1977 dollars per ton)
Overburden ratio[a]		
5	5,193,234	$ 3.57
10	2,596,618	6.17
15	1,731,079	8.78
20	1,298,309	11.38
Seam thickness[b]		
28	279,417	64.16
36	369,051	48.58
42	437,727	40.96
60	649,674	27.60
72	794,982	22.55
90	1,017,762	17.62

Source: M. B. Zimmerman, "Estimating a Policy Model of U.S. Coal Supply," in *Advances in the Economics of Energy and Resources*, ed. R. S. Pindyck, vol. 2 (Greenwich, Conn.: JAI Press, 1979), pp. 59–92.

[a]In feet per foot of coal

[b]In inches

Unlike the intangible scale economies from petroleum and natural gas extraction, the scale economies of coal mining derive clearly from the thickness of underground seams and from the degree of overburden discussed in chapter 5, as can be seen in table 9.11. One indication of these economies is that the larger the size of an underground or strip deposit, the higher will be the output per worker, as R. Moyer (1964) documented among Illinois mines in a study of midwestern coal markets.[27] A basic reason for the higher output per worker among the larger mines is that the larger the deposit, the greater will be the use of mechanized operations. Of course, this greater capital intensity is also a factor in coal costs. However, as noted in section 9.1, whenever scale choices are available and known, firms tend to choose efficient combinations of capital and labor that still lead to a decreasing average cost from larger mining operations.

A more direct method of estimating the scale economies in coal mining is to utilize the direct engineering approach already noted in conjunction with studies of petroleum refining. Based on this type of methodology, M. Zimmerman (1979) estimated from a sample of 111 mines the level and change in average costs of coal extraction in both underground and strip-mine operations, the results of which confirm even further the simple index used by

[27]R. Moyer, *Competition in the Midwestern Coal Industry* (Cambridge, Mass.: Harvard University Press, 1964). Moyer's study documented that for the period between 1934 and 1962, concentration ratios in the midwestern coal markets were significantly higher than for the economy's coal industry as a whole. Moyer's data on scale economies are reported in section I of table 9.11.

Moyer.[28] Zimmerman's analysis provides supporting evidence that for all practical purposes, the size of a deposit is governed by either the thickness of the coal seam (for underground mining) or the degree of soil and rock overburden per unit of strip-mined coal. One other implication from this evidence is that since the largest deposits are the cheapest, they will also tend to be mined first. Since the largest deposits are likely to be mined with relatively capital-intensive methods as well, the economically most efficient size of firms may also be incompatible with perfect competition, particularly if the market is regional rather than national in scope, as is so often the case with coal. Before any assessment of imperfect competition can be made, however, we need to consider to what extent there are other sources of scale economies.

The second major area of economies of scale in coal is distribution. As pointed out in chapter 5, most coal from mines has been distributed by rail. The problem with conventional mixed-freight rail transport is that a given car may spend 90 percent of its time waiting, 6 percent of its time in delivery, and 4 percent in empty transit. However, in a study of unit coal trains, A. J. Bailey (1967) found that in 1965, a single train carrying only some 13,000 tons of coal from a single mine region to a central electricity utility had an average transport cost of 6.33 mills per ton-mile of coal, which was half of the transport cost from conventional mixed-freight trains.[29] Since transportation accounts for between one-quarter and one-half of the final demand costs of coal, the use of unit trains could reduce average costs by as much as 25 percent. Despite this cost advantage, the scale advantages from unit trains have been limited thus far by inadequate regional demand and by administrative and regulatory inefficiencies in the operations of railroads. Thus, while there are potential economies in the operation of unit trains, they are far from full-scale realization.

Apart from unit-train operation, one other method of achieving potential scale economies is the use of coal slurry pipelines. Though originally proposed as early as 1890, the first experimental pipeline did not begin operation until 1952: a 12-inch-diameter pipe owned by Consolidation Coal Company. Since then, a 10-inch, 108-mile slurry pipeline operated between Cadiz, Ohio, and Cleveland, Ohio's Eastlake electric utility from 1957 to 1963, when the New York Central Railroad offered a lower tariff than had been previously available in mixed-freight operations. More recently, a 273-mile, 18-inch slurry line began operating between Black Mesa, Arizona, and the Mohave power plant in southern Nevada in 1970; it is currently the country's only operating slurry pipeline. With only two commerical lines constructed, the magnitude of scale economies have been difficult to assess. The available evidence suggests that it is most likely to be effective in water-abundant and rail-scarce regions; its potential is thus much more severely limited than that of unit trains. The greatest source of scale economies in

[28]M. B. Zimmerman, "Estimating a Policy Model of U.S. Coal Supply," in *Advances in the Economics of Energy and Resources*, ed. R. S. Pindyck, vol. 2 (Greenwich, Conn.: JAI Press, 1979), pp. 59–92.

[29]A. J. Bailey, *The Economics of Unit Trains* (Chicago: A. T. Kearney Co., 1967).

coal, then, is production, and to a much lesser extent, distribution. Though some additional scale efficiency might be gained through vertical integration, under the present industry structure it would be difficult to prove that there would be any net gains above those available from the separate stages of production and distribution.

Despite its economic potential, in recent years the coal industry has not been studied as intensively as have petroleum and natural gas. Consequently, two problems arise in assessing the degree of competition: (1) inadequate data and (2) the operation of regional rather than national markets.

Absent more recent regional data, one way of assessing the degree of competition in coal is to look at national patterns of concentration in production and in reserves (see table 9.12). Several observations stem directly from these figures. First, coal experienced rising concentration in production in the 1955–72 period, but it has since declined to the more moderate levels of the early 1960s. Second, although the degree of concentration in reserves has not changed much for the twenty-five-year period of available data, the level has continued to exceed the overall degree of concentration in production. Third, concentration ratios for coal production and reserves have generally tended to be lower than their counterpart ratios in domestic and international petroleum and natural gas. However, as with petroleum and natural gas, the degree of concentration in coal still exceeds the overall degree of concentration among all manufacturing industry as a whole.

As noted in section 9.3, there is substantial evidence of horizontal integration by petroleum and natural gas firms into the coal industry. At the same time, this integration has been modified to a considerable extent by the entry of both steel and electric utilities into coal production (see table 9.13). If we compare the data for the years 1970 and 1980, we see that as the overall degree of concentration in coal production has declined, so too has the share of petroleum- and natural gas–owned firms among the top fifteen producers. In short, much of the decline in concentration is attributable to mergers and to new entries by non-petroleum and non–natural gas firms, particularly in the opening of many midwestern strip mines.

Because of the industry's heavy degree of integration with non-coal firms, there is no readily observable basis on which to assess industry profitability. Generally available evidence from such sources as Standard and Poor's market profiles do suggest that rates of return to equity in coal are comparable to those in petroleum and natural gas, as well as to those in manufacturing as a whole.[30] Unfortunately, these data do not permit a sufficiently detailed breakdown to determine to what extent size is a factor in profitability. In sum, then, based on currently available evidence, we can say that with its declining levels of producer concentration, coal has become more competi-

[30]Using unweighted rates of return to equity, Standard and Poor's *Coal and Steel Industry Survey* lists the following rates of return to five primarily coal producing firms: 1955, 7.1 percent; 1960, 6.5 percent; 1965, 7.94 percent; 1970, 15.6 percent; 1971, 12.8 percent; 1972, 10.0 percent; 1973, 10.6 percent; 1974, 25.2 percent; 1975, 29.4 percent; 1976, 22.7 percent; 1977, 11.2 percent.

Table 9.12. Concentration Ratios in the U.S. Coal Industry, 1955–80

	1955	1965	1970	1972	1973	1974	1975	1976	1977	1978	1979	1980
Production shares of the largest:												
4 firms	16.5%	26.6%	30.2%	30.4%	29.2%	27.3%	26.1%	24.8%	23.0%	20.9%	22.3%	21.1%
8 firms	24.0	36.4	40.7	40.4	39.3	37.6	35.7	33.5	30.7	27.9	30.4	29.5
15 firms	35.4	46.5	52.8	51.9	49.6	47.5	45.3	43.8	40.5	37.5	40.9	40.3
50 firms	54.7	62.3	66.8	67.0	69.2	65.5	64.5	63.2	65.0	57.9	66.1	64.5
Coal reserves[a] ownership by the largest:												
4 firms	—	—	—	—	30.3	36.7	27.7	29.5	31.3	29.8	29.4	29.6
8 firms	—	—	—	—	51.0	55.9	45.1	46.7	48.2	47.9	47.3	46.6
15 firms	—	—	—	—	66.9	71.0	59.1	60.7	62.3	63.5	62.7	60.5
20 firms	—	—	—	—	73.9	77.8	65.6	67.0	68.4	69.3	68.4	65.9
30 firms	—	—	—	—	82.3	86.7	74.0	75.8	77.5	77.9	77.0	74.5

Sources: T. D. Duchesneau, *Competition in the U.S. Energy Industry* (Cambridge, Mass.: Ballinger Publishing Co., 1975), p. 76; *Keystone Coal Buyers Manual* (New York: McGraw-Hill Publishing Co., selected years). Duchesneau lists the latter as the source for his estimates.

[a]Reserve estimates do not differentiate between recoverable and in-place reserves

Table 9.13. Interindustry Concentration in U.S. Coal Production, 1970, 1980

Coal Company	Parent Company	Thousand Tons Produced	Percentage of U.S. Production
1970			
Peabody Coal	Kennecott	67,850	11.3%
Consolidation Coal	Continental Oil	64,062	10.6
Island Creek Coal	Occidental Petroleum	29,722	4.9
Pittston Coal		20,540	3.4
U.S. Steel		19,631	3.3
Bethlehem Steel		14,605	2.4
Eastern Associated Coal	Eastern Gas and Fuel	14,539	2.4
Ayrshire		14,427	2.4
General Dynamics		14,092	2.3
Old Ben Coal	Standard Oil (Ohio)	11,687	1.9
Westmoreland Coal		11,347	1.9
North American Coal		9,674	1.6
Pittsburg and Midway	Gulf Oil	7,838	1.3
Utah Construction		6,021	1.0
Southwestern Illinois		5,715	0.9
Total above		311,751	51.7
Total U.S.		602,932	100.0
1980			
Peabody Group	Newmont; Williams; Bechtel	59,083	7.2
Consolidation Coal	Continental Oil Company; Dupont	48,955	5.9
AMAX Group	AMAX, Inc.	40,547	4.9
Texas Utilities	Texas Utilities	27,590	3.3
Island Creek Coal	Occidental Petroleum	20,017	2.4
Pittston Coal		17,775	2.1
NERCO	Pacific Power and Light	16,900	2.0
Arch Mineral		15,818	1.9
U.S. Steel	U.S. Steel	14,223	1.7
American Electric Power		14,052	1.7
Peter Kiewit		13,450	1.6
North American Group		12,670	1.5
Westmoreland Coal	Penn-Virginia; Morrison-Knudson	12,657	1.5
Bethlehem Mines	Bethlehem Steel Company	11,707	1.4
Exxon Coal Group	Exxon Corporation	11,400	1.4
Total above		336,846	40.3
Total U.S.		835,400	100.0

Source: Keystone Coal Buyers Manual (New York: McGraw-Hill Publishing Co., selected years).

tive in recent years. Given its relative degrees of concentration and profitability, coal would not appear to be a likely first candidate for some of the procompetitive policy measures that we have noted previously.

9.5. NUCLEAR ENERGY

Five characteristics distinguish the nuclear energy industry from its fossil fuel counterparts. First, as noted in chapter 6, it is devoted almost exclusively to the production of electricity. Second, the number of transformation stages within the nuclear fuel cycle far exceeds those found in the production of petroleum. Third, although there would be economies arising from integrated operations, thus far the nuclear industry remains as one of the least vertically integrated of all energy industries, with much of its activities inextricably intertwined with government ownership, pricing, and production policies. Fourth, to a far greater extent than coal, nuclear energy functions on a national and international basis, at least under current conditions. Finally, despite the absence of significant vertical integration within each stage of production, the nuclear industry is one of the most concentrated of all energy industries, as the concentration ratios in production, reactor sales, and ownership of reserves listed in table 9.14 show. From our present perspective, our concern at this point is whether the nuclear energy industry has economies of scale that could explain the prevailing degree of concentration, and whether the industry could be considered a competitive one.

Studies of the nuclear energy industry have been devoted almost exclusively to the pricing of nuclear reactors and to nuclear fuel costs in the aggregate. Because these studies have focused as often as not on the underlying question of whether a closed (that is, reprocessing-inclusive) or open ("throw-away") nuclear fuel cycle would be used, there has been virtually no hard evidence with which to assess the extent of scale economies within any single stage of the nuclear fuel cycle or across any number of these stages together. Yet, even from the indirect evidence that is available, we can draw some conclusions regarding the structure of the nuclear energy industry.

Table 9.14. Concentration Ratios in the U.S. Nuclear Industry, 1955–75

	1955	1960	1965	1970	1971	1973	1974	1975
Uranium oxide concentrate production by the largest:								
4 firms	79.9%	51.4%	55.4%	55.3%	54.4%	55.7%	55.7%	54.3%
8 firms	99.1	72.4	79.3	80.8	78.5	83.9	82.2	77.9
15 firms	100.0	94.6	98.1	100.0	98.5	98.2	100.0	—
20 firms	100.0	99.6	100.0	100.0	100.0	100.0	100.0	100.0
Cumulative reactor sales by the largest:								
4 firms	—	—	—	98.0	98.0	96.3	96.6	—
8 firms	—	—	—	100.0	100.0	100.0	100.0	—
Ownership of uranium oxide reserves by the largest:								
4 firms	—	—	—	—	—	—	—	72.4
8 firms	—	—	—	—	—	—	—	87.8
10 firms	—	—	—	—	—	—	—	90.9

Sources: Federal Trade Commission, *Concentration Levels and Trends in the Energy Sector of the U.S. Economy, 1974,* Report to the U.S. House Committee on Mines and Mining (Washington, D.C.: U.S. Government Printing Office, 1975); U.S. Atomic Energy Commission, *The Nuclear Industry* (Washington, D.C.: U.S. Government Printing Office, selected years); Mark Gilman, "Investment Opportunities in the Domestic Uranium Industry," (New York: Energy and Research Development Group, Salomon Brothers, 1976), reported in *Petroleum Economist*, October 1976, p. 395.

First, since there are economies of scale to coal extraction, it is reasonable to assume that comparable economies are to be found in uranium oxide and thorium extraction mining and milling as well. However, given the smaller volume of uranium oxide and thorium markets in comparison with coal markets, it is not clear whether the actual scale of mining and milling is one that matches or exceeds the level necessary for their realization.

Second, there is insufficient evidence with which to assess the extent of scale economies in the conversion and enrichment phases of nuclear fuel preparation. At present, conversion is performed by two firms—Allied Chemical in Metropolis, Illinois, and Kerr-McGee in Sequoyah, Oklahoma—while gaseous diffusion enrichment is done at three federal government owned plants—in Oak Ridge, Tennessee, Paducah, Kentucky, and Portsmouth, Ohio. It is reasonable to assume that in both of these stages the capital requirements involved do lead to economies of scale, but as in the case of mining and milling, there is no hard evidence to determine if in fact these plants represent or exceed the optimal scale necessary for their realization.

Third, in the fabrication of fuel and in the construction of nuclear reactors, there is likewise a paucity of data with which to determine the extent of scale economies. Given that a standard 1,000-megawatt reactor now typically costs over 1 billion 1980 dollars, there are undoubtedly some economies that could be derived from large-scale production, in terms both of the number of reactors per unit of time and of their average size. However, for reasons already anticipated in chapter 6, the rate of expansion of nuclear reactors has now approached zero. Thus, whatever scale economies could be realized seem largely to be undermined in light of the limited scale of industry activity and by the absence of standard procedures for reactor design and construction standards. As will be seen in subsequent chapters, even in the most optimistic scenarios involving the expansion of nuclear power, it is likely that whatever scale economies might be available in theory would be only marginally realizable in practice.

Two other factors affecting the degree of competition in the nuclear energy industry are horizontal integration and profitability. While horizontal integration by petroleum firms in uranium reserves and mining has become significant in recent years, in the case of mining at least, it has contributed to the decline of concentration. Second, insofar as tests of profitability are concerned, the prevailing degree of horizontal integration makes it as difficult to isolate the specific returns to any one stage of the nuclear fuel cycle (or the industry as a whole for that matter) as in the case of coal. Limited evidence on profitability does suggest that the returns to nuclear energy have tended to be competitive with those for other energy industries, though the experience since the incident at Three Mile Island has created considerable uncertainty regarding the future.[31] In effect, because commercial nuclear energy has

[31] Standard and Poor's *Coal and Steel Industry Survey* lists returns to equity among the principal reactor producing firms at rates comparable to or exceeding manufacturing industry rates as a whole. Since the two largest firms, General Electric and Westinghouse, are also producers of steam electric turbines and related industrial machinery, there is no readily comparable figure for a pure rate of return to nuclear reactor construction.

been so strongly shaped by government intervention and by horizontal integration, it is fair to say that the industry is far from being a competitively structured one. That it also does not appear to possess significant economies of scale suggests that nuclear energy could well be one of the least efficient of the industries we have examined.

9.6. THE ELECTRICITY INDUSTRY

One problem that affects the assessment of the nuclear energy industry in particular is that its principal function is to generate steam for the production of electricity. As we will see in chapter 11, commercial electricity generation is determined largely by various regulatory commissions which must approve plant licenses, rate structures, and other decisions affecting various aspects of industry behavior. Thus, to understand fully the structure of the energy industry, we need to know to what extent there are economies of scale in electricity production, as well as the extent to which the industry is a competitive one.

The regulation of electricity production is justified traditionally on the assumption that the industry is a natural monopoly. The notion behind a natural monopoly is that there are continually falling average costs throughout all stages of production. Hence, it is argued that the most logical structure of production is a single monopoly in which the most efficient level of production can be derived. The role of regulation is to prevent the accumulation of monopoly profits that might otherwise occur. Clearly, then, the extent to which the actual structure of electricity production exhibits these economies of scale bears directly on the economic efficiency of continued electricity regulation.

Electricity in the United States is produced by three types of firms: federal power authorities, state power authorities, and local public and private utilities. Given the variety of organizational patterns in electricity generation, most observers agree that there are scale economies in the industry.[32] They differ, however, in their estimates of the extent of these economies. As examples, in one study, Hulbert (1969) claimed that scale economies can be achieved for systems of up to 25,000 megawatts, a figure that is over twice the capacity of the country's largest private utility in 1970, American Electric Power, Inc.[33] In contrast, Nerlove (1963) found that these economies are exhausted at relatively modest levels of output.[34]

Differences in estimates of scale economies can be traced to several principal causes: data deficiencies, technological change, and differences in

[32]For a recent review of the literature, see L. W. Weiss, "Antitrust in the Electric Power Industry," in *Promoting Competition in Regulated Markets,* ed. Almarin Phillips (Washington, D.C.: Brookings Institution, 1975).

[33]G. C. Hulbert, "Power Generation in the 1970's," *1969 Future Power Forum: Perspective for the 1970's* (New York: Westinghouse Corporation, 1969).

[34]M. Nerlove, "Returns to Scale in Electricity Supply," in *Measurement in Economics—Studies in Mathematical Economics and Econometrics in Memory of Yehuda Grunfeld,* ed. C. F. Christ (Palo Alto: Stanford University Press, 1963).

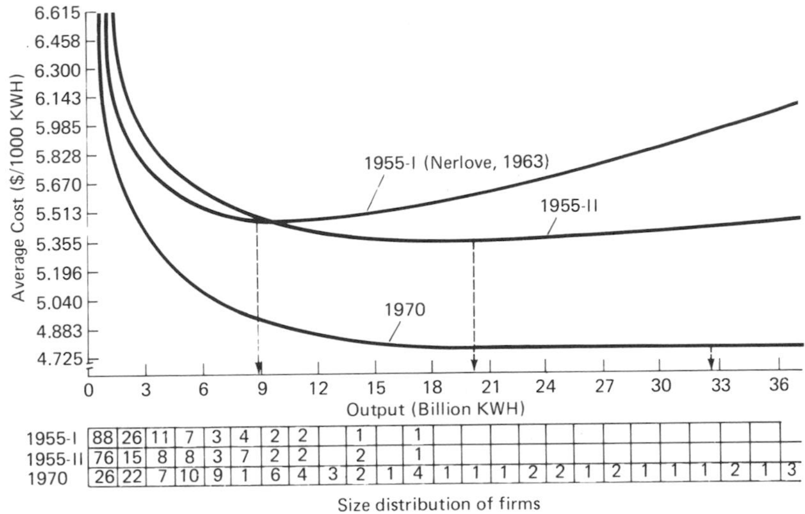

Figure 9.3. Economies of Scale in U.S. Electricity Generation. From L. R. Christensen and W. H. Greene, "Economies of Scale in U.S. Electric Power Generation," *Journal of Political Economy* 84 (August 1976):671.

estimation procedures. In an attempt to reconcile these differences, Christensen and Greene (1976) used a translog cost function to reestimate the scale economies of the 1955 sample used by Nerlove (1963), as well as to provide a more recent estimate of 1970 scale economies.[35] Because the translog cost function imposes no restrictions on the degree of input substitution, Christensen and Greene found that there were significant scale economies in 1955 which exceeded Nerlove's original estimates and which were much closer to the figure cited by Hulbert. However, they found that by 1970 the actual scale of many firms exceeded the level necessary to realize these economies under the current level of technology, as may be seen in reference to the long-run average cost curves derived in figure 9.3.

The implications of the Christensen and Greene study are substantial. For 1970 at least, their estimates suggest that the 15 percent of firms with annual production in excess of 20 billion kilowatt-hours each had capacities beyond the 19.8 billion kilowatt-hours necessary for the realization of economies of scale in the electricity generation industry. Since the seventeen firms in this category accounted for just over half of the 1970 production of 1,534 billion kilowatt-hours, the industry could be substantially restructured with no significant increases in average electricity costs. That it has not been done can be attributed to administrative costs, the absence of significant diseconomies of scale, and bureaucratic inertia. Finally, the study also suggests that among the largest firms at least, there may be significant barriers

[35] L. R. Christensen and W. H. Greene, "Economies of Scale in U.S. Electric Power Generation," *Journal of Political Economy* 84 (August 1976):655–76.

to entry that inhibit the operation of the electricity industry along lines more consistent with the efficiency criteria of perfect competition.

If the size of electricity generating firms exceeds the level necessary for the realization of economies of scale, it also points to a significant degree of concentration. Table 9.15 lists the degree of concentration in output and inputs by size of producing firms and type of fuel among the largest utilities in the country for the year 1969. As in the primary energy industries already reviewed, the degree of concentration at the national level exceeds the degree of concentration among all manufacturing industries as a whole (see table 9.3). Moreover, were these data disaggregated into regional markets more representative of actual electricity-consuming areas, the extent of concentration in any single region would undoubtedly be well above the figures listed here.

One other test of competition is profitability. The profitability of utilities is of course determined by regulation, but during the 1970s at least, the actual levels were below those of manufacturing as a whole. It does not necessarily follow that utilities are more competitive, however, in that the risks to regulated utilities are not everywhere equivalent to those of the manufacturing sector. Thus, we can say that the regulated electrical utility industry is one in which there are economies of scale in production, that the actual scale of the largest firms exceeds the necessary level for their realization, that the industry is relatively concentrated, but that profitability does not exceed the overall degree in manufacturing as a whole. In order to understand how this profitability is determined, in the following chapters we will look at the nature of demand and the determination of energy prices.

9.7. SUMMARY

From an economic perspective, energy policy choices depend critically on the responsiveness of producers to given changes in prices. In the near term at least, they are tied directly to the elasticity of supply in conventional fossil fuels, in nuclear energy, and in the generation of electricity. According to currently available evidence, the supply of these resources is relatively price-inelastic in the short run, suggesting the susceptibility of the economy not only to periodic energy crises but also to the presence of imperfectly competitive producer structures.

The structure of energy markets is best understood with reference to established economic criteria. Drawing on conventional economic analysis, it is possible to utilize two basic tests to assess the responsiveness and efficiency of any given resource producer: the extent of scale economies and the extent of competition. The greater the presence of scale economies, the more we can justify higher degrees of concentration in the organization of production. At the same time, unless they are otherwise constrained, larger scale economies may also be detrimental to competitive economic efficiency. The implication is that where scale economies lead to natural monopoly conditions, regulation may be justified as a way of promotions competitive economic behavior. Absent such scale economies in highly concentrated industries, a restructuring into a more competitive grouping of firms may be necessary.

Table 9.15. Concentration Ratios in the U.S. Electricity Industry, 1969

	Share of the Largest:						
	4 Firms	8 Firms	15 Firms	20 Firms	50 Firms	75 Firms	100 Firms
I. Capacity and generation by firms producing more than 2 billion kwh							
Capacity	—	—	39.8%	47.7%	70.3%	80.7%	87.5%
Generation	—	—	42.2	50.9	75.1	84.8	90.7
II. Concentration in coal consumption by electric utilities	31.6%	45.3%	—	66.8	89.1	99.5	—
III. Concentration in fuel oil consumption by electric utilities	37.2	56.7	75.8	82.8	—	—	—

Sources: Richard L. Gordon, *U.S. Coal and the Electric Power Industry* (Baltimore, Md.: Johns Hopkins University Press for Resources for the Future, 1975), pp. 42, 46, 47, 48, 50; and U.S. Department of Energy, Energy Information Administration, *Annual Report to Congress, 1978* (Washington, D.C.: U.S. Government Printing Office, April 1979).

Three basic methods are available to test the presence of scale economies: survival studies, statistical cost analysis, and engineering process analysis. In energy markets at least, the most reliable are either engineering or statistical cost studies. According to recently available evidence, there are indications of scale economies in petroleum, coal, nuclear power, and electricity generation, based on conventional energy technology. At the same time, virtually all of these resource markets have actual degrees of concentration that appear to exceed the scale which is essential for the realization of economies of scale.

When the actual size of an energy firm exceeds that which is necessary for economies of scale, it is an indication that the behavior of markets may not be competitive. Several criteria have been devised to determine the degree of competition in any given market: concentration ratios, vertical and horizontal integration, joint ventures, advertising, profitability, and the nature of pricing, to name the most important. Evidence from these tests (apart from pricing, which is covered in chapter 11) suggests imperfectly competitive markets. Though profitability does not appear to exceed comparable rates in manufacturing as a whole, larger firms have periodically enjoyed premium rates of return over smaller firms. Moreover, concentration has continued to exceed the levels in manufacturing as a whole. At the same time, there are indications that the degree of imperfect competition has been reduced over time. In order to determine its levels in the future, as well as to assess the social costs of policy alternatives, we must also consider the nature of demand and the determination of energy prices, to which we now turn.

SUGGESTED READINGS

Adelman, M. A. *The World Petroleum Market.* Baltimore: Johns Hopkins Press for Resources for the Future, 1972.

Duchesneau, T. D. *Competition in the U.S. Energy Industry.* Cambridge, Mass.: Ballinger Publishing Co., 1975.

Goldschmid, H. J., Mann, H. M., and Weston, J. F., eds. *Industrial Concentration: The New Learning.* Boston: Little, Brown and Co., 1974.

Gordon, Richard L. *U.S. Coal and the Electric Power Industry.* Baltimore: Johns Hopkins University Press for Resources for the Future, 1975.

Jacoby, N. H. *Multinational Oil.* New York: Macmillan Publishing Co., 1974.

Markham, J. W., Hourihan, A. P., and Sterling, F. L. *Horizontal Divestiture and the Petroleum Industry.* Cambridge, Mass.: Ballinger Publishing Co., 1977.

Pindyck, R. S., ed. *Advances in the Economics of Energy and Resources.* Vol. 1. Greenwich, Conn.: JAI Press, 1979.

10

THE DEMAND FOR ENERGY

All energy consumption is a reflection of demand. As noted in chapters 2 and 3, for the United States at least, the pattern of this demand is a key factor in determining the susceptibility of the economy to periodic energy crises. Beyond its importance to the prediction of energy crises, knowledge of demand is significant in two additional ways: first, all energy production decisions are based on its known or expected pattern; second, demand is a basic factor in the design of appropriate energy policies. Thus, although the technical efficiency of all energy utilization is governed ultimately by the laws of thermodynamics spelled out in chapter 4, any practical measures that may be devised to approach the limits of these laws depend first and foremost on the nature of energy demand and its capacity for change.

In concert with supply, the demand for energy can be viewed on an aggregate or fuel-specific basis. Though national energy policies are framed in aggregate terms, it is on a fuel- and sector-specific microeconomic level that the success of these policies is ultimately determined. With this dual framework of energy demand in mind, our concern at this point focuses on three fundamental questions: (1) To what extent do non-energy goods serve as substitutes for the energy resources presently consumed? (2) To what extent is the demand for individual fuels sensitive to changes in their prices? and (3) To what extent are these energy resources good substitutes for each other? Though these questions pertain in the long run to the alternative energy resources discussed in part II, in the short term at least, they are most relevant to the fossil, nuclear, and renewable energy resources on which the economy presently depends.

10.1. A REFERENCE FRAMEWORK FOR ENERGY DEMAND DECISIONS

The demand for energy derives from the demand for the various non-energy goods and services with which it is consumed. Where the demand for these goods and services changes, there will be some corresponding impact on the demand for the energy required for their production and consumption, in the price of that energy, in its quantity, or in both. Thus, whether on a macro- or

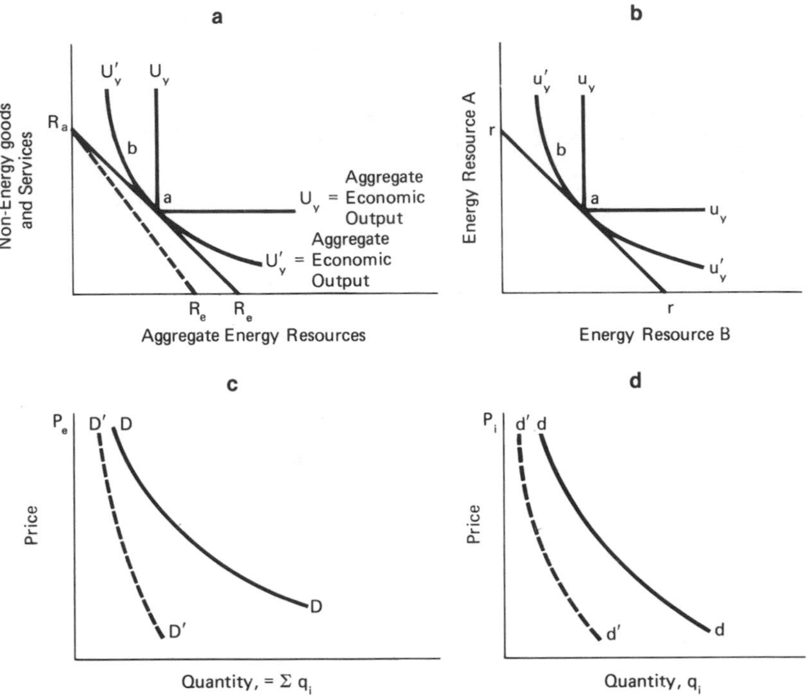

Figure 10.1. The Simple Geometry of Short-Run Energy Demand Decisions: **a.** aggregate energy substitutability; **b.** interfuel energy substitutability; **c.** aggregate energy demand; **d.** individual energy demand.

microeconomic level, we can express the derived demand for energy in terms of the non-energy goods and services associated with its use, as well as in terms of its own price.

Figure 10.1.*a* illustrates the basic consumption linkage between the demand for energy and the demand for non-energy goods and services in the economy. Although there may be differences in this linkage according to type of fuel, geographic region, sector (residential, industrial, transportation), or stage of transformation (intermediate production versus final consumption), in the aggregate it can be expressed as a weighted average of all these individual variations. Indeed, figure 10.1.*a* can be thought of as a more precise way of representing the energy-GNP ratio illustrated in figure 1.3.

At any given time period, the level of output of an economy can be apportioned between its consumption of energy and of non-energy goods. The greater the degree of flexibility, or elasticity, in the substitution of non-energy for energy, the greater will be the range of choices between these two goods.[1] At one extreme is the perfect substitutability case illustrated by the

[1]As noted in chapter 9, the elasticity of substitution measures the relative change in the ratio of one good to another in proportion to the relative change in the ratio of their prices. The elasticity of substitution referred to in figure 10.1.*a* can be expressed in quantitative terms as σ

line R_aR_e. This points to the greatest range of choice between energy and non-energy goods, but it is unrealistic, suggesting as it does that the production and consumption of these goods could be accomplished without any use of energy. Another extreme is zero substitutability, illustrated here by the L-shaped curve U_yU_y. In this case, the assumption that energy is so unique that no substitution is possible ignores the possibility that actual energy use may be well below its thermodynamic limits. This leaves an intermediate range between zero and infinity, typified by the curve $U_y'U_y'$, the interpretation of which calls for some elaboration.

In the short-run terms of figure 10.1.*a*, the substitution of non-energy for energy means essentially that the economy has adopted a technically more efficient use of a given stock of energy. In the reference terms of chapter 4, it means that the actual technical efficiency of energy use has been brought closer to its thermodynamic limits. It can be done in the short run by a variety of conservation measures such as the waste recycling noted in chapter 8, by more optimal use of temperature and thermostat controls, by enforcement of highway speed limits, and by related changes in the use of the given stock of these resources. In the long run, it may affect not only the level of energy resource use but also the types of resources and their associated conversion technologies, about which more will be said in a moment.

If an economy has any degree of technical substitutability, it probably results from a change in the relative prices of energy and non-energy goods. In figure 10.1.*a*, relative prices of energy and non-energy goods are embodied in the economy's given income line R_aR_e.[2] For the given level of output, R_aR_e specified the various combinations of energy and non-energy goods which society could acquire under a given set of prices. Conventional macroeconomic efficiency is attained at point *a*, which is where society's budgetary expenditure attains the highest possible level of output.[3]

In the reference terms of figure 10.1.*a*, an increase in the price of energy will raise the slope of the economy's income line R_aR_e beyond its original tangency position, *a*. The economic consequences of a given increase in energy price will depend on three basic factors: the value share of energy in aggregate economic output, the percentage increase in the price of energy, and the elasticity of substitution of non-energy goods for energy goods. If the substitution possibilities are like those represented by $U_y'U_y'$, an increase in the slope of the income line R_aR_e will result in a new point of tangency such

$= - [\Delta(A/E)/(A/E)]/[\Delta(P_a/P_e)/(P_a/P_e)]$, where A and E refer, respectively, to non-energy and energy goods and P refers to the price.

[2]Accordingly, total income is allocated as follows: $(P_a)(R_a) + (P_e)(R_e) = TR$.

[3]As in the determination of supply, the economic efficiency here can be determined from society's aggregate utility function, $U = f(A, E)$, subject to its income constraint, $P_aA + P_eE = Y$. With a Lagrangian reformulation, the problem then becomes: Maximize $L = f(A, E) - \lambda(P_aA + P_eE - Y)$. The first order optimal conditions are: $(\partial L/\partial A) = (\partial U/\partial A) - \lambda P_a = 0$; $(\partial L/\partial E) = (\partial U/\partial E) - \lambda P_e = 0$; $(\partial L/\partial \lambda) = P_aA + P_eE - Y = 0$. Thus $(\partial U/\partial A)/P_a = (\partial U/\partial E)/P_e = (\partial U/\partial A)/(\partial U/\partial E) = (P_a/P_e)$, i.e., the marginal rate of technical substitution between non-energy and energy goods is exactly equal to the ratio of their prices, which in this case is at position *a*, the point of tangency between the price line and the economy's aggregate utility function.

as at position b, to the left, with no significant effect on the level of economic output. However, if the substitution possibilities are limited, as in the zero degree illustrated by U_yU_y, then an increase in the price of energy will also produce an adverse effect on the level of economic output, as indicated by the shift of the income line from R_aR_e to R_aR_e'.[4] Just how significant these various possibilities might be can be illustrated with a few hypothetical examples.

In the extreme case of a zero elasticity of substitution, by definition an increase in the price of energy cannot be absorbed by a shift into non-energy goods, nor will it result initially in any reduction in the given level of aggregate energy consumption. As a result, this higher cost of energy could be absorbed only by a reduction in the level of aggregate economic output by means of a proportional increase in the cost of energy. Once the reduction in economic activity is attained, there will be a proportional reduction in the physical consumption of energy, though the value share of energy in the economy will have risen by the proportional increase in its price. For example, if the value share of energy in the U.S. economy were 4 percent (which is where it stood in relation to the 1970 U.S. GNP), a doubling of the price of energy would produce at most a 4 percent reduction in the level of aggregate economic production. The 4 percent reduction would then be matched by a proportional reduction in aggregate energy consumption, even though the value share of this new level of energy would double from its initial level to 8 percent. In sum, for a zero elasticity of substitution, the higher the initial value share of energy, the greater will be the reduction in aggregate economic production for a given increase in the price of energy.[5]

Since an infinite elasticity of substitution between non-energy goods and energy goods would be impossible, this leaves three other cases for us to consider: unitary, less than infinity but greater than unitary, and less than one but greater than zero. In the case of a unitary elasticity of substitution, for any given increase in the price of energy, there will be a proportional reduction in its consumption, which is just matched by a proportional expansion in the demand for non-energy goods. The aggregate level of economic activity is unaffected, as is the value share of energy, even though the technical conversion of energy in physical terms will have been raised closer to its thermodynamic limits.

In the case where the elasticity of substitution has a value of less than infinity but greater than unitary, for a given increase in the price of energy, there will be a greater than proportional reduction in energy consumption and its value share, as well as a greater than proportional expansion of the

[4]In order to maintain diagrammatic simplicity, a lower aggregate economic output isoquant has not been included in figure 10.1.a.

[5]In this example, a 4 percent reduction in physical energy consumption would, of course, result in a new level at 96 percent of the previous one. It should also be noted that economic theory suggests that were the value share of energy to become large over time, as has indeed been the case in recent years, the elasticity of substitution would also become larger, much as is the case of the own-price elasticity of demand for any individual good in relation to individual income.

non-energy value share, even though the level of aggregate economic activity remains the same. This suggests an ideal position, resulting as it would in greater thermodynamic efficiency at no loss of aggregate income or of alternative non-energy goods than could be achieved by a unitary elasticity of substitution. Unfortunately, it is only slightly less likely than the implausible case of an infinite elasticity of substitution.

The final case is the most realistic. For values of the elasticity of substitution that range between zero and unity, substitution between energy and non-energy goods is possible, but its extent will always be proportionally less than the given increase in the price of energy. A limited shift into non-energy goods means that there will be an increase in the value share of energy which at the same time will result in some reduction in the level of aggregate economic production. The closer the elasticity of substitution approaches a value of one, for a given increase in price, the smaller will be the adverse impact on aggregate economic production, the more likely will be the constancy in the value share of energy, and the greater will be the thermodynamic efficiency in physical energy use. Indeed, as we will see, practical energy alternatives must inevitably be designed largely on this segment of the demand elasticity continuum.

As we might expect, the aggregate energy elasticity of substitution is tied intimately to its own-price elasticity of demand and to the elasticities of substitution of alternative types of energy resources. Figure 10.1.*c* illustrates the basic inverse relationship between the quantity of aggregate energy consumption and its price. The own-price elasticity of demand in the curve *DD* is greater than that in *D′D′*. To the extent that the elasticity of substitution between energy and non-energy goods is small, so too will be the own-price elasticity of demand for energy as well as for non-energy goods. From a policy perspective, then, any steps that may lead to a more elastic demand for aggregate energy resources will at the same time help to reduce the adverse income effects that may arise from an increase in the relative price of energy.

If the aggregate demand for energy is the sum of demands for individual types of energy, the elasticity of aggregate energy demand is simply a weighted average of the individual elasticities of demand of these resources. Moreover, the own-price elasticity of demand for any individual energy resource, to the extent that it is low, also points to an underlying inelasticity of substitution among its closest alternatives. When the aggregate relations of figures 10.1.*a* and 10.1.*c* are broken down by fuel (and sector), as in figures 10.1.*b* and 10.1.*d*, we can identify the relative importance of individual fuels to aggregate demand for energy and determine the impact of these variables on the level of aggregate production in the economy. Thus, any policy measures designed to alter the aggregate elasticity of energy demand will at the same time be focused in more practical terms on the demand for individual types of fuels in the specific sectors of the economy in which they are consumed.

If there is any flexibility in the demand for energy, its fullest potential is most likely to be realized in the long run. When longer time periods are taken into account, the aggregate demand for energy will be influenced not only by its relative price but also by the extent to which there has been economic growth and technical change (see figure 10.2.*a*). If we set aside the impact of a change in the relative price of energy (examined in figure 10.1.*a*), an increase in aggregate income will shift society's consumption possibilities from R_1R_1 to R_2R_2. One possibility is that the aggregate demand for energy will change in direct proportion to the increase in aggregate economic output, as in the shift in equilibrium positions from *a* to *b*. In this case (since the price of energy has been held constant by virtue of the parallel change in R_1R_1), there is a unitary income elasticity of energy demand, which implies that an economy's energy–GNP ratio is unaltered over time. As noted in chapter 1, in the United States at least, historical experience suggests that the assumption of a unitary income elasticity of energy demand would be most unwarranted, ignoring as it does both relative price changes and the extent of technical change.

Technical change in energy can occur over time whether relative prices change or remain the same. The simplest way of measuring the impact of technical change on energy is to look at the value share of energy in aggregate economic output over time. If relative prices are unchanged (and inflationary distortions have been taken into account), a decline in the value share of en-

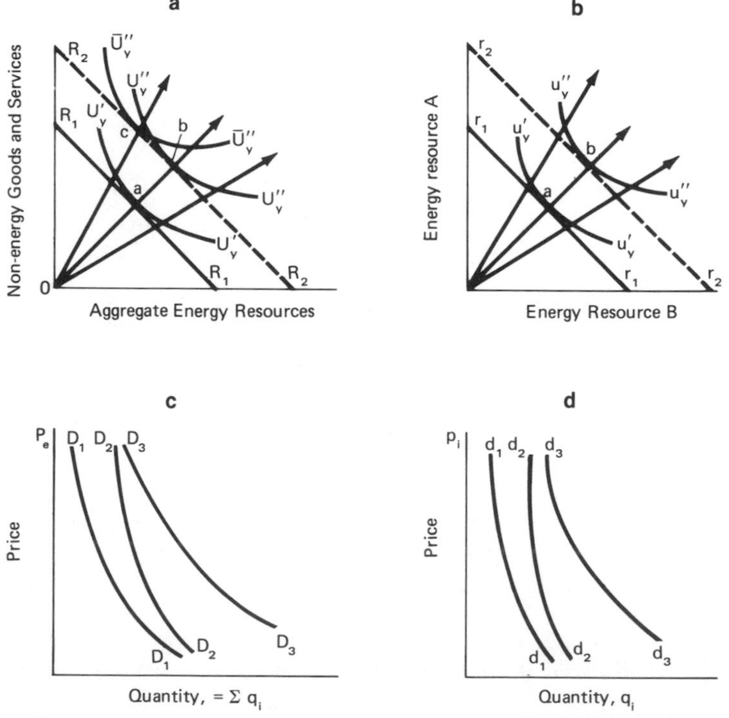

Figure 10.2. The Simple Geometry of Long-Run Energy Demand Decisions: **a.** aggregate energy substitutability; **b.** interfuel energy substitutability; **c.** aggregate energy demand; **d.** individual energy demand.

ergy points to an energy-saving bias from technical change, for example, greater fuel efficiency in new automobiles. In diagrammatic terms, this would be equivalent to a shift in the economy's aggregate energy equilibrium from *a* to *c* rather than its original shift from *a* to *b*. Conversely, an energy-using bias from technical change implies, as economic growth occurs, an expansion path along a ray such as the one furthest to the right in figure 10.2.*a*.

Whether energy-saving technical change will affect the absolute level of energy consumption in physical terms depends on the magnitude of the technical change and on the overall rate of economic growth. In figure 10.2.*a*, in relation to the change in the economy's level of output, the extent of technical change is just sufficient to prevent an increase in the absolute level of energy consumption. The implication of this illustration is that although relative prices do have an important role to play over time, changes in energy demand will also be affected to a great extent by the degree of technical change in energy-resource utilization. Where exhaustible fossil and nuclear resources are concerned, the significance of this change becomes crucial to the long-run growth potential of the economy.

It should be noted that as the economy evolves over time, the interaction of technical change and economic growth will also affect the own-price elasticity of aggregate energy demand, as well as its position (see figure 10.2.*c*). If there is economic growth which causes an increase in the aggregate demand for energy, technical change can also change the extent to which the demand for energy will shift. As figure 10.2.*c* shows, technical change may make aggregate demand more elastic, such as in the shift from D_2D_2 to D_3D_3 (and in so doing cause the isoquants in figure 10.2.*a* to be flatter in their new equilibrium positions). Similarly, where technical change also raises the physical utilization of energy closer to its thermodynamic limits, it could also cause a decline in aggregate energy demand, as well as result in a greater degree of price elasticity, such as the shift from D_2D_2 to D_1D_1.

Finally, behind the aggregate energy changes noted in figures 10.2.*a* and 10.2.*c*, there will be corresponding changes in the demand for the individual energy resources on which the economy depends. In figure 10.2.*b*, interfuel energy substitutability over time is a factor that lies behind the aggregate energy changes already noted. To the extent that interfuel substitution is limited over time, so too will aggregate energy substitution be limited. Similarly, as the demand for individual fuels changes in response to technical change and economic growth, so too may its own-price elasticity of demand be affected (see figure 10.2.*d*). The long-run factors central to aggregate energy demand are thus the level of income, relative prices, and technical change.

10.2. AN OVERVIEW OF AGGREGATE ENERGY DEMAND

As noted in part I, there is a positive relationship between the level of aggregate economic activity and the overall use of energy. At the same time, as long as the technical efficiency of energy resource conversion lies below its thermodynamic limits, it is reasonable to expect that this positive relationship between energy and the economy will be a flexible one, particularly in response to changes in relative prices. To test this proposition, several studies have focused on the aggregate demand for energy as it pertains to both the overall level of output in the economy and to non-energy inputs with which the economy's energy use is combined. Before turning to the available evidence, we need first to define the general framework used in these studies.

Studies of the energy–GNP relationship typically have been based on the use of aggregate production functions.[6] The general form of these functions can be expressed as follows:

$$Y = f(K, L, E, M), \tag{10.1}$$

where Y is the level of production (in the aggregate or by sector) of the economy, measured in real purchasing-power terms, K is the level of capital inputs, L is the level of labor inputs, E is the level of energy inputs, and M is the level of non-energy material inputs. Consistency of aggregation in the measurement of these inputs has met with the usual difficulties involving neoclassical production functions, notably the separation of technical change from changes in the levels of inputs themselves and the estimation of capital stocks independent of the rate of interest, that is the validity of a marginal productivity theory of functional distribution.[7] Difficulties with neoclassical functions notwithstanding, attempts to measure the behavior of energy in relation to non-energy inputs have presented considerable problems in their own right. As will be seen, however, these studies do tend to confirm the general theoretical framework outlined in section 10.1.

In simple terms, the economic theory of section 10.1 suggests that for a given level of income and technology, the energy–GNP relationship is determined by the relative price of energy and the economy's substitution possibilities. If energy becomes relatively less expensive than other inputs, then we would expect more of it to be substituted in place of other available inputs, and vice versa for an increase in the relative price of energy.

[6]Several critical behavioral properties are central to the choice of a particular empirical production function, namely, homogeneity, the extent to which economies of scale can be measured; homotheticity, the extent to which input proportions are independent of the level of output; separability of inputs, the extent to which inputs can vary independently of each other; additivity, the extent to which inputs can be consistently aggregated under alternative transformation patterns, and a priori restrictions on the elasticity of substitution among the input factors of production. Of several types of production functions that have been used in empirical studies, such as Leontief, Cobb-Doublas, CES, and transcendental, the latter imposes the fewest restrictive assumptions and therefore has been used increasingly in the analysis of energy in recent years. For a description of the comparative properties of the transcendental, or translog, production function, see L. Christensen, D. Jorgenson, and L. Lau, "Conjugate Duality and the Transcendental Logarithmic Production Function," *Econometrica* 39 (July 1971):225–56; and idem, "Transcendental Logarithmic Production Frontiers," *Review of Economics and Statistics* 55 (February 1973):28–45.

[7]Though somewhat beyond the central issues of energy policy, this question is nevertheless a basic one in the methodology of economic analysis (see G. C. Harcourt, *Some Cambridge Controversies in the Theory of Capital* [Cambridge: Cambridge University Press, 1972]; E. K. Hunt and J. G. Schwartz, eds., *A Critique of Economic Theory* [Baltimore: Penguin Books, 1972]; and L. Pasinetti, *Lectures on the Theory of Production* [New York: Columbia University Press, 1977], esp. chap. 6).

One of the most common measures of the economy's energy substitution possibilities is the elasticity of substitution. As noted in section 10.1, the elasticity of substitution defines the relative change in input proportions in response to a relative change in their prices. In more specific terms, the extent of this movement along a given isoquant, or constant output level, can be expressed as

$$\epsilon_{ij} = \frac{d\,(x_i/x_j)/(x_i/x_j)}{d\,(p_i/p_j)/(p_i/p_j)}, \tag{10.2}$$

where x_i is the quantity of the ith input (e.g., K, L, E, or M) and p_i is the price of the ith input. Where the elasticity of substitution is positive and exceeds a value of one, for a given increase in the relative price of energy, there will be a greater than proportional reduction in the consumption of energy as non-energy inputs are expanded in its place. Thus, to the extent that the elasticity of substitution between energy and any other single input is positive and statistically significant, we would expect this also to be the case among its non-energy inputs. In contrast, when the coefficient is negative, energy is considered as complementary with the factor that has had a change in its relative price. However, although the elasticity of substitution of any paired set of inputs can be negative, for the production process as a whole, it must have a net value that is either zero or positive, in keeping with the general shape of the isoquants themselves as depicted in figure 10.1.

Table 10.1 lists estimates of the elasticity of substitution among energy and non-energy inputs in four recent studies. The studies all affirm a positive degree of substitution between energy and non-energy inputs, but they differ as to the particular form and magnitude of this substitutability. In the Özatalay-Grubaugh-Long and Griffin-Gregory studies, energy appears to exhibit a significant degree of substitutability with capital and other non-energy inputs; yet in the Berndt-Wood and Hudson-Jorgenson studies, energy is shown to exhibit strong complementarity with capital even though there is some degree of substitutability between energy and other non-capital inputs. Since the form and magnitude of the economy's energy substitution possibilities are essential to the specification of energy policy alternatives, the reasons for these differences merit further elaboration.

There are two basic reasons for differences in the elasticity estimates of table 10.1: data and estimation procedures. Once these differences are taken into account, a common basis exists for interpreting the overall behavior of energy in response to changes in relative prices which is consistent with the theoretical framework of section 10.1. For example, both the Berndt-Wood and Hudson-Jorgenson studies were based on time-series data on U.S. manufacturing for the period 1947–71; the Özatalay-Grubaugh-Long and Griffin-Gregory studies were based on cross-section data pooled from a variety of countries for a much more limited number of years.[8] Since the U.S.

[8]Özatalay, Grubaugh, and Long base their estimates on data for 1963–74 from the United States, Canada, West Germany, Japan, the Netherlands, Norway, and Sweden; Griffin and Gregory base theirs on data for 1955, 1960, 1965, and 1969 from the United States, Belgium,

Table 10.1. Alternative Estimates of the Macroeconomic Elasticity of Substitution between Energy and Non-Energy Resources in the U.S. Economy

Study	Elasticity of Substitution Coefficients Based on Paired Inputs Defined as:					
	Capital-Labor	Capital-Materials	Capital-Energy	Labor-Energy	Labor-Materials	Materials-Energy
Özatalay-Grubaugh-Long (1979)	1.08 (0.07)[a]	0.85 (0.03)[a]	1.22 (0.10)[a]	1.03 (0.30)[a]	1.00 (0.09)[a]	0.58 (0.20)[a]
Griffin-Gregory (1976)	0.06 (0.37)[b]	—	1.07 (0.95)[b]	0.87 (0.16)[b]	—	—
Berndt-Wood (1975)	1.01 (0.27	0.56	−3.22 (1.68)	0.65	0.60 (0.26)	0.75
Hudson-Jorgenson (1974)	1.09	0.25	−1.37	2.16	0.45	−0.77

Sources: S. Özatalay, S. Grubaugh, and T. V. Long II, "Energy Substitution and National Energy Policy," *American Economic Review* 69 (May 1979): 369–71; J. M. Griffin and P. R. Gregory, "An Intercountry Translog Model of Energy Substitution Responses," ibid., 66 (December 1976):845–57; E. R. Berndt and D. O. Wood, "Technology, Prices, and the Derived Demand for Energy," *Review of Economics and Statistics* 56, no. 3 (August 1975):259–68; and E. A. Hudson and D. W. Jorgenson, "U.S. Energy Policy and Economic Growth, 1975–2000," *Bell Journal of Economics and Management Science* 5 (Autumn 1974):461–514.

Note: All estimates of the elasticity of substitution are based on the Allen formulation, after R. G. D. Allen, *Mathematical Analysis for Economists* (New York: St. Martin's Press, 1967), pp. 503–9. Figures in parentheses are estimated standard errors.

[a]All parameters are significant at the 0.05 level

[b]This estimate is based on the approximation method of Lawrence Klein, *A Textbook of Econometrics* (Evanston, Ill.: Row, Peterson and Co., 1953), p. 258

time-series data reflect only year-to-year variations in the economy over a long period of time, the econometric estimates of the elasticity coefficients are most likely to reflect the average of short-run substitution possibilities, as several observers have noted.[9] Moreover, since the real price of energy was falling throughout the 1947–71 period, the time-series estimates of the elasticity of substitution may not necessarily reflect in real terms the extent to which conservation measure could actually be implemented, particularly since the real price of energy has been rising so much in the post-1973 era.

Even if the estimates of table 10.1 were based on a common data sample, differences in estimating procedures would still give rise to alternative elasticity coefficients. In terms of the analytical framework of section 10.1, the problem can be stated in simple terms: although we are interested in identifying the pure impact of a change in relative prices on energy utilization, such a controlled experiment is not possible in the actual economy. Thus, although there may be changes in relative prices, there will also be changes in the level of output of the economy, so that the measurement of input substitutability will be complicated.

One recent effort to reconcile differences among the alternative elasticity estimates already cited has been proposed by Berndt and Wood (1979).[10] Drawing on advances in the theory and measurability of production functions of the type illustrated in equation (10.1), the authors contend that insofar as capital-energy substitutability is concerned, if the level of output, Y, is statistically held constant (in conformity with a single isoquant such as the one illustrated in figure 10.1.*a*), net capital-energy complementarity is more likely than when Y is allowed to vary.[11] They reach this conclusion by formulating what is known as a weakly separable subfunction in which the level of output, Y, depends on the individual inputs, K, L, E, M, but in which an energy production subfunction can also be specified from the master production function.[12] In more practical terms, the energy production subfunction

---

Denmark, France, West Germany, Italy, Netherlands, Norway and the United Kingdom; Hudson and Jorgenson base theirs on U.S. manufacturing data for 1947–71 among nine sectors, including energy-production industries themselves; and Berndt and Wood base theirs on data from twenty-five producing sectors and ten consuming sectors with five categories of final demand.

[9]This point has been stressed not only by Griffin and Gregory but also by R. Pindyck in "Interfuel Substitution and the Industrial Demand for Energy: An International Comparison," *Review of Economics and Statistics* 61 (May 1979):169–79, and in "The Characteristics of the Demand for Energy," in *Energy Conservation and Public Policy*, ed. J. C. Sawhill (Englewood Cliffs, N.J.: Prentice-Hall, 1979), pp. 22–45.

[10]E. R. Berndt and D. O. Wood, "Engineering and Econometric Interpretations of Capital-Energy Complementarity," *American Economic Review* 69 (June 1979):342–54.

[11]By "net" complementarity, Berndt and Wood refer to the fact that the elasticity coefficients have been adjusted to account for any changes in the level of output, Y, or what is equivalent, to estimate the input elasticity of substitution with a constant level of output. Such net estimation is essential to the specification of the production function's partial, or Hicks-Allen, elasticity of substitution, as illustrated in section 10.1. For a more formal derivation, see R.G.D. Allen, *Mathematical Analysis for Economists* (New York: St. Martin's Press, 1967), pp. 503–9.

[12]In the reference framework used by Berndt and Wood, a gross elasticity production function can be expressed as $Y = f(K, L, E, M)$ and the weakly separable formulation can be defined as $Y = f[(K, E), (L, M)]$.

could be thought of as steam generation, which depends in turn in a boiler capital input and a primary energy input such as petroleum, natural gas, or coal.

In the Berndt-Wood gross subfunction formulation, if we are interested in identifying whether capital and energy are substitutes, the empirical model is one in which the output of the subfunction is held constant and the inputs of the energy subfunction adjust to their optimal levels in response to the subfunction's relative price structure. However, the inputs of the master function, which are not part of the subfunction, are held constant, while the master function's output level, Y, is allowed to vary. Berndt and Wood conclude that under such a gross price elasticity formulation, capital and energy are substitutable, but with the caveat that an upward bias may exist to the extent that the level of output, Y, is variable.

Berndt and Wood contrast the gross elasticity formulation with what they refer to as the net price elasticity model. Under a net price model, the output of the master function, Y, is held constant and all inputs, that is, those within the weakly separable subfunction and all other inputs, are permitted to vary in an optimal fashion in response to changes in relative input prices. They find that under this net price elasticity formulation, although there may be some degree of substitution between energy and non-capital inputs, there is net complementarity between energy and capital.

Future research will undoubtedly yield further insights as to the role of energy substitutability in the economy. At this point we can take stock of presently known elasticity estimates and of the Berndt-Wood reconciliation in terms of the analytical framework of section 10.1. First, although there may be differences regarding the form and magnitude of the elasticity of substitution, there is general agreement that energy substitution can occur in response to a change in relative price. In the short run at least, substitution arising from an increase in the relative price of energy is most likely to occur in response to a greater use of labor and material inputs rather than in response to an increased use of capital. The logic of this behavior is not difficult to grasp. Greater materials intensity can occur as both firms and households expand their use of such items as insulation of buildings and related steps designed to raise the technical efficiency of energy conversion. Such measures also create jobs and hence explain the positive degree of labor-energy substitution.[13] However, in the short run, little change is possible in the thermodynamic efficiency of the economy's capital stock. Short-run energy-capital complementarity exists because most capital goods are technically designed to consume given quantities of energy regardless of a change in the relative price of energy, as anyone who has kept a gasoline-guzzling automobile during times of rapid increases in the price of petroleum

[13]The employment-generating consequences of an increase in the price of energy are, of course, more complex than may be evident from an aggregate production function. Thus, the increased demand for labor may appear first in the energy-skills sector, which in turn may filter down to lesser skilled labor, thereby eventually affecting the general rate of unemployment in the economy.

can attest.[14] Yet given sufficient time, once there has been an increase in the relative price of energy, the economy can respond by producing new capital goods with substantially higher thermodynamic efficiency than those already in use.[15] Thus, to the extent that energy-capital complementarity exists in the short run and that overall energy–noncapital input substitution may be limited, there is a need for a more rapid turnover in the present stock of capital as part of an economy's long-run energy policies.

Second, despite evidence of energy substitution possibilities in the economy, in the short run at least, the extent of such substitutions may be limited. The fact that elasticity-of-substitution coefficients between energy and non-energy fall largely between zero and one underscores the continuing sensitivity of the nation's income to the relative price of its depletable energy in general and to the short-run dependence on OPEC oil in particular, much as was suggested in chapter 3. At the same time, although there may be a short-run dependence on the aggregate demand for energy, any policies that may be adopted to reduce this dependence must also take into account the nature of demand on sectoral and fuel-specific bases, each of which can now be examined.

10.3. THE SECTORAL DEMAND FOR ENERGY

The sectoral demand for energy can be measured in a variety of ways. One of the most obvious measures is the own-price elasticity of demand. A second way is in terms of the cross-price elasticity of demand, and a third is in terms of the income elasticity of demand for energy. In general, if there is any degree of substitutability between aggregate energy and non-energy inputs, we would expect to find some flexibility in these specific measures of the demand for energy among individual sectors of the economy. Of course, as in the measurement of the elasticity of substitution, there are problems in the specification of appropriate estimating equations, in both the quantity and the quality of data, and in the estimation procedures. However, when these differences are taken into account, there are several key properties of the sectoral demand for energy, as will be seen in an examination of various estimates.

The own-price elasticity of demand for energy is analogous to the own-price elasticity of supply defined in chapter 9, namely:

$$\epsilon_{ii} = \frac{d\,(x_i)/x_i}{d\,(p_i)/p_i}, \tag{10.3}$$

where x_i is the quantity of energy demanded in the ith sector of the economy per unit of time and p_i is the own-price of energy in the ith sector of the

[14] Of course, there may be some shift to more energy-efficient capital stocks even in the short run, as in the use of railroads and buses. However, where the level of output is relatively fixed, so too will be the slack capacity in any of these alternative capital structures, unless the economy is already operating at substantially less than capacity.

[15] As Berndt and Wood, among others, have acknowledged, the capacity to do so is predicated on the economy's presently low degree of thermodynamic efficiency.

economy per unit of time. Where the absolute value of the own-price elasticity coefficient is greater than one, any given change in the price of energy will produce a significant change in its use. Conversely, where it has a value of one, the change will be proportional, and for values less than one, it will be less than proportional. In general we would expect that the higher the own-price elasticity of demand for energy in a given sector of the economy, the higher the degree of substitutability between energy and non-energy resources (which is much like what we would expect in the case of the aggregate elasticity of substitution).

The cross-price elasticity of demand for energy is defined as the ratio of the relative change in the quantity of energy demanded to the relative change in the price of non-energy alternatives. In more specific quantitative terms, it can be expressed as

$$\epsilon_{ij} = \frac{d\,(x_i)/x_i}{d\,(p_j)/p_j}, \tag{10.4}$$

where x_i is the quantity demanded of the ith good, such as energy, and p_j is the price of the jth non-energy good, such as capital, materials, or labor. In terms of the analytical framework of section 10.1, the higher the own-price elasticity of demand, the higher the cross-price elasticity of demand should be. In turn, the higher the value of these two coefficients, the higher the aggregate elasticity of substitution between energy and alternative resources.

A third measure of the sectoral demand for energy is the income elasticity of demand. The income elasticity of demand for energy can be defined in quantitative terms as

$$\epsilon_{yi} = \frac{d\,(x_i)/x_i}{d\,(y_i)/y_i}, \tag{10.5}$$

where x_i is the quantity demanded of energy in the ith sector of the economy and y_i is the level of income in the ith sector of the economy. In equation (10.5), the income elasticity-of-demand coefficient is based on all other things being held equal, that is, there is no change in the relative prices of energy and non-energy alternative resources. To the extent that there is no change in the relative price of energy, the income elasticity-of-demand coefficient can be used to project the growth in energy demand for a given increment of growth in the economy. However, it should be kept in mind that if we allow for change in the relative price of energy, as has indeed occurred in the post-1973 era, then the energy-income, ratio or even the aggregate energy–GNP ratio, should be a flexible one, at least to the extent that its alternative substitution possibilities are significant.

Table 10.2 lists several recent estimates of the sectoral demand for energy in the U.S. economy. Despite differences in data and estimating procedures, the evidence from these studies points to several underlying characteristics in the demand for energy.

First, whether it is viewed on an aggregate or a sectoral basis, the own-price elasticity of demand for energy is significantly less than one. To be sure, the aggregate elasticity-of-substitution data of table 10.1 lead us to expect this to be the case. If we accept the all-sector own-price elasticity-of-demand estimate of −0.35, then for every 1 percent increase in the price of energy in all of its forms there will be only about a 0.33 percent reduction in its consumption, or what is equivalent, for every 1 percent reduction in energy consumption there would have to be an almost 3 percent increase in its price.

Like the aggregate elasticity of substitution, the own-price elasticity of demand for energy may well be underestimated. The estimate is based on annual time-series data and thus may represent a long-run average of the economy's short-run own-price elasticity of demand. Moreover, since this estimate is based largely on a period in which real energy prices were falling in both absolute and relative terms, it may also contain a secondary source of bias. The reason why this may be so is that if the real price of energy were falling while real income were increasing, the own-price of energy would claim a smaller and smaller share of real income, thereby leaving consumers less and less sensitive to changes in the price of energy.[16] Economic theory states that the own-price elasticity of demand for any commodity will be conditioned by several basic factors: the price and substitutability with alternative goods, the level of income, and the share of income that the purchase of the good represents in one's budget. The higher the share of one's income that is spent for a given commodity, even if it is considered as a necessity and there are relatively few substitutes, the greater will be the likelihood that the own-price elasticity coefficient will also be higher in absolute terms than if the cost share were small. In brief, then, though the historically estimated all-sector own-price elasticity of demand has a value significantly less than one, it may well represent an underestimate of the economy's present and future long-run own-price elasticity of demand, especially in the post-1973 era.

If anything in table 10.2 lends support to the preceding characterization of the demand for energy, it is that the available long-run estimates of the own-price elasticity are invariably higher than the short-run coefficients. Indeed, there is every reason to expect that among all three principal energy-consuming sectors of the economy, the long-run own-price elasticity may well be greater than one. The significance of a long-run relatively elastic demand for energy is that there are economic limits to the seemingly inexorable rise in the price of the economy's conventional fuels. Indeed, once the own-price elasticity rises above one, it is no longer in the interest of producers to raise the price further, since there will be a reduction in total revenue by virtue of the greater than proportional reduction in consumption, a matter which will be examined more closely in part IV.

Beyond the distinctions already noted, it should be pointed out that not every sector exhibits the same degree of response in its own-price elasticity of demand. In the studies listed in table 10.2, whether on a short- or long-run basis, the industrial sector shows mostly the highest degree of flexibility in

[16]For empirical verification among non-energy goods, see H. Schultz, *Theory and Measurement of Demand* (Chicago: University of Chicago Press, 1938); and H. Wold, *Demand Analysis* (New York: John Wiley and Sons, 1953).

Table 10.2. Estimates of Price and Income Elasticities of Aggregate Energy Demand

Study	Elasticity of Demand							
	Own-Price			Cross-Price		Income		
	Short-Run	Long-Run	Time Period Not Specified	Short-Run	Long-Run	Short-Run	Long-Run	Time Period Not Specified
	Residential and Commercial Sector							
Baughman-Joskow (1974)	−0.08	−0.50					+0.80	
FEA (1974)	−0.23	−0.23					+0.64	
Joskow-Baughman (1976)	−0.12	−0.50					+0.60	
Nelson (1975)			−0.28					+0.27
Jorgenson (1974)			−0.40					
Nordhaus (1975)[a]			−0.71				+1.09	
Pindyck (1979)[b]			−1.10				+1.00	
FEA (1976)							+0.30[c] +0.70[d]	
	Industrial Sector							
Baughman-Zerhoot (1975)	−0.05	−0.15					+0.65	
FEA (1974)	−0.41	−0.70					+0.46	
Berndt-Wood (1975)	−0.49			−0.15[e], +0.03[f]				
Halvorsen-Ford (1979)	−0.66 to −2.56							
Griffin-Gregory (1976)[b]	−0.80			+0.13[e], +0.11[f]				
Pindyck (1979)	−0.83 to −0.85			+0.02 to +0.08[e]				

	Transportation Sector		
FEA (1974)	−0.20	−0.80	0.60
	All Sectors		
Hudson-Jorgenson (1974)		−0.35	
Baughman-Joskow (1974); Joskow-Baughman (1976)[g]		−0.31	

Sources: M. L. Baughman and P. L. Joskow, "Energy Consumption and Fuel Choices by Residential and Commercial Consumers in the United States" (Cambridge, Mass.: MIT Energy Laboratory, July 1974); Federal Energy Administration, *Project Independence Report* (Washington, D.C.: U.S. Government Printing Office, November 1974); P. L. Joskow and M. L. Baughman, "The Future of the U.S. Nuclear Energy Industry," *Bell Journal of Economics* 7 (Spring 1976): 3–32; J. P. Nelson, "The Demand for Space Heating Energy," *Review of Economics and Statistics* 57 (November 1975); D. W. Jorgenson, "Consumer Demand for Energy" (Cambridge, Mass.: Harvard Institute of Economic Research, November 1974); William D. Nordhaus, "The Demand for Energy: An International Perspective" (New Haven: Yale University, September 1975); R. S. Pindyck, *The Structure of World Energy Demand* (Cambridge, Mass.: MIT Press, 1979); Federal Energy Administration, *National Energy Outlook, 1976* (Washington, D.C.: U.S. Government Printing Office, February 1976), p. C-7; M. L. Baughman and F. S. Zerhoot, "Energy Consumption and Fuel Choice by Industrial Consumers in the United States" (Cambridge, Mass.: MIT Energy Laboratory, March 1975); E. R. Berndt and D. O. Wood, "Technology, Prices, and the Derived Demand for Energy," *Review of Economics and Statistics* 56, no. 3 (August 1975):259–68; R. Halvorsen and J. Ford, "Substitution among Energy, Capital, and Labor Inputs in U.S. Manufacturing," in *Advances in the Economics of Energy and Resources,* ed. R. S. Pindyck, vol. 1 (Greenwich, Conn.: JAI Press, 1979), pp. 51–75; J. M. Griffin and P. R. Gregory, "An Intercountry Translog Model of Energy Substitution Responses," *American Economic Review* 66 (December 1976):845–57; R. S. Pindyck, "Interfuel Substitution and the Industrial Demand for Energy: An International Comparison," *Review of Economics and Statistics 61* (May 1979):169–79; E. A. Hudson and D. W. Jorgenson, "U.S. Energy Policy and Economic Growth, 1975–2000," *Bell Journal of Economics and Management Science* 5 (Autumn 1974):461–514.

Note: Unless otherwise noted, all estimates are for the United States.

[a]Internationally pooled sample, based on six countries

[b]Internationally pooled sample, based on nine countries

[c]Residential

[d]Commercial

[e]Capital-energy

[f]Labor-energy

[g]Exclusive of the transportation sector

response to a change in the price of energy, while some of the least flexibility appears in the residential, commercial, and transportation sectors. There are several possible reasons for these differences. In the case of transportation, one of the most obvious is that the economy has for a long time developed a dependence on the automobile, a bias reinforced by the Federal Highway Trust Fund, restrictive regulation of railroads, and other energy-intensive practices noted in chapter 2.[17] In the residential and commercial sectors, the own-price inelasticity of demand for energy can be explained in comparable terms. Within any given time period, the stock of housing, including its degree of thermal efficiency in heating and cooling, as well as the energy-using appliances which form part of individual and family social patterns, is little changed. At the same time, the fact that these estimates have been based generally on pre-1973 prices may well underestimate the future capacity for change. Indeed, since the industrial sector's energy-using appliances, or capital stock, show markedly higher own-price elasticities, there is every reason to expect that the long-run capacity for change will be much greater than now appears to be the case.

As noted in section 10.1, if the own-price elasticity of demand is significant, it is likely that the cross-price elasticity of demand also will be significant. Estimate of cross-price elasticities in the industrial sector in table 10.2 confirm this general pattern and provide a further indication of the underlying aggregate elasticity-of-substitution figures cited in table 10.1. However, in the industrial sector at least, the relatively low values of the cross-elasticity coefficients also show that in the short run much of the reduction in consumption for given increases in the price of energy derives from disembodied organizational changes rather than from a substantial shift to capital- or labor-intensive alternatives. As often as not, these changes encompass the technically more efficient use of lighting and temperature controls, as well as the energy-efficient scheduling of production. Indeed, it is this short-run apparent inflexibility in substitution that contributes to the employment and inflationary pressures which so often accompany a given change in the price of energy. Before these employment and inflationary issues are considered in greater detail, we should proceed one stage further to look at the nature of the demand for individual energy resources.

10.4. THE DEMAND FOR INDIVIDUAL ENERGY RESOURCES

The sectoral demand for energy derives ultimately from a combination of individual fuels. Although it is useful to examine the own- and cross-price elasticities of demand of aggregate energy in each sector of the economy, it is on a fuel-specific basis that the conservation and substitution effects are most likely to be clearly understood.

[17]Despite this historical pattern, future energy policies can well adapt to changing relative prices (see Robert F. Hemphill, Jr., "Energy Conservation in the Transportation Sector," in *Energy Conservation and Public Policy,* ed. J. C. Sawhill [Englewood Cliffs, N.J.: Prentice-Hall, 1979], pp. 79–96).

Estimates of the demand for individual fuels within key sectors of the U.S. economy are reported in table 10.3. These elasticities are based on the same measurement procedures noted in the preceding section. Yet within this common empirical framework there are several distinguishing characteristics, each of which merits elaboration.

Not surprisingly, estimates of the own-price elasticity of demand for individual fuels show greater flexibility in the long run than in the short run. At the same time, there is considerable variation in these elasticities when individual fuels are taken into account. For example, in the residential and commercial and the industrial sectors, estimates of the natural gas own-price elasticity point to slightly greater flexibility than do those for oil. In turn, both of these fuels are generally more sensitive to price than is electricity. The relatively higher own-price elasticity of demand for natural gas can be explained partly by the fact that its marketing is relatively recent in comparison with that of oil. Indeed, although individual cross-price elasticities are not shown, there is generally a significant degree of substitutability between these two fuels in comparison with their separate or joint substitutability with coal or electricity.

The relatively low own-price elasticity of demand for electricity in the residential, commercial, and industrial sectors stems directly from the absence of competitive substitutes in several of its end uses. Electricity can be used for space and hot water heating, of course, but oil and natural gas are competitive substitutes. However, where lighting and appliances are concerned, non-electricity substitution is practically impossible without major modification in capital stocks. To the extent that it is possible, then, substitution in electricity turns mostly on the technical efficiency of electricity use for a given task, as in the substitution of solid-state circuitry for vacuum-tube technology during the past twenty years.[18]

Despite the similarities in elasticities in the residential, commercial, and industrial sectors, there is a slightly greater degree of flexibility among fuels in the industrial sector. This is because coal is still a significant fuel in industry, whereas in the residential and commercial sector it has been largely replaced by oil and natural gas, as pointed out in chapter 5. However, coal is not a perfect substitute for oil and natural gas in that as a solid, it is more cumbersome to use with present-day technology. For this reason, the own-price elasticity of demand for coal in the industrial sector generally has a higher absolute value than does any of its alternatives.

Apart from substitution in the consumption of electricity, there is also the question of substitutability of fuels in electricity production. As noted in chapter 6, three-quarters of all U.S. electricity generation is provided by

[18]A more recent invention of comparable importance is the electric synthesizer noted in chapter 8. Such synthesizers could save up to 50 percent of the energy used to operate electric motors. Until recently, the Exxon Corporation was trying to acquire the Reliance Electric Corporation of Cleveland, Ohio, in an effort to enter into commercial production. It has since abandoned the effort to produce electric synthesizers even though they may yet become economically competitive.

coal, oil, and natural gas; the other quarter is provided by nuclear and hydropower. That five different types of energy can be used is one reason to expect that the own-price elasticity of demand for any single fuel will be high. Unfortunately, the complexity of both nuclear-generating technology and the expansion of hydropower capacity does not readily translate into the more direct substitutability that we could observe among individual alternative fossil fuels. However, the fact that there are non-fossil alternatives may well help to explain the relatively high values of own-price elasticities that have been estimated for fossil fuels. Indeed, the estimates of the cross-price elasticities of demand among paired fossil fuels in table 10.3 show a significant degree of substitutability, especially when there is sufficient time for electricity-generating producers to adjust to changes in relative prices.

Of all own-price elasticities of demand for individual fuels, one of the lowest appears to be that for gasoline. The reasons for this relatively inelastic demand have already been noted in conjunction with the sectoral demand for transportation energy. However, it should be stressed that not only were the estimates of table 10.3 based largely on the falling real absolute and relative price conditions of the pre-1973 era but under these conditions, the share of gasoline costs in consumer budgets was declining. What is important for the future is that as the real absolute and relative price of gasoline rises, consumer demand will become more price-elastic. Indeed, it is for this reason that in the more recent study by Pindyck (1979), the own-price elasticity of demand could have a relatively elastic coefficient of −1.30.[19]

Differences in elasticities are due largely to variations in the quantity and quality of data, and to alternative estimation procedures. Although the number of estimates listed in tables 10.2 and 10.3 precludes a more extensive analysis of these differences, we can nevertheless take stock of some of the variables that have given rise to them. In most of the studies, the independent variables used to explain the variation in energy consumption are based on the typical influences already noted in section 10.1: the own-price of energy, the level of income, the price of technically competitive substitutes and complements, and related characteristics appropriate to each type of energy demand. Examples of these related energy characteristics include population densities, the percentage of the population living in rural versus urban sectors, and the number of heating-degree days in a specific area.

Given differences in economic sectors, geographic regions, and types of variables used to estimate elasticities, one thing is clear: with sufficient time, the price elasticity of energy demand will tend to be greater than in the short run. Substitution among differing types of energy resources, and between energy and non-energy resources can occur to a significant degree. Table 10.4 shows to what extent such substitution is possible, summarizing the effects of changing energy prices on energy intensities among some thirteen industries of the United States for the period 1967–74 which includes the 1973

[19]R. S. Pindyck, *The Structure of World Energy Demand* (Cambridge, Mass.: MIT Press, 1979).

Table 10.3. Estimates of Price and Income Elasticities of Individual Energy Demand, by Fuel

Study	Elasticity of Demand							
	Own-Price			Cross-Price		Income		
	Short-Run	Long-Run	Time Period Not Specified	Short-Run	Long-Run	Short-Run	Long-Run	Time Period Not Specified
	Residential and Commercial Sector							
Oil								
Baughman-Joskow (1974)		−0.81						
Anderson (1972)		−1.58						
Baughman-Zerhoot (1975)			−0.64					
Joskow-Baughman (1976)		−1.0 to +1.10						
Hirst-Lin-Cope (1976)		−0.84 to −0.91						
Pindyck (1979)[a]		−1.10 to −1.30						
Natural gas								
Baughman-Joskow (1974)		−0.62						
Anderson (1972)		−1.73						
Baughman-Zerhoot (1975)			−0.37					
Joskow-Baughman (1976)		−1.00 to −1.10						
Liew (1974)		−1.28 to −1.77						
Hirst-Lin-Cope (1976)		−0.84 to −0.91						
Pindyck (1979)		−1.30 to −2.10						
Electricity								
Baughman-Joskow (1974)		−1.31						
Anderson (1972)		−0.84						
Baughman-Zerhoot (1975)			−0.44					
Halvorsen (1975)		−1.00 to −1.20						
Liew (1974)			−0.40					
Hirst-Lin-Cope (1976)		−0.84 to −0.91						
Pindyck (1979)		−0.30 to −0.70						

Table 10.3.—*Continued*

Study	Elasticity of Demand							
	Own-Price			Cross-Price		Income		
	Short-Run	Long-Run	Time Period Not Specified	Short-Run	Long-Run	Short-Run	Long-Run	Time Period Not Specified
	Industrial Sector							
Oil								
Baughman-Zerhoot (1975)		−1.32 to −1.40						
Halvorsen (1975)			−2.82					
Pindyck (1979)		−0.20 to −1.20						
Natural gas								
Baughman-Zerhoot		−0.81 to −1.51						
Halvorsen (1975)			−1.47					
Coal								
Baughman-Zerhoot (1975)		−0.59 to −1.14						
Halvorsen (1975)			−1.52					
Pindyck (1979)		−1.30 to −2.20						
Electricity								
Baughman-Zerhoot (1975)		−1.29 to −1.36						
Halvorsen (1975)			−0.92					
[illegible]		[illegible]						

Gasoline						
Houthakker-Verleger (1974)	−0.32			+0.30	+0.98	
Kennedy (1974)	−0.82					
FEA (1974)	−0.80					
Ramsey-Rasche-Allen (1975)	−0.70					+1.15
Adams-Graham-Griffin (1974)[b]	−0.92					+0.54
Pindyck (1979)[c]	−1.30					+0.80
	Electricity Generation Sector					
Oil						
Griffin (1977)		−1.00 to −4.00	+0.20 to +1.2[d]			
Atkinson-Halvorsen (1976)		−1.50 to −1.60				
Natural gas						
Griffin (1977)		−0.80 to −1.20	+0.20 to −1.2[d]			
Atkinson-Halvorsen (1976)		−1.40				
Coal						
Griffin (1977)		−0.50 to −0.80	+0.2 to +1.2[d]			
Atkinson-Halvorsen (1976)		−0.40 to −1.20	+0.4 to +1.0[d]			

Sources: M. L. Baughman and P. L. Joskow, "Energy Consumption and Fuel Choices by Residential and Commercial Consumers in the United States" (Cambridge, Mass.: MIT Energy Laboratory, July 1974); K. P. Anderson, "Residential Demand for Electricity: Econometric Estimates for California and the United States," Report R-905-NSF (Santa Monica: RAND Corporation, January 1972); M. L. Baughman and F. S. Zerhoot, "Energy Consumption and Fuel Choice by Industrial Consumers in the United States" (Cambridge, Mass.: MIT Energy Laboratory, March 1975); P. L. Joskow and M. L. Baughman, "The Future of the U.S. Nuclear Energy Industry," *Bell Journal of Economics* 7 (Spring 1976):3–32; E. Hirst, W. Lin, and J. Cope, "An Engineering Economic Model of Residential Energy Use," Technical Report TM-5470 (Oak Ridge, Tenn.: Oak Ridge National Laboratory, July 1976); R. S. Pindyck, *The Structure of World Energy Demand* (Cambridge, Mass.: MIT Press, 1979); C. K. Liew, "Measuring the Substitutability of Energy Consumption" (December 1974), cited in R. S. Pindyck, "The Characteristics of the Demand for Energy," in *Energy Conservation and Public Policy*, ed. John C. Sawhill (Englewood Cliffs, N.J.: Prentice-Hall, 1979), p. 40; R. Halvorsen, "Residential Demand for Electric Energy," *Review of Economics and Statistics* 57 (February 1975):12–18; H. S. Houthakker and P. K. Verleger, Jr., "Dynamic Analyses for Gasoline and Residential Electricity," *American Journal of Agricultural Economics* 56 (May 1974):412–18; M. Kennedy, "An Economic Model of the World Oil Market," *Bell Journal of Economics and Management Science* 5 (Autumn 1974):540–77; Federal Energy Administration, *Project Independence Report* (Washington, D.C.: U.S. Government Printing Office, November 1974); J. R. Ramsey, R. Rasche, and B. Allen, "An Analysis of the Private and Commercial Demand for Gasoline," *Review of Economics and Statistics* 57 (November 1975); F. G. Adams, H. Graham, and J. M. Griffin, "Demand Elasticities for Gasoline: Another View," Discussion Paper 279, Department of Economics, University of Pennsylvania, June 1974; J. M. Griffin, "Interfuel Substitution Possibilities: A Translog Application to Pooled Data," *International Economic Review*, October 1977; S. E. Atkinson and R. Halvorsen, "Interfuel Substitution in Steam Electric Power Generation," *Journal of Political Economy* 84 (October 1976):959–78.

Note: Unless otherwise noted, all estimates are for the United States.

[a] Based on an international pooled sample of nine countries

[b] Based on an international pooled sample of twenty countries

[c] Based on an international pooled sample of eleven countries

[d] Oil-gas, oil-coal

Table 10.4. Energy Consumption in U.S. Manufacturing, 1967, 1971, 1974

Standard Industrial Classification[a]		Purchased Energy Consumption (in billions of kilowatt-hours)			Average Energy Cost (in current dollars per 1,000 kilowatt-hours)			Energy Consumption/Output[b]			Percent Change in Energy Consumption/Output[c]	
Code	Industry	1967	1971	1974	1967	1971	1974	1967	1971	1974	1967–71	1971–74
	All manufacturing	3,461	3,847	3,925	$2.22	$2.71	$4.96	34.61	36.57	31.57	5.65%	−13.66%
2911	Petroleum refining	386	445	435	1.08	1.32	2.65	3.87	3.89	3.58	0.52	−7.77
3312	Blast furnaces and steel mills	416	408	448	2.11	2.82	5.45	4.16	4.26	3.84	2.43	−9.82
2869	Industrial organic chemicals	232	251	289	1.13	1.60	2.98	2.33	2.11	1.91	−9.32	−9.39
2621	Paper mills, except building paper	149	171	168	1.67	2.19	4.78	1.49	1.49	1.29	0.70	−14.03
2631	Paperboard mills	126	135	150	1.37	1.91	4.54	1.26	1.08	1.09	−14.06	0.37
3241	Cement, hydraulic	137	134	145	1.39	1.81	3.40	1.37	1.20	1.25	−11.84	3.49
3334	Primary aluminum	86	85	111	2.05	2.56	4.14	0.86	0.70	0.74	−18.38	4.68
2812	Alkalies and chlorine	54	50	53	1.76	2.23	4.38	0.54	0.45	0.43	−17.94	−2.92
2824	Synthetic organic fibers, except cellulose	46	43	45	1.61	2.21	5.47	0.26	0.26	0.19	1.56	−25.67
2865	Cyclic intermediates and crudes	—	40	41	—	2.27	4.50	—	0.32	0.25	—	−23.36
3221	Glass containers	35	42	41	1.92	2.35	4.39	0.35	0.36	0.33	3.76	−9.22
3714	Motor vehicle parts and accessories	31	37	36	3.54	4.35	7.28	0.31	0.32	0.32	2.26	−0.63
3711	Motor vehicles and passenger car bodies	35	33	32	3.03	4.04	6.68	0.35	0.29	0.29	−15.85	−1.71

Source: W. G. Rice and E. Rossidivito, "Changing Energy Consumption Patterns in U.S. Manufacturing," in *How Energy Affects the Economy,* ed. A. B. Askin (Lexington, Mass.: D. C. Heath and Co., 1978), pp. 23–34.

[a]The coding system employed by the U.S. Department of Commerce

[b]Measured as the kilowatt-hours equivalent (KWE) divided by the Federal Reserve Board's Industrial Production Index. No adjustment is made for the industry or the national rate of unemployment, or for shifts due to technical change

[c]Computed from three-decimal-point listings

OPEC oil embargo). In that time period alone, energy consumption per dollar of real manufactured output dropped by almost 14 percent, even though real manufacturing output continued to increase, as did real GNP. Similar patterns could be shown for other sectors of the economy, with even greater gains in light of more recent changes in the real price of energy since 1974.

10.5. AGGREGATE ENERGY DEMAND, ECONOMIC GROWTH, AND INFLATION

Inasmuch as the demand for energy does show a potentially significant degree of flexibility, there is still the question of its impact on the aggregate level of income and on the general level of prices, particularly in the post-1973 era. We would expect that the smaller the value share of energy in the GNP and the higher the degree of the economy's energy substitution possibilities, the smaller would be the adverse impact of an increase in the relative price of energy on the aggregate level of income and on the general level of prices. Moreover, to the extent that these conditions were true over time, we would also expect the economy's energy-GNP linkage, or income elasticity of demand, to be a flexible one. As an empirical proposition, however, much of the validity of these statements depend critically on the time frame within which the anticipated adjustments would be permitted to take place.

A useful way of verifying the preceding propositions is to examine first the available evidence of the economy's income elasticity of demand for energy. Table 10.2 lists several estimates of the income elasticity of demand for energy among principal sectors of the U.S. economy.[20] Though there is significant variation among these estimates, they show for the most part that the long-run income elasticity of demand for energy is consistent with the theoretical framework of section 10.1 as well as with the historical evidence from chapter 2. In effect, given sufficient time, the economy can indeed adjust its energy consumption patterns to technological change and to the structure of relative input prices in ways that enhance overall economic efficiency. Moreover, now that the relative price of energy has been rising in the post-1973 era, a low income elasticity of demand also points to long-run economic growth at rates that do not give rise to proportional increases in the demand for energy—by improvements in the technical efficiency of energy conversion, the potential for which is vast, as noted in chapter 3 and in part II.[21]

As reassuring as a low income elasticity of demand for energy may be for the long run, it does not necessarily follow that the same degree of flexibility will hold true in the short run. Worse yet, even where some short-run flex-

[20]As noted in section 10.3, for constant relative prices, the income elasticity of demand measures the relative change in the demand for energy per relative change in income.

[21]Relative prices provide an incentive to such innovation, but technical change depends on a variety of non-price factors as well. For a recent survey, see E. Mansfield et al., *The Production and Application of New Industrial Technology* (New York: W. W. Norton and Co., 1977).

ibility may exist, the mechanism by which adjustments may take place in response to changes in income, technology, and relative prices may well be one that creates pressure on the overall level of prices. Indeed, in the post-1973 era, there has been a relatively close correlation between increases in the price of energy and the overall rate of inflation. However, to impute all, or even a major part, of the rate of inflation to increases in the price of energy would vastly oversimplify historical experience and the underlying adjustments that a general rate of inflation often tends to obscure.

There are several ways to empirically separate an increase in the price of energy from increases in the general level of prices and output in the economy. One way is to use an aggregate production function of the kind defined in equation (10.1) to simulate the effects of a change in the relative price of energy on the real level of GNP. In one such exercise designed to calculate the effects of required changes in the real price of energy to attain targeted levels of future energy consumption of the U.S. economy for the year 2010, Hogan and Mann (1979) found that if the aggregate elasticity of substitution were as low as 0.1, the incremental real cost of energy per MBtu at 110 quads of gross energy consumption in the year 2010 would be $27.53 (in 1975 dollars), whereas if it were as high as 0.3, the incremental cost of energy would decline to $5.76.[22] A lower elasticity of substitution would not only create greater pressures on the general level of prices in the economy; it would also tend to retard the real potential rate of growth, since higher marginal energy costs would tend to claim an ever larger share of the GNP. For example, with an elasticity of substitution of 0.3, real GNP in the year 2010 could attain a level of approximately $4,200 billion, whereas if the elasticity of substitution were 0.1, real GNP would only reach a level of just over $3,000 billion. If the aggregate elasticity of energy substitution were as high as infinity, then virtually any targeted level of reduction in energy consumption could be achieved with a zero marginal cost and a projected level of real GNP as high as $4,400. Thus, the elasticity-of-substitution estimates noted in section 10.2 suggest that if the value were at a level of one or higher, then higher real energy prices would prove to have relatively negligible effects on the level and rate of growth of real GNP over the long run.

Another way of assessing the inflationary consequences of energy pricing changes is by using a given estimate of the elasticity of substitution in a macroeconomic model: we can simulate the actual behavior of the economy under historical conditions, and contrast these conditions with alternative hypothetical pricing scenarios.[23] Several studies of this kind have been undertaken on the U.S. economy in recent years, particularly in reference to the impact of the 1973 OPEC oil embargo, and many of the results have been

[22]W. W. Hogan and A. S. Manne, "Energy-Economy Interactions: The Fable of the Elephant and the Rabbit?" in *Advances in the Economics of Energy and Resources,* ed. R. S. Pindyck, vol. 1 (Greenwich, Conn.: JAI Press, 1979), pp. 7–26.

[23]For a review of the general methodology used in simulation models, see T. H. Naylor, "Policy Simulation Experiments with Macroeconomic Models: The State of the Art," *Journal of Agricultural Economics* 52 (May 1970):263–71.

reported in a compendium study by A. B. Askin (1978).[24] Since all of the models used in these studies are of the kind outlined in general form in chapter 3, rather than examine the details of each one, we can concentrate on their findings regarding the aggregate level of output, unemployment, and inflation.

Without exception, quantitative studies of the 1973 period show strong evidence that at least half of the changes in output, unemployment, and inflation in the United States economy were due to factors other than the embargo. The most obvious of these other factors were the inflationary consequences of prolonged U.S. military intervention in the Vietnam war, an already aggravated balance-of-payments deficit arising from a still overvalued dollar, and numerous policy controls then in place which had encouraged the U.S. economy's energy intensity and dependence on oil imports.[25] As Serot (1978) noted in a review of several model simulations of the events of 1973–75, because of contractionary policies then directed at reducing the domestic rate of inflation, the U.S. economy was already moving into a recession in the period just prior to the embargo.[26] Indeed, as can be seen in three comparison scenarios of the 1973–75 period based on the Data Resources, Incorporated (DRI) economic model summarized in table 10.5, what the embargo did to the economy was to increase both prices and unemployment, thereby reducing the real level of output even further than it would otherwise have been reduced.

It is always easier to interpret events long after they have occurred than it is to interpret them when they are actually taking place. In the case of the U.S. economy in 1973, it is now obvious that there was no anticipation of an OPEC oil embargo, an oversight whose consequences were compounded by an almost complete ignorance among policymakers of the structural significance of energy to aggregate economic performance. Although in the interim much has been learned about the economy's demand for energy, the translation of this wisdom into appropriate economic policies has been at best imperfect.

What, then, is the significance of energy demand elasticities for energy policy? The studies examined in this chapter have four basic implications. One is that although the demand for energy may appear to be relatively price-inelastic in the short run, given sufficient time, consumers can and do make significant adjustments to changes in the relative prices of goods and services. Thus, the degrees of energy conservation which we looked at in the energy-GNP projections of chapter 3 and in the specific forms of energy conservation in chapter 8 represent technically feasible and economically practical alternatives to the energy-intensive growth of the past.

Though not stressed in most of the studies cited here, a second implication

[24] A. B. Askin, ed., *How Energy Affects the Economy* (Lexington, Mass.: D. C. Heath Publishing Co., 1978).

[25] A more detailed discussion of these changes is presented in chapter 14.

[26] D. Serot, "The Energy Crisis and the U.S. Economy, 1973–75," in *How Energy Affects the Economy*, ed. A. B. Askin (Lexington, Mass.: D.C. Heath Publishing Co., 1978), pp. 7–22.

Table 10.5. Embargo Simulations Based on the DRI Model, 1973–75

Quarter	Base Case	No Disruption	No Disruption, with Tight Money
	Real GNP (in billions of 1972 dollars)		
1973:4	$1,280.8	$1,266.0	$1,271.0
1974:1	1,256.3	1,258.3	1,257.0
1974:2	1,250.7	1,265.4	1,253.9
1974:3	1,243.8	1,268.0	1,245.9
1974:4	1,214.4	1,253.4	1,221.1
1975:1	1,175.8	1,237.1	1,197.8
1975:2	1,180.2	1,257.1	1,211.7
1975:3	1,218.0	1,307.5	1,255.3
1975:4	1,233.8	1,335.0	1,278.8
	GNP Implicit Price Deflator		
1973:4	159.1	158.8	—
1974:1	163.8	162.2	—
1974:2	167.5	165.2	—
1974:3	172.2	167.8	—
1974:4	178.2	171.9	—
1975:1	181.7	173.5	—
1975:2	183.9	173.9	—
1975:3	186.1	174.5	—
1975:4	189.2	176.4	—
	Unemployment Rate		
1973:4	4.7%	4.9%	4.8%
1974:1	5.2	5.3	5.2
1974:2	5.2	5.1	5.2
1974:3	5.6	5.2	5.5
1974:4	6.7	5.9	6.6
1975:1	8.5	7.2	8.1
1975:2	9.1	7.3	8.4
1975:3	8.5	6.4	7.6
1975:4	8.6	6.1	7.4

Source: Federal Energy Administration, *Report to Congress on the Economic Impact of Energy Actions,* NTIS Report PB-256-684 (Springfield, Va.: National Technical Information Service, 1976).

of energy demand elasticities is that if conservation, economic growth, and minimal inflation are mutually possible, so too is environmental protection. As we saw in chapters 4 and 5, much of the problem of environmental pollution can be traced directly to the technically inefficient conversion of energy. If energy conservation can be achieved at relatively low cost, then for the same level of real income, at a lower level of energy consumption there will be some positive degree of reduction in the level of environmental pollution from automobiles, electric utilities, and industrial plants. Indeed, there is likely to be a GNP social dividend from energy conservation, since the regulatory mechanisms used to address this problem under the low energy prices of the past have often proved to be cumbersome, even though effective. Although the Second Law of Thermodynamics rules out the virtual elimination of environmental pollution, relatively high energy demand elasticities offer substantial promise as a cost-effective alternative to traditional and uniquely regulatory approaches.

A third implication of energy demand elasticities is that if energy conservation is economically practical, it also offers an alternative to continued dependence on uncertain supplies of imported energy, notably embargo-prone OPEC oil. As a simplified example, in 1980 petroleum imports accounted for just under 15 percent of aggregate primary energy consumption in the United States, and almost 90 percent of U.S. net energy imports. Now, according to the own-price elasticity-of-demand equation (10.3), if the all-energy aggregate own-price elasticity of demand were as low as the 0.31 estimate given at the bottom of table 10.2, then by increasing the price of aggregate primary energy by 50 percent, the United States would completely eliminate its dependence on all imported energy.[27] Indeed, in the aftermath of the 1979–80 doubling of OPEC oil prices, it is precisely this potential for energy conservation that has given rise to recent divisions among OPEC member countries seeking to maximize their own export revenues.

The fourth implication of energy demand elasticities for energy policy is that increasing relative prices to attain goals of economic growth, environmental protection, and energy security may have adverse effects on the distribution of income. Poorer individuals tend to spend a higher share of their income on energy than do the rich, even though their absolute level of expenditures on energy may be smaller. As an illustration, if the own-price elasticity of demand for energy were the same among all levels of income, then other things being equal, an increase in the relative price of energy would tend to increase the degree of inequality in the distribution of income. To the extent that energy conservation is desirable and economically feasible, the implication for energy policy is that instead of the relative merits of an alteration in the distribution of income being weighed against environmental protection, economic growth, price stability, or energy security, the incidence of taxation on income should be adjusted to ensure that the redistributive effects of changing energy prices are spread proportionally among all levels of income. How this could be accomplished is discussed further in chapter 14.

[27]Mathematically, to reduce energy imports to zero would require a 13.78 percent reduction in primary energy consumption: (1) 1980 net energy imports = 12.077 quads; (2) 1980 gross primary energy consumption = 76.201 quads; (3) 1980 gross primary energy consumption net of 1980 imports = 76.201 − 12.077 = 64.12; (4) 1980 change in energy consumption to achieve zero imports: (76.201 − 64.12)/76.201 = 15.85 percent. Substituting the 15.85 percent change in energy consumption into equation (10.3) yields the required change in price, based on an own-price elasticity of 0.31, that is: 0.31 = (.1585)/% change in price = 51.14 percent increase. This estimate is biased upward in two ways. First, a point elasticity estimate rather than an arc elasticity estimate is used. If an arc elasticity estimate were used, then the required increase in the price of energy would be: $0.31 = [(76.201 - 64.12)/(76.201 + 64.12)/2]/x = 38.97$ percent. Second, if the own-price elasticity is as high as the 0.35 level of table 10.3, then the required price increase would drop even further, to: $0.35 = 0.08609/x = 24.60$ percent. If the own-price elasticity were as high as 0.50, then the required price increase would drop even further, to 17.22 percent.

At this point, we need to examine to what extent economic competition, economic growth, price stability, environmental protection, and energy security have influenced the actual pricing of alternative energy resources.

10.6. SUMMARY

The demand for energy is derived ultimately from the demand for the goods and services with which its use is combined. Though the nature of the demand for energy is a key element in the prediction of future energy use, it constitutes at the same time a primary basis from which appropriate policy response must be made. Before any appropriate policy can be decided upon, it is essential that the determinants of aggregate energy demand, and of the individual fuels and economic sectors in which energy is consumed, be understood.

Several measures can be used to determine the demand for energy. The most common of these are the own-price, the cross-price, the substitution, and the income elasticities of demand. The expected relationships among all of these measures are based on the commonsense logic of conventional economic theory. First, to the extent that the own-price elasticity of demand for aggregate or individual energy resources is elastic, so too should be the cross-price elasticity of competitive substitute resources and thus the elasticity of substitution. Second, to the extent that the own-price, cross-price, and substitution elasticity coefficients are substantial, we would expect to find a loose, or relatively inelastic, income demand for energy. Third, any measure of the long-run elasticity of demand for energy should exhibit a much greater flexibility than its short-run counterpart.

Empirical estimates of the elasticity of demand for energy in the U.S. economy all tend to confirm expected theory. Though the demand for energy is relatively price-inelastic on an aggregate, sectoral, and fuel-specific basis, the apparent insensitivity to price may well be underestimated for two basic reasons. First, the time-series data used in many studies are likely to provide a long-run average of the economy's short-run elasticities. Second, most historical studies of the demand for energy have been based on periods in which the real price of energy was falling in absolute and relative terms, thereby encouraging growth in consumption and insensitivity to its price. Now that the real price of energy is claiming a higher share of income, even the short-run elasticity of demand is likely to show much greater flexibility than has been the case in the past, as international cross-section data all tend to confirm. However, even though the future short-run own-price elasticity of demand may tend to exceed unity, not all fuels and sectors are likely to exhibit the same improvements in flexibility at comparable rates of change, unless otherwise influenced by subsequent changes in technology.

Given the potential flexibility in the demand for energy, demand elasticities point to four basic implications for energy policy choices: first, significant energy conservation is possible within a framework of continued real economic growth and minimal levels of inflation; second, energy conservation is compatible with environmental protection; third, energy conservation represents an economically viable alternative to continued dependence on uncertain supplies of imported energy; and fourth, since energy conservation may create greater inequality in the distribution of income, to the extent that conservation is pursued, it should be accompanied by appropriate adjustments in the incidence of income taxation so that the distribution of income is unaffected by such changes.

SUGGESTED READINGS

Askin, A. B., ed. *How Energy Affects the Economy.* Lexington, Mass.: D. C. Heath and Co., 1978.

Basile, P., ed. *Energy Demand Studies: Major Consuming Countries.* Cambridge, Mass.: MIT Press, 1976.

Halvorsen, R., *Econometric Models of U.S. Energy Demand.* Lexington, Mass.: D. C. Heath and Co., 1978.

Nordhaus, W. D., ed. *International Studies of the Demand for Energy.* New York: Elsevier North-Holland Publishing Co., 1978.

Pindyck, R. S., *The Structure of World Energy Demand.* Cambridge, Mass.: MIT Press, 1979.

Sawhill, J. C., ed. *Energy Conservation and Public Policy.* Englewood Cliffs, N.J.: Prentice-Hall, 1979.

11

THE PRICING OF PETROLEUM AND NATURAL GAS

In most economies, prices perform two basic functions. They ration relatively scarce resources, and they allocate them toward their most productive uses. Though energy prices have been known to function in this way, they have not always done so. Indeed, the gasoline lines of the 1970s, the natural gas shortage of 1977, and the oil surpluses of 1980 and 1981 all suggest that the pricing of energy resources has been strongly influenced by a variety of competing economic concerns. Because market supply and demand are but two elements that influence energy pricing, we need to examine how such factors as OPEC, domestic energy taxation and subsidies, and direct governmental regulation have modified the basic roles of energy pricing. We can then better address the underlying normative issues regarding appropriate energy policy choices.

11.1. A REFERENCE FRAMEWORK FOR ENERGY PRICING DECISIONS

Complex though it may at first appear to be, a useful method of understanding energy pricing is to define a general conceptual framework within which current pricing decisions are made. The simplest point of departure is the interaction of market supply and demand independently of any alternative policy choices. As noted in chapters 9 and 10, there are many determinants of market supply and demand. On the demand side, they include the number of buyers, their level of income, the price of energy, the price of substitute and complementary goods, the level of consumer wealth and debt, and expectations about the future. On the supply side, they include the number of producers, the input costs of production and the associated production technology, the potential selling price of the resource and anticipated profitability, and expectations about the future. Unless otherwise constrained, these determinants will work to eliminate any surplus or shortage that would temporarily arise, a process which is one of the principal virtues of market pricing. However, whether this process is efficient depends on whether the resource is depletable or renewable, the degree of competition, the degree of energy substitution possibilities, and on whether any net external costs or benefits are present. Since these questions are treated more formally in chapters 13 and 14, here we need only to note how they can affect the pricing of energy resources.

As noted in chapter 4, some energy forms are endowed with replacement flows at sufficiently high rates in comparison with feasible consumption possibilities that they are considered as renewable resources. In the case of depletable energy resources, as additional amounts of the resource are consumed, the price will rise. Part of the increased cost of each additional unit reflects the irreversible use of the resource. Thus, the consumption of such resources gives rise eventually to user costs, also known as rents, or royalties. It is important to keep in mind at this point that whether user costs rise rapidly or slowly will be determined by several key factors, namely, the degree of economic competition, the extent of energy substitution possibilities for switching to renewable energy resources, and the rate of technological change in energy conversion processes, that is, the extent to which energy conservation is possible within present and evolving energy conversion technologies. Though these factors are not likely to eliminate user costs, they can serve to prevent the collection of monopoly rents by depletable energy resource producers.

The most universal standard by which economic efficiency is traditionally judged is the model of perfect competition. Under perfectly competitive conditions the market is endowed with full information on all transformation possibilities and their associated prices. Because no single buyer or seller is significant in relation to the market and because there is resource mobility and an absence of artificial restraints, no monopoly gains can be sustained over time (see figures 11.1.*a* and 11.1.*b*). Under these conditions, there is an equality of average and marginal costs and revenues among individual producers. In turn, the competitive rate of return to capital in any individual market will be determined by society's generalized rate of time preference for future versus present goods, and this latter rate also will determine the distribution of income to non-capital factors of production. Society's generalized rate of time preference is thus a measure of its willingness to consume its stock of depletable energy resources, given available information on technology and on alternative energy substitution possibilities.

It should be stressed that a perfectly competitive market is predicated on a significant degree of technical substitution possibilities. Indeed, for truly competitive market conditions to exist, this substitution must be possible not only in product markets but also in factor markets. As we will see, imperfect information, technological rigidity, and imperfect competition can reduce substantially the speed of adjustment in response to changes in relative prices.

Another factor that can affect the efficiency of a perfectly competitive economy is externalities. As noted in chapter 1, external costs and benefits are forms of market failure, that is, unintended consequences on parties other than buyers and sellers in a given market. To the extent that they occur, there will be a divergence between efficiency conditions for private

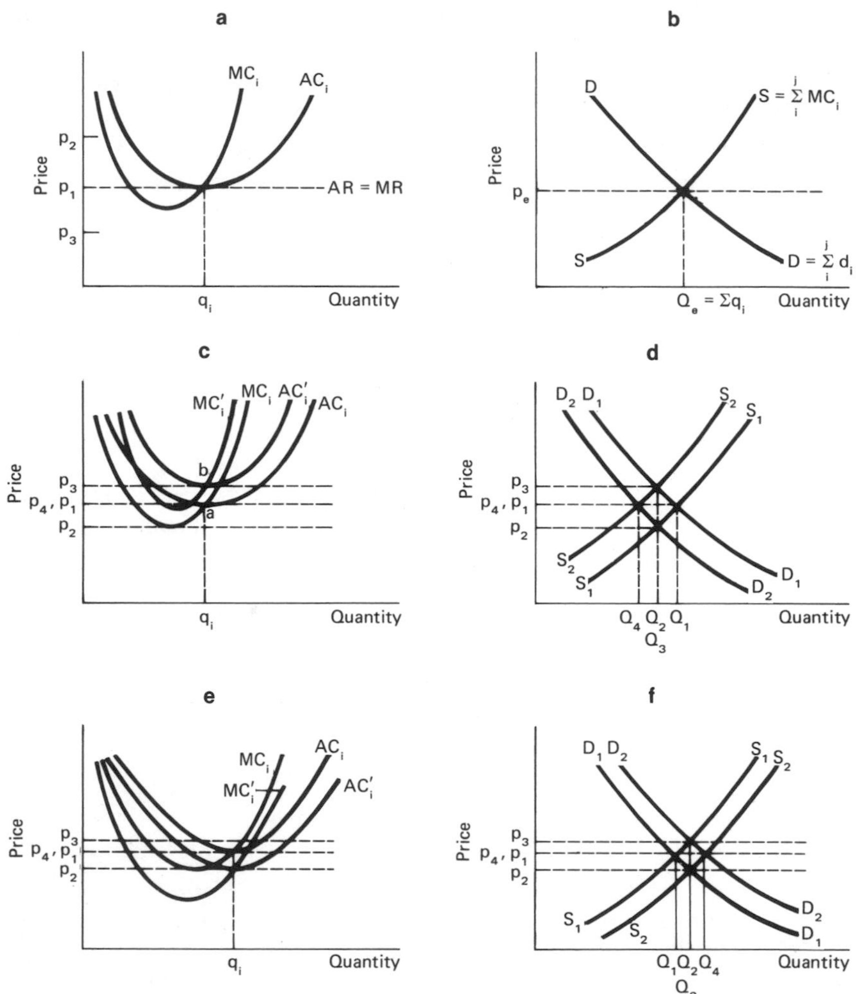

Figure 11.1. The Simple Geometry of Public Intervention in Competitive Energy Markets: **a.** individual producer equilibrium; **b.** market equilibrium; **c.** consequences of taxation-regulation on individual producer equilibrium; **d.** consequences of taxation-regulation on energy market equilibrium; **e.** consequences of subsidy-regulation on individual producer equilibrium; **f.** consequences of subsidy-regulation on energy market equilibrium.

markets and those for society as a whole, as figure 11.2 shows. In figure 11.2.*a*, where net external benefits exist, the inability of producers to charge consumers for them will give rise to a privately produced supply that is less than optimal to society as a whole. In the absence of any adjustments, market supply will be at S_1S_1, with an equilibrium price and quantity of p_1 and Q_1, respectively. However, if subsidies equal to the external benefits were im-

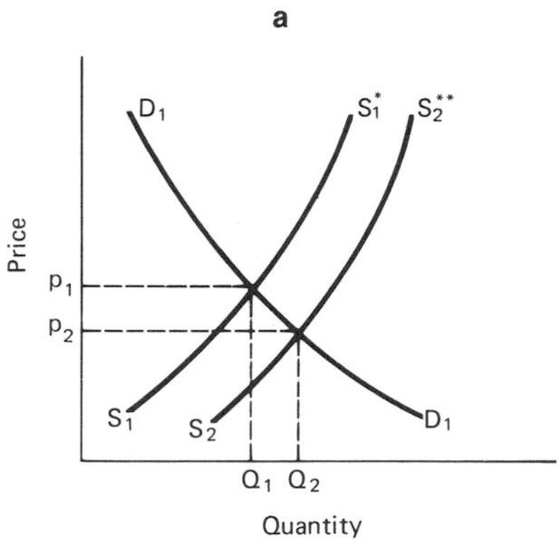

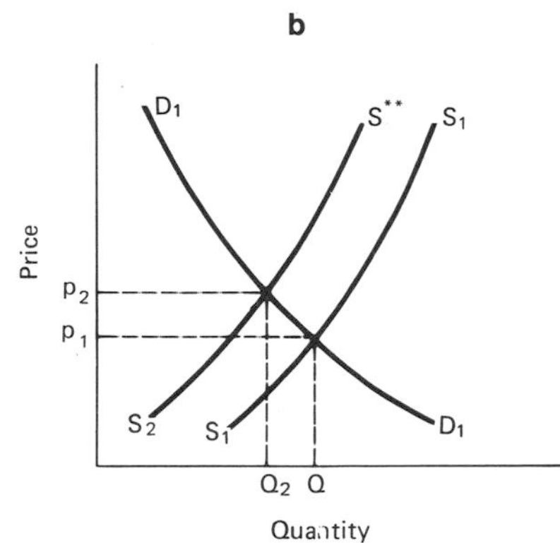

* Unadjusted market supply
** Socially optimal market supply

Figure 11.2. The Simple Geometry of Externalities in Energy Resource Pricing: **a.** net external benefits; **b.** net external costs.

posed, then the optimal supply curve would rise to S_2S_2, and the equilibrium price and quantity would change to p_2 and Q_2, respectively. Conversely, where net external costs are found, as in figure 11.2.*b*, then the privately produced supply would be at S_1S_1, which is higher than the socially optimal level, S_2S_2.[1] To reduce the privately produced oversupply to a socially optimal level would call for taxation or other means of reducing these external costs. A more rigorous analysis of market failure will be given in chapters 12 and 13, but the significance of externalities for efficiency and pricing are clear: unless otherwise corrected by appropriate taxes and subsidies, even perfectly competitive markets can operate at less than socially optimal levels.

As the presence of externalities suggests, the attainment of maximum economic efficiency may require some degree of public intervention in the allocation of resources. Since public intervention can take a variety of forms and can originate for reasons other than externalities alone, we need to spell out here the ways in which this intervention can alter the determination of particular energy prices.

In perfectly competitive markets, one form of public intervention in pricing is to impose taxes or other restrictive regulations. Taxes on the production of energy resources can take a variety of forms, such as income, sales, and excise levies. Though the types of taxes will differ in the way in which they bear on production decisions over time, the general consequence of a tax on a perfectly competitive industry at a particular moment in time is clear.[2]

[1]As can be seen in figure 11.2, the attainment of a socially optimal condition depends in part on the price elasticity of demand. The higher the price elasticity of demand, the smaller will be the cost of bringing about desired adjustments in supply. In turn, this cost must also encompass the administrative costs of the adjustments themselves (see Ronald M. Coase, "The Problem of Social Cost," *Journal of Law and Economics* 3 [October 1960]:1–44).

[2]Though not central to energy pricing as a whole, it is of course possible for government to im-

As figure 11.1.*c* shows, the short-run effect of a tax on energy is to increase a firm's average- and marginal-cost curves upward, as in the shift from AC and MC to AC' and MC', respectively. Since a perfectly competitive firm cannot pass on the burden of the tax to consumers by virtue of readily available substitutes, some firms will now experience losses equal to the amount of the tax. In the reference terms of figure 11.1.*c*, if the market price remains unchanged at p_1, losses to an individual producer will rise by the amount of the tax, to p_1ap_2b. Since these losses will cause some firms to reduce or terminate production, the market supply curve in figure 11.1.*d* will shift to the left, from S_1S_1 to S_2S_2. The market equilibrium quantity will now shift from Q_1 to Q_2, and the movement along the market demand curve D_1D_1 will raise the equilibrium price from p_1 to p_3. In turn, the increase in price will sustain enough firms and production to satisfy the new market equilibrium.

It should be kept in mind that a reduction in the consumption of energy can be influenced not only by taxes on the resource itself. It can also be influenced by a reduction in energy demand, as in the shift from D_1D_1 to D_2D_2 in figure 11.1.*d*. In this case, if the initial supply curve remains at S_1S_1, there will be a decrease in the equilibrium price from p_1 to p_2 and a decline in consumption from Q_1 to Q_2. In turn, on an individual-firm level such as in figure 11.1.*c*, a new price of p_2 will now cause some firms to experience losses, thereby leading to a reduction in the number of firms and total production down to the point of the new market equilibrium in figure 11.1.*d*. For such a reduction in demand to occur, either there must be an energy tax on the income of energy consumers or technological change, new substitution possibilities, or subsidies to alternative energy resources must be brought about.[3] The key distinction between this and a tax on the original energy resource itself is that the reduction in energy consumption will be accompanied by no increase in the equilibrium price of the resource, even though there may well be increases in prices of other resources in other sectors of the economy.

Apart from the use of taxation, one additional means of public intervention in energy use is regulation. Regulation can be used as a form of taxation or as a means of subsidizing the production and consumption of any commodity. Regulation designed to reduce the consumption of a resource can be achieved in a variety of ways. One way is to set allowable prices at higher than conventional market equilibrium levels. This not only will provide an incentive for firms to expand their production of energy but at the same time will encourage energy consumers to reduce their consumption below the initial

---

pose taxes on energy at the same rates as they are imposed on all non-energy resources for purposes other than affecting the particular patter of energy production and consumption, in which case such levies could be thought of as energy-neutral. They nevertheless would have some effects on output and demand.

[3]As noted in chapter 10, the higher the price of energy, the higher will be the share of an individual's income devoted to energy consumption. Consequently, the greater the increase in the price of energy, the greater is the likelihood that its initial price elasticity of demand will become greater through conservation and substitution.

pre-regulated rate; thus a surplus will be generated.[4] In the reference terms of figure 11.1.*d*, if initial supply is S_1S_1 and initial demand is D_2D_2, the initial price and quantity will be p_2 and Q_2, respectively. From this position, regulatory authorities can generate a surplus and at the same time reduce energy consumption by establishing a market price of p_1. Quantity demanded will now decline to Q_4 and quantity supplied will rise to Q_1, resulting in a surplus of $Q_1 - Q_4$. Such a surplus could arise, as in the U.S. decision to establish a crude-oil stockpile in the aftermath of the 1973 OPEC oil embargo, the details of which are spelled out in chapter 15.

A second major way that regulation can be used to restrict energy consumption is by control over the quantity of production. In the United States at least, such controls can determine the physical quantities of various energy resources that any consuming region may be allowed to receive, in addition to any associated restrictions that may be placed on prices. This is perhaps nowhere more true than in the allocation of gasoline and home fuel oil supplies, as will be seen in section 11.2. Beyond these quantity controls, there are also controls of future supplies as well, particularly in the leasing of drilling rights to firms engaged in offshore exploration for oil and natural gas, as well as in the right to exploration on publicly owned continental deposits. In all of these cases, the regulatory impact will be equivalent to shifting the supply curve to the left, thereby raising the equilibrium price and reducing the quantity demanded.

It is always possible that public intervention in even perfectly competitive energy markets can be used to raise consumption beyond what it would otherwise be. One way is to use fiscal subsidies in the form of tax deductions and exemptions. Though some energy consumption could be subsidized directly, more often than not it is on the supply side that these subsidies have been most used. As an example, once a firm is involved in extracting oil or natural gas, it may receive a percentage depletion allowance, along with a tax deduction for intangible drilling expenses, as part of its production and exploration operations. The purpose of these fiscal incentives is to encourage the production and exploration for depletable fossil fuels and, implicitly at least, to forestall the rise in user costs that might otherwise result.[5] Production and consumption will tend to be at higher levels than would be the case were these subsidies not granted in the first place. In the reference terms of figure 11.1.*f*, if the initial demand and supply curves are D_1D_1 and S_1S_1, respectively, percentage depletion and intangible drilling expense tax allowances will cause the supply curve to shift to S_2S_2, thereby lowering the equilibrium price and quantity to p_2 and Q_2, respectively. What enables this shift to take place can be seen in figure 11.1.*e*. The granting of energy pro-

[4]The rationale of such a choice is, of course, more complex than is suggested here. Among other things, we must include the costs of generating and storing such a surplus, which thereby reduces some of an energy stockpile's potential benefits.

[5]As already noted, where a particular depletable energy resource is concerned, whether user costs will exist in the absence of subsidies depends on the price elasticity of demand, and thus on the economy's technical substitution possibilities.

duction subsidies lowers individual producer average- and marginal-cost curves from AC and MC to AC' and MC', respectively. The temporary profits that this provides will induce additional firms to enter into production, and collectively they contribute to the supply-curve shift in figure 11.1.*f*.

Energy consumption can also be subsidized where intervention in non-energy markets raises the prices of all competitive substitutes, thereby increasing the demand for energy. In the reference terms of figure 11.1.*f*, the impact of these changes is to cause the initial demand for energy to shift from D_1D_1 to D_2D_2, thereby increasing the level of consumption as well as the price. In practice, however, this shift is more likely to occur as the result of regulated relative price differentials rather than of direct fiscal measures alone.

Under regulation, individual firms may be given nonfiscal subsidies in the form of preferential access to publicly owned energy deposits, and consumers, in the form of particular pricing ceilings such as for gasoline and natural gas. These regulated conditions can be thought of as subsidies in the following way. Access to publicly owned lands may be gained at a cost below what firms would have to pay for exploration and extraction rights under competitively structured, privately held reserve markets. Moreover, where price ceilings are set below the cost of producing additional supplies, a subsidy to consumption has been permitted. In the first case, a firm's average- and marginal-cost curves will be lowered, thereby shifting the market supply curve to the right (see figure 11.1.*f*). In the second case, with fixed demand and supply curves, such as D_1D_1 and S_1S_1, a price ceiling below the original equilibrium price of p_1, such as p_2, would result in a shortage unless otherwise corrected.

The principal difference between a perfectly competitive market and an imperfectly competitive market is that in the latter case there are sufficient barriers to entry that one firm or a limited number of firms can enjoy higher profitability than would otherwise occur. The steady-state equilibrium on the supply side of an imperfectly competitive energy market in the absence of any intervention is illustrated in figures 11.3.*a* and 11.3.*b*. An imperfectly competitive firm will choose a pricing and output combination in which its marginal cost equals its marginal revenue, just as in a perfectly competitive industry. However, since an imperfectly competitive firm will also have a significant share of the market, its average costs and revenues may not be equal, and the difference between them at the firm's optimal output level is its monopolistic profits, shown in figure 11.3.*a* as p_ebcd. Thus, the market equilibrium under a price of p_e will result in production and consumption of energy at Q_e, but the price will be higher, and the output smaller, than would be the case of in perfectly competitive energy industry.

Public intervention can take place in both perfectly competitive and imperfectly competitive energy markets. Where restrictive taxation or regulation is involved, the purpose of such intervention may be to reduce imperfectly competitive profits or the level of consumption of a particular resource, such as depletable fossil fuels. However, there are differences between the regulatory and taxation approaches that merit some elaboration.

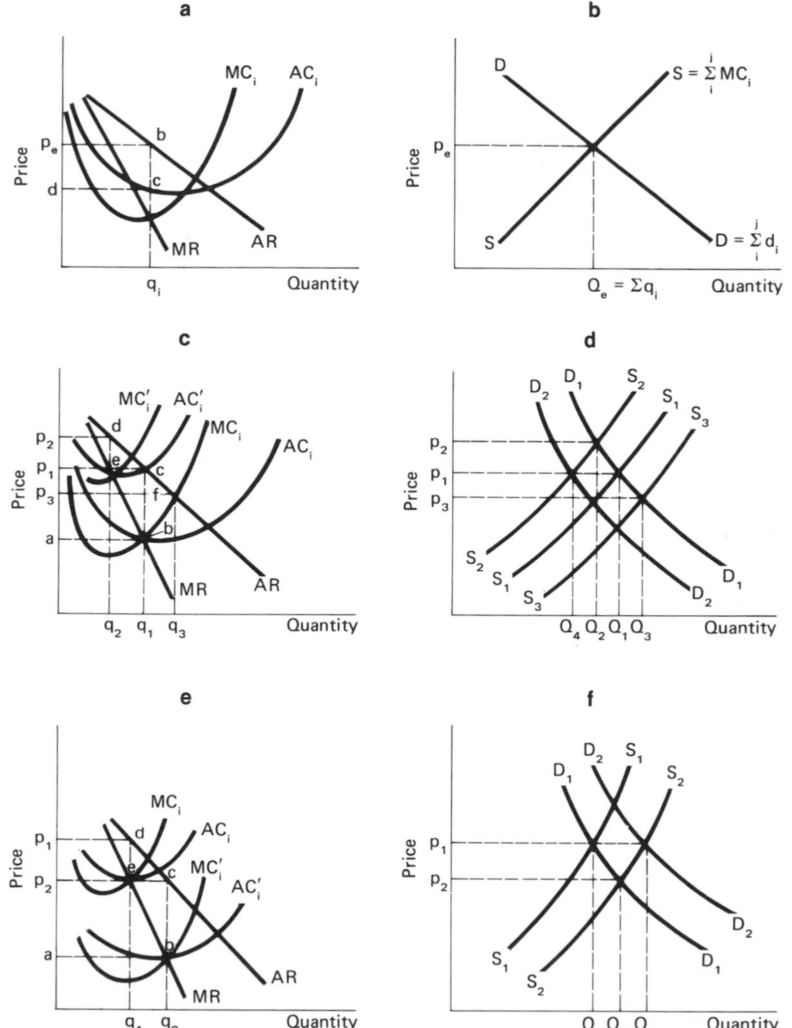

Figure 11.3. The Simple Geometry of Public Intervention in Imperfectly Competitive Energy Markets: **a.** individual producer equilibrium; **b.** market equilibrium; **c.** consequences of taxation-regulation on individual producer equilibrium; **d.** consequences of taxation-regulation on energy market equilibrium; **e.** consequences of subsidy-regulation on individual producer equilibrium; **f.** consequences of subsidy-regulation on energy market equilibrium.

Taxation mechanisms in an imperfectly competitive industry are not significantly different from those in a perfectly competitive industry. Sales, property, and income levies are all commonly used. What distinguishes the taxation of imperfectly competitive industries from taxation of perfectly competitive industries is the rate and incidence of such taxation on producers and consumers. If an excise or sales tax is imposed on the output of an imperfectly competitive industry, the effect will be to raise the firm's average and marginal costs from AC and MC to AC' and MC', respectively, as figure 11.3.*c* shows. Initial output, price, and profits are reduced by the tax from q_1, p_1, and abp_1d to q_2, p_2, and p_1edp_2, respectively. On the other hand, if the tax is imposed on an imperfectly competitive firm's profits, its optimal output will be unaffected at q_1, but its level of profits will decline from abp_1c to a lower level, such as abf_3. If the industry is other than a pure-monopoly imperfectly competitive one, the reduction in profitability among its limited members could result in a decline in the number of firms over time, thereby reducing the market supply position in 11.3.*d* from S_1S_1 to S_2S_2. Thus some of the former degree of profitability could be restored to the remaining members of the industry.[6]

As might be expected, the efficiency of taxation in reducing the rate of profitability and the level of energy consumption depends largely on the market price elasticity of demand. The higher the price elasticity of demand in absolute terms, the greater will be the effectiveness of a given rate of taxation in reducing imperfectly competitive firm profitability and in reducing energy consumption.[7] However, it depends also on the position of the demand curve, for if changes in the determinants of energy demand such as relative prices of energy and non-energy goods cause a decline in the demand for energy, then on an individual-firm level, its average- and marginal-revenue curves will also shift to the left. This will offset some of the degree of effectiveness of the originally proposed rate of taxation. In the reference terms of figures 11.3.*c* and 11.3.*d*, the original demand curve D_1D_1 may decline to D_2D_2 as a result of the aforementioned factors. The equilibrium price will fall (perhaps to the equilibrium level of p_1 in figure 11.3.*d*), as will consumption. On an individual-firm level, the average- and marginal-revenue curves would then shift to the left, thereby reducing the level of profitability to an individual firm.

The regulatory approach to the control of imperfectly competitive industries is based on limits on prices and production. In the reference terms of figures 11.3.*c* and 11.3.*d*, if an imperfectly competitive firm's average- and marginal-cost curves are AC and MC, and if the market supply and demand curves are S_1S_1 and D_1D_1, the market equilibrium price and quantity will be p_1 and Q_1. In order to reduce the imperfectly competitive profitability of a firm or a limited number of firms, regulatory authorities may decide to impose a price ceiling of p_3. Though there are several such ceilings which we could choose, two typical comparison alternatives would be the equating of marginal cost to average revenue, as is shown, or the equating of average cost

[6]It should also be noted that imperfect competition can exist even with a relatively elastic demand, though this is not generally the case in energy-resource markets.

[7]There is a perversity here. Governments may wish to raise revenues through the imposition of excise or sales taxes on energy independently of an energy-conserving strategy. Indirect levies are maximized as long as they do not result in raising the price elasticity of demand above one. Indeed, were they to do so and bring about significant energy conservation, many state and local governments could be adversely affected because of their dependence on energy taxes. Thus, the need by state and local governments to raise revenue may be in conflict with a national energy-conservation strategy.

to average revenue. In either case, individual-firm profitability would be reduced from the firm's optimal level of operations, and its production would be increased, thereby shifting market supply from S_1S_1 to S_3S_3.[8]

Beyond restrictive taxation and regulation in imperfectly competitive markets, there is also the possibility of subsidy-regulation alternatives. The same kinds of subsidy arrangements noted with respect to competitive markets can be applied to imperfectly competitive markets. Such subsidies can be based on attempts to stimulate additional exploration, particularly if there is considerable supply uncertainty, such as domestic-exploration incentives to reduce current dependence on OPEC oil imports. Subsidies will lower individual-firm costs, as shown in the shift of average- and marginal-cost curves in figure 11.3.*e* from *AC* and *MC* to *AC*′ and *MC*′. Individual-firm profitability is raised, but this is accompanied by some lowering of prices, from p_1 to p_2 and an increase in individual production, from q_1 to q_2. In turn, the market supply of figure 11.3.*f* will increase from S_1S_1 to S_2S_2. In regulatory terms, similar results can be otained by a relaxation of restrictions on additional exploration and production permits. Unless otherwise offset by an increase in market demand such as is shown in figure 11.3.*f*, both regulation and subsidies can thus be used to raise the level of energy production and consumption, as well as to lower the price of energy. With this general framework of taxation and regulation in perfectly competitive and imperfectly competitive markets, we can now turn to the specifics of pricing of individual energy resources.

11.2. THE PRICING OF PETROLEUM ENERGY RESOURCES

In the pricing of resources, few industries have deviated from competitive market supply and demand as have petroleum and natural gas. Apart from the underlying operation of supply and demand, three basic factors have influenced the price of petroleum and natural gas: taxation and subsidies imposed by domestic government authorities, pricing and output decisions of OPEC, and direct control of domestic prices and production by national and state regulatory agencies. As we will see, conflicting concerns over market competition, price stability, and energy security have done much to distort the relative prices of petroleum and natural gas. Though there have also been significant changes in how taxation, subsidies, and regulation have been used, and in the behavior of OPEC, it is instructive to see how each of these factors has influenced the pricing of these resources.

[8]This is not to say that the long-run equilibrium would remain the same. If firms were forced to opt for a second-best production level, then if the profitability of this decision were substantially less than that found in other industries, long-run energy exploration and production would be restrained as investment shifted to industries with relatively higher rates of return. The underlying assumption behind the imposition of the second-best level is that this level would provide a rate of return at least as high as that found in competitive alternatives.

11.2.1. Petroleum and Natural Gas Taxes and Subsidies

The short-run supply of petroleum and natural gas is determined conventionally by the aggregation of individual marginal costs of production among all firms in the market. These marginal costs include payments to land, labor, capital, and materials, as well as unique payments of user-cost royalties for the extraction of depletable resources. Uncertainty and risk associated with exploration and extraction, as well as any distortions arising from imperfect competition, are also included in these costs. Since these costs vary from one deposit to another, our concern at this point is to examine the extent to which the resulting market equilibrium from a given level of demand will be altered by the imposition of taxes and subsidies.

Like firms in any industry, petroleum and natural gas firms are subject to a variety of taxes. These include: federal, state, and local income taxes; federal and state excise taxes; state and local property taxes; income, property, sales, and excise taxes imposed by foreign governments on overseas operations; and miscellaneous domestic sales taxes on a subnational level.[9] As complex as this list may at first appear to be, only those levies imposed at greater or less than average rates for all industries are of particular significance to energy policy decisions. In the case of petroleum and natural gas, the taxes that fall into this category are essentially the federal income tax and taxes imposed by foreign governments, notably OPEC member states.

A useful way of understanding the impact of differential taxation on petroleum and natural gas production is by reference to a hypothetical numerical example such as the one illustrated in Table 11.1. For a firm engaged in the exploration and extraction of two deposits, A and B, the firm must first pay a royalty, or user cost, to the owner of the property, be it an OPEC government or any other institution. The gross income after these payments is then adjusted downward for drilling and allied property operating expenses. The net property income after these expense adjustments is then adjusted downward further by a depletion allowance, the significance of which calls for some elaboration.

A depletion allowance is based on the concept of capital-asset depreciation. Under ordinary capital-asset pricing, a firm is allowed traditionally to lower its tax liability by listing in its deductible expenses that portion of its capital assets which is used up in a given reporting period. Where applied to natural resources, this depreciation is estimated as the value of the portion of the deposit depleted during a given reporting period. The only difference between depletion and depreciation of the conventional type is that whereas a typical capital asset is reproducible, a natural resource asset such as petroleum or natural gas is not capable of such reproduction by virtue of the laws of thermodynamics enunciated in chapter 4. Though congressional passage of the Tax Reform Act of 1975 eliminated the benefits of percentage deple-

[9]Dividend and interest income from petroleum and natural gas firms is also subject to personal taxation at the federal, state, and local levels. Moreover, excise and sales taxes are also imposed at various stages of production.

Table 11.1. The Incidence of Taxation on Oil and Gas Independent Producers—An Illustrative Computation

	Properties		
	Deposit A	Deposit B	Total
1. Gross income after royalties	$500,000	$500,000	$1,000,000
2. *Less* costs attributable to property	−200,000	−300,000	−500,000
3. Net property income before depletion	300,000	200,000	500,000
Less allowable depletion, the smaller of:			
4. 22% of gross income	−110,000		
5. 50% of net income		−100,000	−210,000
6. Net property income after depletion	$190,000	$100,000	$290,000
7. *Less* all other costs of doing business (assumed)			−150,000
8. Net taxable income			140,000
9. Ordinary income tax (48%)			67,200
Additional tax on net "preference items"			
10. Percentage depletion allowed			210,000
11. Less unused cost basis (assumed)			−30,000
12. Excess depletion			180,000
13. Less exemption			−30,000
14. Less ordinary tax liability (9)			−67,200
15. Base of tax on net preference items			82,800
16. Tax on preference items (10%)			8,280
17. Total tax liability (14 plus 16)			75,480
Economic income and effective tax rate			
18. Net before taxes per tax return			140,000
19. *Add back* excess depletion (12)			180,000
20. *Add back* excess intangible expenses over amortization charge (assumed)			45,000
21. Economic net before taxes			$365,000
22. Total tax liability (17)			$ 75,480
23. Effective tax rate (22/21)			20.7%

Source: Stephen L. McDonald, "Taxation System and Market Distortion," in *Energy Supply and Government Policy,* eds. R. J. Kalter and W. A. Vogely (Ithaca: Cornell University Press, 1976), p. 32.

Note: Since the passage of the Tax Reform Act of 1975, the benefits of percentage depletion have been eliminated for major vertically integrated petroleum firms and are now applicable only to independent producers with a maximum refining capacity of 50,000 barrels per day.

tion from major integrated firms, its continued applicability to smaller independent firms is still of some significance to aggregate market supply and equilibrium pricing.[10]

To continue with the example in table 11.1 regardless of the particular

[10]The Tax Reform Act of 1975 limits the percentage-depletion allowance to some 10,000 independent producers with no more than 50,000 barrels per day of production. The rate declines to 22 percent through 1980 and then is reduced gradually to 15 percent by 1984. For a more detailed discussion, see Gerard M. Brannon, *Energy Taxes and Subsidies,* Report to the Energy Policy Project of the Ford Foundation (Cambridge, Mass.: Ballinger Publishing Co., 1975); and Stephen McDonald, "Taxation System and Market Distortion," in *Energy Supply and Government Policy,* ed. R. J. Kalter and W. A. Vogely (Ithaca: Cornell University Press, 1976), pp. 25–50. McDonald estimated that the limited repeal of percentage depletion which took place in 1975 was equivalent to a 10–12 percent reduction in the net price received by producers (pp. 48–49).

method used, a depletion allowance will lower the value of a firm's net property income which can be subjected to income taxation. Once the firm then deducts all other allowable business costs such as refining and distribution, the remainder represents the firm's net taxable income which is subject to the prevailing corporate income tax rate, such as the 48 percent figure shown on line 9.

At first glance, the corporate income tax rate shown on line 9 does not appear to differ significantly from any other industry's tax rate. However, when we consider the taxes on net preference items and economic income as a whole, a substantially different picture emerges. In the case of net preference items, the deductions that a firm can make in determining its tax liability may be limited, and anything in excess of its limits may be subject to additional taxation. As is shown in line 16, the amount of the firm's additional taxation is determined by subtracting its unused cost-basis alternative from its allowable percentage depletion to derive its excess depletion. In turn, the amount of the excess depletion is reduced by an allowable exemption equal to its unused cost-basis depreciation alternative and by its ordinary tax liability to arrive at its tax base on net preference items in line 15. This base is then subject to an additional tax at approximately 10 percent, which raises only slightly the firm's total tax liability. This adjusted tax-liability figure must then be compared with the firm's economic income to determine the effective rate of taxation, a figure which is likely to be considerably lower than its nominal rate of taxation.

The economic income of the firm is the sum of its net pre-tax income plus its excess depletion plus the excess of its intangible drilling expenses over its allowable amortization charge on reproducible capital assets. Intangible drilling expenses are based on the costs of drilling and equipping productive wells. They include labor, fuel, materials, supplies, tool rentals, and repairs of drilling equipment, and they account for about three-quarters of the costs of drilling productive wells.[11]

As is suggested in table 11.1, intangible drilling expenses enable a firm to enjoy a considerably higher economic income and a lower effective rate of taxation than would be the case were these expenses not tax-dedutible. The benefits received are actually threefold. First, though a firm could recoup intangible drilling expenses through capitalization of all assets and reliance on a depletion allowance, by not doing so for intangibles and by deducting fully these costs as they arise, a firm can supplement the full amount of benefits from percentage depletion that would occur in any case for a productive well. Second, a firm that incorporates intangible drilling expenses into its deductions enjoys an imputed interest benefit, that is, it allows the firm to enjoy investible income now rather wait until that period when its capitalized value could be written off under a conventional percentage-depletion-allowance alternative. Third, current expensing of intangible drilling costs could also

[11]McDonald, "Taxation System and Market Distortion," p. 29. The remaining share of well costs is accounted for by tangible items such as pipes, pumps, tanks, and any other durable equipment.

lower a firm's tax liability should its subsequent discovery of petroleum or natural gas result in a sale by the firm of the property rights at any significant long-term capital gain. The taxation on long-term capital gains is less than the conventional corporate income tax rate, and the difference represents a potential subsidy to the firm.

The difference between a firm's effective tax rate and the nominal rate of taxation represents a subsidy to that industry. As noted in section 11.1, a subsidy will tend to raise the profitability to firms in the industry, thereby inducing the provision of a larger supply of petroleum and natural gas than would be the case in its absence. Yet before we conclude that these subsidies have indeed had a net positive effect on supply, we should also consider the impact of OPEC pricing and output decisions, as well as the impact of U.S. domestic regulatory activities.

11.2.2. OPEC Pricing and Production Decisions

The Organization of Petroleum Exporting Countries, or OPEC, has influenced in a major way the determination of U.S. and international petroleum pricing and production decisions. To appreciate the significance of OPEC to this process, we can consider the following facts: as of 1980, OPEC accounted for 60 percent of world petroleum production outside of Communist areas; its share of world non-Communist reserves stood at 77 percent; and it accounted for 12 percent of U.S. gross energy consumption, over one-quarter of U.S. gross petroleum consumption, and 62 percent of U.S. petroleum imports.[12] In value terms, the cost of OPEC and non-OPEC oil imports to the United States in 1980 amounted to approximately $80 billion, or the equivalent of one-quarter of all U.S. imported goods and services, and about 3 percent of its GNP. OPEC's share thus amounted to approximately $50 billion and 2 percent of the 1980 U.S. GNP.

OPEC is a cartel. At the same time, its behavior differs in important ways from the classical textbook example of monopoly. To understand its role in the determination of world petroleum and natural gas pricing, we need first to identify the linkages between U.S. fiscal policies and OPEC decisions. We can then consider alternative models of OPEC behavior and take stock of OPEC's likely future role in world energy markets.

Of particular significance to petroleum pricing is foreign taxation, especially its impact on the international distribution of production and income. In general, the United States has adhered to the broadly accepted principle that double taxation of income is contrary to the economic basis for international trade, namely, that it undermines the potential economic gain from specialization through comparative advantage. However, as logical as the principle of no double taxation of foreign income has been in theory, countries' differing definitions of taxation have led to considerable distortions in the allocation of petroleum resources.

The cutting edge of the international taxation of petroleum income lies in

[12] *International Petroleum Encyclopedia* (Tulsa: Pennwell Publishing Co., 1981), pp. 222–23.

the difficulty tax authorities face in distinguishing between the imposition of a royalty charge and the imposition of an income tax by a foreign government. Any foreign charge that can be construed as an income tax is fully creditable against U.S. income taxes, whereas any non-income tax payments can be treated only as tax-deductible expenses. The distinction is an important one, for the effective rate of taxation in the former case is likely to be considerably lower than that in the latter, thereby substantially affecting the profitability of international petroleum operations.

Table 11.2 provides a comparative statement of the fiscal impact on international petroleum income arising from two differing treatments of foreign taxation by a firm's parent tax authority. Under the conventional rule, no distinction has been made between royalty payments and income taxes on the international profits of firms. Royalty payments, which are excise taxes rather than income taxes per se, have thus been included in the total foreign tax payments that petroleum firms have been able to credit against their domestic income tax liabilities, as shown for three different foreign tax rates at left. In effect, as long as these foreign tax levies are imposed at a rate that is equal to or greater than the U.S. tax rate and are admissible as income taxes, they reduce the payment liability of these firms to U.S. tax authorities to zero. Thus the inclusion of royalties as part of a firm's foreign income tax liability represents a subsidy to international petroleum activities. Since this sudsidy is not available to domestic petroleum operations, it increases the differential profitability of foreign operations and thereby encourages the growth of the economy's dependence on imported petroleum beyond what it would attain otherwise.

Before we turn to the specifics of OPEC pricing policies, it should be noted that one additional fiscal distortion can exist under international petroleum taxation. Since there are periodic shifts in the market equilibrium for internationally traded petroleum, there may well be divergences between the posted price of petroleum and the actual transaction price which is paid by a

Table 11.2. The Incidence of International Petroleum Taxation under Alternative Fiscal Regimes

	Foreign Taxes Classified as a					
	Credit, with a foreign tax rate of			Deduction, with a foreign tax rate of		
	50%	60%	70%	50%	60%	70%
1. Foreign taxable income	$1,000	$1,000	$1,000	$1,000	$1,000	$1,000
2. Foreign tax	500	600	700	500	600	700
3. U.S. taxable income	1,000	1,000	1,000	500	400	300
4. U.S. tax (46%)	460	460	460	230	184	138
5. U.S. tax after credit	0	0	0	230	184	138
6. Total taxes	500	600	700	730	784	838
7. *Effective tax rate*	50%	60%	70%	73%	78.4%	83.8%

petroleum firm to a deposit owner.[13] Traditionally, the market for internationally traded petroleum has been based on a common reference price, or marker crude. Given the significance of Middle Eastern petroleum to the international petroleum market, this reference price has most often been Arabian light, that is, the price of Saudi Arabian crude oil with a specific gravity of thirty-four degrees.[14] The key issue is how a divergence in the market price from the posted price affects revenues of petroleum firms and deposit owners.

When the posted price of petroleum exceeds the actual transaction price, it signals two conditions in the market. First, there is inadequate demand to satisfy the prevailing posted price. Unless some adjustment occurs on the supply side, there will be a surplus quantity which will exert downward pressures on the actual price. Second, although higher posted prices can also raise owner royalties, as long as posted-price royalties are admissible as foreign income taxes, they can be used to lower the domestic tax liability of petroleum firms, at the same time, they create even higher earnings for those firms, since the actual transaction price would be lower than the posted price. The subsequent appearance of higher profitability in earnings statements of petroleum firms provides an inducement for deposit owners to reduce their permissible production to a level where the posted and actual prices coincide. Indeed, as long as this adjustment can be made within a moderate range of a producer's general share of the market and consistent with the owner country's revenue absorption capacity, there is every reason to expect such behavior in the market.

The other divergence in the pricing of petroleum arises when the posted price is less than the actual transaction price. In this case, petroleum firms' income will be less than what a spot posted-price equilibrium would be because the higher spot price for oil is only a tax-deductible expense and is not eligible for foreign tax credit. There is thus a sample coincidence of wants: both petroleum firms and oil producing countries stand to gain by an increase in the posted price to the prevailing spot market price.

OPEC's significance to the pricing of petroleum depends on several key factors. First, as may be seen in figure 11.4, although OPEC's share of world petroleum reserves is substantial, its ability to set and enforce prices depends largely on the cooperative behavior of international petroleum firms. Specifically, OPEC countries do not yet possess directly the means of extracting, converting, and marketing crude oil from points of origin to final users—refineries, tankers, pipelines, and distributive organizational capacity. Al-

[13]A more detailed discussion of pre-embargo pricing arrangements is found in M. A. Adelman, *The World Petroleum Market* (Baltimore: Johns Hopkins Press for Resources for the Future, 1972). The conventional linkage between the posted price and the actual transactions price is the spot price, particularly in large spot markets such as Rotterdam.

[14]Given recent divisions within OPEC, this base-point pricing system has given way to a more heterogeneous pricing structure, even though a dominant producer such as Saudi Arabia can strongly influence how much variation there will be by virtue of its ability to adjust its output to enforce some degree of pricing cohesion.

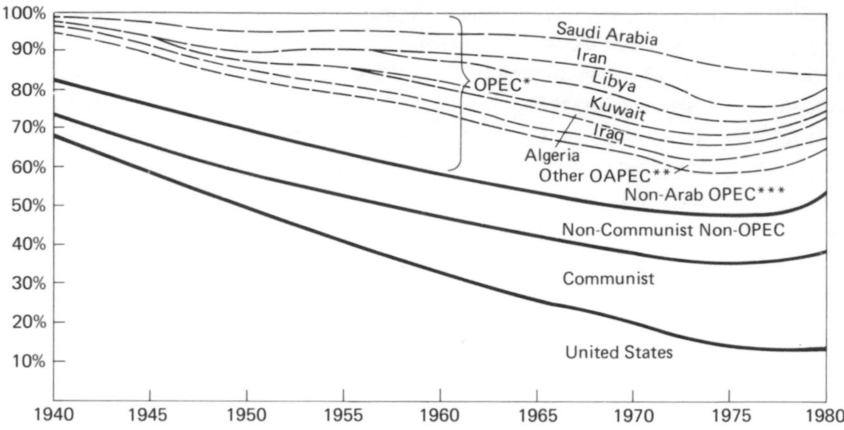

*OPEC was established in September, 1960 by Saudi Arabia, Iraq, Kuwait, Iran, and Venezuela, and expanded its membership in succeeding years to include Algeria, Qatar, the United Arab Emirates (Abu Dhabi, Bahrain, Dubai), Indonesia, Equador, Gabon, and Nigeria. Shares are thus reported on an OPEC-equivalent basis.
**Qatar, Algeria, United Arab Emirates.
***Venezuela, Nigeria, Indonesia, Gabon, Equador.

Figure 11.4. Geographic Distribution of World Petroleum Production, 1940–80. Adapted from data in *International Petroleum Encyclopedia, 1981* (Tulsa: Penn Well Publishing Co., 1981).

though there has been a clear rise in OPEC participation, or nationalization, in refinery and pipeline operations, especially since 1973, most internationally traded world petroleum is still transported by ships belonging to the major consuming countries. Moreover, the extension of reserves among OPEC countries still depends primarily on the technological capacity of non-OPEC firms. Thus, there may be limits to the ability of OPEC countries to capture the profits accruing to international petroleum firms.

Second, an economic limit to OPEC pricing is the elasticity of demand. As noted in chapter 10, the short-run price elasticity of demand may be very small, and the corresponding income elasticity of demand close to unity. However, once the cost of petroleum represents a significant share of consumer income, as its price is raised, even with limited substitution possibilities the elasticity of demand is likely to change. In particular, the price elasticity of demand is likely to rise as consumers engage in conservation. Depending on relative prices and technology, the price elasticity of demand is also likely to rise as domestic substitute fuels become competitive and as other non-OPEC international reserves become economic. Thus, offshore exploration, tar sands, shale oil, and coal gasification and liquefaction do constitute resources which must be taken into consideration in OPEC pricing decisions. Furthermore, the larger a given OPEC increase in the short run, the greater is the likelihood that it will slow down the economic growth rate in consuming countries, thereby lowering the growth of demand for petroleum and hence the ability of OPEC to sustain a given price increase.[15]

The third factor central to OPEC pricing ability is the economic cohesion of its members. Given favorable external conditions, the economic cohesion of OPEC is a function of the number of members, the distribution of reserves and production capacity, and the degree of shared political values. Each of these factors merits some elaboration.

Several factors outside OPEC are favorable to its internal cohesion. What they share in common is their contributory role in the preservation of a relatively low price elasticity of demand, for a relatively inelastic demand is what makes possible the price-increasing income maximization of OPEC in the first place. These favorable factors include: a concentration of world petroleum reserves within a limited number of countries, domestic economic policies among non-OPEC consuming countries which encourage consumption, and non-OPEC petroleum-supply policies that enhance the profitability of petroleum operations within OPEC to the detriment of exploration and development of alternative resources. The evolution of energy policy will be examined in greater detail in chapter 15. At this point we can say that the fundamental consequence of these measures has been to facilitate the organization and operation of OPEC. Indeed, had OPEC itself not existed, it is most likely that a similar organization would have emerged sooner or later, much as was suggested in chapter 1.

Given the favorable external conditions which give rise to a relatively inelastic demand for OPEC petroleum, it does not necessarily follow that the cartel can proceed to maximize its revenue through equalization of marginal costs and revenues in the textbook monopoly fashion outlined in section 11.1. To be sure, OPEC has had considerable success in increasing its revenues far above the levels obtained in the pre-1973 period (see table 11.3). This may provide but cold comfort to principal consuming countries, but it is important to note that the range of subsequent increases even within conditions of persisting inelastic demand for OPEC oil may be more narrow than at first might appear.

The principal economic difficulty with which OPEC must contend in revenue maximization is that it is a cartel, not a single-firm monopoly. Its thirteen member states are likely to face somewhat differing marginal-cost curves, as well as differences in productive capacity, in absorptive capacity, and in domestic economic conditions which give rise to the internal demand for petroleum revenues in the first place. These differences can result in in-

[15] As noted in chapter 10, the short-run price elasticity of demand is relatively low. A given price increase may first lower the level of aggregate economic demand in general, and this lowered demand then lowers the demand for petroleum. Only after adjustments have been made in petroleum use is the level of aggregate economic demand likely to return to its former level, if at all. Until that happens, there may well be weakness in the world demand for oil, particularly insofar as the United States is one of the principal consuming countries of OPEC exports. In turn, higher long-run price elasticities of demand tend to further weaken upward pricing movement, as the events of 1980–81 tended to confirm.

Table 11.3. Estimated Oil Exports and Revenues of Principal OPEC Countries, 1971–80

Country	1971	1972	1973	1974	1975	1976	1977	1978	1979	1980
	Oil Exports (in millions of barrels)									
Saudi Arabia	1,707	2,163	2,769	3,099	2,581	3,030	3,212	2,789	3,395	3,504
Kuwait	1,164	1,218	1,114	938	748	767	694	655	876	584
Iran	1,562	1,752	1,971	2,007	1,825	1,971	1,898	1,768	876	402
Iraq	594	382	668	640	785	767	767	846	1,205	876
United Arab Emirates	339	384	556	604	602	657	694	664	657	621
Qatar	156	176	208	190	160	183	146	200	182	183
Libya	989	813	794	544	531	657	730	728	730	621
Algeria	276	373	371	353	331	365	402	418	402	329
Nigeria	531	628	734	804	622	730	730	619	767	694
Venezuela	1,206	1,133	1,146	999	783	803	730	734	730	657
Indonesia	273	345	370	379	363	438	511	514	475	438
Total	8,807	9,367	10,701	10,557	9,331	10,363	10,514	9,935	10,295	8,909
	Government Oil Revenues (in millions of U.S. dollars)[a]									
Saudi Arabia	2,149	3,107	4,340	22,574	25,676	33,500	37,800	37,191	57,700	104,200
Kuwait	1,400	1,657	1,900	7,000	7,500	8,500	8,500	8,400	16,000	18,300
Iran	1,944	2,380	4,100	17,500	18,500	22,000	23,000	23,780	20,800	11,600
Iraq	840	575	1,843	5,700	7,500	8,500	9,600	11,243	23,400	26,500
United Arab Emirates	[illegible]	[illegible]	[illegible]	[illegible]	[illegible]	[illegible]	[illegible]	[illegible]	[illegible]	[illegible]

Algeria	[illegible]	[illegible]	[illegible]	[illegible]	[illegible]	[illegible]	[illegible]	[illegible]	[illegible]	[illegible]
Nigeria	915	1,174	2,200	8,900	6,570	8,500	9,400	9,174	16,100	20,000
Venezuela	1,702	1,948	2,670	8,700	7,525	8,500	8,000	10,915	12,000	18,900
Indonesia	284	429	950	3,300	3,850	4,500	5,600	7,170	8,100	10,500
Total	11,979	14,374	22,512	90,510	93,296	115,000	127,100	136,783	195,800	269,300
	Government Receipts (in U.S. dollars per barrel of exports)[b]									
Saudi Arabia	1.25	1.43	1.56	7.28	9.94	11.51	12.09	13.33	18.00	32.00
Kuwait	1.20	1.36	1.70	7.46	10.02	11.23	12.87	12.83	21.43	36.00
Iran	1.24	1.35	2.08	8.71	10.13	11.62	12.81	13.45	23.71	36.00
Iraq	1.41	1.50	2.75	8.90	9.55	11.70	12.65	13.29	21.96	36.00
United Arab Emirates	1.27	1.43	1.61	9.16	9.96	11.82	12.45	14.01	21.56	34.00
Qatar	1.26	1.44	1.96	8.42	10.62	11.66	13.19	14.04	21.23	37.00
Libya	1.78	1.96	2.89	11.02	9.60	12.62	13.92	14.59	26.27	41.00
Algeria	1.26	1.87	2.42	10.48	10.19	13.10	14.30	14.78	26.27	40.00
Nigeria	1.72	1.87	2.99	11.06	10.56	13.16	14.63	14.82	26.26	40.00
Venezuela	1.41	1.71	2.33	8.70	9.61	12.80	13.99	14.87	18.93	35.00
Indonesia	1.04	1.24	2.56	8.70	10.60	12.80	13.55	13.95	23.50	35.00
Average	1.35	1.56	2.26	9.08	10.08	12.17	13.31	13.99	22.64	36.55

Sources: For 1971–75, *Petroleum Economist*, September 1976, p. 338; for 1976–78, ibid., July 1977, pp. 254, 277, and *International Petroleum Encyclopedia* (Tulsa: Petroleum Publishing Co., 1979), pp. 254–56, 375–77; for 1979, *New York Times*, 30 January 1980, p. D-1, based on 1 December 1979 prices; and for 1980, *Petroleum Economist*, June 1981, p. 232.

[a]Based on the average price paid during the calendar year rather than on end-of-year figures

[b]Generally end-of-year estimates

creased tension among member countries. Unless some sanction can be invoked, rising tension may result in cheating, which would undermine the basis for coordinated pricing and production decisions by the cartel.

Let us consider the problem of differing marginal-cost curves among individual member countries. In this case, the cartel's price will be well above each member's current average cost, but it may not provide the same margin for each member, nor will it necessarily be high enough to cover the marginal costs of production. For example, differences in the size of proven reserves provide different time horizons before exhaustion is reached under prevailing demand, production, and pricing conditions. Each member is thus concerned with eventual extension of reserves. The marginal cost of new reserve oil will most likely differ according to previous exploration efforts, geological data, and current and evolving exploration and extraction technology of the kind noted in chapter 5. Hence, there will be tension between the high-marginal-cost and low-marginal-cost producers concerning the optimal pricing level, much as occurred in the OPEC strategy meeting in Geneva, Switzerland, in May 1981.[16] The greatest pressure for an increase arose from those states with a relatively small proven reserve base, the greatest pressure for restraint in the increase of prices came from Saudi Arabia, the cartel member with the largest proven reserves. Indeed, Saudi Arabia's 1979 decision to temporarily expand its daily production from 8.5 million to 9.5 million barrels a day derived not only from a desire to encourage a homogeneous pricing system but also because the marginal cost of production to Saudi Arabia was so much lower than that of states such as Algeria, Venezuela, and Indonesia.[17]

A related source of tension among OPEC member states is the distribution of productive capacity. Although there is a significant degree of positive correlation between production capacity and proven reserves, substantial variations in this relationship may exist among individual member countries. The reason why this may provoke tension is that countries with relatively small cartel shares and a substantial margin of productive capacity face a relatively elastic demand curve in relation to larger producers and cartel demand as a whole. There is thus an incentive for a small-share producer to cheat by expanding its production at a time when overall production restraint is being pursued by the cartel. As in the preceding example of marginal-cost variations, the aggravation of tension may result in adjustments to output by a larger member state such as Saudi Arabia, or the possibility of imposing mandatory share arrangements among all members beyond the somewhat amorphous, historical share relationship.

Another source of tension within OPEC is that there may be substantial differences in the revenue absorptive capacity of individual member economies. In the context of OPEC decisionmaking, absorptive capacity is the ability of an individual economy to digest new investment revenue on a scale that does not lower the prevailing rate of return below a minimally acceptable

[16]"A Breather for Oil Prices," *Business Week*, 25 May 1981, pp. 104–15.
[17]*New York Times*, 25 December 1979, p. 1.

level.[18] Of course, a minimally acceptable, or even maximum target, level can have several meanings. On a practical level, there are several good indicators of how absorptive capacity could be determined. In general, the greater the flow of petroleum revenue to a cartel member, the greater is the likelihood that there will be inflationary pressures within the economy. To offset these inflationary pressures, new revenues can be channeled into investment projects which enlarge an economy's productive capacity, and by extension its absorptive capacity. However, the channeling of these funds can by itself create serious strains on the economy's existing resources, thereby aggravating the inflationary pressure. The signs of this strain are: a lack of an optimal mix of unskilled and skilled labor, technical delays in transport and materials, and poor managerial coordination in the face of structural change. In turn, these problems lower the efficiency of the investment process and hence the economic rate of return to a point where any additional revenues can only accelerate domestic inflation. At that point an economy faces a critical choice. On the one hand it can lower petroleum exports, the price of petroleum, or both, to reduce the flow of revenue into the economy in order to stem inflationary pressure. If it does so, it may also lose its bargaining strength within the cartel, particularly if the export price elasticity of petroleum demand is sufficiently low to begin with and if other members can thereby readily expand their production to take up the slack by virtue of their relatively large absorptive capacities. On the other hand, an economy with low absorptive capacity can maintain its output and pricing in such a fashion that its share of cartel revenues remains the same while all incremental revenues to the individual economy are invested abroad. The basis for so doing is, of course, to stem the domestic inflationary pressure, maintain the domestic minimally acceptable rate of return, and at the same time obtain a return on overseas investment at least as high on a real net basis as the domestic minimally acceptable rate of return.

Table 11.4 provides a general profile of some of the factors influencing OPEC cohesion. No one of these characteristics necessarily could explain any particular pricing and production decision, but taken together, they do suggest some of the underlying factors influencing the behavior of the cartel.[19] As one example, though they constitute only one-quarter of the cartel population, Iran and the Arab members of OPEC traditionally have accounted for approximately four-fifths of its production and almost 90 percent of its published proven reserves. The dominant role of Arab oil-producing states suggests one reason why most OPEC countries were willing to impose an oil embargo during the 1973 Middle East war: with the exception of Egypt,

[18]For a more detailed discussion, see John H. Adler, *Absorptive Capacity: The Concept and Its Determinants* (Washington, D.C.: Brookings Institution, 1965).

[19]There is a substantial literature on cartel behavior too numerous to cover in detail here. For an exposition of dynamic limit pricing, see D. W. Gaskins, Jr., "Dynamic Limit Pricing: Optimal Pricing under Threat of Entry," *Journal of Economic Theory* 3 (1971); and S. W. Salant, "Staving off the Backstop: Dynamic Limit Pricing with a Kinked Demand Curve," in *Advances in the Economics of Energy and Resources*, ed. R. S. Pindyck, vol. 2 (Greenwich, Conn.: JAI Press, 1979), pp. 187–205.

Table 11.4. Economic Indicators of OPEC Member Countries

Country	1980 Share of OPEC Oil Production	1980 Share of OPEC Oil Reserves	1980 Mid-year Population (in millions)	1978 Per Capita GNP (in current U.S. dollars)[a]	Rate of Increase in Consumer Prices	1980 Relative Index of Oil Production Capacity[b]
Saudi Arabia	35.8%	38.0%	8.37	$ 7,690	2.21%	47.7%
Iraq	9.8	6.9	13.08	1,860	7.94[f]	72.7
United Arab Emirates	8.5	8.4	0.80	(12,200)	10.91	52.3
Venezuela	8.1	4.1	13.91	2,910	20.24	100.0
Nigeria	7.6	3.9	77.08	560	8.55	102.3
Libya	6.6	5.3	2.98	6,910	14.55[c]	63.6
Indonesia	5.9	2.2	151.89	360	16.90	138.6
Iran	5.5	13.2	37.45	2,160	26.90	20.5
Kuwait	5.1	14.9	1.36	14,890	8.03	18.2
Algeria	3.8	1.9	19.77	1,260	14.59[d]	102.3
Qatar	1.8	0.8	0.22	(12,105)	9.00[d]	109.1
Ecuador	0.8	0.3	8.35	880	14.80	168.2
Gabon	0.7	0.1	0.55	(3,160)	11.09[g]	297.7
Total	100.0	100.0	335.81	—	—	—
Unweighted average	7.7%	7.7%	25.83	$3,948[b]	12.75%	100.0%

Sources: United Nations, *Monthly Bulletin of Statistics*, June 1981, pp. 1–4; World Bank, *World Development Report, 1980* (New York: Oxford University Press, 1980), pp. 110–11; International Monetary Fund, *International Financial Statistics*, June 1981; *International Petroleum Encyclopedia* (Tulsa: Penn Well Publishing Co., 1981), pp. 222–23.

[a]Data in parentheses are for 1977

[b]The relative index is computed as $\alpha_i = \dfrac{(p_i/r_i)}{\left[\sum_{i=1}^{n} (p_i/r_i)/n\right]}$, where p_i is the annual oil production rate of the ith country, r_i is the proven reserves of the ith country, and α_i is the production-to-reserves ratio of the ith country relative to the simple mean production-to-reserves ratio

[c]First quarter, 1978–first quarter, 1979

[d]Fourth quarter, 1978–fourth quarter, 1979

[e]Second quarter, 1978–second quarter, 1979

[f]Third quarter, 1978–third quarter, 1979

[g]First quarter, 1979–first quarter, 1980

[h]Exclusive of figures in parentheses

Arab states have generally been hostile to Israel.[20] Against the apparent solidarity of Arab oil producers, however, there are considerable differences in the productive and absorptive capacities even among these individual member states. Differences in populations, real growth rates of income, and inflation point to potential weaknesses in cartel unity. States with relatively high productive capacity such as Saudi Arabia and Kuwait could readily alter production to enforce some degree of unity in overall OPEC pricing, particularly if they expanded their output to support cartel price unity and moderation. At the same time, they may have limited domestic revenue absorption capacities for maintaining such production increases over a sustained period of time, for an expansion of their output would tend to aggravate greatly domestic inflation and create social and economic unrest. Indeed, apart from the political dimensions of the Shah's regime, one factor which undoubtedly hastened the Iranian revolution was the relatively limited ability of the Iranian economy to absorb petroleum revenues at the rate at which they were being acquired, especially when we consider the short-run impact of these revenues on the personal distribution of income.

As a third illustration from table 11.4, some countries with relatively limited production capacity are often under considerable domestic pressure to increase prices and limit the expansion of production because of high population growth rates, relatively small reserves, and short-term limits to non-oil sources of economic growth. Algeria, Libya, Nigeria, and Venezuela are typical examples.

Each of the foregoing characteristics of OPEC pricing and production decisions can now be combined in general graphic form. With the exception of the 1973 embargo, OPEC has not generally pursued a supply-reducing income-maximization strategy. Rather, it has most often tended to restrain the growth of production, which in relation to the growth of world petroleum demand has enabled it to obtain substantially higher prices and net revenues than has historically been the case. As has been noted, the demand for OPEC oil depends on the extent to which a price-increasing strategy will raise the elasticity of demand for OPEC oil to a point where such a strategy is no longer viable (see figure 11.5).

In figure 11.5.*a*, the world oil supply curve is a function of OPEC, the competitive fringe of non-OPEC oil-producing states, and synthetic oil technology. As long as OPEC is the lowest-cost producer with a relatively large market share, and the demand for oil is relatively price-inelastic, cartel revenues can be maximized by restraining the growth of production relative to the growth of demand. However, the higher the world price of oil, the greater is the likelihood that there will be increased production by the competitive fringe, which would thereby reduce OPEC's share of world oil supplies and thus its ability to pursue a price increasing strategy. Non-OPEC

[20] As a non-Arab Moslem country, Iran under the Shah did not support the 1973 embargo and generally maintained its export levels throughout that period. However, the Shah did press vigorously for the ensuing quadrupling of oil prices, thereby promoting the essential unity for subsequent OPEC pricing decisions.

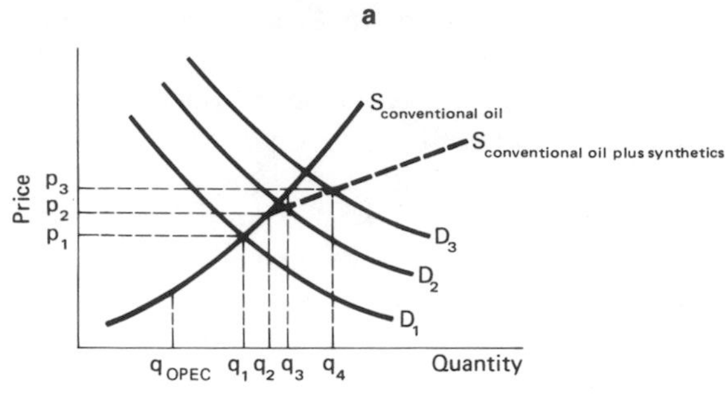

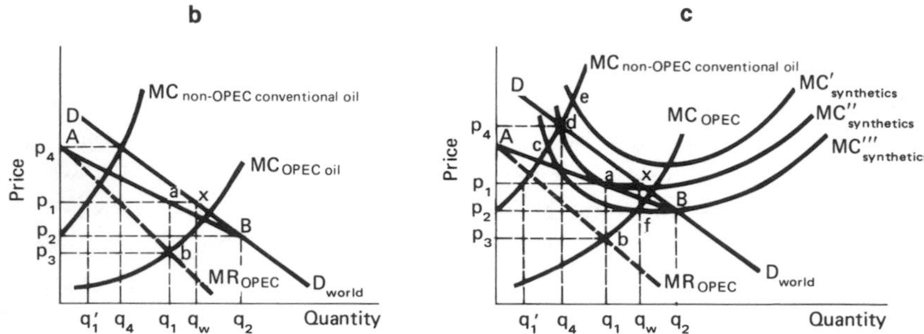

Figure 11.5. OPEC External Limit Pricing: **a.** synthetic fuels and world petroleum equilibrium; **b.** the competitive fringe and OPEC; **c.** the competitive fringe, OPEC, and synthetic fuels.

fruinge producer countries such as the United States, the European North Sea states, Canada, and Mexico find that increases in the real price of oil make it economical to engage in offshore exploration, as well as in secondary and tertiary recovery methods for existing wells. There is thus a limit to OPEC's ability to raise prices. This limit is shown in greater detail in figure 11.5.*b*.

In figure 11.5.*b*, OPEC faces a kinked demand curve for its oil, *ABD*, relative to that for world demand as a whole, *DD*. If the profit-maximizing level of OPEC production is q_1, the cartel average price and production levels will be p_1 and q_1, respectively. The supply of higher-cost non-OPEC oil will be only q_2', which will give a total world production level of q_w. If the profit-maximizing price of OPEC oil goes higher than p_1, then the share of non-OPEC oil will go higher than p_1 the share of non-OPEC competitive-fatigue oil will become larger, and the ability to obtain additional cartel revenues will be reduced.

The significance of synthetic oil to OPEC pricing decisions is illustrated in figure 11.5.*c*. As long as the marginal cost of synthetic oil technology lies beyond world petroleum demand, as in MC', synthetic oil technology will exert no influence on the ability of OPEC to pursue cartel revenue and profit maximization. On the other hand, if the world demand for petroleum were to increase, or what is equivalent, if the technology of synthetic oil were to lower its relative marginal cost, as in the shift from MC' to MC'' or MC''', then the intersection of synthetic oil technology costs with conventional petroleum costs would begin to have a significant impact on OPEC decisions. For example, if the price of conventional world petroleum were to rise from p_1, the initial cartel profit-maximizing price of OPEC in figure 11.b.*c*, to p_4 and if the relative marginal cost of synthetic technology might be able to enjoy economies of scale by expanding production from q_4 out as far as q_w, OPEC profits would be reduced from p_1abp_3 to p_ixfp_2. Thus, to the extent that synthetic technology is endowed with economies of scale, it can substantially erode cartel profitability once the threshhold price is reached, thereby establishing a more elastic supply curve for world oil as a whole, as in indicated in figure 11.5.*a*.

Beyond the potential limits to OPEC pricing and production profit maximization, there are also productive and absorptive capacity constraints of individual member countries (see figure 11.6). An individual member of OPEC will first seek to maximize its profits by choosing a pricing and production level consistent with the equalization of its own marginal costs and revenues, illustrated in the lower lefthand diagram of figure 11.6 as position *a*. Though the elasticity of demand could vary, this optimal position will generate a given amount of revenue such as at position *a* on an iso-revenue curve for the individual member country. In turn, the revenues of the individual country are invested under a priority scheduling of projects from most to least pro-

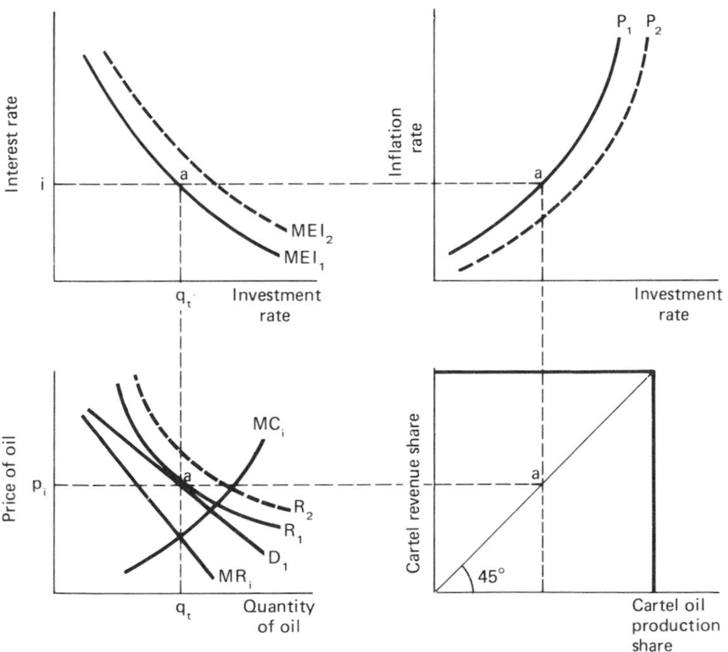

Figure 11.6. Individual OPEC Member Productive and Absorptive Capacity

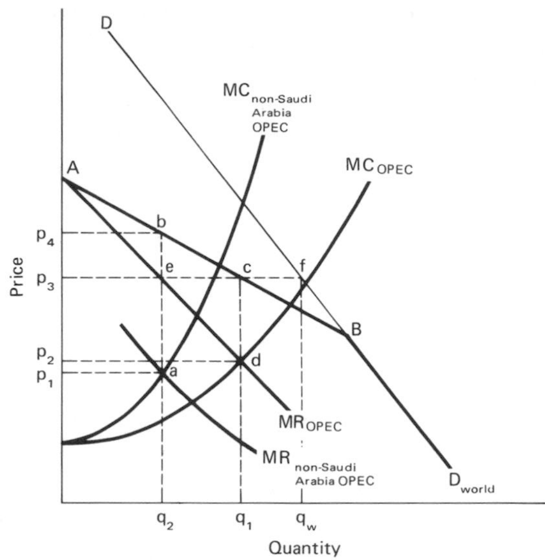

Figure 11.7. OPEC Dominant Firm Pricing by Saudi Arabia

fitable. This schedule of project profitability is shown in the marginal-efficiency-of-investment (MEI) curve in the upper lefthand diagram of figure 11.6. At the same time, for a given MEI schedule, the greater the investment rate, the lower will be the prevailing rate of return and most likely the higher the domestic rate of inflation. Declines in the rate of return to investments plus additions to the marginal rate of inflation together place limits on the ability of an individual member of the cartel to accelerate the rate of revenue generation, even with the individual cartel members' overseas revenue investment.

Despite the potentially large share of cartel profit-maximizing revenues which a single OPEC member might wish to obtain, the unequal distribution of existing production and revenue shares within the cartel will lead to some degree of dominance by the state which produces the most at the lowest cost. Saudi Arabia is the largest single producer within the cartel (see figure 11.7). Though it could reduce its production to achieve a single-country optimal pricing and production profit-maximizing position, it might accept for itself a second-best position in the interest of pursuing overall cartel pricing uniformity. Optimal profits to the cartel as a whole would dictate a production level of q_1 and a price level of p_3, with the non-OPEC world petroleum production level left at $q_w q_1$. Absent Saudi Arabia, the non-OPEC optimal strategy would be a price of p_4 and an output of q_2. This would tend to lower the non-OPEC share of world production, particularly in that some non-OPEC oil might then become more competitive. Saudi Arabia could then expand its production to a level at which it might be operating at a less than optimal level for itself but at which cartel revenues as a whole are maximized. Non-

Saudi Arabian OPEC member countries might thus be forced to accept a lower level of profitability than might be otherwise possible.

Given the operational constraints on OPEC's profit-maximizing opportunities, we should not underestimate the ability of the cartel to raise prices and limit the growth and level of production. As long as secondary and tertiary oil marginal costs, non-OPEC fringe-producer marginal costs, and synthetic oil marginal costs exceed the prevailing world price of petroleum, and as long as the average price of petroleum in principal consuming countries does not raise the elasticity of its demand through effective conservation, there is every reason to expect OPEC to be able to enjoy, in the near term at least, substantial rates of growth of real income. What makes this especially true is the combined influence of cartel organizational ability, the international tax policies already noted, and the domestic petroleum and natural gas regulatory policies of a principal consuming country such as the United States.

11.2.3. The Regulation and Deregulation of Petroleum

As noted in section 11.1, the price of an energy resource may be influenced substantially by regulatory decisions. Nowhere has this been more true than in the United States, especially in the impact regulation has had on petroleum and natural gas prices. Though petroleum and natural gas pricing are now being substantially modified, it is instructive to examine in some detail how regulation has influenced the pricing of these resources.

Regulation of petroleum in the United States has taken a variety of forms, including: prorationing, import quotas, entitlements, and mandatory allocation of available supplies.[21] Though it has since been abandoned, prorationing was first initiated in the United States during the 1930s by the Texas Railroad Commission as a device for limiting the then relative glut of oil from recent domestic discoveries and the decline in relative demand brought about by the Great Depression.[22] In essence, principal producing states such as Texas would assign extraction rates to producers in such a way as to minimize protracted rate wars and accelerated depletion, much as OPEC has sought to do in the post-1973 era.

Prorationing persisted in the United States until the early 1970s. Though

[21]Though since abandoned, regulation of petroleum has also included tariffs and import fees. During the OPEC pre-embargo era, until 1 May 1973, crude oil was subject to a 10.5 percent tariff, at which time it was replaced by a 10.5 percent import fee. This fee was replaced during the Ford administration by a $2.00 per barrel flat import fee until 1 August 1975, when it was eliminated as a result of a Supreme Court decision.

[22]There have been two types of prorationing: maximum-efficient-recovery, or MER, and market-demand. In the MER type, production rates are assigned in such a way as to approximate the maximum efficient recovery for a particular reservoir. Market-demand prorationing, which would not necessarily be compatible with MER rates, operated on revenue-maximizing principles of the kind referred to in sections 11.1 and 11.2.2 (see W. J. Mead, "Petroleum: An Unregulated Industry?" in *Energy Supply and Government Policy,* ed. R. J. Kalter and W. A. Vogely [Ithaca: Cornell University Press, 1976], pp. 130–60; and Stephen L. McDonald, *Petroleum Conservation in the United States: An Economic Analysis* [Baltimore: Johns Hopkins Press for Resources for the Future, 1971]).

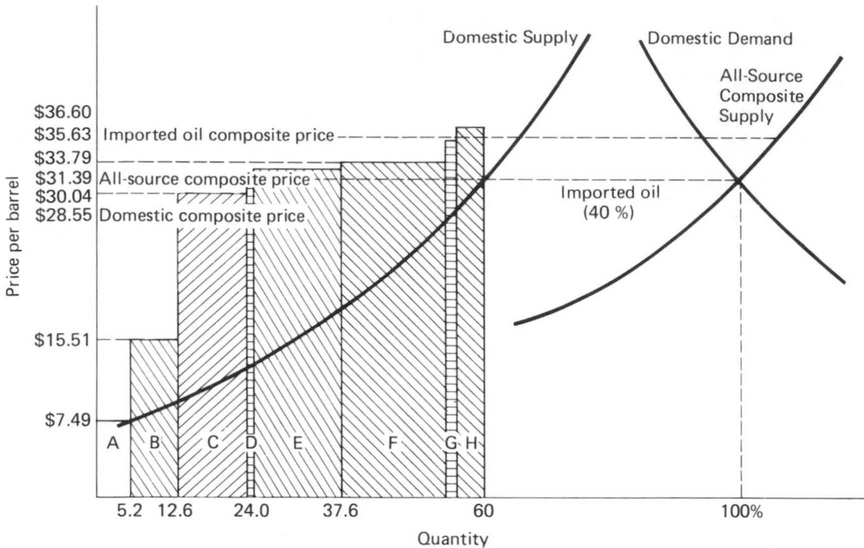

Figure 11.8. U.S. Crude-Oil Demand, Domestic Supply, and Imports, December 1980. *A*, lower-tier oil; *B*, upper-tier oil; *C*, Alaskan oil; *D*, naval petroleum reserve; *E*, stripper oil; *F*, decontrolled heavy oil; *G*, tertiary oil; *H*, newly discovered oil.

the 1973 Arab OPEC embargo had much to do with its demise, one factor that helped it to last as long as it did was the use of import quotas by successive administrations dating from the second term of President Eisenhower in 1959 until 1 May 1973.[23] Since these quotas, and their subsequent replacement by import fees during the Ford administration, have also been terminated, what is most important at this point is to spell out the panoply of alternative controls which until very recently have governed the price of oil.

Though the practice was ended completely by the Reagan administration in February 1981, the petroleum industry operated as a regulated industry throughout most of the 1970s, beginning in August 1971 when President Nixon imposed a mandatory freeze on wages and prices to combat the then accelerating inflation associated with expanding U.S. military involvement in Southeast Asia. The freeze was soon lifted, in early 1972, but comprehensive controls were kept in place until the Arab OPEC embargo of October 1973. However, although controls were lifted from other sectors of the economy by 1974, they were retained for petroleum and natural gas.

Figure 11.8 provides a profile of the various classes of regulated U.S. domestic oil supplies and their relationship to imported oil and the domestic market equilibrium. Lower-tier oil refers to domestic production from wells in existence prior to 1972 at rates not in excess of average production during that year but at a minimum rate of more than ten barrels per well per day.

[23]A more extensive discussion of the historical background and rationale of these decisions and their relation to the evolution of national energy policy is found in chapter 15.

Upper-tier oil includes production from wells that came into operation after 1972 plus any production from pre-1972 wells in excess of 1972 rates at a minimum of more than ten barrels per well per day. Stripper oil refers to production which began after 31 December 1972 on a twelve-month consecutive basis at a rate of no more than ten barrels per well per day. And newly discovered oil refers to any petroleum produced from wells that began operation after 1978.[24] Apart from miscellaneous sources of domestic production, imports, the largest share of which comes from OPEC producer states, account for the remainder of U.S. supply. Though none of the categories of domestic production had a permanent price freeze, until the termination of controls in 1981, the composite price of domestic oil remained at levels generally far below the price of all OPEC and non-OPEC sources of imported crude oil and equivalent refined products, which thereby accelerated the consumption of domestic supplies and simultaneously discouraged domestic exploration and production efforts.

As figure 11.8 suggests, variations in the price of oil at any given time can affect greatly not only domestic producer profitability but also the profitability of domestic refining and marketing operations. Not surprisingly, when the Arab OPEC oil embargo was imposed, Congress passed the Emergency Petroleum Allocation Act, which was used between November 1973 and February 1981 to attempt to minimize the adverse cost impact of embargo-prone and domestically produced supplies to both refiners and distributors. Under this legislation, the Department of Energy, like its predecessor, the Federal Energy Administration, determined on a calendar quarterly basis the flow of crude oil through each domestic refinery. At the same time, it gathered data on the supply-to-capacity ratio of each refinery, as well as calculated the national average supply-to-capacity ratio. It then published a "buy-sell" list according to which refiners with less than the national average supply-to-capacity ratio were authorized to purchase crude oil from those refiners with more than the national average ratio. The value of these authorizations, or entitlements, thus varied according to the variation in refinery capacity rates.

Following a fifteen-day adjustment period, the Department of Energy could order mandatory sales based on the merits of individual appeals. The price under both types of transactions would be determined by the Department of Energy and was based on its estimate of the average cost of crude oil. Any refining firm that had been obligated under either arrangement to sell any of its supply of crude had to then make up its own requirements from what free market crude oil there may have been for sale in the United States, or from foreign suppliers such as OPEC. Since those companies that had acquired more than national average supplies would have to obtain replacement supplies at prices most certainly higher than their original sources, they would be effectively penalized, regardless of whether foresight or local domestic marketing conditions would have justified the decision to the firm in

[24]Upper-tier oil thus refers to production and discoveries between 1972 and 1978.

the first place. Refined products such as gasoline and home fuel oil were allocated in a similar fashion.

To facilitate the operation of the entitlements system, an entitlement coupons market was established with a federally regulated price. In theory, since certain refiners were required to purchase entitlements from other less-favored refiners, the variation in refiner costs among firms could be reduced. This supposedly would enhance competition and at the same time minimize the adverse effects of the existing mandatory reallocation system. The entitlements transactions would alter the distribution of purchasing power among refining firms by purely financial transfers instead of by immediate physical transfers of crude-oil supplies. Once entitlements reallocations had taken place, the physical reallocation of crude-oil supplies could be implemented with far fewer cost penalties to refiner crude-oil purchasers than would otherwise be the case. In practice, entitlement coupons created the illusion of a freely operating market while at the same time accelerating domestic petroleum demand and discouraging even further domestic-exploration incentives.

A final component in the regulation of petroleum is the impact of federal and state exploratory leasing decisions. As noted in chapter 1, conventional leasing of property for petroleum and natural gas exploration could give rise to substantial external benefits from changing discovery rates. To prevent overdrilling of properties, firms are often required to unitize reservoirs, that is, to designate one principal operator to develop a deposit, determine a technically and economically efficient rate of extraction, and distribute the benefits among contributing firms. Regulation in this regard has encompassed the size of lease tracts, spacing of wells, production rates, gas flaring, and similar requirements. By themselves, these regulations have helped to lessen the problem of potential overdrilling and excessive rates of depletion, but they should not be construed as a conscious effort to promote conservation in the overall use of petroleum.

Beyond the question of external benefits in petroleum exploration, it should also be noted that half or more of all potentially recoverable domestic petroleum reserves now lie in public onshore and offshore regions.[25] Though no firm estimate has yet been made, what is critical to the development of future conventional petroleum supply is the rate of leasing by federal and state authorities. Since no more than 5 percent of offshore locations have been explored thus far, public decisions regarding the rate of exploration can affect substantially not only conventional domestic supply but also the relation of the competitive-fringe petroleum regions to OPEC pricing decisions.

Taken together, international taxation, OPEC pricing and production decisions, and domestic regulation of petroleum have had three primary consequences. First, until recently, the domestic price of petroleum and refined

[25]See R. J. Kalter and W. E. Tyner, "Disposal Policy for Energy Resources in the Public Domain," in *Energy Supply and Government Policy,* ed. R. J. Kalter and W. A. Vogely (Ithaca: Cornell University Press, 1976), pp. 51–75.

products has been less than its domestic replacement cost, which has encouraged the growth of imports and international dependence. Second, the use of depletion allowances, deductibility of intangible drilling expenses, and the foreign tax credit has subsidized the exploration and production of petroleum but with a differential benefit to foreign operations, thereby promoting even further international dependence and accelerated depletion of world petroleum supplies. Third, as long as the particular combination of regulation, tax incentives, and relatively low international petroleum costs were to remain in effect, the United States would have little incentive to conserve its energy. This lack of incentive has resulted in the past in an energy-intensive economy, aggravated pollution of the environment from relatively low technical conversion of energy, and a more rapid exhaustion of depletable petroleum supplies that would otherwise have occurred.

Given the consequences of the pricing of petroleum energy resources, it is not surprising that many of the incentives previously described are being eliminated. As already noted, since February 1981, petroleum prices have been deregulated entirely. In addition, most of the production subsidy from the percentage-depletion allowance has been removed, even though there may still be marginal benefits to international exploration. As the price of petroleum has attained its domestic cost of replacement, so too has there been an increase in energy conservation, as pointed out in previous chapters. Since the deregulation of petroleum in the United States has been tied to the imposition of a national windfall profits tax, we should examine what the impact of such a tax is likely to be on the pricing process already described.

A windfall profits tax is based on two notions. First, any substantial deregulation of petroleum would result in a significant increase in its price. Because the short-run elasticity of demand noted in chapter 10 is likely to be low, this increase in price would provide a substantial increase in revenue gains to producers not unlike the gains that have been accruing to OPEC. Second, because the price elasticity of supply of a depletable resource such as petroleum is likely to be relatively small, deregulation would tend to generate substantial windfall gains to producers, without any proportional increase in production. Windfall gains to producers in the absence of any corresponding increase in production would only result in an unwarranted redistribution of income. In contrast, a windfall profits tax would enable government to cushion the adverse impact of an increase in the price of oil on low-income groups, promote the development of alternative energy resources such as synthetic fuels and renewable energy technologies, and accelerate the increase in conservation choices in transportation, industry and the housing sectors of the economy by use of selected tax credits for energy-efficient capital investments. The tax income forgone from the granting of these credits would be recouped from revenues derived from the windfall profits tax.

Table 11.5 provides an illustration of the impact to two alternative proposals for windfall profits taxation which were presented to the U.S. Congress in 1979, as well as a rough estimate of the compromise legislation passed in March 1980. As we would expect, the higher the tax, the smaller

Table 11.5. Aggregate Effects of Alternative Windfall Profits Taxation under Deregulation of U.S. Petroleum Prices, 1980-90

Legislative Proposal	Total Producer Revenues (in billions of current dollars)	Total Federal Tax Liabilities (in billions of current dollars)[a]	Total State and Local Tax Liabilities (in billions of current dollars)	Total Taxes as a Percent of Total New Revenues[b]	Production of Crude Oil (in millions of barrels per day)	
					1985	1990
No windfall profits tax	$831.8	$197.5	$115.1	38%	8.3	7.9
House of Representatives bill	722.9	442.8	99.1	75	7.9	7.1
Senate bill	793.2	315.5	112.3	54	8.2	7.6
1980 Law[c]	800±	227-304	83-112	38-45	8.1	7.5

Source: Congressional Budget Office, *The Windfall Profits Tax: A Comparative Analysis of Two Bills* (Washington, D.C.: U.S. Government Printing Office, November 1979), p. xviii.

[a]Includes windfall profits tax liabilities and additional corporate income tax liabilities

[b]Includes federal, state, and local taxes

[c]Weighted average of the three alternatives

will be the estimated level of future oil production. At the same time, even if there were no tax, under ordinary regulation, domestic oil production would be expected to eventually peak and then decline. In effect, the windfall profits tax would extend the economic life of the remaining petroleum deposits beyond what they would be otherwise. Perhaps most important, the windfall profits tax and the deregulation of petroleum together are likely to offset to a considerable degree the many consumption incentives which characterized the past pricing of petroleum energy and which were so instrumental to the growth of dependence on uncertain imported supplies.

11.3. THE PRICING OF NATURAL GAS

As noted in section 11.2, the U.S. natural gas market has been subject to many of the economic incentives affecting the production and consumption of petroleum. For example, natural gas has had the benefits of the depletion allowance, deductibility of intangible drilling expenses, and foreign tax credits illustrated in tables 11.1 and 11.2. However, the United States has not had the same degree of dependence on natural gas imports that it has had on petroleum imports. Consequently, despite a relatively inelastic demand, and even though it does purchase significant quantities of natural gas from an OPEC producer state such as Algeria, there have been too many substitution opportunities for an OPEC type of natural gas cartel to emerge. What this leaves as the heart of natural gas pricing is essentially the domestic regulation of its pricing and production.

Natural gas first came under regulation with the passage of the Natural Gas Act of 1938, which placed it under the jurisdiction of the Federal Power Commission. Whereas the early regulation of petroleum was state-based, only the interstate sales of natural gas were controlled by the Federal Power Commission. With the exception of indirect controls over natural gas from the state-based prorationing of associated natural gas and petroleum wells, interstate sales of natural gas were determined essentially by unregulated market prices alone. However, in a landmark decision, the Supreme Court ruled in the 1954 *Phillips* v. *Wisconsin* case that the Federal Power Commission would henceforth have control over the regulation of natural gas wellhead pricing as well as its traditional control over interstate pricing.

The current system of natural gas pricing derives from the passage of the Natural Gas Policy Act of 1978. In the 1954–77 period, prices for natural gas sold on an intrastate basis began to exceed these allowed by the Federal Power Commission for interstate sales.[26] Under such a two-tiered pricing system, domestic producers became increasingly reluctant to commit sales to

[26]For an analysis of the pre-1978 natural gas market, see P. W. MacAvoy and R. S. Pindyck, *Price Controls and the Natural Gas Shortage* (Washington, D.C.: American Enterprise Institute for Public Policy Research, May 1975); R. B. Helms, *Natural Gas Regulation: An Evaluation of FPC Price Controls* (Washington, D.C.: American Enterprise Institute for Public Policy Research, July 1974); and S. G. Breyer and P. W. MacAvoy, "Regulating Natural Gas Producers," in *Energy Supply and Government Policy*, ed. R. J. Kalter and W. A. Vogely (Ithaca: Cornell University Press, 1976), pp. 161–92.

the interstate market, so that by 1977 physical shortages began to appear in the principal consuming regions of the northeastern United States. Moreover, the importation of natural gas from abroad often meant the payment of marginally higher prices than were available to domestic interstate sellers, thereby increasing the reluctance of domestic producers to service the interstate market and thus accelerating domestic physical shortages. A profile of this condition as of 1977 is presented in figure 11.9.

The 1978 Natural Gas Policy Act extends federal pricing authority to intrastate gas sales, thereby eliminating in theroy the two-tiered market system. At the same time, the natural gas proven reserves and domestic production rates noted in chapter 5 have continued to decline, suggesting that even the price increases permitted by the 1978 act have been insufficient to cover the marginal costs of production. Although newly discovered gas and certain interstate gas controls are to be lifted by 1 January 1985, the pricing of most categories of domestic gas production under the 1978 legislation suggests that the potential for a shortage of the kind which took place in 1977 still exists. For this reason, remaining price controls on natural gas could be removed before the 1985 deadline.

What, then, could be said of the consequences of petroleum and natural gas pricing on the U.S. economy? First, until 1973 the combined effects of international production subsidies and domestic pricing restraints accelerated the consumption of these depletable energy resources at rates much faster than market pricing alone would have permitted. Indeed, as figure 3.5 shows, until the OPEC oil embargo, the constant-dollar domestic price of

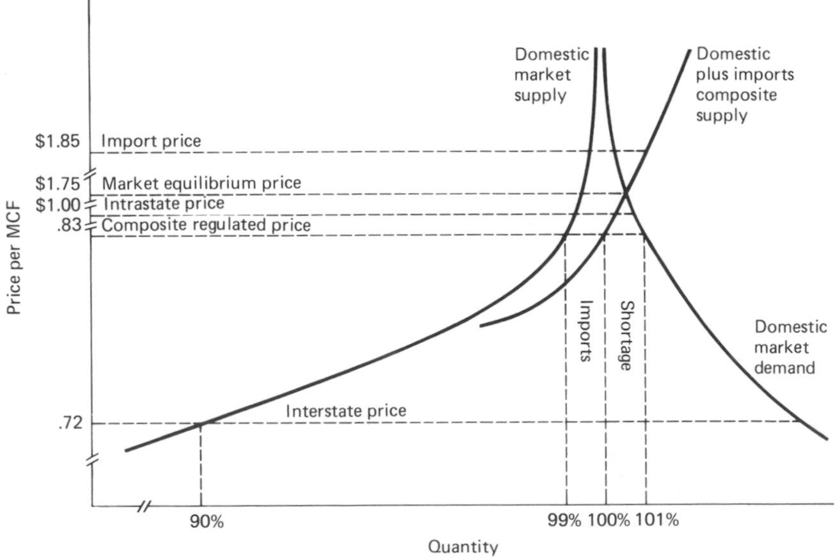

Figure 11.9. The U.S. Natural Gas Market, 1977. The import price is based on weighted imports from Canada and Algeria.

petroleum and natural gas actually fell throughout most of the 1950s and 1960s.

Second, regulated domestic price restraints and international production subsidies accelerated the growth of U.S. dependence on imported supplies of oil. As long as OPEC did not succeed in raising the real price of oil, the U.S. economy could enjoy relative stability in the price of energy. Moreover, it could do so with few adverse effects on the distribution of income, and with the illusions of a pro-competitive policy. Yet the OPEC decisions of the 1970s showed just how tenuous the notions of competition, the stability of prices, and the distribution of income could be when imported energy dependence reached a significant enough level.

Finally, petroleum energy pricing has biased the economy toward energy-intensive activities in general and toward petroleum and natural gas consumption in particular. Market price incentives to conserve, to minimize environmental pollution, and to develop alternative synthetic and renewable energy technologies could hardly exist as long as the consumption of petroleum and natural gas was as subsidized as it had become. Though recent increases in the real prices of these resources have tended to reduce part of this imbalance, in the nearterm at least, the potential for recurring energy crises still remains.

11.4. SUMMARY

The pricing of petroleum and natural gas resources in the United States has been influenced by a wide range of taxes, subsidies, and controls. As noted in chapter 9, these industries are not perfectly competitive. At the same time, the particular fiscal choices that have been adopted have resulted in peculiar consequences far removed from pro-competitive considerations.

In the case of petroleum, the pricing of crude oil and refined products has benefitted from a variety of fiscal incentives, including the percentage-depletion allowance, the deductibility of intangible drilling expenses, the foreign tax credit, import quotas, and the domestic regulation of prices and production. Given the differential benefits of these mechanisms for domestic and international operations, they have encouraged the expansion of overseas exploration and production and the acceleration of domestic consumption through reduced prices to consumers below their opportunity costs of production and they have facilitated the operational effectiveness of OPEC by lowering the domestic and world price elasticities of demand for petroleum. The rise of international dependence and the adverse consequences for the U.S. balance of payments and domestic rates of inflation have created pressures for altering these incentives, resulting most recently in the deregulation of domestic petroleum pricing and the imposition of a windfall profits tax to promote conservation and to reduce international dependence.

Though largely unaffected by international markets, the pricing of natural gas in the United States has been influenced substantially by fiscal incentives and regulation. The production of natural gas has benefitted from many of the same fiscal incentives as has petroleum. At the same time, regulation at the national and state levels has led periodically to shortages and allied disruptions. The net effect of these combined incentives has been to accelerate the domestic consumption of this depletable energy resource beyond what would otherwise be the case. As in the case of petroleum, recent legislation has resulted in real increases in its price, thereby eliminating some of the historical market imbalances, promoting a more technically efficient use of natural gas, and forestalling the potential emergence of international natural gas dependence on the scale that has influenced the production and marketing of petroleum.

Any increase in the price of petroleum or natural gas can have inflationary, windfall, and energy-conserving consequences. What remains to be examined is the extent to which these consequences of higher energy prices can be reconciled within the context of efficient energy choices, a matter which is examined in the following chapters.

SUGGESTED READINGS

Brannon, Gerard M. *Energy Taxes and Subsidies*. Report to the Energy Policy Project of the Ford Foundation. Cambridge, Mass.: Ballinger Publishing Co., 1975.

Edens, David G. *Oil and Development in the Middle East*. New York: Praeger Publishers, 1979.

Abdel-Fadil, Mahmoud, ed. *Papers on the Economics of Oil: A Producer's View*. London: Oxford University Press, 1979.

Kalter, R. J., and Vogely, W. A., *Energy Supply and Government Policy*. Ithaca: Cornell University Press, 1976.

Landis, Robin C., and Klass, Michael W. *OPEC: Policy Implications for the United States*. New York: Praeger Publishers, 1980.

MacAvoy, Paul W., and Pindyck, Robert S. *The Economics of the Natural Gas Shortage, 1960–1980*. New York: Elsevier North-Holland Publishing Co., 1975.

McDonald, Stephen L. *Petroleum Conservation in the United States Economy*. Baltimore: Johns Hopkins Press, 1971.

12

THE PRICING OF ELECTRICITY AND ALTERNATIVE ENERGY RESOURCES

In an economy dependent on depletable energy resources, as more of those resources are consumed over time, the real price must rise. As noted in earlier chapters, given that the U.S. and the world economies depend substantially on depletable energy resources, at some point rising real prices of these resources will bring about two types of consequences. One is that other things equal, the relative prices of depletable energy resources will bring about a shift from those that are closer to exhaustion to those that are less so, as in a shift from petroleum and natural gas to conventional and synthetic fuels from coal, shale oil, and tar sands. At the same time, rising real prices of these conventional and alternative depletable energy resources will also make renewable energy resource technologies economically more competitive. The other consequence is that depending on the relative costs of depletable and renewable energy technologies, conservation will become competitive as a third alternative resource.

Now that we have looked at the degree of competition in energy markets, at the nature of energy demand, and at the determinants of petroleum and natural gas pricing, let us consider the pricing of alternative energy resources. As we will see, the questions of competition, externalities, energy security, and the effects of relative energy prices on the distribution of income are important considerations which enter into the determination of the prices of these alternative energy resources. Because electricity is the principal consumer of conventional coal and nuclear energy, we can begin with an examination of the various ways that it is priced and look at some of the implications of these pricing mechanisms for energy policy choices.

12.1. THE PRICING OF ELECTRICAL ENERGY

As noted in chapter 4, the production of commercial electricity claims over one-quarter of all U.S. primary energy consumption. Moreover, until the Arab OPEC embargo of 1973, electricity consumption in the United States grew at annual rates approximately twice the overall rate of growth of primary energy end-use alternatives. Because decisions concerning the production and pricing of electricity are made largely by federal and state authorities, electricity's role in the economy depends substantially on the ways in which regulatory decisions can affect its relative price.

The commercial electricity industry is one of the most regulated industries in the United States. As figure 12.1 shows, electricity pricing and production decisions are shaped by direct and indirect controls imposed at the federal and state levels. A useful way of understanding the nature and consequences of regulation is to begin with the retail pricing of electricity and then to trace the determinants of this pricing to differences in types of fuels and electricity-generation technologies.

Underlying many forms of regulation is the notion of natural monopoly. As noted in chapter 9, a natural monopoly exists where declining average costs are found over the dominant, if not exclusive, range of production. Under this condition, it is "natural" to permit a monopoly firm to operate, since this configuration would result in the economically most efficient pattern of production. However, in order to prevent the adverse monopolistic behavior which might otherwise result, such natural monopolies should also be regulated according to competitive-equivalent economic conditions (see figure 12.2). An unregulated monopolistic firm would maximize its profits by adopting a level of output at q_m and a price of p_m, which would give it profits of $p_m abp_c$. Were the firm to be regulated, the adoption of output level q_n and price p_c would result in not only an output increment equal to $q_n - q_m$ but also a lowering of average cost from v to d. Moreover, when this principle is combined with the imposition of constraints designed to reduce external costs and benefits, regulated utilities could be made to conform even more to the ideal conditions of a perfectly competitive economy. Thus, the rationale for regulation is essentially that of economic efficiency, regardless of the type of utility ownership involved. Whether this principle is upheld in fact depends on the nature of costs and the demand for electricity.

For a given level of demand, electricity costs can be classified into three basic segments: generation, transmission, and distribution. Table 12.1 lists sample data based on this classification for the United States in the early 1970s and underlines the significance of capital-intensive fixed costs in the generation of electricity. For example, even if we do not include equipment costs associated with electricity generation, fixed costs associated with transmission and distribution can account for between one-half and two-thirds of delivered electricity costs. Consequently, the average and marginal costs which underlie these figures will be influenced at least as much by the cost of capital equipment as they are by the fuel essential to the generation of electricity.

In chapter 7 we saw how the consumption of electricity tends to vary significantly according to the time of day, the day of the week, or the season of the year. If a relatively invariant pricing structure is adopted for a given period of time, then utilities must keep in reserve a considerable degree of spare capacity not only to service baseload consumption requirements but also to satisfy

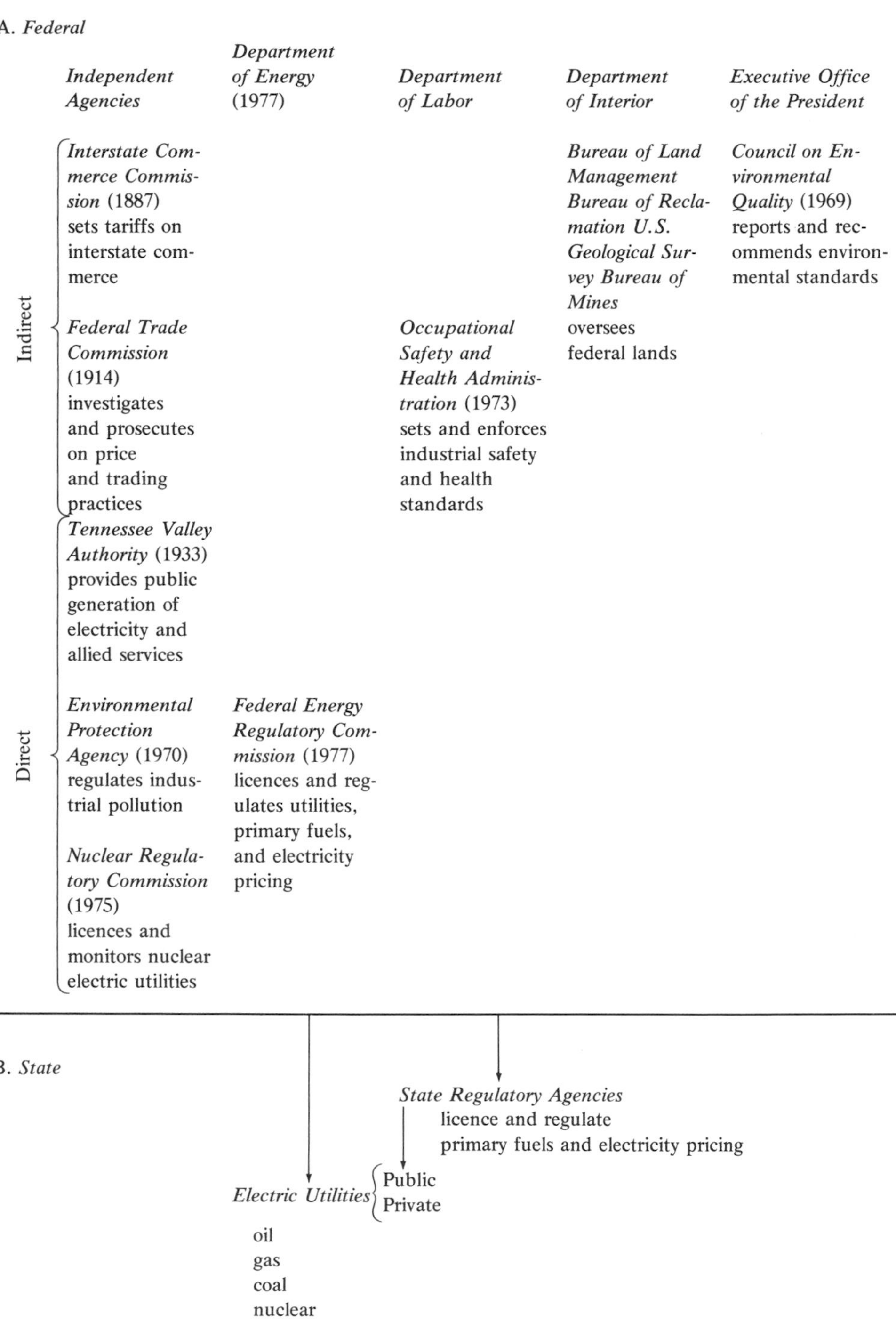

Figure 12.1. Regulatory Dimensions of Electric Utility Pricing

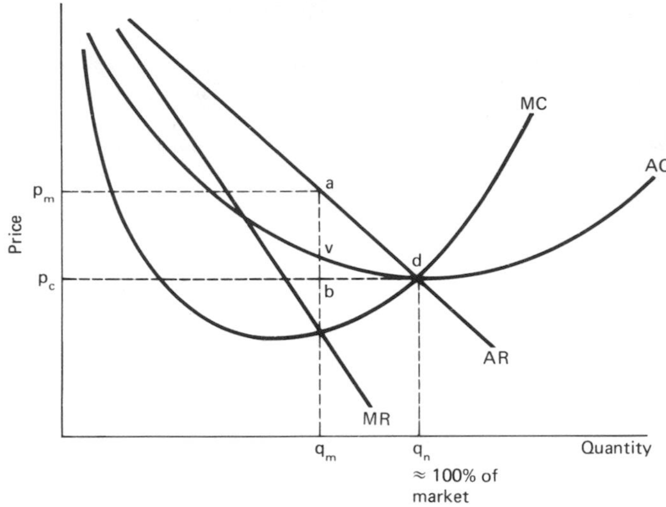

Figure 12.2. Pricing Choices under Natural Monopoly

any incremental variations in demand. Moreover, given that electricity cannot be stored except by conversion to an alternative energy stock, the capital-intensive nature of electrical costs is easier still to understand.

At this point, one fundamental characteristic of electricity generation is clear: though there are alternative generating technologies with differing degrees of thermodynamic efficiency, optimum economic efficiency with a given technology will depend largely on the selection of prices in response to particular patterns of demand. Four principal pricing systems merit elabora-

Table 12.1. Representative Cost Components of Electricity Bought from U.S. Private Utilities, 1972

Item	Residential and Commercial Consumers		Industrial Consumers	
	(cents/kwh)	(%)	(cents/kwh)	(%)
Transmission equipment	0.45¢	20%	0.43¢	34%
Distribution equipment	0.58	26	0.06	5
Operation and maintenance of transmission and distribution equipment	0.50	22	0.08	6
Total transmission and distribution	1.54	69	0.57	45
Electricity generation (fuel and equipment)	0.69	31	0.69	55
Delivered total cost	2.23	100	1.26	100
Average revenue	2.37		1.17	

Source: M. L. Baughman and D. J. Bottaro, "Electric Power Transmission and Distribution Systems: Costs and Their Allocation," National Science Foundation, RANN 75-107 (Austin: Center for Energy Studies, University of Texas, July 1975).

Table 12.2. Illustration of Regulated Electricity Rates

Customers	Winter	Summer
Residential[a]		
Customer charge per month	$3.33	$3.33
Energy charge per month		
0–359 kwh	$0.07788 / kwh	$0.09288 / kwh
360–780 kwh	$0.05460 / kwh	$0.09033 / kwh
Commercial and industrial[b]		
Demand charge per month[c]		
0–100 kw	$12.49	$15.49
101–200 kw	$11.40	$14.40
201–9,700 kw	$10.73	$13.73
9,701–15,000 kw	$10.25	$13.25
Excess over 25,000 kw	$ 9.25	$12.25
Energy charge per month		
0–40,000 kwh	$0.0506 / kwh	$0.0506 / kwh
40,000–1,460,000 kwh	$0.0427 / kwh	$0.0427 / kwh
Excess of 1,500,000 kwh	$0.0407 / kwh	$0.0407 / kwh

Source: Consolidated Edison Company of New York, Public Service Commission no. 8—Electricity service classifications 1 (Residential and Religious) and 4 (Commercial and Industrial—Redistribution), both effective 11 August 1979.

[a]Declining-block tariff

[b]Two-part, declining-block tariff

[c]Low tension only

tion in some detail, since they cover both past and evolving policies adopted by various regulatory authorities.

The simplest and one of the oldest systems of regulated pricing is to adopt a uniform price of electricity regardless of the variation in consumption. Under such a system, utilities would be permitted to charge a single unit price to all customers, with revisions based on long-run average costs and average long-run demand. Since this type of policy would reflect only the long run, it would usually be inefficient in the short run, given the demand variations already noted. Consequently, it serves mostly as a point of departure rather than as an example of widespread practice.

A second, and more typical, system of pricing adopted by regulatory authorities is to use declining-block, two-part tariffs and what economists refer to as third-degree price discrimination.[1] A typical example of this configura-

[1]Economists generally have classified price discrimination into three categories. Price discrimination of the first degree exists when a customer pays a different price for each unit of a good that is purchased, which eliminates, in theory at least, any consumer surplus. This type of discrimination is not generally practical to implement and is useful largely as a frame of reference. A more common practice is price discrimination of the second degree, which exists when a consumer is charged a different price for each block of units of a product, as occurs in declining-block and two-part tariff structures of the kind illustrated in table 12.2. Price discrimination of the third degree exists when different consumers are charged different prices on a group market basis, as occurs in the pricing of electricity to industrial versus residential consumers. Third-degree price discrimination was so identified first by A. C. Pigou, *The Economics of Welfare*, 4th ed. (London: Macmillan Publishing Co., 1950).

tion is presented in table 12.2. Residential customers are charged according to a declining-block tariff for incremental consumption. A two-part tariff for industrial and commercial customers is similar to the declining-block system, except that the lower unit cost charge is based also on a customer's consumption capacity. When cheaper rates for larger capacity are combined with a declining-block tariff, such as in table 12.2, the net effect is clearly one of systematic price discrimination in favor of commercial and industrial customers over residential consumers.

A logical question which arises from looking at this second type of electricity pricing is whether it is in any way more efficient than the constant tariff system. The answer is yes, though the gain in efficiency is not as substantial as could be obtained by adopting other alternatives. To see how the second type of pricing is more efficient than the first, we need to answer two specific questions: (1) At what stage of production are the economic gains to be found within a declining price-rate structure? and (2) to that extent is efficiency enhanced by systematic price discrimination.

A declining-block structure, and its commercial and industrial counterpart, the two-part tariff, can be more efficient than a constant rate structure in that it induces customers to consume at a rate sufficiently large to bring about lower average transmission and distribution costs as utilities operate closer to capacity.[2] The difficulty with this pattern, however, is that it encourages ever-expanding consumption with little regard for the variation in costs from reserve generating units which must be kept operable on a stand-by basis. Consequently, although a declining-block structure could result in lower transmission and distribution costs, part of the economic gain at this stage of production would be dissipated because utilities would still have an incentive to increase stand-by generating capacity. Thus, a declining-block structure would do little to relieve the capital-intensive nature of the industry. The remaining source of efficiency is systematic price discrimination of the third degree.

The economic basis for systematic price discrimination is found directly in differences in the elasticity of demand for electricity among principal classes of consumers. As the demand studies of chapter 10 generally confirm, though the overall demand for electricity tends to be price-inelastic, the own-price elasticity of demand of industrial consumers tends to be relatively higher than the own-price elasticity of demand among residential and commercial users. Moreover, the underlying reasons for these differences in the elasticity of demand are not difficult to fathom: because energy is a significant production cost in the industrial sector, consumers will choose technologies and fuels

[2]This will be seen more clearly in reference to alternative electricity technologies, but table 12.1 suggests one obvious reason for declining-block, two-part tariffs: transmission and distribution costs account for at least half of total delivered costs of electricity, and any pricing that could increase the utilization rate of the fixed capital structures could also lower up to a point delivered average costs. Declining-block, two-part traiffs are also an underlying factor in the application of rate-of-return regulation within the industry, though there is now a shift toward marginal-cost pricing.

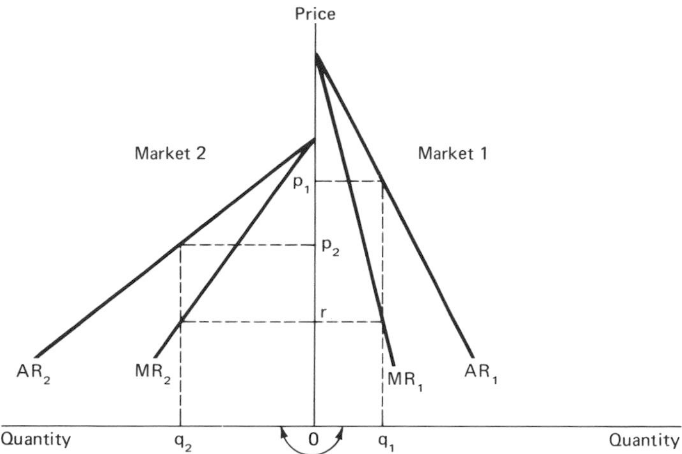

Figure 12.3. Allocation of Production under Price Discrimination

that have the lowest relative costs, particularly in that technological and energy substitution possibilities may be substantial over time. In contrast, residential customers tend to spend a relatively smaller share of their incomes on electricity, and to face fewer substitution opportunities, than do industrial consumers.

A geometric formulation of systematic price discrimination is presented in figure 12.3. Consumers in market 1 exhibit a relatively inelastic demand in comparison with consumers in market 2. Absent any regulatory constraint, a firm would maximize its profits by the equalization of marginal revenues and marginal costs in each market, charging p_1 and producing q_1 in market 1 and charging p_2 and producing q_2 in market 2. However, if we now recall the natural monopoly conditions illustrated in figure 12.2 and the accompanying rationale for regulation, a somewhat modified pricing structure might be imposed. In figure 12.4, both markets under price discrimination are displayed within the first quadrant, along with their summed average- and marginal-revenue curves. Unregulated third-degree price discrimination would result in the utility's adoption of a production level of q_m, which is where its summed marginal-revenue curve intersects its marginal cost curve.[3] Since natural monopoly conditions similar to those illustrated in figure 12.2 may be present, regulatory authorities could achieve a larger total level of production at q'_m, lower the utility's average cost from v to d, and still permit systematic discrimi-

[3]Unregulated profits can be expressed as: $\pi = p_1q_1 + p_2q_2 - c(q)$. Changes in profits are $(\partial\pi/\partial q_1) = (\partial(p_1q_1)/\partial q_1) - (\partial c(q)/\partial q_1) = (d(p_1q_1/dq_1) - (dc(q)/dq)(\partial q/\partial q_1) = (d(p_1q_1)/dq_1) - (dc(q)/dq) = 0$ and $(\partial\pi/\partial q_2) = (\partial(p_2q_2)/\partial q_2) - (\partial c(q)/(\partial q_2) = d(p_2q_2)/dq_2) - (dc(q)/dq)(\partial q/\partial q_2) = (d(p_2q_2)/dq_2) - (dc(q)/dq) = 0$. For profits to be at a maximum, $(d(p_1q_1/dq_1) = (d(p_2q_2)/dq_2) = (dc(q)/dq)$, i.e., $MR_1 = MR_2 = MC$. Since $MR_1 = p_1(1 - (1/\epsilon_1))$, $MR_2 = p_2(1 - (1/\epsilon_2))$, then $p_1/p_2 = (1 - (1/\epsilon_2))/(1 - (1/\epsilon_1))$, where ϵ is the price elasticity of demand coefficient of the respective market.

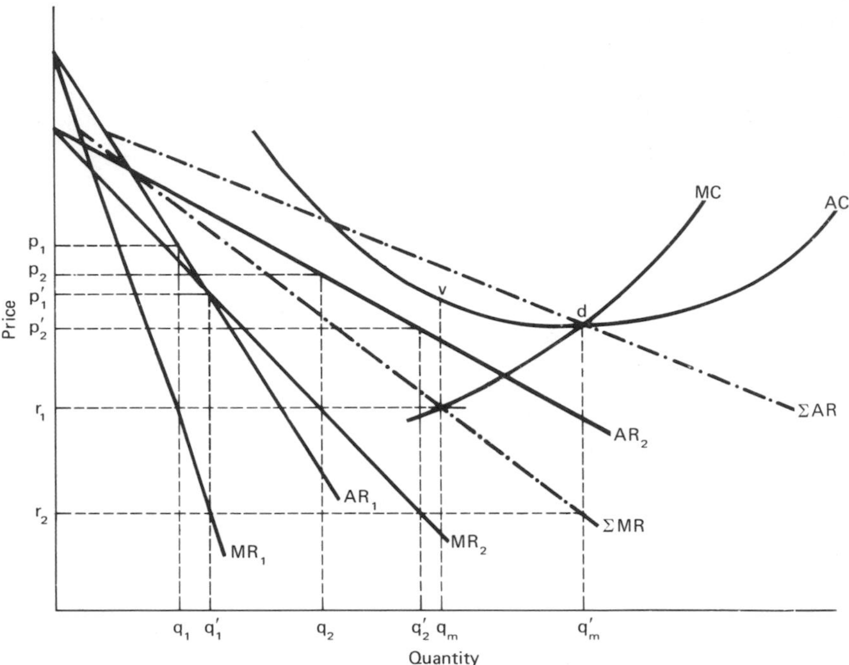

Figure 12.4. Price Discrimination under Regulatory Constraint

nation.[4] Market 1 would have a q_1' level of production priced at p_1', and market 2 would have an even lower price at p_2' corresponding to its expanded level of production at q_2'.

A third system of regulated utility pricing combines declining-block, two-part tariffs and market discrimination with an allowance for peak-load consumption. As already noted, because of variations in electricity demand, utilities often must keep considerable reserve capacity on hand. One pattern of this variation in demand is the consumption of higher amounts of electricity during the summer period than during the winter, especially for such appliances as air conditioners in the residential and industrial sectors. What this variation in demand represents is a substantial difference in the cost of generation, since the incremental electricity production during the peak-load period will come from units that otherwise would be idle. Peak-load pricing would thus reflect the baseload cost of generation and the higher marginal cost of generation from stand-by units. Typical of this pattern is the pricing

[4]Obviously, several refinements could be elaborated on even within this type of pricing. One important conclusion is that if pricing under regulation can not be set equal to marginal costs, then some form of price discrimination may be necessary to the attainment of economic efficiency. For an elaboration on this point, see William J. Baumol and D. J. Bradford, "Optimal Departures from Marginal Cost Pricing," *American Economic Review* 60 (June 1970):265–83.

differential between the summer and winter periods for residential, commercial, and industrial customers illustrated in table 12.2.

The last system of electrical utility pricing combines the third type with the use of time-of-day and time-of-week variations. Under this system, prices are allowed to reflect even more precisely the marginal costs of generation and distribution, with daytime and during-the-week rates generally higher than nighttime and weekend rates. An example of this type of pricing is shown in table 12.3. Taken together, the various elements of this fourth pricing system would lead to a greater degree of economic efficiency in the electric utility industry than has been the case in the past. This would help to lessen the variations in consumption, thereby reducing some of the capital requirements so characteristic of the industry. Since marginal-cost pricing has not necessarily been the basis for specific regulatory decisions, before we look at the fuels and technologies now in use, we need to identify more closely the nature of nonmarginal cost pricing and its significance to the performance of regulated electrical utilities.

There is at present no comprehensive theory that could be used to explain the actual behavior of regulated industries. Political considerations do play a role in regulatory decisions, to be sure, as a numer of recent studies have shown. Yet with or without political pressure, there is no a priori basis for assuming that regulatory agencies will adopt economically efficient pricing choices, particularly if natural monopoly conditions are present or where information on efficient choices may be inadequate.[5] Without presuming to construct a comprehensive theory of regulation, we can at least point out some of the complexities of utility rate determination by looking at two theories of

Table 12.3. Representative Time-of-Day Electricity Rates

Commercial and Industrial Customers[a]	Rate
Transmission	$10.70 / kw
Primary distribution	6.39 / kw
Energy generation	
Peak hours[b]	0.0387 / kwh
Off-peak hours[c]	0.0274 / kwh

Source: Consolidated Edison Company of New York, Public Service Commission no. 8—Electricity Service Classification 4 (Commercial and Industrial—Redistribution), effective 30 August 1979.

[a]Low tension only

[b]Monday through Friday, 8:00 A.M.–10:00 P.M.

[c]All other hours

[5]See. R. L. Hagerman and B. T. Ratchford, "Some Determinants of Allowed Rates of Return on Equity to Electric Utilities," *Bell Journal of Economics* 9 (Autumn 1978):46–55; W. J. Baumol and A. G. Walten, "Full Costing, Competition, and Regulatory Practice," *Yale Law Journal* 82 (March 1973):639–55; and Elizabeth E. Bailey, *Economic Theory of Regulatory Constraint* (Lexington, Mass.: Lexington Books, 1973).

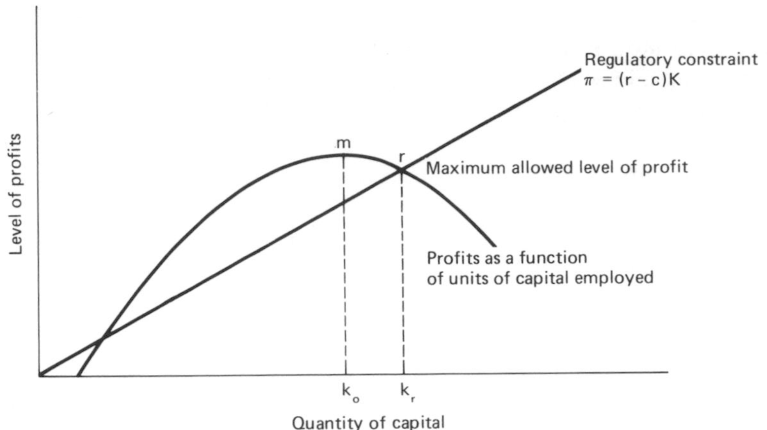

Figure 12.5. Input Distortions under Utility Regulation

economic behavior: the Averch-Johnson hypothesis and what Harvey Leibenstein has labeled X-inefficiency.[6]

The Averch-Johnson hypothesis states that regulated firms such as electric utilities are constrained by rate-of-return policies which distort the relative costs of inputs and that this distortion leads firms to adopt an inefficient combination of resources which results in higher costs and prices to the public. The argument rests on the premise that regulatory authorities are prone to favor the interests of the regulated industries and generally permit a rate of return above what would be found in a competitive, risk-equivalent non-regulated industry. In turn, regulated utilities then perceive capital as relatively inexpensive and adopt a capital-intensive, inefficient pattern of production.

A diagrammatic formulation of the Averch-Johnson hypothesis is presented in figure 12.5. Conventional economic theory states that an unregulated firm will maximize its profits by choosing that combination of inputs in which the marginal-revenue product of each input is equal to its price. For a given production function, the unregulated optimal quantity of capital equipment would be at k_0, since this is the level corresponding to the maximum level of profits. Once regulation is imposed, the allowed rate of return on capital is set at a level, r, which will tend to be greater than its competitive cost, c. Given the regulated differential in the price of capital, $r - c$, utilities now expand their use of the resource up to k_r, which corresponds to the firm's regulated rate of return, r, In the reference terms of figure 12.4, the Averch-Johnson effect would be expressed as an upward shift in the utility's cost curves, which would thereby reduce the range of regulatory choices until such time as a shift in demand were to occur.

[6]Harvey Averch and Leland L. Johnson, "Behavior of the Firm under Regulatory Constraint," *American Economic Review* 53 (December 1962):1052–69; and Harvey Leibenstein, "Allocative Efficiency versus 'X-Efficiency,' " *ibid.*, 55 (June 1966):392–415.

Though it may have similar consequences for costs and prices, X-inefficiency does not depend directly on the existence of an Averch-Johnson type of regulatory constraint. Instead, X-inefficiency encompasses a broader range of situations in which nonoptimizing behavior can arise and thereby increase the costs of production above what a traditional profit-maximizing firm would experience. As Leibenstein has argued, in the absence of more complete information and a sufficient level of motivation, managers of firms may adopt incomplete contracts for resources which permit a variety of suboptimal patterns of behavior; moreover, the production function that a firm employs may not be completely known; and finally, not all inputs may be marketed, or even if they are, they may not be marketed on equal terms to all buyers. In more direct terms, X-inefficiency implies that the notion that either a regulatory commission or the management of a utility could achieve economic efficiency in the fullest technical and allocative sense may not be borne out in practice.

Studies of both Averch-Johnson bias and X-inefficiency provide mixed evidence on the extent of these distortions in the behavior of firms. Evidence in support of the Averch-Johnson overcapitalization bias has been reported by Courville (1974) and Spann (1974).[7] At the same time, Smithson (1978) and Baron and Taggart (1977) noted that when allowance is made for adjustment lags, the overcapitalization phenomenon may not exist at all and undercapitalization may be present.[8] Baumol and Klevorick (1970) went even further in an early assessment of the literature, suggesting that Averch-Johnson bias may not be as significant as X-inefficiency, especially if firms pursue non-profit-maximizing objectives such as sales maximization.[9] X-inefficiency is more difficult to measure, but Primeaux (1977) and Shen (1973) report evidence that it does exist, particularly in industries where competition may be limited.[10] In the reference terms of the four pricing systems already noted, and the extent of their use, because electric utilities have relied until recently largely on nonmarginal cost-pricing choices, the general pattern within the

[7]Leon Courville, "Regulation and Efficiency in the Electric Utility Industry," *Bell Journal of Economics and Management Science* 5 (Spring 1974):53–74; Robert M. Spann, "Rate of Return Regulation and Efficiency in Production: An Empirical Test of Regulatory Effects," *Bell Journal of Economics* 6 (Spring 1975):111-26.

[8]C. W. Smithson, "The Degree of Regulation and the Monopoly Firm: Further Empirical Evidence," *Southern Economic Journal* 44 (January 1978):568-80; D. P. Baron and R. A. Taggart, "A Model of Regulation under Uncertainty and a Test of Regulatory Bias," *Bell Journal of Economics* 8 (Spring 1977):151-67.

[9]William J. Baumol and Alvin K. Klevorick, "Input Choices and Rate-of-Return-Regulation: An Overview of the Discussion," *Bell Journal of Economics and Management Science* 1 (Autumn 1970):162–90. See also Paul L. Joskow, "Pricing Decisions of Regulated Firms: A Behavioral Approach," *ibid.*, 4 (Spring 1973):118–40.

[10]Walter J. Primeaux, Jr., "An Assessment of X-Efficiency Gained through Competition," *Review of Economics and Statistics* 59 (February 1977):105–7; Tsung-Yuen Shen, "Technology, Diffusion, Substitution, and X-Efficiency," *Econometrica* 41 (March 1973):263–84. See also Harvey Leibenstein, "X-Inefficiency Xists—Reply to an Xorcist," *American Economic Review* 68 (March 1978):203–11; and P. L. Joskow and R. G. Noll, "Regulation in Theory and Practice: An Overview," Working Paper 218 (Cambridge, Mass.: MIT Department of Economics, April 1978).

industry has been one of greater capitalization than otherwise would have occurred, regardless of the sources of inefficiency we may adduce.

Taken together, what do the various mechanisms of electricity pricing imply for energy policy choices? Had the regulatory commissions and utilities known the precise contours of their average and marginal costs at each and every moment in time, and had they been able to translate these cost variations into corresponding prices, there would be a much wider variation in electric rates per unit of time than has been the case in the past. Such variations would have three basic consequences. First, the need for excess capacity by utilities would be reduced to some extent, which over time could restrain the growth of the industry's long-run average cost beyond what it would be otherwise. This would occur because consumers would become much more sensitive to differences in electricity costs per unit of time and would make some corresponding degree of adjustment in consumption, given prevailing elasticities of demand. Second, since the variation in prices needed to match electricity consumption more closely to capacity could be substantial, there would undoubtedly be some effect on the distribution of income, with poorer individuals affected more adversely than the rich, since they would have fewer opportunities to adjust to changes in these prices. If we were interested in preserving the preexisting distribution of income, then there would be some need to adjust the incidence of taxation to reflect these changes. Finally, even under conditions of uncertainty, because marginal-cost principles could lead to a wider variation in pricing, central-station conventional electricity technology might not be as competitive in the future as many decentralized alternatives. Indeed, as we will see, co-generation based on conventional fuels and on renewable energy technologies could be far more competitive under a regime of fully distributed marginal costs, particularly in handling peak-load demand.

Thus far, none of the discussion of the pricing of electrical energy has addressed the issues of externalities and resource depletion. To address these issues, we need to shift the focus from the determinants of pricing at the consumer level to the types of fuels and generation technologies employed. Although petroleum, natural gas, and hydropower systems fall within this range, most of our attention will be devoted to coal and nuclear energy, because these two resources account for approximately three-fifths of all primary energy used to generate electricity in the United States and because until recently nuclear energy was projected to account for the bulk of incremental generation capacity in the coming decades.

12.1.1. The Pricing of Coal-Based Electricity Generation

With conventional technology, any fuel that is suitable for the production of steam is a theoretical competitor in the electricity industry. What makes a particular fuel such as coal or nuclear energy an actual competitor is, of course, its price relative to that of the next available alternatives. Given the recent price increases in petroleum and natural gas discussed in chapter 11, it is perhaps not surprising that coal and nuclear energy have come to be viewed as the principal near-term resources for the generation of electricity. Yet the degree of competition between coal and nuclear energy, and between these resources and other alternatives, is very much affected by the determination of their own prices as well.

Like petroleum and natural gas pricing, the pricing of coal is influenced by both market competition and regulatory constraints. Though less than perfectly competitive, coal firms must still contend not only with each other in a given region but also with competing fuels. Yet, even with inter-firm and inter-fuel competition, coal is subject to widespread regulation by various federal and state agencies. Much of this regulation derives less from a concern for competition than from a concern for the significant external costs associated with its production and consumption.

Coal is dirty. Even with the mechanization technologies noted in chapter 5, coal is often hazardous to extract, and it frequently contains substantial impurities such as sulfur and nitrogen oxides. When coal is burned by an electric utility or by any other consumer, these impurities are ejected into the atmosphere along with particulate residues associated with the relatively low thermodynamic efficiencies of conventional combustion technologies. The result is smog and, where precipitation occurs, acid rain. In fact, so substantial is the potential pollution from the burning of coal that it could produce a greenhouse effect.[11] Under such conditions, the burning of coal and similar fuels increases the proportion of carbon dioxide in the atmosphere. During the day, short-wave radiation from the sun continues to reach the earth at its usual rate, but when it is transformed to heat on the earth's surface, much of the re-radiated infrared energy is absorbed by the carbon dioxide in the atmosphere, thereby increasing the average temperature on earth. Increasing the temperature on earth by only a few degrees could bring about major climatic changes, including the melting of polar ice caps, substantial flooding of lowlands, and a significant increase in respiratory diseases.

Though potentially destructive, the greenhouse effect does not need to be an inevitable consequence of the continued use of coal. Pollution can be minimized by an appropriate adjustment in the price of coal. Of the two principal means by which this minimization of pollution could be accomplished, taxation and regulation, the latter has been the most widely used thus far in the U.S. economy. Rather than assess the relative merits of these two approaches at this point, we can proceed initially with an enumeration of the specific ways in which regulation affects the pricing of coal and point out its significance to the containment of external costs.

Direct federal and state regulation of coal production and consumption is focused on three principal types of external costs: safety, health, and environmental. As figure 12.1 indicates, agencies such as the Department of Labor's Occupational Safety and Health Administration establish and promulgate standards affecting the safety and health of workers in industry. These stan-

[11]For further analysis, see George M. Woodwell, "The Carbon Dioxide Question," *Scientific American* 242 (January 1978):34–43; and U. Sigenthaler and H. Oeschger, "Predicting Future Atmospheric Carbon Dioxide Levels," *Science*, 27 January 1978; pp. 388–95.

dards include protective clothing requirements and equipment safeguards, and available evidence indicates that they have had an effect on lowering industrial accidents and sickness whose risks had hitherto been largely assumed by employees in relatively highly hazardous occupations such as coal mining. Similarly, by defining permissible impurity limits of coal to be consumed by utilities and by the establishment of emission standards for industrial firms, the Environmental Protection Agency and its state counterparts can also have an impact on the level of atmospheric and environmental pollution. Current EPA air-emissions standards stipulate an upper limit of 0.55 kilos (1.2 pounds) of sulfur dioxide, 0.014 kilos (0.03 pounds) of particulates, and 0.23–0.36 kilos (0.5–0.8 pounds) of nitrogen dioxide per million Btu's of fuel consumed.[12]

Another external cost of coal extraction is alteration of the environment, in particular its impact on alternative uses of land arising from strip-mining technologies and on water supply and quality. The cutting edge of this aspect of coal use is that strip mining using market prices alone with no accounting for environmental effects is generally far less expensive per ton of product than the older deep-mining methods, even when deep mining is as mechanized as strip mining. Investigations of coal pricing by Spore and Nephew (1974), Gordon (1976), Habicht (1974), and the National Academy of Sciences (1974) have pointed out the risks of noncontainment of the environmental cost of coal extraction and have made various proposals to solve the problem.[13] In turn, Congress and affected states have established standards for reclamation of coal fields, most notably with congressional passage of the Surface Mining Control and Reclamation Act of 1977.

Indirect regulation also affects the pricing of coal, though not with the specific objective of containing external costs. Perhaps the most prominent example in this context is the regulation of railroads. Given that coal mines may be at substantial distances from electric utilities, the price of delivered coal is affected by tariff decisions imposed on railroads and other less frequently used modes of transport by the Interstate Commerce Commission. It should also be noted in this context that decisions by the Interstate Commerce Commission could affect the use of unit trains discussed in chapter 5, particularly for noncaptive marketed production between mining firms and utilities. As to coal slurry pipelines still under consideration, any positive decision to

[12]U.S. Environmental Protection Agency, "Electric Utility Steam Generating Units: Proposed Standards of Performance and Announcement of Public Hearing on Proposed Standards," pt. 5, *Federal Register* 43 (19 September 1978):42154–84.

[13]Robert L. Spore and E. A. Nephew, "Opportunity Costs of Land Use: The Case of Coal Surface Mining," in *Energy: Demand, Conservation, and Institutional Problems*, ed. M. S. Macrakis (Cambridge, Mass.: MIT Press, 1974), pp. 209–24; Richard L. Gordon, "Coal—The Swing Fuel," in *Energy Supply and Government Policy*, ed. R. J. Kalter and W. A. Vogely (Ithaca: Cornell University Press, 1976), pp. 193–215; E. R. Habicht, Jr., "The Northern Plains Coal Resource—Case Study in Public Nonpolicy," in *Energy: Demand, Conservation, and Institutional Problems*, ed. M. S. Macrakis (Cambridge, Mass.: MIT Press, 1974), pp. 249–60; and National Academy of Sciences, *Rehabilitation Potential of Western Coal Lands*, Report to the Energy Policy Project of the Ford Foundation (Cambridge, Mass.: Ballinger Publishing Co., 1974).

proceed with their expansion would involve not only the Interstate Commerce Commission but also the Department of Energy, the Environmental Protection Agency, and the Department of the Interior, as well as associated state-level agencies.

A logical question at this point is, to what extent does direct regulation of coal production and consumption result in the internalization of its associated costs to society? As tables 12.4 and 12.5 show, in the United States at least, there has been a significant reduction in particulate emissions, as well as smaller improvements in sulfur oxide and volatile organic compound pollution in the atmosphere. At the same time, the level of nitrogen oxide and carbon monoxide emissions appears to have increased, resulting in a fairly mixed outcome. What these figures also suggest is that the continued use of coal even under regulation is still generating costs to society above those charged in the market.

It would be useful to know precisely how far below the costs to society as a whole the marketed costs of coal are. To be sure, research in this area has sought to measure these costs. Though estimates are subject to uncertainty, evidence from a recent study by William Ramsey (1979) shown in table 12.6 provides some indication of the order of magnitude of these costs. Since a more detailed methodology for assessing these costs is presented in chapter 13, we can conclude the discussion of external costs in coal pricing with one summary observation. As long as there are divergences between the marketed costs of coal and its total social costs, market pricing will lead at best to inefficient solutions regarding the allocation of resources in electricity generation and in other energy-consuming sectors of the economy.

As noted in chapter 11, one characteristic of a depletable energy resource is the element of user costs. The closer a resource approaches depletion, the greater the likelihood that this cost will be in absolute terms and as a propor-

Table 12.4. Emissions from Combustion in the United States, 1940–78
(in millions of metric tons per year)

Year	Particulates	Sulfur Oxides	Nitrogen Oxides	Volatile Organic Compounds	Carbon Monoxide
1940	27.1	21.5	7.9	19.1	85.4
1950	25.9	23.8	10.4	25.6	103.0
1960	25.3	23.8	14.0	31.6	127.4
1970	23.3	29.8	19.9	28.4	102.8
1974	17.9	28.5	21.8	27.2	99.8
1975	14.6	26.3	20.9	25.4	97.4
1976	14.1	27.5	22.5	27.1	103.1
1977	13.6	27.3	23.5	27.2	102.5
1978	12.5	27.1	23.4	27.8	102.3

Sources: U.S. Environmental Protection Agency, *Nationwide Air Pollutant Emission Trends, 1940–1970* (Washington, D.C.: U.S. Environmental Protection Agency, 1973); idem, *National Air Quality, Monitoring, and Emissions Trends Report* (Washington, D.C.: U.S. Environmental Protection Agency, 1978).

Table 12.5. Sources of Air-Pollution Emissions in the United States, 1978

Source	Particulates	Sulfur Oxides	Nitrogen Oxides	Volatile Organic Compounds	Carbon Monoxide
Transport	10.1%	3.0%	40.5%	38.6%	83.6%
Fuel combustion (stationary)	10.2	16.6	24.5	1.0	1.2
Industrial	49.3	15.1	3.5	49.0	7.5
Solid waste disposal	4.3	—	0.4	2.9	2.7
Electric utilities	20.3	65.3	30.7	42.5	78.1
Miscellaneous	5.8	—	0.4	8.5	5.0
Total	100.0	100.0	100.0	100.0	100.0
All energy use share	44.9%	100.0%	96.1%	42.5%	78.1%

Source: U.S. Environmental Protection Agency, *National Air Pollutant Emission Estimates, 1970–78* (Washington, D.C.: U.S. Government Printing Office, 1979).

[a]Based on the sum of transport, fuel-combustion, electric-utilities, and solid-waste shares.

tion of its private and social costs.[14] There is some indication that user costs have become significant in the cases of petroleum and natural gas, but current rates of coal consumption in relation to discovery and production rates are so low that user costs for this resource are not presently a significant element, at least using current technology. However, a more complicated picture emerges in the case of nuclear energy pricing.

12.1.2. The Pricing of Nuclear Energy Resources

The pricing of nuclear energy is determined by four principal factors. First, unlike coal, petroleum, natural gas, or hydropower, commercial nuclear energy is devoted exclusively to the production of electricity. Because nuclear energy has accounted for a relatively small share of overall primary energy used in the generation of electricity, the market for reactors has been limited at any given moment, which has constrained the ability of the industry to achieve economies of scale such as the standardization of parts which one finds in many established industries. Second, as noted in chapter 9, with but a handful of firms, the nuclear industry is far from being a perfectly competitive one. Yet although intra-industry competiton may be somewhat limited, nuclear power must contend with its principal alternative technologies, as well as comply with the extensive regulation to which the industry has become subjected. Third, nuclear energy is endowed with significant contingent external costs. These costs are in the form of health and environmental hazards arising from routine and reactor accident conditions and the risks of nuclear weapons proliferation and terrorism. Finally, as noted in chapter 6, historically the private market costs of nuclear energy have been lowered by a vast program of government subsidies. As we will see, these subsidies have been most pronounced in research and development assistance, and, through the Price-Anderson Act, in establishing accident-liability insurance coverage limits for

[14]A formal treatment of this question is presented under energy policy criteria of chapter 13.

Table 12.6. Private and Social Costs of Delivered Coal-Based Electricity for the United States, 1975

Item	Physical Cost per USW[a]	Imputed Monetary Cost[b]	Equivalent Monetary Cost in Terms of Typical Residential Monthly Electricity Bill, 1975[c]
1. Monthly residential electricity bill (actual)	—	—	$21.97 (per 681 Kwh)
2. Sulfur-oxides			
Fatalities	0–8,000	0–$699,630,991	0–0.70
Asthma attacks	0–12 million	0–10,494,360,000	0–10.94
Chronic respiratory attacks	0–5.5 million	0–4,809,915,000	0–4.81
Child respiratory attacks	0–2.5 million	0–10,931,625,000	0–10.93
Aggravated heart-lung symptoms[d]	0–55 million	0–857,290,921	0–0.86
3. Nitrogen-oxides fatalities	0–300	0–26,235,900	0–0.026
4. Property damage		200,000,000–2,000,000,000	0.20–2.00
5. Crop damage		200,000,000–630,000,000	0.20–0.70
6. Strip-mining damage		150,000,000–600,000,000	0.15–0.60
7. Rail transport fatalities	200–500	17,490,600–43,726,500	0.0174–0.0437
8. Mining fatalities	0–350	0–30,608,550	0–0.0306
9. Mining nonfatal accidents	0–40,000	0–1,749,060,000	0–1.749
10. Total social costs per monthly bill			22.41–55.36
11. Total social costs per kilowatt-hour of electricity			0.032907–0.081292
12. Total social costs per million Btu's			$9.64–23.82

Source: William Ramsey, *Unpaid Costs of Electrical Energy* (Baltimore: Johns Hopkins University Press for Resources for the Future, 1979).

Note: Cost comparisons are average cost equivalent. They do not reflect nonlinearities implicit in marginal cost relationships such as exponential increases in atmospheric pollution associated with a substantial expansion in coal production.

[a] One USW is equal to 2 trillion kilowatt-hours of electricity, the amount of power generated by all means in the United States in 1975. Since approximately one-half of all electricity during that year was generated by coal, monetary estimates have been adjusted accordingly by Ramsey in the cases of property, crop, and strip-mining damage. Other monetary estimates are derived from Ramsey's physical cost per USW data and translated accordingly into the typical residential monthly bill.

[b] Imputed monetary costs are based on the present value of per capita national income of $5,689 per year, discounted at 5 percent over a thirty-year period, or $87,453 per capita, and this figure was used in the valuation of all per capita fatalities. For asthma and chronic respiratory attacks, 1 percent of the present value of per capita national income was used. For child respiratory attacks, 5 percent of per capita national income was used, and for nonfatal mining accidents, 50 percent of discounted per capita national income was used.

[c] Following Ramsey, a conversion ratio of $2 billion per USW to $2.00 per average monthly electric bill was used to express total imputed social costs in these terms. The base-line average residential monthly bill for 1975 was derived from an average residential monthly level of electricity consumption of 681 kilowatt-hours, a figure Ramsey took, from figures supplied by the Edison Electric Institute (pp. 22, 31). Per-kilowatt-hour electricity costs are derived from this base-line level of consumption. None of these costs reflects the discounted value of increases in real national income per capita, insurance, hospitalization, or related market and nonmarket expenses incurred by individuals, families, or affected institutions, including the operating costs of government regulatory agencies themselves. Since they refer only to the direct opportunity costs of the present value of constant-dollar per capita national income, they are likely to represent an underestimate of the range of social costs.

[d] In person-days

nuclear electric utilities below what would be the case under a purely private market insurance program.

A useful way to integrate the economic determinants of nuclear energy into a unified discussion of pricing is to use a systematic reference to the various stages of the nuclear fuel cycle. As table 12.1 shows, the price of delivered electricity from the current mix of technologies in the U.S. economy is dominated essentially by transmission and distribution expenditures, with plant generating and fuel components accounting typically for less than half of total costs. So it is with nuclear energy. What distinguishes the marketed price of nuclear-based electricity from its alternatives is that generation costs are based predominantly on capital construction and operating expenditures rather than on fuel, as table 12.7 shows. For example, if we use the national average estimates, fuel and fuel inventories account for between one-quarter and one-third of nuclear generating costs, whereas in the case of coal-based electricity, fuel accounts for from 40 percent to just under 50 percent of its generating costs.

Table 12.7 points to another important characteristic of nuclear electricity pricing. Since fuel accounts for a relatively smaller share of nuclear generating costs than it does in the case of conventional coal technology, the competitive position of nuclear electricity depends largely on the interest charged for capital construction. Before we look at differences in the pricing of fuel, therefore, it is important to consider first the differences in capital-generating technologies.

Table 12.8 provides a profile of overnight capital cost comparisons between a conventional light water nuclear reactor steam plant and two competing versions of coal-based systems. What is important to note from these esti-

Table 12.7. National Average and Regional Variations in Coal and Nuclear Electricity-Generating Costs for 1985
(in 1975 mills per kwh)

	Coal		Nuclear	
Cost Item	National Average	Regional Variation	National Average	Regional Variation
Capital costs				
At 10%	7.9	7.2–8.6	9.6	8.8–10.8
At 15%	11.9	10.8–13.0	14.4	13.2–16.1
Fuel inventory	0.1	0.1	0.7	0.7
Fuel	8.7	7.5–13.1	4.8	4.8
Operation and maintenance	2.1	2.1	1.5	1.5
Total				
At 10%	18.8	16.9–23.9	16.6	15.8–17.8
At 15%	22.8	20.5–28.3	21.4	20.2–23.1

Source: University of Texas Center for Energy Studies, "Future Central Station Electric Power Generating Alternatives" (Austin: University of Texas for Resources for the Future, 1978), listed in Sam H. Schurr, *Energy in America's Future: The Choice before Us* (Baltimore: Johns Hopkins University Press for Resources for the Future, 1979), p. 288.

Table 12.8. Overnight Nuclear and Coal-Fired Capital-Cost Comparisons for a 1,000-Megawatt Electric Steam Plant
(in thousands of 1975 dollars)

	Pulverized Coal-Fired Plant		
Cost Item	With Flue Gas Desulfurization	Without Desulfurization	Light Water Reactor
1. Site improvement	$2,000	$2,000	$1,700
2. Earthwork plus pilings	4,100	4,100	10,200
3. Circulating water system	21,000	18,000	23,000
4. Concrete	9,600	9,000	44,900
5. Structural steel, lifting equipment, stacks	28,600	26,000	43,600
6. Buildings (indoor)	12,100	11,600	16,600
7. Turbine generator	29,600	29,600	41,600
8. Boiler, fuel handling, pollution control	147,700	95,000	72,300
9. Other mechanical equipment	14,700	14,700	20,900
10. Piping	17,300	16,000	45,900
11. Insulation and lagging	10,900	10,900	3,700
12. Instrumentation	2,700	2,500	2,900
13. Electrical equipment	25,400	24,000	43,200
14. Painting and finishing	1,800	1,700	2,100
15. Land (excluding cooling system)	600	600	400
Total direct	$328,100	$265,700	$373,000
16. Indirect construction	28,600	27,000	38,300
17. Architect-engineer fees	41,800	38,000	62,600
Total direct and indirect	$398,500	$330,700	$473,900
18. Contingencies	47,800	39,600	56,900
Total estimate	$446,300	$370,300	$530,800

Source: University of Texas Center for Energy Studies, "Future Central Station Electric Power Generating Alternatives" (Austin: University of Texas for Resources for the Future, 1977, 1978), reported in Sam H. Schurr, *Energy in America's Future: The Choice before Us* (Baltimore: Johns Hopkins University Press for Resources for the Future, 1979), pp. 276, 285.

Note: "Overnight" estimates are exclusive of any costs over time such as interest and delay cost escalations.

mates is that a conventional light water reactor would cost almost 20 percent more than an environmentally sensitive coal-based system. There are three possible reasons for this differential in costs. One is that the degree of seller competition in the nuclear reactor industry historically has been limited. Another is that because of its limited size, the nuclear industry has not been in a position to realize economies of standardization so typical of many other industries in the economy. Finally, there is also the cost of containing the danger of radioactive emissions of the kind enumerated in chapter 6 and the incorporation of several levels of safeguards in reactor operations to minimize the likelihood of a serious nuclear accident. We will examine whether in fact these costs are adequately accounted for in marketed capital costs once we have looked at pricing within the nuclear fuel cycle's preparation and disposal phases.

As noted in chapter 6, conventional light water reactor nuclear energy in the United States is based on an open fuel cycle. The current share of delivered nuclear electricity accounted for by fuel may be small, but it is this phase of

Table 12.9. Representative Nuclear Fuel Cycle Costs in the United States, 1975

Cost Component	Cost (mills/kwh)	Percentage Distribution: No Recycle	Percentage Distribution: Recycle
1. Mining and milling (\$24.70/lb U_3O_8)	1.49	27.24%	26.42%
2. Conversion to UF_6 (\$1.65/lb U)	0.10	1.83	1.77
3. Enrichment (\$187.82/kg SWU)	2.66	48.63	47.16
4. Reconversion and fabrication (\$77/kg U)	0.30	5.48	5.32
5. Spent-fuel shipping (\$24.75/kg)	0.10	1.83	1.77
6. Waste management (\$606,250/1,000 MWe plant)	0.11	2.01	1.95
7. Fuel inventory carrying charge (at 15 percent)	0.71	12.98	12.59
8. Total open-cycle fuel cost per kwh	5.47	100.00%	96.99%
9. Reprocessing (\$124.29/kg U)	0.46		
10. Mining and milling not required	(0.29)		
11. Conversion to UF_6 not required	(0.02)		
12. 15 percent carrying charge	0.02		
12. Total reprocessing cost	0.17		3.01
14. Total closed-cycle fuel cost per kwh	5.64		100.00%

Source: Saunders Miller, *The Economics of Nuclear and Coal Power* (New York: Praeger Publishers, 1976), p. 82.

nuclear energy which may be the most critical to the future of commercial nuclear energy, as table 12.9 shows. In an open nuclear fuel cycle, fuel that has been used and removed from a reactor core is kept in storage pools adjacent to a utility's operating plant. As long as the price of uranium ore does not escalate faster than the price of competing fuels, utilities may have a short-term incentive to rely on the throwaway cycle, particularly if the marginal cost of reprocessing exceeds the cost of storage by a significant amount.

The logical way to solve the problem of reprocessing is, of course, through empirical investigation. Unfortunately, studies to date show that our conclusions depend critically on the quality of the data we can assemble, and this in the nuclear industry has had such limited operating experience as to throw some degree of doubt on whatever conclusions we might reach. With this caveat in mind, mention should still be made of some of the work done in this area. Evidence in favor of the continued short-run use of the open nuclear fuel cycle has been advanced by Murray (1976), Gordon and Baughman (1979), and Landsberg (1979); more critical assessments have been made by Miller (1976) and by the National Academy of Sciences (1979).[15] Given that there is at present no firmly established technology for long-term waste disposal, and that the risks of weapons proliferation and terrorism associated

[15]R. Michael Murrary, Jr., "The Economics of Electric Power Generation, 1975–2000," in *The Nuclear Power Controversy*, ed. Arthur W. Murphy (Englewood Cliffs, N.J.: Prentice-Hall, 1976), pp. 55–85; John B. Gordon and Martin L. Baughman, "The Economics of the Throwaway Nuclear Fuel Cycle," in *Advances in the Economics of Energy and Resources*, ed. R. S. Pindyck, vol. 1 (Greenwich, Conn.: JAI Press, 1979), pp. 213–56; Hans H. Landsberg, *Energy: The Next Twenty Years*, Report sponsored by the Ford Foundation and administered by Resources for the Future (Cambridge, Mass.: Ballinger Publishing Co., 1979); Saunders Miller, *The Economics of Nuclear and Coal Power* (New York: Praeger Publishers, 1976); and Philip Handler, *Energy in Transition, 1985–2010* (San Francisco: W. H. Freeman and Co., 1980).

with reprocessing are not readily measurable with a high degree of confidence, it is difficult to determine with precision whether mining and reprocessing costs will behave over time in such a way that reprocessing will become economic. Perhaps it is for this reason that some studies have avoided any conclusive evaluation of the merits of reprocessing, and have instead placed the issue within the confines of research and development priorities. What is clear from all of these studies, though, is that a substantial expansion of conventional nuclear power based on the open fuel cycle could not proceed for more than a few decades, since by that time temporary storage costs of wastes would tend to outweigh even some of the most pessimistic supply predictions for nuclear fuel.

At various stages in the discussion of nuclear electricity pricing, reference has been made to risks associated with conventional commercial production technology. Unless otherwise contained, these risks constitute direct and contingent external costs borne by parties other than the buyers and sellers of nuclear electric power. As in the case of coal, nuclear risks encompass damage to human health and to the environment. Despite difficulties in assessing these risks, the results of William Ramsey's (1979) study have been translated into equivalent monetary costs, based on the year 1975, and are reported here in table 12.10.

As in the case of coal-based electricity, it is difficult to estimate with precision the differences between the private and social costs of nuclear energy. Two factors that accentuate this difficulty in the case of nuclear energy are that the probability-severity relationships of nuclear risks are not normally distributed and that government subsidies such as those that resulted from the Price-Anderson Insurance Act tend to make nuclear-based electricity cheaper than it would otherwise be. Figure 12.6 illustrates the skewed distribution of risk arising from a worst-case nuclear reactor accident.[16] Given past operating experience, the likelihood of a worst-case nuclear reactor meltdown accident would appear to be relatively small, even given the experience at Three Mile Island. At the same time, should a worst-case accident occur, it could cause thousands of fatalities, as well as associated environmental damage for extensive periods of time.

The conventional response to risk is insurance. Ordinarily, we would multiply the probability of an event by its severity and then estimate the monetary cost to arrive at the amount of insurance needed to compensate for such

[16]A distribution of the kind illustrated in figure 12.6 that is used for the analysis of rare events is the Poisson distribution. It can be expressed as $P(x) = e^{-\lambda} \lambda^x/x!$, where $x > 0$ and $\lambda > 0$ and where e is 2.71828, the base of natural logarithms; x is the hypothesized number of occurrences; and λ is the mean rate of occurrences of an event. In a relationship with such a limited likelihood, the mean of the Poisson distribution turns out also to be equal to its variance. However, as in Bayesian statistics, accuracy in the determination of the probability of an event depends critically on prior information regarding the value of the mean rate, λ, which in the case of a nuclear accident is difficult to determine given the limited operating time of commerical nuclear technology and the observed relatively low probability of a worst-case disaster, for example. For an introductory exposition of the properties and uses of the Poisson distribution, see Donald L. Harnett and James L. Murrow, *Introductory Statistical Analysis*, 2d ed. (Reading, Mass.: Addison-Wesley Publishing Co., 1980), pp. 161–72.

Table 12.10. Private and Social Costs of Delivered Nuclear-Based Electricity for the United States, 1975

Item	Physical Cost per USW[a]	Imputed Monetary Cost[b]	Equivalent Monetary Cost in Terms of Typical Residential Monthly Electricity Bill, 1975[c]
1. Monthly residential electricity bill (actual)			$21.97
2. Routine health hazards			
Cancer fatalities	0–1.3	0–$113,689	0–$0.0001
Thyroid tumors	0–1.8	0–157,415	0–0.0002
Carbon-14 fatalities	0–300[d]	0–26,235,900	0–0.0262
Radon fatalities	0–225,000[d]	0–19,676,925,000	0–19.68
3. Routine nuclear wastes			
Processed fuel waste			0–0.10
Low-level processed wastes			0–0.025
Reactor decommission and disposal			0–0.20
4. Reactor accident health hazards			
Latent-cancer fatalities[e]	0–20–308	0–26,935,524	0–0.026936
Thyroid-tumor fatalities[e]	0–175–2,692	0–235,423,476	0–0.235423
Radiation illnesses[e]	0–2.25–35	0–1,530,428	0–0.001530
Genetic illnesses[e]	0–6–92	0–8,045,676	0–0.008046
Worst-case-disaster immediate fatalities	0–48,000	0–4,197,744,000	0–4.197744
5. Nuclear proliferation and terrorism casualties	0–3,000	0–262,359,000	0–0.262
6. Environmental costs			
Thermal water pollution		0–3,000,000,000	0–3.00
Land alteration	0–25,000 acres	0–20,830,000	0–0.02083
7. Occupational hazards			
Conventional accident fatalities	20–70	1,749,060–6,121,710	0.001749–0.006122
Radiation-induced illness	0–50	0–4,372,650	0–0.004373
Non-fatal illness and accidents[f]	4,000–7,000	87,523–153,165	0.000088–0.000153
8. Total social costs (undiscounted) per monthly bill			21.97–49.76
9. Total social costs (undiscounted) per kilowatt-hour of electricity			0.032261–0.073069
10. [illegible]			[illegible]

Note: The table refers to light water reactors and high-temperature gas converter reactors only. Cost comparisons are average cost equivalent. They do not reflect nonlinearities implicit in marginal cost relationships such as exponential increases in cancer fatality rates associated with a substantial expansion in nuclear power plants.

[a]One USW is equal to 2 trillion kilowatt-hours of electricity, the amount of power generated by all means in the United States in 1975. Since approximately 9 percent of all electricity during that year was generated by nuclear power, monetary estimates have been adjusted accordingly by Ramsey in the cases of routine nuclear wastes. Other monetary estimates are derived from Ramsey's physical cost per USW data, and translated into the typical residential monthly bill.

[b]Imputed monetary costs are based on the present value of 1975 dollar per capita national income of $5,689 per year, discounted at 5 percent over a thirty-year period, or $87,453 per capita, and this figure was used in the valuation of all per capita fatalities. For radiation illnesses, 50 percent of the discounted value was used, and for genetic illness 75 percent, with a conversion of nonfatal illness and accident person-day costs into person-years and the corresponding amount of aggregated per capita national income.

[c]Following Ramsey, a conversion ratio of $2 billion per USW to $2.00 per average monthly electric bill was used to express total imputed social costs in these terms. The base-line average monthly residential bill for 1975 was derived from an average residential monthly level of electricity consumption of 681 kilowatt-hours, a figure Ramsey took from figures supplied by the Edison Electric Institute (p. 22, 31). Per-kilowatt-hour electricity costs are derived from this base-line level of consumption. None of these costs reflects the discounted value of increases in real national income per capita, insurance, hospitalization, or related market and nonmarket expenses incurred by individuals, families, or affected institutions, including the operating costs of government regulatory agencies themselves. At the same time, since contingent social costs such as nuclear reactor accidents and terrorism are not weighted by the probability of occurrences or of the time frame in which all costs are incurred (i.e., future fatalities are not discounted), it is not possible to state whether the range of social costs is greater or less than the estimates cited here.

[d]Such fatalities are incurred over several generations. The figures cited here are undiscounted for purposes of comparison.

[e]Intermediate physical costs are based on WASH-1400, the Rasmussen Report prepared for the Nuclear Regulatory Commission in 1975. The upper range of physical costs refers to figures considered by the Ford Foundation's *Nuclear Power Issues and Choices* examination of the Rasmussen report and an allowance for underestimation in WASH-1400.

[f]In person-days.

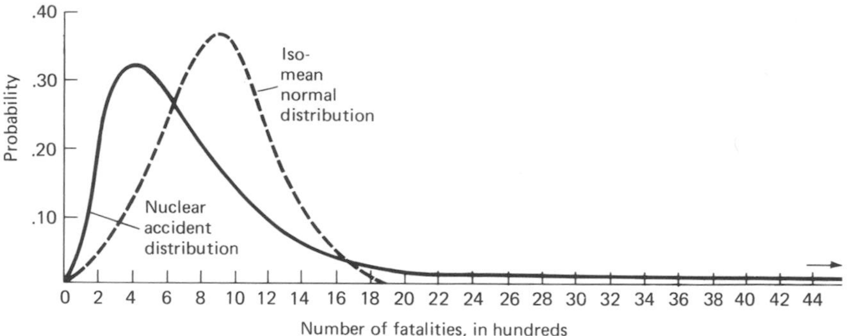

Figure 12.6. Hypothetical Probability Distribution of Fatalities Associated with a Nuclear Reactor Accident

risk. Yet when considering events that have never occurred, we must base such cost estimates on hypothetical rather than observed data. In the case of the Price-Anderson Insurance Act, the federal government has set a limit of $560 million per worst-case reactor accident, of which $435 million would be provided directly by the federal government and $125 million would be provided by all electric utilities. The subsidy embodied in this liability limit may be seen by comparing it with the current estimates of a less-than-worst-case accident such as occurred at Three Mile Island. With cleanup costs there estimated at over $1 billion, the difference between the liability limit of the Price-Anderson Act and what a commercial insurance company alone would charge represents an effective public subsidy to nuclear energy which lowers its market price below what it would otherwise be.

What do these various pricing mechanisms imply for energy policy choices? As we might expect, failure to account for divergences between the private and social costs of alternative energy resources leads to distorted production choices, which reduce the general level of community welfare. These distortions affect more than comparisons between coal and nuclear energy. They also affect comparisons between either of these resources and the many alternative electricity-generating technologies examined in chapters 7 and 8.

12.1.3. The Pricing of Alternative Electrical Technologies

Despite their current significance in the U.S. economy, coal and nuclear energy are by no means the exclusive sources of commercial electricity. Nor, for that matter, should we assume that these resources will maintain their present role in the future. Indeed, until the 1970s, petroleum and natural gas were both relatively cheaper and possessed far fewer risks and environmental hazards, so much so that they constituted highly competitive fuels for incremental electricity-generating plants. Since petroleum and natural gas price increases may well have precluded a return of that role for the immediate future, an important question at this point is, to what extent will price increases in conventional resource systems affect the emergence of alternative energy technologies? In addition to conventional hydroelectricity, the alternative electricity-generating technologies which bear some degree of attention in this context are breeder reactors, fuel cells, magnetohydrodynamics, nuclear fusion, wind generators, tidal power, hydrothermal power, geothermal power, and photovoltaic systems.

Of all conventional electricity-generating technologies, hydropower appears to be, on the surface at least, one of the most attractive. After all, it does not involve combustion of an environment-polluting fuel, and it contains no radioactive elements which threaten community health and safety. At the same time, the economic competitiveness of hydropower is affected by several unique cost considerations. First, hydropower does pose some degree of operating risk, though not as severe as in the case of fossil-fired or nuclear electricity. In addition to worker accident risk, the possibility of a dam failure, small though it may be, is unique to hydropower.[17] Second, hydropower imposes a significant cost on the environment. Eutrophication, the deoxygenation of slowly running water to a point where only plants tend to survive, and the accompanying silting of waterways reduce marine animal life, alter commercial navigation, and eliminate alternative uses of floodlands, even though hydroelectric reservoirs may provide some recreational and allied benefits to affected communities. Third, technically optimal hydropower sites which are well endowed with good water flow rates and height configurations are often at a considerable distance from principal consuming markets, which limits the ability of hydroelectricity to compete on a geographic scale with many alternative technologies.

Table 12.11 provides partial evidence of the competitive position of hydroelectricity in the U.S. economy. As the range of estimated generating costs suggests, hydropower appears to be superior to many of its competitors, especially in mountainous, water-abundant, principal electricity-consuming regions of the economy. However, if we consider transmission and distribution costs, along with the associated external costs of conventional technologies, the competitive position of delivered hydroelectricity is likely to be much more limited in scale and in geographic scope than the private generating costs of table 12.11 suggest.[18]

One alternative technology with demonstrated technical feasibility for the commercial generation of electricity is the breeder reactor. As pointed out in chapter 6, a breeder reactor is one which creates more fuel than it consumes, notably by the joint production of electricity and usable plutonium as a by-prod-

[17]See Handler, *Energy in Transition*, pp. 430, 459–60. The National Academy of Sciences noted that for 1972, routine accidents in hydroelectric plants were half as frequent and one-tenth as severe as the average for all electricity-generating plants, and that the failure rate of dams in the United States was about 8×10^{-4} per dam-year, with a major disaster rated at 1.3×10^{-4} per dam-year.

[18]A standard reference is K. Inouye et al., *Water Use Policies and Power Plant Economics* (Washington, D.C.: National Technical Information Service, June 1974). Given the environmental and transport costs of large-scale projects, a more likely alternative is small-scale hydro projects.

Table 12.11. Marginal Private Generating Costs of Alternative Conventional Electricity Technologies
(in 1976 dollars)

Technology	Construction and License Time	Overnight Capital Cost per KWe	Fuel Cost in Mills/Kwh	Capacity Factor	Capital Cost per Kwh[a]	Capital[b] and Fuel-Generating Cost Per Kwh
Nuclear	10 yrs.	$700	6	60–65%	$ 0.0187–0.0202	$ 0.0247–0.0262
Coal with flue gas desulfurization	6	600	12	60–65	0.0160–0.0174	0.0280–0.0294
Oil, steam generation	5	450	21	60–65	0.0120–0.0130	0.0330–0.0340
Oil, combined cycle	5	370	16	60–65	0.0099–0.0107	0.0259–0.0267
Oil, gas turbine	3	200	24	60–65	0.0053–0.0058	0.0293–0.0298
Hydroelectric	3–6	592–1,014	0	60–75	0.0158–0.0294	0.0158–0.0294

Sources: Exclusive of hydroelectric data, data for construction and license time, overnight capital cost and fuel cost in mills per kilowatt-hour are taken from Hans H. Landsberg, *Energy: The Next Twenty Years* (Cambridge, Mass.: Ballinger Publishing Co., 1979), p. 416. Hydroelectric capital costs are based on 1978 data reported in Sam H. Schurr, *Energy in America's Future: The Choices before Us* (Baltimore: Johns Hopkins University Press for Resources for the Future, 1979), p. 316, and have been converted with a GNP deflator to 1976 dollars.

Note: Estimates are exclusive of cost escalations due to delays and do not include operating and maintenance costs. In addition to these factors, marginal private delivered electricity costs must include incremental transmission and distribution costs. Delivered marginal private costs of electricity would thus be in the neighborhood of 40–70 percent more than the estimates listed under capital and fuel-generating cost per kilowatt-hour.

[a]Capital costs per kilowatt-hour are based on a thirty-year life of capital equipment, a 15 percent discount rate, and the indicated capacity factors, as follows: generating cost per Kwh = [Annual Capital Payment/hours per year]/capacity factor, where Annual Capital Payment = $\frac{PV \cdot i(1+i)^n}{(1+i)^n - 1}$, PV = the overnight capital cost, i = the discount rate, and n = the number of years of equipment loan life.

[b]Exclusive of operation and maintenance costs.

uct of the fissioning of primary uranium fuel. The economic rationale of the breeder is straightforward. With its capacity to generate a plutonium fuel by-product, the breeder could forestall the increase in the demand for conventional enriched uranium fuel. Traditional converter and developing breeder fission reactors could together retain their jointly competitive economic position in relation to fossil and hydroelectric technologies and thereby satisfy the bulk of the economy's requirements for incremental electricity generating capacity.

As noted in chapter 6, the most developed breeder technology in the United States is the liquid-sodium model. Although some commercial experience has been gained with the Fermi station in Lagoona Beach, Michigan, the closing of this reactor because of malfunctioning and the uncertain status of the experimental model at the Oak Ridge, Tennessee, Clinch River site makes it difficult to arrive at an adequate estimate of the commercial generating cost of breeder reactor technology. Yet, on the basis of available studies to date, the breeder does not now appear to be a competitive electricity-generating technology, particularly if we include the public subsidies, environmental risks, and private market costs thus far known.

Table 12.12 lists marginal private cost estimates of competing fission reactor generating technologies undertaken for the Oak Ridge National Laboratory in 1977. Although it appears that the liquid-metal fast breeder's private generating costs are below those of the CANDU heavy water reactor, they are still significantly above the generating costs of conventional light water reactors. As the figures also show, the principal reason for the higher cost dif-

Table 12.12. Marginal Private Generating Costs of Conventional and Advanced Fission Reactors (in 1976 dollars)

System	Capital Cost per Kilowatt	Capital Cost Per Kilowatt-Hour	Fuel Cost in Mills per Kilowatt-Hour	Total Costs per Kilowatt-Hour
1. Light water reactor	\$590[a]	\$0.0158–0.0171	6	\$0.0218–0.0231
2. High-temperature gas reactor	675	0.0181–0.0196	6	0.0241–0.0256
3. Liquid-metal fast breeder reactor	755	0.0202–0.0219	4	0.0242–0.0259
4. CANDU heavy water reactor	863	0.0231–0.0250	4	0.0271–0.0290

Source: Adapted from estimates cited by the National Academy of Sciences, *Energy in Transition, 1985–2010* (San Francisco: W. H. Freeman and Co., 1980), p. 248.

Note: Capital costs of the National Academy study are based on Resources Planning Associates, *The Economics of Utilization of Thorium in Nuclear Reactors—Textual Annexes 1 and 2*, Oak Ridge National Laboratory, and expressed originally in 1977 dollars. Capital cost estimates above have been converted into 1976 dollars and are expressed in terms of kilowatt-hours using a 15 percent discount rate, a thirty-year plant-life cycle, and a 60–65 percent capacity factor, based on the calculation illustrated in note *a* to table 12.11.

[a] As an indication of the uncertainty in these figures, it should be noted that the 1976 dollar estimate of a light water reactor given by the Ford Foundation study in Table 12.11 is \$700/kw, whereas the Oak Ridge National Laboratory cites a figure of \$590/kw, including interest during construction. Other than adding an interest charge to the Oak Ridge estimate and deriving the capital cost per kilowatt-hour, no attempt has been made to reconcile the outstanding 15–18 percent capital cost differential between the two figures.

ferential of the breeder is that its lower relative fuel costs are more than offset by higher capital costs. The two basic reasons for higher capital costs are (1) the technology essential to the containment of a fast neutron reaction is different from that of a conventional light water reactor and (2) the capital cost of breeder technology, with little production experience, is burdened by uncertainty and absence of any standardization economies from large-scale production. Moreover, the liquid-metal fast breeder may not even be as competitive as more advanced models such as the molten salt and gas-cooled breeder systems also under development. Yet what may be most significant of all is that the contingent risks of nuclear weapons proliferation and nuclear terrorism which are more acute in the case of breeder technology eliminate for the present time at least the social-cost competitiveness of breeder reactors for the commercial generation of electricity.[19] What this leaves for consideration is whether continued research in breeder technology should be maintained and at what rate, questions which are taken up in greater detail in chapters 13 and 14.

Beyond the breeder reactor, there are several experimental and developing commercial electricity-generating technologies. As the estimates in table 12.13 show, some of these systems are based on depletable energy resources such as fossil or nuclear fuels, while others depend on renewable energy flows. These technologies may be grouped according to a broad range of resource choices, and they may be further grouped according to their degree of centralization. Magnetohydrodynamics, nuclear fusion, tidal, hydrothermal, and geothermal technologies are essentially large-scale centralized technologies not largely different in capacity from the conventional generating plants now in use. Fuel cells, photovoltaics, wind generators, and biomass electric units are more modular in nature. They could be designed as single residential or commercial on-site units, or scaled up to the existing capacities of their conventional counterparts. What they all share in common, though, is that the less economically established any particular technology may be, the less certain we can be as to its marketed costs of production. Despite this uncertainty, it is still essential to consider the range of costs of these technologies, for these systems may well come to perform a substantive role in future commercial electricity generation.

As in the case of conventional electricity systems, the delivered market price of an alternative technology comprises three principal elements: generating costs, transmission costs, and distribution costs. For a centralized technology, the critical issue is the extent to which an alternative generating system is economically competitive with conventional generating costs. For a decentralized technology, which is likely to be based on renewable energy flows, the critical issue is whether its marginal storage costs will exceed the transmission and distribution marginal costs of conventional and alternative cen-

[19]For a critical study, see Thomas B. Cochran, *The Liquid Metal Fast Breeder Reactor: An Environmental and Economic Critique* (Baltimore: Johns Hopkins University Press for Resources for the Future, 1974).

tralized technologies. Since these relationships may not be immediately obvious, a useful way of expressing them is in basic quantitative terms.

The marginal private cost of a technology is derived in a number of steps. At the generation stage, the estimated overnight capital cost of a plant must first be converted into an annualized marginal capital cost per kilowatt-hour of electricity produced.[20] This conversion can be expressed as

$$MC_{kwh} = \left[\frac{PMT}{\text{Hours per year}}\right] \Big/ \text{Capacity Factor,} \tag{12.1}$$

where PMT is the annualized payment of the capital cost of the generating plant, Hours per year equal 24 × 365, or 8,760 hours, and Capacity Factor is the estimated fraction of time that a generating plant will be in operation, to reflect refueling, routine maintenance, and the accident failure rate per unit of time, <1. In turn, the annualized capital payment can be expressed as

$$PMT = \frac{PV \cdot i(1 + i)^n}{(1 + i)^n - 1}, \tag{12.2}$$

where PV is the overnight cost of capital, i is the discount rate used to evaluate the project's economic value over time, and n is the number of years involved in the plant's economic life. Obviously, the choice of the discount rate and the estimated life of a project is critical to the valuation of estimated annualized generating costs. The economic implications of these variables will be examined more closely in chapter 13; at this point, we should assume that private marginal cost estimates will be based largely on the opportunity cost of investment resources, that is, on what a competitive investment's estimated life and corresponding rate of interest will be.

In order to assess the impact of cost escalations on the estimated annualized marginal private generating cost of a project, equation 12.1 can be reexpressed as

$$MC_{kwh} = \left[\frac{PMT(1 + r)^p C}{\text{Hours per Year}}\right] \Big/ \text{Capacity Factor,} \tag{12.1.a}$$

where r is the average estimated inflation rate for capital costs, p is the number of years involved in project construction, (with allowances added for delays), and C is the distributed-construction-cost coefficient, defined as $\Sigma_{j=1}^{p} (1 + i)^j \cdot (\alpha)_j$, with i equal to the interest rate chosen for project evaluation, and α_j equal the share of project construction funds allocated in the jth year, ≤ 1, and all other terms have the same interpretation as in equation (12.1).

To the annualized capital cost per kilowatt-hour must be added the annu-

[20]As used elsewhere in this chapter, an overnight capital cost is exclusive of any cost escalation and of the interest charge affecting the completion of the project. A more realistic assessment would include these charges, along with maintenance, depreciation, insurance, and taxation, to determine its private net present value, rate of return, or other measure of profitability. Of course, private profitability may well diverge from social returns to such a project. Whether private or social costs and benefits should be used depends on whether the question is being approached from the point of view of the individual firm or from that of the economy as a whole. For our present purposes, we are concerned with the economy as a whole.

Table 12.13. Marginal Private Generating Costs of Alternative Developing Electricity Technologies
(in 1976 dollars)

Reference	Capital Cost Kilowatt	Total Generating Cost per Kilowatt-Hour	Estimated Feasible Commercialization Date
Fuel cells			
Aaronson (1971)	—	$ 0.0163	1980–85
Dorf (1978)	$ 440	—	—
Schurr (1979)	376	0.037–0.040	—
Magnetohydrodynamics			
Aaronson (1971)	—	0.0163	1990
Nuclear fusion			
Mills (1975)	630	0.0157	2000
Schurr (1979)	1,000–3,000	0.040–0.060	—
Wind generation			
Banks (1977)	500–700	—	1977
Clark (1975)	700	0.010	1975
Commoner (1979)	450	—	1985
Dept. of Energy (1978)	700	0.010	1978
FEA (1974)	290–2,305	—	—
Handler (1980)	825	0.0349	1977
Inglis (1978)	1,212–68,880	0.025–0.24	1978
Lovins (1977)	520–620	0.021–0.0235	1976
Schurr (1979)	250–1,400	0.021–0.040	1978
Wade (1974)	461–692	—	1974
Tidal			
Banks (1977)	106	—	1980
Dorf (1978)	400–800	—	—
Schurr (1979)	807–1,616	0.022–0.0646	1980
Hydrothermal			
Anderson-Mayer (1979)	405	—	1984
Dept. of Energy (1978)	3,000	0.330	—
FEA (1974)	750	0.014	1976
Handler (1980)	—	0.070	1985
Schurr	1,500–2,000	0.028–0.042	1980
Zener (1973)	121–505	—	1973
Geothermal			
Banks (1977)	170	—	—
Dorf (1978)	200–250	—	—
Handler (1980)	268–2,500	0.110–0.600	1975
Schurr (1979)	500–600	0.015–0.030	1979
Photovoltaics			
Decentralized and centralized			
Commoner (1979)	500	—	1982
FEA (1974)	4,609	0.046–0.092	—
Gervais-Box (1975)	1,500	—	1975
Handler (1980)	1,000–2,000	—	1980
Landsberg (1979)	—	0.030–0.040	—
Miller (1976)	700–1,180	0.108	—
Schurr (1979)	1,600–2,650	0.070–0.100	1980
Satellite solar			
Glaser (1977)	1,600–3,500	0.030–0.120	1980
Schurr (1979)	1,143–1,500	0.013–0.037	—
Biomass electric			
Handler (1980)	—	0.010–0.028	1980
Schurr (1979)	500	0.023–0.052	1980
Average cost composite of conventional generating technologies			
Dept. of Energy (1978)	—	0.014–0.024	1976[a]

alized costs of fuel, operation, and maintenance. These costs may be expressed as:

$$(12.3) \qquad \overline{MC}_{fom} = F(1 + r_f)^n + OM(1 + r_{om})^n,$$

where F is the base-year fuel cost per kilowatt-hour, r_f is the expected inflation rate for fuel (where appropriate), n is the number of years from the base period to the start of commercial electricity generation from the plant, OM is the operation and maintenance base-year cost per kilowatt-hour, and r_{om} is the expected rate of inflation in operation and maintenance costs. Adding together equations (12.1.*a*) and (12.3) gives the estimated marginal private generating cost of a technology. To translate this figure into an estimate of the marginal private cost of delivered electricity, we must derive the annualized capital and operating-maintenance costs of existing and incremental transmission and distribution facilities, each of which can be obtained from application of an equation comparable to 12.1.*a*. Once these estimates have

---

Sources: Terri Aaronson, "The Black Box—Fuel Cells," *Environment* 13 (December 1971): 10–18; J. Hilbert Anderson and David F. Mayer, "Sea Thermal Power—Competitive Electricity and Chemicals from the Sea," in *Advances in Energy Systems and Technology*, ed. Peter Auer, vol. 2 (New York: Academic Press, 1979), pp. 50–101; Ferdinand Banks, *Scarcity, Energy, and Economic Progress* (Lexington, Mass.: Lexington Books, 1977); Wilson Clark, *Energy for Survival* (Garden City, N.Y.: Doubleday Anchor Books, 1975); Barry Commoner, *The Politics of Energy* (New York: Alfred A. Knopf, 1979); J. B. Dicks, "Magnetohydrodynamic Central Power: A Status Report," *Mechanical Engineering* 94 (May 1974):14–20; Edward M. Dickson, John W. Ryan, and Marilyn H. Smulyan, *The Hydrogen Energy Economy* (New York: Praeger Publishers, 1977); R. C. Dorf, *Energy, Resources, and Policy* (Reading, Mass.: Addison-Wesley Publishing Co., 1978); Federal Energy Administration, *Project Independence Blueprint* (Washington, D.C.: U.S. Government Printing Office, November 1974); R. L. Gervais and P. B. Box, "Solar Thermal Electric Power," *Astronautics and Aeronautics*, November 1975, pp. 38–45; Peter E. Glaser, "The Development of Solar Power Satellites," in *Advances in Energy Systems and Technology*, ed. Peter Auer, vol. 2 (New York: Academic Press, 1979), pp. 2–48; Philip Handler, *Energy in Transition, 1985–2010* (San Francisco: W. H. Freeman and Co., 1980); H. C. Hottel and J. B. Howard, *New Energy Technology: Some Facts and Assessments* (1971; reprint ed., Cambridge, Mass.: MIT Press, 1974); David R. Inglis, *Wind Power and Other Energy Options* (Ann Arbor: University of Michigan Press, 1978); Hans H. Landsberg, *Energy: The Next Twenty Years,* Report sponsored by the Ford Foundation and administered by Resources for the Future (Cambridge, Mass.: Ballinger Publishing Co., 1979); Amory B. Lovins, *Soft Energy Paths: Toward a Durable Peace* (Cambridge, Mass.: Ballinger Publishing Co., 1977); Saunders B. Miller, *The Economics of Nuclear and Coal Power* (New York: Praeger Publishers, 1976); R. G. Mills, "Problems and Promises of Controlled Fusion Power," *Mechanical Engineering* 95 (September 1975):20–25; Harry Perry, "Coal Conversion Technology," *Chemical Engineering* 81 (22 July 1974):88–102; Sam H. Schurr, *Energy in America's Future: The Choices before Us,* Study prepared for the Resources for the Future National Energy Strategies Project (Baltimore: Johns Hopkins University Press for Resources for the Future, 1979); Robert Stobaugh and Daniel Yergin, eds., *Energy Future,* Report of the Energy Project at the Harvard Business School (New York: Random House Publishers, 1979); U.S. Congress, Congressional Research Service, "Fusion Power: Potential Energy Source," in *What Should be the Energy Policy of the United States?* (Washington, D.C.: U.S. Government Printing Office, 1978); U.S. Department of Energy, Energy Information Administration, *Annual Report to Congress,* vol. 2, 1977 (Washington, D.C.: U.S. Government Printing Office, April 1978); N. Wade, "Windmills: The Resurrection of an Ancient Technology," *Science*, 7 June 1974, pp. 1055–58; Clarence Zener, "Solar Sea Power," *Physics Today*, January 1973.

Note: Variations in estimates are a function of the state of technology at the time the assessments were made, differences in the assumed scale of production and underlying learning curves, and alternative costs of financing, including discount rate differentials, equity versus debt financing, and the extent of assumed taxes and subsidies. Since the estimates have not been adjusted for these differences, they are not strictly comparable. Caution should therefore be exercised in their interpretation.

[a]Actual

been obtained, an adjustment must then be made for transmission and distribution losses as follows:

$$(12.4) \qquad \overline{MC}_{kwh,\,d} = \overline{MC}_{kwh,\,g,\,t,\,d}(1 + a),$$

where a is equal to the transmission and distribution losses as a percentage of generated electricity.

In the case of total on-site generation technologies, transmission and distribution costs are deleted and replaced by the marginal cost of storage technology per kilowatt-hour of electricity. The marginal cost of such delivered electricity is then expressed as

$$(12.5) \qquad \overline{\overline{MC}}_{kwh,\,d} = MC_{kwh,\,g} + \beta\,\overline{\overline{MC}}_{sto},$$

where $\overline{\overline{MC}}_{sto}$ is the marginal cost of storage technology per kilowatt-hour, derived from a variation of 12.1.*a,* and β is the average fraction of total generated electricity which must be converted and stored, adjusted for losses. Finally, the marginal cost of delivered electricity from decentralized systems which must rely on a centralized backup system can be expressed as

$$(12.6) \qquad \overline{\overline{MC}}_{kwh,\,d} = \gamma(\overline{\overline{MC}}_{kwh,\,g} + \alpha\overline{\overline{MC}}_{sto}) + \delta\overline{MC}_{kwh,\,d},$$

where γ is the share of on-site decentralized delivered marginal electricity costs and δ is the share of delivered marginal electricity costs provided by conventional centralized backup system $\gamma + \delta = 1$.

With the above framework in mind, we can draw several conclusions from the various estimates of private marginal generating costs of table 12.13. First, with due allowance for differences in the time when the estimates were made, it appears that several alternative generating technologies are quite competitive with the estimated average cost of conventional generating technologies. Second, because many of these estimates refer only to the experimental phase of development, many of the systems are not currently available in any significant quantities, if at all, and consequently, the range of uncertainty may be even higher than the upper and lower limits already shown. Third, the renewable technologies at least, some allowance must be made for a potential divergence between the marginal cost of storage and the marginal cost of transmission and distribution from centralized alternatives.

Estimates of marginal private costs of electricity storage among several competitive technologies are listed in table 12.19. As these figures suggest all too clearly, many decentralized technologies may have competitive marginal generating costs, but the economic advantage of these systems may well be offset by disproportionately high conversion and storage costs, at least if we rely only on the private market prices used in these estimates. Indeed, it is essentially for this reason that many commercial designs of decentralized systems more often than not use a conventional generating system as a backup electricity technology. At the same time, should there be significant advances in the reduction of energy storage costs, then there is every reason to expect a more vigorous role for decentralized independent electricity systems as part of the economy's evolving energy mix. Since the answer to this question depends largely on actual energy policy and specific energy criteria, we can defer further consideration of the issue until the following chapters.

12.2. THE PRICING OF ALTERNATIVE FOSSIL ENERGY RESOURCES

Given the pricing of conventional fossil fuels and the collusive pricing pressures of OPEC, it is not surprising that there should be a vivid interest in the costs of competitive alternatives. For the United States at least, fossil-based alternatives include secondary and tertiary recovery methods from existing wells, accelerated exploration of continental and offshore sites, and synthetic fuels. At currently rising prices of oil, there is undoubtedly a greater physical yield from existing wells. Moreover, higher prices raise the incentive to bring hitherto geologically feasible deposits of oil into economically competitive reserve status. However, it is also true that the known fossil resources in greatest relative abundance are still coal, shale oil, and tar sands. Because these resources are not readily suited in their natural state for direct conversion into the usable forms consumed within the economy, the underlying question is, to what extent are synthetic technology costs competitive with the conventional counterpart prices of these resources?

If coal is to perform an expanded role in the economy's energy mix, at least two basic questions must be addressed at the outset. First is the question of the health and environmental costs noted in section 12.1, for these costs form a significant portion of coal used in electricity consumption and in virtually all of its alternative end uses. Second is the the question of the costs of conversion of coal into the liquid and gas fossil fuels on which the economy is now so largely dependent. Setting aside for the moment the external costs of coal, our initial concern is with the private marketed costs of coal-conversion technologies.

Table 12.14 lists several recent estimates of the marginal private costs of synthetic liquid and gas fuels derived from coal. Like the estimates for electricity conversion and storage technologies, these figures are based on some degree of uncertainty. The reasons for this uncertainty are familiar enough: apart from their associated health and environmental costs, none of these technologies has acquired the necessary commercial experience to account for potential economies of scale and competitive market forces. Yet even given this level of uncertainty, the estimates thus far available do point to the potential competitive ability of coal gasification and coal liquefaction as substitutes for their domestic conventional alternatives. Moreover, if we consider the fact that the price of imported oil from OPEC and non-OPEC sources is higher than several of these estimates and contains an uncertainty of supply contingent cost as well, then the apparent private market price advantage of synthetics is even stronger.

In contrast to the optimism of comparative market prices, the social costs of synthetics present a far different picture. If we consider that the health, safety, and environmental costs of these synthetic fuels may be at least pro-

Table 12.14. Marginal Private Costs of Alternative Fossil Energy Technologies
(in 1976 dollars)

Reference	Cost in Standard Units[a]	Cost per MBtu	Estimated Feasible Commercialization Date
Coal liquefaction			
FEA (1976)	$ 12.00-30.00	$ 2.06-5.17	1984
Handler (1980)	24.00-29.00	4.14-5.00	1985-90
Laoussine (1979)	16.04	2.77	1985-90
Nordhaus (1979)	16.62	2.86	1990
Perry (1974)	7.50-11.10	1.29-1.91	—
Schurr (1979)	15.31-64.03	2.64-11.04	1985-90
Stobaugh-Yergin (1979)	10.55-18.00	1.82-3.10	1985-90
Coal gasification			
FEA (1976)	2.94-4.14/Mcf	3.03-4.27	1985
Handler (1980)	4.12/Mcf	4.25	1987-90
Hottel-Howard (1971)	1.15/Mcf	1.18	—
Landsberg (1979)	3.92-5.49/Mcf	4.40-5.66	—
Laoussine (1979)	2.96/Mcf	3.06	1985-90
Nordhaus (1979)	2.82/Mcf	2.91	1985-90
Perry (1974)	1.12-1.68/Mcf	1.15-1.73	—
Schurr (1979)	1.45-5.31/Mcf	1.50-5.47	1985-90
Stobaugh-Yergin (1979)	1.74-2.21/Mcf	1.79-2.28	1985-95
Tar sands			
Hottel-Howard (1971)	4.04	0.70	1975-80
Laoussine (1979)	14.63	2.52	1985-90
Shale oil			
Handler (1980)	18.91-24.18	3.26-4.17	1985-90
Hottel-Howard (1971)	4.46	0.71	—
Landsberg (1979)	22.00	3.79	—
Laoussine (1979)	16.25	2.80	1985-90
Nordhaus (1979)	11.62-16.80	2.00-2.84	1990
Schurr (1979)	24.07-51.44	4.15-8.87	1985-95
Stobaugh-Yergin (1979)	8.79	1.52	1985-95
Average cost of conventional resources (Dept. of Energy, 1980)			
Domestic			
Coal	21.40/short ton	0.82 minemouth	December 1979
Petroleum	16.16	2.78 refiner acquisition cost	December 1979
Natural gas	1.04/Mcf	1.01 wellhead	December 1979
Imported			
Petroleum	21.50-28.37	3.71-4.89/FOB	June 1980
	11.00-12.00	1.89-2.07/FOB	December 1976
Liquified natural gas	2.81	2.90/FOB	1977

Sources: Federal Energy Administration, *National Energy Outlook, 1976* (Washington, D.C.: U.S. Government Printing Office, February 1976); Philip Handler, *Energy in Transition, 1985-2010* (San Francisco: W. H. Freeman and Co., 1980); H. C. Hottel and J. B. Howard, *New Energy Technology: Some Facts and Asssessments* (Cambridge, Mass.: MIT Press, 1974); Hans H. Landsberg, *Energy: The Next Twenty Years,* Report sponsored by the Ford Foundation and administered by Resources for the Future (Cambridge, Mass.: Ballinger Publishing Co., 1979); Nordine Laid Laoussine, "Pricing Policy as an Instrument for the Optimum Management of the World's Energy Endowment," in *Papers on the Economics of Oil—A Producers' View,* ed. Mahmoud Abdel-Fadil (London: Oxford University Press, 1979), pp. 67-78; William D. Nordhaus, *The Efficient Use of Energy Resources* (New Haven: Yale University Press, 1979); Harry Perry, "Coal Conversion Technology," *Chemical Engineering* 81 (22 July 1974): 88-102; Sam H. Schurr, *Energy in America's Future: The Choices before Us,* Study prepared for the Resources for the Future National Energy Strategies Project (Baltimore: Johns Hopkins University Press for Resources for the Future, 1979); Robert Stobaugh and Daniel Yergin, eds., *Energy Future,* Report of the Energy Project at the Harvard Business School (New York: Random House Publishers, 1979).

Note: Variations in estimates are a function of the state of technology at the time assessments were made, differences in the assumed scale of production and underlying learning curves, and alternative costs of financing, including discount rate differentials, equity versus debt financing, and the extent of assumed taxes and subsidies. Since the estimates have not been adjusted for these differences, they are not strictly comparable. Caution should therefore be exercised in their interpretation.

[a]Unless otherwise indicated, the cost is per barrel

portional to the comparable costs of unconverted coal, then the range of costs from table 12.6 would suggest that the marginal social costs of coal-based synthetic fuels would range as much as two and a half times the private cost estimates for coal liquefaction and gasification in table 12.14. Thus, when the external costs are included, the marginal social costs of synthetics may be at least as high as the contingent risks and associated social costs of imported oil, and comparable to the range of marginal social costs of newly discovered conventional supplies of petroleum. Clearly, then, the way in which the price of coal-based synthetics is determined is crucial to the competitive position of these fuels in the economy's evolving energy mix.

Beyond coal liquefaction and gasification, tar sands and shale oil represent two additional fossil fuel alternatives. On the basis of marginal private cost estimates alone, these fuels are well within the range of estimates derived for coal-based synthetics. At the same time, there is little comparable basis on which to assess the associated external costs of these technologies. What is relatively well known is that the water requirements for shale oil are especially significant, particularly in the drier midwestern part of the United States, where the most concentrated deposits of shale oil are found.[21] Absent more concrete evidence from experimental or commercial production, what this suggests is that the higher uncertainty of shale oil would indicate an even greater range of underlying social costs than for coal-gasification and coal-liquefaction technologies. Taken together, then, although synthetic fuels are not yet a significant element in U.S. energy supplies, if private market prices alone are used, there is some evidence that these technologies are competitive with conventional fossil fuel alternatives. If, on the other hand, social marginal costs are used, the competitive basis of synthetic fossil fuels is much smaller than the estimates of table 12.14 suggest.

As one final element in the pricing of synthetic fossil fuels, it should be noted that the development of these technologies has been designated to receive substantial federal subsidies through the recently established Synthetic Fuels Corporation. Much of the impetus to subsidize fossil fuel development has come from the dramatic increases in OPEC oil since 1973, and the associated risks of uncertain imported supplies. Subsidies can undoubtedly lower the marginal private costs of synthetics, but if we are to compare the pricing of these resources with such alternatives as renewable energy resources or energy conservation, then we must combine the marginal private costs with any external environmental costs, and with the magnitude of direct government outlays or tax subsidies that may be used.

[21]Harry Perry, *Production of Liquids and Gases from Other Resources* (Washington, D.C.: Resources for the Future, 1978), pp. 17–101. Perry's estimates of the water requirements of shale oil production are for 2–6 cubic feet per second per effective plant-year equivalent, whereas the mining of coal alone with reclamation would require 0.2–3 cubic feet per second per effective plant-year equivalent. Perry's estimates of water requirements for coal are for 2–7 cubic feet per second per plant-year equivalent.

12.3. THE PRICING OF ALTERNATIVE RENEWABLE ENERGY TECHNOLOGIES

As pointed out in chapter 7, because renewable energy resources are based almost exclusively on flows rather than on stocks, they are frequently suited to the generation of electricity. Indeed, as we have seen, many of the alternative electricity-generating technologies of table 12.13 involve renewable energy resources. At the same time, not all renewable energy resources are appropriate only to electricity generation. The two principal exceptions to this pattern are direct solar space and water heating, cooling, and biomass energy for heating and storage. Because these resources can be used in alternative ways, it is important to compare the pricing of their associated technologies with that of their conventional competitive counterparts.

While it lacks the energy density of conventional fossil fuels, biomass energy does possess one competitive quality in that it can be stored as a solid, a liquid, or a gas. As the marginal private costs of biomass resources in table 12.15 illustrate, the source costs of consumable forms of this energy appear to be competitive with the average market price of many conventional resources now used in the economy. This is particularly true in the rural and agricultural sectors of the economy, where wood-stove heating, biogas digesters, and alcohol fuels can and do compete effectively with many conventional fossil fuel and electricity counterparts. Yet what the estimates of table 12.15 do not show are the delivered marginal social costs of biomass energy resources. To find these costs, we must add transportation costs and an allowance for the health and environmental costs of these resources, thereby yielding a figure which would be somewhat higher than, and less competitive with, that for conventional fuels now in use. Moreover, if we include the opportunity costs of expanded biomass energy in terms of the supply of agricultural food crops and industrial products, then the economic advantages of biomass may be even smaller, if they exist at all, in relation to many conventional and other alternative energy technologies. As a U.S. Department of Energy recent policy review on alcohol fuels notes, not all of the impacts of biomass energy have been adequately accounted for.[22] Thus, the potential role of this resource in the economy will depend to a great extent on the clarification of these costs in relation to the costs of competing energy resource technologies.

One way to understand the significance of pricing methods for the competitiveness of alternative energy technologies is to take a more detailed look at one of them, in this case solar-heating costs and benefits. As the estimates of table 12.15 suggest, solar space and hot-water heating does appear to be competitive with many conventional heating technologies now in use. Yet it is not entirely clear whether solar heating can compete with these technologies in all cases. To illustrate the issues, we can spell out with a numerical exam-

[22]U.S. Department of Energy, *The Report of the Alcohol Fuels Policy Review* (Washington, D.C.: U.S. Government Printing Office, June 1979).

Table 12.15. Marginal Private Costs of Alternative Renewable Energy Technologies

Reference	Cost per MBtu (1976 dollars)	Estimated Feasible Commercialization Date
Residential solar heating		
Chapman (1978)	$ 6.48–7.36	1980
Clark (1975)	2.00–6.00	1970–75
FEA (1974)	2.30–3.46	1975–90
Handler (1980)[a]	6.06–32.31	1980–2000
Lovins (1977)	2.50–3.57	1975–85
Morrow (1973)	3.64–6.67	1974
Schurr (1979)[a]	9.69–26.37	1985–2000
Biomass energy[b]		
Wood-equivalent heat		
FEA (1974)	0.75	1970
Handler (1980)	0.44–1.76	1970
Schurr (1979)	0.88–2.64	1975–2000
Stobaugh-Yergin (1979)	2.00–3.50	1978
Biogas from waste		
FEA (1974)	2.29–2.54	1980
Handler (1980)	1.97	1980
Schurr (1979)	0.47–17.59	1980–2000
Synthetic liquid fuels		
FEA (1974)	2.30–4.61	1980
Handler (1980)	1.06–4.84	1980
Robinson (1974)	2.36	1980
Schurr (1979)	4.40–8.00	1985–2000
Domestic average cost of conventional resources (Dept. of Energy, 1980)		
Coal	0.82/minemouth	1979[c]
Electric resistance heat	11.60 delivered	1979[c]
Natural gas	2.76 delivered	1979[c]
Residential fuel oil	5.01 delivered	1979[c]

Sources: Duane Chapman, "Taxation, Energy Use, and Employment," Testimony delivered to the U.S. Congress, Joint Economic Committee, Subcommittee on Energy, 15 March 1978; Wilson Clark, *Energy for Survival* (Garden City, N.Y.: Doubleday Anchor Books, 1975); Federal Energy Administration, *Project Independence Blueprint* (Washington, D.C.: U.S. Government Printing Office, November 1974); Philip Handler, *Energy in Transition, 1985–2010* (San Francisco: W. H. Freeman and Company, 1980); Amory B. Lovins, *Soft Energy Paths: Toward a Durable Peace* (Cambridge, Mass.: Ballinger Publishing Co., 1977); Walter E. Morrow, Jr., "Solar Energy: Its Time Is Near," *Technology Review* 76 (December 1973):30–42; A. L. Robinson, "Energy Storage," *Science*, 17 May 1974, pp. 785–87; Sam H. Schurr, *Energy in America's Future* (Baltimore: Johns Hopkins University Press for Resources for the Future, 1979); Robert Stobaugh and Daniel Yergin, eds., *Energy Future,* Report of the Energy Project at the Harvard Business School (New York: Random House Publishers, 1979).

Note: Variations in estimates are a function of the state of technology at the time assessments were made, differences in the assumed scale of production and underlying learning curves, and alternative costs of financing, including discount rate differentials, equity versus debt financing, and the extent of assumed taxes and subsidies. Since the estimates have not been adjusted for these differences, they are not strictly comparable. Caution should therefore be exercised in their interpretation.

[a] Heat and hot water

[b] Source pricing

[c] Actual, in 1976 dollars

Table 12.16. Private Costs and Benefits of a Residential Solar Heating and Hot-Water

Year	Annualized Capital Cost of $8,000 Unit at Interest Rate of 10%	Annualized Capital Cost of $8,000 Unit at Interest Rate of 15%	Annualized Maintenance Cost, at 2% of Base Price	Tax Deductible Interest Charges at Interest Rate of 10%	Tax Deductible Interest Charges at Interest Rate of 15%	Energy Tax Credits at Interest Rate of 10%	Energy Tax Credits at Interest Rate of 15%
1	$1,051.79	$1,368.14	$10.67	$774.82	$1,174.78	$315.54	$410.44
2	1,051.79	1,368.14	10.67	747.12	1,145.77	305.18	410.44
3	1,051.79	1,368.14	10.67	716.16	1,112.42	305.18	410.44
4	1,051.79	1,368.14	10.67	683.14	1,074.07	305.18	410.44
5	1,051.79	1,368.14	10.67	646.28	1,029.96	305.18	410.44
6	1,051.79	1,368.14	10.67	605.73	979.23	305.18	410.44
7	1,051.79	1,368.14	10.67	561.12	920.89	305.18	410.44
8	1,051.79	1,368.14	10.67	512.06	853.81	305.18	410.44
9	1,051.79	1,368.14	10.67	458.08	776.66	305.18	410.44
10	1,051.79	1,368.14	10.67	398.71	687.93	305.18	410.44
11	1,051.79	1,368.14	10.67	333.46	585.90	305.18	410.44
12	1,051.79	1,368.14	10.67	261.56	468.57	305.18	410.44
13	1,051.79	1,368.14	10.67	182.54	333.63	305.18	410.44
14	1,051.79	1,368.14	10.67	95.62	178.45	305.18	410.44
15	1,051.79	1,368.14	10.67	0	0	305.18	410.44

Note: Figures are for a unit with 800 square feet of collector space with water storage and tubing included. Based on a technology of the kind illustrated in figure 7.5, an 800-square-foot unit would have a gross absorption rate of 440 MBtu's per year, with a 13 percent conversion efficiency, yielding a net residential input of 57 MBtu's, out of a total heating load of 84 MBtu's, the difference to be supplied by an auxiliary heating system.

ple the underlying conditions necessary for solar heating to be a commercially competitive energy technology.

Tables 12.16, 12.17, and 12.18 list representative financial data for a 1979–80 residential heating and hot-water technology system. A typical single-family residence ordinarily consumes about 84 million Btu's per year for heating and hot water.[23] With routine service and fuel, the cost of a conventional mixed-fuel system can amount to just under $900 per year at current base-year prices, or approximately $10.50 per delivered MBtu. A solar space and hot-water heating system costs approximately $8,000, inclusive of tubing and water-storage components. This system, which is based on 800 square feet of collector space, has a gross absorption rate of 440 million Btu's per year with a conversion efficiency of 13 percent, yielding a net residential heating input of 57 million Btu's per year, or approximately two-thirds of the residential annual heating and hot-water requirements. Estimated maintenance of the solar unit is expected to be minimal at 2 percent of the base price of the unit, which yields an annual cost of $10.67 per year.

Exclusive of any tax and subsidy considerations, the base-year annual

[23]Heating and hot-water data are based on Albert Weinstein, "Technical and Heating Consideration for Solar Heating and Cooling of Buildings: A Report by Westinghouse Electric Corporation," in *Proceedings of the Workshop on Solar Heating and Cooling of Buildings*, ed. F. Anthony Iachetta (Washington, D.C.: National Science Foundation, 1975), p. 37.

System—Basic Data

Interest-Credit Tax Benefits of 25% Tax Bracket at Interest Rate of		Interest-Credit Tax Benefits of 50% Tax Bracket at Interest Rate of		Fuel Savings with Fuel Price Increase Per Year at		
10%	15%	10%	15%	0%	5%	8%
$509.25	$704.14	$702.95	$997.83	$600	$600	$600
491.96	696.88	678.74	983.33	600	630	648
484.22	688.55	663.26	966.65	600	662	700
475.97	678.96	646.75	947.18	600	695	756
466.75	667.93	628.32	925.12	600	729	816
456.61	655.25	608.05	899.76	600	766	882
445.46	640.66	585.74	870.59	600	804	952
433.20	623.89	561.21	837.05	600	844	1,028
419.70	604.61	534.22	798.47	600	886	1,111
404.86	582.42	504.54	754.11	600	931	1,199
388.53	556.92	471.88	703.09	600	977	1,295
370.57	527.58	435.96	644.43	600	1,026	1,399
350.82	493.85	396.45	576.96	600	1,078	1,511
329.09	455.05	352.99	499.37	600	1,131	1,632
305.09	410.44	305.18	410.44	600	1,188	1,762

operating cost of the delivered solar heating and hot-water system can be derived by dividing the annualized capital and maintenance cost of the unit by the amount of net delivered heat. For capital charges of 10–15 percent, the annual cost of base-year net delivered solar heat would thus amount to between $18.64 and $24.19 per million Btu's per year, a figure significantly higher than the estimated $10.53 per million Btu's per year for the conventional mixed-fuel system already in place. However, we must also consider the impact of rising prices from conventional energy resources, the fiscal incentives affecting solar energy investment, and the time frame in which a solar unit could operate.

One way to sort out the significance of these variables is to compare alternative net benefits streams based on various underlying assumptions. Several of these net benefit streams have been calculated from the data in table 12.16 and are listed in table 12.17. As the streams clearly show, the value of solar-heating technology can be influenced significantly by the tax deductibility of interest payments, by the rate of interest on a solar loan, by solar-energy tax credits, and by the rate of increase in price of conventional energy resources. Yet, in order to make a meaningful comparison, we must consider discounting of future net benefits.[24] Once a particular discount rate has been chosen, the net present value of the investment stream can be calculated as follows:

[24]A discount rate is based on the simple proposition that a cost or a benefit in the future is worth less than is available today. However, there are important efficiency and equity implications involved in the choice of a particular discount rate for energy pricing decisions. These questions are taken up in chapter 13.

$$Z = \sum_{t=1}^{n} \frac{(B - C)_t}{(1 + i)^t}, \tag{12.7}$$

where Z is the discounted net present value, B is gross benefits, C is gross costs, i is the discount rate, and n is the number of time periods used to evaluate the investment.

Several hypothetical interest rates have been used to discount the ten net benefit streams of table 12.17. Because there are negative net benefits at different points among the streams, the largest, or optimum, stream is critically dependent on the particular rate chosen, as the net present value figures listed in table 12.18 show. If we adopt as a comparison rule of thumb that the discount rate lies between the 10 percent and the 15 percent hypothetical range of capital costs, then the choice of a particular investment stream is simplified. What this example suggests is straightforward: with no fiscal incentives and with conventional fuel increases of up to 8 percent a year, solar heating would not make sense, since the net present value is negative, even for discount rates as high as 50 percent. On the other hand, if interest charges are tax-deductible and if the current energy tax credit is available, then a solar-heating system does become economical.[25] It makes even greater sense the higher one's tax bracket and the lower the cost of capital. Thus, solar heating becomes viable only under particular circumstances and is more likely to be acquired first by higher-income individuals.

Three basic conclusions can be drawn from the preceding example. First, a first-cost comparison of alternative technologies rather than a life-cycle-cost comparison can be misleading. Where capital costs are a significant component in total delivered costs, a discounted life-cycle comparison is the relevant measure to use. Second, changes in relative energy prices can have important distributive consequences. These changes encompass the choice of specific energy technologies, as well as their effects on the personal distribution of income. Third, the competitive economic position of renewable energy resources should be judged on the same basis as that used for fossil and nuclear energy resources. The important consideration to keep in mind is that when such a consistent basis is used, as the real social costs of conventional depletable resources rise over time, solar and other renewable energy resource technologies will most certainly have a stronger role to play in the economy's aggregate energy mix. As the example we have used here suggests, the rate at which this occurs depends partly on the social rate of discount, a matter which we will consider more formally in chapter 14.

12.4. THE PRICING OF CONSERVATION ENERGY TECHNOLOGIES

To complete our discussion of alternative technology pricing, we need to consider the costs and benefits of energy conservation. As noted in chapters 10

[25]Under choices 7 and 8 of table 12.17, the 10 percent discounted present value of solar energy per MBtu is $7.36 and $5.70, respectively, exclusive of fuel savings and inclusive of tax and subsidy benefits.

Table 12.17. Alternative Net Benefit Streams for a Residential Solar Heating and Hot-Water System

Year	(1) 5% Fuel Increase, 10% Capital Charge	(2) 8% Fuel Increase, 10% Capital Charge	(3) 0% Fuel Increase, 10% Capital, Interest and Tax Credit, 25% Bracket	(4) 0% Fuel Increase, 10% Capital, Interest and Tax Credit, 50% Bracket	(5) 0% Fuel Increase, 15% Capital Charge, Interest and Tax Credit, 25% Bracket	(6) 0% Fuel Increase, 15% Capital Charge, Interest and Tax Credit, 50% Bracket	(7) 5% Fuel Increase, 10% Capital Charge, Interest and Tax Credit, 25% Bracket	(8) 5% Fuel Increase, 10% Capital Charge, Interest and Tax Credit, 50% Bracket	(9) 5% Fuel Increase, 15% Capital Charge, Interest and Tax Credit, 25% Bracket	(10) 5% Fuel Increase, 15% Capital Charge, Interest and Tax Credit, 50% Bracket
1	−$611.79	−$611.79	$ 46.79	$240.49	−$74.67	$219.02	$46.79	$240.49	− $74.67	$219.02
2	− 581.79	− 563.79	29.50	216.28	− 81.93	204.52	59.50	246.28	−51.93	234.52
3	− 549.79	− 511.79	21.76	200.80	− 90.26	187.84	83.76	262.80	−28.26	249.84
4	− 516.79	− 455.79	13.51	184.29	− 99.85	168.37	108.51	279.29	− 4.85	263.37
5	− 482.79	− 395.79	4.29	165.86	−110.88	146.31	133.29	294.86	18.12	275.31
6	− 445.79	− 329.79	− 5.85	146.59	−123.56	120.95	160.15	311.59	42.44	286.95
7	− 407.79	− 259.79	−17.00	123.28	−138.15	91.78	187.00	327.28	65.85	295.78
8	− 367.79	− 183.79	−29.26	98.75	−154.92	58.24	214.74	342.75	89.08	302.24
9	− 325.79	− 100.79	−42.76	71.76	−174.20	19.66	243.24	357.76	111.80	305.66
10	− 280.79	− 12.79	−57.60	42.08	−196.39	−24.70	273.40	373.08	134.61	306.30
11	− 234.79	83.21	−73.93	9.42	−221.89	−75.72	303.07	386.42	155.11	301.28
12	− 185.79	187.21	−90.89	−26.50	−251.23	−134.38	334.11	399.50	174.77	291.62
13	− 133.79	299.21	−111.64	−66.01	−284.96	−201.85	366.36	411.99	193.64	276.15
14	− 80.79	420.21	−133.37	−109.47	−323.76	−279.44	397.63	421.53	207.24	251.56
15	− 23.79	550.21	−157.37	−157.28	−368.37	−368.37	430.63	430.72	219.63	219.63

Note: The alternative net benefit streams have been calculated from the basic data in table 12.16.

Table 12.18. Alternative Present Values of Net Benefit Streams for a Residential Solar Heating and Hot-Water System

Net Benefit Stream[a]	Discount Rate				
	0%	5%	10%	15%	50%
(1)	−$5,229.85	−$4,006.45	−$3,188.92	−$2,618.47	−$1,090.86
(2)	−1,885.85	−2,060.70	−1,998.73	−1,855.81	−999.76
(3)	−422.04	−290.50	−131.18	−46.93	46.28
(4)	1,139.34	1,040.22	924.52	741.86	399.47
(5)	−2,695.02	−1,681.98	−1,116.76	−784.50	−188.09
(6)	132.23	457.45	566.87	583.97	358.69
(7)	3,342.18	2,052.48	1,333.22	911.77	176.20
(8)	5,086.34	3,383.95	2,388.93	1,775.33	529.40
(9)	1,252.58	661.74	347.64	174.40	−58.16
(10)	4,079.23	2,801.17	2,031.27	1,542.86	488.62

Note: Estimates have been calculated from net benefit streams in table 12.17.
[a]From table 12.17

and 11, an increase in the price of a conventional energy resource will lead to a reduction in the quantity consumed if the demand is not completely price-inelastic. In turn, the price elasticity of demand depends directly on the availability of substitute forms of energy and on whether it is possible to make a technically more efficient use of the given quantity of energy. The logic of the latter proposition is straightforward: as long as the cost of energy conservation is less than the price of conventional or alternative energy resources, there is an obvious basis for improving the technical efficiency of energy use.

Energy conservation can occur at any stage of the conversion and storage of energy. Because there are so many ways to achieve conservation, there is no single technology that could be classified as the archtypical system. At the same time, there are many representative examples that can be cited to illustrate the range of conservation energy costs.

Table 12.19 lists the marginal private costs of several alternative storage and conservation technologies. As noted in section 12.1.1, marginal private storage costs of energy converted from electricity are currently relatively expensive. However, since the amount of storage needed per unit of electrical consumption may represent a small share of total electrical consumption, there may be lowered costs in the delivered price of electricity. The net gain may arise from the lowered generating costs made possible by higher-capacity operating factors and may help to offset some of the higher marginal costs of storage. Because there is at present only limited experience with these storage systems, the potential economic gain is not as well established as in some other areas of energy conservation technology.

Four examples of alternative conservation technologies are also listed in table 12.19, and a diagrammatic profile of one of them is shown in figure 12.7. Like the private marginal cost of solar heating, the private marginal cost of conservation is subject to a number of technical and economic variables. Yet according to studies already noted, the costs of conservation in

Table 12.19. Marginal Private Costs of Alternative Storage and Conservation Technologies (in 1976 dollars)

Reference	Capital Cost per Kilowatt	Cost per MBtu (Kwh)	Estimated Feasible Commercialization Date
Pumped hydro			
Dorf (1978)	$ 188	—	1975
FEA (1974)	278–348	—	1975–80
Inglis (1978)	135–5,020	—	1975
Kalhammer (1979)	222	$ 3,550 (12.12)	1979
Compressed air			
FEA (1974)	1,016	—	1975–85
Kalhammer (1979)	238	1,184 (4.04)	1979
Flywheel			
Clark (1975)	200–600	—	1980
FEA (1974)	550	—	1980–85
Inglis (1978)	325–175,000	—	1980–85
Kalhammer (1979)	384	23,671 (80.8)	1980–85
Post-Post (1973)	139	—	1980–85
Advanced battery			
Clark (1975)	80–1,500	—	1975
FEA (1974)	250–1,393	—	1975–85
Kalhammer (1979)	80	12,882–25,764 (40.1–80.8)	1982–85
Hydrogen storage			
Dickson-Ryan-Smulyan (1977)		20–3,945	1980–85
FEA (1974)	300	—	—
Inglis (1978)	283–372	—	1978–85
Kalhammer (1979)	485	4,735 (16.2)	1980
Conservation			
Heat pumps			
Lovins (1977)	200	—	—
Schurr (1979)	—	9.60 (0.0327)	1975
Co-generation			
Schurr (1979)	200–760	5.45–9.96 (0.019–0.034)	1978
Widmer-Hatsopoulos (1977)	790		
In new and old buildings			
Schurr (1979)	—	2.50 (0.0085)	1975
Automobile fuel efficiency			
Adapted from Schurr (1979)	—	4.50–5.70 (0.015–0.019)	1980–90
Domestic average cost of conventional resources (Dept. of Energy, 1980)			
Electric resistance heat	—	11.60 delivered	1979[a]
Gasoline ($ 1.20/gallon)	—	7.69 delivered	1979[a]
Natural gas	—	2.76 delivered	1979[a]
Residential fuel oil	—	5.01 delivered	1979[a]

Sources: Wilson Clark, *Energy for Survival* (Garden City, N.Y.: Doubleday Anchor Books, 1975); Edward M. Dickson, John W. Ryan, and Marilyn H. Smulyan, *The Hydrogen Energy Economy* (New York: Praeger Publishers, 1977); R. C. Dorf, *Energy, Resources, and Policy* (Reading, Mass.: Addison-Wesley Publishing Co., 1978); Federal Energy Administration, *Project Independence Blueprint* (Washington, D.C.: U.S. Government Printing Office, November 1974); David R. Inglis, *Wind Power and Other Energy Options* (Ann Arbor: University of Michigan Press, 1978); Fritz R. Kalhammer, "Energy Storage Systems," *Scientific American* 241 (December 1979):56–65; Amory B. Lovins, *Soft Energy Paths: Toward a Durable Peace* (Cambridge, Mass.: Ballinger Publishing Co., 1977); R. F. Post and S. F. Post, "Flywheels," *Scientific American* 229 (December 1973):17–23; Sam H. Schurr, *Energy in America's Future: The Choices before Us,* Study prepared for the Resources for the Future National Energy Strategies Project (Baltimore: Johns Hopkins University Press for Resources for the Future, 1979); Thomas F. Widmer and George N. Hatsopoulos, "Summary Assessment of Electricity Cogeneration in Industry" (Waltham, Mass.: Thermo Electron Corp., 15 March 1977).

Note: Variations in estimates are a function of the state of technology at the time assessments were made, differences in the assumed scale of production and underlying learning curves, alternative costs of financing, and the extent of assumed taxes and subsidies. Since the estimates have not been adjusted for these differences, they are not strictly comparable. Caution should therefore be exercised in their interpretation.

[a]Actual, in 1976 dollars

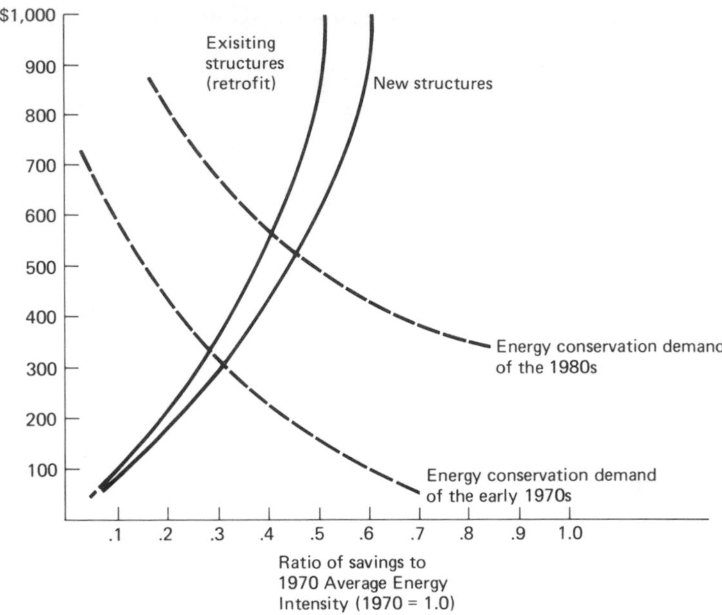

Figure 12.7. Marginal Private Capital Costs of Single-Family Residences Adopting Space-Heating Conservation Technologies, in 1975 Dollars. Adapted from E. Hirst et al., *An Improved Economic-Engineering Model of Residential Energy Use,* ORNL/CON-8 (Oak Ridge, Tenn.: Oak Ridge National Laboratory, 1977).

many cases do appear to be highly competitive with delivered energy costs of conventional resource technologies.

The economic basis for energy conservation decisions is the same as in the comparison used in equation (12.7). In the case of conservation, we can first use a variant of equation (12.1) to obtain the marginal cost of an energy-conserving investment. In this case costs reflect the investment in energy savings capacity rather than in energy generating capacity. In turn, the benefits of conservation can be expressed as the discounted flow of energy not consumed because the investment was undertaken. However, as in other types of comparisons we have examined, we should use social costs and benefits for purposes of energy policy choices rather than market prices alone. If the price elasticity of energy demand is as high as the estimates of chapter 10 suggest, then even with the energy production subsidies and pricing distortions of the recent past, conservation represents a highly competitive alternative energy resource to the social costs of imported energy or to some of the social costs of domestically produced alternatives.

12.5. SUMMARY

The pricing of electricity and alternative energy resources is dependent on a variety of factors. Regulation, the degree of competition, the state of technology, historical experience, uncertainty, and divergences between private and social costs contribute in fundamental ways to the determination of existing and projected energy prices. Any effort to formulate appropriate energy policies can only proceed with sufficient understanding of the nature of existing energy pricing and the underlying assumptions which affect its behavior.

The electricity industry, like the natural gas industry, is highly regulated. The rationale for electricity regulation is the presumption of a natural monopoly. In making actual pricing decisions, regulatory commissions can contribute to an inefficient use of resources. The adoption of nonmarginal cost pricing tends to lead to overcapitalization of the industry. In turn, given relative prices, this pattern of regulation tends to accentuate the expansion of nuclear and coal-based generating technologies, posing serious risks to health, safety, and the environment. Because the pricing of these resources does not accurately reflect their associated external costs, fundamental distortions can arise regarding the adoption of conventional and alternative energy technologies.

Though commercially less established, the costs of many alternative electricity generating technologies appear to be economically competitive with the private and social costs of conventional resources. The difficulties in measuring the costs of alternative electricity-generating technologies are that many of them are not currently available in sufficient quantities to displace existing resources or accommodate future growth, that they may have relatively high storage costs, and that their social marginal costs are subject to the uncertainties of any developing technology. Consequently, the pricing of an alternative energy technology is particularly sensitive to the fiscal incentives and to the research and development effort inherent in its adoption.

Non-electricity energy technologies represent important alternatives to existing domestic production and to the uncertainty of imported energy, especially petroleum. The private marginal costs of fossil and renewable energy resources suggest that they are strongly competitive with existing energy resources. Yet, as in the case of alternative electricity technologies, these resources are not yet available in significant quantities to have an immediate impact, and their associated prices are bounded by uncertainty and external costs. Thus, their prices are intimately tied to particular energy policy choices.

Energy conservation is an essential part of the range of alternative energy technologies. If we consider the social costs and benefits of alternative energy technologies, energy conservation may well be one of the most competitive of these choices. Whether conservation or other technologies perform such a role depends critically on how these resources are priced, and ultimately on the policy criteria by which they are to be judged.

SUGGESTED READINGS

Baughman, Martin L., Joskow, Paul L., and Kamat, Dilip P. *Electric Power in the United States: Models and Policy Analysis.* Cambridge, Mass.: MIT Press, 1979.

Cicchetti, Charles J., Gillen, W. J., and Smolensky, Paul. *The Marginal Cost and Pricing of Electricity.* Cambridge, Mass.: Ballinger Publishing Co., 1977.

Gaines, Linda, Berry, R. Stephen, and Long, Thomas Veach, II. *TOSCA: The Total Social Cost of Coal and Nuclear Power.* Cambridge, Mass.: Ballinger Publishing Co., 1979.

Kneese, Allen V., and Bower, Blair T. *Environmental Quality Analysis: Theory and Method in the Social Sciences.* Baltimore: Johns Hopkins Press for Resources for the Future, 1972.

Krutilla, John V., and Fisher, Anthony C. *Economic and Fiscal Impacts of Coal Development.* Baltimore: Johns Hopkins University Press, 1978.

Ramsey, William. *Unpaid Costs of Electrical Energy.* Baltimore: Johns Hopkins University Press for Resources for the Future, 1979.

Schmalensee, Richard. *The Control of Natural Monopolies.* Lexington, Mass.: Lexington Books, 1979.

Schurr, Sam H. *Energy in America's Future: The Choices before Us.* Study prepared for the Resources for the Future National Energy Strategies Project. Baltimore: Johns Hopkins University Press for Resources for the Future, 1979.

PART IV

THE DESIGN AND IMPLEMENTATION OF ENERGY POLICY

13

ENERGY POLICY CRITERIA—I

To judge energy policy, we need an appropriate frame of reference. As should be obvious by now, energy technologies and prices are important elements in this process. Yet these elements make sense only in relation to particular policy criteria. The preceding chapters have utilized underlying technical and economic concepts to explain the nature of existing energy conversion and storage patterns; we are now in a position to integrate these notions within a normative, or prescriptive, analytic perspective.

An energy decision can be evaluated in terms of four basic criteria. First, is it economically efficient? Second, is it equitable? Third, does it reduce the uncertainty which would occur were it not adopted? Finally, is it adequate in relation to broader economic and social objectives? Although any energy decision is likely to invoke several of these criteria, for our present purpose we can consider them in a step-by-step fashion.

13.1. THE EFFICIENT ALLOCATION OF ENERGY RESOURCES

The aspect of energy policy that has drawn the greatest attention of economists, is the question of efficiency in the use of energy resources. The reason for this degree of attention is simple enough: of the four basic policy criteria cited above, efficiency is the one which appears most amenable to the means-and-ends methodological perspective at the heart of traditional economic analysis. As we will see, although conventional economic analysis can bring much insight to bear regarding the efficient use of energy resources, there are limitations to this approach, particularly insofar as the efficient use of resources is inconsistent with associated energy policy objectives. However, before we can consider these limitations, we need first to spell out the conditions of allocative efficiency in energy resource use.

We can think of allocative efficiency in two fundamental ways: as static efficiency at a given point in time or as dynamic efficiency over time. If efficiency is to be applied at all as a criterion for energy policy decisions, the conditions of static efficiency must also be consistent with dynamic allocative efficiency. Whether in fact this is possible depends on several underlying assumptions which are set forth in the following sections.

13.1.1. Static Economic Efficiency

At several points throughout this book, reference has been made to the model of perfect competition. Since this model also conforms to static optimum allocative efficiency, we need initially to summarize the key assumptions which lie behind perfect competition. First is the assumption that there is a well-defined homogeneous and perfectly divisible product market. Second is the assumption that there are so many buyers and sellers that no single buyer or seller can have a significant influence in the determination of either the quantity produced and consumed or the price. Third, perfect competition assumes that individual consumers and producers act out of self-interest, that is, that they seek to maximize individual economic welfare. Fourth, it assumes that individual preferences are independent and additive. Finally, it assumes that markets are informationally efficient, that is, that everyone has full and immediate knowledge of any changes in production or price, that all cost and benefits are embodied in market prices, and that all resources can be switched instantly from less satisfactory to more satisfactory uses.

We can further express the model of perfect competition in terms of what economists call Pareto optimality.[1] In its simplest terms, Pareto optimality states that an efficient allocation of resources has been attained when it is no longer possible to make any futher reallocation of resources without adversely affecting someone's welfare. Conversely, there is less than a Pareto optimum when it is still possible to reallocate resources and improve economic welfare of some individuals without adversely affecting any single individual's welfare.

The relationship of Pareto optimality to a perfectly competitive economy may be understood more clearly with reference to the geometric illustration presented in figure 13.1. For purposes of graphic presentation, the economy is portrayed here as a two-person, two-good example. According to this model, the economy can produce two goods, *A* and *B*, in varying combinations up to the production-possibilities frontier, *PP*. *A* and *B* can be thought of as two types of energy, or as an energy aggregate and a non-energy aggregate.

The shape and position of the production-possibilities frontier is based on two underlying notions. The first is that technology, like the endowment of capital, labor, material, and energy inputs available to the economy, is fixed at a given point in time. The second is that whether we are considering the production of only alternative types of energy or of energy versus non-energy

[1]Named after Italian economist and sociologist Vilfredo Pareto (1848–1923), in particular, the methodology outlined in his *Manuel d'economie politique*, 2d ed. (Paris: V. Giard and E. Brière, 1909). Much of the exposition here is based on the general framework outlined in Francis M. Bator, "The Simple Analytics of Welfare Maximization," *American Economic Review* 47 (March 1957):22–59.

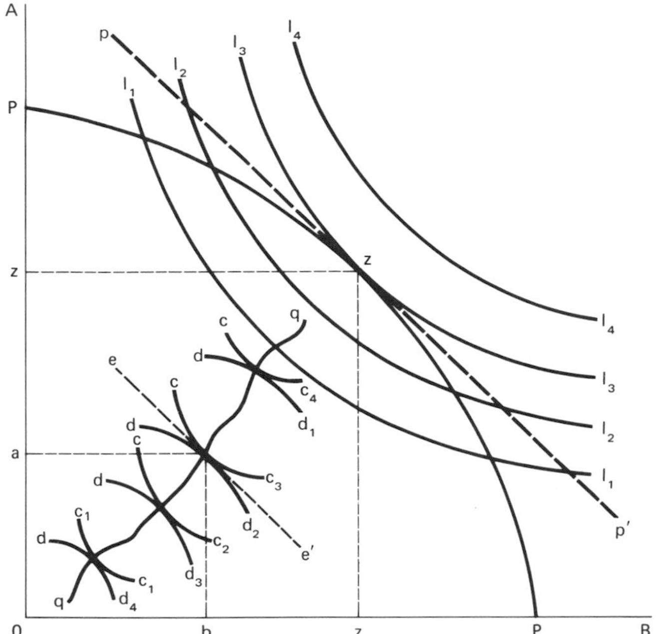

Figure 13.1. Pareto-Optimum Static Efficiency

goods, there are diminishing marginal returns from input substitution; that is, as we shift inputs away from the production of one good, such as from *A* to *B*, smaller and smaller quantity of output can be obtained from each additional input. The reason for this diminishing return is that inputs used to produce good *A* are assumed to be imperfect substitutes for the inputs needed to produce good *B*, particularly if there is some degree of specialization, as in the case of the inputs needed to produce wind-generated electricity versus those needed to produce nuclear-based electricity.

Given an economy's production possibilities, the first step in the determination of Pareto optimality is the selection of a particular output combination. Although some combination of *A* and *B* inside the production-possibilities frontier could be chosen, the assumption that self-interested individuals will seek economic-welfare maximization will tend to eliminate this possibility in favor of some point along the frontier itself.[2] The question is where this point will be and why.

[2]The assumption of informationally efficient markets is critical to this condition. Where imperfect-information conditions exist, it is relatively easy to arrive at a point corresponding to what Harvey Leibenstein has classified as "X-Inefficiency" (see his "Allocative Efficiency versus 'X-Inefficiency,' " *ibid.*, 55 [June 1966]:392–415; and Sanford J. Grossman and Joseph E. Stiglitz, "On the Impossibility of Informationally Efficient Markets," *ibid.*, 70 [June 1980]:393–408). Grossman and Stiglitz contend that a necessary condition for efficient markets is that information be costless, but in a competitive economy this requirement contradicts the notion of relative scarcity.

The simplified two-product economy of figure 13.1 is based on two individuals, *c* and *d*. Each of these self-interested individuals seeks to maximize his or her economic welfare, even though one may differ from the other as to tastes and preferences regarding the choice of alternative combinations of goods *A* and *B*. The portrayal of these tastes and preferences is given here in the individual indifference curves shown in the boxed region, *Ozzz*. At income level 1, curve cc_1 expresses the various combinations of goods *A* and *B* which yield equal satisfaction to individual *c*. In turn, curve cc_2 expresses the varying combinations of goods *A* and *B* that yield equal satisfaction to individual *c* at income level 2. Similarly, if we express individual *d*'s choices as increasing from point *z* on the production-possibilities curve toward each axis, curve dd_1 represents the various combinations of goods *A* and *B* which yield equal satisfaction at an income level 1. Curve dd_2 expresses the various combinations of goods *A* and *B* yielding equal satisfaction to individual *d* at income level 2, and so on for higher income levels.

For a given level of aggregate, or community, income, Pareto-optimal static efficiency can be attained under various patterns of income distribution. Setting aside at this point the equity issues involved in the determination of the distribution of income, for any particular level of community income as a whole we can use one hypothetical distribution to complete the selection of a Pareto-optimal allocation.

In figure 13.1, given the distribution of income between individuals *c* and *d* along their contract, or conflict, curve *qq*, the optimal mix of goods *A* and *B* will be where each individual's highest possible indifference curve is tangent to the other's. As shown here, individual *c* will consume *ca* of good *A* and *cb* of good *B*, while individual *d* will consume *za* of good *A* and *zb* of good *B*. The point of tangency of these two indifference curves is where the marginal rate of substitution of goods *A* and *B* for individual *c* is equal to the marginal rate of substitution of goods *A* and *B* for individual *d*.

When the indifference curves of individuals *c* and *d* are joined together, they can be expressed as the community indifference curve, which is part of the community's social-welfare function.[3] Given the initial level of income and its distribution between individuals *c* and *d*, community indifference curve $I_1 I_1$ represents various combinations of goods *A* and *B* that yield equal community satisfaction. Similarly, community indifference curve $I_2 I_2$ expresses the various combinations of goods *A* and *B* that yield equal community satisfaction at income level 2, and so on for higher income levels. Com-

[3]Despite its conceptual simplicity, the joining of individual indifference curves to derive the community's social-welfare function is no simple matter. Whether we can do so depends on whether individual preferences are independent, and therefore additive. If they are not independent, then the community-welfare function depends more critically on the particular pattern of income distribution that may be adopted. Thus, unlike the conventional model of Pareto optimality, economic efficiency will vary to some extent according to the distribution of income (see M. J. Farrell, "The Convexity Assumption in the Theory of Competitive Markets," *Journal of Political Economy* 62 [August 1959]:377–91; Jerome Rothenberg, "Non-Convexity, Aggregation, and Pareto Optimality," ibid., 63 [October 1960]:435–68; and M. J. Gorman, "Are Social Indifference Curves Convex?" *Quarterly Journal of Economics*, August 1959, pp. 485–96).

munity economic welfare is maximized at the point of tangency between the highest community indifference curve and the economy's production-possibility frontier *PP*. In figure 13.1, this is found at point *z* on the production-possibilities curve.

Under the given assumptions, point *z* represents the Pareto-optimal efficient allocation of resources, since the marginal rate of transformation (*MRT*) of good *A* to good *B* is just equal to the marginal rate of substitution (*MRS*) of good *A* for good *B* in the community's social-welfare function. Moreover, the individual marginal rate of substitution of good *A* to good *B* of individual *c* is equal to that of individual *d*, and each is also equal to the marginal rate of transformation. In terms of costs, since in a perfectly competitive economy price is equal to marginal cost, and since marginal cost is equivalent here to the opportunity cost of production, or the marginal rate of transformation of good *A* to good *B*, Pareto optimality is equivalent to the equalization of marginal costs to the marginal utility per unit of expenditure by the individuals who consume these two goods.[4] In algebraic terms:

$$MRT = -\frac{\Delta A}{\Delta B} = \frac{MC_B}{MC_A} \tag{13.1}$$

and

$$MRS = -\frac{\Delta A}{\Delta B} = \frac{\Delta U / \Delta B}{\Delta U / \Delta A} = \frac{MU_B}{MU_A} = \frac{P_B}{P_A}. \tag{13.2}$$

Since $P_B/P_A = MC_B/MC_A$, Pareto optimality thus becomes

$$MRS = MRT. \tag{13.3}$$

In diagrammatic terms, these conditions are equivalent to the equalization of the slopes of lines *pp*′ and *ee*′.

The appeal of Pareto optimality is that it appears to answer in a convenient form the best possible combination of goods production based on an initial endowment of resources and an associated level and distribution of income. At the same time, because there are differences between this model and the real-world economy, Pareto optimality serves largely as a frame of reference for considering policy alternatives when its underlying assumptions are not realized. The question is, To what extent can we relax these assumptions and still arrive at a Pareto-equivalent level of allocative efficiency?

[4]Pareto optimality traditionally comprises three conditions. In addition to the stipulation that the marginal rates of substitution between any pair of consumer goods be the same for all consumers and that the marginal rate of transformation in production be equal to the marginal rate of substitution in consumption for each pair of commodities and for each individual who consume both of these commodities, Pareto optimality also requires that the marginal rate of technical substitution between any two inputs must be the same for all producers who consume both inputs, e.g., $MRTS^x{}_{kl} = MRTS^y{}_{kl} = P_k/P_l$, where *k* and *l* refer respectively to individual inputs. Although the generalization may be true for an individual unit in the economy, there is a difficulty in applying it to the economy as a whole in that the marginal productivity of capital can not be readily determined independently of the interest rate (see G. C. Harcourt, *Some Cambridge Controversies in the Theory of Capital* [Cambridge: Cambridge University Press, 1972]).

13.1.2. Static Market Failure

Pareto-optimality conditions may be violated by five basic types of market failure. First, there may be substantial imperfect competition. Second, externalities may be present. Third, decreasing cost conditions may arise. Fourth, some goods may be available only through public-goods intervention. Finally, markets may be informationally incomplete, and therefore uncertain. Uncertainty is treated separately in chapter 14; our concern here is with the implications of the four types of static market failure and with the choices available to remedy them.

As noted in part III, if we use established measures of pricing, profitability, and concentration as test, energy markets in the United States and international markets such as the OPEC cartel can hardly be said to conform to the model of perfect competition. At the same time, neither do these markets exhibit the other extreme of pure monopoly. Rather, they are more typically representative of the gray worlds of oligopoly and monopolistic competition. Before we can consider alternative remedies, however, it is instructive to point out how imperfect competition leads to a distortion of the Pareto-optimal conditions just enumerated.

Where imperfect competition exists, production will be smaller and prices will be higher than would otherwise be the case.[5] How this leads to a breakdown of Pareto optimality can be seen in figure 13.2. Let us first consider the case where only sector *B* of the economy is imperfectly competitive. Initially, the increase in relative price of good *B* will tend to shift consumer preferences from the initial equilibrium at z to somewhere to the left of z, such as at v. However, there is also a reduction in quantity arising from sector *B*'s imperfectly competitive production. This has the effect of reducing the production-possibilities curve from *PP* to *PP'*, since the same level of resources will now yield a smaller level of good *B* than before. Community welfare is thus lowered from point z on I_2I_2 to a second-best point such as z' on I_1I_1. Because the relative-price line which passes through points such as v or z' will be steeper than the original line *pp*, individuals *c* and *d* will no longer be at an optimum level of welfare. Pareto optimality is violated, because the economy's marginal rate of substitution along I_2I_2 at point z is no longer equal to the marginal rate of product transformation of good *A* to good *B* along its new

[5]In more formal terms, let the monopolist's profit-maximizing revenues and costs be expressed as functions of the quantity produced: $\pi = qf(q) - c(q)$. Profit maximization requires that the rate of change in profits as a function of output be zero, i.e., $\partial\pi/\partial q = f(q) + af'(q') - c'(q) = 0$, where $f(q) + af'(a)$ is marginal revenue and $c'(q)$ is marginal cost. A second-order condition for profit maximization is that the slope of the marginal-revenue curve be less than the slope of the marginal-curve, i.e., that $\partial^2\pi/\partial^2 q = sf'(q) + af''(q) - c''(q) < 0$. The difference between a competitive and a monopolistic firm is that profit maximization (or loss minimization) requires that the slope of its marginal-cost curve be positive in the former case, whereas it can be positively or negatively sloped in the latter as long as its absolute value exceeds the value of the slope of the marginal-revenue curve. Given the nature of cost and revenue curves, a monopolist will thus choose a point of output which is lower than that of a perfectly competitive firm, and the corresponding price will therefore tend to be higher.

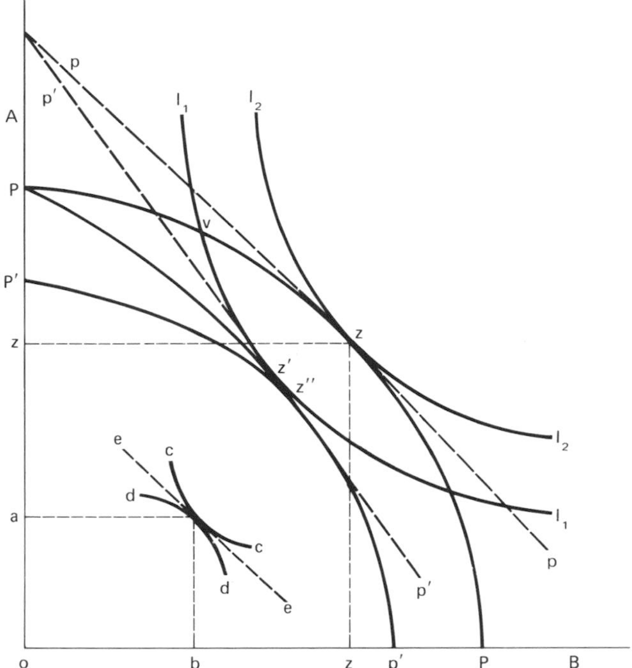

Figure 13.2. Consequences of Imperfect Competition on Pareto-Optimum Static Efficiency

production-possibilities curve PP' at point z'. Moreover, with its lower level of economic welfare of I_1I_1 at z', the distribution of goods A and B between individuals c and d may also be altered.

A second case to consider is where imperfect competition prevails in both product markets. Here, it is possible to achieve a pseudo Pareto optimum. A pseudo Pareto optimum occurs where there is an equality of the marginal rate of substitution and the marginal rate of transformation of good A to good B, but at a lower level of aggregate economic welfare than could be achieved under a perfectly competitive market structure. It is shown here by the point of tangency z'' of the imperfectly competitive production-possibilities curve $P'P'$ to the community welfare curve I_1I_1. Though not shown here, it has a relative-price line with a slope just equal to the original relative-price line pp. What is more, the equalization of individual marginal rates of substitution of good A to good B may be accompanied by a further redistribution of income between individuals c and d. Taken together, the two cases of deviations from Pareto optimality point to an important theorem of welfare economics in general and to energy policy in particular: if one attempts to correct the deficiency of imperfect competition in energy markets, an improvement in economic welfare as a whole will occur only if the same standard is applied

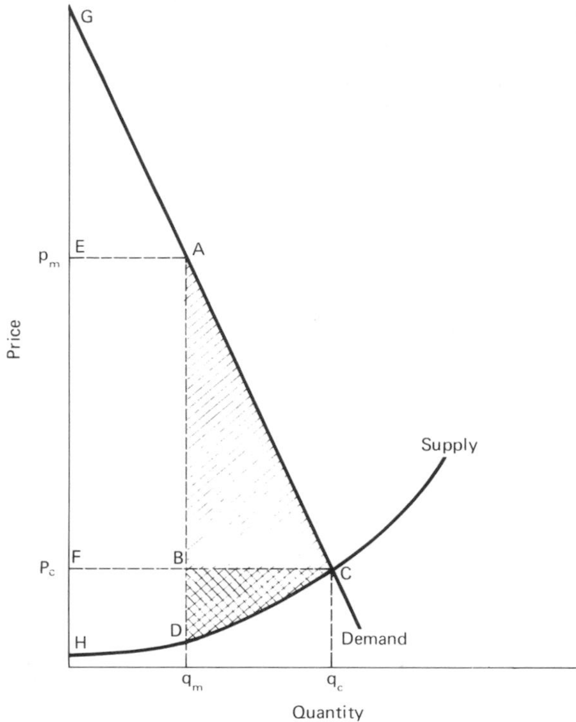

Figure 13.3. Welfare Losses under Imperfect Competition

to all other sectors of the economy.[6] Piecemeal measures will perpetuate, if not worsen, the existing degree of allocative inefficiency.

With the preceding framework in mind, we can further express the impact of imperfect competition in terms of the distributive gains and losses among producers and consumers. Figure 13.3 illustrates the welfare impact of imperfect competition based on private market equilibrium conditions. Under perfectly competitive market conditions, equilibrium price and quantity would be at p_c and q_c, respectively. Imperfect competition results in a higher price and lower quantity, at p_m and q_m, respectively. The triangular region *ACD* represents the private economic-welfare loss from imperfect competi-

[6]The standard reference for this proposition is R. G. Lipsey and Kelvin Lancaster, "The General Theory of Second Best," *Review of Economic Studies* 24 (1956–57):11–33. In terms of figure 13.2, if we were to undertake measures to make only the energy sector of the economy more competitive, the relative price of energy would decline, thereby inducing the economy to adopt a more energy-intensive pattern of production and consumption than it would were all sectors equally competitive (or equally non-competitive). Pareto optimality would be violated in that the marginal rate of substitution would be greater than the marginal rate of transformation obtainable under universally competitive conditions. Stated more rigorously, the Lipsey-Lancaster conclusion stipulates that if one or more of the first-best conditions is not met, second-best choices are attainable only if all other Pareto first-best conditions are abandoned. Moreover, as long as one or more Pareto first-best condition remains unmet, we can not conclude a priori that a minimization of all other departures will represent a Pareto-optimal improvement.

tion. It consists of two elements, consumers' and producers' surplus, each of which merits brief elaboration.[7]

Consumers' surplus is a measure of the value of a good to consumers and is defined as the difference between what an individual actually pays and what the individual would be willing to pay for the given quantity of the good. Similarly, producers' surplus is a measure of the value of a good to producers and is defined as the difference between what a producer can actually charge and the minimum necessary price needed to induce firms to provide a given quantity of a good. In figure 13.3, under a perfectly competitive equilibrium, consumers who would be willing to purchase q_m of a good would be willing to pay a price of p_m in accordance with a given level of demand, GC, and its associated income, relative-price, tastes, and preference determinants. Yet, if the actual equilibrium price is only p_c, then there is a consumers' surplus, segment AB, that is, a benefit which consumers are not actually required to pay even though they would be willing to do so. As we move along the demand curve, the complete range of consumers' surplus is represented by the triangular region FGC, given the existing equilibrium price p_c.[8] Similarly, the range of producers' surplus consists of the region HFC. In the context of imperfect competition, the region ACD thus represents a loss to both producers and consumers.

Given the welfare losses illustrated in figure 13.3, we also need to understand why it makes sense for firms to seek monopolistic gains in the first place. Profit maximization, sales maximization, and individual-firm economic security concerns all enter into such a decision, to be sure.[9] Rather than elaborate on the relative effects of these factors on individual-firm behavior, we need here to translate the gain to producers from imperfect competition in the diagrammatic terms of figure 13.3. Since there is a loss of producers' surplus equals to the triangle BCD, there must be a gain at least as great in order for it to make sense to pursue monopolistic behavior. In this case, the gain to producers consists of the rectangle $FEAB$, a region much larger in area than that of the loss BCD. As figure 13.3 also suggests, the

[7]Consumers' and producers' surplus were formulated, respectively, by Jules Dupuit (1804–66) and Alfred Marshall (1842–1924) (see Jules Dupuit, *De l'Utilité et de sa mesure* [Turin: Editions Marie de Bernardi, 1933], first published in 1844; and Alfred Marshall, *Principles of Economics*, 9th ed. [London: Macmillan Publishing Co., 1961], first published in 1890).

[8]If the demand curve is linear, we can derive the amount of consumers' surplus as $S = 0.5\Delta P\Delta Q$. In actuality, demand curves are often nonlinear. Consequently, consumers' surplus can be expressed as $Z = \int_a^b Z(Q)dQ$, where $Z(q)$ is the given demand function and a and b represent the range of prices of the given segment of the demand curve.

[9]Differences in firms' objectives obviously can affect our estimate of the degree of economic inefficiency arising from imperfect competition. In addition to the theory of X-inefficiency referred to in note 2 and the conventional profit-maximizing hypothesis, for a theory of economic security, see J. K. Galbraith, *The New Industrial State* (Boston: Hougton-Mifflin, 1967). For a theory of sales maximization, see W. J. Baumol, *Business Behavior*, 2d ed. (New York: Macmillan Publishing Co., 1959). For a non-optimizing theory of "satisficing" behavior, see Henry Simon, "Theories of Decision-Making in Economics and Behavioral Science," *American Economic Review* 49 (June 1959). For a more recent survey, see Oliver Williamson, *Markets and Hierarchies: Analysis and Antitrust Implications* (New York: Free Press, 1975).

more inelastic the demand for a good, the easier it becomes to obtain monopolistic gains, much as was suggested in chapters 10 and 11.[10]

Externalities can also lead to a breakdown of Pareto optimality, even when all other conditions of a perfectly competitive economy are met. As noted in previous chapters, externalities are unpaid costs or benefits accruing to third parties from a given market transaction. In the present context, these consequences are known as technological externalities in the sense that they are not priced directly through market transactions.[11] Their value must therefore be imputed on the basis of their opportunity costs. It is for this reason that economists often use the term "shadow prices" when attempting to measure the value of these external costs and benefits and their associated private market costs and benefits.

External costs and benefits can be found in both production and consumption. In the reference terms of the Pareto optimality diagram figure 13.1, they create distortions in both the production-possibilities transformation curve and in the individual and community indifference curves. In summary terms, we can note the following modifications of Pareto-optimality conditions arising from the impact of technological externalities. Let us first consider the general case where externalities exist only in the case of one good, such as B in figure 13.1. An external cost such as environmental pollution in the production of good B is equivalent to a downward shift in the production-possibilities curve from PP to PP', as shown in figure 13.2. In turn, community welfare is now lowered from its original level of $I_2 I_2$ to $I_1 I_1$, and at a new point of tangency such as z', on its altered production-possibilities curve. Pareto optimality no longer holds, because the economy's marginal rate of substitution along $I_2 I_2$ at z is no longer equal to its marginal rate of transformation of good A to good B along its new production-possibilities curve PP' at z'. In the more practical terms of this example, since environmental pollution derives partly from a technically inefficient conversion of energy, a reduction in pollution would yield a greater quantity of good B, whether it is net energy itself or an associated energy-consuming good. In the case of a production external economy, the initial production-possibilities curve would be PP' and each of the preceding conditions in the external-production-cost example would be reversed.

Externalities in consumption are reflected in the alteration of individual and community indifference curves rather than in alterations in the shape and position of the production-possibilities curve. Let us consider again the case where consumption externalities are found only in one sector. If there is an external consumption cost such as the rejected heat and particulate emis-

[10]The less elastic a demand curve, the greater will be the vertical distance between the equilibrium price and the demand curve itself at positions other than the intersection of market demand and supply.

[11]For elaborations on these distinctions, see James E. Meade, "External Economics and Diseconomies in a Competitive Situation," *Economic Journal* 62 (1952):54–67; and Tibor Scitovsky, "Two Concepts of External Economies," *Journal of Political Economy* 62 (April 1954):143–51.

sions from the burning of gasoline, good *B*, then the private preferences of individuals for gasoline will be greater than the social one. In the reference terms of figure 13.1, if there were pollution, the community indifference curve would show a smaller relative preference for gasoline than if pollution were controlled. This would be equivalent to a community preference between goods *A* and *B* somewhat to the left of the original equilibrium of $I_2 I_2$ and *PP* at *z*, such as at *v* in figure 13.2. Yet the non-market external costs, unless otherwise internalized within the price of gasoline, would lead to the continued adoption of point *z* along *PP*. In the converse case of a consumption external economy, the reverse condition would hold.

It should be noted that external economies and diseconomies can also occur under pseudo Pareto-optimal conditions. In this case, a pseudo Pareto optimum can occur as long as the net external economies or diseconomies in the production of good *A* are equal to the net external economies or diseconomies in the production of good *B*. Similarly, it can occur as long as the net external economies or diseconomies in the consumption of good *A* are equal to the net external economies or diseconomies in the consumption of good *B*. If there are equal net consumption external economies, community welfare would be enhanced by an augmented production of both up to some limit along the production-possibilities frontier. Realization of the net production external economies would be equivalent to the potential expansion of the production-possibilities frontier itself. The policy implication of these cases is that as in the case of market failure through imperfect competition, measures to correct externalities distortions in the energy sector of the economy will lead to an improvement in community economic welfare only if the same standards are applied to all sectors of the economy.

The distorting effects of externalities can also be expressed in terms of the distributive gains and losses among producers and consumers. The various diagrams of figure 13.4 illustrates the welfare consequences of alternative externalities configurations on market equilibrium conditions. In figure 13.4.*a*, an initial private market equilibrium with production external economies exists with price p_1 and quantity q_p. Because the production of the particular good, let us say hydroelectricity, also makes possible a hitherto unfeasible irrigation system for bringing adjacent lands under cultivation, there is a potential production external economy. From the farmer's point of view, as long as the costs of irrigation are less than the costs of not farming, there is an advantage in paying the owner of the hydroelectric unit some compensation for the amount of water consumed. From the hydroelectric plant operator's point of view, as long as the water payments by the farmer are greater than the benefits of electricity not produced, there is an equal incentive to enter into an agreement with the farmer to permit irrigation. The welfare gain consists of the sum of net benefits to both parties from undertaking a joint cooperative project.

With no irrigation, the private market equilibrium of the demand and supply of electricity alone would have a welfare level equal to the region *PDA*. This consists of Pp_1A producer surplus and p_1DA consumer surplus. Now if

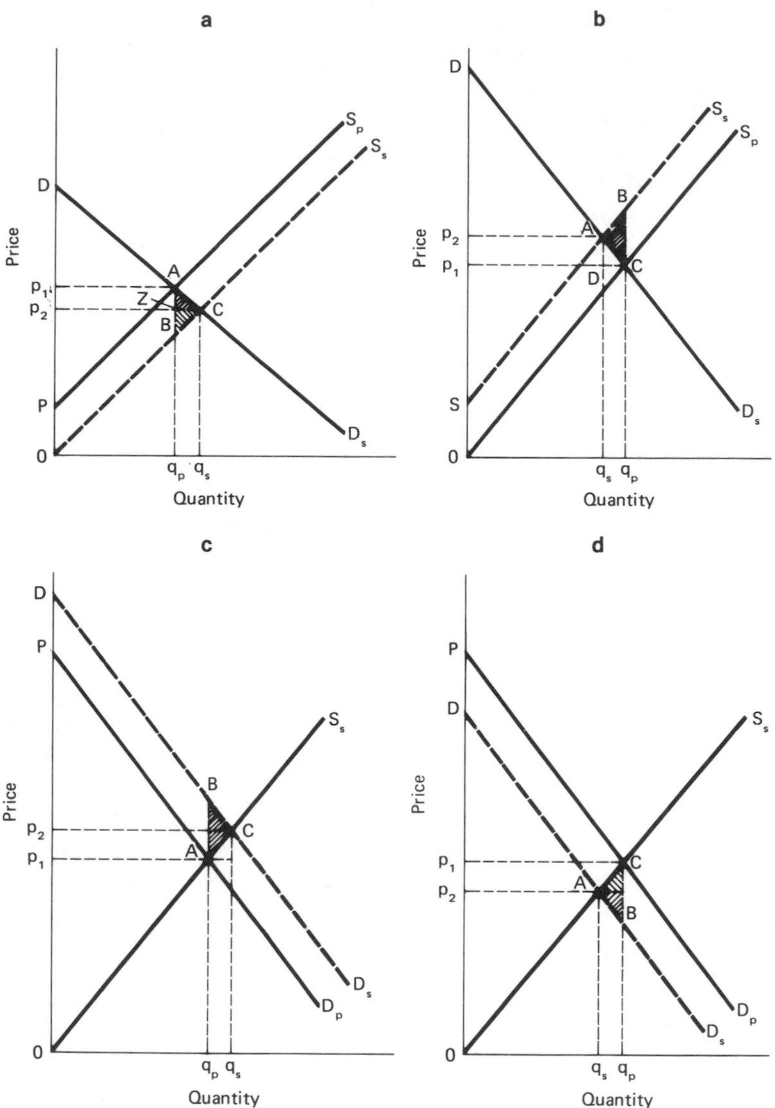

Figure 13.4. Welfare Effects of Alternative Externalities Configurations: **a**. production external economies; **b**. production external diseconomies; **c**. consumption external economies; **d**. consumption external diseconomies.

payments by the farmer amounting to AB per unit of water consumed are undertaken, the value of joint electricity and farm production will be augmented from the original supply curve S_p to S_s, and a new, socially optimal equilibrium will be achieved at price p_2 and quantity q_s. The gain in community economic welfare is equal to the difference between the social benefits and social costs throughout the range of production and consumption under consideration. In this case, the social cost with the farmer's subsidy is equal to q_pBCq_s, and the social benefit is equal to ACq_sq_p, leaving a net social benefit of ABC, which comprises the increments of consumers' and producers' surplus.[12] Conversely, if we were considering a production external diseconomy such as environmental pollution from a coal-fired electricity-generating plant, the region ABC of figure 13.4.*b* could be interpreted as the gain in social welfare from the imposition of a tax per unit of electricity produced equal to AB.

Static market failure can also exist under conditions of decreasing-cost industries.[13] As noted in previous chapters, decreasing-cost industries are those in which a firm has a long-run declining average-cost function. If the declining-cost function exists throughout the range of marketable production, then the industry could be considered as a natural monopoly, that is, there is an economic basis for permitting a single firm in the industry to operate in order to obtain the lowest possible average cost of production under the greatest possible volume of output. However, unless the industry is regulated to achieve this maximum level of economic efficiency, it could simply adopt the conventional profit-maximizing rule of choosing a price-output combination where marginal cost equals marginal revenue, thereby reducing the level of social welfare.

The potential welfare consequences within a decreasing-cost industry are illustrated in figure 13.5. If a regulated price of p_c rather than p_m is adopted, production will increase from q_m to q_n, leading to an increase in consumers' surplus of the region *avd*. However, as in the other categories of static market failure, Pareto optimality will be attained only if measures designed to maximize the social-welfare gains from decreasing-cost industries in the energy sector are applied in equal degree to all other sectors of the economy.

The final category of static market failure is public, or social, goods. In previous chapters we saw that this category of goods encompasses both quasi-public and pure public goods. The breakdown of Pareto optimality occurs because all (pure public) or a portion (quasi-public) of the benefits from a good yield external pecuniary benefits which can not be captured on the basis of market prices alone by the producers who could provide them. In terms of

[12]Since the increase in consumers' surplus of p_1AZp_2 is equal to the loss in producers' surplus, our concern is with the net change in social welfare at the margin. The welfare gain in this case is equal to ZAC of consumers' surplus and ABC of producers' surplus. A quality unique to this example is that if the affected parties of a potential project are few enough in number, then it may be possible to arrange a local-order solution independently of specific governmental intervention. Some writers such as Ronald Coase and James M. Buchanan contend that these local-order opportunities are likely to be more widespread than a general advocate of public intervention might be willing to admit (see Ronald M. Coase, "The Problem of Social Cost," *Journal of Law and Economics* 3 [October 1960]:1–44; and James M. Buchanan and William Craig Stubblebine, "Externality," *Economica* 29 [November 1962]:371–84).

[13]E. D. Lowrey, in "Justification for Regulation: The Case for Natural Monopoly," *Public Utilities Fortnightly* 92 (8 November 1973):17–23, attributed the origin of natural monopoly to John Stuart Mill (1806–73). The modern formulation dates from Allyn Young, "Pigou's Wealth and Welfare," *Quarterly Journal of Economics* 27 (1913):672–86; and Piero Sraffa, "The Law of Returns under Competitive Conditions," *Economic Journal* 36 (1926):535–50.

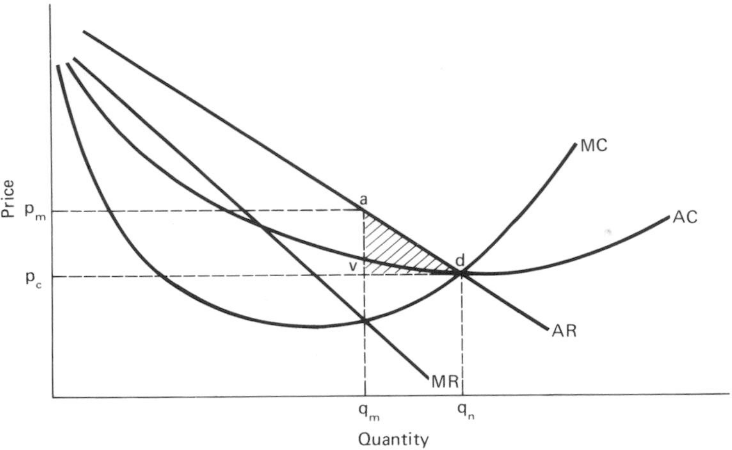

Figure 13.5. Static Welfare Effects of Decreasing-Cost Industries

the Pareto-optimality framework of figure 13.1, to the extent that public goods are a significant element in the economy, under a given production-possibilities frontier, the economy's individual indifference curves will be tangent at points where their marginal rates of substitution are not equal to the marginal rate of transformation.[14] Typical of this type of market failure is the question of basic energy research. Unlike applied energy research, basic research may be difficult if not impossible to appropriate through private markets alone, since many if not all of the potential benefits may redound to society as a whole rather than to well-defined markets with specific, well-behaved pricing structures. Hence, the principal way in which these public goods must often be produced is by direct government intervention. Again, however, for Pareto optimality to be achieved, the degree of intervention in energy markets must be accompanied by application of the same standards to non-energy markets.

The welfare dimensions of quasi-public goods are analogous to the consumption external economies illustrated in figure 13.4.*c*. However, the case of pure public goods is somewhat more complicated. Figure 13.6 illustrates the welfare conditions existing in the case of pure public goods. Unlike the private-good market demand curves, derived as the horizontal summation of individual demand curves, the demand curve for pure public goods is derived as the vertical summation of individual demand curves.[15] What this means is

[14]In this case, consider *A* as units of private good and *b* as a pure public good. At any particular level of income distribution, consumers tend to adjust their mix of purely private goods to arrive at a Pareto-optimal allocation. However, when one or more goods are indivisible pure public ones, then each individual will adopt a public-private preference marginal rate of substitution that may not be equal to the marginal rate of substitution of any or all other cumsumer. For an exposition of this point, see Paul A. Samuelson, "The Pure Theory of Public Expenditures," *Review of Economics and Statistics* 36 (November 1954):387–89; and idem, "Diagrammatic Exposition of a Theory of Public Expenditures," 37 (November 1955):350–6.

[15]This definition was first given by Howard R. Bowen in *Toward Social Economy* (New York: Rinehart, 1948), p. 177.

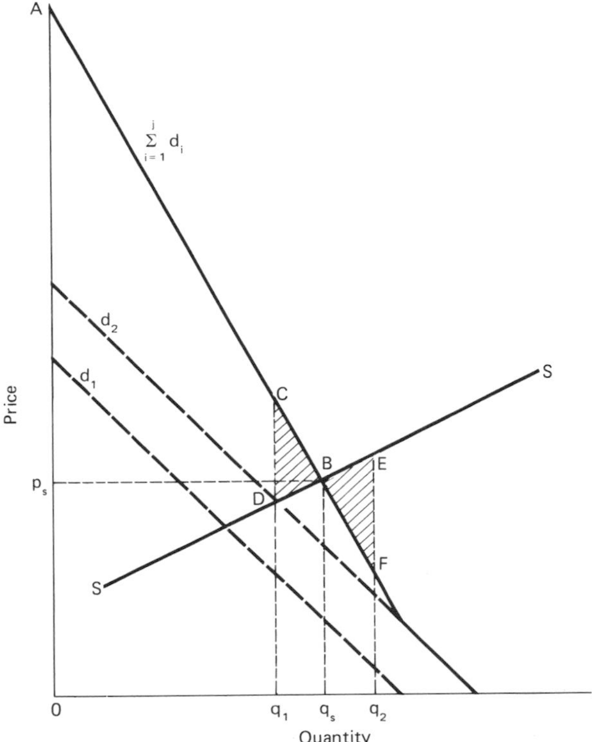

Figure 13.6. Static Welfare Conditions for Pure Public Goods

that the marginal social cost of an extra unit of consumption of a public good is zero, that is, the benefits are indivisible. If, as in the proverbial lighthouse example, the benefits are indivisible, then there is no way that anyone can be excluded from consumption of the good, and it is therefore not in any individual's interest to produce it. In figure 13.6, the welfare level corresponding to a Pareto approximate optimum is where the vertical sum of the individual demand curves is equal to the marginal social cost of production, shown here are price p_s and quantity q_s, respectively. However, there is no guarantee that the economy will actually attain this optimum. The reason why it may fail to do so is that equal per capita consumption of the pure public good in relation to heterogeneous consumer preferences may not result in the equalization of individual marginal rates of substitution between private and public goods.[16] Worse yet, if there are imperfections or inconsistencies in the political process by which pure-public-goods preferences are expressed, it is very possible that a less than or greater than socially optimal quantity of a pure public good may be produced, shown here by points q_1 and q_2, respec-

[16]Whether this equalization can be achieved depends partly on how public goods are to be financed, that is, on how taxation and borrowing choices affect consumer preferences for individual private goods. For a more detailed treatment, see Richard W. Tresch, *Public Finance: A Normative Theory* (Plano, Tex.: Business Publications, 1981), esp. chaps. 13–20.

tively. The shaded areas *BCD* and *BEF* represent the corresponding degrees of social-welfare losses arising from such choices.

13.1.3. Policy Choices for Static Market Failure

A logical question of concern to policymakers is whether, and under what conditions, public intervention can bring about an improvement in allocative efficiency. The policy rule which economists have adopted is that any change in which the marginal social benefits are greater than the marginal social costs is an improvement in allocative efficiency. A corollary to this rule is that any change which yields no increase in allocative efficiency but which satisfies other criteria is also worth undertaking. In cases where a decrease in allocative efficiency accompanies the fulfilling of one or more other policy criteria, no conclusion can be drawn without a full specification of the weights society attaches to various policy objectives, in other words, its social-welfare function. Since we are concerned here with static allocative efficiency, we still defer any consideration of the third alternative until chapter 14.

The effects of any change in welfare can be traced to four economic agents: producers, consumers, government, and third parties. In terms of the general policy rule, an improvement in allocative efficiency can be said to occur as long as the sum of the changes in these variables is greater than zero. To illustrate the application of this rule, we can consider two of four types of market failure discussed under section 13.1.*b*, namely, imperfect competition and externalities.

Figure 13.7 illustrates the welfare and distributive consequences of imperfect competition referred to in figure 13.6. An imperfectly competitive industry will maximize profits by lowering production from q_c to q_m, by raising prices from p_c to p_m, and will enjoy an increase in producers' surplus of $p_c p_m AB$ minus *BCD*. In turn, the loss of consumers' surplus $p_c p_m AC$ leaves a net welfare loss of the triangular region *ACD*. Now, in an effort to restore this loss, government may consider the imposition of taxes, regulation, antitrust, or nationalization. Let us consider, for example, the use of taxation. Government can impose a tax on the industry up to a limit of $p_m - p_c (= AD)$ at the imperfectly competitive production level q_m. Government would thus receive revenues equal to the shaded area $p_1 p_m$AD, which is far greater than the welfare-loss region *ACD*. Yet it does not follow that an improvement in allocative efficiency has occurred. Government could distribute $p_c p_m AB$ of its revenues to consumers to restore some of the loss in consumers' surplus, and it could apportion an amount equal to *ABC* to make up for the remainder. However, while these revenues could certainly eliminate the net gain in producers' surplus of the imperfectly competitive industry, they would also eliminate part or all of the producers' surplus of $p_1 p_c BD$, which would have existed even under competitive economic conditions. Furthermore, if we include the transactions costs of government intervention, the net redistributive potential would be even less than the amount $p_1 p_m BD$. Consequently, even under costless redistribution, there is still a net welfare loss equal to *ACD*, the amount which the original intervention was designed to

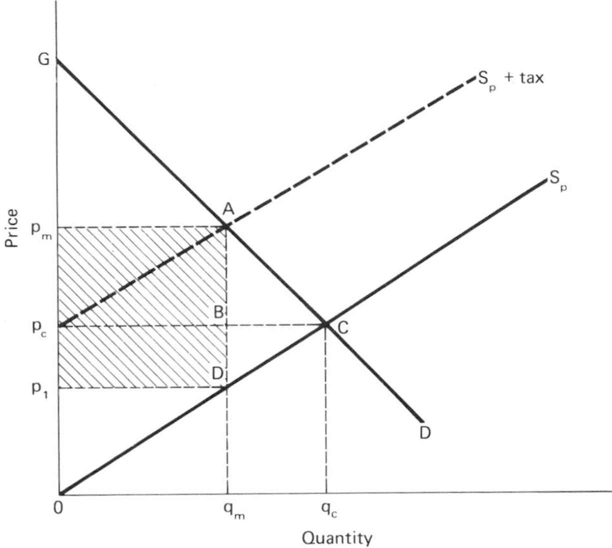

Figure 13.7. Welfare Effects of Taxation on Imperfect Competition

eliminate. It is for this reason that ACD is considered a deadweight loss, that is, it is impossible to eliminate within a static allocative framework.

As should be obvious by now, static welfare criteria are traditionally applied in marginal, or incremental, units. The key to potential welfare gains and losses turns largely on the size of the triangular regions defined by the intersection of private and social demand and supply curves. These regions could be measured by geometry, but because nonlinearities exist in many demand and supply curves, the technique most often used is numerical integration. The traditional way of measuring the triangular area ACD in figure 13.7 is:

(13.4) $$Z = \int_{q_1}^{q_2} (P_d - \bar{P}_s)dQ,$$

where P_d is the prevailing market demand function and P_s is the imperfectly competitive industry's supply function. For example, if the competitive market demand and supply curves for daily petroleum production, in barrels per day, are defined as[17]

[17]It should be kept in mind that these equations are based on *ceteris paribus* conditions. In a more realistic econometric equation, other influences should be allowed for and held statisically constant. The degree of bias in statistical demand curves will be smaller the greater the substitution effect over the income effect, and the smaller the share an item is in consumer budgets. An index of statistical bias in demand curves has been proposed by J. M. Henderson and R. E. Quandt as: $e_i - E_i = S_i n_{iy}$, where e_i is the price elasticity of demand of an adjusted demand schedule, E_i is the price elasticity of demand of an unadjusted demand schedule, S_i is the share of income spent on the particular item, and n is the income elasticity of demand (see their *Microeconomic Theory* [New York: McGraw-Hill, 1971], pp. 31–37).

(13.5) $$P_d = 87 - 0.0000085\, Q$$

and

(13.6) $$P_s = 2 + 0.0000015\, Q,$$

this yields a competitive equilibrium price of \$14.75 per barrel and a domestic production and consumption rate of 8.5 million barrels per day. However, given imperfectly competitive conditions, an alternative industry supply curve can be defined as

(13.7) $$\bar{P}_s = 12 + 0.0000015\, Q,$$

which when combined with the market demand curve of equation (13.5) results in an equilibrium price of \$23.25 per barrel and an equilibrium quantity of 7.5 million barrels per day.

To calculate the welfare loss using equation (13.4), we must first subtract equation (13.7) from equation (13.5):

(13.8) $$P_d - \bar{P}_s = 75 - 0.00001\, Q.$$

Then, taking the antiderivative of (13.8) and subtracting the values of the upper and lower quantity levels yields:[18]

(13.9) $$\int_{8,500,000}^{7,500,000} (75 - 0.00001\, Q)dQ = 75Q - \frac{0.00001\, Q^2}{2}\Bigg|_{8,500,000}^{7,500,000}$$

$$= \left[75(7,500,000) - \frac{0.00001(7,500,000)^2}{2}\right]$$

$$- \left[75(8,500,000) - \frac{0.00001(8,500,000)^2}{2}\right]$$

$$= 5,000,000.$$

[18]As a comparative exercise, since the example is based on linear equations, we can also measure the welfare region *BCD* in geometric terms. *BCD* comprises two triangles, *BCE* and *CDE*. The welfare gain or loss can be defined as $0.5\Delta Pd\Delta Q(BCE) + 0.5\Delta Ps\Delta Q(CDE)$. Multiplication of the first term by $\Delta P_d P_0 Q_0 P_0/\Delta P_d P_0 Q_0 P_0$ and the second term by $\Delta P_s P_0 Q_0 P_0/\Delta P_s P_0 Q_0 P_0$ yields $0.5(\Delta P_d/P_0)^2(P_0Q_0)(\Delta Q P_0/\Delta P_d Q_0) + 0.5\,(\Delta P_s/P_0)^2 P_0 Q_0(\Delta Q P_0/\Delta P Q_0)$, which simplifies to $0.5(\Delta P_d/P_0)^2$ (volume of competitive production sales) $\times\ \epsilon_d + 0.5(\Delta P_s/P_0)^2$ (volume of competitive production sales) $\times\ \epsilon_s$, where ϵ_d and ϵ_s refer to elasticities of demand and supply, respectively. ΔP_d is the difference between the competitive and imperfectly competitive equilibrium price; ΔP_s is the difference between the competitive price and the industry supply price at the imperfectly competitive level of production. The magnitude of these two changes in price can be derived from the price elasticities of demand and supply, since the ratio of the price elasticity of demand to the price elasticity of supply is equal to the inverse ratio of the change in the supply price to the change in the demand price. In the example used here, $\epsilon_d = 0.20588235$ and $\epsilon_s = 1.1666667$, so that the changes in the supply and demand prices are $\Delta P_s = 1.5$ and $\Delta P_d = 8.5$. Plugging these values into the expanded formula, we have: $0.5(1.5/14.75)^2(125,375,000)(1.166667) + 0.5(8.5/14.75)^2(125,375,000)(.20588235) = \$5,042,372 \approx \$5,000,000$. The appeal of the integral calculus formulation is that while it may be less subject to immediate economic interpretation, it is far easier to apply in computational terms.

The 5,000,000 derived from equation (13.9) represents a daily welfare loss of $5,000,000 arising from the presence of imperfect competition.

What do static welfare losses from imperfect competition imply for energy policy choices? Based on the static allocative efficiency criterion that we have thus far examined, the main implication is that no intervention in the form of taxation, regulation, antitrust, or public ownership would increase social welfare, since there would still be inevitable deadweight losses. However, before we conclude that no intervention would be justified under any circumstances, let us consider four important qualifications.

First, once there is a shift from static to dynamic conditions, the welfare effects of intervention become more complex. If the costs of intervention lead to deadweight losses in one time period, they may be offset by gains in subsequent periods. As long as the discounted net present value of social-welfare changes from pro-competitive intervention is positive, then in dynamic terms, there may be grounds for proceeding with some form of action. Second, the dynamic behavior of an energy industry, if it is increasingly consistent with competitive economic behavior, may limit to some degree, or even offset, the basis for public intervention. To recall the competitive tests examined in chapter 9, we would need to combine evidence from horizontal and vertical integration over time with dynamic tests for economies of scale, profitability, and technological change. The difficulty in applying such tests may be illustrated by the fact that we would need some basis for evaluating the decline in concentration ratios of various energy industries and the absence of exceptional rates of return within a dynamic framework to justify pro-competitive measures. Third, to the extent that pro-competitive measures might appear warranted within a dynamic framework, and that the energy industry were also an international one, Pareto-efficient changes would be obtained only to the extent that such pro-competitive measures were adopted on the same scale among all other international firms as well. Finally, even when pro-competitive measures may be unwarranted in Pareto-efficiency terms, depending on a society's social-welfare function, the redistributive gains from public intervention might still be justified in terms of distributive justice.[19] Obviously, for such a move to be justified, equity considerations

[19]The basis for such an option usually proceeds first from the measure of the welfare loss as a percentage of the value of competitive economic welfare. In figure 13.7, under competitive conditions, *OGC* has a value of $361,250,000. The welfare loss of $5,000,000 represents 1.384 percent of this amount, a relatively small distortion. However, there has been much debate among economists as to the significance of the apparently small amount of welfare loss. One aspect of this debate is the possibility of X-inefficiency already noted, in which case the degree of welfare loss appears smaller because of increases in average costs. Another issue is the redistributive implications of imperfect competition. In the example we have used here, the gain of $31,125,000 in producers' surplus amounts to 8.62 percent of the total amount of economic welfare under competition; and the $36,125,000 loss of consumers' surplus amounts to 10 percent of competitive economic welfare, figures well in excess of the allocative efficiency welfare loss of 1.384 percent. For an exposition of this point, see Abram Bergson, "On Monopoly Welfare Losses," *American Economic Review* 63 (December 1973):853–70. Bergson points out that where goods may have relatively inelastic demand curves and account for a significant share of consumer budgets, the redistributive implications from imperfect competition may be substantial.

would have to outweigh efficiency considerations in the static framework that we have used here. However, as we will see in chapter 14; there may be more efficient ways to achieve distributive justice, particularly through the exercise of direct taxation.

As a second illustration of policy choices, let us consider the effects of net external diseconomies in production, as in the case of environmental pollution. As noted previously, the consumption of energy can impose environmental costs. The combustion of coal increases the level of carbon dioxide, sulfur dioxide, and nitrogen oxides in the atmosphere, just as the routine operation of a nuclear power plant imposes thermal pollution by its rejected water. In the reference terms of figure 13.4.*b*, the external welfare loss ABC borne by third parties could be reduced by imposition of environmental standards on plant emissions, or in equivalent terms, a tax on pollution. A unit tax on pollution would increase the industry's cost curve from S_p to S_s, lower production from q_p to q_s, and increase the market price from p_1 to p_2. However, since the increase in market price also represents a reduction in the external cost imposed on third parties, there will have been a net gain in allocative efficiency. In this example, the reduction in production from q_p to q_s in figure 13.4.*b* brings about a decrease in social costs of q_sABq_p and a reduction of social benefits of q_sACq_p. Since the reduction in social costs is greater than the reduction in social benefits, there is an increase in net social benefits. Though some adjustment must also be made for the transactions costs of taxation, there may still be a reasonable range of potential net positive welfare gain.

With the general framework just outlined, let us consider briefly two more specific formulations that economists have used to approach questions of environmental policy, namely, marginal social damage-benefit analysis, and materials-balance models. Figure 13.8 illustrates how these approaches can be used to arrive at environmental policy choices. A marginal damage function expresses society's willingness to pay for the removal of various quantities of pollutants per unit of time, as in the reduction of sulfur dioxide emissions from the operations of a coal-fired electric utility. As the quantity of sulfur dioxide removed per unit of time approaches q_2 units, the willingness of the public to pay for additional removal declines to zero. This demand function is based on the assumption that the marginal or extra utility from each increment of pollution removed is less than the preceding. Similarly, to eliminate larger and larger quantities of sulfur dioxide involves increasing marginal costs, shown here by a marginal cost control function. In less abstract terms, we might think here of the fluidized bed and scrubber technologies examined in chapter 5. A socially desirable optimum would be achieved at the point where the marginal damage function intersects the marginal cost-control function, yielding an equilibrium unit price of p_1 and a quantity of pollution abatement of q_1.

As appealing as this marginal analysis may be for environmental policy choices, a number of difficulties arise when we attempt to translate this framework into practice. First, contrary to the impression given by figure

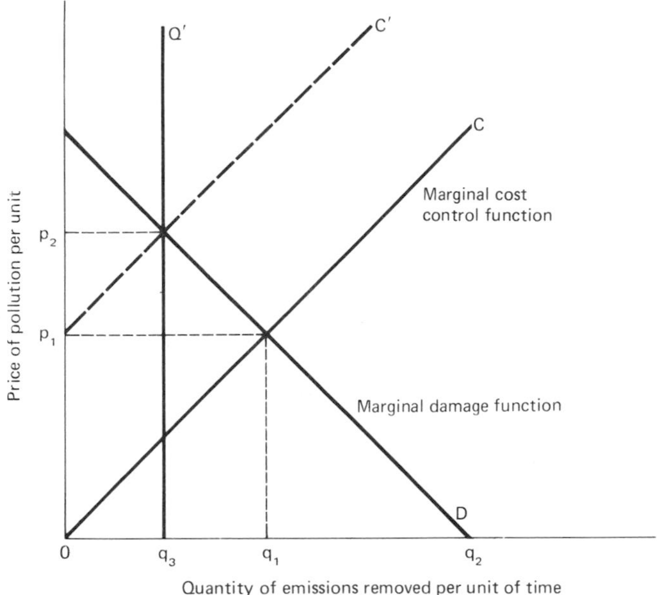

Figure 13.8. Policy Choices for Environmental Protection

13.8, there are no well-defined markets by which these choices can be readily exercised. When there are many individual buyers and sellers in a market that involves environmental pollution as a by-product, like the automobile market, marginal damage functions become difficult to estimate. The reason for this difficulty is that while health and aesthetic benefits from pollution abatement are generally agreed upon, translating them into specific rates of reduction of sickness and fatalities is a complicated task dependent on a number of variables. Unless the public is persuaded of specific linkages between abatement and particular health indicators, its willingness to allocate resources to reduce environmental pollution is likely to be only as strong as the evidence provided. Second, even where there may be evidence of specific linkages between pollution-abatement efforts and health indicators, because the net benefits may be so diffused, the only way that pollution control can proceed is by direct government taxation or regulation. The difficulty with this procedure is that the political process may fail to reflect accurately the level of public demand for pollution control. Third, because environmental protection is likely to require government intervention, there is no guarantee that the instruments used will be economically efficient. The regulatory standards that government has so often been prone to use often impose higher costs of controlling pollution than do other alternatives. For this reason, many economists have tended to prefer pollution taxes to direct regulatory controls, since they offer greater flexibility to industry and consumers as to how best to eliminate particular levels of pollution.

Because information about the effects of pollution is so poorly organized and distributed, one alternative that some economists have proposed is the use of a materials-balance model. A materials-balance model combines energy conversion rates and economic activities with the dynamics of environmental stocks and flows. It posits an upper limit of environmental pollution, illustrated in Figure 13.8 at q_3, based on the underlying assumption that this represents the ability of the environment to absorb various pollutants without imposing irreversible damage. Thus, a lake could absorb so many tons of particulates per year before it would choke off aquatic life, and soils could absorb only so many chemicals before they would no longer be usable for the production of food. Given the limit Q', government would then sell "rights to pollute," the price of which would vary with the demand for using the lake or soil as an emissions site.

A pollution-rights model poses three basic difficulties in adopting specific environmental policy choices. First, the tolerance limits of the environment may be as difficult to estimate as the benefits of pollution abatement. Second, even if such tolerance limits were known with some degree of certainty, it does not follow that such a limit would correspond to the public's demand for environmental protection. Society may well prefer a much higher standard than one that permits the choking off of the aquatic life of a stream. Thus, there is likely to be a spectrum of points along society's demand for environmental protection, of which the pollution-rights limit is but one point. Finally, if our scientific understanding of the environment is at all correct, and such principles as evolution have any meaning, then the concept of an environmental steady-state equilibrium could not exist. Indeed, the entropy principle from the Second Law of Thermodynamics suggests that the quality of the environment is always exposed to some degree of change. Thus there remains the relevant question: To what extent will human intervention in the form of pollution-environmental protection choices affect the rate of environmental change, and in what direction? For all of these reasons, then, the appeal of a social cost-benefit approach inherent in marginal damages-benefits models is readily understandable.

What do alternative approaches to environmental protection imply for the optimal pricing of energy resources? In general, since relative prices are a key factor in the determination of the technical efficiency of energy conversion, to the extent that the relative price of energy is greater than the relative price of non-energy resources, there will be some corresponding degree of improvement in environmental protection. If thermal, sulfur dioxide, carbon dioxide, nitrogen oxide, hydrocarbon particulates, and nuclear and chemical wastes are key pollutant by-products of economic activity, then part of the incentive for their reduction lies in the relative price of energy itself rather than with the pricing of pollution by-products alone. To be sure, not all environmental pollution can be attributed exclusively to relatively cheap energy. At the same time, to approach environmental policy questions independently of the pricing of energy resources would make little sense. In effect, while these observations do not posit a specific optimal relative price of energy, they do stress the underlying linkages between energy policy choices and environmental protection.

Using the static welfare allocative criterion, are there limits to the potential welfare gains? Of course there are, even when the potential gains may be positive. One limit is the problem of transactions costs. If they are substantial enough, they may eliminate potential gains altogether. Another is the difficulty inherent in the measurement of external costs and benefits. Since externalities are not readily observable on the basis of market prices, policymakers must rely on accounting, or shadow, prices, which may be subject to some degree of error. The measurement questions noted in the divergences between private and social costs in chapter 12 are good illustrations of this problem. A third limit is the presence of inefficient market prices under imperfect competition and in regulated industries, even when externalities may not be present. As pointed out in chapter 12, where the Averch-Johnson effect and X-inefficiency exist, they may underestimate the potential gains implied by standard welfare analysis, at least insofar as a competitive standard is needed to determine policy alternatives. Finally, even where corrective action may be warranted, in order for the public authority to apply the principles of Pareto optimality, it must also have the requisite jurisdiction. An oil spill in the Gulf of Mexico which imposes environmental damage to Texas beaches and marine life can be corrected only through negotiations between the U.S. and Mexican governments. Still, all of these limits are problems of degree rather than of substance. To use them as a rationalization for policy inaction is to adopt wholesale the net welfare losses of static market failure.

13.1.4. Dynamic Economic Efficiency

If energy policy is to be effective, it must be consistent. As applied to the criterion of economic efficiency, what this requirement means is that the normative principles for a static Pareto optimum must also be applicable over time. Though it is easy enough to envision dynamic efficiency within a comparative static framework, there is one important difference from the efficiency conditions spelled out in section 13.1.*a*. It is the question of depletable energy resources. The issue of depletion has loomed significantly in preceding chapters; our concern at this point is to examine the extent to which the Pareto-efficiency criterion can be applied with consistency to both depletable and renewable energy resources. We can then identify the conditions of dynamic market failure and point out the implications of alternative policy choices.

As noted in previous chapters, where depletable energy resources are concerned, there is in addition to conventional production costs what economists refer to as a user cost. This cost is a rent which reflects the relative scarcity price of a commodity. As incremental units of a depletable energy resource are consumed, the user cost will rise. The question is, How can this user cost be measured, what determines its rate of increase, and to what extent is it sufficient to satisfy the Pareto conditions of dynamic economic efficiency?

Figure 13.9 provides a simplified framework to illustrate the optimal pric-

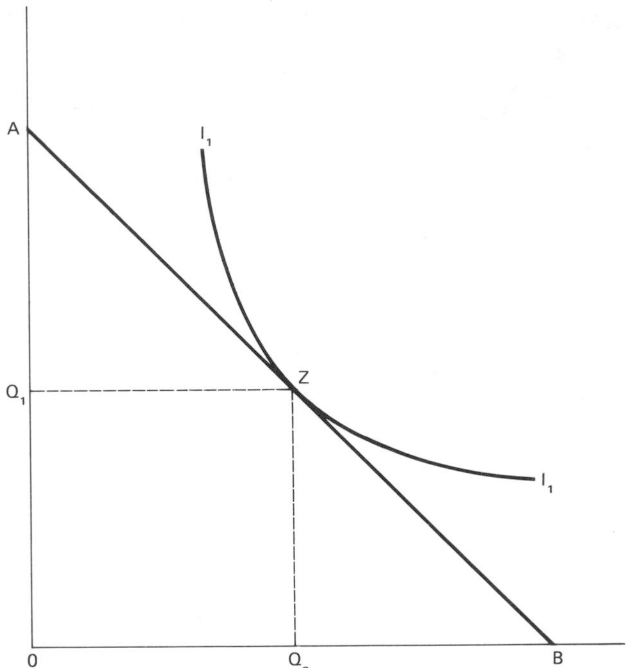

Figure 13.9. Intertemporal Valuation of a Depletable Energy Resource

ing of a depletable resource over time. As an initial condition, let us assume that we are looking at a perfectly competitive economy which has a known finite stock of a depletable energy resource. In addition, to facilitate graphical representation, let us assume that depletion occurs along a spectrum of only two time periods. If all of the resource is consumed today, the amount will be *OB*. If all is consumed tomorrow, the amount will be *OA*. The segment *AB* thus represents the economy's intertemporal set of consumption possibilities. Society must choose the particular rate of depletion which maximizes community economic welfare. In figure 13.9 this level corresponds to the point of tangency *Z* of society's marginal rate of transformation between present and future depletion to society's rate of time preference along its highest community indifference curve, I_1I_1.

To translate the geometry of figure 13.9 into an elementary numerical example, we need first to elaborate on the underlying assumptions of the model of perfect competition within a dynamic framework. According to the initial assumptions, perfectly competitive firms will allocate resources in order to maximize profits. Although the absolute level of profits may vary from firm to firm and from industry to industry, competition works to ensure that the rate of profit among all industries and firms is equalized. In turn, the rate of profits under perfect competition is equal to society's rate-of-time preference for present versus future goods, that is, the rate of interest. Though the rate of interest is derived from the intersection of investment demand and the supply of savings, because the amount of savings is influenced by the supply of money, perfect competition assumes that monetary and fiscal authorities in the economy will behave in such a way that the equilibrium rate of interest will reflect society's rate-of-time preference between present and future goods. Thus, from a single firm's perspective, the rate of interest is given, and will determine what types of investment and production that firm will undertake and at what rate, given the quantity and prices of available resources and markets.

As long as the rate of interest is positive, a dollar's worth of production in the future will by definition be worth less then a dollar's worth of production today, even under a regime of zero inflation. Consequently, in order to compensate for this difference, the level of future profits must be larger than the level of today's profits.[20] Thus, the condition of profit maximization can be expressed as

$$PV_{\max} = \sum_{o}^{n} \frac{V_i}{(1+r)^i}, \tag{13.10}$$

where PV is the discounted present value of current and future profits flows and V_i is $P_iQ_i - C_iQ_i$, the difference between revenues and costs at the profit-maximizing level of production in each time period. In the case of a depletable energy resource, we can refine equation (13.10) further to distinguish the value of production costs from that of scarcity rents, or user costs. Under perfect competition, marginal cost is equal to the price of a commodity. However, the price will consist of the marginal cost of production plus an implicit cost which reflects the scarcity value of the depletable resource. In the extreme case where marginal production costs were zero, the price of a depletable energy resource would be equal only to the user cost. Whether marginal production costs are zero or positive, however, profit maximization requires that user costs be equalized in each time period of the consumption horizon.[21] This condition can be expressed as:

$$UC_0 = \frac{UC_1}{(1+r)} = \frac{UC_2}{(1+r)^2} = \ldots . \frac{UC_n}{(1+r)^n}. \tag{13.11}$$

[20]Equation (13.10) also permits uneven and negative net benefits in some future periods as a condition for profit maximization. As long as the sum of net discounted present values from all flows is positive, there is a standard basis with which to compare alternative investment opportunities, provided appropriate adjustments have been made for the presence or absence of externalities. For a standard reference, see E. J. Mishan, *Cost-Benefit Analysis*, 2d ed. (New York: Praeger Publishers, 1976).

[21]For early formulations of this condition, see L. C. Gray, "Rent under the Assumption of Exhaustibility," *Quarterly Journal of Economics* 28 (May 1914):466–89; and Harold Hotelling, "The Economics of Exhaustible Resources," *Journal of Political Economy* 39 (April 1931):137–75. For more recent formulations, see Anthony D. Scott, "Notes on User Cost," *Economic Journal* 63 (1953):368–84; Richard L. Gordon, "A Reinterpretation of the Pure Theory of Exhaustion," *Journal of Political Economy* 75 (June 1967):274–86; and William D. Nordhaus, "The Allocation of Energy Resources," *Brookings Papers on Economic Activity* 3 (1973):529–70.

To clarify our understanding of equations (13.10) and (13.11) in relation to Pareto optimality, let us now consider the two-period depletion problem illustrated in figure 13.9.[22] We can facilitate matters by adopting temporarily assumption that production costs are zero in all time periods and that the demand for the depletable resource in each time period is given by the following hypothetical equations:

(13.12) $$P_0 = 10 - 0.05\, Q_0$$

and

(13.13) $$P_1 = 10 - 0.04\, Q_1 .$$

If society's rate of time preference is 5 percent and its finite stock of the depletable energy resource is 150 units, for example, MBtu's, we can derive the perfectly competitive quantity and price in each period using two equations and two unknowns, as follows:

(13.14) $$(10 - 0.05\, Q_0) = (10 - 0.04\, Q_1)\ /\ (1.05)$$

and

(13.15) $$Q_0 + Q_1 = 150.$$

Solving for Q_0 and Q_1 gives 70.27 and 79.73, respectively. Inserting these quantities in the corresponding demand equations, (13.12) and (13.13), yields an initial price of \$6.49 and a terminal price of \$6.87. Because we have assumed that production costs are zero in this example, these prices reflect the user cost of the resource in each time period. As it turns out, the price in period one is 5 percent greater than the price in the initial period, satisfying the condition defined in equation (13.11). However, in order to determine whether this pricing and production pattern is everywhere a theoretically efficient one, we need to consider the impact of technological change, positive extraction costs, changes in the pattern of demand, and the role of renewable, or backstop, energy technologies.[23] Each of these variations will be considered in turn.

[22]Obviously, a two-period model can provide only an elementary first-order approximation of real-world conditions. A more general formulation used in the literature on exhaustible resources is the constrained maximization problem: max $NPV = \int_0^t \pi(q(r),t)e^{-rt}dt - \lambda(\int_o^t q(t)dt - v)$, where NPV is the net present value, π = profits as a function of costs, production, and time, and λ is the cumulative production constraint reflecting the finite limit of the resource, v. Under perfectly competitive conditions, marginal revenue is equal to price, which consists of the marginal cost plus the user cost of the resource. Mathematically, $\pi_{max}(t) = MR(t) - MC(t) = \lambda e^{rt}$, which when dated from the initial time period is equivalent to stating that $\pi_{max}(t) = \pi_{max}(0)e^{rt}$, or that the royalty, or user cost, will rise exponentially at the rate of interest or discount rate adopted by society. This rule would guarantee that the present value of future discounted profits would be equal to the value of current profits, i.e., an optimum allocation of resources over time.

[23]A "backstop technology" is one in which the production costs are relatively constant over time. It usually refers to renewable energy technologies such as the solar energy configurations noted in chapter 7, though it has also been used in reference to nuclear fusion. Since the Second Law of Thermodynamics precludes the possibility of a truly constant cost energy technology, a backstop system becomes meaningful only in the context of the more limited time horizon in which most decisions involving resource allocation are made. This question will be taken up in further detail in chapter 14.

Technological change in a depletable energy resource industry is equivalent to an increase in the proven recoverable stock of reserves. A typical example is where secondary and tertiary methods enhance the quantity of petroleum and natural gas reserves. Apart from the increase in reserves, the effects of technological change on the pricing and production of depletable energy are twofold: first, there will be an increase in the current price relative to the previous competitive current price, but the rate of increase in the user cost will be smaller; second, some production will be deferred to future periods. In effect, technological change will tend to stretch out the economically useful life of a depletable energy resource.

To illustrate in numerical terms the impact of technological change, we can modify the simplified model defined in equations (13.14) and (13.15). Let us assume that the rate of technological change is 3 percent and is realized in the terminal time period. Equations (13.14) and (13.15) are now altered to

$$(10 - 0.05\,Q_0) = (10 - 0.04\,Q_1)(1.03)\,/\,(1.05) \tag{13.14.a}$$

$$Q_0 + Q_1 = 150 + 0.03\,Q_1. \tag{13.15.a}$$

The optimal solution is that Q_0 will be 69.19, Q_1 will be 83.31, P_0 will be \$6.54, and P_1 will be \$6.67. Total reserves are increased from 150 to 152.50, and some of the previous current level of production is now shifted forward. Though the initial price is now higher than the previous current price, the rate of increase over time is smaller, and the terminal price will be less than the previous terminal price. The equalization of user costs rule is now defined as

$$UC_0 = \frac{UC_1\,(1 + \alpha)}{(1 + r)}, \tag{13.11.a}$$

where α is the rate of technological change.

Increasing costs for a depletable energy resource will tend to shift current production forward and increase the current period price relative to the zero-production-cost current period price. In turn, the increasing-cost case will have a higher terminal period price relative to the zero-production-cost case.[24] Again, as in the zero-production-cost case, the reason for this pricing and production pattern is that it is necessary in order to equalize user costs over time. To expand on the numerical example, let us assume that each additional unit of the depletable resource defined in equations (13.14) and (13.15) will now cost \$0.04. With no technological change, the equilibrium price and production pattern is now determined as

$$10 - 0.05\,Q_0 - 0.04\,Q_0 = (10 - 0.04\,Q_1 - 0.04\,Q_0)\,/\,(1.05) \tag{13.14.b}$$

[24]See Donald A. Hanson, "Increasing Extraction Costs and Resources Prices," in *Advances in the Economics of Energy and Resources*, ed. R. S. Pindyck, vol. 2 (Greenwich, Conn.: JAI Press, 1979), pp. 171–86; and Robert M. Solow and F. Y. Wan, "Extraction Costs in the Theory of Exhaustible Resources," *Bell Journal of Economics* 7 (Fall 1976):359–70.

and

$$Q_0 + Q_1 = 150. \tag{13.15.b}$$

The solution is that Q_0 will be 68.78 units, Q_1 will be 81.22 units, P_0 will be \$6.56, and P_1 will be \$6.75. It is a Pareto-optimal equilibrium in that the incremental cost of the 68.78th unit will be \$2.75, which when subtracted from the equilibrium price in each period leaves a user cost of \$3.81 in the first period and \$4.00 in the second. The user cost in the terminal period is 5 percent greater than the initial user cost, which satisfies the requirement of equalization of user costs over time defined in equation (13.11).

As noted in chapter 10, changes in demand are a function of the level of income, technical substitution possibilities, and relative prices. Let us consider here the possibility of an increase in the demand for the depletable resource. Under competitive economic conditions, with no technical change and zero production costs, the effect of an increase in demand will be to increase the price of the resource in both periods and to shift some production from the current period to the future. Since production costs are zero in the example, the terminal price must be equal to the initial price multiplied by the given rate of interest. In terms of our numerical example, let the terminal-period demand equation now increase from the level defined in equation (13.13) to

$$P_1 = 10 - 0.02\,Q_1. \tag{13.13.a}$$

The dynamic equilibrium price and quantity pattern will now be defined as

$$10 - 0.05\,Q_0 = (10 - 0.02\,Q_1)\ /\ (1.05) \tag{13.14.c}$$

$$Q_0 + Q_1 = 150. \tag{13.15}$$

The solution is that the initial quantity will be 48.28, Q_1 will be 101.72, the initial price will be \$7.59, and P_1 will be \$7.97. Dividing P_1 by the 5 percent discount rate just equals P_0; thus user costs are equalized over time.

The final variation in the dynamic pricing of depletable energy resources is the impact of renewable, or backstop, energy technologies. Unless the price of a renewable energy technology is competitive with the current or future price of a depletable energy resource, there will be no impact on the prevailing pricing and production pattern. Where a backstop technology becomes competitive, both current and future prices of the depletable resource will decline.[25] In addition, the more competitive the price and the sooner the backstop is introduced, the greater will be the tendency of firms in the depletable-resource industry to shift future production to the present, thereby shortening the economically useful life of the resource. Of course, if the renewable technology is available soon enough and at a competitive enough price, the de-

[25]For an exposition of this relationship, see Geoffrey Heal, "The Relationship between Price and Extraction Costs for a Resource with a Backstop Technology," *ibid.*, pp. 371–8; and Stephen W. Salant, "Staving Off the Backstop: Dynamic Limit Pricing with a Kinked Demand Curve," in *Advance in the Economics of Energy and Resources*, ed. R. S. Pindyck, vol. 2 (Greenwich, Conn: JAI Press, 1979), pp. 187–204.

mand for the depletable resource can be reduced to a point where physical exhaustion is never reached.

To illustrate the impact of a renewable energy technology, let us assume that its price is set at \$6.49 (the lower-boundary price of the original model) and that it will be introduced in the terminal period of the two-period model defined in equations (13.14) and (13.15). By substituting the limit price of the backstop technology for the demand equation in the terminal period, we can determine the new pricing and production configuration of the depletable resource, as well as derive how much of the terminal-period consumption of energy can be met by the backstop. Equation (13.14) is now defined as

$$(13.14.d) \qquad 10 - 0.05\ Q_0 = \$6.49\ /\ (1.05),$$

and equation (13.15) will be the same as in the original case. We need only equation (13.14.*d*) to derive the initial quantity and price, which turn out to be 76.38 and \$6.18, respectively. Then, if we set the demand equation (13.13) of the terminal period equal to the backstop price of \$6.49, terminal-period consumption will be 87.75. Since total consumption in the two periods is 164.13 and the backstop technology becomes available only in the terminal period, terminal consumption will comprise 73.62 units of the depletable resource and 14.13 of the renewable energy resource. However, since the backstop is competitively priced with the renewable resource in the terminal period, it is more likely that terminal consumption will be supplied by an even greater amount of the renewable resource; thus a residual amount of the depletable resource will be conserved further into the future. In any case, the present value of user costs in each time period has been equalized.

We can now recapitulate the conditions of Pareto optimality within a dynamic setting. Basically, Pareto optimality will be attained as long as the present value of user costs in each time period is equalized, that is, as long as the value of user costs increases with the rate of interest. Though the present value of the competitive price of a depletable energy resource will vary according to technology, production costs, demand, and the competitive position of renewable energy technologies, allocative efficiency over time will be maximized by the rule of user-cost equalization. Thus, as the alternative trajectories of (figure 13.10) suggest, there may be a variety of efficient pricing and production patterns for a depletable energy resource. However, even though these conditions can exist in theory, there is no guarantee that they will exist in practice.

13.1.5. Dynamic Market Failure and Alternative Policy Choices

As suggested in section 13.1.2, market failure is not limited to static conditions alone. Indeed, it is much more realistic to view imperfect competition, externalities, decreasing costs, and public goods within a dynamic setting. The question here is, To what extent are the forms and magnitude of market failure altered over time and to what extent do dynamic conditions lead to policy choices which differ from those under static market failure?

The conditions of dynamic market failure are distinguished from their

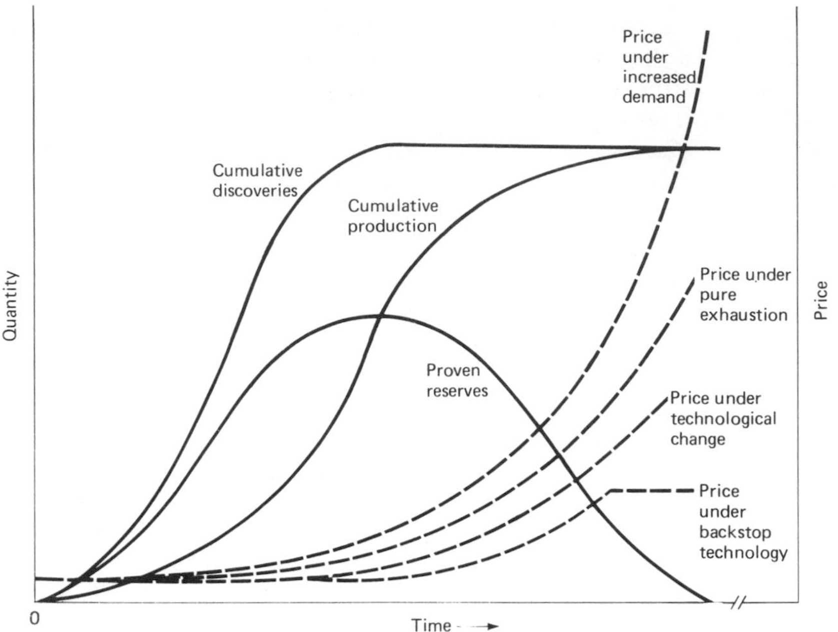

Figure 13.10. Alternative Life Cycles of a Depletable Energy Resource. For each price trajectory there will be a unique set of relations for cumulative discoveries, cumulative production, and proven reserves.

static counterparts in two basic areas. First, imperfect competition in a dynamic setting differs from that in the static market in that in the former case, welfare losses and equity considerations may be affected by technological change. Moreover, with the higher price and reduced production arising from profit-maximizing behavior, imperfect competition will also enhance the conservation of a depletable energy resource more than in the case of a perfectly competitive economy.[26] Second, intertemporal economic efficiency depends critically on the choice of an appropriate rate of discount, or interest rate. Where depletable resources are concerned, market-determined rates of interest may fail to reflect socially optimal choices.[27] We will consider each of these areas of dynamic market failure in turn, as well as discuss alternative policy choices.

We can illustrate the consequences of imperfect competition for depletable energy resources, as well as assess technological change, in terms of the sim-

[26]As Robert Solow sarcastically phrased this observation, "the monopolist is the conservationist's friend" (see "The Economics of Resources or the Resources of Economics," *American Economic Review* 64 [March 1974]:1–14). What this generalization ignores, of course, are the redistributive consequences of imperfectly competitive markets as a vehicle for conservation.

[27]The distinction between depletable and renewable resources is not always clear-cut. For an elaboration of this issue, see Colin W. Clark, Frank H. Clarke, and Gordon R. Munro, "The Optimal Exploration of Renewable Resource Stocks: Problems of Irreversible Investment," *Econometrica* 43 (March 1979):25–47.

ple two-period model utilized in section 13.1.4. Though allowance can also be made for rising extraction costs, changes in demand, and the introduction of backstop technologies, our primary concern is to contrast the pricing and depletion path under imperfect competition with that under perfect competition.

Under imperfect competition, firms maximize profits by setting marginal revenues equal to marginal costs, just as occurs within a perfectly competitive industry. However, under imperfect competition, the price will exceed both marginal revenue and marginal cost. This condition, and the gain associated with it, can be represented by taking the first derivative of the demand equations (13.12) and (13.13) to obtain the respective marginal-revenue functions. Since production costs are assumed initially to be zero, these marginal-revenue equations can then be inserted into equation (13.14) and combined with equation (13.15) to determine the level of production in each period with a 5 percent discount rate and a finite reserve of 150 units. Then, once production has been allocated in the two periods, we can insert the respective quantities into the original demand equations, (12.12) and (13.13), to solve for initial and terminal prices. The problem now is expressed as

$$(13.12.a) \quad MR_0 = \frac{\partial R}{\partial Q_0} = \frac{d[(10 - 0.05\, Q_0)Q_0]}{dQ_0} = \frac{d(10\, Q_0 - 0.05\, Q_0^2)}{dQ_0}$$

$$= 10 - 0.1\, Q_0,$$

$$(13.13.b) \quad MR_1 = \frac{\partial R}{\partial Q_1} = \frac{d[(10 - 0.04\, Q_1)Q_1]}{dQ_1} = \frac{d(10\, Q_1 - 0.04\, Q_1^2)}{dQ_1}$$

$$= 10 - 0.08\, Q_1.$$

$$(13.14.e) \quad (10 - 0.1\, Q_0) = (10 - 0.08\, Q_1)\ /\ (1.05)$$

$$(13.15) \quad Q_0 + Q_1 = 150.$$

The solution is that Q_0 is 67.57, P_0 is \$6.62, Q_1 is 82.43, and P_1 is \$6.70, which also is the pricing and production pattern which maximizes the present value of the resource.[28] Yet, market failure has arisen, since from society's point of view, redistribution and equity aside, the net marginal social benefits from greater present consumption exceed those in the future.

The marginal net social benefit is the difference between the market price and user cost in each time period. Under the assumptions of imperfect competition and zero production costs in this example, the user cost is equal to marginal revenue. If we substitute the imperfectly-competitive-equilibrium quantities in their respective marginal-revenue equations, (13.12.*a*) and (13.13.*a*),

[28]In this elementary model, the present value of the imperfectly competitive equilibrium is \$973.62, which is only slightly greater than the \$972.97 under perfect competition. The key to market failure is not so much the difference in the present value of the resource as it is how production and prices are determined over time. For a more formal treatment, see Joseph Stiglitz, "Monopoly and the Rate of Extraction of Exhaustible Resources," *American Economic Review* 66 (September 1976):655–61.

the initial-period user cost is \$3.24 and the terminal-period user cost is \$3.41. Subtracting these values from the corresponding market prices of the imperfectly competitive equilibrium yields a net marginal social benefit of \$3.38 in the first period and a 5 percent discounted net marginal social benefit of \$3.14 in the second. In contrast, under our perfectly competitive zero-production-cost reference case, price would be equal to the user cost in each time period. Since the net marginal social benefit would also be zero, it would be Pareto-optimal.

Imperfect competition presents an obvious dilemma. On the one hand, it leads to welfare losses and substantial redistribution of income, while on the other, it tends to conserve the economically useful life of a depletable energy resource. In the hands of the OPEC cartel, the appeal to petroleum conservation is thus used by its members to justify the massive redistribution of income which its imperfectly competitive structure brings about. However, what should be kept in mind is that conservation and redistribution can be achieved in a variety of ways. Before we can consider what these policy choices are, however, we should also examine the importance of technological change within the context of a dynamic market failure.

One peculiar aspect of dynamic market failure is the question of technological change. Unlike the rarefied equations (13.11.*a*), (13.14.*a*), and (13.15.*a*), technological change involves costs both in direct terms as well as in risk. As Joseph Schumpeter argued long ago, differential profitability is a reward for the risk of innovation, thereby justifying imperfect competition in a dynamic setting.[29] Considering the redistributive and efficiency implications, it is not surprising that this question has drawn much debate among economists. Since risk and uncertainty are treated in chapter 14, rather than expand on the arguments of this debate, we can spell out here in basic terms the implications of technological change within the context of dynamic market failure.

For a given interest rate, regardless of the degree of competition, technological change in an increasing marginal-cost industry that involves the production of a depletable energy resource will tend to increase the net present value of the resource. The reason for this change is obvious: no firm would deliberately pursue an innovation if it would reduce the value of the resource.[30]

[29]Joseph A. Schumpeter, *The Theory of Economic Development* (New York: Oxford University Press, 1961), first published in German in 1911. For some evidence in support of the Schumpeter thesis, see Partha Dasgupta and Joseph Stiglitz, "Uncertainty, Industrial Structure, and the Speed of R and D," *Bell Journal of Economics* 11 (Spring 1980):1–28; and G. Loury, "Market Structure of Innovation," *Quarterly Journal of Economics* 93 (August 1979):395–410.

[30]As an illustration, consider the difference in net present value from technological change using the simplified two-period competitive industry model of equations (13.14.*a*) and (13.15.*a*). For each demand equation, insert a negative linear marginal-cost function, MC = \$0.04 Q_0, and derive the user-cost equilibrium. The solution is that $Q_0 = 68.61$, $Q_1 = 83.92$, $P_0 = \$6.57$, and $P_1 = 6.64$. At equilibrium, Q_0's marginal cost is \$2.7444, and the marginal cost of the 152.52d unit is \$6.10. Inserting the corresponding price, cost, and quantity values into equation (13.10) yields a *NPV* of \$305.83, which is just under 5 percent less than the *NPV* of a zero-technological-change case of \$320.15. Obviously, technological change must affect the economically useful life of a resource and in so doing, it must offset to a significant extent the impact of rising marginal extraction costs.

However, since technological change would at the same time increase economic life of the resource, we can pose the Schumpeterian argument in straightforward terms: as long as the rate of technological change in a perfectly competitive economy is less than the rate of technological change in an imperfectly competitive one, then there is some basis for justifying a less than perfectly competitive market structure, and the associated differential profitability which such a structure would imply. However, if we look at the performance indicators of the U.S. energy industry covered in part III, the evidence in support of this proposition is sketchy at best. In addition to the pricing distortions that past government policies themselves have brought about, for the U.S. energy industry at least, there has been no compelling evidence that the rate of technological change could by itself justify the degree of current market concentration.

Beyond the question of imperfect competition, the choice of a social rate of discount can also lead to market failure. Whereas we assume that there is perfect information and foresight in a competitive economy, no one is truly so endowed in reality. Among others, Frank Ramsey and Arthur C. Pigou long ago contended that under these circumstances the discounting of future conditions was an inappropriate way to provide an efficient allocation of resources over time.[31] Since we are concerned especially with depletable energy resources, let us consider how the rate of discount will affect the allocation of energy resources over time in the reference terms of our simplified two-period model.

An increase in the discount rate will shorten the economic life of a depletable energy resource by shifting future production toward the present and lowering the current price below its previous level while allowing the future price to exceed its previous level. To illustrate this change, consider an increase in the rate of interest from 5 percent to 10 percent. With no technological change, no change in demand, and no backstop technology, the competitive economy with zero extraction costs of equation (13.14) now becomes:

$$(10 - 0.05\, Q_0) = (10 - 0.04\, Q_1) \;/\; (1.10), \tag{13.14.f}$$

which when combined with the existing reserve equation (13.15) yields a Q_0 of 73.68, a P_0 of \$6.32, a Q_1 of 76.32, and a P_1 of \$6.95. Not only does the current period price fall relative to the current period price of a lower rate of discount but the net present value of the resource is also decreased.[32] What this example suggests is that there is a tradeoff between the benefits of lower current energy prices and a decline in the net present value of the resource. Though the efficiency criterion is satisfied, whether the rate of discount should be increased depends also on the opportunities for future technologi-

[31]Frank Ramsey, "A Mathematical Theory of Saving," *Economic Journal* 38 (December 1928):543–59; and Arthur C. Pigou, *The Economics of Welfare*, 4th ed. (London: Macmillan Publishing Co., 1950).

[32]In the case of a competitive industry with zero extraction costs and zero technological change, the net present value of the two-period model of equations (13.14) and (13.15) with a 5 percent discount rate is \$973.16. Under a 10 percent discount rate, the net present value becomes \$947.17, a decrease of almost 3 percent.

cal change, on the role of renewable energy resources, and on the criterion of intertemporal equity, to which we now turn.

13.2. SUMMARY

From the issues thus far examined, several policy choices emerge. First, where imperfect competition exists, as long as technological change and scale economies have been allowed for, allocative efficiency will be improved by a competitive market structure. As noted in chapter 1, regulation, antitrust, and public ownership are potential instruments to achieve this objective, to which taxation may be added as a fourth. Yet, the decision of whether to apply any of these instruments should be based on a careful analysis of the discounted costs of correction in relation to the discounted increases in benefits over time. If costs are substantial enough, they will obviously reduce or eliminate the net gain over time. In the limiting case where the net present value of incremental allocative efficiency is zero, we must consider whether any action would be justified on equity grounds, as already noted in section 13.1.3. At the same time, though some form of intervention might bring about an improvement, the gain would still be confined to the individual economy in which it was applied. OPEC and other forms of market failure in the international economy could still remain. Second, though externalities can exist as much in a dynamic setting as they do in the static terms of section 13.1.2, any proposals to promote the reduction of these consequences should be based on similar cost-benefit considerations. Indeed, although regulation has been the most widely used instrument to correct environmental pollution, taxation may be at least as efficient a means, as a number of writers have contended. Third, where decreasing costs lead to natural monopoly conditions, allocative efficiency can be promoted by public utility ownership as well as by regulation of private firms. However, as noted in chapter 12, the success of these choices will depend on the extent to which marginal cost-pricing principles and average cost minimization over time can be achieved. Averch-Johnson input distortions and X-inefficiency conditions can exist among publicly owned firms, much as they can arise in the regulation of privately owned ones. Fourth, where public energy goods such as basic research in new technologies are concerned, the choice of specific programs and levels of funding is very much dependent on the institutional mechanisms by which these preferences must inevitably be expressed. The speed with which U.S. policymakers choose to emphasize programs to reduce current dependence on imported energy is also dependent on the time horizon which reflects society's attitude toward the future. To place these choices within a more integrated framework requires that the criterion of economic efficiency be viewed along with related policy criteria.

SUGGESTED READINGS

Dasgupta, Partha S., and Heal, Geoffrey M. *Economic Theory and Exhaustible Resources.* Cambridge: Cambridge University Press, 1979.

Herfindahl, Orris C., and Kneese, Allen V. *Economic Theory of Natural Resources.* Columbus, Ohio: Charles E. Merrill Publishing Co., 1974.

Krutilla, John V., and Fisher, Anthony C. *The Economics of Natural Environments: Studies in the Valuation of Commodities and Amenity Resources.* Baltimore: Johns Hopkins University Press, 1975.

Mills, Edwin S. *The Economics of Environmental Quality.* New York: W. W. Norton and Co., 1978.

Smith, V. Kerry. *Technical Change, Relative Prices, and Environmental Resource Evaluation.* Baltimore: Johns Hopkins University Press, 1974.

14

ENERGY POLICY CRITERIA—II

14.1. THE EQUITABLE ALLOCATION OF ENERGY RESOURCES

As we might expect, the efficient allocation of resources is an important ingredient in the formulation of energy policy alternatives. At the same time, efficient policy choices often carry important equity consequences. From an economic perspective, this presents an uncomfortable dilemma. On the one hand, questions of efficiency are readily subject to the means-and-ends methodology of scientific economic investigation. On the other hand, if there are important redistributive consequences arising from economically efficient energy choices, then the decision is no longer purely economic. It is not surprising, therefore, that economists often tend to avoid the issue of equity on the grounds that it involves value judgments which cannot be subjected to objective evaluation.[1] Indeed, this is a defensible position to adopt if the question of efficiency is to be given the attention that it deserves in the specification of energy policy alternatives. Yet, for the energy policymaker, who must by definition invoke such value judgments, the issue of equity cannot be avoided, even in the pursuit of efficiency. Since Pareto optimality is consistent with various patterns of income distribution, it is instructive to spell out the relationship between allocative efficiency and alternative notions of equity. In this way, efficiency-equity alternatives can acquire a greater degree of coherence.

14.1.1. Static Equity Choices

We have already seen how imperfect competition can have important consequences for the distribution of income. Some writers have proposed that rather than invoke the Pareto criterion alone on this issue, policymakers should adopt a utilitarian welfare function based on subjective and explicit distributive value

[1]Perhaps the most notable statement of this position is found in Lionel Robbins, *An Essay on the Nature and Significance of Economic Science* (London: Macmillan Publishing Co., 1932). At the same time, one should be wary of assuming that economics is value-free or that its concerns have not been strongly guided by value judgments. For an elaboration on this point, see Gunnar Myrdal, *The Political Element in the Development of Economic Theory* (New York: Simon and Schuster Clarion Books, 1969), first published in 1930.

judgments to complement an established emphasis on allocative efficiency.[2] In this way, at least the subjective value judgments employed might be applied in a consistent fashion. The choice of explicit distributive criteria is no simple task. Indeed, it requires policymakers to make interpersonal comparisons of utility, which raises the question of whether consistent equity preferences of society can be expressed in a democratic fashion.[3] In other words, under a utilitarian rule, redistribution could be considered an improvement only if it could be shown that the gains to recipients exceeded the losses which others would have to bear. Since there is no known scientific basis for proving or refuting this proposition, our examination of equity in energy policy must proceed with due allowance for a range of alternative equity criteria which encompasses the political spectrum of individual and social preferences.

Table 14.1 illustrates the equity problem as it pertains to static policy choices in the U.S. economy. In addition to the fact that personal income is unequally distributed to begin with, because the short-run demand tends to be relatively price-inelastic, poorer individuals are likely to spend a higher share of their income on energy than the rich, even though the absolute level of consumption and expenditures by the poor may be smaller. Yet, in order to decide whether this pattern, or any other one resulting from deliberate policy decisions, is in any way socially optimal, we need first to define a measure of the degree of inequality.

For some time, economists and statisticians have proposed a number of measures of the degree of inequality.[4] A measure which has particular appeal for our purposes is the index first defined by A. B. Atkinson in 1970.[5] Atkinson's index of inequality draws on the notion that all individuals attach some value to risk aversion. Since the degree of inequality of income distribution is one element of risk, Atkinson's index expresses society's willingness to tolerate inequality as analogous to its willingness to tolerate risk. The index which incorporates this explicit subjective weight is defined as

$$I = 1 - [\sum_i (Y_i / \bar{Y})^{1-\epsilon} f(Y_i)]^{1/1-\epsilon} \tag{14.1}$$

where I is the index of inequality, which ranges from zero (absolute equality) to one (absolute inequality), Y_i is the income of the ith individual, $\bar{Y}$ is the mean

[2] This conclusion is brought out forcefully in Abram [Bergson] Burk, "A Reformulation of Certain Aspects of Welfare Economics," *Quarterly Journal of Economics* 52 (1938):310–34.

[3] For an elaboration of the first issue, see I.M.D. Little, *A Critique of Welfare Economics*, 2d ed. (1957; reprint ed., New York: Oxford University Press, 1973), first published in 1950. The problem of inconsistency in social preferences has been stated in axiomatic terms by K. J. Arrow in *Social Choice and Individual Values* (New Haven: Yale University Press, 1951).

[4] The indices of inequality proposed all derive from the geometric formulation of inequality known as the Lorenz curve. Among the most notable of these measures are the Gini, the Champernowne, the Theil, the Kuznets, variance of logarithms, and entropy. For an elaboration of the properties of some of these measures, see Nanak C. Kakwani, *Income Inequality and Poverty* (New York: Oxford University Press, 1980).

[5] Anthony B. Atkinson, "On the Measurement of Inequality," *Journal of Economic Theory* 2 (September 1970):244–63. For a nontechnical exposition and applications, see idem, *The Economics of Inequality* (New York: Oxford University Press, 1975).

Table 14.1. Energy Consumption and the Distribution of Family Income in the United States, 1972-73

	(1) Percentage of U.S. Families	(2) Average Family Income[a]	(3) Per Capita Energy Consumption[b]	(4) Share of Family Income Spent on Energy	(5) Family Income Net of Energy Expenditures[c]
	13.2%	$ 2,500	207	15.2%	$ 2,120
	46.9	8,000	294	7.2	7,424
	28.4	14,000	403	5.9	13,174
	11.5	24,500	478	4.1	23,495
Average	25.0%	$10,875.5	334.6	7.5303%	$10,205

Sources: Washington Center for Metropolitan Studies Lifestyle and Energy Surveys, 1972-73, published in Ford Foundation Energy Policy Project, *A Time to Choose* (Cambridge, Mass.: Ballinger Publishing Co., 1974), p. 118; and data from the U.S. Department of Commerce, Bureau of the Census, *Current Population Reports,* series P-60 (Washington, D.C.: U.S. Government Printing Office, 1974).

[a]Current dollars, based on census model of family of four.

[b]In millions of Btu's. No attempt has been made to reconcile the average per capita consumption figure listed here with the data reported in chapter 2.

[c]Derived as the product of the number in column 2 and the corresponding number in column 4, subtracted from the number in column two. No attempt has been made to reconcile the differences in average energy prices paid by each family grouping. The higher unit price of energy paid by higher-income groups may be a reflection of the differing proportions of energy forms consumed by these groups relative to lower-income groups, e.g., electricity and premium gasoline.

level of per capita income, and ϵ is the subjective weight which reflects the social aversion to inequality. The value of the inequality aversion parameter, ϵ, ranges from zero to infinity. The higher the value, the greater is the aversion that society attaches to inequality. Consequently, we can incorporate explicit distributive criteria ranging from the inegalitarian elitism of a Gaetano Mosca to the equalitarian maxi-min principles of a John Rawls.[6]

The distributive-welfare function of equation (14.1) may be more readily understood in terms of an elementary numerical example. Let us assume that the distributive weight which expresses society's degree of aversion to income inequality is 0.5. Inserting this value and the data of the first two columns of table 14.1 in equation (14.1) yields an inequality index of 0.07769. Following Atkinson, the interpretation of the index is that the same level of social welfare could be achieved with just over 92 percent of the present level of average income if all income were equally distributed. Similarly, an equalization of the distribution of the present level of income would be equivalent to an increase in income of just under 8 percent.

Given society's subjective degree of aversion to income inequality, we are

[6]Gaetano Mosca, *The Ruling Class*, trans. Hannah D. Kahn (New York: McGraw-Hill, 1967), translation of the 1898 edition; John Rawls, *A Theory of Justice* (Cambridge, Mass.: Harvard University Press, 1971). Rawls's maxi-min criterion is a concept of equity in which welfare is improved as long as changes benefit the least advantaged in society; Mosca's theory of elites is considered to have been an intellectual precursor to fascism.

now in a position to examine the role of equity in energy policy decisions. In the static terms of table 14.1, we can utilize the example of imperfect competition to determine alternative equity choices.[7] For purposes of comparison, let us assume that the average price of energy paid by all consumers under imperfect competition is twice the price which would exist under perfectly competitive conditions and that the data of table 14.1 represent an initial condition of perfect competition. In order to draw any equity comparisons between these two states, we need to derive the degree of inequality of residual family income, that is, the income net of energy consumption expenditures. Residual income can thus be defined as

$$Y_i' = Y_i - P_{ei}Q_{ei}, \tag{14.2}$$

the levels of which are reported in column 5 of table 14.1.

According to microeconomic theory, the extent to which any increase in the price of energy will affect the degree of inequality of residual income is a function of the price elasticity of demand, which in turn is influenced by the degree of consumer technical-substitution possibilities, the price of substitute goods, the level of income, and the share of income which is devoted to the consumption of the good, energy. Now even though the share of income devoted to energy consumption is not uniform in table 14.1, let us consider the impact of the doubling of the price of energy under alternative hypothetical price elasticities of demand.

Table 14.2 summarizes the impact on inequality of family residual income arising from a doubling of the average price of energy paid by each income class under alternative hypothetical price elasticities of demand. Under an extreme case of a zero iso-inelastic demand among all income classes, case A shows that with a given inequality-aversion preference, the degree of inequality of family residual income becomes greater than before the doubling of the average price of energy. Were the cause of the increase in the price of energy due to imperfectly competitive domestic industry behavior alone, a tax on profits could be used to restore the preexisting degree of inequality in family residual income by implementing a declining schedule of tax rebates to the affected income classes. On the other hand, if an increase in the price of energy were to occur under a condition of perfectly inelastic demand and a competitive market structure, than an alternative method of preserving the original degree of equity would be by a progressive redistribution of the existing level of tax resources to compensate for the adverse income effects on

[7]The principle of equity is by no means confined only to the case of imperfect competition. For example, the taxation principles that apply to the case of declining-cost industries apply equally to the means of financing the regulatory structure charged with the responsibility of establishing marginal cost pricing. Similarly, where external costs are pervasive and can not be internalized readily within a local contractual framework, the distribution of tax revenues should conform properly to the same equity rules, as should the progressivity of taxes which may be imposed to finance such public goods as basic energy research and development expenditures. The term used by economists to generalize the principle illustrated here is "vertical equity" (see Richard A. Musgrave and Peggy B. Musgrave, *Public Finance*, 3d ed. [New York: McGraw-Hill, 1980], esp. pt. 2).

Table 14.2. Static Equity Choices under Alternative Price Elasticities of Demand Based on a Doubling of the Average Price of Energy

Item	Reference Case	Case A		Case B		Case C		Case D	
	Family Residual Income	Elasticity of Demand[a]	Family Residual Income[b]	Elasticity of Demand[a]	Family Residual Income[b]	Elasticity of Demand[a]	Family Residual Income[b]	Elasticity of Demand[a]	Family Residual Income[b]
Percentage of U.S. families									
13.2%	$ 2,120	0	$ 1,740	1	$ 2,120	1.00	$ 2,120	0.25	$ 1,857
46.9	7,424	0	6,848	1	7,424	0.75	7,309	0.50	7,177
28.4	13,174	0	12,348	1	13,174	0.50	12,820	0.75	13,009
11.5	23,495	0	22,491	1	23,495	0.25	23,068	1.00	23,495
Weighted average	$10,205		$ 9,534.7		$10,205		$10,001.1		$10.007.6
Atkinson inequality-aversion coefficient	0.5		0.5		0.5		0.5		0.5
Atkinson inequality index	0.083466039		0.090505478		0.083466039		0.082447018		0.0898162

Sources: Data for 1972–73 are from Table 14.1.

[a]Hypothetical values

[b]Since ϵ_d, the price elasticity of demand, is the relative change in quantity demanded divided by the relative change in price, if ϵ_d and $\%\Delta P(= +100\%)$ are given, it is possible to derive Q_2 from Q_1 and the percentage change in Q. Then, using equation (14.2), family residual income can be derived from the product of the new values of P and Q.

the relatively poor. Regardless of the cause of an increase in the price of energy, even though the preexisting degree of equity may be preserved, since the administrative costs of taxation are greater than zero, the level of family income would not in any case be restored to its previous position.

In case B, under unitary iso-elastic demand among all income classes, a doubling of the average price of energy would lower the average level of income to a lesser extent than in the zero iso-elastic case, but at the same time it would not worsen the preexisting degree of inequality of family residual income. If the doubling of the price of energy were due to an imperfectly competitive market structure, an excess profits tax could be imposed to recapture some of the income losses, particularly if redistribution of these tax revenues were allocated proportionately among all income classes.

Cases C and D are more complicated in that the assumption of an iso-elastic demand for energy among all income groups is now dropped in favor of two monotonic alternatives. In case C, though the average level of income is lower than before, the doubling of the price of energy leads to a reduction in the degree of inequality of family residual income. In this case, if the goal is to arrive at a preexisting degree of income inequality, a tax on the imperfectly competitive domestic industry's profits would call for a redistribution of revenues which is slightly regressive in comparsion with that of case B. In case D, the opposite conclusion would hold.

The static equity choices thus far enumerated point to an important conclusion for energy policy alternatives. Where the income effects of changing prices of energy are large, equity should be preserved through alterations in the level and incidence of income taxation. Regulation of the price of energy may be appropriate to the achievement of allocative efficiency, but it is an inappropriate tool for achieving specific degrees of equity. The reason for this distinction should be obvious: regulation-induced equity choices may conflict with the efficient allocation of resources. In more direct terms, if society is interested in both efficiency and equity, then the price of energy should be based on its marginal social cost, and any adverse income consequences adjusted where necessary through alteration of the existing mix of taxation. Moreover, if equity-efficiency choices are to be everywhere consistent, they must also be applicable in dynamic terms as well.

14.1.2. Dynamic Equity Choices

Just as equity considerations affect static energy policy choices, so too do they bear on the allocation of energy resources over time. They do so even where the conditions of allocative efficiency enumerated in chapter 13 have been attained. Though any allocation of energy resources over time must account ultimately for the question of uncertainty, we will proceed here with the temporary heroic assumption of complete information about present and future conditions.

The assumption of complete information about the future is profound in its simplicity. It means, after all, that policymakers today know with precision the stock of ultimately recoverable energy resources. This means, in turn, that they know the rate of technological change throughout the economy, and therefore the ways in which the First and Second Laws of Thermodynamics will influence the forms of future energy technologies, as well as the rate of change and level of future population. In institutional terms, all of this information would be available to policymakers through well-behaved futures markets.

Under the foregoing conditions, the question of intertemporal equity can now be viewed as the basic problem of adopting a particular rate of social discount.[8] As one alternative, if we adhere to the Pigou-Ramsey position that a zero discount rate must be applied to investment decisions, we are confronted with an uncomfortable dilemma. On the one hand, if we adopt any rule regarding the consumption of energy resources, the time frame cannot be infinite. The reason for this limitation should be obvious: by virtue of the Second Law of Thermodynamics, even the flow of renewable energy resources in the universe is not infinite. Consequently, as pointed out in chapter 4, because there is degradation of the quality of available energy over time, allocation of this energy over an infinite time period becomes mathematically impossible. On the other hand, if the date for the end of the world were known, we could use an Atkinson type of inequality-aversion welfare index to allocate the finite stock of energy resources among all generations. Yet, to do so would also require a satisfactory explanation for stipulating a specific date for the end of the world. Indeed, if such a date were known, policymakers might just as well abandon their concern for the allocation of energy resources and concentrate instead on the metaphysical significance of their teleological knowledge.

Suppose instead that we were to adopt a positive rate of discount. While a positive discount rate would enable us to avoid the philosophic burdens just described, it would carry an implicit intertemporal equity judgment. In effect, if future conditions were discounted, the dilemma of a finite or infinite future would be avoided, but so too would be the value which today's society attaches to the preferences of future generations. If the preferences of future generations are to count less than those of the present one, is some form of conservation appropriate? To answer this question, we should look briefly at the arguments against and in support of this proposition, and at the underlying assumptions on which they are based.

One way of considering the issue of energy conservation is to look at the argument posed by the nineteenth-century English economist William Stanley Jevons (1835–82).[9] In his 1865 book, *The Coal Question*, Jevons tried to

[8]It is important to emphasize here that the use of a social rate of discount differs from a private one in that it incorporates intertemporal external costs and benefits, which enables us to focus more directly on the question within a dynamic setting. At the same time, use of a social rate of discount does not correct for other forms of market failure, notably pure public goods, decreasing-cost industries, and imperfect competition. For purposes of discussion, we will temporarily assume that these other forms of market failure do not exist. Obviously, specific policies to allow for intertemporal equity must take these three types of market failure into account.

[9]Apart from his role in the development of neoclassical marginal economic analysis, Jevons is known for his study of coal exhaustion and his sunspot theory of business cycles, neither of which gained widespread acceptance. See his book, *The Coal Question*, ed. A. M. Flux (1865; reprint ed., New York: A. M. Kelley, 1965).

predict the exhaustion of England's coal resources. On the basis of the evidence then available, he concluded that conservation was essential to sustain these reserves beyond a few generations. Despite public interest in Jevons's study, no conservation plan was adopted. Moreover, as more recent critics have pointed out, oil, natural gas, and nuclear power have together displaced much of the potential value of England's coal reserves in any case. Thus, contend these critics, for England to have engaged in substantial conservation of coal during the nineteenth century would have lowered the economic welfare of Jevons's generation in favor of the present one. Yet, as should also be evident, the notion that conservation today would also be unjustified is based on the underlying assumption that comparable energy substitution opportunities will be available in the future. Consequently, any argument in favor of expanded conservation today must be based on the extent to which energy substitution opportunities are in some way adversely and irreversibly affected over time. In other words, even with a positive discount rate, the argument for conservation is tantamount to the position that current economic welfare is dependent on the quality of future energy choices.

The world of continuing energy substitution possibilities is, in effect, the world of neoclassical economics.[10] To defend this view as a realistic one of future energy opportunities, many neoclassical economists have drawn on three pieces of evidence. One is the energy-GNP ratio referred to in chapter 1. As long as the energy-GNP ratio is constant or falling, there is little need to worry about general energy scarcity. A second piece of evidence, which is based directly on the first, is that the price of natural resources in real terms does not appear to have risen over time. As Harold J. Barnett noted in a recent update of his widely cited study of natural resource scarcity, technological change and a shift in the composition of output from a manufacturing-agricultural mix to a service-based economy are two important reasons why this stable behavior appears to have persisted.[11] The third piece of evidence in support of the neoclassical view is that even where the relative price of energy may rise, the elasticity of substitution between energy and non-energy resources can be

[10]Though hardly concerned only with the economics of energy and natural resources, neoclassical economics is most characteristic of current mainstream economic theory. Its predilection for a market-oriented allocation of resources is based on the twin assumptions of significantly high substitution elasticities in all sectors of the economy and the relative insignificance of market failure, at least when viewed in terms of its opportunity costs of government intervention. It differs from the classical economics of Adam Smith (1723-90), Thomas Malthus (1766-1834), David Ricardo (1772-1823), and John Stuart Mill (1806-73) in that problems of natural resource scarcity, overpopulation, and the very long run are not considered important within the time frame in which finite decisions regarding resource allocation are made. Economists whose writings on the issues of energy resource allocation have tended to reflect these neoclassical views include R. M. Solow, W. D. Nordhaus, J. E. Stiglitz, A. C. Fisher, H. J. Barnett, J. L. Sweeney, R. S. Pindyck, V. K. Smith, and H. Hotelling, among others too numerous to list here.

[11]Harold J. Barnett, "Growth and Scarcity Revisited," in *Scarcity and Growth Reconsidered*, ed. V. K. Smith (Baltimore: Johns Hopkins University Press for Resources for the Future, 1979), pp. 163-217. See also H. J. Barnett and Chandler Morse, *Scarcity and Growth: The Economics of Natural Resource Availablity* (Baltimore: Johns Hopkins Press for Resources for the Future, 1963).

positive over time. Indeed, the evidence on the demand for energy noted in chapter 10 lends some support for this proposition.[12]

As appealing as the neoclassical position appears to be, there is also a compelling case for conservation. Central to the conservationist position are four key arguments.[13] First, by virtue of the Second Law of Thermodynamics, the technical possiblities for energy conservation will tend to become more limited over time. Thus, if energy conservation can now be made to be relatively efficient in both economic and technical terms, then society's self-interest will be better served by extending the technically and economically useful life of today's relatively low-entropy resources for as long as possible. The second argument, similar to the first, is that because market rates of discount are used so widely to determine the relative pricing of alternative energy resources, there is an inherent tendency for the economy to consume relatively low-entropy depletable energy resources now and to defer into the future the eventual shift to renewable and conservation energy technologies. Because the consumption of today's depletable energy resources by definition precludes the possibility of their being consumed in the future, there is a conflict between what would appear to be economically efficient market rates of discount and qualitative notions of intergenerational equity. Third, energy conservation is compatible with environmental protection. Without a corresponding emphasis on energy conservation, measures to promote environment protection would tend to be irrational and unproductive. Finally, for the United States at least, energy conservation may be an economically efficient route to energy security. To the extent that the technical efficiency of energy conversion can be raised now, the degree of dependence on uncertain supplies of imported energy can be reduced. What is needed at this point is to determine to what extent the conservationist view is compatible with the conventional neoclassical model of the economy.

If the conservationist view has any validity, then we must be able to explain why the energy–GNP ratio has been relatively stable over time and why the long-run elasticity of substitution between energy and non-energy resources could be as high as the studies of chapter 10 suggest. There are two possible reasons for the apparent stability of the energy–GNP ratio: an increase in the social rate of discount over time, and technological change. As noted in chapter 13, an increase in the rate of discount will tend to shift future energy production and consumption of depletable resources toward the present, thereby enlarg-

[12]See esp. tables 10.1, 10.2, and 10.3.

[13]Though differing in the degree to which they are opposed to particular neoclassical theories, prominent critics in the field of energy include not only economists but also writers in allied professions, notably those in the natural sciences. Economists whose writings have tended to express varying degrees of emphasis on conservation include E. J. Mishan, Nicholas Georgescu-Roegen, Herman E. Daly, Barbara Ward, Kenneth Boulding, E. F. Schumacher, Dennis Goulet, Talbot Page, Fred Hirsch, O. C. Herfindahl, A. Kneese, and others too numerous to list here. Among notable non-economists we should include Paul Ehrlich, Barry Commoner, Amory Lovins, Garrett Hardin, Jay Forrester, Dennis Meadows, Donella Meadows, Hazel Henderson, Wilson Clark, Rachel Carson, Frederick Soddy, Eugene and Howard Odum, M. King Hubbert, Harrison Brown, Denis Hayes, John Holdren, Nathan Keyfitz, and others too numerous to list here.

ing today's supply sufficiently to offset or dampen what would otherwise be an increase in its real price to reflect its underlying user cost. Such a shifting of future consumption toward the present would enable the present generation to offset the adverse consequences of the Second Law of Thermodynamics, that is, the tendency for the economy's ratio of net available, or usable, energy to its gross input energy to fall.[14] Consequently, as long as the price of energy did not increase by any significant amount, and as long as the share of the GNP accounted for by expenditures were not large, then it would be possible to enjoy a short-term stable, or even declining, energy–GNP ratio.

Have real interest rates risen? To be sure, there are many determinants of the level of interest rates at any particular moment in time. Yet the key issue here is whether they have risen over time. To provide one test of this question, data on one- and five-year prime corporate bonds in the United States for the period 1946–75 were regressed as a function of time.[15] In order to make multiyear comparisons, both sets of data were converted to real rates of interest using a 1972 base-year GNP price deflator. Although regressions using linear and nonlinear equations were both significant, the form that best accounted for the trends in real interest rates was logarithmic time series. The results are:

$$\text{One-Year Real Interest Rate (1946–75)} = \underset{(4.031226)}{-5.936413} + \underset{(4.307272)}{2.381895} \log(i)_t \qquad (14.3)$$

$$\bar{R}^2 = 0.377049$$
$$F = 18.552595$$

and

$$\text{Five-Year Real Interest Rate (1946–75)} = \underset{(4.281492)}{-2.867101} + \underset{(4.386773)}{1.312521} \log(i)_t \qquad (14.4)$$

$$\bar{R}^2 = 0.394513$$
$$F = 19.243774,$$

where the statistics in parentheses are the computed t ratios. The key to both equations is that the signs of the dependent variables are positive, that is,

[14]As an example, consider an economy with a GNP of $100, of which 5 percent is spent on energy. The composition of this expenditures is a consumption of 5 units of energy at a price of $1.00 per unit. Now an increase in the discount rate permits the level of energy consumption to increase to 10 units at $0.50 per unit, or $5.00. In turn, the level of GNP now increases from $100 to $200, of which 2.5 percent is spent on energy. The energy share of GNP expenditures has fallen to half of its previous level, while the energy–GNP ratio remains the same. What has made it possible is the decline in the price of energy brought about by an increase in the rate of discount.

[15]Interest rates on U.S. Government securities are used commonly to estimate the social rate of discount, since government is not constrained by profit-maximization considerations. In the use of the corporate rates here the level of government rates is thus probably overestimated to some extent, but the trends exhibited in figure 14.1 would not be markedly different from the trends for U.S. government securities.

factors other than time may have influenced interest rates, but time alone shows that there has been a gradual upward trend, at least for the postwar period used by most neoclassical models of energy relationships referred to in previous chapters.

Does the stability of the energy–GNP ratio depend critically on an increase in the real rate of discount over time? An increase in the discount rate can be a factor in the determination of a stable, or even a declining, energy–GNP ratio. However, over time, the shifting of future resources toward the present should run up eventually against the law of diminishing marginal returns as lower-quality resources are consumed. The energy–GNP ratio would rise, since the price of energy would reflect both rising marginal extraction costs and a steepening path of user-cost increases. Yet, as we saw in chapter 13, technological change can offset the projected rise in user costs, thereby perpetuating a stable or falling energy–GNP ratio. Before we could conclude that the rate of discount was the primary determinant in the energy–GNP ratio, then, we would also have to consider the opportunities for energy-conserving technological change.

There are two ways in which technological change can sustain a relatively stable energy–GNP ratio. One is that at any given moment in time, if the First Law efficiency is sufficiently below the Second Law efficiency, then it is perfectly possible to increase the technical efficiency of energy conversion and have a relatively stable or falling pattern of prices. The shape of this relationship is similar to the conventional relationship between average- and marginal-cost curves in microeconomic theory, shown here in figure 14.1. As long as the marginal cost of improved energy-conversion efficiency is less than the marginal cost of alternative non-energy inputs, a stable or even falling energy–GNP ratio can be maintained. Given the relatively low levels of

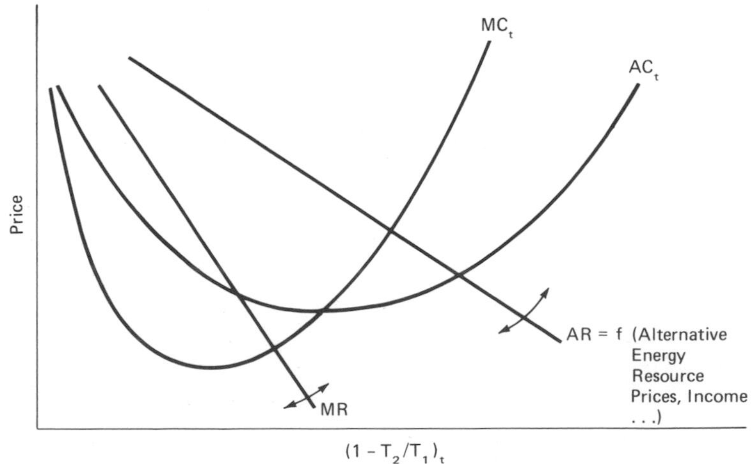

Figure 14.1. Second Law Thermodynamic Efficiency and the Static Price of Energy Conservation

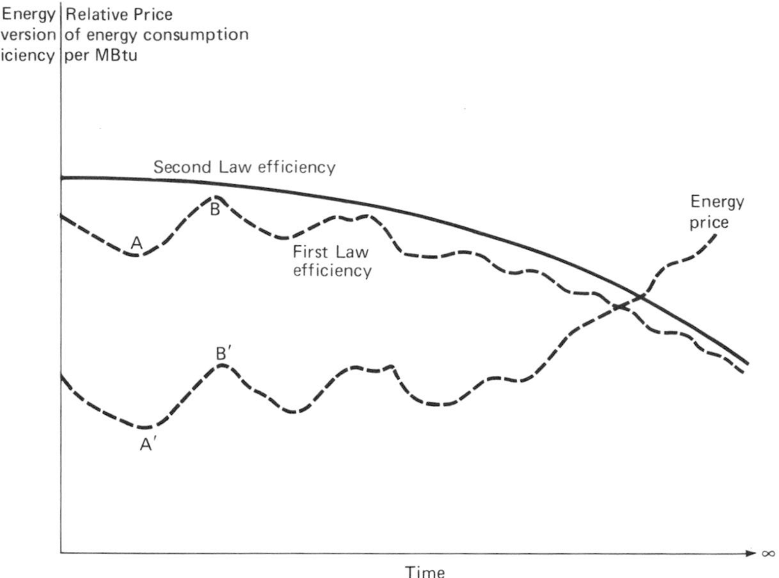

Figure 14.2. Technological Change, Thermodynamics, and Energy Prices

technical efficiency of energy conversion in the U.S. economy during the periods covered by the energy demand studies of chapter 10, it is not surprising that a relatively stable energy–GNP ratio has been observed.

The second way in which technological change could be used to explain a relatively stable energy–GNP ratio is more subtle. Some writers have argued that it is misleading to suggest that the world has moved continuously from lower- to higher-entropy forms of energy conversion. After all, it is pointed out, petroleum has a lower entropy than the wood energy which preceded it, and nuclear energy has a much lower entropy than fossil energy resources. The paradox in these examples is that an economy can acquire lower-entropy energy technologies at a given moment in time, but only at the price of increasing the global level of entropy sometime farther into the future.[16] As a practical illustration, the relatively efficient energy yields one obtains from commercial nuclear fission are obtained by deferring the problem of nuclear wastes for up to thousands of years into the future. Consequently, although there may be local-order exceptions to the Second Law of Thermodynamics, on a global level the principle still holds, much as is illustrated in figure 14.2. In terms of intertemporal equity, the quality of energy available to future generations will still tend to dissipate over time.

Figure 14.2 also illustrates the third argument for energy conservation. To the extent that the relative price of energy is low, not only will it promote an

[16]For an elaboration of local-order exceptions to the Second Law of Thermodynamics, see Ilya Prigogine, "Time, Structure, and Entropy," in *Time in Science and Philosophy*, ed. Jiri Zeman (Amsterdam: Elsevier Publishing Co., 1971), pp. 89–99.

energy-intensive economy but it will tend to produce higher levels of environmental pollution than would otherwise occur. As pointed out in chapters 12 and 13, much environmental pollution can be traced directly to the technically inefficient conversion of energy. With a lower relative price of energy such as at A', the First Law technical efficiency of energy conversion at point A will tend to be well below the Second Law limit. The gap between these two measures of technical efficiency provides a relative measure of the extent to which environmental pollution will occur within the economy. In contrast, at a higher relative price B', the technical efficiency of energy conversion is raised to B, and environmental pollution is correspondingly lowered. Although market prices could determine the degree of energy conversion, in the economic-efficiency terms of the equalization of marginal social costs and benefits and in terms of intergenerational equity, there is a case to be made for a higher relative price of energy. Indeed, the neoclassical model of economic efficiency calls for the equalization of marginal social costs and benefits but does not make the direct connection between the relative price of energy conversion and environmental protection. Since energy security, the fourth argument in support of energy conservation, is treated in section 14.2, we will examine its merits at that point within the context of economic uncertainty.

Given the foregoing considerations, it is not difficult to see why the economy's energy–GNP ratio could be as variable as the neoclassical model suggests. Yet because part of this flexibility is dependent on the social rate of discount, on opportunities for technological change, and on the presence or absence of externalities, the question of intertemporal equity still remains.

Is there an optimal rule for intertemporal equity? Unfortunately, no such rule exists, since any equity choice must still be based on subjective value judgments. In its simplest terms, the policy implication here is that the greater the extent to which one weighs future energy choices relative to those of today, the greater will be the emphasis on the consumption of higher-entropy resources now and the deferral of consumption of some lower-entropy resources into the future. Under such conditions, if the rate of social discount were lowered to give greater weight to the future, today's energy mix would lean more heavily in favor of solar as opposed to nuclear energy, and there would be an opposite mix of technologies (see figure 14.3). Because information about the future is so often laden with uncertainty, the choice of an optimal rate of discount depends partly on how questions of uncertainty are addressed.

14.2. THE CERTAIN ALLOCATION OF ENERGY RESOURCES

Until now, the examination of energy policy criteria has been based on a critical simplifying assumption, namely, that regardless of the level of allocative efficiency and associated degree of equity, energy decisions operate in a world of perfect information. To assume that these decisions are made in a real-world setting of perfect information contradicts both common sense and historical experience. Indeed, the very nature of energy crises discussed in part one con-

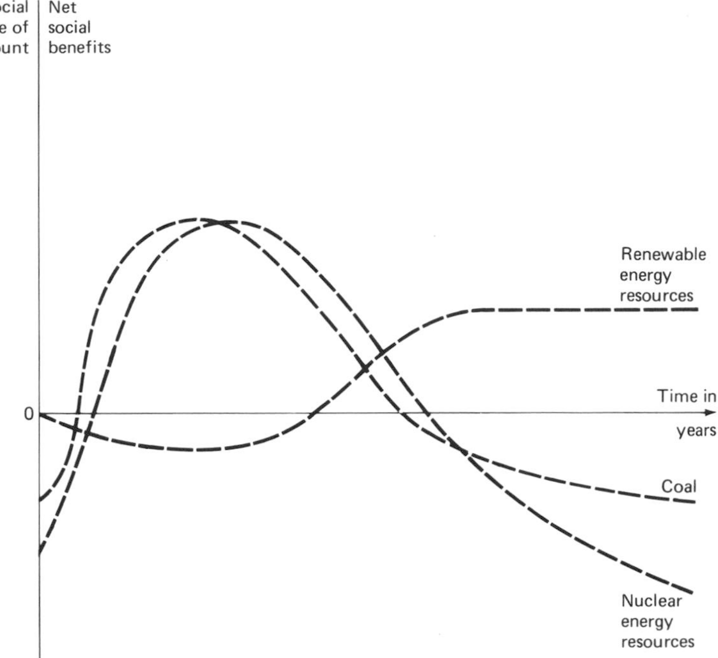

Figure 14.3. Intertemporal Equity Choices in Electricity Investments

firms just how important the quality of information can be to making energy policy choices. At this point, then, we need to identify the various ways in which imperfect information can affect energy policy alternatives.

14.2.1. Uncertainty in Energy Resource Allocation

The problem of decisionmaking under uncertainty is least a twofold one. On one level, as long as we possess some degree of knowledge regarding probabilities of particular outcomes and as long as we have some knowledge regarding decisionmakers' attitudes toward risk, there is still a rational basis with which to proceed with the allocation of resources. On the other hand, in some types of decisionmaking, so little is known about the particular risks that even if we are prone to taking risks, there may be little, if any, reasonable basis for adopting one alternative over another.[17] The examples that follow illustrate the nature of energy decisionmaking under various degrees of uncertainty. They will enable us to define an appropriate mix of incentives

[17]In economics, the distinction between assignable risk and unassignable uncertainty derives largely from the writings of Frank H. Knight (see his *Risk, Uncertainty, and Profit* [Boston: Houghton Mifflin, 1921]). Much of the discussion in this section is based on more modern formulations. For an illustration, see Howard Raiffa, *Decision Analysis: Introductory Lectures on Choices under Uncertainty* (Reading, Mass.: Addison-Wesley Publishing Co., 1970).

consistent with an efficient allocation of resources, covered in chapter 13, and the equity criteria of section 14.1.

As has been shown in previous chapters, the allocation of energy resources abounds with examples of uncertainty. Since we are interested here in differentiating the impact of varying degrees of uncertainty on the nature of energy allocation decisions, we can simplify matters by concentrating on three representative examples which are of central importance to contemporary policy: incremental petroleum-reserve discoveries, nuclear power safety, and sudden disruptions of international petroleum supplies. For reasons spelled out below, these examples can be viewed as an ascending hierarchy of the degree of uncertainty in energy resource allocation decisions.

Though basic information regarding the technology and economics of petroleum extraction, conversion, and consumption is reasonably well known, there is always some degree of risk associated with any investment in incremental capacity. Nowhere is this uncertainty greater than at the level of discovery of additional reserves. We can best appreciate the problem of risk in this case by assuming that the level of demand for refined petroleum is clearly defined, as are the costs of refining and distribution. Moreover, the decision to invest in incremental capacity is based on a competitive market structure with none of the types of market failure enumerated in chapter 13.

Figure 14.4 illustrates the problem of uncertainty arising in petroleum exploration. For a single firm, prediction of an additional deposit prior to drilling within an existing oil field is a function of several key variables: the mean and variance of previous discoveries, the ratio of dry to successful holes drilled,

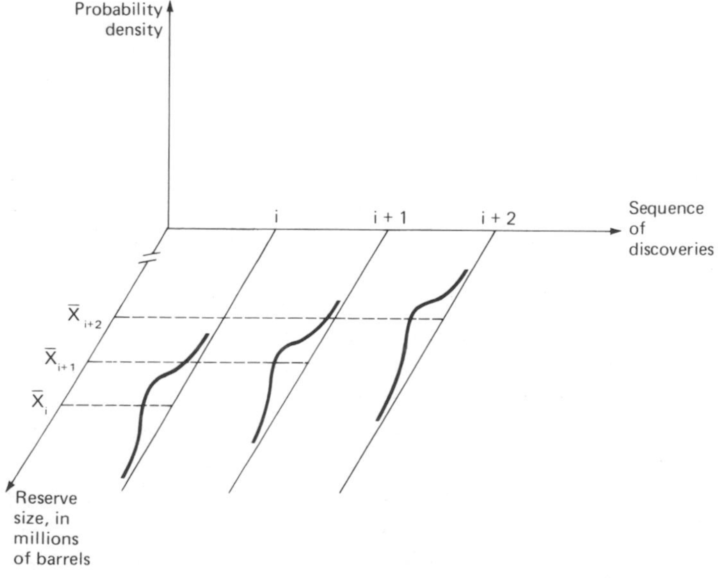

Figure 14.4. Geological Uncertainty in Petroleum Exploration

the depth pattern of sequentially drilled successful wells, the pressure level and decline rate among sequentially drilled successful wells, cumulative extraction to date, and the time lags among previously drilled successful wells. Now even if all of these data were known with precision, the likelihood of discovering an additional barrel of oil with a specific well pressure at a particular depth and location would still be subject to some degree of risk.[18] Yet the advantage of this prior information is that it enables the firm to reduce the level of uncertainty down to an assignable-risk investment decision.

The conventional way of deciding whether to proceed with an uncertain investment is to compare the utility of such a decision with the utility of a certainty-equivalent alternative. For an individual firm engaged in petroleum exploration, the comparative utility in question is the discounted net present value of its alternative investment choices as a function of the degree of risk which the firm is willing to take. To make such a decision, the firm must first take the given technical information on the probability of discovery of a specific quantity of the resource and compute the net discounted present value of the investment under probable successful and probable unsuccessful outcomes. The probability-weighted value of the uncertain investment can then be expressed as

$$NPV_u = (\pi)(X) - (1 - \pi)(Y), \tag{14.5}$$

where π is the probability of a successful outcome if the investment is undertaken, X is the discounted net present value of a successful investment, $1 - \pi$ is the probability of an unsuccessful outcome if the investment is undertaken, and Y is the discounted net present value of an unsuccessful investment. For example, if under competitive market conditions the probability of a successful drilling were estimated at 0.5, the discounted net present value from a successful drilling were estimated at $2,000,000, and the discounted net present value of costs from an unsuccessful drilling were estimated at $500,000, then the probability-weighted discounted net present value of the uncertain investment would be $750,000.

A firm would then compare the expected value of an uncertain investment with a certainty-equivalent alternative. Since a certainty-equivalent alternative would yield a smaller discounted net present value than would the uncertain alternative, as long as the difference in expected value were sufficient to compensate the firm for not adopting its certainty-equivalent alternative, then the firm would proceed with the uncertain investment. As should be obvious, though, the utility of any investment to the firm is a function of its willingness to tolerate such risk. Thus, even if the certainty-equivalent alternative were to provide a discounted net present value of only $500,001 on an investment of $500,000, an extremely risk-averse firm might still prefer such a minimal return to the fifty-fifty chance of a $750,000 alternative.

As should be obvious, risk aversion can have a profound effect on the

[18]To keep the issue in perspective, we are ruling out by temporary assumption the possibility of potential external benefits in this example.

allocation of energy resources. The policy implication here is that where risk is unevenly distributed among alternative energy resource technologies, as well as between energy and non-energy resource choices, there may be some grounds for public intervention to reduce the disparities in the pursuit of associated policy objectives. Yet before we can consider any such measures, we should examine the nature of energy resource allocation under greater degrees of uncertainty than in the examples thus far cited.

An area of considerable uncertainty in energy decisionmaking is that of the safety of conventional commercial nuclear fission reactors. As noted in chapters 6 and 12, the technical characteristics and pricing of nuclear energy can be substantially affected by uncertain conditions such as reactor safety, radioactive waste disposal, nuclear terrorism, and nuclear weapons proliferation. An important distinction in each of these cases is that the quality of information necessary to their prediction and control is likely to be inferior to the quality of information available in the area of a more established technology such as petroleum exploration. The question here is, To what extent does a relatively higher degree of uncertainty alter the decisionmaking of individual firms?

Under conditions of uncertainty where it appears impossible to assign specific outcome probabilities to a proposed investment project, a decisionmaker has three choices. One is to reject an investment project altogether on the basis of extreme risk aversion. Of course, firms that opt periodically for this alternative do so only because some other alternative possesses a higher expected value. When such alternatives are not available, a second choice is to seek to reduce the existing degree of uncertainty down to a level more suitable for accepting or rejecting the project. A third alternative is to adopt subjective probabilities and then weigh the consequences against the decisionmakers' willingness to assume the risk. Though realistic in certain cases, the first choice is interesting only as a polar case. Since the third is discussed in the context of disruptions to the international petroleum supply, our concern at this point is with the second alternative, particularly as it applies to commercial nuclear power.

Of the four types of uncertainty in commercial nuclear power, the one which appears most readily amenable to systematic risk assessment is reactor safety. Studies such as the Rasmussen Report, or WASH-1400, noted in chapter 6, attempt to predict the likelihood of a serious but unobserved reactor accident by construction of a sequential series of possible events leading to such an outcome. To minimize the probability of a worst case, a firm would compute the costs of safety mechanisms such as an emergency core cooling system and automated control rods, which must then be weighed against the benefits that such protection would provide. The degree of redundancy of these safety systems is a function of the seriousness of the worst-case accident and of the costs of alternative control mechanisms in relation to the expected stream of benefits discounted at the prevailing rate of interest.

Figure 14.5 illustrates one of two commonly used methods of estimating the degree of risk of an event with no prior historical occurrence, in this case

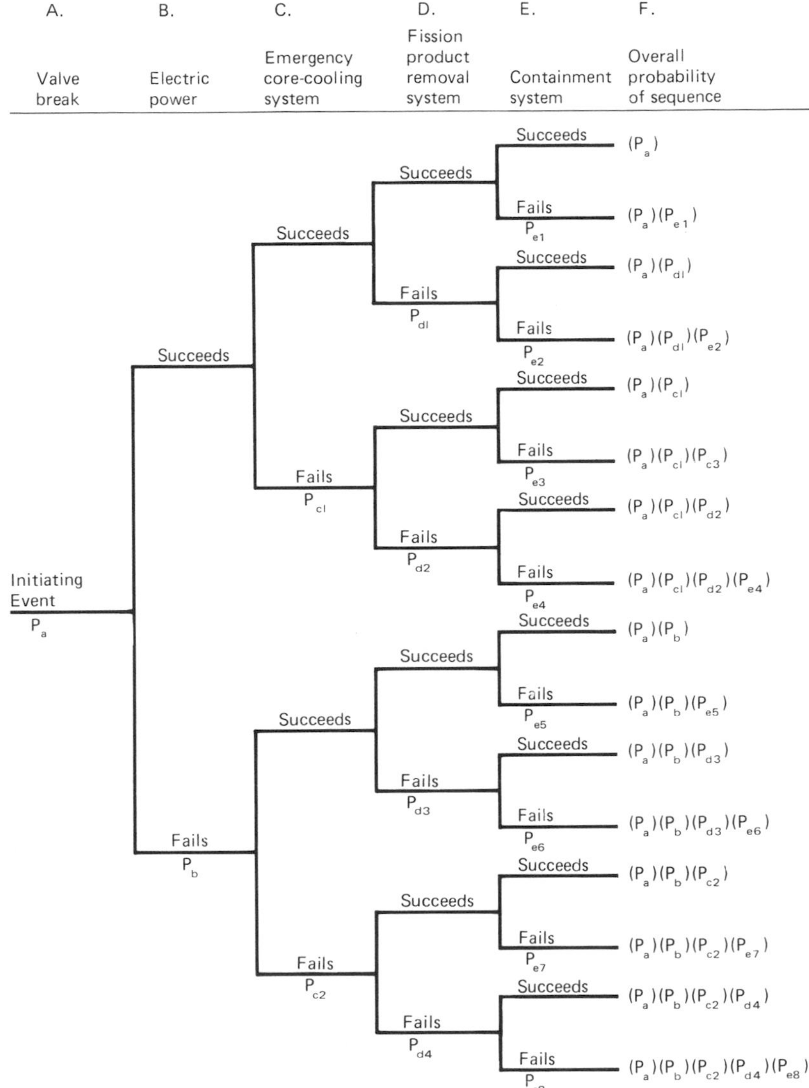

Figure 14.5. Nuclear Reactor Risk-Assessment Event Tree

the sequence of consequences associated with a possible worst-case nuclear reactor accident caused by a cooling-valve malfunction. Unlike its fault-tree-analysis counterpart, event-tree analysis is designed to show how various types of overlapping safety systems can reduce the probability of a worst-case accident down to an assignable-risk level. The probabilities at each stage of an event are based on the technical characteristics of the safety equipment and on the required skill level of reactor personnel responsible for accident prevention and control. If personnel and equipment are performing at their stipulated levels, the likelihood of a worst-case accident is the product of failure possibilities from all safety systems. In figure 14.5, the worst-case sequence is shown in the lower envelope of the tree and is expressed as

$$P_{\text{worst-case}} = (P_a)(P_b)(P_{c2})(P_{d4})(P_{e8}). \tag{14.6}$$

For each type of possible accident, including the worst-case one, the firm will compute the associated costs. If available, the costs of insurance necessary to cover these potential accidents will then be included in the firm's stream of discounted investment costs. If no such insurance exists, then the firm must include in its estimates the costs of each of the various types of accidents weighted by the estimated probabilities of their occurrence in a fashion similar to the method expressed in equation (14.5). In effect, through simulation of alternative possible outcomes, the firm has attempted to reduce an unobservable event down to the type of specific risks involved in the petroleum-exploration problem. However, because the risks faced by a firm engaged in petroleum exploration are likely to be known with greater certainty and because the social consequences of a worst-case nuclear reactor accident are likely to be far more serious than the loss of income from unsuccessful exploration, insurance subsidies such as those available to nuclear electric utilities under the Price-Anderson Act tend to bias the allocation of resources toward nuclear energy. Whether such publicly subsidized risks are justifiable in terms of Pareto optimality depends on the relevant opportunity costs, notably the extent to which nuclear energy provides an efficient solution to depletable or uncertain alternative resources. What is clear is that if utilities were to bear the full risks of radioactive waste disposal, nuclear theft, and weapons proliferation, even were insurance available for each of these contingencies, the investment costs of nuclear power would undoubtedly be much higher than the comparative estimates indicated in chapter 12.

The most difficult type of risk exists where no amount of technical information can permit decisionmakers to assign specific probabilities to a possible event. Typical of this type of risk is the possibility of disruptions to the international petroleum supply such as occurred in the 1973 OPEC embargo, the 1979 Iranian revolution, and the 1980 Iraqi-Iranian war. The difficulty here is that while human behavior may be predictable up to a point, it is far less certain than the largely technical risks involved in petroleum exploration or nuclear reactor operations. In this case, decisionmakers can adopt subjective probabilities of an event and weigh the consequences of these uncertain conditions against their willingness to tolerate risk.

Table 14.3 illustrates in hypothetical terms the problem of uncertainty concerning the international petroleum supply as it applies to a firm considering investment in liquid fuels. If no embargo were to occur, investment in overseas exploration for conventional petroleum would provide the firm with the highest expected discounted net present value. Under a partial embargo, domestic biomass alcohol fuels would provide the next highest net discounted present value; and under a total embargo, investment in domestic shale oil would provide the next highest value. Since the firm has no basis for

Table 14.3. International Petroleum Supply Risks in Liquid Fuel Investments

Investment Choice	No Embargo	Partial Embargo	Total Embargo
	A. Hypothetical Discounted Net Present Values		
1. Overseas exploration	600	100	0
2. Domestic shale oil	140	260	280
3. Domestic biomass alcohol	130	290	230
	B. Hypothetical Discounted Net Present Opportunity-Cost Values		
1. Overseas exploration	0	190	280
2. Domestic shale oil	460	30	0
3. Domestic biomass alcohol	470[a]	0	50

[a]Derived as: 470 = 600 − 130.

assuming that any one of the three conditions is more likely than any other, it must decide under what criteria it would be willing to adopt any of the three alternatives. Three typical criteria illustrate the complexity of arriving at this choice.

One method of deciding among the three investments is to adopt the maxi-min criterion. Under this rule, a firm chooses to maximize the value of the minimum possible payoff among the possible alternative investments. In this case, the firm would choose domestic shale oil, since in a worst-case scenario among all three investments, domestic shale oil would provide the firm with the largest minimum possible return.[19] On the other hand, the firm may prefer to arrive at its decision on an opportunity-cost basis, that is, by use of the mini-max regrets criterion. In this case, the firm seeks to minimize the maximum value of the investment opportunity forgone. Part B of table 14.3 illustrates the opportunity-cost basis of the mini-max regrets criterion. If a firm chooses biomass alcohol fuel and no embargo occurs, its opportunity cost of investment is 600 minus 130, or 470. If this rule were adopted, the choice that minimized the value of investment opportunities forgone would be the biomass-alcohol-fuel alternative. Finally, we could simply assume that the probabilities of the three embargo states are equal, in which case the firm would choose the investment that maximized the weighted average value of the investment under each possible state. Based on the estimated values shown in part A of table 14.3, the expected values of the three investments would be

$$\text{(14.7)} \qquad \text{Overseas exploration} = (600)(0.33333) + (100)(0.33333)$$
$$= 233.33,$$

[19]The respective minimum values of choices 1, 2, and 3 are 0, 140, and 130, respectively. Since 140 is the highest minimum value, domestic shale oil would be preferred. The key issue in formulating a practical policy alternative is to decide how to weigh the degree of public generalized risk aversion.

$$\text{(14.8)} \qquad \text{Domestic shale oil} = (140)(0.33333) + (260)(0.33333) + (280)(0.33333) = 226.66,$$

and

$$\text{(14.9)} \qquad \text{Domestic biomass alcohol} = (130)(0.33333) + (290)(0.33333) + (230)(0.33333) = 216.66.$$

Overseas exploration would be chosen as the preferred alternative. The point in each of these examples is that where risk cannot be determined with any degree of confidence, there is no longer any objective basis for choosing one investment over any other. Yet since most firms, like the individuals who manage them, are likely to be risk-averse, the presence of generalized uncertainty can create serious distortions which may call for some degree of corrective intervention.

14.2.2. Policy Choices to Reduce Uncertainty

Risk is a cost. Where it originates, who bears it, and how it is distributed can be influenced by energy policy choices. Although risk can never be eliminated from any decision, to the extent that one policy minimizes the degree of risk at the lowest possible cost, we can adopt some choices as superior to others. In effect, risk minimization can be thought of as a variation on the allocative-efficiency criterion covered in chapter 13.

To be consistent, policy choices to promote a risk-efficient allocation of energy resources depend on three normalizing principles. First, prior to any policy decision, the prevailing degree of risk in energy markets should be greater than the degree of risk in non-energy markets. Unless this is so, any measure that lowers the relative costs of risk in energy markets is equivalent to a subsidy for the production and consumption of energy at the expense of non-energy goods and services. Such a measure would violate the Pareto allocative-efficiency criterion, stipulated in chapter 13, and it could also alter the existing degree of equity, spelled out in section 14.1.

Second, government intervention to reduce risks in energy markets is warranted only to the extent that market-based choices are unavailable to existing firms in the industry. Many, if not most, types of energy risks can be routinely handled within prevailing institutions. These institutions include insurance markets, futures markets, and research and development activities by individual firms. Where these institutions operate at a less than perfectly competitive level, there may be some basis for public intervention. The reason for such intervention is straightforward: absent any corrective measures, the failure of private firms to attain a perfectly competitive allocation of risk-laden resources would violate one or more conditions of a Pareto-optimal allocation, discussed in chapter 13. Moreover, it could also result in a distribution of income other than what society would consider as optimal.

Third, the types of intervention used to minimize the degree of risk in energy markets should match directly the specific forms of market failure. As is often the case, risk and uncertainty often carry widespread net external costs or benefits. Where net external costs prevail, the appropriate policy measure is to restrict that type of energy decision up to the point where the marginal social costs of restriction are equal to the marginal social benefits of reduced levels of external risk. Conversely, where net external benefits can arise, the appropriate policy choice is to subsidize that type of investment up to the point of equalization of marginal social costs and benefits. To see how all of these principles can be applied to specific types of energy decisions, let us now return to the risk examples cited in section 14.2.1.

Where specific risks can be assigned to an energy decision, as long as they do not exceed the risks in alternative choices and as long as no net external costs and benefits are involved, there is no reason for any form of risk-adjusting public intervention. Nowhere is this more true than in the case of petroleum exploration. In areas such as offshore exploration, it is appropriate on efficiency grounds for government to unitize reservoir development to minimize the possibility that external benefits will arise to individual firms. It is also appropriate for government to use cash bidding or royalty agreements in such offshore exploration to achieve a desired degree of current and intergenerational equity. However, once these conditions have been satisfied, there is no basis for any additional action such as geological exploration by government itself in these publicly owned areas. Were government to take such action, unless production were somehow restrained over time by equity-preserving relatively higher cash bidding or royalty requirements, such geological knowledge would lower the costs of risk relative to other alternatives faced by petroleum exploration firms. Since petroleum is also a depletable energy resource, such a decision would also carry significant equity consequences along the lines noted in sections 14.1.1 and 14.1.2.

As we have seen, commercial nuclear power involves potentially serious environmental and political risks. There are three possible policy instruments which can be used to contain these risks: regulation, research and development expenditures, and insurance subsidies. As the following discussion will show, the first two instruments are appropriate under certain conditions to contain existing nuclear risks, but the third is not.

Regulation of nuclear power can promote a risk-efficient use of this resource in several basic ways. First, by stipulating specific design and maintenance configurations, regulation can promote the satisfaction of a desired level of reactor operating safety. Regulation can also be used to minimize some of the associated nuclear risks of radioactive waste disposal, nuclear terrorism, and nuclear weapons proliferation, even though the latter two problems extend beyond direct regulation of commercial nuclear reactors. Whether these risks are in fact minimized is a function of the type of regulation undertaken, as the counterexample of the Middletown, Pennsylvania, 1979 accident at Three Mile Island illustrates all too well. Since no amount of regulation is likely to eliminate these nuclear risks, a complementary policy measure is the use of research and development expenditures to determine to what extent the external costs of residual risks in a regulated environment can be further contained. As in other types of allocative-efficiency questions, the rule here is that the marginal social benefits of research and development should determine the marginal social costs of undertaking these expenditures; the degree of regulation over commercial nuclear reactors should be guided by the same operating principle.

A different conclusion arises in the case of nuclear insurance. As noted in section 14.2.1, commercial nuclear power in the United States receives a peculiar type of operating subsidy under the Price-Anderson Act. Figure 14.6 illustrates the distorting consequences of this legislation for the distribution of risk and for the degree of allocative efficiency. The problem here is that under this legislation, a ceiling level of liability to commercial nuclear utilities is set at a level below what would be the case were firms required to obtain coverage in purely private insurance markets. Consequently, a subsidized price of p_1 results in a level of nuclear energy production of q_1, whereas if firms were to carry the associated risks through private-market alternatives, the comparable costs of insurance would shift the industry supply curve from S_1S_1 to S_2S_2, resulting in a price of p_2 and a quantity of q_2. In other words, the imposition of an insurance subsidy results in an external cost of ABC, which is now borne by taxpayers. The irrationality of such a decision is that

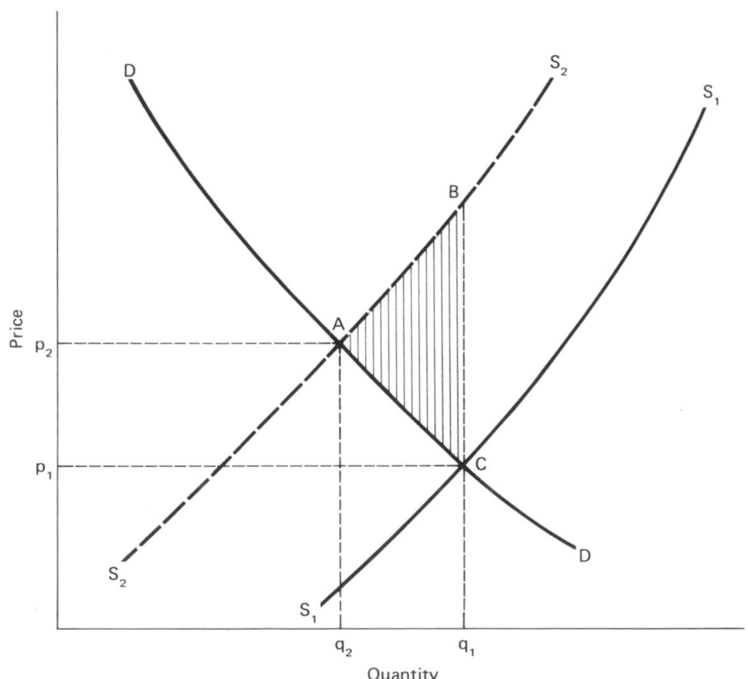

Figure 14.6. Allocative Distortion of Nuclear Reactor Safety Risks under Publicly Subsidized Insurance.

public revenues are utilized to create an external production diseconomy, that is, the public is paying to have an existing level of risk redistributed at large, and at a price which the public itself would not be willing to assume under purely private markets. In sum, where external costs such as risk are involved, the appropriate policy choice is not to subsidize but to require that the costs of risk be fully embodied in the price of the resource itself.

A third type of energy policy choice involving risk is how to handle the uncertainty of international energy supply. To the extent that an economy depends on imported energy from a source which may inpose an embargo on supplies, undergo a revolution, or experience a debilitating military conflict, the risk-inclusive price of that energy resource will be far greater than the price imposed by a competitive market or even a cartel would suggest. Since the costs of risk in this case are equivalent to an external consumption diseconomy, unless otherwise corrected, international supply uncertainty leads to a breakdown of a Pareto-optimal allocation of resources. There are many alternatives that a consuming economy could adopt in response to this uncertainty; we will focus on six common alternatives: domestic-production subsidies, tariffs, quotas, shut-in capacity, strategic petroleum reserves, and domestic-consumption taxes.

Introduction of a domestic-production subsidy could be brought about by a number of means, such as accelerated-depletion allowances, a tax-deduction allowance for intangible drilling expenses in domestic exploration, or a lower tax rate applied only to producers of the closest domestic substitute resource. To be sure, any or all of these measures would tend to lower the cost of the domestically produced substitute resource relative to that of its risk-prone imported alternative. Dependency on imported energy would tend to decline. The difficulty in adopting this solution is that it may perpetuate or even worsen the original Pareto-inefficient allocation of resources, as well as alter the prevailing degree of equity. In the Pareto comparative reference terms of figure 13.2, a domestic-production subsidy would tend to promote an energy-intensive pattern of production in the economy which would bear no relation to the domestic opportunity costs of this resource. Consequently, a Pareto-efficient solution would require that the level of subsidy extended to domestic producers of an import-dependent resource also be extended simultaneously to all other sectors of the domestic economy, or that no subsidy be permitted in the first place in favor of some other alternative. Furthermore, even if a Pareto-efficient generalized subsidy, or tax cut, were extended to all sectors of the economy, should the domestically produced energy alternative be a depletable energy resource such as petroleum, intergenerational equity would also be affected.

Tariffs and quotas are two alternative instruments which can be used to reduce the uncertainty of imported-energy dependence. However, they will produce at least three distorting consequences. One is that the artificial alteration of the terms of trade will lead to a lowering of real income in both the exporting and the importing countries. Another is that the distribution of income between the exporting and importing countries is likely to be altered.

Perhaps most important of all is the fact that once they are imposed by one country, retaliatory tariffs are likely to be imposed by the affected energy-exporting countries, which would lead to successive rounds of reductions in the value of international trade and real-world income. Indeed, contraction of international trade precipitated by protectionist measures could bring about a world economic depression even greater than the great contraction of the 1930s, especially since the world's economies have become so much more interdependent since that time.

Figure 14.7 illustrates the distorting effects of tariffs and quotas on international economic welfare. In figure 14.7.*a*, prior to imposition of a tariff, the prevailing international price of a traded commodity such as petroleum is

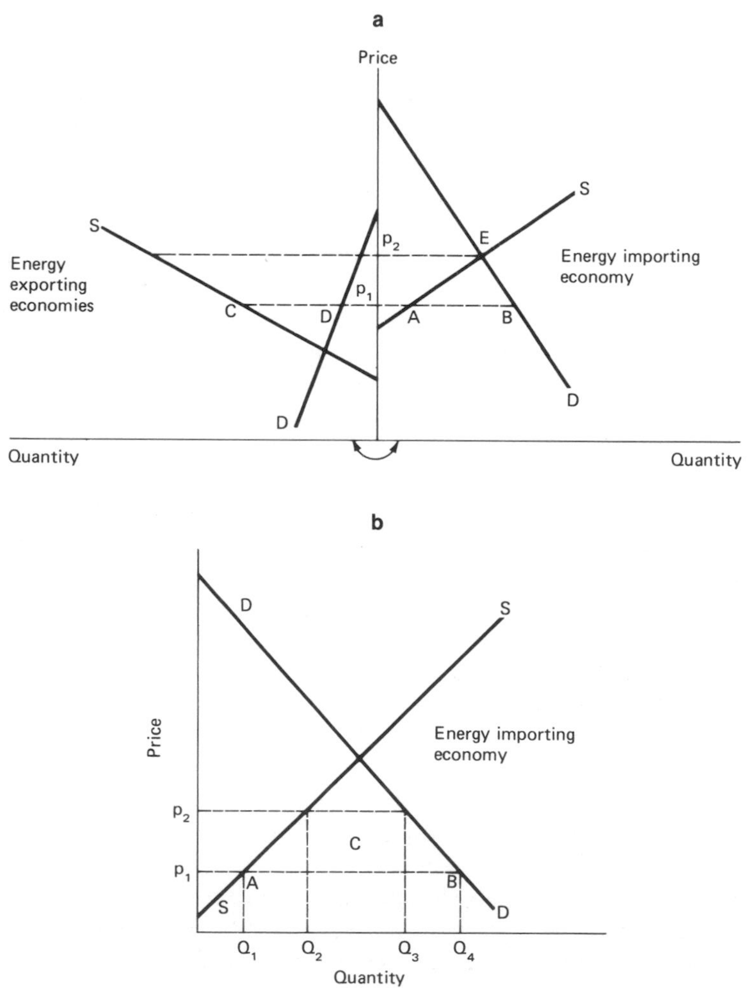

Figure 14.7. Welfare Consequences of Tariffs and Quotas on Energy-Import Dependence: **a**. tariffs; **b**. quotas.

p_1. At this price, energy-exporting economies produce a surplus quantity shown here as the segment *CD*. In turn, an energy-importing economy (or group of economies) consumes at a price of p_1 a quantity *B* but produces only quantity *A*; thus energy imports are equal to segment *AB*. However, faced with a potential sudden interruption of supply, the importing country decides to impose a tariff equal to $p_2 - p_1$ per barrel, thereby raising the price of the resource from p_1 to p_2 and eliminating its dependence on the uncertain international supply. If this happens, several specific distortions will occur. First, the real income of both economies will be lowered by the unilateral tariff decision. Although the tariff will generate some revenue to the government of the energy-importing economy, to the extent that the marginal social cost of domestically protected energy along the segment *AE* exceeds the uncertainty-inclusive marginal social cost of the imported alternative, real income in the consuming economy will be less than under a free trading regime. In turn, income of the exporting economies will be lowered to the extent that their domestic demand for the previously exported commodity is price-elastic and that energy exports account for a significant share of their gross national production. The second distortion follows directly from the first. To the extent that the sum of the price elasticities of demand and supply of the traded commodity is greater in one economy than in the other, imposition of a tariff will alter the distribution of income between the two trading units.[20] For example, if the sum of these price elasticities is greater in the importing economy than in the exporting economies, then the loss of real income in the importing economy will be less than the loss of income in the exporting economies. Moreover, the magnitude of this relative loss of income will be greater the larger the share of energy-based trade in the gross national production of exporting economies in comparison with the share of trade in the energy-importing economy. Third, successive rounds of tariff retaliation on both sides among all categories of trade can be viewed as an extension of the first two effects. Finally, if the domestic price elasticity of supply is greater than the domestic price elasticity of demand, and if the commodity is a depletable energy resource such as petroleum, then the tariff will also affect intertemporal equity, at least insofar as the consumption mix of depletable and renewable energy resources in the importing economy is altered.

In terms of broad distorting consequences, quotas are no different from tariffs, as may be seen in figure 14.7.*b*. Under free trade, an economy dependent on energy imports will consume Q_4 units of energy, produce only Q_1, and make up the difference by imports equal to the segment *AB* at the internationally traded price of p_1. Let us assume now that concern over international-supply uncertainty results in the imposition of a quota of $Q_2 - Q_3$ units of imported energy. Even though no direct price restriction has been imposed under the quota, the equilibrium price will rise from p_1 to p_2. At a price of p_2, consumption is reduced from Q_4 to Q_3, and domestic production

[20]This conclusion is based on the Marshall-Lerner conditions for international trade adjustments through alteration of relative prices.

increases from Q_1 to Q_2. Quotas may differ from tariffs, since unless the government of the importing country imposes a fee equal to the revenue that a tariff would have provided, equal in figure 14.7.*b* to region *C*, any importer who pays less than the tariff-equivalent rate receives a windfall gain. Indeed, it is not surprising that an industry seeking protection would much prefer a quota over a tariff, particularly if it were also able to control those imports with an inexpensive licence.

Like tariffs, quotas are inefficient instruments to reduce the costs of international-energy-supply uncertainty. They are rigid and difficult to administer, they hide real economic costs, and under most circumstances they do not even possess the superficial attraction of generating the benefit of public revenue to any significant extent. Where they are imposed, they often lead to retaliatory quota action, thereby reducing the opportunities for an efficient allocation of resources.

Shut-in capacity and strategic petroleum reserves represent two additional alternatives to uncertainty in imported energy supplies. Shut-in capacity refers to unextracted known recoverable reserves from an existing reservoir, strategic petroleum reserves have been pumped into a separate storage unit such as an abandoned salt mine for subsequent reextraction. In thermodynamic terms, the level of entropy will be greater in the case of a strategic petroleum reserve than in the case of shut-in capacity. Thus, to the extent that a strategic petroleum reserve is utilized relative to shut-in capacity, intertemporal equity will again be affected. At the same time, because neither of these instruments would be used except during the case of an actual interruption of imported supplies, they both represent economically superior choices to any of the preceding alternatives thus far discussed.

We can illustrate further the efficiency basis of shut-in capacity and strategic petroleum reserve policy choices in terms of a simplified numerical example. Let us assume that the present value of a shut-in petroleum reserve can be expressed as

$$NPV = \int_o^\infty PQe^{-(r+q)t}dt = \frac{PQ}{(r+k)}, \tag{14.10}$$

where *NPV* is the discounted net present value of the resource, *Q* is the quantity of the resource, *P* is the price of the resource, *k* is the maximum rate of physical extraction of the resource, and *r* is the rate of discount. The cost of shut-in capacity is the opportunity cost, or forgone income, from not extracting and consuming the resource. In this case, the one-year cost of this capacity for any given level of production can be expressed as

$$K = NPV - NPV \,/\, (1+r) = NPV\left[\frac{r}{1+r}\right]. \tag{14.11}$$

This storage cost, *K*, must then be compared with the expected utility which society attaches to a given degree of supply certainty. As an illustration, if the average current price of domestically produced and internationally traded petroleum is thirty dollars a barrel, the rate of feasible extraction is 10 percent, and the prevailing rate of discount is also 10 percent, then the one-year cost of covering completely the daily flow of imports of five million barrels per day is

$$K = \left[\frac{(30)(5{,}000{,}000 \,/\, \text{day} \times 365 \text{ days})}{(1 + 0.1)}\right]\left[\frac{0.1}{1.1}\right], \tag{14.12}$$

$$= \$24.89 \text{ billion.}$$

It is this sum that government would have to pay private firms to develop but not to produce for one year, given the prevailing degree of uncertainty of imports and society's degree of risk aversion.

A sixth alternative instrument which could be used to reduce the degree of uncertainty in imported energy is a tax on consumption. Its appeal is simple: a tax on consumption would not have the discriminatory quality of tariffs or quotas and would reduce the level of imported energy, as may be seen in figure 14.8. Given an initial position of energy dependence on imports, an economy consumes Q_1, produces Q_2, and imports $Q_2 - Q_1$ units of energy at a price of p_1. The imposition of a unit tax of $p_2 - p_1$ would shift the domestic supply curve to the left from S_1 to S_2. Since the unit tax would apply equally to imported and domestic energy, the average price would rise from p_1 to p_2,

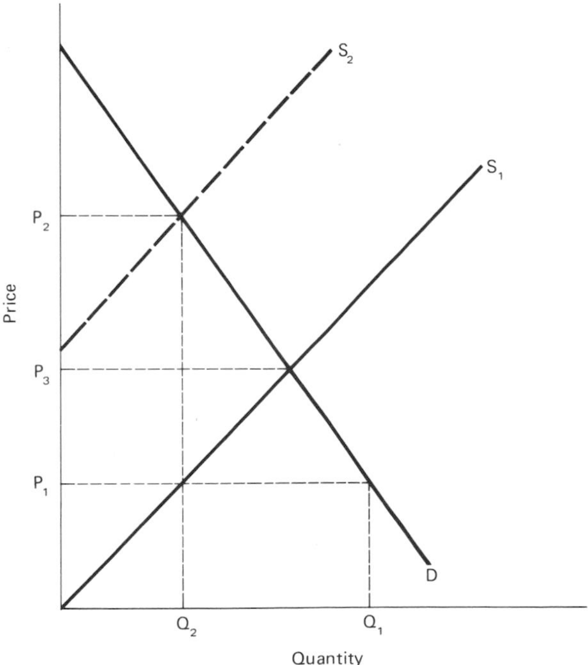

Figure 14.8. Welfare Consequences of a Consumption Tax on Energy

and thus the new equilibrium quantity of Q_2 would be provided from domestic production alone. Any price below p_2, such as at p_3, would leave some degree of import dependence. Regardless of the desired level of independence, as long as the revenues from an energy-consumption tax were used to preserve the preexisting static degree of equity, a tax on consumption would be compatible with a risk-inclusive efficient allocation of energy resources.

The aforementioned policy instruments represent a far from exhaustive list. After all, we have said nothing about the possibility of a government agency with exclusive rights to purchase energy imports on a sealed-bid basis, mandatory rationing of domestic and imported supplies, or subsidies for domestic synthetic-fuel substitutes, each of which could lower the level of energy imports.[21] In brief, the principal difficulty with a government import-purchasing monopoly is that although the price of a cartel-based resource could be lowered to some degree by this countervailing force, as long as the cartel persisted, the problem of a potential disruption of supply would remain. Moreover, it could also result in the creation of similar types of purchasing monopolies among the various economies to which the energy-dependent economy sends its own exports, much as would occur under a worldwide regime of tariffs or quotas.

Mandatory rationing would preserve the prevailing market price, but it would contain a public cost of administration and thus would fail to improve the degree of allocative efficiency available from other alternatives. Moreover, when the costs of administration are included, there is no guarantee that the preexisting degree of equity could be preserved. Finally, while synthetic fuels could become competitive under a regime of increasing market prices, to the extent that they benefitted from government subsidies not available to alternative energy and non-energy resources, Pareto-optimal allocation of resources would tend to break down. In this regard, publicly supported research and development expenditures to determine the external costs and benefits of synthetic fuels could be justified on grounds of allocative efficiency, whereas the extension of such subsidies to commercial production facilities would not.

As should be obvious from the preceding examples, the choice of policy instruments to reduce the level of uncertainty in imported energy supply bears directly on allocative efficiency and on the prevailing degree of equity. Of all these instruments, shut-in capacity, strategic petroleum reserves, and a tax on consumption are most consistent with an efficient allocation of resources and the preservation of the prevailing degree of equity. The principal difference between a tax on energy consumption and the use of strategic petroleum reserves or shut-in capacity is that in the former case the fiscal effect is embodied directly in the pricing of the resource itself whereas in the

[21]Apart from specific measures to ration gasoline in the United States by use of coupons, and subsidies to establish a domestic synthetic-fuels industry, some attention has been given to the possibility of establishing a government agency for purchasing petroleum imports, a proposal advocated most prominently by M. A. Adelman of MIT.

latter two cases the fiscal effects are diffused among all other sectors of the economy. To the extent that the price elasticity of demand is high, that is, to the extent that conservation and resource substitution are possible and significant, a tax on consumption would be superior to either of the stand-by-reserve alternatives. The second principal difference between these alternatives is that a tax on consumption would tend to encourage greater conservation today, thereby affecting in a potentially significant way the degree of intertemporal equity, particularly insofar as the resource in question is a depletable resource such as petroleum.

14.3. THE ADEQUATE ALLOCATION OF ENERGY RESOURCES

Adequacy is the fourth basic criterion which one can use to evaluate energy policy decisions. Here the question is to what extent can an efficient, equitable, and certain allocation of resources be consistent with such associated economic goals as price stability, full employment, and economic growth. As will be seen, all of these objectives are compatible, but only if there is consistency in the application of appropriate policy instruments.

14.3.1. The Linkage between Energy and Alternative Economic Policy Objectives

By definition, questions of full employment, price stability, and economic growth are macroeconomic in nature. As noted in chapter 3, since the demand for energy is a function of the demand for goods and services which it is used to produce and consume, macroeconomic decisions to stabilize the economy or to promote a particular rate of economic growth will of necessity affect to some degree the energy sector of the economy. Whether the energy sector will limit the ability of the economy to achieve its broader goals depends directly on the extent to which questions of allocative efficiency, equity, and uncertainty have been addressed in a mutually consistent fashion. How this may occur can be understood in terms of each of these criteria.

Figure 14.9 illustrates the linkage between a Pareto-optimal allocation of resources and macroeconomic stability. In figure 14.9.*a*, a Pareto-optimal allocation of resources enables the economy to attain a full-employment equilibrium with price stability, shown here at point *a*, the intersection of aggregate demand and supply. Although macroeconomic monetary and fiscal policies could lead to alternative unemployment or inflationary equilibria such as at *b* or *c*, other than for reasons of incompetence, no one would deliberately choose these positions over point *a*. Position *a* is thus a macroeconomic optimum that depends on the simultaneous satisfaction of a Pareto-efficient allocation of resources.

In contrast to the Pareto ideal conditions of figure 14.9.*a*, figure 14.9.*b* illustrates the consequences of microeconomic inefficiency on aggregate economic equilibrium. Whether for reasons of imperfect competition, external costs or benefits, or informational uncertainty, where market failure occurs, the allocation of resources will exhibit far less flexibility as the economy

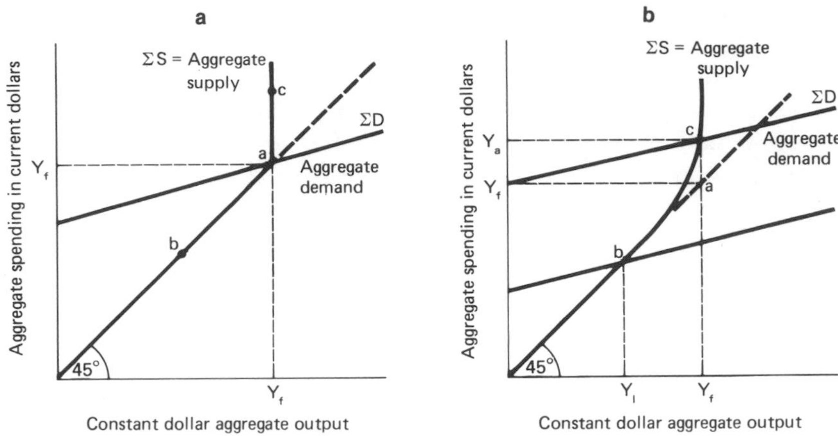

Figure 14.9. Microeconomic Allocative Efficiency and Aggregate Economic Equilibrium: **a.** Pareto optimality; **b.** static market failure.

approaches its full-employment level of capacity than if a Pareto-optimal structure were to exist. Consequently, expansion of aggregate demand to attain a full-employment level of production generates pressures on the general level of prices, much as efforts to reduce inflation by a lowering of aggregate demand generate an increase in unemployment. Moreover, to the extent that microeconomic policies further weaken the degree of allocative efficiency, even under a relatively constant level of aggregate demand, the resulting leftward shift in aggregate supply would simultaneously increase the prevailing rates of inflation and unemployment. Such stagflation, it is fair to say, is the utlimate cost to society of failure to achieve a Pareto-optimal allocation of resources.[22]

Not only is Pareto optimality a necessary condition for macroeconomic stability but it applies to economic growth as well. Figure 14.10 illustrates the linkage between energy and economic growth. At any single point in time, under a Pareto-efficient allocation of resources, an economy can achieve an equilibrium between aggregate demand, ΣD, and aggregate supply, ΣS, with stable prices and full employment, shown here in the upper diagram. For each of these equilibrium conditions, the economy will consume a given quantity of energy, which under present prices and technologies consists mostly of depletable fossil and nuclear resources. As the rate of production of depletable energy resources begins to exceed the rate of discovery of incremental supplies, an increase in the price of the resource begins to appear, shown in the lower diagram as the shift from p_1 to p_2 in period t_n. Such an increase in price would generate an increase in the general level of prices within the economy; under a Pareto-optimal allocation of resources, however, an increase in the price of energy would be offset to a large extent by two types of

[22]Allocative efficiency here refers to both domestic and international markets.

change: an increase in the technical conversion of energy and the production of alternative energy resources such as the backstop technologies referred to in chapter 13.

As figure 14.10 shows, to the extent that the competitive marginal social costs of energy conservation and backstop technologies are lower than the competitive marginal social costs of depletable energy resources, an increase in the level of aggregate income could be accommodated within a full-employment, relatively stable price dynamic equilibrium. However, where

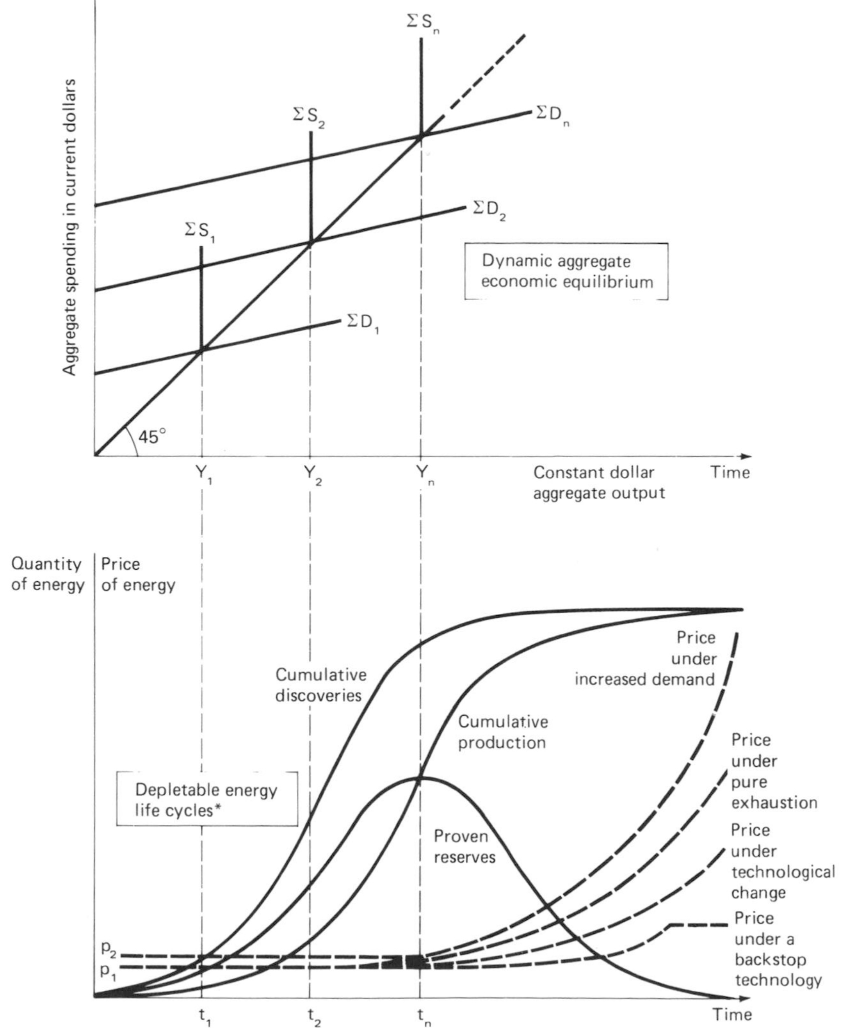

*For each price trajectory there will be a unique set of relations for cumulative discoveries, cumulative production, and proven reserves.

Figure 14.10. Dynamic Economic Equilibrium and the Consumption of Exhaustible Energy Resources

Pareto optimality is not realized, in order to sustain relatively stable energy prices today, an economy might decide to accelerate its consumption of depletable energy resources now in exchange for a much higher rate of increase in user costs tomorrow. This would occur because the extent of substitution opportunities for both conservation and a shift to backstop or renewable energy technologies under prevailing economic conditions would be less than those which would obtain under a Pareto-efficient allocative structure. Such an acceleration of consumption of depletable energy resources today would be tantamount to an increase in the social rate of discount, as noted in section 14.1. Thus, the failure to achieve Pareto optimality would have a twofold consequence: a more dramatic change between present and future energy prices than would otherwise be the case, and as a consequence of a change in the mix of present and future depletable energy consumption, a more substantial shift in the degree of intertemporal equity.

14.3.2. Defining the Public-Private Sector Mix in Energy Policy

The principles of a Pareto-efficient economy are central to the selection of appropriate energy policies. As we have seen, along with society's equity preferences, these principles provide a consistent normative basis by which policymakers may adopt sector-specific and aggregate economic decisions regarding the production and consumption of energy and non-energy resources. Since we have referred periodically to alternative types of policy instruments which could be used to achieve these objectives, it is useful at this point to see how they help to define the mix of public and private decision-making within a comprehensive policy setting.

A useful way of distinguishing between the private and public allocation of resources is to imagine an initial condition of Pareto optimality prior to any government action. In such an economy there would be perfect competition, perfect foresight, and zero net external costs and benefits. The appropriate role of the public sector would be to ensure that the resulting degree of equity in the distribution of income conformed to social preferences and that the supply of money within the economy grew at a rate sufficient to ensure a steady-state equilibrium of full employment and stable prices. After all, public goods would not exist, pollution would not exist, and since all economic agents would have perfect information, they would adjust the production and consumption of goods and services with a level of efficiency that would leave each individual satisfied within his or her level of income at all moments in time. The problem is that such a utopian economy does not now exist, has not existed in the past, and is not likely to exist in the future. The task of the policymaker, then, is to see to what extent specific types of intervention can enable the real-world economy to resemble the ideal economic model of Pareto optimality.

As defective as actual economic conditions may be at any moment in time, any or all forms of public intervention will not necessarily be justified. Indeed, as we have seen in numerous examples, many of the defects within a private market economy are as much a product of specific government actions as they are the product of the weaknesses these actions were designed to eliminate. If we are to arrive at an appropriate mix of public and private choices, we need a summary classification of market pricing defects and the corresponding types of policy instruments suitable to their correction.

Table 14.4 provides a summary of alternative energy policy instruments and the specific types of conditions which they are designed to correct. While the list is far from exhaustive, it illustrates in general under what conditions public intervention may be justified in the design and implementation of appropriate energy choices. Because each of these instruments will carry varying levels of administrative costs, we can never expect the adoption of any one of them to fully achieve a Pareto-optimal, equitable, certain, and adequate allocation of energy resources. At the same time, since a failure to respond to specific policy issues may carry far greater costs, the value of including an appropriate mix of these measures becomes all too clear. How and just what mix should be proposed depends on the particular problems and on existing policy measures.

14.3.3. Neoclassical Growth versus the Steady-State Economy

As may be fairly evident, the adequate allocation of energy resources depends ultimately on the level of allocative efficiency, the level of economic uncertainty, and the associated degree of equity. Since none of these conditions may be ideal at any given moment, the choice of a particular mix of measures today will affect to some extent the level of resource adequacy sometime in the future. It is therefore useful at this point to compare the conventional neoclassical model of economic growth with what its detractors suggest as a normative alternative, namely, the steady-state economy.

As we have seen, the neoclassical model is essentially indifferent to the Second Law of Thermodynanics. This is not surprising. By discounting future conditions and relying empirically on past and present economic performance, it usually avoids the pessimistic dimensions of increasing global entropy. As a model of hope, it is thus much more appealing to a policymaker, whose success may be governed largely by the same discounted time horizon. Indeed, it is occasionally said, the future will take care of itself. Rising energy consumption will bring about rising real incomes, so that for each degree of future energy liabilities, there will also be at least the same degree of benefits available to each successive generation.

The principal alternative to the conventional neoclassical model is what may be generally called the steady-state economy.[23] Unlike a world of continuing energy substitution opportunities, the steady-state economy operates on the fundamental premise that there are limits on the ability of an economy to sustain ever-increasing levels of real per capita income. The origins of the steady-state economy are found in the classical economic ideas of Adam Smith, David Ricardo, Thomas Malthus, and John Stuart Mill. A central

[23]There is no unique model of a steady-state economy. For one well-known essay, see Herman E. Daly, *Steady-State Economics* (San Francisco: W. H. Freeman and Co., 1977).

Table 14.4. Energy Policy Instruments

Policy Issue	Alternative Policy Instrument	Scope and Limitation of Policy Instrument
1. *Imperfect competition*		
Domestic only	Antitrust	Must be applied simultaneously to all comparable economic sectors; imperfect competition may subsequently reappear; may forsake some economies of scale in production and innovation.
	Regulation	Must be applied simultaneously to all comparable economic sectors; may violate competitive-equivalent marginal-cost pricing through Averch-Johnson and X-inefficiency distortions; may be wrongly used to achieve specific degrees of equity; may create perpetual shortages or surpluses through adoption of disequilibrium prices and quantities; may forsake some economies of scale in production and innovation.
	Taxation	Must be applied simultaneously to all comparable economic sectors; may have burden shifted to consumers if demand is relatively price-inelastic; may promote X-inefficiency if applied only to profits; allocation of tax revenues may be used to create distortions elsewhere in the economy; may reduce economies of scale in production and innovation.
	Public ownership	Must be applied simultaneously to all comparable economic sectors; may do nothing to achieve competitive marginal-cost allocative efficiency; may be used wrongly to achieve specific degrees of equity; may reduce economies of scale and innovation; may require periodic or continuing subsidies; may behave as a privately owned imperfectly competitive firm would do.
International only	Domestic-consumption taxes	Must be applied simultaneously to all comparable economic sectors; may not reduce distortion to domestic economy if demand is price-inelastic; may affect existing degree of equity.
	Domestic-production subsidy	Must be applied simultaneously to all comparable economic sectors; may promote accelerated depletion of exhaustible resource; may produce retaliatory measures among other trading industries; may promote domestic imperfect competition; may affect existing degree of equity.
	Tariffs and quotas	May promote domestic imperfect competition; will likely lead to international retaliation; undermines further the opportunity-cost basis of international trade; is likely to affect the existing degree of equity insofar as the demand is price-inelastic.
2. *Externalities*		
External costs	Taxation	Must be applied simultaneously to all comparable economic sectors; the incidence of taxation may be shifted to consumers if demand is price-inelastic while leaving external costs unaffected; may be at a higher or lower rate than socially optimal for economic efficiency; tax revenues may be used to create economic distortions elsewhere in the economy; may affect the existing degree of equity insofar as the demand is price-inelastic.
	Regulation	Must be applied simultaneously to all comparable economic sectors; may violate competitive-equivalent marginal-cost pricing through Averch-Johnson and X-ineffi-

Table 14.4.—*Continued*

Policy Issue	Alternative Policy Instrument	Scope and Limitation of Policy Instrument
		ciency distortions; may create perpetual shortages or surpluses through adoption of disequilibrium prices and quantities; may forsake some economies of scale in production and innovation.
External benefits	Subsidies	Must be applied simultaneously to all comparable economic sectors; may create input-output pricing distortions in imperfectly competitive industries; may promote accelerated depletion of exhaustible resources; may promote domestic imperfect competition; may affect existing degree of equity.
	Regulation	Must be applied simultaneously to all comparable economic sectors; may promote accelerated depletion of exhaustible resources; may promote domestic imperfect competition; may affect existing degree of equity.
3. *Natural monopoly*		
Domestic only	Regulation	Must be applied simultaneously to all comparable economic sectors; may violate competitive-equivalent marginal-cost pricing through Averch-Johnson and X-inefficiency distortions; may be wrongly used to achieve specific degrees of equity; may create perpetual shortages or surpluses through adoption of disequilibrium prices and quantities; may forsake some economies of scale in production and innovation.
	Taxation	Must be applied simultaneously to all comparable economic sectors; may have burden shifted to consumers if demand is relatively price-inelastic; may promote X-inefficiency if applied only to profits; allocation of tax revenues may be used to create distortions elsewhere in the economy; may reduce economies of scale in production and innovation.
	Public ownership	Must be applied simultaneously to all comparable economic sectors; may do nothing to achieve competitive marginal-cost allocative efficiency; may be used wrongly to achieve specific degrees of equity; may reduce economies of scale and innovation; may require periodic or continuing subsidies; may behave as a privately owned imperfectly competitive firm would do.
International only	Domestic-consumption taxes	Must be applied simultaneously to all comparable economic sectors; may not reduce distortion to domestic economy if demand is price-inelastic; may affect existing degree of equity; the choice depends largely on how natural monopoly is treated in the international market.
	Domestic-production subsidy	Must be applied simultaneously to all comparable economic sectors; may promote accelerated depletion of exhaustible resource; may produce retaliatory measures among other trading industries; may promote domestic imperfect competition; may affect existing degree of equity; the choice depends largely on how natural monopoly is treated in the international market.
4. *Public goods*		
Domestic only	Subsidies	Must be applied simultaneously to all comparable economic sectors; may create input-output pricing distortions among affected private producers; may promote imperfect competition; may affect existing degree of equity.

Table 14.4.—*Continued*

Policy Issue	Alternative Policy Instrument	Scope and Limitation of Policy Instrument
	Public ownership	Must be applied simultaneously to all comparable economic sectors; may do nothing to achieve competitive marginal-cost allocative efficiency; may be used wrongly to achieve specific degrees of equity; may reduce economies of scale and innovation; may require periodic or continuing subsidies; may behave as a privately owned imperfectly competitive firm would do.
International only	Subsidies	Must be applied simultaneously to all comparable economic sectors; may create input-output pricing distortions among affected private producers; may promote international imperfect competition; may affect existing degree of equity; depends largely on how public goods are treated within the international economy and on the extent to which benefits redound to the domestic economy.
	Joint public ownership	Must be applied simultaneously to all comparable economic sectors; may do nothing to achieve competitive marginal-cost allocative efficiency; may be used wrongly to achieve specific degrees of equity; may reduce economies of scale and innovation; may require periodic or continuing subsidies; may behave as a privately owned imperfectly competitive firm would do; may create input-output pricing distortions among affected private producers; may promote international imperfect competition; may affect existing degree of equity; depends largely on how public goods are treated within the international economy and on the extent to which benefits redound to the domestic economy.
5. *Equity*		
Static	Taxation	Should be exercised by direct taxation and redistribution of incomes rather than through selective fiscal incentives; subjective basis and institutional voting procedures complicate selection of optimal degree of equity.
Dynamic	Taxation	Same as for static.
	Discount-rate selection	If Pareto optimality holds, no degree of alteration is justified; where irreversibilities and uncertainty are significant, some adjustments may be appropriate.
6. *Uncertainty*		
Domestic external costs	Regulation	Must be applied simultaneously to all comparable economic sectors; may violate competitive-equivalent marginal-cost pricing through Averch-Johnson and X-inefficiency distortions; may create perpetual shortages or surpluses through adoption of disequilibrium prices and quantities; may forsake some economies of scale in production and innovation.
Domestic external benefits	Subsidies	Research and development expenditures may be justified where specific risks can not be assigned.
International external costs	Strategic reserves	The level of strategic reserves should match the public's degree of risk aversion.
	Consumption taxes	Must be applied simultaneously to all comparable economic sectors; the incidence of taxation may be shifted to consumers if demand is price-inelastic while leaving external costs unaffected; may be at a higher or lower rate than socially optimal for economic efficiency; tax revenues may be used to create economic distortions elsewhere in the economy; may affect the existing de-

Table 14.4.—*Continued*

Policy Issue	Alternative Policy Instrument	Scope and Limitation of Policy Instrument
		gree of equity insofar as the demand is price-inelastic; may promote X-inefficiency if applied only to profits; may reduce economies of scale in production and innovation.
International external benefits	Subsidies	Must be applied simultaneously to all comparable economic sectors; may create input-output pricing distortions among affected private producers; may promote international imperfect competition; may affect existing degree of equity; depends largely on how public goods are treated within the international economy and on the extent to which benefits redound to the domestic economy.
	Joint public ownership	Must be applied simultaneously to all comparable economic sectors; may do nothing to achieve competitive marginal-cost allocative efficiency; may be used wrongly to achieve specific degrees of equity; may reduce economies of scale and innovation; may require periodic or continuing subsidies; may behave as a privately owned imperfectly competitive firm would do; may create input-output pricing distortions among affected private producers; may promote international imperfect competition; may affect existing degree of equity; depends largely on how public goods are treated within the international economy and on the extent to which benefits redound to the domestic economy.

preoccupation of these writers was to discover the sources of economic growth and development to which they were witness during the English industrial revolution. Whether they were the impact of the specialization and division of labor, comparative advantage in international trade, active fiscal policies, or competitive economic markets, there was little doubt that England was experiencing at that time unprecedented growth in its real per capita income. Yet beyond the various explanations for this industrial transformation, each of these classical economic writers also perceived limits to continued economic growth. While it is doubtful that any of them was familiar with Sadi Carnot's discovery of the Second Law of Thermodynamics, the answers which they gave to explain these limits were all consistent with this basic law of physics. For example, the upper limits to the Smithian specialization and division of labor are a direct reflection of organizational entropy. Moreover, Ricardo's theory of rents for a fixed but ongoing resource such as land anticipated the theory of user costs in the case of depletable energy resources, and Malthus's theory of population dynamics is but an extension of the limits of natural resources to sustain an ever-growing world population. How, then, would a steady-state economy function, and to what extent is it a plausible alternative to the traditional neoclassical model so prevalent in today's society?

As a normative economic model, a steady-state economy is based on several basic principles. First, because the level of entropy will always tend to increase, conservation should be given greater priority over consumption, particularly as it applies to depletable energy resources. Second, the rate of growth of population should be reduced to at least zero. Third, under a steady-state level of population, the only source of rising per capita income would be technological change in the conversion and storage of energy and non-energy resources. Allocative efficiency, equity, informational certainty, and adequacy would still be appropriate criteria for the allocation of resources, but intertemporal equity and adequacy of resources would play much more prominent roles. In effect, the steady-state economy would be tantamount to a zero or near-zero rate of social time preference.

Despite the attractiveness of a steady-state economy, it is laden with many of the difficulties of the neoclassical model, three of which merit brief elaboration. One is that if the contemporary world of positive discounted time horizons is so limited, how could we expect to create the necessary institutional structures appropriate to a very long-run allocation of resources under a steady-state economy? In more prosaic terms, how would we make superior allocative decisions today for affected populations which are as yet unborn? A second difficulty is that even if we were able to define and operate such long-term institutions in an equitable and efficient form, by virtue of the Second Law of Thermodynamics, we would still be subject to some positive rate of entropy over time. Thus, a truly steady-state economy could not even exist in the fullest sense. The third difficulty is that even in a steady-state economy, questions of allocative efficiency and uncertainty regarding future conditions could well still remain. In effect, there is nothing in a steady-state economy that would prevent the possibilities of future energy crises. In sum, then, although the steady-state economy does represent in many ways an appealing alternative to the neoclassical model, the question of an adequate and equitable allocation of resources would still exist. To provide concrete answers to some of these questions, we need to shift our attention from the normative principles thus far discussed to the specific policies adopted by individual economies.

14.4. SUMMARY

Energy policy decisions can be judged by four basic criteria: allocative efficiency, equity, certainty, and adequacy. If energy policy decisions are to be coherent, these principles must be applied consistently to all sectors of the economy. Given an efficient allocation of resources, equity, certainty, and adequacy can be defined in specific static and dynamic terms.

The equitable allocation of energy resources depends ultimately on subjective value judgments. If such subjective value judgments have been clearly determined, equity in energy decisions requires that the income effects of shifting resource prices preserve the desired distribution of income, whether in static or dynamic terms. One important corollary of this rule is that if an efficient and equitable allocation is to be achieved, the appropriate mechanism of adjustment is through direct taxation and redistribution of income rather than through indirect controls, even where the demand for a resource is relatively price-inelastic.

The certain allocation of resources depends on the nature of risk. Like any question involving the future, the allocation of energy resources will involve some degree of uncertainty. Since risk is embodied in any decision, the choice of policy measures should be guided by the extent to which external costs and benefits may be present. Under this rule, it is possible to determine under what conditions such instruments as regulation, taxation, subsidies, and research and development expenditures may be justified.

The adequate allocation of resources links the level of energy production and consumption to associated economic objectives. Where full employment, price stability, and economic growth are concerned, an adequate allocation of energy resources will be guided first and foremost by the principles of allocative efficiency, reduction of uncertainty, and equity. Where questions of economic growth are concerned, the adequate allocation of resources raises the fundamental issue of the extent to which a neoclassical model of decisionmaking is a satisfactory alternative to a conservation-based steady-state economy. The question of adequacy thus turns ultimately on the principles of thermodynamics and on corresponding subjective value judgments.

SUGGESTED READINGS

Chao, H. *Economies with Exhaustible Resources.* New York: Garland Publishing, 1979.

Daly, Herman E. *Steady-State Economics.* San Francisco: W. H. Freeman and Co., 1977.

Hirsch, Fred. *The Social Limits to Growth.* Cambridge, Mass.: Harvard University Press, 1976.

Hitch, Charles J., ed. *Energy, Conservation, and Economic Growth.* Boulder: Westview Press, 1978.

Page, Talbot. *Conservation and Economic Efficiency.* Baltimore: Johns Hopkins University Press for Resources for the Future, 1977.

Raiffa, Howard. *Decision Analysis: Introductory Lectures on Choices under Uncertainty.* Reading, Mass.: Addison-Wesley Publishing Co., 1970.

Smith, Kerry V., ed. *Scarcity and Growth Reconsidered.* Baltimore: Johns Hopkins University Press for Resources for the Future, 1979.

15

U.S. ENERGY POLICY IN AN INTERDEPENDENT WORLD

Energy policy is determined by the interaction of technology, economics, and institutions. We have examined the nature of energy technology and the economic factors that influence its forms; it is appropriate that we round out our understanding of energy decisions by looking more closely at the evolution of specific policies and what they suggest for the future. Since the energy policies of any single economy are linked ultimately to those of all other economies, our perspective in this examination will be an international one. We will begin by tracing the evolution of U.S. energy policies, and then we will compare them with the energy policies of other members of the world community.

15.1. THE EVOLUTION OF U.S. ENERGY POLICY

For the greater part of the twentieth century, U.S. energy policy has sought to provide resources that were cheap, secure, and environmentally benign.[1] In many respects, these objectives are similar to the energy policy criteria enumerated in chapters 13 and 14, particularly if we consider "cheap" and "environmentally benign" as expressions of static allocative efficiency, and "secure" in terms of the certain allocation of resources. Yet, before we can understand how these three objectives have been pursued and the uneven

[1]The three objectives have not been pursued with equal intensity nor always simultaneously. Unfortunately, there is no single account of all areas of present U.S. energy policy. For a study of energy policy since the 1950s, see Craufurd D. Goodwin, ed., *Energy Policy in Perspective* (Washington, D.C.: Brookings Institution, 1981). See also Stephen L. McDonald, *Petroleum Conservation in the United States: An Economic Analysis* (Baltimore: Johns Hopkins Press, 1971); Wallace F. Lovejoy and Paul T. Homan, *Economic Aspects of Oil Conservation Regulation* (Baltimore: Johns Hopkins Press, 1967); Stephen G. Breyer and Paul W. MacAvoy, *Energy Regulation by the Federal Power Commission* (Washington, D.C.: Brookings Institution, 1974); Robert J. Kalter and William A. Vogely, eds., *Energy Supply and Government Policy* (Ithaca: Cornell University Press, 1976); Gerald D. Nash, *United States Oil Policy, 1890–1964* (Pittsburgh: University of Pittsburgh Press, 1968); John M. Blair, *The Control of Oil* (New York: Pantheon Books, 1976); and Irvin C. Bupp and Jean-Claude Derian, *Light Water: How the Nuclear Dream Dissolved* (New York: Basic Books, 1978).

consequences they have wrought, three initial qualifying statements are in order.

First, despite many similarities, "cheap," "environmentally benign," and "secure" are not identical to allocative efficiency and economic certainty. The pursuit of cheap energy for its own sake can result in shortages and the accelerated depletion of exhaustible resources in ways that could hardly be equated with allocative efficiency. Second, even when these three objectives have been defined and pursued in mutually consistent terms, because they have not encompassed such related questions as dynamic allocative efficiency, equity, and adequacy, they have often failed to minimize the possibilities of a recurrent energy crisis and the associated paralysis of social and economic institutions which such a crisis represents. Finally, despite the emergence of a comprehensive energy policy in the United States in recent years, future U.S. energy choices will depend increasingly on the extent to which domestic policy objectives are consistent with the international policies and conditions of other countries within the world economic community.

15.1.1. U.S. Energy Policy in the Pre-OPEC Era

If cheap energy has been a hallmark of U.S. energy policy, it was never more pronounced than in the first six decades of the twentieth century. Despite the effects of two world wars and the Great Depression of the 1930s on the U.S. and the world economy, the commitment to cheap energy remained relatively strong and consistent during this era. So strong was this emphasis that the provision of environmentally benign and secure energy resources was often given only secondary consideration, and questions of resource adequacy and equity over time were rarely raised. Rather than attempt to provide an exhaustive analysis of these issues here, we can provide a basic documentation of the policy of cheap energy in terms of key historical decisions.

The policy of cheap energy in the United States has been most evident in the treatment of petroleum and natural gas. An important reason for this emphasis on petroleum and natural gas is that while coal has functioned as an important resource in many sectors of the economy, its use has been far from environmentally benign. Moreover, in its primary form, coal has been ill-adapted for use in many energy-consuming technologies of the twentieth century, notably in such areas as motor highway and aviation transportation. Thus, until quite recently, coal was often benignly neglected. At the same time, when it became clear that petroleum and natural gas could not forever remain relatively cheap, let alone environmentally safe or secure, the policy of cheap energy began to shift toward the promotion of commercial nuclear power. Indeed, until its environmental and political hazards became more obvious to policymakers, nuclear power was widely viewed as the ultimate cheap energy resource. Curiously, this view persisted even though the near-term substitution possibilities between conventional nuclear energy and increasingly uncertain supplies of oil were limited to the electricity-generation sector of the economy. As we will see, since oil consumption in this sector represented less than one-fifth of all U.S. oil consumption by 1970, the emphasis on nuclear energy turned out to be a less than satisfactory route to cheap and secure energy supplies.

Table 15.1 provides a useful frame of reference for identifying key U.S. energy policy decisions. In the pre-1973 OPEC embargo era, the principal instruments used to promote cheap energy were antitrust, production subsidies, and regulation, though not always simultaneously nor with the same degree of emphasis. Yet the net effect of these decisions was to facilitate the rise of OPEC and the sudden disruption of a fossil-based cheap energy policy.

An early step in the promotion of cheap energy was the 1911 United States Supreme Court decision which ordered the dissolution of the Standard Oil Company. Since its formation by John D. Rockerfeller in 1870, the Standard Oil Company had established by 1900 a position of overwhelming dominance in the U.S. domestic petroleum industry. With extensive vertical and horizontal integration and substantial international operations, Standard Oil soon became a powerful symbol of economic monopoly in the United States. In turn, rising public criticism of Standard Oil, reflected partly in congressional passage of the Sherman Act of 1890 and culminating in the publication of journalist Ida Tarbell's *History of the Standard Oil Company* in 1904, gradually set the stage for radical antitrust action.[2]

The Supreme Court decision of 1911 broke the Standard Oil Company into thirty-eight separate corporations, each firm's assets being defined by the geographic boundaries of the state in which it had been operating. Yet although antitrust and independent discoveries of new reserves in Texas did much to facilitate the rise of new competition, three of the thirty-eight firms from the old Standard Oil company were to join subsequently with two other American and two European firms to establish an international petroleum cartel during the 1920s.[3] The structure and operation of this cartel was to serve as a model for the founders of OPEC several decades later. These seven firms—Standard Oil of New Jersey (Exxon), Standard Oil of California (Socal), Standard Oil of New York (Mobil), Gulf Oil, Texaco, Anglo-Persian Oil (British Petroleum), and Royal Dutch Shell—soon became known as "the Seven Sisters," a title reflecting both admiration and resentment made popular by the Italian oil competitor Enrico Mattei during the 1950s and early 1960s.

The dissolution of Standard Oil and the subsequent rise of the international petroleum cartel illustrate a fundamental difficulty in the pursuit of a

[2]Ida M. Tarbell, *History of the Standard Oil Company* (1904; reprint ed., New York: Macmillan Publishing Co., 1925). See also Bruce Bringhurst, *Antitrust and the Oil Monopoly: The Standard Oil Cases, 1890–1911* (Westport, Conn.: Greenwood Press, 1979). The principal criticism of the Standard Oil Company was not so much that it engaged in the classical textbook model of monopoly through price-increasing profit-maximizing behavior as that it eliminated its competitors through predatory price-cutting practices.

[3]Details on the formation and operation of the cartel are reported in Blair, *The Control of Oil*; in Anthony Sampson, *The Seven Sisters* (New York: Viking Press, 1975); and in Federal Trade Commission, *The International Petroleum Cartel*, Senate Small Business Committee, 22 August 1952 (Washington, D.C.: U.S. Government Printing Office, 1952).

cheap energy policy. Because the sovereignty of a country limits the jurisdiction of international antitrust actions, to the extent that the affected industry is an international one and to the extent that other countries impose no comparable pro-competitive measures, we are confronted with a Pareto second-best-policy dilemma. On the one hand, if the domestic operations of firms are restructured to perfectly competitive conditions while imperfect competition continues to prevail elsewhere, the domestic industry could well become vulnerable to bargaining pressures from international firms. Thus, imports could quickly dominate the newly restructured domestic competitive market, and domestically competitive firms could find themselves at a disadvantage in international trade. On the other hand, to do anything less would make it impossible to arrive at a competitive determination of the price of a resource. Indeed, imperfectly competitive firms could drive the price of internationally purchased crude oil down to well below the price of its nearest substitute. Then the imperfectly competitive profitability to such an industry would tend to accelerate the depletion of resources at a rate which the domestic consuming economy would undoubtedly find intolerable were such a resource provided entirely from deposits within its own national boundaries. For the United States and other principal consuming countries at least, cheap energy from petroleum thus meant a willingness to accept the structural imperfections of international markets, at least until these conditions were interrupted by the influx of newly competitive forces and the rise of OPEC.

A second step in the promotion of a U.S. cheap energy policy was the introduction of specific production subsidies. These incentives, which comprised the percentage-depletion allowance and provision for the deduction of intangible drilling expenses from a firm's tax liabilities, were unique to U.S. natural resource industries. Following the introduction of percentage-depletion allowances at the federal government level in 1918, these incentives were gradually narrowed to rates strongly favoring petroleum and natural gas production over alternative resources. By 1926 the statutory rule granted to oil and natural gas producers provided for an allowance of 27.5 percent of gross income, with 15 percent to shale oil producers and 10 percent to coal producers. These differential rates, which remained in effect until 1975, were much more indicative of the relative importance of these resources to energy demand than of their relative scarcity or their marginal costs of production. In any case, when considered in light of the international expansion of worldwide petroleum discoveries then under way, the resurgence of domestic competition and the introduction of production subsidies did much to accelerate the growth of market supplies and periodically falling prices. So strong was the growth of supply that by the late 1920s there were substantial pressures from within the petroleum industry to find some way to restrain the flow of production. The international solution was the petroleum cartel already noted; in the U.S. domestic economy it took the form of state-level programs of petroleum prorationing.

A third step in the promotion of a policy of cheap energy has been regulation. However, because it has also been used to achieve other energy policy

Table 15.1. Key U.S. Energy Policy Decisions

Year	Environment	Renewable Resources	Coal	Oil	Natural Gas	Nuclear Energy	Conventional Electricity	Synfuels
1885–1905				1890—Sherman Act	1885—Interstate Commerce Act			
1905–10							1907—Wisconsin Regulation	
1910–15				1911—*U.S.* v. *Std. Oil Company*				
1915–20		1917—U.S. Army Corps of Engineers						
1920–25		1920—U.S. Federal Power Commission (FPC)						
1925–30			{1926—U.S. percentage-depletion allowances}					
1930–35		1933—U.S. Tennessee Valley Authority		1930—state-level prorationing			1933—U.S. Tennessee Valley Authority	1930—Shale oil leasing restricted
1935–40				1935—U.S. Connally "Hot Oil" Act	1938—U.S. FPC Natural Gas Regulation		1935—Public Utilities Regulatory Act, Rural Electrification Administration	
1940–45				{1942–45 U.S. wartime rationing}				1944—U.S. Synthetic Fuels Act
1945–50						1946—U.S. Atomic Energy		

			Outer Continental Shelf Lands Act	*Phillips* v. *Wisconsin*	"Atoms for Peace"		
1955-60			1955-73—U.S. import quotas on oil		1957—U.S. Price-Anderson Act		
1960-65	1963—U.S. Clean Air Act						
1965-70	1967—U.S. Clean Air Act						
1970-74	1970—U.S. Environmental Protection Agency	1973—U.S. Mining Safety Administration	1973—U.S. Emergency Petroleum Allocation	1974—U.S. FEA, ERDA			
1975			1975—U.S. Tax Reduction Act		1975—U.S. Nuclear Regulatory Commission		
		{1975—U.S. Energy Policy and Conservation Act}					
1977	1977—U.S. Strip Mine Act	{1977—U.S. Department of Energy}				1977—U.S. Federal Energy Regulatory Commission	
1978		1978—U.S. National Energy Conservation Policy Act		1978—U.S. Natural Gas Policy Act		1978—U.S. Public Utilities Regulation Act	
1979			1979-80—U.S. Standby Gasoline Rationing Plan				
1980			1980—U.S. Windfall Oil Profits Tax and Deregulation				1980—U.S. Synfuels Corporation

objectives, we need to distinguish among three distinct types of regulation: the reduction of externalities, which has been embodied partly in the use of state-level programs of petroleum prorationing just cited; the promotion of economies of scale; and the control of monopoly. Since regulatory success in achieving any one of these objectives has often meant a tradeoff with one or both of the other two objectives, we need to consider the separate ways in which each of them has been pursued.

Prorationing is a relatively simple form of regulation. As practiced by the Texas Railroad Commission and other state regulatory agencies, each well was assigned a ceiling rate of extraction based on an estimate of current market demand. Production was stabilized, as were prices. Apart from the renewal of domestic market competition and the decline in the demand for oil during the Great Depression of the 1930s, a principal reason for the implementation of prorationing was the "rule of capture." This rule, which had long governed petroleum and natural gas exploration, meant that a firm could sell any and all oil or natural gas extracted from its wells even though the deposit might extend beyond the property rights acquired by the firm. By moving gradually in the direction of unitization of reservoir development, prorationing tended to eliminate the rule of capture even as it restricted the level of production and kept prices from falling. Thus, while prorationing represented an early effort to apply marginal social cost pricing, it also had an anticompetitive dimension.

During the 1930s the anticompetitive nature of state-level prorationing almost proved to be its undoing. Continuing domestic market competition among firms within the industry soon weakened the effectiveness of mandated production quotas. Individual firms dissatisfied with their market shares sought to circumvent these restraints by arranging for secret sales on an interstate basis. These shipments soon undermined prorationing to such an extent that many states appealed to the federal government for their elimination. Congress responded to these appeals by outlawing "hot oil" shipments, as they were called, under the Connally Act of 1935. When this legislation was renewed in 1942 it sustained the use of state-level prorationing commissions until the early 1970s.

As framed in the Interstate Commerce Act of 1887, the initial focus of regulation was on monopoly, particularly on controlling the anti-competitive behavior of railroad firms then creating an interstate transportation network. As embodied in such agencies as the Army Corps of Engineers and the Federal Power Commission, regulation meant not only the control of potential energy monopolies but also a concern for economies of scale and external economies and diseconomies. Indeed, formal development of social cost-benefit analysis first arose in the United States from the need for project evaluation by the Army Corps of Engineers and the Federal Power Commission. How some of these functions evolved may be seen in terms of a few key decisions.

The policy of cheap energy was by no means limited to petroleum. Insofar as electricity was concerned, both production subsidies and regulation were employed to promote the inexpensive pricing and production of this resource. Two federal government agencies instrumental to this process were the Army Corps of Engineers and the Federal Power Commission, established in 1917 and 1920, respectively. The Corps of Engineers has focused on both energy and non-energy projects. The Federal Power Commission was given the basic responsibility for the expansion and regulation of hydropower capacity for interstate systems; later it was to assume primary responsibility for the price regulation of natural gas. In regard to hydropower development, one project in Tennessee was so large in scope that in 1933 Congress established a separate Tennessee Valley Authority as a publicly owned electric utility. TVA, which would serve as a model for public power-generation systems elsewhere in the economy, combined hydro with coal resources to become one of the largest electric utilities in the country. Moreover, with the development of the atomic bomb during the Second World War, TVA functioned as the principal energy source for the government research laboratory at Oak Ridge, Tennessee. Indeed, since its establishment, the Oak Ridge National Laboratory has continued to function as a major center for U.S. military- and energy-related research.

The Federal Power Commission was later given responsibility for regulation of monopoly behavior by a key decision of 1938. Just three years after congressional passage of the Connally Act, there was a growing concern that prorationing was inadequate to handle the pricing of natural gas transmission sales, particularly since most shipments were based on interstate pipeline facilities. For this reason, Congress passed the Natural Gas Act of 1938, granting to the Federal Power Commission authority to regulate all interstate shipments of natural gas. Unlike prorationing, this legislation governed both quantities and prices. However, no federal regulation of intrastate shipments of natural gas was adopted until 1954, under the Supreme Court *Phillips* v. *Wisconsin* decision, to which we will return. The reason why natural gas was not regulated at the intrastate level originally is straightforward: since oil and natural gas were frequently joint products of exploration, prorationing of petroleum would serve as an effective restraint over intrastate natural gas as well.

Regulation as a competitive policy instrument was also applied in other energy markets. Beginning with legislation in Wisconsin in 1907, state-level regulation was used to restrain monopoly behavior by electric utilities and to achieve economies of scale from central-station electricity generating and distribution systems. At the same time, the rapid growth of electric utilities in the following years led to efforts by some utilities to circumvent state-level regulatory constraints through holding-company operations. For this reason, Congress avoided direct federal regulation of most utilities in favor of a more generalized regulatory reform. The Public Utilities Regulatory Act of 1935 greatly limited the ability of utilities to operate holding companies, which reinforced the authority of state-level electric and natural gas regulatory commissions. Indeed, state-level regulation of electricity and natural gas has persisted down to the present, even though it has often been plagued with inefficient administration and nonmarginal pricing and production decisionmaking of the kinds analyzed in chapters 11 and 12.

Apart from the pursuit of cheap energy, another objective in U.S. energy policy has been energy security. This objective first became evident during the Second World War. Faced with a need to reallocate scarce resources in support of wartime rearmament, in 1942 Congress approved a system of coupon rationing encompassing energy and other key sectors of the economy. It lasted until 1945 and did manage to keep consumer prices from increasing as rapidly as they would have otherwise. Though the United States was relatively self-sufficient in energy during this period, because some energy resources were redirected in support of allied war efforts, in 1944 Congress passed a Synthetic Fuels Act to accelerate the development of alternative supplies (the war's end in the following year led to termination of the program). The 1944 decision contrasted strongly with a 1930 decision in which the federal government had restricted shale oil leasing on federal lands. That decision had been made to complement the many state-level prorationing programs being put into operation at the onset of the Great Depression.

Despite the postwar growth in world petroleum supplies, after 1948 the United States was no longer self-sufficient in this resource. Although import dependence is not necessarily tantamount to supply uncertainty, because of the patterns of resource discoveries then under way, there were questions of energy security which for a critical period of time U.S. policymakers chose largely to ignore. Worse yet, when specific measures were adopted to address the problem of uncertain supplies, they frequently led to additional distortions in the allocation of resources. Two areas of decisionmaking indicative of these distortions were the promotion of nuclear energy and regulation-induced distortions in the pricing of petroleum and natural gas.

As noted previously, the technical potential of commercial nuclear power emerged directly from the development of nuclear weapons. With pioneer experience in these weapons, Congress decided in 1946 to establish permanent central control over the development of nuclear energy by creating the Atomic Energy Commission (AEC). Much of the original focus of the AEC was on the control over the various stages of the open nuclear fuel cycle essential to the continued production of weapons, but there was also a concerted effort to apply nuclear energy to other areas as well. Nuclear-powered submarines, aircrafts carriers, and satellites demonstrated some of the potential nonlethal uses of nuclear power. Yet it was the commercial development of nuclear power as an alternative to fossil and hydropower electricity that became a major concern of the AEC in the following years.

The principal method of promoting the commercial use of nuclear power has been through subsidies. The AEC, and then its successor, the Nuclear Regulatory Commission, maintained control over the fuel cycle through exclusive public ownership of gaseous-diffusion enrichment plants even though their management was on a contract basis with private firms. In tandem with fuel enrichment, the AEC also sponsored accelerated research in the development of alternative light water reactor technologies, a program publicized as "Atoms for Peace" during the mid-1950s. The next step, which was critical to the opening of the first commercial nuclear reactor in Shippingport, Pennsylvania, and its successors, was the 1957 Congressional decision to provide a regulated insurance subsidy to commercial electric utilities under the Price-Anderson Act. As noted previously, with the establishment of a financial limit to the insurance liability of nuclear-based electric utilities and the underwriting of a substantial proportion of the regulated limit of $560 million per single nuclear reactor accident, nuclear fission reactors were soon in a position to compete with established electricity-generation technologies. Moreover, since the AEC also accepted financial responsibility for disposal and potential recycling of spent nuclear fuel, commercial nuclear power was made even more attractive in comparative pricing terms. That the disposal of nuclear waste, the safety of nuclear reactors, the potential of nuclear weapons proliferation, and terrorism still remain as unique external costs of commercial nuclear power has raised serious questions as to the marginal social costs of this resource in relation to other alternatives.

If commercial nuclear power provided an illusion of U.S. energy security, the illusion was magnified by the perpetuation of subsidies and regulation in petroleum and natural gas markets. For example, continuing state-level prorationing of petroleum tended to increase even further the price of domestic production relative to foreign supplies. While it also enhanced domestic profitability, as long as prorationing was in force, the expected profitability from overseas exploration still exceeded that which was available from expanded domestic activity. Petroleum-import dependence grew accordingly. In fact, until the 1973 Arab OPEC oil embargo, the only notable efforts to check this dependence were the Outer Continental Shelf Lands Act of 1953 and the oil import-quota program that began in 1956.

The 1953 Outer Continental Shelf Lands Act established federal jurisdiction over resource utilization by industry beyond the traditional three-mile limit reserved to the states. Consistent with the general policy of cheap energy, the federal government adopted a competitive sealed-bid leasing system, much like that which had been applied to onshore federally owned lands. Under this system, depending on existing industry preferences, firms could bid for lease permits from the Department of Interior on a cash bonus or royalty basis, with royalty payments to be set at a minimum of 12.5 percent of the market value of resource discoveries. However, even though the differential tax benefits provisions remained in effect until 1975, offshore costs were still in excess of costs prevailing in international markets, particularly those in the Middle East. Consequently, the import share of domestic oil consumption was little affected by the opening up of offshore drilling during this period, which is why a federal government oil import-quota program was imposed beginning in 1956.

The federal oil import-quota system of the Eisenhower administration was based on the Trade Agreements Extension Act of 1955.[4] Under this legisla-

[4]See James C. Burrows and Thomas A. Domenich, *An Analysis of the United States Oil Import Quota* (Lexington, Mass.: Lexington Books, 1970); and D. R. Bohi and M. Russell, *U.S. Energy Policy—Alternatives for Security* (Baltimore: Johns Hopkins University Press, 1975).

tion, the president had authority to impose quotas on imports if national security were impaired. To be sure, "national security" is a nebulous concept, particularly as it pertains to the certain allocation of resources. In the case of petroleum, past U.S. policy had already done much to promote the very dependence which a quota system would ostensibly reduce. Worse yet, in terms of domestic production, what the quota system did was to accelerate the depletion of domestic low-cost oil resources, which weakened state-level prorationing programs in effect since the 1930s. With this combination of subsidies and regulations in place, changes in international petroleum markets soon set the stage for the emergence of OPEC.

Beyond the decisions thus far cited, two other factors also led to rising petroleum dependence during the post-World War II era. One was the expansion of the cheap energy regulatory policy over natural gas in 1954.[5] In a controversial decision, the Supreme Court ruled in *Phillips* v. *Wisconsin* that the Federal Power Commission, which had hitherto regulated only interstate natural gas shipments, also had authority to regulate the wellhead price of interstate-based natural gas production. Ostensibly, the purpose of this decision was to enhance the ability of the Federal Power Commission to promote the competitive delivery of natural gas to interstate consumers. The concentration ratios among natural gas producers examined in chapter 9 do point to an increase in concentration, but it is curious that the expansion of jurisdiction under the *Phillips* decision did nothing to reverse this trend. Moreover, what the 1954 decision would later demonstrate all too clearly was that domestic exploratory drilling would decline and that lags in price adjustments by the Federal Power Commission would lead to a severe natural gas shortage by the mid 1970s. Even though the relative scarcity of natural gas did not translate directly into an increase in its price, it did increase the demand for substitute petroleum resources, thereby aggravating the already precarious degree of import dependence. Again, as noted in previous chapters, when combined with antitrust or taxation, deregulation would be much more likely to lead to a solution of competitive marginal social cost pricing of natural gas than would the shortage-prone regulatory approach which was adopted.

The other contributory factor to rising petroleum dependence was a growing concern for environmentally benign energy resources within the United States. As we have seen, state-level prorationing represented an early effort to minimize the external benefits arising from the rule of capture in petroleum and natural gas exploration. At the same time, the general policy of cheap energy also posed external costs on the economy, notably environmental pollution and occupational safety. Key early steps to counter environmental pollution were the Federal Clean Air Acts of 1963 and 1967 and the establishment of the Federal Environmental Protection Agency in 1970.

[5]See Paul W. MacAvoy and R. S. Pindyck, *Price Controls and the Natural Gas Shortage* (Washington, D.C.: American Enterprise Institute for Public Policy Research, May 1975); and K. C. Brown, *Regulation of the Natural Gas Producing Industry* (Baltimore: Johns Hopkins Press, 1972).

Since then, the EPA has been largely responsible for the imposition of emission standards on consumer vehicles, industry, and other sources of environmental pollution. The 1973 establishment of the Mining Safety Administration applied the principle of reducing external costs borne by workers, and the 1977 Strip Mine Act applied it to the reclamation of surface-mined coal lands.

Apart from the question of whether regulation is the most cost-effective method of reducing external costs, one thing is clear: as in the question of antitrust, to the extent that the United States has imposed environmental standards where other countries have not, we are confronted with the familiar Pareto second-best problem. For the United States at least, higher environmental-quality standards during the 1960s and 1970s came at a time when the relatively cleanest conventional resources, petroleum and natural gas, were also the most shortage-prone. Thus, until relative prices were drastically altered by OPEC, relatively abundant supplies of less than environmentally benign coal reserves and commercial nuclear power were hardly in a position to address the problem of energy security.[6]

15.1.2. The Rise of OPEC in the Allocation of Energy Resources

Of the many factors that have contributed to the rise of OPEC in world petroleum markets, three have been central to its success: the impact of U.S. domestic energy policies on international petroleum resource allocation, the evolution of the international petroleum cartel, and the emergence of international petroleum energy dependence in world energy markets. Since OPEC decisions have been crucial to the evolution of recent U.S. energy policy alternatives, we need to examine briefly how OPEC has evolved.

From our overview of pre-OPEC U.S. domestic energy policies, one conclusion stands out, namely, that the emphasis on cheap and environmentally benign energy tended to accelerate consumption of domestic petroleum supplies. Moreover, cheap energy also meant increasing dependence on imported oil, since few substitute resources could then compete with conventional petroleum energy, at least insofar as the final demand for refined products was concerned.

There are several ways to analyze the impact of the U.S. cheap energy policy on the international allocation of petroleum resources. One way is in terms of profitability. In terms of economic theory, if petroleum firms behave as profit maximizers, they will allocate their resources among alternative types and regions of production such that the risk-adjusted rate of return is equalized among all available investment alternatives. Unfortunately, since the published records of most firms do not indicate profitability by region, we have no readily available way to apply conventional economic theory in direct terms.

[6]For example, in 1975 nuclear power accounted for 2.4 percent of U.S. gross primary energy consumption, and 8.62 percent of gross primary energy used to produce electricity. Had nuclear energy replaced all oil used to produce electricity, there would still have been net oil imports equal to approximately 28 percent of gross oil consumption (see figure 4.4).

Despite limited data, it is nevertheless worth noting two published studies concerned with differential returns to alternative petroleum investments. One of these studies is the annual survey of some thirty international petroleum firms published by the Chase Manhattan Bank.[7] The Chase sample shows that for the 1965–79 period at least, the mean rate of return to investment capital in the United States was 12.5 percent, and for the rest of the world, 14 percent. Moreover, while the trend in this rate for the United States was at an annual increase of 0.34 percent, for the rest of the world it was 0.79 percent, which suggests that firms would shift petroleum investment away from the United States toward other regions of the world.

A second study of profitability is one published in the mid-1960s by Zuhayr Mikdashi.[8] Mikdashi's data are based on Middle Eastern oil concessions and cover the period up to the early 1960s. For specific firms and countries at least, Mikdashi reports rates of return on invested capital at levels of no less than 30 percent during the mid-1950s and early 1960s, a period, it should be noted, when OPEC was first establishing itself. For the Middle East at least, then, the profitability to petroleum investment appears to have far exceeded the worldwide rates of the Chase survey and to have achieved levels well in excess of those available to domestic U.S. petroleum investments at that time.

In lieu of more comprehensive data on differential profitability, there are two other indicators of the impact of the U.S. cheap energy policy on international resource markets: the geographic allocation of investment expenditures and the differential price of petroleum energy, shown here in figures 15.1 and 15.2, respectively. In figure 15.1, one basic trend is clear: the U.S. share of international exploration and development expenditures has tended to fall substantially since the end of World War II. A good reason for this decline is, of course, the fact that until very recently the price of international petroleum was usually well below the level of domestically produced resources. Indeed, until the 1973 Arab OPEC oil embargo, post–World War II Middle Eastern and Venezuelan wellhead prices were never as high as U.S. prorationed and import-quota–protected domestic production. Thus, despite transportation costs, imported oil could readily compete with domestic production, as the quota alone showed all too clearly.

The rise of OPEC has depended on more than the cheap energy policy of the United States. A second contributing factor was the international petroleum cartel referred to in section 15.1.1. While this cartel has since disintegrated, during the period from the 1920s until the 1950s at least, it did exert substantial influence on the international petroleum market. Moreover, along with the U.S. system of state-level oil prorationing, the cartel did much to inspire the founders of OPEC in the years that followed.

As noted in chapter 11, a cartel can seek to maximize the income of its

[7]Chase Manhattan Bank, *Financial Analysis of a Group of Petroleum Companies* (New York: Chase Energy Economics Division of the Chase Manhattan Bank, published annually).

[8]Zuhayr Mikdashi, *A Financial Analysis of Middle Eastern Oil Concessions, 1901–1965* (New York: Praeger Publishers, 1966).

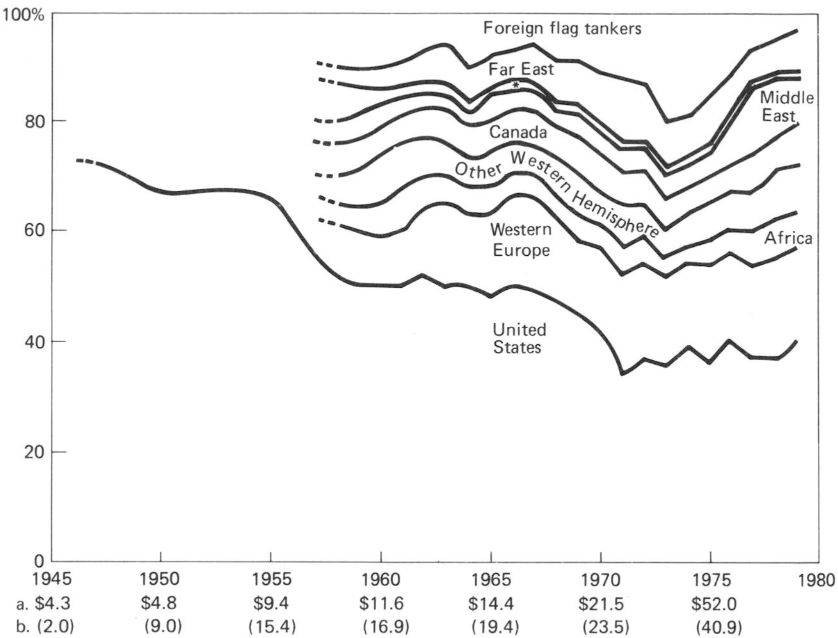

Figure 15.1. Geographic Distribution of World Capital and Development Expenditures Exclusive of Eastern Europe, the Soviet Union, and China. Data from Chase Manhattan Bank, *Capital Investments of the World Petroleum Industry*, 1963, 1968, 1972, 1978, 1979.

members through restraints on production and increases in the price of the good that it sells. It can also accomplish this objective by exerting downward pressure on the prices of the inputs that it employs, in which case it behaves as a monopsonist. Both of these approaches were characteristic of the international petroleum cartel. Rather than retrace the many details of the cartel's operations during its heyday, we can illustrate its influence in terms of four major decisions: the 1938 Mexican nationalization, the 1948 Venezuelan agreement, the 1950 Saudi Arabian royalty agreement, and the 1951 Iranian nationalization.

The decision by Mexico to nationalize the assets of international oil firms in 1938 stemmed from a dispute over how best to resolve a strike by oil-field workers who were demanding improved housing and working conditions. After refusing informal government requests to accede to the basic demands of the striking workers, the firms referred the case to the Mexican Supreme Court. In turn, popular sentiment in favor of the workers led Mexican President Lazaro Cardenas to expropriate the holdings of the seventeen firms involved in the dispute. These holdings were then consolidated under a newly formed Mexican national oil company, Pemex. In retaliation, the affected

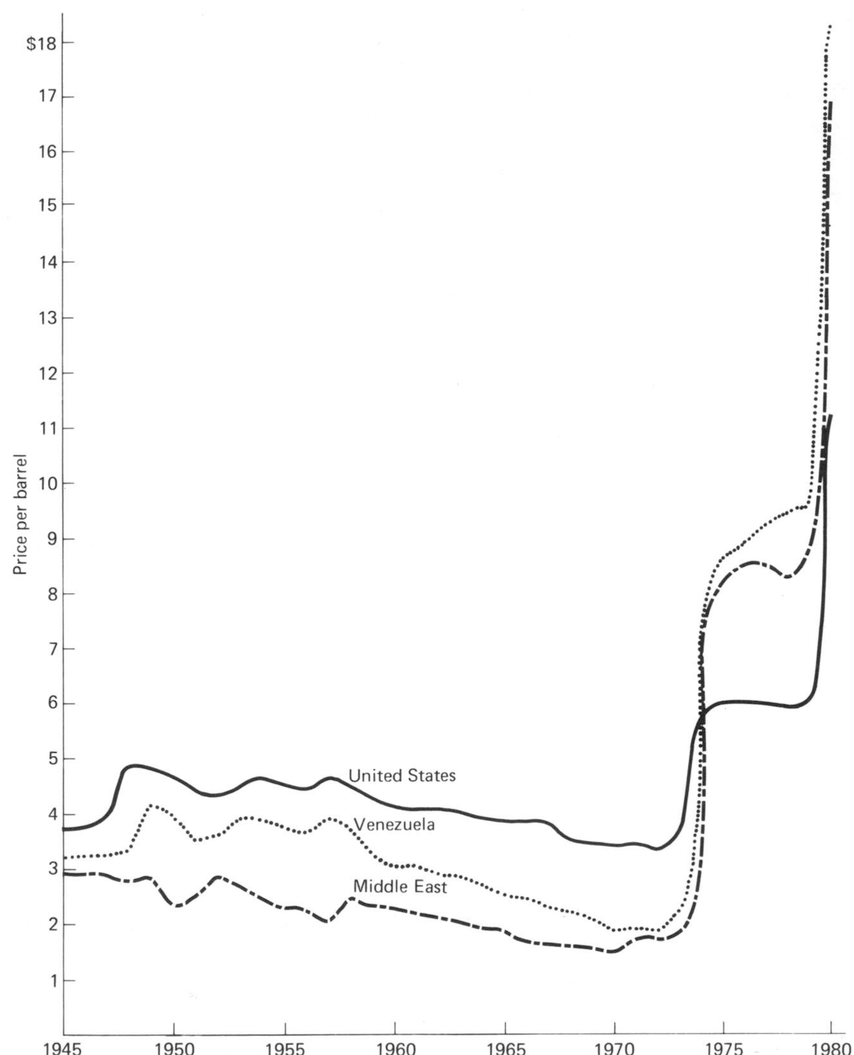

Figure 15.2. Constant-Dollar Wellhead Prices of Crude Oil in the United States, the Middle East, and Venezuela, in 1972 Dollars. Data from Department of Energy, Energy Information Administration, *Annual Report to Congress III* (1980); idem, *Monthly Energy Review*, April 1981; M. A. Adelman, *The World Petroleum Market* (Baltimore: Johns Hopkins Press for Resources for the Future, 1972), pp. 141, 342, 388–93. Given the degree of integrated operations and the use of base-point pricing, wellhead prices tend to underestimate differences in incremental production costs.

firms began a boycott against Pemex exports, which though interrupted by subsequent litigation and the Second World War, resulted in eventual compensation to the companies of some $130 million dollars. That such a boycott was able to be organized in the first place and then effectively enforced by the affected firms provided ample evidence of imperfect competition, much as nationalization represented an exercise of imperfect competition on the side of the Mexican government.

The other three decisions, of 1948, 1950, and 1951, illustrate the peak and subsequent decline of cartel bargaining strength in the world petroleum market. Following the removal of wartime rationing, because firms were wary of becoming entangled in confrontation such as occurred in Mexico, major firms began to demonstrate a much greater willingness to share petroleum revenues with producing countries. One crucial decision which reflected these changing conditions was the 1948 Venezuelan law requiring that profits from petroleum concessions henceforth be shared with the Venezuelan government on a fifty-fifty basis. Since this decision represented a major departure from historical patterns, it soon led to pressures for parity agreements by other major producing countries, notably those in the Middle East.

Had the degree of concentration among international petroleum firms remained unchanged from the 1920s through the 1950s, the spread of fifty-fifty agreements might not have occurred as fast as it did, if at all. At the same time, if there were substantial increases in payments to producing countries, they would soon begin to show up in declining profit rates in the balance sheets of major firms. If these firms were to raise the prices of refined products to any significant degree in the United States, there would be renewed criticism of the industry, particularly in light of already existing production subsidies and the persistence of state-level prorationing. Instead the subsidy granted to petroleum firms was enlarged, a measure first instituted in Saudi Arabia in 1950.

The Saudi agreement called for the designation of royalty payments as an income tax. As noted in chapter 11, as a result, the foreign "income tax" payments by U.S. international petroleum firms could be claimed as a credit against their domestic U.S. tax liability. Moreover, by using posted prices of petroleum rather than the traditionally discounted actual selling price to compute these taxes, U.S. firms were able to raise the payments level to producing countries, preserve the relatively low prices central to a cheap energy policy, and at the same time maintain profitability. The only difficulty with this agreement was that it was unique to the petroleum industry and posed an opportunity cost to the United States Treasury. By the 1960s, these foreign tax credits were growing by 12 percent a year and were worth well over a billion dollars annually.[9]

[9]U.S. Department of Energy "An Analysis of Federal Incentives Used to Stimulate Energy Production" (Washington, D.C.: U.S Government Printing Office, June 1978), p. 222. In 1962, the value was estimated at $815 million. By 1968 it reached an estimated annual level of $1.6 billion.

The Saudi agreement of 1950 was possible largely because of the preponderance of U.S. firms operating Saudi concessions.[10] A less successful conclusion emerged in the case of Iran, which since the early 1900s had permitted the development of its oil fields almost exclusively by the Anglo-Persian Oil Company, known subsequently as British Petroleum (BP). British Petroleum had made an offer to provide payments to the Iranian government at rates at least as generous as those agreed to in the 1950 Saudi–U.S. agreement, but the Iranian government of Prime Minister Dr. Mohammed Mossadegh, reacting to growing nationalist sentiment, expropriated the assets of BP, the first such nationalization since the Mexican decision of 1938. NIOC, the National Iranian Oil Company, formed to operate the oil fields, soon was beset with a boycott by BP and other members of the old petroleum cartel.

With half of BP's shares owned by the British government, reflecting an even greater dependence on imported petroleum in Britain than in the United States, and joint U.K. and U.S. concern that the Soviet Union might occupy northern Iran as it had done during the Second World War, there were considerable external pressures to resolve the Iranian oil crisis in an expeditious fashion.[11] The solution was the lending of U.S. and U.K. governmental support to the petroleum boycott, which undermined the Mossadegh government to the point of collapse by 1953. In the interim, Shah Mohammed Riza Pahlevi, who had been the titular head of the government since 1941, was then able to gain effective control over the government in a coup staged with covert U.S. support.[12] Then, following a decision to retain ownership of the oil fields and refineries, the Iranian government paid compensation to BP and authorized an enlarged consortium of firms to develop and market its production.[13]

The Iranian decision was critical to the subsequent role of OPEC in two important ways. First, although the boycotting firms took satisfaction that nationalization had not gone uncompensated, by enlarging the marketing consortium, Iran had established a model by which a producing country

[10]Aramco, the Arabian-American Oil consortium company formed in the early 1930s, consisted originally of the joint firm of Socal and Texaco, or Caltex, and was enlarged in 1948 to include Mobil and Exxon. By 1972, Socal's shareholding was 30 percent, Texaco's was 30 percent, Exxon's 30 percent, and Mobil's 10 percent.

[11]The Soviet Union and Great Britain had jointly occupied Iran from 1941 to 1946 since the then ruler of Iran, Reza Khan, had expressed sympathy with Nazi Germany. English dependence on imported petroleum was especially acute in the navy, a legacy from earlier years when Winston Churchill had made an exclusive agreement with Iran to provide oil for the fleet.

[12]For a recent account of Iran under Shah Mohammed Riza Pahlevi, see Robert Graham, *Iran: The Illusion of Power* (New York: St. Martin's Press, 1979). The 4 November 1979 capture of American diplomatic personnel by militant students supporting the revolutionary Islamic regime of Ayatollah Khomeini was tied directly to the past dependence of the Shah on U.S. military support and to the authoritarian nature of his regime.

[13]Production of oil in Iran resumed its pre-boycott levels by 1954. The consortium of firms consisted of a 40 percent share allocated to BP, a 14 percent share to Shell, 7 percent shares to Exxon, Mobil, Gulf, Texaco, and Socal, a 6 percent share to CFP, and 5 percent shares to all others. These firms, and the consortium as a whole, continued to market Iranian oil until the revolution of 1979.

could more readily negotiate favorable terms for its concessions, as revolutionary Libya would demonstrate all too clearly in 1970. Second, by broadening the number of firms, Iran provided an added competitive incentive for accelerating the development of its oil resources, which thereby increased Iran's role as a major petroleum-exporting country to the United States and other major industrial countries. Indeed, in the years that followed, the continuing decline in worldwide concentration ratios tended to enhance the role of international supplies, particularly among the economies that subsequently made up OPEC.

If a single underlying factor led to the establishment of OPEC in September 1960, it was the continuing downward pressure on crude-oil prices exerted by expanding world supply relative to demand. As figure 15.2 shows clearly, this downward trend in prices was quite pronounced during the 1950s. Then, frustrated over declining petroleum revenues, representatives from Venezuela, Iran, Saudi Arabia, Iraq, and Kuwait met in Baghdad to establish the Organization of Petroleum Exporting Countries, or OPEC, as a counter-cartel to the major Western oil firms, which they perceived as the principal cause of declining petroleum revenues.

During the 1960s OPEC exerted relatively little control over the real price of petroleum. Producer-country revenues continued to stagnate accordingly. At the same time, OPEC's membership continued to expand such that once demand growth was more closely matched by supply growth, there would be a better opportunity to increase prices. Qatar joined OPEC in 1961, Indonesia and Libya in 1962, Abu Dhabi (later renamed the United Arab Emirates) in 1967, Algeria in 1969, Nigeria in 1971, and Ecuador and Gabon in 1973. When Libyan leader Colonel Moummar el-Khadaffi toppled the regime of King Idris in the coup of 1969, he set into motion oil-production restraints on the smaller, less-integrated Western firms least able to obtain alternative supplies. The strategy was effective in raising the real price of Libyan crude supplies. Thereafter, agreements on increased real prices soon spread to other OPEC members.[14] Increased producer-country participation, or gradual nationalization, agreements which had already been taking place over the years, also began to accelerate during this period.[15]

[14]In 1970, Libya cut back the permissible production of Occidental Petroleum from 680,000 to 500,000 barrels a day until Occidental agreed to pay Libya $0.30 more per barrel, a $0.02 per barrel annual rate of increase over five years, and to increase its tax rate payment from 50 percent to 58 percent. At its 9 December 1970 Caracas meeting, OPEC then stipulated that all firms would have to pay taxes at a rate of 55 percent rather than at the then prevailing average rate of 50 percent.

[15]In 1964, Iraq established the Iraq National Oil Company, INOC, as a counterweight to be Iraqi Petroleum Company, whose membership comprised a 23.75 percent share held by BP, a 23.75 percent share held by Shell, 11.875 percent shares held by Exxon and Mobil, a CFP share of 23.75 percent, and all other shares 5 percent each. In February 1971, Algeria nationalized 51 percent of French interests in its oil fields. In December 1971, Libya nationalized all of BP's Libyan assets. In June 1972, Iraq nationalized the Iraq Petroleum Company. In October 1972, Saudi Arabia nationalized 25 percent of its concessions. In 1973, prior to the embargo, Libya nationalized 51 percent of all remaining oil companies in Libya, including subsidiaries of Exxon, Mobil, Texaco, Shell, and Socal. In 1974, Saudi Arabia raised its ownership of Aramco to 60

As pointed out in chapter 1, the October 1973 Middle East war between Israel and the combined forces of Egypt and Syria provided the catalyst for the Arab members of OPEC to impose an oil embargo on key industrialized consuming countries. Though such an embargo had been tried unsuccessfully in the 1967 Middle East war, by 1972, Arab oil-embargo states accounted for some 60 percent of world petroleum exports, certainly enough to exert substantial leverage on the major oil-importing countries of Western Europe, the United States, and Japan. In the upward surge of world petroleum prices which accompanied and followed the embargo, the U.S. cheap energy policy could no longer be sustained.

15.1.3. The Emergence of a Comprehensive U.S. Energy Policy

In the years since the Arab OPEC oil embargo, the United States has shifted from its primary reliance on cheap energy in favor of greater energy security. The two basic ways of achieving greater energy security are by rationing relatively scarce supplies and preserving low prices as long as possible, or by permitting prices to rise to a point where substitution and conservation can reduce the dependence on uncertain imported energy. Because of the short-run relatively inelastic demand for energy and the widespread suspicion within the United States that anticompetitive elements within the U.S. petroleum industry lay behind the quadrupling of OPEC oil prices during 1973–74, there has been considerable hesitation to rely primarily on the use of market prices to reduce U.S. dependence on energy imports. Yet, as will be seen, the alteration of relative energy prices has been one of the most effective approaches to recent energy policy decisions, the reasons for which are set out below.

Because of the swiftness with which the 1973 Arab OPEC oil embargo was imposed, the United States was clearly ill-prepared to redress the sudden shortage that followed. Apart from all other contributory factors thus far noted, one immediate reason for this lack of preparedness was that well prior to the embargo, the Nixon administration had implemented wage-price controls throughout the economy in the fall of 1971. With regard to petroleum, when combined with the fact that imported oil was still subject to a quota, the average price of petroleum products was still substantially below market equilibrium. Moreover, by this time U.S. dependence on imported oil was so substantial that the quota system was not longer of any practical significance other than for preserving some measure of stability to domestic petroleum prices.

To contend with the embargo, Congress passed the Emergency Petroleum Allocation Act of 1973. The United States Federal Energy Administration, formed as a separate unit to allocate energy supplies during this period, im-

---

percent. In October 1975, Venezuela nationalized all foreign oil concessions. In February 1979, Iran renounced its agreement to market its oil through the consortium of firms listed in note 13 above. By mid-1980 the equity interest share of foreign oil firms operating in the Middle East had fallen to 8.5 percent, substantially below the 94 percent share which existed at the beginning of 1972.

mediately set up a rationing system and undertook an intensive investigation of energy policy alternatives. The conclusions of this study were published subsequently as *Project Independence Blueprint.* To complement the work of the FEA, Congress also established the Energy Research and Development Administration, or ERDA, in 1974 to accelerate research and development of alternative technologies in the coming years. Yet what *Project Independence Blueprint* made all too clear was that under the traditional cheap energy policy, reduction of U.S. energy dependence would be impossible. Moreover, a comprehensive approach to energy policy decisions would be needed to acheive any appreciable degree of energy independence. Indeed, the decision to accelerate the commercial production of Alaskan North Slope oil (discussed in chapter 1) provided ample evidence of the complexity of energy policy decisionmaking.

To sustain the short-run rationing of petroleum, in November 1974 the Federal Energy Administration instituted a program known as entitlements. This program, which lasted until the deregulation of petroleum in February 1981, had two simple objectives. One was to give small-scale refiners, particularly nonintegrated firms, access to some of the still relatively inexpensive domestically produced crude oil, whose price was less than that of imported oil. In so doing, it would provide regulated support to preserving an ostensibly more competitive market structure, since any precipitous increase in the price of crude oil would undoubtedly drive many of the smaller firms out of business. The second objective was to control inflation, and toward this end, the Federal Energy Administration sought to retain control over the price of oil for as long as possible. Unfortunately, given short-run price elasticities of demand and supply, the entitlements program could only defer for a while the eventual adjustment in prices.

One major decision that would work toward the long-run reduction in imported-energy dependence was the elimination of the petroleum-depletion allowance. For most oil and natural gas producers, this allowance was removed by the United States Tax Reduction Act of 1975. Though it eliminated neither the expensing privileges discussed in chapter 11 nor depletion for other mineral resources, by raising the price of oil and natural gas closer to their actual replacement costs, it clearly represented a step toward greater allocative efficiency.

Another step in the shift of U.S. energy policy was the Energy Policy and Conservation Act of 1975. Although it kept some oil under continued price controls, certain categories of oil such as "newly discovered" and "stripper" oil were granted price ceilings much closer to prevailing world prices. The assumption was that if various classes of oil were denominated under alternative regulated price ceilings, individual market prices would more accurately reflect marginal costs and at the same time prevent the accumulation of any windfall gains to low-cost producers. The 1975 act also called for mandatory improvements in fuel-consumption levels of new automobiles such that within a decade average fuel efficiency would be doubled.

Additional upward adjustments in the pricing of petroleum were made under the Energy Conservation and Production Act of 1976. Yet by 1977 it was clear that U.S. dependence on imported petroleum and the appeal of cheap energy were still largely unreconciled to any significant degree. It was at this point that the Carter administration unveiled a national energy plan consisting of more than a hundred interrelated proposals, key versions of which are summarized here in table 15.2. Although Congress readily agreed to a Carter administration proposal to consolidate key federal agencies under a newly established Department of Energy, at first there was considerable reluctance to permit U.S. energy prices to rise to prevailing world levels, particularly since the price of crude oil was so dependent on the OPEC cartel. Yet by 1981 most of these proposals had become law, if for no other reason than that accelerating prices of OPEC oil and international supply uncertainty were increasing.

Three aspects of recent U.S. energy policy referred to in table 15.2 merit brief elaboration in terms of future energy choices. One is U.S. energy leas-

Table 15.2. Comprehensive Energy Policy Proposals of the Carter Administration, 1977–80

Issue	Proposal(s)	Congressional Action
1. Gasoline tax	Standby tax of $0.05–0.50 to take effect if consumption exceeded targets (1977)	Never acted on; a key policy proposal of unsuccessful Anderson 1980 presidential campaign
	Oil import fee to be passed through to consumers at $0.10 per gallon (1980)	Rejected
2. Conservation	Residential, commercial, and industrial tax credits for spending related to conservation (1977)	Adopted with minor change
	Federally mandated utility rate reform to encourage conservation (1977)	Energy Department given authority only to propose rate reforms to states
	Special federal banks to provide loans for solar and conservation investments (1979)	Adopted with minor changes
3. Oil prices	Extension of price controls on some oil, combined with decontrol of "new" oil and a crude-oil "equalization" tax to bring U.S. consumer prices to world levels (1977)	Rejected
	Gradual decontrol of crude-oil prices by executive order, combined with windfall profits tax (1979)	Accepted with some changes; complete decontrol approved by President Reagan in February 1981
4. Natural gas	New gas to be priced on a par with crude oil, with controls extended to intrastate sales and higher prices charged initially to industrial users (1977)	Gradual phaseout of price controls by 1985, with controls extended intrastate in the interim; industrial users to pay more initially
5. Coal conversion	New plants fired by oil or gas to be barred, and conversion of all coal-capable plants to be mandated: utilities to be banned from burning gas after 1990 (1977)	Passed with discretionary use of mandatory coal conversion
	$10 billion in grants to utilities to pay for conversion and to build new plants (1980)	No final action

Table 15.2.—*Continued*

Issue	Proposal(s)	Congressional Action
6. Gasoline rationing	Stand-by plan for allocation of fuel to all registered vehicles plus a "white market" for coupons (1979)	Rejected
	More complex stand-by plan allowing some "white market" coupons and providing for regional differences in driving and some special tax treatment (1980)	Approved
7. Synthetic fuels	$88 billion in federal subsidies to aid development, with funding administered by a government corporation (1980)	Accepted with variable funding arrangements
8. Expedited licensing	Energy mobilization board to be set up to eliminate redundant approval requirements (1979)	No final action
	Licensing for nuclear plants to be speeded, and incentives to be established to standardize reactors (1978)	No final action
9. Strip mining	Standards to be established for reclamation and restoration of strip-mining tracts (1977)	Approved
10. Strategic petroleum reserve	Target level to be raised from the 1975 congressional one of 750 million barrels to 1 billion (1978)	Actual level in 1980 at 91.7 million barrels—no change in policy of limited stockpiling
11. Breeder reactors	Development of breeder reactor to be deferred as a means of limiting the use of plutonium for nuclear weapons (1977)	Substantial reduction in funding down to a token level, with no final action taken
12. Nuclear fusion	$20 billion to be used over 20 years for fusion research	Approved

Sources: U.S. Congress, *Surface Mining Control and Reclamation Act of 1977*, 95th Cong., with amendment under Public Law 95-343, 1978; 96th Congress, *The National Energy Act*, 1979, consisting of the U.S. *National Energy Conservation Policy Act of 1978*, the U.S. *Natural Gas Policy Act of 1978*, the *Powerplant and Industrial Fuel Act of 1978*, and the *Energy Tax Act of 1978*; *Business Week*, 14 July 1980, p. 41; *New York Times*, 21 September 1977 and 26 August 1980.

ing policy. Despite the closer realignment of U.S. energy prices with prevailing world levels, for the near term at least, U.S. energy policy remains committed basically to the consumption of depletable energy resources. Indeed, the funding of a Synthetic Fuels Corporation provides ample evidence of this commitment. Although changes in relative prices have brought about significant increases in conservation, incremental supplies of synthetic depletable resources will depend largely on the rate of change in energy technology and on the leasing of federally owned resources.

Table 15.3 provides a summary of known federally owned and corporate leased energy resources in the United States as of 1975. There is still some scope for expanded leasing of petroleum reserves, but the least developed of the economy's fossil fuel resources are in coal and shale oil. Any accelerated development of these alternatives to imported oil will depend not only on technological limitations involving environmental pollution and water consumption in the drier areas of the country where these deposits are located but largely on increased leasing of deposits. Assuming that the environmen-

Table 15.3. Known Federally and Corporate-Controlled Energy Reserves, 1975

Resource	Nonleased Federal Reserves	Corporate-held or Leased Reserves	Total Reserves	Corporate Share of Total Reserves
Coal	118.4×10^9 tons	131.6×10^9 tons	250×10^9 tons	52.6%
Geothermal	1,146,941 acres	271,408 acres	1,418,349 acres	19.1
Natural gas	negligible	228.2×10^{12} ft^3	228.2×10^{12} ft^3	100.0
Oil	11.1×10^9 bbls	39.0×10^9 bbls	50.1×10^9 bbls	77.8
Shale oil	480×10^9 bbls	120×10^9 bbls	600×10^9 bbls	20.0
Uranium	negligible	441.5×10^3 tons	441.5×10^3 tons	100.0

Source: J. W. Markham, A. P. Hourihan, and F. L. Sterling, *Horizontal Divestiture and the Petroleum Industry* (Cambridge, Mass.: Ballinger Publishing Co., 1977), p. 21.

tal costs of coal and shale oil could be contained, there is still a question of intertemporal equity which such a decision represents. In its most basic terms, this question can be posed in the following way: To what extent does the accelerated development of the economy's currently known and publicly owned depletable energy resources enhance present-day energy security more than it reduces future energy security?

As noted in chapter 14, the market-based positive discount rates likely to be used to make intertemporal economic decisions are prone to justify the accelerated consumption of low-entropy depletable energy resources rather than greater investment in conservation or renewable energy resources. Moreover, if external costs are ignored as well, then market prices alone will tend to justify even further the accelerated consumption of depletable energy resources. Yet from an efficiency and equity perspective, the appropriate way of choosing among these alternatives is by the use of marginal social cost pricing and by an appropriate downward adjustment in the market rate of discount to reflect the irreversible consequences of consuming depletable energy resources. Were such adjustments made, then the expected economic advantage of synthetic fuels or accelerated use of coal would tend to be far less compelling, if at all, as a route to greater energy security.

Alternative energy choices depend partly on the rate of technological change. Yet technological change can be influenced partly by research and development efforts. Since technological change itself is determined largely by investment alternatives, a second aspect of future energy choices which bears closer examination is the evolution of research and development expenditures.

Table 15.4 shows the evolution of U.S. federal expenditures on research and development for several categories of energy resources during the period 1963–80. As noted in section 15.1.1, in the public sector at least, there has been a concerted effort to promote the development of commercial nuclear power, and the nuclear energy share of public research and development expenditures provides ample testimony of this policy. Although a sizeable proportion of nuclear energy research has also been devoted to breeder and nuclear fusion technologies, in the near term at least, greater U.S. energy in-

Table 15.4. Federal Budget Obligations for Energy Research and Development, 1963–81
(in millions of current U.S. dollars)

Category	1963	1969	1972	1974	1976	1978	1979	1980	1981[a]
Nuclear	235 (71%)	308.9 (86%)	375.3 (72%)	1,034 (80%)	753 (59%)	1,378 (54%)	1,452 (43%)	1,254 (36%)	1,067 (32%)
Fossil	51 (16)	36.8 (10)	100.6 (19)	110 (9)	323 (25)	684 (27)	826 (25)	743 (22)	653 (20)
Solar	—	—	—	45 (3)	93 (7)	368 (14)	456 (14)	507 (15)	581 (17)
Geothermal	—	—	—	—	31 (2)	106 (4)	136 (4)	112 (3)	131 (4)
Conservation	43 (13)	15.3 (4)	48.8 (9)	105 (8)	66 (5)	31 (1)	504 (15)	827 (24)	881 (27)
Total	329 (100)	361.0 (100)	524.7 (100)	1,294 (100)	1,266 (100)	2,567 (100)	3,374 (100)	3,443 (100)	3,313 (100)

Sources: U.S. Office of Management and Budget, *The Budget of the United States,* and *Special Analysis of the Budget* (Washington, D.C.: U.S. Government Printing Office, 1976, 1978, 1979, 1980); U.S. Office of Science and Technology, *Energy R and D and National Progress* (Washington, D.C.: U.S. Government Printing Office, 1964); John E. Tilton, *U.S. Energy R and D Policy: The Role of Economics* (Washington, D.C.: Resources for the Future, 1974); idem, "The Public Role in Energy Research and Development," in *Energy Supply and Government Policy,* ed. R. J. Kalter and W. A. Vogely (Ithaca: Cornell University Press, 1976), pp. 99–129; National Science Foundation, *Research and Development in Industry, 1978,* NSF 80-307 (Washington, D.C.: U.S. Government Printing Office, 1979); and idem, *Federal R and D Funding by Budget Function, Fiscal Years 1979–81* (Washington, D.C.: U.S. Government Printing Office, May 1980).

Note: The energy R and D share of the federal budget was as follows: in 1963, 0.29 percent; in 1969, 0.19 percent; in 1972, 0.22 percent; in 1974, 0.46 percent; in 1976, 0.34 percent; in 1978, 0.57 percent; in 1979, 0.68 percent; in 1980, 0.59 percent; and in 1981, 0.50 percent. The federal budget share of total R and D expenditures was 35 percent in 1963; 42 percent in 1974; and 45 percent in 1978. The federal public and private energy R and D expenditure share of the GNP was 0.16 percent in 1963; 0.22 percent in 1974; and 0.26 percent in 1978.

[a]Preliminary estimates

dependence from uncertain supplies of imported oil is much more likely to come from nonnuclear technologies. As pointed out in section 15.1.1, the reason for this conclusion is straightforward: commercial nuclear energy's current and future role is tied directly to the production of electricity. Even if electricity-sector consumption of primary energy continues to rise, in the near term at least, significant reductions in imported energy dependence are more likely to be achieved in the transportation, residential, and industrial sectors of the economy, which claim some three-quarters of all primary energy consumption. Insofar as future research and development is concerned, then, continued diversification of research into alternative energy technologies is likely to accelerate the development of greater energy security. Whether this diversification should be focused more on conservation and renewable energy resources than on synthetic fossil technologies depends again on whether the use of marginal social cost pricing and the question of an appropriate social discount rate are taken into account.

A third aspect of future U.S. energy choices that we need to examine is the linkage between commercial nuclear power and nuclear weapons proliferation. In previous chapters we have seen that in the conventional open nuclear fuel cycle currently used in the United States, apart from the question of nuclear reactor safety, the disposal of spent nuclear fuel poses at least two serious problems: the long-term disposal of radioactive waste and the dispersion of nuclear weapons. At present, several storage technologies are under development, but none of them has been considered sufficiently stable to endure the thousands of years necessary for the most toxic wastes to become environmentally benign. At the same time, as long as commercial nuclear power continues to expand, either a decision must be made regarding the disposal of these wastes or it will be necessary to shift toward reprocessing, or toward reprocessing plus the use of breeder reactor technology. Yet reprocessing and the use of breeder reactor technology mean that the nuclear fuel cycle would contain a much higher proportion of plutonium, or ^{239}Pu, than is now the case. Now, apart from its toxicity and its 24,000-year half-life, plutonium is the primary fuel used in the production of nuclear weapons.

Table 15.5 illustrates the nuclear weapons potential posed by the international expansion of commercial nuclear reactor technology. Based on prevailing reactor designs and on the current predominance of light water converter fission reactors, the Stockholm International Peace Research Institute estimates that under ordinary operating conditions, for each unit of approximately forty net megawatts of capacity, enough plutonium would be available to construct one twenty-kiloton atomic bomb per year. What is striking from the data in the table is that under this theoretical conversion ratio, the 1975 potential production rate of some 1,800 weapons per year would reach a rate of over 5,000 per year by 1980. The potential for producing nuclear weapons would more than double in a little over three years, and the problem of radioactive waste disposal would be increased substantially.

There is no necessary chain of causality between the ability to produce nuclear weapons and the actual decision to do so. Most of the countries listed in table 15.5 have entered into various agreements that either pledge the pro-

Table 15.5. Commercial Nuclear Power and International Nuclear Weapons Potential

Country	Nuclear Power Capacity, 1975 Mwe (Net)	Nuclear Power Capacity, 1980 Mwe (Net)	Number of Power Reactors with Capacity of more than 20 Mwe, 1980	Theoretical Annual Bomb Production Capacity for 20-kt Explosives
United States	36,593	86,690	103	1,880–2,360
Soviet Union	5,464	19,624	36	425–535
France	2,706	14,462	22	315–90
United Kingdom	4,539	10,697	39	230–90
China	—	—	—	—
Japan	6,287	19,066	28	450
West Germany	4,060	13,320	18	330
Spain	1,073	8,365	11	210
Sweden	3,184	8,264	11	210
Canada	2,539	7,802	15	200
Switzerland	1,006	5,933	8	150
Belgium	1,650	3,446	5	85
Taiwan	—	2,156	3	50
South Korea	—	1,769	3	45
East Germany	926	1,786	5	45
Czechoslovakia	110	1,838	5	45
Bulgaria	864	1,728	4	45
Finland	—	1,500	3	35
Italy	542	1,422	5	35
Yugoslavia	—	1,400	2	35
Mexico	—	1,308	2	30
India	587	1,229	6	30
Iran	—	1,200	1	30
Argentina	319	919	2	25
Hungary	—	864	2	20
Brazil	—	626	1	15
Austria	—	692	1	15
Netherlands	499	499	2	12
Rumania	—	432	1	10
Pakistan	125	125	1	3
Australia	50	50	1	1
Denmark	50	50	1	1
Israel	50	50	1	1
Norway	50	50	1	1
South Africa	50	50	1	1
Total	73,273[a]	220,414[b]	350	5,040–5,765

Sources: World Armaments and Disarmament, SIPRI Yearbook, 1976 (Stockholm: Almqvist and Wiksell, Stockholm International Peace Research Institute, 1976), p. 42; William Epstein, "Why States Go—and Don't Go—Nuclear," *Annals of Political and Social Science* 430 (March 1977): 16–28.

[a]Twenty-five countries

[b]Thirty-five countries

hibition of nuclear weapons production or promise to use nuclear weapons only in retaliation to an act of agression.[16] Still, there is no guarantee that written agreements will be upheld unless there are appropriate economic and

[16]For a more detailed discussion of the weapons-linkage issue, see "Nuclear Proliferation: Prospects, Problems, and Proposals," *Annals of the American Academy of Political and Social Science* 430 (March 1977).

political incentives, and well-established safeguards, to do so. Thus, some countries may simply decide to acquire nuclear-enrichment facilities suitable to the production of plutonium, or they may enter into alternative reprocessing agreements with other countries that give them equivalent access to nuclear weapons technology.

For the United States, the international expansion of commercial nuclear power presents a fundamental policy dilemma. On the one hand, if fossil fuel prices, and the prices of OPEC oil in particular, continue to increase as rapidly as they have since 1973, there is likely to be a parallel growth of interest in commercial nuclear reactor technology. Moreover, for countries that have already achieved a relatively high level of technical efficiency in energy conversion and have relatively limited fossil or renewable energy alternatives to which they can turn, the immediate appeal of commercial nuclear energy becomes even greater, which thus raises the risk of nuclear weapons proliferation. On the other hand, for these same countries to attempt to avoid commercial nuclear power may increase even further their dependency on uncertain supplies of imported energy, at least in the near term. The result could be a substantial redistribution of income, substantial economic stagnation, or both. The prospect of heightened international tension could well be just as great as it would be were commercial nuclear technology adopted. Alternatives to this dilemma thus depend on the geographical dispersion of new energy discoveries, the rate of change in conservation and renewable energy technologies, and the prospects for the international reduction of nuclear weapons potential. Since these decisions depend on and in turn influence the choices in international energy markets, we need now to examine the basic energy policies of key other regions within the global economic community.

15.2. INTERNATIONAL ENERGY POLICIES AMONG NON-OPEC DEVELOPED ECONOMIES

Among economies with relatively high levels of per capita income there is a wide variation in patterns of energy production and consumption. Some of these differences can be explained by the geographic distribution of energy resources; others can be attributed to specific energy policies. How both of these factors distinguish conditions of other countries from those of the United States may be seen in terms of two broad groupings, the OECD countries and Eastern Europe and the Soviet Union.

15.2.1. Energy Policies in OECD Countries

In addition to the United States, the Organization of Economic Cooperation and Development (OECD) countries of Western Europe, Canada, and Japan have highly similar and economically interdependent economies. They are among the most industrialized economies of the world and account regularly for well over two-thirds of world trade. Yet, with the exception of the United Kingdom, the OECD countries of Western Europe and Japan are generally dependent on energy imports to a far greater degree than the United States and Canada.

Table 15.6 provides a first-order approximation of the geographic evolution of world regional energy balances between 1965 and 1978. Although these groupings do not correspond directly to organizational configurations such as the OECD, they do permit a proxy comparison. Europe, which comprises both OECD and Eastern Bloc countries, shows the greatest degree of regional imported-energy dependence. For example, between 1965 and 1978, the import share of aggregate primary energy consumption rose from 34 percent to 44 percent. By 1978, oil accounted for 90 percent of this imported-energy dependence, with Arab OPEC countries of North Africa and the Middle East providing over three-fourths of external supplies. At the same time, because of this greater dependence on imported energy, many of these countries have pursued specific energy policies that place considerable emphasis on conservation and on the promotion of alternative energy technologies.

Among OECD countries, energy conservation has been promoted largely by the use of taxes on consumption and in efforts to apply the marginal social cost pricing principles discussed in chapter 13. Evidence of the impact of energy taxation on consumption can be seen in table 15.7. Keeping in mind that during the 1970s the countries listed in the table all had per capita incomes lower than that in the United States, with the exception of Canada, all of them utilized taxes to raise the delivered price of most forms of petroleum energy well above their counterparts in the United States. Thus, there has been a strong correlation between the share of income devoted to the consumption of energy and the degree to which energy conservation has been achieved, as pointed out in the comparative demand studies of chapter 10.

Although marginal cost pricing has long been practiced in such OECD countries, relatively high levels of energy conservation have by no means insulated them from growing dependence on imported energy. For OECD countries of the North Sea region, there has been an accelerated development of offshore natural gas and petroleum resources, which for the United Kingdom at least is likely to provide virtual energy self-sufficiency for the next few decades.[17] However, for continental European economies such as France, relief from uncertain supplies of imported energy has been sought through accelerated research and development of alternative energy technologies, notably renewable and nuclear energy resources.[18] Whereas there has been a slowdown in the emphasis on nuclear energy in the United States, the French have proceeded with the development of advanced breeder reactor systems, so that policymakers expect half of all French electricity generation

[17]For studies of United Kingdom energy policies, see Kenneth W. Dam, *Oil Resources—Who Gets What How?* (Chicago: University of Chicago Press, 1976); and A. J. Surrey, "Energy Policy in Britain: A Case Study of Adaptation and Change in a Policy System," in *The Energy Syndrome,* ed. Leon A. Lindberg (Lexington, Mass.: D. C. Health and Co., 1977), pp. 33–62.

[18]For a study of French energy policy, see Dominique Saumon and Louis Puiseauz, "Actors and Decisions in French Energy Policy," in ed. Leon A. Lindberg, *The Energy Syndrome* (Lexington, Mass.: D. C. Heath and Co., 1977), pp. 119–72.

Table 15.6. The Evolution of International Energy Balances, 1965–78
(in quadrillion Btu's)

Geographic Area	1965					1978				
	Coal	Oil	Natural Gas	Hydro-Nuclear	Total	Coal	Oil	Natural Gas	Hydro-Nuclear	Total
Production										
North America	15.5 (0.21) (0.26)	22.4 (0.31) (0.38)	19.7 (0.69) (0.34)	1.2 (0.32) (0.02)	58.8 (0.33) (1.00)	18.3 (0.20) (0.25)	26.2 (0.18) (0.36)	25.8 (0.46) (0.35)	2.9 (0.35) (0.04)	73.2 (0.24) (1.00)
Europe	25.4 (0.35) (0.84)	1.8 (0.02) (0.06)	1.7 (0.06) (0.06)	1.3 (0.36) (0.04)	30.2 (0.17) (1.00)	22.6 (0.25) (0.58)	5.1 (0.03) (0.13)	9.1 (0.16) (0.23)	2.4 (0.29) (0.06)	39.2 (0.13) (1.00)
Soviet Union	13.8 (0.19) (0.45)	11.4 (0.15) (0.37	5.5 (0.19) (0.17)	0.3 (0.08) (0.01)	31.0 (0.17) (1.00)	16.7 (0.19) (0.28)	27.7 (0.20) (0.47)	14.2 (0.26) (0.24)	0.8 (0.10) (0.01)	59.4 (0.20) (1.00)
Africa	1.7 (0.02) (0.26)	5.0 (0.07) (0.72)	0.1 (—) (0.01)	0.1 (0.03) (0.01)	6.9 (0.04) (1.00)	3.0 (0.03) (0.17)	13.5 (0.09) (0.77)	0.9 (0.02) (0.05)	0.2 (0.02) (0.01)	17.6 (0.06) (1.00)
Asia-Oceania	16.0 (0.22) (0.41)	21.6 (0.29) (0.56)	0.5 (0.02) (0.01)	0.6 (0.16) (0.02)	38.7 (0.22) (1.00)	28.0 (0.31) (0.30)	61.9 (0.42) (0.65)	3.7 (0.07) (0.04)	1.3 (0.16) (0.01)	94.9 (0.32) (1.00)
Latin America	0.3 (0.01) (0.02	11.5 (0.16) (0.88)	1.0 (0.04) (0.08)	0.2 (0.05) (0.02)	13.0 (0.07) (1.00)	0.5 (0.01) (0.03)	11.5 (0.08) (0.79)	1.9 (0.03) (0.13)	0.7 (0.08) (0.05)	14.6 (0.05) (1.00)
Total	72.7 (1.00) (0.41)	73.7 (1.00) (0.41)	28.5 (1.00) (0.16)	3.7 (1.00) (0.02)	178.6 (1.00) (1.00)	89.1 (1.00) (0.30)	145.9 (1.00) (0.48)	55.6 (1.00) (0.19)	8.3 (1.00) (0.03)	298.9 (1.00) (1.00)
Consumption										
North America	14.4 (0.20) (0.24)	26.2 (0.42) (0.43)	19.4 (0.69) (0.31)	1.2 (0.32) (0.02)	61.2 (0.37) (1.00)	17.5 (0.19) (0.20)	41.4 (0.33) (0.47)	25.9 (0.46) (0.30)	2.8 (0.35) (0.03)	87.6 (0.31) (1.00)
Europe	26.4 (0.36) (0.58)	16.4 (0.26) (0.35)	1.8 (0.06) (0.04)	1.3 (0.36) (0.03)	45.9 (0.27) (1.00)	24.0 (0.27) (0.35)	32.0 (0.25) (0.46)	10.9 (0.20) (0.15)	2.5 (0.30) (0.04)	69.4 (0.25) (1.00)
Soviet Union	13.2 (0.18) (0.49)	8.2 (0.13) (0.30)	5.5 (0.20) (0.20)	0.3 (0.08) (0.01)	27.1 (0.16) (1.00)	16.1 (0.18) (0.35)	16.3 (0.13) (0.34)	13.2 (0.24) (0.29)	0.7 (0.09) (0.02)	46.3 (0.17) (1.00)
Africa	1.7 (0.02) (0.61)	1.0 (0.02) (0.35)	0 (0) (0)	0.1 (0.03) (0.04)	2.8 (0.02) (1.00)	2.7 (0.03) (0.47)	2.5 (0.02) (0.44)	0.3 (0.01) (0.05)	0.2 (0.02) (0.04)	5.7 (0.02) (1.00)
Asia-Oceania	16.3 (0.23) (0.66)	7.3 (0.12) (0.30)	0.5 (0.02) (0.02)	0.6 (0.16) (0.02)	24.7 (0.15) (1.00)	28.7 (0.32) (0.49)	25.7 (0.20) (0.43)	3.4 (0.06) (0.06)	1.2 (0.05) (0.02)	59.0 (0.21) (1.00)
Latin America	0.4 (0.01) (0.07)	3.9 (0.06) (0.72)	0.9 (0.03) (0.17)	0.2 (0.05) (0.04)	5.4 (0.03) (1.00)	0.8 (0.01) (0.06)	9.0 (0.07) (0.73)	1.9 (0.03) (0.15)	0.7 (0.09) (0.06)	12.4 (0.04) (1.00)
Total	72.4 (1.00) (0.43)	62.9 (1.00) (0.38)	28.1(1.00) (0.17)	3.7 (1.00) (0.02)	167.1 (1.00) (1.00)	89.8 (1.00) (0.32)	126.9 (1.00) (0.45)	55.6 (1.00) (0.20)	8.1 (1.00) (0.03)	280.4 (1.00) (1.00)

Source: United Nations, *World Statistics in Brief* (New York: United Nations, 1979), pp. 199, 213.

Table 15.7. Energy Taxes, Energy Prices, and Energy Intensity in OECD Countries

Country	Per Capita GDP, 1975	Gasoline Price per U.S. Gallon[a]	Taxes as Percentage of Delivered Prices on[b]				Primary Energy Consumption per U.S. Dollar of GDP[c]
			Gasoline	Heating Oil	Heavy Fuel Oil	Coal	
Greece	$2,305	$2.93	—	—	—	—	22,668
France	6,360	2.45	54.1%	49.2%	0	—	15,503
Spain	2,848	2.40	58.8	20.0	8.7%	1.5%	18,847
Italy	3,084	2.23	64.6	14.6	10.8	0	24,416
Japan	4,437	1.98	30.8	43.9	0	0	20,408
West Germany	6,871	1.98	54.8	12.6	0	0	19,448
Ireland	2,492	1.69	50.0	0	0	0	31,069
United Kingdom	4,089	1.53	52.7	3.5	4.5	0	32,190
United States	7,087	0.85	20.5	0	0	0	38,800
Canada	6,995	0.79	39.4	0	0	0	35,411

Sources: New York Times, 3 May 1977, p. L-63, 19 May 1979, p. 8; U.S. Department of the Interior, Bureau of Mines, *International Petroleum Annual, 1975* (Washington, D.C.: U.S. Government Printing Office, 1977), pp. 30–36; World Bank, *World Tables, 1980* (Baltimore: Johns Hopkins University Press, 1980); United Nations, *Statistical Yearbook, 1976* (New York: United Nations Publications, 1977).

[a] Data based on premium gasoline for April 1979, as reported in the *New York Times* in May 1979.

[b] Data are for mid-1976

[c] Energy intensity is expressed in terms of Btu's consumed per U.S. dollar of GDP

to be provided by nuclear energy by as early as 1985. Moreover, based on the argument that worldwide diversification from the current acute dependence on petroleum is more likely to be acheived under the expansion of a nuclear energy alternative, French have also promoted the export of nuclear reactor technology to such countries as Iraq. What this suggests for the United States is that among OECD countries alone, disparities in the technical efficiency of energy use and in the geographic dispersal of alternative energy resources and technologies is likely to do little to reduce the demand for nuclear energy technology in the near term. Thus, the growth of demand for nuclear energy is likely to increase the risk of nuclear weapons proliferation (as discussed in section 15.1.3). What makes this continuing divergence more crucial for the future, however, is the evolution of energy policy alternatives in Eastern Europe and the Soviet Union, as well as the emerging energy alternatives among the non-OPEC developing countries.

15.2.2. Energy Policies in Eastern Europe and in the Soviet Union

Like other major industrialized countries, over the past fifty years the Soviet Union has undergone a substantial shift from coal-based to a petroleum- and natural gas-based economy. It has done so essentially through implementation of successive multiyear development plans which have emphasized accelerated industrialization at the expense of agriculture and consumer goods and in which considerable emphasis has been given to the internal mobilization of resources. Thus, unlike OECD countries, the Soviet Union and its Eastern allies, or COMECON, have enjoyed relative self-sufficiency in energy and other industries, especially in the period since the Second World War. At the same time, the goal of self-sufficiency has carried a particular economic cost in forgone alternatives, especially when we consider the relative economic efficiency of many Soviet industries. Perhaps more important for the future is that the regional energy equilibrium so characteristic of past Soviet economic development may be increasingly difficult to maintain in the years ahead. The implications of this bear some elaboration.

As can be seen in table 15.6, between 1965 and 1978 the Soviet Union maintained a position as a net exporter of energy. Net exports as a percentage of aggregate energy consumption stood at 14 percent in 1965 and reached a level of 28 percent by 1978. Except for limited shipments of petroleum and natural gas to Italy, West Germany, and Japan, almost all of the Soviet Union's energy exports have been channeled to the COMECON countries, who themselves have shifted from an earlier position of net energy exporters to net energy importers.[19] Although a regional energy equilibrium still exists, three basic factors are critical to the continuation of regional energy self-sufficiency.

[19]See Marshall I. Goldman, *The Enigma of Soviet Petroleum— Half Empty or Half Full?* (London: George Allen and Unwin, 1980); Robert W. Campbell, *Soviet Energy Balances*, Report R-2257-DOE (Santa Monica: RAND Corporation, December 1978); and U.S. Office of Technology Assessment, *World Petroleum Availability* (Washington, D.C.: U.S. Government Printing Office, October 1980).

First, even though there has been an emphasis on such energy-conserving measures as mass transit, the Soviet Union remains as one of the world's more energy-intensive economies. For example, in 1978 the Soviet Union consumed 42,513 Btu's for each dollar of Gross Domestic Product, a figure approximately 10 percent higher than in the United States and substantially greater than in the other OECD countries listed in table 15.7. The significance of these comparisons is that unless greater energy conservation is achieved, the future growth of Soviet and Eastern European income will require a more accelerated development of Siberian oil and natural gas resources than has been the case until now, or else the region will risk losing its energy self-sufficiency. Yet much of the technology suitable to the most efficient development of Siberian energy fields is still found among Western European and North American firms. To the extent that Soviet economic expansion depends on the importation of Western technology and capital, it poses a potential weakening of the traditional Soviet policy of economic and energy independence. Thus, depending on the status of East-West relations under détente, unless more conservation is achieved, the ability of Soviet policymakers to acquire Western technology poses a major dilemma: traditional energy equilibrium versus continued economic growth.

A second factor influencing Soviet energy alternatives is commercial nuclear power. As in the OECD countries, the Soviet Union is accelerating its development of nuclear-based electricity as an alternative to its fossil fuel–based economy and to the potential of dependence on imported energy, particularly OPEC petroleum. Although the Soviet Union already possesses an extensive nuclear weapons arsenal, recent economic plans have projected the nuclear share of primary energy consumption to reach over 1 percent by 1980 and 5 percent by 1990.[20] To the extent that the Soviets emphasize reprocessing of nuclear fuel and to the extent that breeder reactor technology is accelerated, consumption of fossil fuel resources can be stretched further into the future. Yet, as in the case of all OECD countries, the ability of commercial nuclear power to serve as a significant substitute for conventional fossil fuels is substantially limited to the electricity sector of the economy. Indeed, if as of 1980 all Soviet electricity were generated by nuclear power, it would account for at most 20 percent of all primary energy consumption. Moreover, since half of Soviet electricity is dependent on coal, the savings in the Soviet Union's traditional energy exports, oil and natural gas, would amount to no more than 10 percent, at least in the near term.[21] Nuclear power thus risks nuclear weapons proliferation.

The third factor in Soviet energy alternatives follows directly from the first two: To what extent would a shift to a status of being a net energy importer

[20]Emily Jack, J. Richard Lee, and Harold H. Lent, "Outlook for Soviet Energy," in U.S. Congress, Joint Economic Committee, 94th Cong. *Soviet Economy in a New Perspective* (Washington, D.C.: U.S. Government Printing Office, 14 October 1976), p. 474. Most Soviet commercial nuclear power plants are being concentrated in the energy-scarce western regions of the country, where they are projected to be used for industrial and residential co-generation.

[21]Goldman, *The Enigma of Soviet Petroleum*, p. 153.

result in greater pressure on OPEC oil suppliers? More specifically, would it cause the Soviet Union to expand beyond its current military occupation of Afghanistan into a greatly weakened Iran and then proceed to take over part if not all of its oil- and natural-producing fields? Such questions tend to be somewhat speculative, but they have not gone unnoticed among Middle Eastern OPEC countries, nor have they been overlooked by the petroleum-importing OECD countries. The implications of such expansion for the OECD countries, and the United States in particular, is the likelihood of even greater Western military involvement in the Middle East, which would divert additional resources from the development of energy and non-energy alternatives. What this suggests for countries with advanced petroleum and natural gas technology such as the United States is that efforts to restrain the development of Soviet energy alternatives may carry far greater costs than the potential cooperation such restraints would ostensibly bring about. Moreover, even if such pressures could be shown to exert any specific restraint on the part of the Soviet Union, they would be successful only to the extent that they were applied in a concerted fashion by all OECD countries. Perhaps most important of all, any such pressures would be operating on the assumption that there are no areas of mutual self-interest between the Soviet Union and OECD countries, an assumption that even in the light of nuclear armaments, Third World conflicts, and an expanded Soviet presence in Afghanistan, overlooks a continuing Soviet concern for economic and political stability among its Eastern European allies, the need to obtain advanced Western technology, and the periodic demand for agricultural imports which OECD countries in general and the United States in particular are still in the best position to supply. Since many of these energy policy issues are also tied to energy alternatives in the Third World, we need to complete these comparisons of international energy policies by looking more closely at the non-OPEC developing countries.

15.3. INTERNATIONAL ENERGY POLICIES AMONG NON-OPEC DEVELOPING COUNTRIES

The part of the world most affected by recent changes in the production, pricing, and consumption of energy resources comprises the non-OPEC developing economies of the Third World. These countries account for approximately two-thirds of world population and have the lowest per capita incomes among all of the economic groupings we have thus far examined. Moreover, they have the smallest shares of proven depletable energy resources and the lowest levels of per capita energy consumption. Given the growth of international trade over the past few decades and the economic interdependence that it has brought about, it is therefore essential that we identify several of the key factors that are central to the future energy policy alternatives of the non-OPEC developing economies.

Table 15.8 illustrates the energy–Gross Domestic Product relationship as it applies to several developing Third World economies. Most of the coun-

Table 15.8. The Evolution of Energy Intensities among Selected Non-OPEC Developing Economies, 1960–75

	1960			1975		
Country	Per Capita Energy Consumption (in MBtu's)	Per Capita GDP in 1972 Dollars	Btu's per 1972 Constant Dollars of GDP	Per Capita Energy Consumption (in MBtu's)	Per Capita GDP in 1972 Dollars	Btu's per 1972 Constant Dollars of GDP
Brazil	9.49	$494	19,221	19.17	$893	21,467
China	1.95	95	20,526	1.98	162	12,222
Ethiopia	0.23	87	2,644	0.70	73	9,589
Ghana	3.03	261	11,609	4.98	396	12,576
Jamaica	13.00	869	14,960	35.70	953	37,461
Morocco	3.96	226	17,522	7.29	278	26,223
Senegal	2.80	322	8,696	4.90	290	16,897
Sudan	1.44	136	10,588	4.41	214	20,607
Tunisia	4.20	353	11,898	11.20	418	26,794
Zambia	9.80	273	35,897	12.60	399	31,579
GDP-weighted per Capita Average Energy Intensity			16,016			25,253

Sources: World Bank, *World Tables, 1976 and 1980* (Baltimore: Johns Hopkins University Press, 1976, 1980).

Note: Figures are based on current market prices converted into U.S. dollars at official exchange rates and adjusted to 1972 constant dollars using the U.S. 1972 base-year GDP price deflator. Per Capita energy consumption is based on 28,600 Btu's per kilogram of coal-equivalent commercial energy consumption, from IBRD and U.N. data reported in the *World Tables*.

tries in the sample experienced increases in real per capita GDP between 1960 and 1975, but many of them also encountered rising energy intensities. What these rising energy intensities suggest is that despite relatively low per capita incomes and relatively expensive energy, price elasticities of demand in these countries have remained relatively low. Rising energy prices, particularly those brought about by OPEC production and pricing decisions, thus pose an added constraint on developing countries' economic opportunities, leading to potentially widening disparities in the world distribution of income and in intra-country income distribution.[22]

Relatively low price elasticities of demand and limited stocks of proven depletable energy resources point to three fundamental energy policy alternatives for non-OPEC developing economies. Apart from the possibility of accelerated exploration and development of incremental domestic supplies of depletable energy resources, the two other basic alternatives involve raising the price elasticity of demand for these resources. One approach is to find ways to promote a more technically efficient conversion and storage of existing energy resources in ways that increase the price elasticity of demand to a point where the adverse income effects of rising real energy prices are minimized, if not offset altogether. The other alternative is to accelerate the development of renewable energy resources, with the same desired effects on the price elasticity of demand. There is widespread evidence that many non-OPEC developing economies are expanding exploration and development of depletable energy resources, but we will concentrate here on the potential of conservation and renewable energy resources, largely because conservation and renewable energy resources are so often considered as exotic but uneconomical alternatives but also because the known stocks of depletable energy resources among non-OPEC developing countries suggest a limited base from which to promote economic growth and development.[23]

To appreciate the basis for conservation among non-OPEC developing economies, we need to make an important qualification in the interpretation of the data in table 15.8. Unlike OECD and COMECON countries, non-OPEC developing economies consume significant quantities of what is known as noncommercial energy. Noncommercial energy consists of biomass and animal resources such as firewood, charcoal, ox-driven agriculture, and comparable resources within the rural sector of developing economies. Indeed, many, if not most, developing countries consume almost all of their depletable and renewable commercial energy within the urbanized and industrialized sectors of their economies. Electricity, automobiles, and most

[22]Another way of expressing this relationship is in terms of the income elasticity of demand. Based on the equation log Energy $= a + b$ log GDP per capita, the income elasticity of demand for the ten countries was 1.36891 in 1960 and 1.4288 in 1975.

[23]Based on data in the *Oil and Gas Journal*, outside of OECD, COMECON, and OPEC economies, as of 1 January 1980, non-OPEC developing economies were estimated to account for 10.5 percent of proven oil reserves, and 12.5 percent of proven world natural gas reserves. The MIT Workshop on Alternative Energy Strategies (WAES) estimated that as of 1977, non-OPEC developing economies held 25.6 percent of proven coal reserves (see WAES, *Energy: Global Prospects, 1985–2000* [New York: McGraw-Hill, 1977], p. 171).

forms of industry that require the conventional use of commercial energy are largely, if not wholly, absent from the rural sectors of these economies. Consequently, if we are to understand more clearly the particular energy alternatives involving conservation and renewable energy resources, we must go further than the data of table 15.8 and examine the role of noncommercial energy within the framework of total energy production and consumption balances.

Studies on the mix of energy resources among developing economies indicate that the proportion of noncommercial energy relative to all primary energy consumption ranges from some 30 percent to 70 percent.[24] Though some of this variation can be attributed to differences in per capita incomes among countries, the economy's degree of urbanization and industrialization are also important determinants. Based on available evidence, as real per capita incomes rise, the share of noncommercial energy tends to fall. The reason for the shift to commercial energy is that accelerated urbanization creates an additional demand for relatively low-entropy resources that until fairly recently has been most readily satisfied by coal, natural gas, and conventional petroleum products. Since rising real prices of these resources have slowed down the opportunities for real per capita incomes to rise, if historical experience is any guide, one energy policy alternative is the potential role of noncommercial energy resources.

Table 15.9 illustrates the significance of noncommercial energy in five developing economies. Although Nigeria and Mexico are both oil-exporting countries and Nigeria is a member of OPEC, the role noncommercial energy plays in these economies is strikingly similar to its role in other developing economies. For example, in the rural sector of the economy, noncommerical energy accounts for at least four-fifths of all primary energy consumption. And while noncommercial energy provides the largest source of supply, it is overwhelmingly inefficient as compared with commercial energy. Indeed, the noncommercial share of useful energy is well under one-third of all rural useful energy, and the energy intensity of these rural economies is far greater than that of the United States, the Soviet Union, or other energy-intensive industrialized economies. The question for developing economies is: To what extent can the technical efficiency of rural noncommercial energy be increased as an alternative to rising real prices of commercial energy resources?

Improving the technical efficiency of rural noncommercial energy resources is possible for developing economies, but only if the technology is adapted, or appropriate, to existing and evolving economic conditions. For example, in

[24]See Jose M. Miccoles, "Alternative Energy Technologies in Brazil," in *Renewable Energy Resources and Rural Applications in the Developing World*, ed. Norman L. Brown (Boulder: Westview Press, 1978), pp. 53–73, in which the noncommercial share of primary energy was estimated to range between 27 percent and 54 percent from 1952–1972; P. D. Henderson, in "Energy Resources, Consumption, and Supply in India," estimates that the noncommercial share of primary energy in India has ranged from 48 percent to 68 percent during the 1953–71 period (in Vaclav Smil and William E. Knowland, eds., *Energy in the Developing World—The Real Energy Crisis* [New York: Oxford University Press, 1980], pp. 208–14; other figures cited in Smil and Knowland are 69 percent for Bangladesh and 30 percent in Turkey).

Table 15.9. Sector Distribution and Technical Efficiency of Per Capita Energy Use in Rural Areas of Developing Countries, ca. 1975

	India		China		Tanzania		Nigeria		Mexico	
	Distri-bution	Effi-ciency	Distri-bution	Effi-ciency	Distri-bution	Effi-ciency	Distri-bution	Effi-ciency	Distri-bution	Effi-ciency
Noncommercial Energy										
Residential	0.265	5.0%	0.635	5.0%	0.880	5.0%	0.819	5.0%	0.276	9.4%
Agricultural	0.510	6.5	0.263	16.9	0.092	2.6	0.131	6.7	0.666	32.9
Transportation	0.225	2.9	0.102	3.1	0.028	2.9	0.050	3.3	0.058	2.8
Total	1.000		1.000		1.000		1.000		1.0000	
Amount[a]	15.1		31.5		25.0		18.3		61.6	
Useful energy[a]	0.8	5.3%	2.5	7.9%	1.2	4.8%	0.9	4.9%	15.2	24.7%
Commercial energy[a]										
Inputs	2.5		8.0		1.0		0.7		15.0	
Useful energy	0.5	20.0%	1.6	20.0%	0.2	20.0%	0.14	20.0%	3.0	20.0%
Total Energy[a]										
Inputs	17.2		39.5		26.0		19.2		75.6	
Useful energy	1.3	7.6%	4.1	10.4%	1.4	5.4%	1.1	5.9%	18.2	24.1%
Energy Mix										
Noncommercial share of total energy	85.8%		79.7%		96.2%		96.3%		80.4%	
Noncommercial share of useful energy	27.8%		28.1%		12.5%		10.9%		14.2%	
Energy Intensity										
In megajoules										
Rural	202.32		282.09		273.64		119.98		167.97	
Total[b]	49.01		12.88		14.76		9.27		35.56	
In Btu's										
Rural	191,952		267,641		259,617		113,832		159,364	
Total[b]	46,501		12,222		14,000		8,799		33,737	

Sources: Arjun Makhijani, "Energy in the Rural Third World," in *Energy in the Developing World—The Real Energy Crisis*, ed. Vaclav Smil and William E. Knowland (New York: Oxford University Press, 1980), p. 18. Per capita GDP figures used to estimate energy intensities have been derived from World Bank, *World Tables, 1980* (Baltimore: Johns Hopkins University Press, 1980).

[a]Unless otherwise noted, energy units given are in Gigajoules (10^9 joules).

[b]Total energy intensity, or energy consumption per 1975 U.S. dollar of GDP, is based only on commercial energy. Given that rural per capita GDP estimates are based only on commercially realized income, reported energy intensities are biased upward relative to total energy intensities.

the residential sector of rural economies, much of the firewood, charcoal, and dung used for heating and cooking is wasted because of the use of open hearths. Stoves made of clay or metal can raise the useful energy yield of noncommercial energy far above the relatively low conversion efficiencies shown in table 15.9. Moreover, such energy-conserving measures would forestall the depletion of existing forests caused by rising real energy prices and thereby minimize the adverse consequences on the environment. Yet although there are many ways to adopt such energy-conserving measures in rural developing areas, increasing the useful energy for transportation and agriculture can be far more difficult. This is because rural transport depends on horses, mules, or camels, and to raise the useful energy in agriculture often depends on changing the mix of crops, fertilizers, and patterns of tillage traditionally practiced in ways that may be difficult for many communities to accomplish.

Another policy choice for developing economies is to promote the use of alternative renewable energy technologies—to develop hydropower resources for the production of electricity, to extend the use of wind electricity-generating systems, to develop the use of biogas digesters for the production of low-Btu gas, and to use some biomass energy as a source of liquid fuels, notably alcohol—to minimize the adverse income effects of rising real prices of commercial energy resources. Yet the financial burden of the transition imposes a considerable strain on the developing economies. For this reason, we need to place the energy alternatives of developing economies within the context of evolving and future international energy policies.

15.4. INTERNATIONAL ENERGY POLICIES AND THE FUTURE

The one link among all of the various energy policies thus far discussed is economic and energy interdependence. Under normal economic conditions, interdependence is a logical and desirable consequence of trade based on comparative advantage and specialization in production, since the degree of trade affords higher world incomes than would otherwise be possible. However, what distinguishes the current degree of global energy interdependence from the traditional model of trade is the extent to which depletable energy resources establish user costs, or rents, as the principal medium of exchange. To the extent that trade is based on these rents rather than on differences in opportunity costs of production, shifts in the relative price of energy will tend to redistribute the existing level of world income more than it adds to the total. Thus, until such time as conservation and the emergence of alternative energy resources reduce the magnitude of depletable energy rents, the near-term nature of international energy trade will depend to a critical extent on alternative patterns of distribution, a process that has come generally to be known as petroleum revenue recycling.

Figure 15.3 illustrates the institutional structure of world energy trade and the problem of recycling. Given the relative self-sufficiency in energy and related production among the Eastern European economies, the principal channels of income redistribution involve the energy import dependent

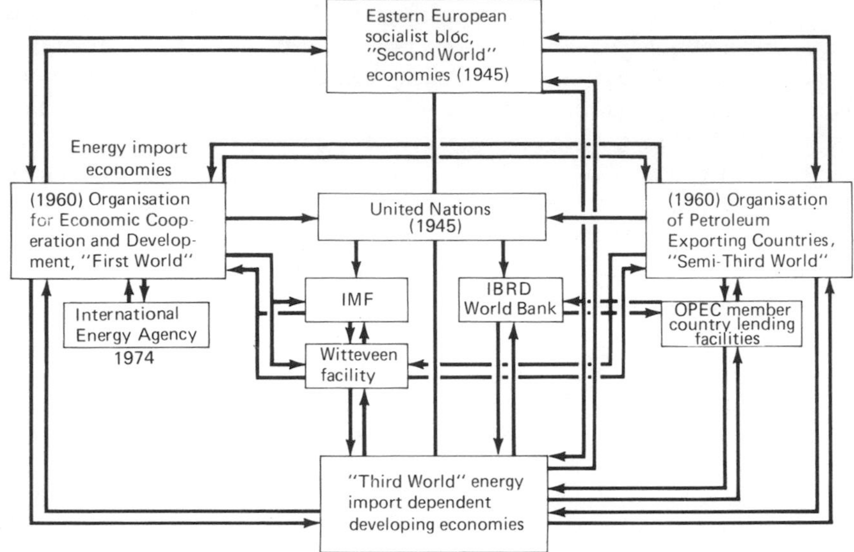

Figure 15.3. Energy Dependency and the Institutional Structure of International Trade

developing economies of the Third World. As of 1980, the current account balances for all energy and non-energy trade of OPEC countries reached an estimated surplus of $125 billion dollars, whereas the current account balances of OECD and non-OPEC developing countries reached deficits of $75 billion and $50 billion, respectively. At the same time, in order to minimize the adverse redistributive effects of rising real energy prices, both OECD and OPEC countries have implemented a number of institutional innovations to accommodate the process of recycling.

Within the OECD, the International Energy Agency has been created to address the impact of rising real prices and potential shortfalls in world energy supplies. Established in the aftermath of the 1973 Middle East war, its primary function is to distribute existing supplies in the event of a sudden disruption of OPEC oil exports. While it could yet be required to do so at some point in the future, in the interim it has functioned largely as an energy information agency for OECD member countries, leaving the problems of energy policy coordination to established political and economic channels.

Another measure undertaken by OECD countries to address the problem of petroleum revenue recycling has been participation in the International Monetary Fund's Witteveen facility, a $10 billion fund created after the 1973–74 quadrupling of oil prices, and named after the then director of the IMF, Johannes Witteveen. With funding participation by OPEC member countries, the primary purpose of the Witteveen facility has been to provide concessionary assistance to developing countries whose balance of payments deficits have been most adversely affected by increasing real prices of OPEC oil.

A third institutional innovation shown in figure 15.3 is the OPEC member-country direct lending facility. Unlike the OECD International Energy Agency, the lending facility channels some of OPEC's revenues into direct bilateral loans to developing countries affected by rising oil prices.

Finally, there are the traditional sources of international financial transfers within the United Nations, namely, the IMF and the World Bank. Although neither agency has focused exclusively on petroleum revenue recycling, the magnitude of recent oil price increases has caused a shift in their operations toward greater concern with this process, a trend which may well accelerate in the future.

What do these various changes in international energy markets imply for future U.S. policy? First and foremost, the prices of alternative energy resources should always be set as closely as possible to equalize their marginal social costs and benefits. As we have seen in preceeding chapters, this principle encompasses a series of economic tests. If market prices exceed marginal private costs because of imperfect competition, as long as the social costs of intervention are less than or equal to the social benefits, then some form of public intervention to restructure energy markets would be justified. At the same time, if market prices are less than competitive private marginal costs because of regulatory constraints, then deregulation would be fully warranted. Similarly, if competitive marginal social costs were to exceed current market prices because of environmental pollution, then taxes on pollution to equate prices to marginal social costs would be fully justified.

What about uncertainty? Although competitive insurance markets represent an efficient way to handle problems of risk, when these risks are unknown, to the extent that the degree of uncertainty in energy decisions exceeds the degree in non-energy decisions, some public intervention could be justified. Yet because uncertainty can not be expressed in specific quantitative terms, the level of public subsidies or taxes that would be consistent with the principle of allocative efficiency is likely to invoke potentially controversial value judgments. Moreover, the degree of uncertainty is rarely fixed long enough for efficient policies to be implemented. Thus, the uncertainty of oil prices which led the Carter administration to promote the development of synthetic fossil fuels with fiscal subsidies appears greatly diminished in light of the expanded degree of energy conservation which higher relative prices have brought about in the intervening time.

Another implication for future U.S. energy policy is that equity and economic stabilization can be achieved more effectively through conventional tools of income distribution and the use of fiscal and monetary policy than through specific intervention in energy markets. As we have seen, regulation of energy prices to protect the poor or to control inflation tends to create additional distortions with little or no net gain in social welfare. Thus, if individuals are adversely affected by rising energy prices because they are poor, then we should apply taxation and income transfers from the rich to ensure that the preexisting degree of equity is at least preserved. Moreover, to the extent that intergenerational equity is involved, as long as market rates of discount exceed society's rate of time preference, energy policy should include the use of conservation, or severance, taxes on depletable resources. The burden of these taxes should also be distributed in accordance with prevailing standards of equity. As to economic stabilization, the regulation of energy prices is more likely to lead to repressed inflation and a future energy crisis than it is to satisfy this fundamental macroeconomic objective. To use regulation as a substitute for fiscal and monetary policy would only tend to compound the difficulty of achieving stabilization over a longer period of time.

As these observations suggest, the mix of public and private roles in energy decisions can not be reduced to simple choices between a free market and a controlled economy. Although it is tempting to embrace completely private markets as the most effective form of energy policy, they provide no guarantee that competitive economic efficiency will prevail at home and abroad, that the environment will be protected from pollution, or that an equitable distribution of income will prevail. On the other hand, the fact that government can intervene in energy markets does not ensure that it will necessarily solve these same problems. Between these two positions is the underlying premise that some forms of public intervention may be necessary if the United States is to avoid a protracted energy crisis. Though none of these choices will necessarily be simple to resolve, through increased understanding of energy economics and technology, efficient and equitable solutions are possible. That task is now before us.

15.5. SUMMARY

Energy policies depend ultimately on technology, economics, and institutions. For the United States at least, gradual changes in world energy balances have caused a fundamental shift from the traditional policies of cheap, secure, and environmentally benign energy toward greater recognition of international energy interdependence. In the process, U.S. energy policies have become more consistent with international energy markets and institutions.

Of the many factors that have shaped the evolution of U.S. energy alternatives, three have been most important. One has been the past policy of cheap energy. Percentage-depletion tax allowances, intangible drilling-expense deductions, and peculiarities in the treatment of foreign tax credits have encouraged domestic energy intensity and have increased the dependence of the United States on imported energy. Another factor has been the structure and behavior of international energy markets, notably the ability of international firms in the past to perpetuate for many years the prevailing policy of cheap energy through favorable concession terms in producing countries. The third factor has been the rise of OPEC, which through its ability to withhold production and increase the real price of petroleum has brought about the shift from cheap energy.

The speed with which the United States can adjust to a regime of higher real energy prices depends on several considerations, such as the degree of leasing of public lands to increase the supply of conventional energy resources, research and development efforts in alternative energy resources and technologies, and efforts to reconcile the marginal social costs of individual energy resources with an equitable distribution of income. These choices also encompass whether the concern for environmentally benign and secure energy resources will result in greater energy conservation, as well as in greater or lesser dependence on nuclear energy technologies.

There is also growing energy interdependence outside the United States. Although the Eastern European economies have remained relatively self-sufficient in energy, the ability to preserve this position depends partly on the state of East-West relations as it affects the transfer of energy technology. For OECD countries, even though they are generally far less energy-intensive than the United States, to the extent that either the United States or the Eastern European economies become more dependent on imported energy, there is likely to be a more rapid shift toward the use of nuclear energy resources, which under prevailing economic conditions may also add to the problem of nuclear weapons proliferation.

Of all groups in the world economy, the non-OPEC developing countries have been the most adversely affected by rising real energy prices. In addition to efforts that these countries have made to promote enhanced conservation and alternative energy resource utilization, in the interim they face potentially significant losses of income, which increases the degree of inequality in the world distribution of income. To cushion these effects, both OECD and OPEC countries have contributed resources toward alleviating the burden of petroleum revenue recycling.

SUGGESTED READINGS

Dunkerley, Joy; Ramsay, William; Gordon, Lincoln; and Cecelski, Elizabeth. *Energy Strategies for Developing Nations.* Baltimore: Johns Hopkins University Press for Resources for the Future, 1981.

Goldman, Marshall I. *The Enigma of Soviet Petroleum—Half Empty or Half Full?* London: George Allen and Unwin, 1980.

Goodwin, Craufurd D., ed. *Energy Policy in Perspective.* Washington, D.C.: Brookings Institution, 1981.

Harrison, Selig. *China, Oil, and Asia: Conflict Ahead?* New York: Columbia University Press, 1977.

Mikdashi, Zuhayr. *The Community of Oil Exporting Countries: A Study in Government Cooperation.* Ithaca: Cornell University Press, 1972.

Smil, Vaclav, and Knowland, William E., eds. *Energy in the Developing World—The Real Energy Crisis.* New York: Oxford University Press, 1980.

APPENDIX

STANDARD ACCOUNTING UNITS

I. Energy Conversion Factors

	Calorie[a]	Therm	Watt-hour	Joule
Calorie[a]	—	3.97×10^{-5}	1.16279	4,184.1
Therm	25,201.6	—	29,299.7	1.05×10^{8}
Watt-hour	0.860	3.41×10^{-5}	—	3,600
Joule	0.000239	9.49×10^{-9}	2.77×10^{-4}	—
Btu	0.252	10^{-5}	0.293	1,054
Photon[b]	11.8×10^{-23}	4.68×10^{-32}	1.37×10^{-27}	4.9×10^{-24}
Hph[c]	641.559	1.87×10^{-30}	746	2.6×10^{6}
Foot-pound	3.2×10^{-4}	3.61×10^{-24}	3.8×10^{-4}	1.40

	Btu	Photon[b]	Hph[c]	Foot-pound
Calorie[a]	3.968	8.47×10^{21}	1.56×10^{-3}	3,100
Therm	10^{5}	2.13×10^{31}	5.34×10^{29}	2.77×10^{23}
Watt-hour	3.413	7.29×10^{26}	1.34×10^{-3}	2,679
Joule	9.49×10^{-4}	2.03×10^{23}	3.73×10^{-7}	0.7143
Btu	—	2.14×10^{26}	3.93×10^{-4}	780
Photon[b]	46.8×10^{-28}	—	1.84×10^{-25}	1.66×10^{-6}
Hph[c]	2,500	5.44×10^{24}	—	2×10^{6}
Foot-pound	1.3×10^{-3}	600,000	5.1×10^{-7}	—

[a] Calorie units are based on kilocalories.
[b] Photon units are based on blue light at 4,000 Angstroms.
[c] Horsepower per hour.

II. Approximate Btu Content of Selected Energy Resources

1. Coal (per short ton)
   - Anthracite 25.4×10^{6} Btu's
   - Bituminous 25.0×10^{6} Btu's
   - Sub-bituminous 20.0×10^{6} Btu's
   - Lignite 14.0×10^{6} Btu's

   Crude coal oil, 1 gallon 130,000 Btu's
   Crude coal tar, 1 gallon 150,000 Btu's

2. Natural gas (per cubic foot)
   - Dry 1,031 Btu's
   - Wet 1,103 Btu's
   - Liquid (average) 4,100 Btu's

   Liquid per barrel 4,011,000 Btu's
   1 cubic meter 37,000 Btu's

3. Petroleum (per 42-gallon barrel)
   - Crude oil 5.8×10^6 Btu's
   - Residual fuel oil 6.29×10^6 Btu's
   - Distillate fuel oil 5.83×10^6 Btu's
   - Gasoline 5.25×10^6 Btu's
   - Jet fuel (kerosene) 5.67×10^6 Btu's
   - Jet fuel (Naptha) 5.36×10^6 Btu's
   - Kerosene 5.67×10^6 Btu's

   1-lb. gas 21,000 Btu's
   6-lb. gas = 1 gallon = 126,000 Btu's

4. Nuclear
   - 1 gram fissioned U-235 = 74×10^6 Btu's (= 3.364 fuel pellets)
   - 1 ton uranium oxide (U_3O_8) = 580×10^9 Btu's

III. Aggregate Energy-Unit Equivalents

1. 1 MBDOE = 1 million barrels per day of oil equivalent
   = 50 million tons of oil equivalent per year
   = 76 million metric tons of oil equivalent per year
   = 57 billion (57×10^9) cubic meters of natural gas per year
   = 2.2 exajoules (10^{18}) per year
   = 530×10^{12} kilocalories per year
   = 2.1×10^{15} Btu's per year = 2.1 quads
   = 620 terrawatt-hours (10^9 kwh) per year
2. 1 Quad = 1 quadrillion Btu's = 10^{15} Btu's
   = 500,000 petroleum barrels a day per year = 182,500,000 barrels
   = 40,000,000 short tons of bituminous coal = 36,363,636 metric tons
   = 1 trillion (10^{12}) cubic feet of natural gas
   = 100 billion (10^{11}) kwh (based on 10,000 Btu/kwh heat rate)
3. 1 Kilowatt-hour hydropower = 10×10^3 Btu's
   = 0.88 lb. coal
   = 0.076 gallon crude oil
   = 10.4 cubic feet of natural gas
4. 1 MTCE = one million short tons of coal equivalent
   = 4.48×10^6 barrels of crude oil
   = 67 tons of crude oil
   = 25.19×10^{12} cubic feet of natural gas
5. 1 Terawatt-hour (electric) = 3.75 million metric tons of oil equivalent
   = 0.103618 quads
   = 2.25 million metric tons of coal equivalent
   = 0.0001 terajoules
6. 1 Terawatt-hour (thermal) = 12.50 million metric tons of oil equivalent
   = 0.345395 quads
   = 7.49 million metric tons of coal equivalent
   = 3.33 terawatt-hours electric
   = 0.0003 terajoules

7. Solar densities:
   1 Langley = 1 calorie of radiant energy per square centimeter
   1 Watt/cm^2 = langleys per minute multiplied by 0.0698
8. Biomass:
   1 cord of wood (128 ft^3) = 19.5×10^6 Btu's

IV. Metric and Scientific Conversion Units
1. Area
   1 square foot = 0.0929 square meters
   1 acre = 4,047 square meters
2. Length
   1 inch = 2.54 centimeters
   1 foot = 0.3048 meter
   1 mile = 1,609 meters
   1 Angstrom = 10^{-10} meters
3. Mass
   1 ton = 2,000 pounds = 909.09 kilograms
   1 tonne = 1 metric ton = 2,200 pounds = 1,000 kilograms
   1 pound = 0.4536 kilogram
   1 ounce = 28.571429 grams
4. Speed
   1 mile per hour = 0.4470 meters per second
5. Temperature
   Absolute zero = 0°K = 0°R = −273.15°C = −459.67°F
   Kelvin temperature = T(°C) + 273 = T(°R)/1.80
   Rankine temperature = T(°F) + 460
   Centigrade = (°F − 32)5 / 9
   Fahrenheit = (°C)9/5 + 32
6. Volume
   1 gallon = 3.785 liters
   1 acre-foot = 1,233 cubic meters = 43,560 cubic feet
   1 quart = 0.946 liter
   1 pint = 0.473 liter
   1 fluid ounce = 29.574 milliliters
7. Scientific notation
   1 million = 10^6 (prefix: giga)
   1 billion = 10^9 (prefix: mega)
   1 trillion = 10^{12} (prefix:tera)
   1 quadrillion = 10^{15}
   1 quintillion = 10^{18}

GLOSSARY

Anaerobic digestion—The decomposition of organic material by bacteria in the absence of air or oxygen.

Anthracite—A relatively hard type of coal whose combustion yields comparatively high amounts of heat and little environmental pollution per unit consumed. In the United States it is located typically in eastern Appalachian deposits.

Atkinson inequality—An index of inequality defined by Anthony B. Atkinson in 1970. It is expressed as $I = 1 - [\Sigma_i (Y_i / \bar{Y})^{1 - \epsilon} f(Y_i)]^{1 / 1 - \epsilon}$, where Y_i is the income of the ith individual, $\bar{Y}$ is the mean level of per capita income, ϵ is the subjective weight which reflects the social aversion to inquality, and $f(Y_i)$ is the frequency of income of individuals at the ith level.

Atomic Energy Commission (AEC)—Established by Congress in 1946 as a national agency to promote the commercial application of nuclear energy. Served as the focal point of nuclear regulation and nuclear power subsidies to commercial electric utilities until 1975, when it was renamed the Nuclear Regulatory Commission (NRC). *See also* Nuclear Regulatory Commission.

Averch-Johnson hypothesis—A theory published by Harvey Averch and Leland Johnson in 1962 regarding the distorting effects of rate-of-return regulation, it stresses that since regulatory commissions do not possess sufficient information to adopt efficient pricing choices, excess capacity and overcapitalization tend to arise, resulting in higher costs and prices to consumers than there would be otherwise.

Balance of payments—An accounting statement listing all international transactions of an economy at a particular moment in time. The net balance of the current and capital accounts forms the basis for either an alteration of an economy's exchange rate or some method of payment or receipt of income between the debtor or surplus economy and its trading partners.

Baseload—A unit of electricity-generating capacity for a public-utility. Refers to capacity continuously in use. Baseload capacity contrasts with peak-load, or standby, capacity, which is used only part of the time.

Beta emission—The emission of electrons from the nucleus of an atom during a nuclear reaction.

Binding energy—The quantity of energy released when nucleons (protons and neutrons) combine to form an atomic nucleus or when a given nucleus is disrupted, as in the case of nuclear fission. Generally measured in terms of atomic mass units, or amu's, one unit of which is equal to one-sixteenth of the atomic mass of one atom of oxygen, or 1.6603×10^{-24} grams. In terms of energy, one amu is equal to 931.8 megavolts, or 1.49×10^{-3} ergs.

Biomass—Potential energy which through photosynthesis is accumulated in organic material, of which firewood is the most typical example.

Bituminous—Containing bitumens, or asphaltic tar. Usually refers to soft coal.

Boiling water reactor (BWR)—A nuclear reactor in which steam is formed by passing water through the reactor chamber, where it is used to operate an electricity-generating turbine; the steam is then cooled, and the water recycled back through the reactor chamber.

Boltzmann's constant—A measure of energy defined by Ludwig Boltzman as having a value of 1.38×10^{-23} joules per degree of Kelvin temperature.

Breeder reactor—A nuclear reactor in which the emission of neutrons is sufficiently fast that the quantity of fissile energy isotopes released in the reaction exceeds the quantity of energy in the parent fuel.

British Thermal Unit (Btu)—The amount of heat needed to raise the temperature of one pound of water one degree Fahrenheit from its maximum density temperature of 39.2 degrees Fahrenheit. As a common unit of energy measurement, it is often expressed in aggregate units as a quad, one of which is equal to 10^{15}, or 1 quadrillion, Btu's.

Calorie—The amount of energy needed to raise the temperature of one gram of water by one degree Centigrade either from 3.5 to 4.5 degrees or from 14.5 to 15.5 degrees.

Capital consumption allowance—The difference between gross and net private domestic investment as used in national income accounting. Consists almost exclusively in the depreciation of capital assets.

Capital-output ratio—The ratio of an economy's capital stock to output per unit of time. Often expressed as the incremental capital-output ratio, or the amount of additional investment needed to increase the productive capacity of the economy by one unit.

Carbonization—Any process that results in the addition of carbon, e.g., partial combustion of fossil fuel.

Clayton Act of 1914—A cornerstone of U.S. antitrust legislation that declares as illegal any price discrimination, tying contracts, intercorporate stockholdings and directorates that are deemed to lessen the degree of competition, the only exception to which is price discrimination that can be attributed to differences in grade, quality, or quantity sold, with due allowances for selling and transport cost differentials.

Coal gasification—Any chemical process that converts coal into a gas form suitable for use as a fuel. The most common examples are the Lurgi process, developed in Germany in the 1930s; the Koppers-Totzek process, Hygas, the Carbon Dioxide Acceptor process, and the Synthane process.

Coal liquefaction—Any chemical process that converts coal into a liquid form suitable for use as a fuel. The four most common examples are carbonization, direct hydrogenation, Fisher-Tropsch synthesis, and solvent refinement.

Coal slurry—Coal that has been pulverized and mixed with a common liquid such as water, which is then suitable for pipeline transport or for use in synthetic fuel conversion processes.

Coefficient of performance (*C.O.P.*)—an index of the technical efficiency of energy conversion defined as the ratio of input energy to the amount of energy converted into work, given the Second Law Efficiency, and expressed as C.O.P. $= Q_1/W =$

$\chi/(1 - T_2 / T_1)$, where χ is the Second Law Efficiency, Q_1 is the quantity of input energy, W is the amount of energy converted into work, T_1 is the inside warm-air absolute temperature in degrees Kelvin, and T_2 is the outside cool-air absolute temperature in degrees Kelvin.

Co-generation—Any process that uses the rejected energy from an initial conversion technology as input energy for a secondary energy conversion or for a series of subsequent energy conversions. An example is the use of rejected industrial steam for space heating.

Comparative advantage—A principle involving the comparison of the relative opportunity, or forgone, costs of production of goods of two or more economies. The conclusion of this comparison is that the economy with the lowest relative opportunity costs should specialize in the production of those goods and services and that it should trade with other countries whose opportunity costs—or comparative advantage—lie in other types of production. The distribution of gains from such trade depend on the magnitude of difference in the respective countries' own opportunity costs, the degree of specialization undertaken by each country, and the terms of trade.

Concentration ratio—An index of the degree to which a single firm—or x largest number of firms in an industry—accounts for total industry sales, assets, or comparable measure of economic activity. For a given number of largest firms, the higher the concentration ratio, the less is the presumed degree of competition within the industry. The ratio is thus one test of the existence of competitive markets.

Consumers' surplus—The difference between what an individual would be willing to pay for a good and what the individual actually pays. Refers to the area between the equilibrium market price of a commodity and the demand curve and is a key element in the formation of optimal economic policies.

Consumption function—A systematic relationship between the level of consumption expenditures and other economic variables such as income, expectations, the level of consumer debt, the stock of consumer durables and liquid assets, and the level of taxation. Often expressed as the relationship between consumption expenditures and income when these other variables are held constant.

Convection—The transmission of heat or electrical energy by currents of the moving particles of a gas or liquid.

Critical mass—The minimum quantity and configuration of a fissile material such as uranium-235 or plutonium-239 needed to sustain a fission process in a nuclear reactor.

Cross-price elasticity—A ratio of the relative change in quantity demanded of a particular good to the relative change in price of any other good. Expressed as $\epsilon_{xy} = (\Delta Q_x / (Q_{x1} + Q_{x2}))/(\Delta P_y / (P_{y1} + P_{y2}))$, where Q_{x1} and Q_{x2} refer to the initial and the terminal quantity demanded of good x, and P_{y1} and P_{y2} refer to the initial and the terminal price of good y. In general, the higher the cross-price elasticity of demand for a good, the higher will be its own-price elasticity of demand. The scale of the price elasticity of demand ranges between zero and infinity.

Curie—A measure of the degree of radioactivity. One curie is equal to the quantity of any radioactive isotope that undergoes 3.7×10^{10} disintegrations per second. It is equal to the radioactivity of one gram of radium-226.

Depletion allowance—A form of depreciation used by owners of exhaustible natural resources which lowers the owner's tax liability by a stipulated percentage.

Historically, such depreciation has been greatest for oil and natural gas, though recently it has been substantially reduced in magnitude.

Depreciation—See Capital consumption allowance.

Deuterium—An isotope of hydrogen known as heavy hydrogen which has an atomic weight of 2 and an atomic mass of 2.0147 (or approximately twice the frequency of the common isotope of light hydrogen), and exists in nature at approximately 0.02 percent of natural hydrogen. Heavy water based on deuterium has been used as a moderating element in some types of nuclear reactor designs, notably the Canadian deuterium-uranium, or CANDU, design.

Discount rate—An interest rate used to express the time value of money or any other economic benefit or cost in terms of present value. The present value of a dollar to be received in year n with an interest rate of r can be expressed as $\$1 / (1 + r)^n$.

Dominant-firm theory—A theory of oligopolistic industry behavior in which the pricing and production of a leading firm tends to shape the behavior of the industry as a whole. Also applicable to certain types of cartel organization.

Economies (and Diseconomies) of scale—Decreases (or increases) in a firm's long-run average costs as the size of the plant is increased over time which are attributable to greater specialization, a more efficient utilization of capital equipment, reduced costs of inputs, and opportunities for joint production.

Elasticity of demand—A measure of the sensitivity of the quantity demanded of a good to changes in another variable, namely, the own-price, or income, or the price of a related good (*see* Cross-price elasticity). The own-price elasticity of demand is the ratio of the relative change in quantity demanded to the relative change in its price. It is expressed as $\epsilon_{px} = (\Delta Qx/(Q_{x1} + Q_{x2})) / (\Delta Px/(P_{x1} + P_{x2}))$. The income elasticity of demand is expressed as $\epsilon_{yx} = (\Delta Qx/(Q_{x1} + Q_{x2})) / (\Delta Y/(Y_1 + Y_2))$. Values of ϵ that are $> 0 < 1$ are relatively inelastic; for $\epsilon = 1$, demand is unit-elastic, and for > 1, demand is elastic.

Elasticity of substitution—A measure of the sensitivity of factor inputs to relative changes in their prices. For two goods, x and y, it can be expressed as $\epsilon_{xy} = (\Delta(x/y)/(x/y)) / (\Delta(P_x/P_y) / (p_x/p_y))$.

Elasticity of supply—A measure of the sensitivity of the quantity supplied of a good to changes in another variable, usually the own-price of the good. Defined as the relative change in quantity supplied per relative change in the own-price of the good.

Electrical Generator—A machine that converts mechanical energy into electricity.

Electron—A negatively charged elementary particle that forms a part of all atoms. The number of electrons circulating around a nucleus is equal to the number of positive charges on the nucleus. Any transfer or rearrangement of electrons between atoms underlies all chemical reactions.

Emergency core cooling system (ECCS)—A safety coolant backup system designed to prevent a nuclear reactor meltdown when the normal reactor coolant does not function.

Employment Act of 1946—Stipulates that government shall accept some degree of responsibility for maintaining high levels of employment and price stability through the exercise of fiscal and monetary policy. The Council of Economic Advisors and the Joint Economic Committee are to assist in its implementation.

Entropy—A thermodynamic measure of the quantity of energy unavailable for useful work in a system that is undergoing change. As defined by Rudolf Clausius and

Ludwig Boltzmann, a measure of the degree of disorder within a particular physical system. Universal entropy always tends to increase over time.

Entropy principle—States that the quality of energy in the universe is always tending to deteriorate, since with each conversion, the forms of energy are increasingly disordered.

Eurodif—A joint venture by France, Italy, Belgium, and Spain involving the contruction and operation in France of a gaseous-diffusion plant for nuclear fuel enrichment.

Eutectic—A mixture of two or more elements which solidifies out of the liquid at a minimum freezing point and which can also be reversed, as in eutectic salt compounds for solar-heating storage.

Exhaustible resources—Resources whose ultimate quantities may not be presently known but are assumed to exist in finite amounts, whose remaining deposits tend to be of lesser quality than preceding units consumed, and whose conversion into other forms yields successively lower-quality resources with each successive transformation.

Externalities—Unintended benefits or costs imposed on third parties rather than on buyers and sellers. If left uncorrected, they may lead to a socially inefficient allocation of resources in the economy.

Fast neutron—High energy neutron used to accelerate the process of nuclear fission. As used in commercial nuclear reactors, fast neutrons differentiate the operation of breeder reactors from their slower-neutron thermal- or converter-reactor counterparts.

Federal Energy Regulatory Commission (FERC)—Established in 1977. Consolidated the functions of the former Federal Power Commission and the Nuclear Regulatory Commission under the jurisdiction of the federal Department of Energy.

Fertile nuclear fuel—Any material which is not susceptible to fission by thermal neutrons but which can be converted into fissile material within a nuclear chain reaction. Two common examples are uranium-238 and thorium-232.

First Law of Thermodynamics—States that energy can be neither created nor destroyed. *See also* Thermodynamics.

Fission—In nuclear transformation, the splitting of atoms by neutron bombardment in which relatively high amounts of energy are released. Though fission can occur in nature, it can also be induced through the operation of a controlled or uncontrolled nuclear chain reaction.

Flue-gas desulfurization—The chemical treatment of stack exhaust gases to remove environmental pollutants such as sulfur and sulfuric compounds.

Fluidized-bed combustion—The chemical treatment of crushed coal and calcium carbonate in a pressurized or atmospheric steam chamber to separate sulfur impurities in the form of calcium sulfate, leaving relatively purified coal which can be consumed with low levels of environmental pollution.

Flywheel—An energy-storage device that can be charged mechanically or electrically. Modern lightweight forms that operate in relative vacuum chambers could substantially increase the technical efficiency of energy conversion.

Foreign tax credit—Tax credit granted to firms or individuals in some proportion to the foreign taxes that they have paid, resulting in parent-country tax liability.

Fossil fuel—Any organically based essentially hydrocarbon fuel formed naturally or by a synthetic process. Examples are coal, oil, natural gas, and any synthetic fuel derived from these naturally occurring forms.

Fuel cell—A mechanism that performs a chemical reaction to produce electricity, usually at approximately normal environmental temperatures.

Fuel cycle—Any system involving the conversion of one form of energy into another, one or more steps of which will be applied to economically useful tasks. The nuclear fuel cycle involves mining, refining, fabrication, fission, recovery, potential reprocessing, and ultimate waste storage.

Full Employment and Balanced Growth Act of 1978—A federal law requiring the President to set long- and short-term production and employment targets, requiring the Federal Reserve to declare its monetary policies on a semiannual basis, and requiring the government to undertake fiscal and monetary policy actions which will attain by 1983 an unemployment rate of 4 percent, with no higher levels thereafter, and an inflation rate of 3 percent, which is to decline to 0 percent by 1988 and thereafter. Also known as the Humphrey-Hawkins Act.

Fusion—The joining of atomic nuclei from relatively light elements to form relatively heavier elements, the by-product of which is the release of substantial quantities of energy. The most common approaches to nuclear fusion are magnetic confinement and inertial confinement.

Game theory—The study of strategic options and consequences of actions under uncertainty, the subjects of which have varying degrees of conflict regarding the actions of others.

Gas—Matter that is in a fluid state, is low in relative density, possesses relatively high compressibility, and has neither definite shape, volume, nor free surface.

Gaseous diffusion—The most common method of enrichment of nuclear fuel to permit a controlled nuclear reaction.

Geothermal energy—Energy stored under pressure as steam, hot water, or heat in rocks deep below the earth's surface.

Gini coefficient—A measure of the degree of inequality in a particular distribution. Defined on a Lorenz curve as the ratio of the area between the curve of inequality and the 45-degree line to the entire area beneath the diagonal line. Ranges in value from 0 (complete equality) to 1 (complete inequality). *See also* Atkinson inequality.

Half-life—The period of time required for the level of radioactivity of a substance to decline to half of its original amount.

Heat engine—A machine that transforms heat into mechanical energy.

Heat exchanger—Any device that transfers heat from one liquid or gas to another or to the environment.

Heat pump—A machine that follows the principle of refrigeration to heat rather than cool a building. An expanding refrigeration fluid such as freon removes heat from the outside air, and the subsequent compression of the fluid releases the heat to an exchanger, which distributes the heat to the interior surroundings of a room or building.

Heat sink—The medium or location where rejected heat from energy conversion is discharged. In many conventional energy technologies, the environment serves as the heat sink for rejected energy; thus external costs are imposed on society.

Heavy water—Deuterium oxide (D_2O), or water formed by heavy hydrogen atoms combining with oxygen atoms instead of ordinary light hydrogen. Heavy water has a density of 1.105 and a molecular weight of 20, as against the density of 1.000

and the molecular weight of 18 of ordinary water (H_2O), and is found in nature at approximately one part per five thousand. It is particularly suitable for use as a moderator substance to slow down the emission of neutrons in a nuclear reactor, notably in the Canadian deuterium-uranium, or CANDU, model. *See also* Deuterium.

High-temperature gas reactor (HTGR)—A graphite-moderated, helium-cooled reactor that uses highly enriched uranium as its initial fuel and thorium as a source of new fuel.

Humphrey-Hawkins Act—See Full Employment and Balanced Growth Act of 1978.

Hydrocarbon—Any compound that consists only of hydrogen and carbon. The most common examples are found in fossil fuels whose relative purity is defined by the ratio of hydrocarbons to total compounds.

Hydroelectricity—Electricity formed by the energy of falling water which is used to turn a turbine generator.

Hydrogenation—The combination of any element or compound with hydrogen.

Hydrothermal energy—Energy stored and converted by an process that relies on the temperature differences between surface and deep water, notably in the generation of electricity.

Implicit GNP price deflator—A weighted average of the price indices used to deflate the components of GNP. Defined as the ratio of the current-dollar GNP to constant-dollar GNP.

Income effect—A change in the quantity of a good demanded that is due solely to a change in an individual's real income resulting from a change in the price of the commodity. *See also* Substitution effect.

Income Elasticity of Demand—See Elasticity of demand.

Indifference curve—A graphical portrayal of the various combinations of any two goods that yield the same level of total satisfaction to a consumer, or set of consumers.

Insolation—The rate of solar radiation reaching a given area of the earth's surface. A key measure in determining the technical feasibility of solar energy systems.

Intangible drilling expenses—Expenses incurred by a firm in the exploration for natural resources even though no discovery may occur. Considered as tax-deductible expenses.

International Bank for Reconstruction and Development (IBRD)—A U.N. agency established in 1945 to assist in postwar reconstruction which has since become a principal funding agency for developing countries' development projects for which privately financed funds are not available, or are available only in such limited quantities that such projects would not otherwise be undertaken.

International Monetary Fund (IMF)—A U.N. agency established in 1944 for purposes of eliminating exchange-rate restrictions, encouraging exchange-rate stability, and promoting the worldwide convertibility of currencies to encourage the growth of international trade.

Ionization—A process in which an atom becomes electrically charged by gaining or losing one or more of its extranuclear electrons. An atom that has lost one or more extranuclear electrons is a positive ion; an atom that has gained one or more extranuclear electrons is a negative ion.

Irradiated fuel—Nuclear fuel that has been exposed to nuclear radiation within a reactor. Known as spent fuel if the net energy yield of the fuel has reached a sufficiently low point.

Isoquant—A graphical portrayal of the various combinations of two inputs, or factors of production, that yield the same level of total production, or output.

Isotope—Any of two or more forms of a chemical element which have the same number of protons in the nucleus, or the same atomic number, but different numbers of neutrons in the nucleus, or different atomic weights.

Joule—A unit of energy or work that is equal to one watt-second, or 0.239 calories. Named after the scientist James Joule.

Kerosene—A petroleum derivative that contains hydrocarbons which are slightly heavier than those in gasoline.

Kilocalorie—The amount of energy needed to raise the temperature of one kilogram of water by one degree Centigrade.

Kilowatt—A standard measure of electrical-power capacity equal to 1,000 watts, or 1,000 joules per second.

Kinetic energy—Energy available by virtue of its motion. Defined as $mv^2 / 2$ per unit of time, where m is the mass of the particle and v is its path velocity at that instant.

Lawson criterion—A law formulated by the physicist J. D. Lawson to determine the necessary condition for a succesful sustained nuclear fusion reaction. Defined as $n\tau > 10^{14}$ atoms/second/cm^3, where n is the number of particles per cubic centimeter and τ is the confinement time, in seconds.

Light water reactor—A nuclear reactor in which ordinary (light) water functions as the principal coolant, or moderator, with enriched uranium fuel. The two principal types of light water reactors are the Boiling water reactor (BWR) and the Pressurized water reactor (PWR).

Lignite—Low-grade coal that has an energy content between those of bituminous coal and peat.

Liquefied natural gas (LNG)—Natural gas which has been sufficiently cooled to substantially reduce its volume in order to facilitate its transmission from the extraction site to consumer markets. Commercial LNG is generally transported in ocean tankers at temperatures as low as −140°C.

Liquid-metal fast breeder reactor (LMFBR)—A nuclear reactor that uses a liquid metal such as molten sodium as a moderator and whose uranium-238 fuel is irradiated by fast neutrons to yield conventional steam heat and fissile plutonium-239, which can be used in commercial nuclear reactors or in nuclear weapons.

Lithium—An element whose sixth isotope could serve as a fuel for nuclear power plants.

Lorenz curve—A curve that illustrates the cumulative-percentage relationships between two variables, notably population and income distribution, which can then be compared to a 45-degree diagonal line connected to the two axes and is a measure of absolute equality. *See also* Atkinson inequality; Gini coefficient.

Loss of coolant accident (LOCA)—A reactor accident in which the primary coolant no longer moderates the fission within a reactor core.

Lurgi process—The oldest commercial process of coal gasification, developed in Germany in the 1930s. It has received renewed interest as the price of conventional petroleum has risen.

Magnetic-confinement fusion—A method of achieving a sustained nuclear fusion reaction by passing atoms through an ionized, heated zone, or plasma.

Magnetohydrodynamics (MHD)—The conversion of energy by the initial passage of fuel through a magnetic chamber that ionizes the fuel as it is heated. The resulting plasma can then be converted into electrical energy at much higher conversion efficiencies than are obtainable from conventional processes. MHD technologies are still in the development stage.

Man-rem—The total dose in rem (Roentgen-equivalent man) received by individuals in a given population, where one rem is the product of the absorbed dose of radiation absorbed and the relative biological efficiency of the radiation.

Marginal cost—The change in total cost (or revenue) resulting from a one-unit change in quantity. When the marginal cost is set equal to price, as long as the marginal costs and benefits include all external costs and benefits, socially optimal allocation of resources generally has been attained.

Marginal rate of substitution—The rate at which a consumer is willing to substitute one commodity for another along an indifference curve, or that rate of substitution of goods which yields the consumer the same level of total satisfaction. *See also* Indifference curve.

Marginal rate of technical substitution—The amount of input resource that a firm is able to give up in return for an additional unit of another resource with no loss in output, as in the movement along a firm's isoquant.

Marginal rate of transformation—The quantity of one output that must be given up in order to produce an additional unit of another output, as in the movement along a production-possibilities curve (or frontier). For any given combination of outputs along a production-possibilities curve, the slope of a line that is tangent to the curve at that point is equal to the marginal rate of transformation. Also known as the opportunity cost of production.

Marginal revenue—The change in total revenue resulting from a one-unit change in quantity produced and sold.

Marshall-Lerner condition—The principle formulated by Alfred Marshall and Abba Lerner according to which under a condition of a deficit or surplus in the balance of payments, as long as the sum of a deficit or surplus country's import-demand and export-supply elasticities is greater than one, an alteration in the country's exchange rate will automatically lead to the elimination of the deficit or surplus.

Megawatt—A common measure of energy capacity, particularly with regard to electric utilities, equal to 1 million watts.

Methane—A gaseous hydrocarbon, CH_4, which is colorless, odorless, and inflammable and is formed by the decomposition of vegetable matter or is produced artificially. It is a common energy fuel.

Milling—A process in the uranium nuclear fuel cycle in which ore containing only a very small percentage of uranium oxide (U_3O_8) is converted into material containing a relatively high percentage of U_3O_8, which because of its color and consistency is commonly referred to as yellowcake.

Minemouth plant—A steam-electric or coal gasification-liquefaction plant that is built and operated near a coal mine, requiring as it does relatively long transmission lines to final markets.

National Energy Act of 1978—A series of energy pricing and regulatory reforms promoting conservation, marginal-cost pricing of electricity, and reduced reliance on petroleum energy. It comprises the National Energy Conservation Policy Act, the Powerplant and Industrial Fuel Use Act, the Public Utility Regulatory Policies Act, the Natural Gas Policy Act, and the Energy Tax Act.

National Environmental Policy Act of 1970—An act requiring that large-scale industrial projects include an assessment of environmental impact and alternative choices available before funding proceeds. The agency responsible for the determination and implementation of these standards is the Environmental Protection Agency.

Natural Gas Act of 1938—An act which granted to the Federal Power Commission the right to regulate interstate pipeline sales of natural gas. It was amended to include wellhead pricing of interstate gas under the Phillips decision of 1954.

Natural monopoly—A firm that possesses economies of scale over such a wide range of output that it can supply an entire industry at a lower average cost than two or more firms. Typified historically by electric and natural gas utilities and railroads.

Natural uranium—Uranium as found in nature. It generally contains 0.7 percent uranium-235, 99.3 percent uranium-238, and small quantities of uranium-234. Because of the relatively small share of uranium-235, natural uranium is not generally suited for direct used in a conventional nuclear reactor.

Nernst's heat theorem—A theorem formulated by Walter Nernst, which states that the change in entropy when temperatures have reached absolute zero is zero, and is expressed as

$$\lim_{T \to 0} [\partial(\Delta g) \,/\, \partial T] = \lim_{T \to 0} [\partial(\Delta h) \,/\, \partial T] - \lim_{T \to 0} (\Delta s),$$

where Δg = Gibb's measure of the energy change, adjusted for the degree of mechanical pressure, and Δh = the change in enthalpy, the heat content per unit of mass of constant mechanical pressure.

Net present value—The value today of a sum of benefits minus costs to be received as a stream of net benefits over time, in which future costs and benefits are discounted by a particular interest rate and which can be expressed as

$$NPV = \sum_{i}^{n} \{(B - C)_i/(1 + r)^i\}.$$

Neutron—A subatomic particle with a mass of 1.6848×10^{-24} grams and no electric charge, which is essential to the fission of atomic nuclei, since it is not repelled by the positively charged protons in the atomic nuclei.

Nitrogen oxides—Chemical forms of nitrogen and oxygen which are frequently the byproduct of the combustion of fossil fuels and which when concentrated in the atmosphere contribute to environmental pollution.

Nuclear fuel enrichment—The process of increasing the degree of concentration of fissile uranium-235 in uranium from its natural state of approximately 0.7 percent to approximately 2.5–3.0 percent. The three most prominent means are gaseous diffusion, the gas centrifuge, and more recently, laser enrichment.

Nuclear reactor moderator—A material such as graphite, water, or helium that is used to slow down the thermal velocity of neutrons in a reactor, thereby causing them to collide repeatedly with the nuclei of the atomic fuel without being captured, or absorbed, by the moderator. Slow neutrons are essential to the fission of uranium-235 in a controlled nuclear reaction.

Nuclear Regulatory Commission (NRC)—Established in 1975 as the successor to the Atomic Energy Commission. It is the principal federal agency responsible for licencing nuclear power plants, for setting reactor safety standards, for determining standards to be used in the preparation of nuclear fuel, and for the disposal of nuclear wastes, including the reprocessing of spent nuclear fuel. In 1977 it became part of the FERC.

Nuclear waste—Spent fuel from a nuclear reactor which is either stored at the reactor site, reprocessed to extract usable nuclear fuel components, or moved to semipermanent storage location. At present, no permanent sites for nuclear waste storage have been established in the United States.

Oil shale—Sedimentary rock impregnated with petroleum, which can be extracted when heat is applied to the rock.

Oligopoly—An industry characterized by a limited number of firms producing either homogeneous or differentiated products in which there are likely to be higher prices and smaller equilibrium outputs than under perfectly competitive market conditions.

On-site generation—The production of electricity nearest the point of consumption rather than by purchase from a central-station generating unit of a utility, in which net-deficit energy is purchased from the central-station utility and surplus energy is sold to the utility. On-site generation can also involve co-generation.

Open fuel cycle—The nuclear fuel cycle in which spent fuel is not reprocessed but consigned to waste-disposal sites.

Opportunity cost—The value of a choice forgone by undertaking an alternative, or the amount of one good which must be sacrificed in order to obtain one additional unit of an alternative good. *See also* Marginal rate of transformation.

Organization of Economic Cooperation and Development (OECD)—A group of twenty-four largely industrialized and developed economies in North America, Western Europe, and Japan, known also as the developed capitalist, or "First World," economies and as part of the North group of developed economies. Established in December 1960.

Organization of Petroleum Exporting Countries (OPEC)—A group of thirteen petroleum-exporting countries established in September 1960 by Saudi Arabia, Iraq, Kuwait, Iran, and Venezuela. Its membership was expanded to include the United Arab Emirates (Abu Dhabi, Bahrain, Dubai), Indonesia, Algeria, Libya, Nigeria, Ecuador, Qatar, and Gabon. Because its Arab members imposed an oil embargo on key importing industrialized countries in 1973–74 and because it has been successful in increasing the price of crude oil by over 1,000 percent between 1973 and 1981, it is often referred to as a cartel.

Pareto optimality—A condition in which no change can be made to improve the welfare of one individual without making at least one other individual worse off. A Pareto-optimal improvement is thus a change that makes at least one individual better off without making anyone else worse off. The standard of Pareto optimality has been used to characterize the economically efficient allocation of resources and to formulate economic policy alternatives.

Particulates—Particles of solid waste material such as ash that are released into the atmosphere by the combustion of energy resources, notably in the exhaust gases of automobiles and fossil fuel plants.

Peak-load—The greatest amount of power generated by an electricity-generating system. Consists of baseload and stand-by capacity. Peak-load pricing refers to the distribution of fixed and variable costs to users in a way that is consistent with marginal-cost pricing principles.

Phillips curve—A curve formulated by A. W. Phillips which expresses the presumed trade-off between the rate of unemployment and the rate of inflation.

Phillips Petroleum Case of 1954—A case in which the Supreme Court granted the Federal Power Commission authority to regulate the wellhead price of interstate natural gas sales.

Photon—A quantum, or unit, of visible light which is regarded either as a wave or as a particle having the mass of hv / c^2, where h is Planck's constant (the product of energy and time, with a number value of 6.624×10^{-27} erg-seconds), v is the frequency of vibration, and c is the speed of light in a vacuum.

Photosynthesis—A process performed by green plants in which carbohydrates are formed under the influence of light, with chlorophyl functioning as a catalyst.

Photovoltaic conversion—The transformation of solar radiation into electricity by means of a solid-state instrument such as a silicon solar cell.

Plasma—A fourth state of matter known as "electrified gas." As the hottest and swiftest of magnetic fluids, since plasma contains nearly equal numbers of positive ions and electrons, it is electrically neutral. Plasmas are essential to the operation of magnetohydrodynamic generators and to controlled nuclear fusion.

Plutonium—A relatively heavy element that except for minute traces (approximately one part in 10^{14} in pitchblende and carnotite due to the accidental absorption of neutrons by uranium-238 nuclei in these ores) is produced artificially, usually as a by-product of the fission reaction in a uranium-fueled nuclear reactor. Plutonium-239 is a key fuel in the fabrication of nuclear weapons, is highly toxic, and has a halflife of 24,300 years.

Power—The rate at which energy is converted, or the rate at which work is accomplished, usually measured in watts or horsepower units.

Pressurized water reactor (PWR)—A nuclear reactor in which pressurized water is passed through a heat chamber (and because it is pressurized is not permitted to boil) and a secondary feed-water system passes through a heat exchanger connected to the pressurized water circuit, where the secondary feed-water is then converted into steam, which is used to operate a turbine generator.

Price-Anderson Act of 1957—A law mandating insurance coverage for commercial nuclear reactors on a joint public-private funding basis. A ceiling per reactor accident was established at $560,000,000, a figure which since has been considered substantially below the costs of a minimum-damage accident such as occurred in 1979 at Three Mile Island, in Middletown, Pennsylvania.

Price discrimination—Charging two or more buyers (sellers) different prices for the same product. Price discrimination is possible as long as markets can be segmented and as long as the price elasticities of demand (supply) at each price level differ among markets.

Producers' surplus—The difference between what an individual would be willing to sell a good for and what the selling price actually is. Refers to the area between the equilibrium market price of a commodity and the supply curve and is a key element in the formulation of optimal economic policies.

Production function—The technical relationship between a firm's resource inputs and output of goods and services per unit of time.

Proton—A subatomic particle that is positively charged and has a mass of approximately 1.7×10^{-24} grams, or approximately 1,840 times the mass of an electron. Protons are part of the nucleus of atoms and are emitted in some types of nuclear reactions. The nuclei of atoms are considered to consist of protons and neutrons, known collectively as nucleons; the number of protons in the nucleus is always equal to the atomic number of the isotope, and the combined total of the nucleons is the mass number.

Proven Reserves—The quantity of natural resources that can be recovered with present-day technology and prices.

Pumped storage—An electricity generation system in which water is pumped into a storage reservoir at a higher elevation when surplus electricity is available from a convention fossil fuel or nuclear power plant and then allowed to pass through a hydroelectric generation system in times of peak-load demand. Pumped storage may be economical to the extent that the marginal cost of electricity generation from the combined hydro and depletable energy generating systems is lower than the marginal cost of a conventional peak-load reserve system.

Pyrolysis—The decomposition of organic substances by heat.

Quad—A measurement unit of energy equal to 10^{15}, or 1 quadrillion, Btu's.

Rad—A measure of the radiation absorbed in tissue, corresponding to an energy absorption of 100 ergs per gram.

Radiation—The electromagnetic emission of energy from matter. Ionizing radiation involves the emission of alpha particles, beta particles, and gamma rays.

Radioactive decay—The gradual emission and dilution of the quantity of a radioactive substance caused by the spontaneous disintegration of nuclei by the emission of alpha or beta particles, gamma rays, or positrons. The degree of radioactive decay of a substance is often expressed in terms of its halflife. *See also* Halflife.

Radioactive waste—Material that continues to undergo radioactivity, usually the spent-fuel by-products of commercial and military nuclear reactors.

Rankine—A temperature scale in which zero is absolute zero, and degrees are separated by the same temperature difference as in the Fahrenheit scale.

Rasmussen Report—One of a series of nuclear reactor safety studies authorized by the Atomic Energy Commission. Named after its research director, Norman Rasmussen, it tended to discount the risks of a significant nuclear reactor accident, was widely criticized in the years following its publication in 1975, and has since been disowned by the Nuclear Regulatory Commission.

Refinery—Generally in reference to petroleum, the processing mechanism for the transformation of a primary energy resource into a usable energy form within the economy.

Rem (Roentgen-equivalent man)—The unit of biological dose given by the product of the absorbed dose in rads and the relative biological efficiency of the radiation.

Reprocessing—In reference to spent nuclear fuel, the chemical and mechanical processes by which plutonium-239 and the unused uranium-235 are recovered for subsequent use.

Resources—Deposits known to exist in geologically measureable amounts but not presently recoverable using present-day technologies, or deposits which are suspected or probable on the basis of indirect evidence.

Scrubber—*See* Flue-gas desulfurization.

Secondary recovery—In petroleum extraction, the augmentation of reservoir pressure by the injection of air, gas, or water.

Second Law of Thermodynamics—States that when heat exchange takes place between two bodies, the heat is always transferred from the warmer to the cooler body, thereby reducing the quality of available energy. *See also* Entropy principle; Thermodynamics.

Separative work unit (SWU)—A measure of the work required to separate the isotopes of uranium by enrichment. Used to measure the capacity of an enrichment plant. Approximately 100,000 SWU's are required per year to operate a 1,000-MWe light water reactor at its normal capacity factor for a year, and 2,500 SWU's to fabricate a nuclear weapon.

Shadow prices—Prices imputed to a good, service, or resource that is not priced in market terms or is incorrectly priced by the market because of regulation, imperfect competition, or other pricing distortions.

Sherman Act of 1890—A key antitrust law which prohibits contracts, combinations, and conspiracies in restraint of trade, as well as monopolization or attempts to monopolize interstate trade or foreign trade. The Sherman Act provided the legal framework for the 1911 Supreme Court decision that ordered the dissolution of the Standard Oil Company.

Slow neutron—A neutron with a relatively low amount of energy, or roughly 0.025 electron volts in comparison with the 1,000 or more electron volts of a fast neutron. Slow, or thermal, neutrons are key elements in commercial nuclear reactor configurations.

Solar cell—A fabricated material such as a silicon wafer that converts solar radiation into an electrical current.

Solar constant—The average intensity of solar radiation reaching the atmosphere, which has a value of 1.36 kilowatts per square meter.

Solar Furnace—A mechanism which uses focusing mirrors to direct the sun's rays on a small point to produce relatively high temperatures.

Solvent-refined coal (SRC)—The chemical treatment of coal to produce liquid petroleum by-products.

Spillovers—*See* Externalities.

Steady-state Economy—An economy that is neither growing nor contracting over time. Noted first by classical economists and more recently by proponents of energy and environmental resource conservation.

Steam power plant—A plant in which steam is used to move turbine blades used to generate electricity.

Strategic special nuclear Materials (SSNM's)—Special nuclear materials such as plutonium, uranium-233, enriched uranium-235, and other materials so designated by the Nuclear Regulatory Commission. Materials with at least 20 percent purity of these elements receive this designation primarily because of their potential as nuclear weapons.

Strip mining—Method of coal mining in which the overburden is first removed and the entire underlying seam of coal is scraped away, in contrast with underground and auger mining. Strip mining tends to be privately cheaper than other methods, but imposes higher environmental costs.

Substitution effect—A change in quantity of a good demanded by a buyer resulting from a change in the good's price while the buyer's real income, tastes, and the prices of other goods remain the same. *See also* Income effect.

Tailings—In reference to the nuclear fuel cycle, the rejected material after uranium ore is processed; in contrast, tails are the uranium-235 remaining after the production of enriched uranium. A tails assay consists of the percentage of uranium-235 in tails; since natural uranium contains approximately 0.71 percent uranium-235, the tails assay is likely to be 0.3 percent or lower.

Tar sands—Sedimentary rocks containing heavy, or viscous, petroleum which require special chemical and heating techniques for separation and refinement.

Tertiary recovery—The use of heat and other methods other than fluid injection to increase oil recovery from a reservoir, particularly since the residual oil is likely to be heavier than earlier amounts extracted.

Thermal neutron—*See* Slow neutron.

Thermal pollution—An increase in environmental temperatures of air or water resulting from the release of rejected heat from a thermal electric power plant.

Thermodynamics—The quantitative and qualitative relations governing the convertibility of heat and other forms of energy, often referred to in terms of the laws of thermodynamics. *See also* First Law of Thermodynamics; Second Law of Thermodynamics.

Theta-pinch reactor—A type of fusion reactor in which magnetic lines of force circling a plasma compress it by their tension.

Thorium—A naturally radioactive element of atomic weight 232 which by neutron irradiation can be transformed to fissionable uranium-233, which is suitable for use as a nuclear reactor fuel.

Tidal energy—Energy in waves, caused essentially by the changing gravitational force of the moon on the earth's water bodies. Tidal energy is suitable for the generation of electricity.

Tokamak—A type of nuclear fusion experimental reactor, named after its Soviet origins, which operates on the principle of magnetic confinement. A Tokamak type of reactor has been used in research in the United States as well, at Princeton University.

Total energy system—An energy system that seeks to maximize all possible forms of energy conversion in their thermodynamically most efficient uses. It relies strongly on the optimum use of Second Law thermodynamic principles and in many cases on co-generation technologies.

Tritium—An artificial radioactive isotope of hydrogen which has two neutrons and one proton in the nucleus.

Turbine—An engine operated by the rotation of a stream of water, steam, air, or fluid by a nozzle forced against the blades of a wheel connected to a shaft that is used to convert energy.

Unit train—A train having but one type of cargo, usually coal, and operating continuously between a utility and the source.

Uranium—A radioactive element with an average atomic weight of approximately 238, the two most important isotopes of which are uranium-235 (0.7 percent natural uranium) and uranium-238 (99.3 percent natural uranium). Uranium-235 when sufficiently enriched is the principal fuel in commercial nuclear reactors; uranium-238 can be converted into plutonium. Enriched forms of uranium include uranium oxide (U_3O_8) and, subsequently, uranium hexafluoride (UF_6).

URENCO—A joint British-Dutch-West German organization which operates centrifuge isotope-separation plants.

User cost—Rents or royalties that become incorporated into the price of a depletable energy resource as successive quantities are consumed. User costs exist above and beyond marginal costs of extraction and conversion of a depletable energy resource and depend on the degree of competition in the industry, the social rate of time preference, or discount rate, and the level and rate of change in the demand for the depletable energy resource.

WASH-1400—See Rasmussen Report.

Waste heat—Heat rejected into the environment as a by-product of the conversion of energy from one form to another. Waste heat results in thermal pollution.

Water leaching—A water-focused process of cleaning coal to separate sulfur and other impurities.

Wellhead—The surface point of extraction of petroleum or natural gas from a reservoir. This term is used extensively in pricing decisions by firms and by regulatory authorities.

Windfall profits—Profits above a firm or industry's normal rate of return which are due to a sudden shift in the price of the resource or in the price of related resources and are presumed to exert no influence in the short run over the quantity of the good demanded or supplied. The deregulation of petroleum prices in 1980–81 was accompanied by a windfall profits tax designed to remove the gains that would otherwise have accrued to firms in the industry.

Work—The transfer of energy from one body to another, or the form of energy in the process.

World Bank—See International Bank for Reconstruction and Development.

X-efficiency (inefficiency)—The degree of technical efficiency (or inefficiency) achieved by firms under conditions of imperfect competition, imperfect information, or other distorting influences in comparison to the standard model of competitive efficiency.

Yellowcake—Uranium oxide ore that has been mined and cleaned prior to enrichment.

INDEX